Iowa History Reader

Iowa History Reader

EDITED BY MARVIN BERGMAN

State Historical Society of Iowa
in association with
Iowa State University Press
Ames, Iowa

MARVIN BERGMAN is editor of *The Annals of Iowa* for the State Historical Society of Iowa. He lives in Iowa City.

The Great Seal of Iowa depicted on the cover symbolizes Iowa past and present. The seal was created by the first General Assembly in 1847. It presents a citizen soldier standing in a wheat field, surrounded by farming and industrial tools, with the Mississippi River in the background. An eagle holds a scroll bearing the state motto: "Our liberties we prize, and our rights we will maintain."

The state seal is retained in the custody of and under the control of the governor and can only be used with the governor's permission.

© 1996 Iowa State University Press, Ames, Iowa 50014
All rights reserved

All chapters reprinted with permission. See the bottom of the first page of each chapter.

No part of this book may be reproduced in any form or by any electronic or mechanical means, including information storage and retrieval systems, without permission in writing from the copyright holder, except for brief passages quoted in a review.

∞ Printed on acid-free paper in the United States of America

First edition, 1996

International Standard Book Number: 0-8138-2177-0

Cataloging-in-Publication information is available.

CONTENTS

	Acknowledgments	vii
	Introduction	ix
1.	Iowa: The Middle Land DOROTHY SCHWIEDER	1
2.	"We Dance in Opposite Directions": Mesquakie (Fox) Separatism from the Sac and Fox Tribe MICHAEL D. GREEN	19
3.	The Frontier in Process: Iowa's Trail Women as a Paradigm GLENDA RILEY	37
4.	Farming in the Prairie Peninsula, 1830–1890 ALLAN G. BOGUE	61
5.	The Political Culture of Antebellum Iowa: An Overview ROBERT COOK	86
6.	"Men Did Not Take to the Musket More Commonly than Women to the Needle": Annie Wittenmyer and Soldiers' Aid ELIZABETH D. LEONARD	105
7.	Iowans and the Politics of Race in America, 1857–1880 ROBERT R. DYKSTRA	129
8.	Town Development, Social Structure, and Industrial Conflict SHELTON STROMQUIST	159
9.	Iowa's Struggle for State Railroad Control JOHN LAURITZ LARSON	197
10.	Why the Populist Party Was Strong in Kansas and Nebraska but Weak in Iowa JEFFREY OSTLER	241

11.	Iowa, Wet or Dry? Prohibition and the Fall of the GOP RICHARD JENSEN	263
12.	To Whom Much Is Given: The Social Identity of an Iowa Small Town in the Early Twentieth Century THOMAS J. MORAIN	291
13.	Rural Iowa in the 1920s and 1930s DOROTHY SCHWIEDER AND JOSEPH F. WALL	327
14.	World War II and Rural Women DEBORAH FINK	347
15.	The Modernization of Iowa's Agriculture Structure in the Twentieth Century MARK FREIDBERGER	375
16.	The Evolution of the Iowa Precinct Caucuses HUGH WINEBRENNER	397
17.	Iowa's Abortion Battles of the Late 1960s and Early 1970s: Long-Term Perspectives and Short-Term Analyses JAMES C. MOHR	411
	Index	433

Acknowledgments

MANY PEOPLE have provided support, offered criticism, or acted as sounding boards as I have prepared this collection of essays. I would not have completed it without them. Bill Silag offered encouragement and sound advice when I first proposed the idea in 1993. Laura Moran continued to support me and my proposal after she joined Iowa State University Press. Rebecca Conard, Christie Dailey, David Ferch, Loren Horton, Jack Lufkin, Tom Morain, Malcolm Rohrbough, Tom Ryan, Dorothy Schwieder, and Bill Silag graciously responded to a proposal and list of essays that were early candidates for inclusion in this collection. Most of them will be disappointed that I have not done more to incorporate their suggestions into the final product, but I do appreciate their thoughtful responses and took them more seriously than the product may seem to indicate. The administration and staff of the State Historical Society of Iowa have been unfailingly supportive. I'm especially grateful to Mary Bennett, Christie Dailey, Loren Horton, and Ginalie Swaim for faithfully playing the roles of sounding board and hand-holder, especially when I became nearly overwhelmed with what seemed to be the awesome responsibility of narrowing down my "short list" of 35 or so essays closer to my goal of 12–15, while also taking into account the many additional suggestions from my consultants. Thanks, too, to Brad Kearney for his quietly efficient technical help in preparing the book for publication, and a very special thanks to Bob Burchfield for volunteering his skills as a proofreader. Finally, I'm grateful, as always, for my primary supporting cast (when I'm not serving as part of *theirs*): Jessica, Ruth, Leah, Philip, and — most of all — Darlene.

Introduction

IN 1973 Dorothy Schwieder, frustrated by "the lack of usable classroom materials in Iowa history," compiled a set of essays that she hoped could serve "either for basic or supplemental reading in Iowa history."[1] Now she has gone even further to fill that gap by publishing her long-awaited survey of Iowa history, *Iowa: The Middle Land*. With three very different survey texts now available, the need for *basic* reading material on Iowa history has diminished significantly.[2] But these basic texts should not represent the last word for those who are interested in Iowa history, either for personal reasons or as a subject of formal study. Survey texts sometimes implicitly suggest that history is a static body of material to be mastered. As recent controversies over multiculturalism and "political correctness" have reminded us, however, history is contentious ground that shifts under our feet just when we think we are firmly planted in it.

Iowa history has been a part of some dramatic and some not-so-dramatic interpretive shifts in American history in the past three decades. The essays compiled here reflect those shifts. With the availability of good survey texts, such a collection no longer needs to substitute for a survey of Iowa history, offering comprehensive coverage of the major topics. And this one certainly does not. Rather, these essays offer perspectives on important topics in Iowa history, introducing readers to major debates and inviting further reflection and study of the issues involved. The intended audience, then, is people with a serious interest in Iowa history, those who want to pursue some topics in more depth and with more attention to interpretive issues than they can find in a survey text. These essays, I hope, will help readers see that while history is memory of the substance of the past, it is always a filtered memory; whatever else history is, it is always interpretation.

Too often, history is presented as a chronicle of facts, and readers are treated as passive vessels who receive and store the facts as presented. History as interpretation, on the other hand, engages readers themselves in history making. The author tries to understand the *meaning* of the past and *interpret* it for readers, recognizing that those readers may choose to marshall their own evidence in support of an alternative interpretation. These

---

1. Dorothy Schwieder, ed., *Patterns and Perspectives in Iowa History* (Ames, 1973), viii.

2. The three texts are Dorothy Schwieder, *Iowa: The Middle Land* (Ames, 1996); Leland L. Sage, *A History of Iowa* (Ames, 1974); and Joseph Frazier Wall, *Iowa: A Bicentennial History* (New York and Nashville, 1978). See also the survey text for young people by Dorothy Schwieder, Thomas Morain, and Lynn Nielsen, *Iowa, Past to Present: The People and the Prairie* (Ames, 1989).

essays, then, are not the last word on their respective subjects. Almost all have been written consciously to revise or refine previous interpretations of the subject and implicitly recognize that others may further revise or refine their interpretations.[3]

Several criteria guided the selection of the essays to be included. The primary criterion, in keeping with the overall goal for the collection, was that the essays be *interpretive*. There are many essays, especially in the old *Iowa Journal of History and Politics*, that offer surveys of important topics that historians will rely on for years to come.[4] It's hard to leave them out, but this collection is intended to reflect the existing state of the interpretation of Iowa history more than to provide comprehensive accounts of topics in Iowa history. Second, essays that engage broader historiographical issues in American history received preferential consideration. Many of these essays have been cited by others doing work on similar topics in other locales, states, or regions, or in the nation at large; the others easily could be. I also gave preference to essays that cross subdisciplinary boundaries and cover more than one significant topic. For example, the chapter from Shelton Stromquist's book addresses issues in railroad, labor, and community history. Finally, with so many outstanding essays that shed light on Iowa's history to choose from, I decided not to include essays on "famous Iowans" who made their careers primarily outside of the state, the most prominent of those being Iowa's only presidential son, Herbert Hoover. There were still many individual candidates for inclusion, however. Although much biographical work is more concerned with narrative than interpretation, there is certainly much to choose from: Louise Noun's work on "strong-minded women," Tom Colbert's on James Baird Weaver, George McDaniel's on Smith Wildman Brookhart, Richard Kirkendall's and others' on Henry A. Wallace, and James Larew's on Harold Hughes, among others.[5]

---

3. For a challenging critique of professional historians' tendency to privilege interpretation and explanation over "mere description," see Allan Megill, "Recounting the Past: 'Description,' Explanation, and Narrative in Historiography," *American Historical Review* 94 (1989), 627–53.

4. One of those that I have relied on repeatedly, for example, is Dan Elbert Clark's three-part article, "The History of Liquor Legislation in Iowa," *Iowa Journal of History and Politics* 6 (1908), 55–87, 339–74, 501–68. Myrtle Beinhauer's overview of the Grange, "Development of the Grange in Iowa, 1868–1930," which appeared in the *Annals of Iowa* 34 (1959), 597–618, and was reprinted in Dorothy Schwieder's *Patterns and Perspectives in Iowa History*, 209–30, serves a similar function.

5. Louise Noun, *Strong-Minded Women: The Emergence of the Woman Suffrage Movement in Iowa* (Ames, 1969); idem, *More Strong-Minded Women: Iowa Feminists Tell Their Stories* (Ames, 1992); Tom Colbert, "Disgruntled 'Chronic Office Seeker' or Man of Political Integrity: James Baird Weaver and the Republican Party in Iowa, 1857–1877," *Annals of Iowa* 49 (1988), 187–207; George McDaniel, "New Era Agrarian Radicalism: Smith W. Brookhart and the Populist Critique," *Annals of Iowa* 49 (1988), 208–20; Richard S. Kirkendall, "The Mind of a Farm Leader," *Annals of Iowa* 47 (1983), 138–53; idem, "The Second Secretary Wallace," *Agricultural History* 64 (1990), 199–206; Don S. Kirschner, "Henry A. Wallace as Farm Editor," *American Quarterly* 17 (1965), 187–202; Mark L. Kleinman, "Searching for the 'Inner Light': The Development of Henry A. Wallace's Experimental Spiritualism," *Annals of Iowa* 53 (1994), 195–218; and James C. Larew, "A Party Reborn: Harold Hughes and the Iowa Democrats," *Palimpsest* 59 (1978), 148–61.

Finally, I chose to include only Annie Wittenmyer, primarily because Elizabeth Leonard's chapter is an especially rich interpretive account, but also because it said more about the effect of the Civil War on Iowa than any other essay I found. It also, characteristically, addressed a couple of important topics besides the Civil War, namely, social reform and the changing role of women in nineteenth-century American society.

I also wanted to choose essays that model the craft of creating a historical essay. That model is not a timeless one, but it has been fairly consistent from the 1960s into the 1990s. I will not try to define it here but will let the essays in this volume define it. My choice has meant the exclusion of any essay on Iowa's natural history or essays about pre-contact Indian cultures based on archeological evidence or valuable work by historical geographers, all of which deserve the attention of Iowa historians seeking a comprehensive understanding of the state's history. The essays included here have contributed substantially to shaping or refining historiographical debates at the national level at the same time that they have shed light on Iowa's distinctive culture. These essays, then, indicate that even as concerns about parochialism within the historical profession robbed state and local history of a degree of professional legitimacy, the engagement with broader historiographical issues that professional concerns promoted has greatly enriched work at the state and local levels.

Readers may follow several story lines through the following essays. After Michael Green and Glenda Riley discuss aspects of the story of the displacement of native peoples by European-American settlers, Allan Bogue describes the farming practices that were established in "the prairie peninsula" (Iowa and Illinois) in the nineteenth century. The story of Iowa agriculture is continued for the 1920s and 1930s by Dorothy Schwieder and Joseph Wall, and for the remainder of the twentieth century by Mark Friedberger.

Robert Cook opens the story of Iowa politics with a general description of Iowa's antebellum political culture. Robert Dykstra then traces Iowa's political development on the issue of race. For the key decades at the end of the nineteenth century, there are accounts of Iowa's evolving political views on railroads (John Larson), prohibition (Richard Jensen), and Populism (Jeffrey Ostler). The focus on politics reemerges (except for the references to farm policy in Joseph Wall's essay) only after World War II, as Hugh Winebrenner describes the emergence of Iowa's best-known contribution to contemporary national politics, the precinct caucuses, and James Mohr analyzes Iowa's participation in one of the most contentious issues in contemporary political life, abortion.

The role of women appears at three points of transition: settlement (Glenda Riley), the Civil War (Elizabeth Leonard), and World War II (Deborah Fink). And two essays focus on the dynamics of Iowa communities: Shelton Stromquist compares how two communities along the Burlington Railroad responded to labor conflict in the 1880s, and Thomas Morain offers a general analysis of the social identity of Jefferson, Iowa, during the first third of the twentieth century.

This is not to say that agriculture, politics, women, and communities are the only topics addressed in this volume. The richness of the essays ensures that many other topics emerge. Within the constraints imposed by the criteria employed, I have made some effort to offer chronological balance and some coverage of the most important topics in Iowa history. Perceptive readers will notice, however, significant omissions and imbalances. To take the most obvious example, two-thirds of the essays deal with the nineteenth century, just the reverse of what the case should be if the distribution were to correspond to the state's time span. My choices here reflect not my own preferences but the existing state of the literature. In addition to an unfortunate bias among many historians against recent history, there are understandable reasons for the preponderance of nineteenth-century studies. In the existing academic climate, few professional historians can afford to be so parochial as to be seen as "Iowa historians." They are, first, American historians, with interest in topics that happen to play themselves out in Iowa, perhaps among other places. For most American historians, the twentieth century is a much smaller piece of the pie than it is for Iowa historians.

Professional and present-minded concerns may also help to explain the predominance of agricultural and political history. In the twentieth century, with fears about the depopulation of rural America and the collapse of family farming, people have naturally focused on issues related to agriculture and rural life. This is not to mention Iowa's identity as primarily an agricultural state, perhaps the premier agricultural state in the nation.

Historian Carl Ubbelohde, commenting on the decline and reemergence of interest in the midwestern region as a construct for historical inquiry, may help to account for why many of the best essays tend to focus on political history. "The political historians," he claims, "have stayed the course as long as any, continuing to find the Midwest . . . an interesting arena for analysis."[6] The recent focus on Progressive-era Iowa politics in particular has something to do with sources. As government services expanded after the Civil War, the volume of reporting to and from state government, with the ready access to that material, along with the availability of manuscript census material (both state and federal) now up to 1920, encourage research in that era. Historians have also looked to Iowa for evidence about frontier settlement issues, Populism, prohibition, the origins of the Republican party, and subsequent political realignments, but historians of newer topics—particularly in what used to be the "new" social history—have tended to look to the urban East, while the "new" western historians generally do not include Iowa as part of the West. Good work is being done in new areas in Iowa history, but it is not setting the terms of the debate as some earlier work in other areas did; it tends rather to be more like case studies applying or amplifying findings in other areas.

---

6. Carl Ubbelohde, "History and the Midwest as a Region," *Wisconsin Magazine of History* 78 (1994), 42.

Among the most significant topics missing from this collection is the history of education. Education is and long has been extremely important to Iowans, and it has received serious interpretive treatment by historians. Carroll Engelhardt and Keach Johnson have led the way, mining instructive details and insights from the official reports of the Iowa Department of Public Instruction, the proceedings of the Iowa State Teachers Association, and the writings of the state's educational administrators. Polly Welts Kaufman and Mary Hurlbut Cordier have broadened the reach to encompass the schoolwomen who assumed most of the teaching responsibilities in the state. In addition to excellent overviews in both books of the roles of women teachers, Kaufman edits the diary of Arozina Perkins, who taught in Iowa in the mid-nineteenth century, and letters from other midwestern schoolwomen on the frontier. Cordier's overview is more extensive, and she offers narrative accounts of the lives and careers of five midwestern teachers, including Sarah Gillespie Huftalen, whose long teaching career included stints as a teacher in a rural one-room schoolhouse, a county superintendent, and a supervisor of teacher training in the normal department at Muscatine High School. As for higher education, Stow Persons has written an outstanding book-length account of the University of Iowa in the twentieth century. Dorothy Schwieder extended the notion of education further to include the educational materials and information supplied to rural farm women by farm journals, farm organizations, and the Extension Service.[7] Most of the work thus far on education has focused largely on political, administrative issues. That provides a necessary foundation for our

---

7. Carroll Engelhardt, "Citizenship Training and Community Civics in Iowa Schools: Modern Methods for Traditional Ends, 1876–1928," *Mid-America* 65 (1983), 55–69; idem, "Religion, Morality, and Citizenship in the Public Schools: Iowa, 1858–1930," in *Ideas in America's Cultures: From Republic to Mass Society,* ed. Hamilton Cravens (Ames, 1982), 45–57; idem, "Schools and Character: Educational Reform and Industrial Virtue in Iowa, 1890–1930," *Annals of Iowa* 47 (1985), 618–36; idem, "Henry Sabin (1829–1918): 'The Aristocracy of Character' and Educational Leadership in Iowa," *Annals of Iowa* 48 (1987), 388–412; idem, "Compulsory Education in Iowa, 1872–1919," *Annals of Iowa* 49 (1987), 26–57; Keach Johnson, "The State of Elementary and Secondary Education in Iowa in 1900," *Annals of Iowa* 49 (1987), 26–57; idem, "Roots of Modernization: Educational Reform in Iowa at the Turn of the Century," *Annals of Iowa* 50 (1991), 892–918; Polly Welts Kaufman, *Women Teachers on the Frontier* (New Haven, CT, 1984); Mary Hurlbut Cordier, "Prairie Schoolwomen, Mid-1850s to 1920s, in Iowa, Kansas, and Nebraska," *Great Plains Quarterly* 3 (1988), 102–119; idem, *Schoolwomen of the Prairies and Plains: Personal Narratives from Iowa, Kansas, and Nebraska, 1860s to 1920s* (Albuquerque, NM, 1992); Stow Persons, *The University of Iowa in the Twentieth Century: An Institutional History* (Iowa City, 1990); Dorothy Schwieder, "Education and Change in the Lives of Farm Women, 1900–1940," *Agricultural History* 60 (1986), 200–215; idem, *Seventy-Five Years of Service: Cooperative Extension in Iowa* (Ames, 1993). Sarah Gillespie Huftalen's life and career are detailed more fully in Suzanne L. Bunkers, *"All Will Yet Be Well": The Diary of Sarah Gillespie Huftalen, 1873–1952* (Iowa City, 1993). See also Tom Morain, "Departure of Males from the Teaching Profession," *Civil War History* 26 (1980), 161–70; George S. May, "Iowa's Consolidated Schools," *Palimpsest* 37 (1956), 1–64; and Richard Jensen and Mark Friedberger, *Education and Social Structure: An Historical Study of Iowa, 1870–1930* (Chicago, 1976). A standard reference work for the history of education in Iowa is Clarence R. Aurner, *History of Education in Iowa,* 5 vols. (Iowa City, 1914–1920). A noteworthy exception to the "inevitable wave of progress" school is Wayne E. Fuller, *The Old Country School: The Story of Rural Education in the Middle West* (Chicago, 1982).

understanding of the history of education in Iowa. But to match the insights being provided in other areas, historians of education need to probe more deeply into the ideology and social consequences of the developments usually described as an inevitable wave of progress.

The absence of any essay on immigration or ethnicity (except for Richard Jensen's ethnocultural analysis of voting behavior in the late nineteenth century) is harder to account for. Some of the most fruitful work in American history—even in the history of the Midwest—in recent years has been devoted to the study of immigration and ethnicity.[8] Iowa has participated in this trend with a fairly large volume of work on Iowa's ethnic groups.[9] Curtis Harnack has done some interesting work on an upper-class English settlement in northwestern Iowa. Dorothy Schwieder has described the experience of Italian-American coal miners. Nancy Derr, Steven Wrede, and Peter Petersen have recounted the persecution of Germans and Danes during World War I. Jette Mackintosh has offered a broader look at the Danish experience. Lowell Soike's analysis of the political experience of Norwegian Americans challenges the ethnocultural model of voting behavior espoused by Richard Jensen and others. Béla Vassady offered a fascinating account of the settlement of Hungarian Forty-eighters in Decatur County. And Suzanne Schenken read Mary Treglia's work at the Sioux City Community House into the recent literature on settlement houses. Iowa's Dutch immigrants have been the focus of much attention. Particularly noteworthy is Brian Beltman's longitudinal study of a Dutch-American family in Sioux County.[10] For the most part, however, his-

---

8. For a sampling and response to some of the rich recent work on ethnicity in the rural Midwest, see Suzanne Sinke, "Ethnicity, Gender, Family, and Community in the Rural Midwest: A Review Essay" (reviewing Carol K. Coburn, *Life at Four Corners: Religion, Gender, and Education in a German-Lutheran Community, 1868–1945* [Lawrence, KS, 1992]; Jane Marie Pederson, *Between Memory and Reality: Family and Community in Rural Wisconsin, 1870–1970* [Madison, WI, 1992]; and Sonya Salamon, *Prairie Patrimony: Family, Farming, and Community in the Midwest* [Chapel Hill, NC, 1992]), *Annals of Iowa* 53 (1994), 356–67. See also the historiographical essays by Kathleen Conzen in *Agriculture and National Development: Views on the Nineteenth Century*, ed. Lou Ferleger (Ames, 1990); and Carlton C. Qualey in *American Frontier and Western Issues: A Historiographical Review*, ed. Roger L. Nichols (Westport, CT, 1986).

9. Patricia Dawson and David Hudson list about two hundred items in *Iowa History and Culture: A Bibliography of Materials Published between 1952 and 1986* (Ames, 1989), 183–92, and in "Iowa History and Culture: A Bibliography of Materials Published from 1987 through 1991," *Annals of Iowa* 52 (1993), 426–30.

10. Curtis Harnack, *Gentlemen on the Prairie* (Ames, 1985); Dorothy Schwieder, "Italian-Americans in Iowa's Coal Mining Industry," *Annals of Iowa* 46 (1982), 263–78; Nancy Derr, "Lowden: A Study of Intolerance in an Iowa Community During the Era of the First World War," *Annals of Iowa* 50 (1989), 5–22; Steven Wrede, "The Americanization of Scott County, 1914–1918," *Annals of Iowa* 44 (1979), 627–38; Peter L. Petersen, "Language and Loyalty: Governor Harding and Iowa's Danish-Americans During World War I," *Annals of Iowa* 42 (1974), 405–17; Jette Mackintosh, "Ethnic Patterns in Danish Immigrant Agriculture: A Study of Audobon and Shelby Counties, Iowa," *Agricultural History* 64 (1990), 59–77; idem, "'Little Denmark' on the Prairie: A Study of the Towns Elk Horn and Kimballton in Iowa," *Journal of American Ethnic History* 7 (1988), 46–68; idem, "Migration and Mobility among Danish Settlers in Southwest Iowa," *Journal of Historical Geography* 17 (1991), 165–89; Lowell Soike, *Norwegian Americans and*

torians of Iowa's immigrant and ethnic experience have not fully explored the intersections of ethnic persistence and change and the community and gender dynamics that characterize the richest ethnic history of recent years.

Serious historical interpretation of Iowa's cultural history is even more lacking. Of course, except for a brief flourishing in the 1930s, Iowa has not been known for its contributions to literature and the arts.[11] It is harder to account for the absence of serious treatment of religion, an acknowledged factor in shaping the lives and cultures of Iowans. Richard Jensen's essay in this volume does show how religious affiliation affected voting behavior. And those who have studied Dutch immigration, as well as those who have written about Iowa's famous Amana colonies, have found it nearly impossible to avoid discussing religion. But as historians of American religion have escaped the narrow confines of filiopietistic congregational and denominational history to interpret religion as a part of the larger history of American life and culture, while still treating religion as something other than a mere function of other concerns, religion in Iowa has unfortunately not attracted their attention.[12]

---

the Politics of Dissent, 1880–1924 (Northfield, MN, 1991); Béla Vassady, "New Buda: A Colony of Hungarian Forty-eighters in Iowa," *Annals of Iowa* 51 (1991), 26–52; Suzanne O. Schenken, "The Immigrants' Advocate: Mary Treglia and the Sioux City Community House, 1921–1959," *Annals of Iowa* 50 (1989/1990), 181–213; Brian Beltman, "Ethnic Persistence and Change: The Experience of a Dutch-American Family in Rural Iowa," *Annals of Iowa* 52 (1993), 1–49. See also Richard L. Doyle, "Wealth Mobility in Pella, Iowa, 1847–1925," in *The Dutch in America: Immigration, Settlement, and Cultural Change*, ed. Robert P. Swierenga (New Brunswick, NJ, 1985); Gary H. Koerselman, "The Church and Community Life in Early Middleburg History," *Annals of Iowa* 40 (1971), 631–40; and Ronald D. Rietveld, "Hendrick Peter Scholte and the Land of Promise," *Annals of Iowa* 48 (1986), 135–54. For valuable earlier work, see Flora Dunlap, "Roadside Settlement of Des Moines," *Annals of Iowa* 21 (1938), 161–89; Hildegard Binder Johnson, "German Forty-eighters in Davenport," *Iowa Journal of History and Politics* 44 (1946), 3–53; Lillian May Wilson, "Some Hungarian Patriots in Iowa," *Iowa Journal of History and Politics* 11 (1913), 479–516; Jacob Van der Zee, *The British in Iowa* (Iowa City, 1922); idem, *The Hollanders of Iowa* (Iowa City, 1912).

11. Grant Wood has certainly received his share of attention. Patricia Dawson and David Hudson turned up 36 items about Wood for their bibliography and the update, covering the years 1952–1991. Finally, the larger flowering of Iowa's literary life from the 1890s through the early 1940s is the subject of a book-length treatment by E. Bradford Burns in *Kinship with the Land: Regionalist Thought in Iowa, 1894–1942* (Iowa City, 1996).

12. Exceptions include Cynthia Grant Tucker, *Prophetic Sisterhood: Liberal Women Ministers of the Frontier, 1880–1930* (Boston, 1990); Dewey D. Wallace, Jr., "Charles Oliver Brown at Dubuque: A Study in the Ideals of Midwestern Congregationalists in the Late Nineteenth Century," *Church History* 53 (1984), 46–60; Robert M. Crunden, "George D. Herron in the 1890s: A New Frame of Reference for the Study of the Progressive Era," *Annals of Iowa* 42 (1973), 81–113; Thomas D. Hamm, "Joel Bean and the Revival in Iowa," *Quaker History* 76 (1987), 33–49; Roger D. Launius, "The Mormon Quest for a Perfect Society at Lamoni, Iowa, 1870–1890," *Annals of Iowa* 47 (1984), 325–42; and Michael J. Bell, "'True Israelites of America': The Story of the Jews of Iowa," *Annals of Iowa* 53 (1994), 85–127. It is noteworthy that historians of American religion, while drawing on the lessons learned from years of engagement with broader historical issues, and from the results of local history done by social historians, have rediscovered the value of local congregational studies. See James Wind and James Lewis, *American Congregations*, 2 vols. (Chicago, 1994); and, for a hint of the promise of this new, old approach, Randall Balmer, "Washington Prairie Lutheran Church, Decorah, Iowa," *Christian Century* 108 (30 October 1991), 996–1000.

A couple of developing areas of study might have been represented here, but are not. Material culture has been receiving increasing attention in recent years, particularly by public and local historians. As part of the historic preservation movement, studies of historic architecture have proliferated. But little of that material represents the kind of interpretation of broader historical forces that is represented in the other essays in this volume.[13] Even more recently, environmental history has been emerging into its own. Not surprisingly, much of that literature focuses on the West, but William Cronon's provocative work on Chicago's hinterland shifted some focus to the Midwest. Philip Scarpino had earlier drawn attention to the effects of humans' choices on the Mississippi River. Rebecca Conard has subsequently traced the development of Iowa's state parks system.[14] Much remains to be done in both areas.

These, of course, represent just a sampling of the issues that could benefit from more interpretive history. In general, all topics since World War II need more attention. But the essays compiled here represent some of the richest interpretive work from the past three decades, along with some of the key interpretive issues that the investigation of Iowa history has helped to shape. For those who want to explore further the issues that are raised here, the historiographical notes following each essay direct readers to additional material. The *Annals of Iowa,* which is well represented in the notes to this introduction and in the essays that follow, continues to engage current historiographical issues; it deserves the attention of students of Iowa history.

If much remains to be done, it is nonetheless true that historians have taught us much in the past several decades about the Iowa experience. We have come to appreciate more fully the role of voters in shaping the politics of this

---

13. Sally McMurry, *Families and Farmhouses in Nineteenth-Century America: Vernacular Design and Social Change* (New York, 1988), shows the potential of this kind of work. For examples of work on the history of Iowa's material culture, see Fred W. Peterson, "Tradition and Change in Nineteenth-Century Farmhouses," *Annals of Iowa* 52 (1993), 251–81; idem, *Homes in the Heartland: Balloon Frame Farmhouses of the Upper Midwest, 1850–1920* (Lawrence, KS, 1992); Wesley Ivan Shank, "The Demise of the County Courthouse Tower in Iowa: A Study of Early Twentieth-Century Cultural and Architectural Change," *Annals of Iowa* 51 (1992), 337–62; Signe T. Nielsen Betsinger, "Danes in Iowa and Minnesota," in *To Build in a New Land: Ethnic Landscapes in North America,* ed. Allen G. Noble (Baltimore, 1992); Keith A. Sculle, "Amana's First Decisions about Roadside Architecture: An Index of Cultural Change," *Annals of Iowa* 49 (1988), 462–74; Richard H. Thomas, "From Porch to Patio," *Palimpsest* 56 (1975), 120–27; Lowell Soike, *Without Right Angles: The Round Barns of Iowa* (Des Moines, 1983); and Nancy J. Brcak and Jean W. Sizemore, "The 'New' University of Iowa: A Beaux-Arts Design for the Pentacrest," *Annals of Iowa* 51 (1991), 149–67.

14. William Cronon, *Nature's Metropolis: Chicago and the Great West* (New York, 1991); Philip V. Scarpino, *Great River: An Environmental History of the Upper Mississippi, 1890–1950* (Columbia, MO, 1985); Rebecca Conard, "Hot Kitchens in Places of Quiet Beauty: Iowa State Parks and the Transformation of Conservation Goals," *Annals of Iowa* 51 (1992), 441–79. For the ramifications of Cronon's book for scholarship on Iowa, see Malcolm J. Rohrbough, Timothy R. Mahoney, David B. Danbom, Philip V. Scarpino, and William Cronon, "Perspectives on *Nature's Metropolis:* A Book Forum," *Annals of Iowa* 51 (1992), 480–525. For another perspective on the environmental issues involving the Mississippi River, see John O. Anfinson, "Commerce and Conservation on the Upper Mississippi River," *Annals of Iowa* 52 (1993), 385–417.

place; we know more about the importance of urban places, industrial workers, diverse ethnic groups, and rural women, even as new questions and historical methods have cultivated a fuller understanding of the significance of traditional agriculture for the state's development. This new knowledge about Iowa history has, in turn, refined — and at times necessarily complicated — our understanding of the shape of American history and Iowa's place in it.

Appreciation of the complexity and diversity of the forces that have shaped the state does not undermine the conclusion reached by Dorothy Schwieder in the first essay in this collection that Iowa remains "the middle land," a place that has experienced many of the problems (and opportunities) of the more urban, industrial states to its east and of the more rural states to its west, but not to the same extent as either. It seems fitting to conclude the introduction to a book dedicated to the interpretations of the state's most accomplished historians by quoting one of their most eloquent spokespersons, the late Joseph Frazier Wall. The introduction to his history of the state for the U.S. bicentennial eloquently supports Dorothy Schwieder's characterization of Iowa as "the middle land."[15] After quoting Ruth Suckow, who wrote in 1926 that Iowa was "on the fence geographically, politically, religiously and aesthetically," Wall claimed that Iowa, in 1976,

> was still peculiarly in the middle, still seeking to assert its own identity, still hoping there may be virtue in the average. Part of that middleness, to be sure, is simply an inescapable geographical fact of location. Iowa is the middle ground, a Mesopotamia lying between the two great rivers that drain the continent, bisected by the 42nd parallel, John Dos Passos's latitudinal line of middleness, the line that was roughly followed by the first transcontinental railroad and then later by the transcontinental highway, so that for over a hundred years the constantly moving Americans have had to cross Iowa from New York and Chicago to San Francisco. Partly that middleness is the accident of history, of drawing boundary lines and of carving the land up into the family-sized farms, so that today of the fifty states in the Union, Iowa ranks twenty-fifth in area, twenty-fifth in population. It meets perfectly the Supreme Court's standard of political units conforming to the one-person–one-vote principle, the only state whose U.S. senatorial representation could not be questioned by any equal-representation test. Iowa occupies the middle ground partly out of desire, having an almost instinctive fear and distrust of the extreme, whether in politics, economics, or in social structure. Among fifty states, Iowa ranks twenty-sixth in personal income, and in politics, historically, Iowa's Republicanism has been moderately liberal, its Democracy, moderately conservative. It has no real center where the elite of either power, wealth, or culture may congregate. Iowa, in short, is middle America. Some, including many Iowans, as Suckow indicates, would call that dull average. Others, who have now become increasingly more assertive in an America that is dominated by the extremism of California and Texas, would prefer to call it the blessed golden mean.

---

15. Joseph Frazier Wall, *Iowa: A Bicentennial History* (New York, 1978), xvii–xviii.

Iowa History Reader

1

Iowa:
The Middle Land

DOROTHY SCHWIEDER

> One would be hard pressed to find—or even imagine—a more apt, more elegant, more balanced summary of Iowa's history and character than one finds in the following essay by Dorothy Schwieder, the current dean of Iowa historians.

IN 1930 a relatively unknown artist painted a rather stark portrait of two Iowans entitled *American Gothic*. The portrait captured first prize that year at the Chicago Art Institute and Grant Wood's art career was launched. For the next decade, Wood produced painting after painting in which he depicted his native state. His characterizations of Iowa with its velvety smooth, softly rounded hills, its fat globular trees, its 1930s-vintage farmhouses, and its fastidiously neat rows of corn came to be widely recognized around the region and around the world. Through his paintings, Wood proclaimed to the world that Iowa was a state of natural beauty, a state with great agricultural bounty, and a state of rather staid, conservative folks who tolerated little nonsense.

At the same time, whether intended or not, Wood presented a far wider view of the state. Wood's paintings depicted a state filled with modest farmhouses, hard-working people, and neat, well-kept towns. His *Spring in Town* captured Iowans dutifully performing a multitude of tasks associated with the rituals of spring. In a mural, *Dinner for Threshers,* he depicted an important but typical summer activity in Iowa when farm wives prepared robust meals for threshing crews. Through lithographs, he documented the seasonal rhythm of agricultural work performed throughout the year. His paintings of farmsteads, rural countrysides, small towns, and ordinary people presented a view of a state and a people that could be described with a variety of adjectives: moderate, stable, regular, and consistent. Certainly he portrayed a land isolated

---

Reprinted by permission of Indiana University Press from *Heartland: Comparative Histories of the Midwestern States,* edited by James Madison (Bloomington: Indiana University Press, 1988), 276–95. Copyright © 1988 by Indiana University Press.

from the cities, far from the East and West coasts, a land devoid of excesses or extremes, yet a land of beauty and a land of plenty. Out of these images and impressions perhaps the term *middle land* might best capture the mood as well as the subject matter of Wood's work.

The term has infinite applications to Iowa's location, to its people, and to its history. In a physical sense, Iowa is indeed the middle land, lying at the center of the Middle West and therefore at the center of the nation. If the Middle West is the nation's heartland, then perhaps Iowa is the heart itself, pulsating quietly, slowly, and evenly, blending together the physical and social features of the entire region. Iowa itself is very much a homogeneous region, both in landform and in population. While the topography of the northeastern part of the state is uneven, the remainder of Iowa is mostly composed of gently rolling terrain, crisscrossed with many rivers and streams. Every section of the state is under cultivation, and agricultural interests permeate Iowans' thinking.

Iowa's population, too, is fairly homogeneous, still composed mostly of the descendants of nineteenth-century settlers. In fact, according to the 1980 census, three out of every four Iowans are natives. With only a few large urban centers and less industry than states of the Old Northwest, Iowa has not developed the same degree of ethnic pluralism. During the nineteenth century Iowa attracted large numbers of people from the northeastern United States and immigrants from northern and western Europe. After the Civil War several thousand blacks migrated from the South, and after 1900 a limited number of southern and eastern Europeans arrived, all to work in coal mining. Even with these additions, however, the great majority of Iowans trace their roots to the British Isles or to northern and western Europe.

Iowa achieved statehood in 1846, and the society that later emerged in many ways reflected New England influences. Although mostly moderate, Iowans in the nineteenth century had strong commitments to education, religion, and numerous social and political causes, particularly the prohibition of alcohol and the abolition of slavery. By 1900 Iowans had come to embrace Protestantism, prohibitionism, McGuffeyism, and Republicanism, four conditions that had great significance for the state's people and their institutions.

Grant Wood's most consistent theme, rural life, has been and continues to be the most important and pervasive element in Iowa. Known in the 1800s for its rich agricultural land, the state came to be shaped in its economic and social order by this resource. The land originally attracted settlers to the state, and the resulting farm economy in turn shaped most political issues in the nineteenth and early twentieth centuries. Farm people tended to be sober and hard working, with a strong work ethic, and they took their work and families seriously, attended church on Sunday morning, spoke out against the social evils of liquor, and resided very much in the middle of the social and political spectrum. Although Iowa's farm families have had their belief in the superiority of farm life severely tested, the belief has always been retained.

For the most part, then, Wood's image of a comfortable people living in the middle of the nation has correctly portrayed Iowans through the years. Blessed with some of the best agricultural land in the nation, Iowans have labored long and hard to make the land produce. Moreover, Iowans have been fortunate to experience a relative freedom from a harsh environment and capricious climate, so common in the plains states, a freedom that has given them more time and energy to be concerned with issues beyond mere survival. Although Iowa has always had a few large cities, the politics and social concerns of its urban areas would not come front and center until after World War II. Today, Iowa retains a strong nineteenth-century legacy in its views on education, morality, and the value of rural society. The state, it seems, has aged gracefully, remaining true to its early roots while absorbing and adjusting with a minimum of difficulty to new trends and conditions. Continuity is a fact of life in the Hawkeye state.

THE LAND that Grant Wood painted so gracefully in the 1930s was home first to at least seventeen Native American groups, including the Potawatomi, Santee Sioux, Oto, Missouri, Sauk, Mesquakie, and Ioway. (The latter three tribes were the most visible in the Iowa region in the eighteenth and nineteenth centuries.) These Native Americans were a part of the prairie and plains culture. Tribes moving into the Iowa region from the northeast brought along a woodland culture, including a partial reliance on agriculture; the Plains Indians, who by the 1600s were dependent on the horse and buffalo, embraced a nomadic way of life. In the Upper Mississippi Valley, of which Iowa is a part, these two cultures blended together, combining farming and hunting to produce the basis for a seminomadic existence. For all these tribes, Iowa was a bountiful place to live, providing the opportunities to hunt, fish, pursue agriculture, and gather the natural produce of the land.

By the mid-1800s, however, the Native American phase of Iowa history had essentially ended. In 1830 the federal government concluded treaties with the Missouri, Oto, and Omaha Indians, removing them from the western portion of the Iowa region. The most prolonged removal process was with the Sauk and Mesquakie Indians, who finally left Iowa in 1845. The Santee Sioux relinquished their land in Iowa in 1851. In effect, Indian tribes in Iowa did not retard white settlement. In each section of the state, Indians had officially been removed before whites began settlement. A brief encounter between a small band of Santee Sioux and white settlers in northwest Iowa in 1857, known as the Spirit Lake Massacre, marks the only violent confrontation of any importance between the two groups in Iowa.

Not all Indians left Iowa in 1845, however, as some Mesquakie managed to elude government officials. About a decade later, after convincing Iowa's governor James Grimes to act as their trustee, the Mesquakie began to buy back land that had originally been held jointly by themselves and the Sauk. This land, located in Tama County, became known as the Mesquakie Settlement and eventually included about three thousand acres. Today the Mesquakie hold an annual powwow, where they interpret their history and culture to outsiders. The Mesquakie Settlement is the only Native American location in the state; there are no Indian reservations. As a result, the history of Indian tribes in Iowa — and the interaction between Indians and whites — is quite different from that in other midwestern states, particularly South Dakota.

One year after the Sauk and Mesquakie were removed from extreme eastern Iowa, federal officials opened the area for white settlement. On June 1, 1833, frontiers people hurried across the Mississippi River to stake out their land claims. The first settlers moving into extreme eastern Iowa encountered an environment similar to what they had known in the Northeast. Most importantly, the area included sufficient timber for newcomers to build log cabins and to provide themselves with fuel and fencing. Once they moved farther into the region, however, timber was not sufficient to sustain this lifestyle. In central Iowa only the earliest settlers found adequate timber along the rivers and streams; others had to find substitutes to provide the basic essentials of settlement. People who later located in northwest Iowa encountered an area that approximated the Great Plains to the west: fewer trees, a more level terrain, and rainfall averages ten inches less than in the southeastern part of the state. Because of these physical and climatic conditions, Iowa provided the transitional zone for people moving from the woodland regions into the Great Plains. In effect, settlers in the prairie region were forced to modify their farming techniques and settlement practices. For those moving beyond Iowa into the Great Plains proper, adjustments would be of a far more radical nature.

Like settlers in other midwestern states, Iowa's nineteenth-century settlers were a mix of native- and foreign-born people. Before the Civil War most settlers migrated from Pennsylvania, Indiana, and Ohio, along with substantial numbers from the South. By 1870 the southern-born element had declined considerably and taking their place were more northeasterners and immigrants from northern and western Europe. By 1890, when the number of immigrants reached its highest point, 19 percent of Iowans were foreign born. Germans constituted the largest immigrant population, but Irish, Swedes, Norwegians, and English also settled in substantial numbers.

Settlement in Iowa proceeded in methodical fashion from east to west. In the 1830s the extreme eastern portion of Iowa was settled; by the 1850s newcomers had moved into central Iowa; and by the 1870s extreme northwestern Iowa, the state's last frontier area, was attracting native-born and foreign-born alike. Newcomers took advantage of cheap federal land and also purchased land from Iowa's four land-grant railroads. The Homestead Act of 1862, so significant in states to the west, accounted for only 2.5 percent of Iowa's total land sales. As in other midwestern states, surveyors moved from east to west, marking off uniform sections and townships in preparation for the first land sales. Perhaps of all midwestern states, Iowa with its more uniform terrain and its somewhat rectangular shape—324 miles long and 210 miles wide in its greatest distances—best displays the regularity of the township system.

Given the rapidity and compactness of settlement, Iowa's frontier experience approximated that of the Old Northwest more than that of the midwestern plains states. In the Great Plains families often settled some distance apart, leading to isolation and loneliness, especially for pioneer women. Iowa's early settlers did not experience the degree of isolation described so ably by Middle Border writers Hamlin Garland and Mari Sandoz. In the Hawkeye state, with many farmsteads of eighty acres and with rapid contiguous settlement, isolation or long-term separation from others was not typical.

The rapidity of settlement—in effect, the state was settled in less than forty years—was possible mainly because there were no physical features to disrupt the steady, methodical movement of people. Only one part of the state, a small area in the northwest, was avoided temporarily. That resulted not from irregular terrain or the presence of land barriers but because the area was so level that it remained wet much of the year. In contrast, some midwestern states' dominating physical features slowed settlement and left indelible marks on their later social and economic institutions. Missouri, for example, has its Ozarks, Nebraska its Sand Hills, and South Dakota its East and West River areas. Richard Power, in *Planting Corn Belt Culture*, points out that very real physical differences exist between the northern and southern parts of Ohio, Indiana, and Illinois, resulting in differences also in population and economic enterprise. By contrast, Iowans in nearly every part of the state exhibit a commonality of interests and concerns that reflects the lack of sharp physical differences throughout the state.

Of particular importance to Iowans' shared experience is the role played by the native prairie, the state's most dominant physical feature. Early nineteenth-century explorers recorded that the prairie, with its gentle, undulating surface, its tall grass, and its general absence of trees, covered roughly four-fifths of the region. Iowa was not unique, since the states on all sides also contained prairie land, but the Hawkeye state was blessed with the largest amount, prompting one expert to call Iowa the truest of the prairie states. The large expanse of original prairie, moreover, has determined to a large degree Iowa's eventual preeminence as an agricultural state.

THE SOCIETY that evolved in Iowa was clearly the product of earlier developments in the Northeast. Some historians have used the term *New England belt* to describe a wide path made by New Englanders or their descendants as they migrated across the northern half of the United States. Iowa lay within this belt and soon came to include institutions and values that New Englanders believed to be important. Religious and educational institutions developed quickly in Iowa, both strongly influenced by Protestant church groups and their clergy. In general, Iowa fits the same religious pattern as other middle western states in that it was settled primarily by Protestants whose influence remained dominant throughout the nineteenth century.

Along with a plethora of Protestants, Catholics also became active in Iowa at an early date. Bishop Mathias Loras, a priest from France, established Iowa's first Catholic diocese in Dubuque. Bishop Loras's work paid excellent dividends; by 1850 the Dubuque area served as the center of Catholicism in Iowa and contained two colleges and several sister orders. The bishop was also instrumental in attracting an Irish Trappist monastery to the Dubuque area in 1849. Unlike the Protestant clergy, who were typically native born, Catholic priests and sisters were usually from foreign countries.

All religious groups in Iowa, Protestant and Catholic alike, quickly erected colleges. The Catholics set up separate colleges for men and women throughout eastern Iowa. By 1880 the Methodists had created five colleges, conveniently located so that Methodist young people in almost every part of the state could attend a Methodist institution of higher learning. Other Protestant groups followed suit, establishing colleges everywhere in the state, including Des Moines, Wartburg, Oskaloosa, Fairfield, and Lamoni. By 1900 church colleges numbered more than twenty-five while state institutions of higher learning numbered only three.

Iowa's nineteenth-century educational system developed simultaneously with religious institutions. Like other midwesterners, Iowans quickly erected common schools in rural areas and towns. Believing strongly in the need to provide youngsters with both formal learning and proper moral guidance, Iowans hired teachers not only for their ability to teach but also for their suitability as moral examples. Iowans' concern about both education and morality went hand in hand with the views expressed by William Holmes McGuffey in *McGuffey's Readers*. Countless generations of nineteenth-century Iowa schoolchildren learned to read from one of the many editions of this reader. McGuffey used the device of "constant open moralizing" whereby he continually advised students about proper moral behavior. McGuffey's stories especially admonished children to love God, their parents, and their country. No doubt most Iowa parents would have nodded approvingly when McGuffey observed: "Little children, it is better to be good than to be wise."[1]

Some people who advocated proper moral behavior were even closer to home. Henry Wallace, commonly known as Uncle Henry, wrote innumerable columns of advice for Iowa's rural children in the late nineteenth and early twentieth centuries in which he further expounded on McGuffey's main tenets. Wallace, a native of Pennsylvania and a former Presbyterian clergyman, had moved to Iowa in the 1870s and taken up farming. He soon started writing agricultural columns for the state's farmers. Later he and his son, Henry Cantwell Wallace, a professor at Iowa State College, established a farm

---

1. Quoted in Lewis Atherton, *Main Street on the Middle Border* (reprinted New York, 1975); see 65–88 for a discussion of McGuffey's views.

publication, *Wallaces' Farmer*. With his own publication under way, Uncle Henry had advice for everyone. In his column, "Letters to Farm Folks," Wallace wrote articles with such titles as "Getting the Boy Started Right," "The Proper Brain Food for Farm Folks," and "Girls for the Scrap Heap." Wallace cautioned young people about the dangers lurking in cities and specifically warned about the evils of alcohol and tobacco. Like so many of his midwestern contemporaries, Wallace believed that the farm was the cradle of democracy and decency while the city was a place of sin, corruption, and sloth.

Nineteenth-century Iowa children were also thoroughly imbued with the Protestant work ethic. But beyond that, attitudes toward different kinds of work filtered through. In his classic study *Main Street on the Middle Border*, Lewis Atherton insightfully described the "Cult of the Immediately Useful and Practical" that dominated the Middle Border. The cult proclaimed that behavior was judged by whether or not it had "immediate, practical utilitarianism." The belief had a corollary related to income: "Every art and profession must justify itself financially." Therefore lawyers, bankers, and businessmen were obviously justified in making substantial incomes. Teachers and preachers were accepted because they "buttressed law and order," but unfortunately for them, although respected, their work did not justify a good remuneration. A second corollary stated that if an action was not immediately useful and practical, it would be tolerated if practiced by women but not by men. Music and art were therefore fine for daughters but unacceptable for sons. Atherton points out that young men who were inclined to follow the fine arts or even a writing career "escaped to the cities" because they found little support or acceptance in the rural areas or small towns of middle America.[2]

By the end of the nineteenth century, Iowa's social, moral, and educational mentality was firmly in place. Its public school system had earned a national reputation, based to a large extent on a high literacy rate. But in addition to receiving a solid basic education, Iowa schoolchildren had absorbed the values and morals inherent in both McGuffey's constant open moralizing and the Cult of the Immediately Useful and Practical. Iowans viewed hard work as good, but along with this perception went a value-laden system that included strong gender distinctions and an implied social and economic class structure resulting from the degree of practicality of one's work.

THE SOCIETY which nineteenth-century Iowans constructed, however, went beyond evangelical Protestantism, McGuffeyism, and the admonitions of individuals like Uncle Henry Wallace. This society also contained a strong impulse toward social reform that became evident as early as the 1840s. Before the Civil War Iowans passed their first prohibition law and took a strong stand against slavery. After the war the reform impulse reasserted itself as Iowans

---

2. Ibid., 112–17.

resumed their war on alcohol, moved to grant full constitutional rights to black men, and labored to create various institutions that reflected reformist thinking. An integral part of these changes was the fact that in the 1850s Iowans left behind the party of Andrew Jackson and embraced Republicanism.

The controversy over slavery, so evident in the 1840s, strongly influenced the young state. Given the state's northern location and such laws as the Missouri Compromise and the Northwest Ordinance, there was never any question that Iowa would remain a free state. Although Iowa contained some southern-born individuals in the 1840s and 1850s — a small minority that might have favored slavery — in general Iowans strongly supported abolition. Quakers and Congregationalists were especially active in the abolitionist crusade and in supporting the underground railroad. Quakers created many communities in central and eastern Iowa, including West Branch, Salem, New Providence, and Springdale, that served as centers for their antislavery work.

While Quakers, Congregationalists, and others favored the abolition of slavery, Iowans were of a different mind regarding legal and constitutional rights for blacks. Opposing slavery with its profoundly degrading consequences was one thing, but accepting blacks as social, political, or economic equals was quite another. Iowa followed along the path trod by most northern states before the Civil War in repudiating slavery but withholding constitutional rights from blacks. Iowans, moreover, erected many barriers to keep free blacks out of the state.

In the 1850s Iowa underwent political change. From 1846, when Iowa achieved statehood, to 1854, Iowans had consistently voted Democratic. This habit was broken in 1854 when James Grimes, a bright, energetic easterner who had recently settled in Burlington, was elected governor on the Whig ticket. Like many Whigs, Grimes soon aligned himself with the Republican ticket and was reelected in 1856 as a Republican. Iowans fiercely embraced Republicanism, finding the party's programs of free soil, free labor, and free men much to their liking. At the same time the Democrats seemed to do nothing right. The national leadership of the party did not respond to westerners' requests for free land and money to make internal improvements. Party leadership, moreover, seemed tired and lacking in new ideas. The result of the switch in political parties was long term: with a few temporary lapses, Iowans remained safely within the Republican fold for a century, until the 1950s.

During the latter half of the nineteenth century, the Republican party considered a series of important reform measures that reflected the social concerns of Iowans. Not least among them was the question of a prohibition on alcohol. Iowa contained many Methodists who were increasingly insistent that the state adopt a prohibition law. Responding to this pressure, Republicans in 1855 passed the state's first antiliquor legislation. While Methodists may have approved, however, German immigrants in eastern Iowa reacted with anger. Quick to sense an impending loss at the next election if the Germans deserted them, Republicans negated their action, changing the law to one of local option.

The legislation put the Republican party in the difficult position of trying to please several opposing constituencies. On one hand, the ever-growing Methodist denomination strongly supported total abstinence, as did Congregationalists, Presbyterians, Baptists, and Scandinavian Lutherans. On the other hand, the state's German Lutherans, Catholics, and Episcopalians opposed prohibition. From 1855 until national prohibition was adopted in 1920, Iowa Republicans vacillated, usually unsuccessfully, between strong and weak prohibition measures in an effort to placate all their constituents.

While Iowans debated the prohibition issue and state Republicans enjoyed their newfound power, the nation entered its most cataclysmic period. Caught up in this national crisis while part of the state was still undergoing settlement, Iowans responded to Lincoln's call for troops, and most Iowans supported the Union cause. While the Civil War signaled major economic change for the state, social change was less consistent. Continuity characterized many social movements, including prohibition. In at least one area, however, that of black rights, Iowans repudiated their prewar stance. In 1868, perhaps responding to the national leadership of the Republican party, the Iowa General Assembly approved an amendment to strike out the word *white* from the state constitution—in effect granting suffrage to black men—and voters later approved the measure in a popular referendum. In the process Iowa became one of only two states in the 1860s to take such action. State officials also opened the public schools to black children as a result of three state supreme court decisions between 1868 and 1875. By 1880, moreover, black men had been given the right to serve in the state legislature.

After the Civil War Iowa continued to display progressive action in higher education. The University of Iowa, which had opened its doors in the decade before the Civil War, is recognized as the first state university to admit women. Iowa State College (now Iowa State University) held its first classes in 1869, also admitting women on an equal basis with men. Iowa had been one of the first states to take advantage of the Morrill Act, which granted land for the creation of a land-grant institution. Carrie Chapman Catt (then Carrie Lane) was a product of Iowa State's coeducational policy. Grinnell College (then Iowa College) was one of the first private coeducational schools in the country.

Reform efforts also affected the political sphere. At the turn of the century the Progressive Era influenced Iowans as well as other midwesterners. Republican governor Albert Cummins was especially influential in pushing through legislation to regulate railroads and lessen the railroads' influence in the state. Moreover, the Cummins administration successfully worked for a pure food and pure drug bill and a direct-primary law. Iowa's Progressive movement filtered down to the city level as well. In 1907 Des Moines changed its form of city government, initiating the Des Moines Plan, which eventually was adopted by several other cities.

While the Civil War only temporarily disrupted social development, it affected the state's economy in quite a different way, signaling the end of

Iowa's total domination by agriculture and the beginning of significant industrial development. Railroads served as the necessary prerequisite for this development. Railroad construction had started in eastern Iowa before the war, but not until 1870 did all four major railroad lines reach Iowa's western border. With year-round transportation assured, Iowans began to develop larger and greater numbers of industrial operations.

Coal mining serves as an excellent example of a major industry beholden to railroads for both its initial development and its continued well-being. As railroads expanded in the state, Iowans began to open coal mines to supply the railroads with fuel. By 1900 Iowa contained approximately four hundred underground mines, placing the state fifteenth in terms of national production. Iowa's coal industry remained fairly prosperous until the early 1920s, when the state's railroads began to buy coal out of state. The railroads had originally brought about the growth of the industry in the 1870s and 1880s, and their failure to support the industry in the 1920s led to its decline.

While Iowa's coal industry filled a major economic need, the mining industry also brought considerable social change in its effect on Iowa's ethnic composition. Before 1900 most Iowa coal miners had emigrated from the British Isles and Sweden, but after that date southern and eastern Europeans moved into the industry. Once an Italian or Croatian arrived, money was soon going back home to finance the trip of another family member or friend to the United States. Through this chain migration, many members of one European village ended up living in the same coal camp in central or southern Iowa. The result of the continual need for additional mine workers and the response of people in southern and eastern Europe was that Iowa contained at least a small number of Italians, Croatians, Hungarians, Austrians, Poles, and Russians.

Railroads also acted as an impetus to expansion in other areas. Shortly after the Civil War, meat-packing plants began to open in Iowa. In the 1870s John Morrell and Company located in Ottumwa, while Sinclair Meat Packing opened its doors in Cedar Rapids. In the western part of the state, Sioux City quickly became a major meat-packing center. In effect, Iowa's industrial development centered on its main activity of agriculture. Along with meat-packing, farm implement industries also appeared in several Iowa cities and Quaker Oats began production in Cedar Rapids. Through the years most industrial production has taken place in the eastern half of Iowa, which has the heaviest concentration of population.

After 1900 the state developed greater industrial diversity. In 1909 Frederick Maytag, apparently disappointed with other manufacturing pursuits, began producing washing machines. The company developed a number of innovations such as the seamless tub that quickly made its product the best-selling washer in the country. A short time later the Sheaffer Company began selling fountain pens. Another product that gained a national reputation was Amana refrigeration, first developed in the 1930s. Also in the depression years, Collins Radio began operations in Cedar Rapids, later being bought out by Rockwell International. A more recent development is Winnebago Industries, makers of recreational vehicles. Products from Iowa's factories, like products from Iowa's farms, soon earned a reputation for quality and dependability. Today, product names like Amana and Maytag are recognized around the world. Along with quality products, Iowa has also been recognized for a quality work force. A manufacturer who recently opened a small factory in eastern Iowa explained that he preferred to locate his business there rather than in a city like Chicago for two reasons: Iowans' willingness to work hard and their low rate of absenteeism.

Because of the relatively early development of industry in the state, Iowa has never been viewed as a hinterland, subservient to large cities in other states in the Middle West. Through innovation and quality production, and through the good fortune of having an extensive railroad system and a central location in the nation, Iowa has competed equally in some production areas and gained a reputation for excellence in others. Iowa seems to stand midway between the region's more industrialized states to the east and the region's agricultural states to the west.

THROUGHOUT THE NINETEENTH CENTURY as Iowans created churches and schools, fought a Civil War, and campaigned to close saloons, agriculture dominated the state, economically and politically. By the 1870s, after some thirty years of agricultural experience, Iowa's farmers had developed an agricultural pattern that would have long-term implications. Soon after the Civil War, state agriculturalists like "Tama Jim" Wilson urged Iowa farmers to diversify, planting a variety of crops rather than just wheat. By the seventies, given this advice and some experimentation, Iowa farmers concurred: they could raise corn and hogs more profitably than other crops. This view produced the corn-hog complex which, along with soybeans, still describes most Iowa agriculture today.

Even with some of the best soil in the world, however, Iowa farmers experienced difficult times between 1870 and 1900. For farmers who wished to expand, interest rates were high. Farmers, moreover, faced high transportation costs and low prices for their products. Like farmers in other parts of the Middle West, Iowa farmers blamed their troubles on the railroads and sought ways to curb the railroads' power. While some Iowa farmers registered their unhappiness in the 1870s by joining the Grange and forming the Anti-Monopoly party, overall Iowa's agriculturalists displayed little militancy and avoided joining the more radical farm organizations. Even in the 1880s, when the Greenback party selected Iowan James B. Weaver as its presidential candidate, Iowa farmers did not desert the Republican party in any appreciable numbers. In the 1890s, when Weaver again was selected as a presidential candidate, this time by the Populists, Iowa farmers tended to look the other way. Even though they were hard hit by the depression in the 1890s, the difficulties of Iowa farmers were considerably less than those suffered by farmers in the Great Plains or in the South. Iowa's farm people were able to blunt the harsh impact of the farm depression through their diversified farming practices. The advice given by "Tama Jim" Wilson and other Iowa agriculturalists in the 1870s had served the state well.

After 1900 and continuing through World War I, Iowa farmers, like their counterparts elsewhere in the nation, experienced the "golden years" of agriculture. Exports increased, prices rose, and during the war farmers received federal guarantees of fair prices. Many farmers expanded by purchasing land on credit. The future for agriculture looked bright, indeed, as farmers reflected on their recent prosperity. A nagging concern, however, was the "flight to the cities" whereby high numbers of people left the farm and headed toward urban areas, often outside Iowa. The 1910 federal census reflected this movement; the state's population was 7,082 less than it had been in 1900.

By the end of World War I the state had reached another major watershed. Before then, Protestantism, McGuffeyism, Republicanism, and prohibitionism had largely shaped and defined the state's predominantly rural social order. After 1918 these influences, particularly Republicanism, were still present, but they were more and more muted. The prosperity of the war years, moreover, quickly faded, placing agriculture among the nation's sick industries in the 1920s. A crisis of faith in rural life resulted, only to be followed by the Great Depression. The twenties, in effect, marked the end of the old order in which rural values and concerns dominated the state.

In the 1920s many of Iowa's rural residents seemed to have reservations about the advisability of remaining on the farm. While the ideas of agricultural superiority espoused by Thomas Jefferson were still widely accepted, on a more practical level farm people could see little cause for optimism. The prosperity of the war years had been short-lived and everywhere farm life was negatively compared with town and city life. *Wallaces' Farmer,* the Midwest's leading farm journal, ran advertisements galore proclaiming that farm people should rid themselves of the isolation, monotony, and dreariness of farm living by buying the modern products advertised in the journal. When farm people visited relatives and friends in nearby towns, they could not avoid contrasting their own unmodernized dwellings with town homes, often complete with electricity, indoor plumbing, and other comforts. Town residents, moreover, had a wide range of social activities to attend. To many farm people in the 1920s, farm life might be good, but it was not good enough.

Farm life in the 1920s was still labor intensive, with most members of the family working from dawn to dusk. The men certainly labored long and hard, but they had opportunities to socialize with neighboring farmers and to handle business matters in town. Farm women, tied down to caring for home, children, chickens, and garden, often had little time or opportunity to socialize with outsiders. The Country Life Commission had recognized this problem as early as 1909, urging farm people to develop more social outlets for farm women. The commission was particularly concerned because it recognized that if farm women were unhappy, they often urged their children to leave the farm and seek other work. One Iowa author, Herbert Quick, called the exodus to the cities a "woman problem" because of women's general unhappiness with farm life.

The 1930s brought greater difficulties for Iowa's farm economy, and for a brief time some Iowa farmers reacted militantly. They first took exception to a mandatory program of testing cattle for bovine tuberculosis, and that led to a brief encounter between farmers and state authorities known as the Cow War. The major outburst came a year later in northwest Iowa, where some farmers had joined the Farm Holiday Association. In responding to a high rate of mortgage foreclosures, farmers first tried a withholding action, urging everyone to keep agricultural products temporarily off the market in an effort to raise prices. When this tactic did not work, members resorted to another approach: interference with legal proceedings to stop foreclosures. The most dramatic incident took place in LeMars when farmers pulled Judge Charles Bradley from his courtroom and threatened to hang him if he did not stop issuing foreclosure notices. While the two actions produced little economic relief, they certainly foreshadowed a political revolt by Iowa's rural population. In November 1932 Iowans voted in large numbers for Franklin Roosevelt. As the temporary militancy of the 1930s indicates, Iowa's farm population has never displayed the same radicalism as farmers in the plains states. In effect, strong reaction has always been blunted by the fairly short-term nature of economic dislocations and the return of stable, consistent weather and production patterns. Although Iowa might produce a James B. Weaver, the typical quick return of "dependable agriculture" would soon lead the farming population back to their traditional political alignments and away from radical reaction and third-party candidates.

By the 1930s, even though economic dislocations had become more severe in some ways, the quality of farm life was improving, particularly for farm women. Of considerable importance were changes that made farm living more comfortable. Iowa's transportation officials began to gravel and hard surface more country roads so farm families could get to town more easily and even begin to take short vacations. The Cooperative Extension Service at Iowa State College, initiated in World War I, had become more and more visible throughout the Iowa countryside, providing farm women with both social outlets and information on how to improve the quality of rural life. Of great importance, farm families began to get electricity, made possible by passage of the Rural Electrification Act of 1935. One farm woman described the electricity as a wonderful fairy who came into her home and transformed her life. By the end of the 1930s, though the state had been through the most devastating depression in history, the quality of life for many rural Iowans had improved.

Even with the changes, however, the flight to the cities continued. Curtis Harnack, raised on a farm in northwest Iowa, wrote about his youth in *We Have All Gone Away*. The title captures a terrible contradiction in the Harnack family: farm life had served them well during their developing years, but when they reached maturity the city held out more promise. Harnack's mother, college-educated and a former teacher, frequently told her four children: "Farm life can kill you."[3] She sacrificed much to send her children to college so they might leave the farm far behind. Like countless other rural Iowans, Harnack speaks lovingly and nostalgically about his childhood on the farm, but he never entertained the idea of remaining there. In effect, *We Have All Gone Away* serves as a poignant testimony to Iowa's rural past. Like Harnack, many Iowans pay tribute to the moral and physical advantage of being reared on the land but look to the cities for a fuller social life and greater monetary rewards. The Cult of the Immediately Useful and Practical is still alive and well in the Hawkeye state.

World War II brought great prosperity to Iowa farm families, as it did to farm families throughout the nation. With greater profits, however, came expansion and greater debts. Until the late 1970s, even though there had been some dislocations, Iowa's farm population seemed secure. After all, with land prices rising rapidly, how could anyone go wrong by purchasing more land and enlarging one's operation? Nevertheless, by the early 1980s many things had gone awry and the farm economy had fallen on hard times. Perhaps the most visible evidence of changing times was the decline in farm units. In 1935, the peak year for farms in Iowa, the state contained 221,986 farm units. By 1985 the number had fallen to 115,000, even though almost 94 percent of the state was still under production.

Since World War II Iowa has become a state with a more visible urban population and more ethnic pluralism. Today the state has three cities with populations over 100,000 (Des Moines is close to 200,000) and a total population of 2,913,387. The cities symbolize Iowa's change from a state once totally dominated by agriculture to a state where industry now generates about three times as much revenue as agriculture. At the same time it should be stressed that Iowa is still a state filled with small towns. Since 1930 there has actually been an increase from 123 to 154 in towns with a population range of one thousand to twenty-five hundred. There has also been only a small decrease in towns of under one thousand population, from 713 in 1930 to 669 in 1980. In effect, Iowa's rural society has not been replaced, but rather must now share center stage with an ever-growing urban society.

Since the turn of the century, the number of minority groups has gradually been growing, with most minorities now residing in cities. Before World War I Iowa had a limited number of southern and eastern Europeans, most of whom worked in the coal mines. Around World War I Mexicans came to work in industries in the Quad Cities area and for the railroad in West Des Moines. Since World War II the number of Hispanics in Iowa has risen slowly. Responding to this increase, the General Assembly in 1978 created the Spanish

---

3. Curtis Harnack, *We Have All Gone Away* (Ames, Iowa, 1981), 129.

Speaking Peoples' Committee to provide an advocacy agency for the group. Moreover, in the 1970s Iowa became home to several thousand Southeast Asians. The population of blacks in Iowa has gradually increased, and today they number about 1.4 percent of the population.

In keeping with the trend toward urbanization, Iowa has become a state that can no longer be taken for granted by one political party. Republicans reasserted their domination in the later New Deal years and continued this domination into the 1950s. But by the end of the decade, the Democratic party had picked up considerable strength, particularly in the cities, and successfully challenged the Republicans for both state and national offices. One political scientist, Charles Wiggins, believes that as early as 1955 Iowa had become a two-party state. The reapportionment of Iowa's legislature in 1972 to conform with the "one man, one vote" principle brought rural and urban areas into better balance and in the process gave Iowa the most equitably apportioned legislature in the nation.

Even with considerable change, however, Iowa of the eighties retains characteristics of an earlier time. It is still possible to define Iowa as the middle land where rural and urban values blend together. More and more farmers have taken jobs in nearby cities and towns, often necessary not only to aid in supporting families but to avoid losing the land altogether. Iowans still are a remarkably homogeneous people in regard to cultural values. In keeping with its rural legacy, Iowa is still a state where kinship networks are greatly valued, where family ties are strong, where family members often settle close to one another, and where most social events revolve around members of the family. In small towns across the state, invitations to bridal showers are often printed in local newspapers; in other words, come one, come all. Iowa is still a state with numerous rural churches, many of which are attended by the third or fourth generation of the same families. Families gather to celebrate the rites of passage for the young, including baptisms, birthdays, graduations, confirmations, and marriages. In Iowa, like other parts of the Middle West, summer is filled with family reunions, some attracting two or three hundred people.

THROUGH THE YEARS Iowa has been a relatively stable state, with few upheavals or dramatic changes. Like its physical features, which are quite uniform, and its climate, which is fairly consistent, Iowans politically, socially, and economically have tended to display moderate qualities. Extremity in any form is usually not a fact of life in Iowa. There has rarely been either great wealth or great poverty. Moreover, Iowans have retained many traits first apparent in the nineteenth century. They still place great emphasis on quality education for their young people. In 1985–86, for example, nearly 55 percent of the state's budget went for education. Iowans are a people, moreover, who expect high moral conduct and the exercising of good, common sense on the part of their public officials. Iowa has always had a "squeaky clean" reputation concerning its public officials and state institutions and there is little reason to think that these practices will not continue.

At the same time, the state's rural legacy can have negative as well as positive connotations. For people who live here as well as away, Iowa often conjures up a rather bland image. On a recent popular comedy show, the main character announced that he was going to Des Moines on his vacation. After the looks of disbelief had passed from his associates' faces, one asked: "I hope you've had your shots." This implication that Iowa is in the middle of nowhere has long been apparent. Perhaps it rests partly on the fact that Iowa is indeed the middle land and therefore has no sharply distinguishing physical features. While Iowans themselves often perceive a beauty in the land, others may view it as a region of sameness. Perhaps the negative image rests partly on the state's rural character. Hamlin Garland's *Main Traveled Roads,* published in the 1890s, served as the first realistic portrayal of midwestern farm life. For some, this image remains firmly in place, portraying rural life as still devoid of cultural, economic, or social diversity.

These views of the state have naturally had an impact on Iowans as well as other Americans. Older Iowans seem to accept this situation in a rather stoic manner, but the state's young people are perhaps more vulnerable. Even today, when Iowa's young men and women repeatedly score at the very top of the standardized college entrance exams, they are often reticent about applying to the country's top educational institutions and pursuing the widest range of vocations. Surprisingly, with all its natural gifts, its high quality of life and its greatest resource—its well-educated, hard-working people—Iowa is still a place where some people tend to deprecate themselves and have less than a positive self-image.

As part of the Middle West, Iowa continues to share many similarities with other midwestern states. As something of a microcosm of the region, Iowa has characteristics—topographical, climatic, social, and political—of states located on all four sides. Perhaps once again Iowa is the transition zone between East and West. States to the east have undergone more social and economic change, while states to the west have retained more of their rural agricultural flavor.

Because of its location within the Middle West, Iowa really has two faces. One face looks to the East, responding to the industrial-urban world, tempted to move in that direction. At the same time, one face looks to the West, seeking to remain true to the agrarian past. The problem, of course, is that Iowa is neither totally one nor the other. As Iowa historian Joseph Wall correctly pointed out, each state must develop its own culture, because it cannot survive for long on one that is imported. Even with many similarities to other midwestern states, Iowa has clearly etched out a distinctive place for itself with its particular prairie environment, its reformist social nature, its political moderation, and its agrarian stability. Iowa remains the middle land.

BIBLIOGRAPHICAL NOTE

[This bibliographical note, unlike the notes following each of the essays in the remainder of this volume, was prepared by the author of the essay and published with the original essay.—Ed.]

A bibliographical survey on Iowa can be divided into three parts: general studies and reference guides, standard monographs published before 1970, and monographs published after 1970. Materials published in the state history journals *Iowa Journal of History* (discontinued in 1961), *Annals of Iowa*, and *Palimpsest* should also be acknowledged for their wealth of information on Iowa history, although articles from these journals are not included in this bibliography.

A number of general studies have been written on Iowa, including three multi-volume series. The oldest is Benjamin Gue's four-volume *History of Iowa* (New York, 1903). In the early thirties Edgar Harlan published the five-volume *Narrative History of the People of Iowa* (Chicago, 1931), and in 1952 William Petersen wrote a four-volume study, *A History of Iowa* (New York, 1952). Two recent single-volume histories are Leland Sage, *A History of Iowa* (Ames, Iowa, 1974), basically a political history, and Joseph Wall, *Iowa: A History* (New York, 1978), an interpretive essay written as a part of the bicentennial state history series. Dorothy Schwieder's *Patterns and Perspectives in Iowa History* (Ames, 1973) is a collection of articles dealing mainly with social and economic history. Two useful reference guides are William J. Petersen, *Iowa History Reference Guide* (Iowa City, 1942), and *Guide to Manuscripts* (Iowa City, 1978), a listing of holdings of the State Historical Society in Iowa City.

Older but still highly useful monographs include Earle Ross, *Iowa Agriculture* (Iowa City, 1951); Allan G. Bogue, *From Prairie to Cornbelt: Farming on the Illinois and Iowa Prairies in the Nineteenth Century* (Chicago, 1963); Louise R. Noun, *Strong-Minded Women: The Emergence of the Woman-Suffrage Movement in Iowa* (Ames, 1969); Donald Jackson, ed., *Black Hawk: An Autobiography* (Urbana, Ill., 1969); and Lewis Atherton, *Main Street on the Middle Border* (Bloomington, Ind., 1954).

Since 1970 there has been a significant increase in the number of books published in Iowa history. In keeping with trends in national historiography, many of these books deal with topics related to the new social history. A sampling include Clarence Andrews, *A Literary History of Iowa* (Iowa City, 1972); Elmer and Dorothy Schwieder, *A Peculiar People: Iowa's Old Order Amish* (Ames, 1975); James Larew, *A Party Reborn: The Democrats of Iowa, 1950–1974* (Iowa City, 1980); Hubert H. Wubben, *Civil War Iowa and the Copperhead Movement* (Ames, 1980); Glenda Riley, *Frontierswomen: The Iowa Experience* (Ames, 1981); Dorothy Schwieder, *Black Diamonds: Life and Work in Iowa's Coal Mining Communities, 1895–1925* (Ames, 1983); Diane L. Barthel, *Amana: From Pietist Sect to American Community* (Lincoln, Nebr., 1984); Curtis Harnack, *We Have All Gone Away*, the story of farm life in northwest Iowa in the 1940s (Garden City, N.Y., 1973); Curtis Harnack, *Gentlemen on the Prairie,* an account of English settlement in northwest Iowa in the 1870s (Ames, 1985); and Deborah Fink, *Open Country, Iowa: Rural Women, Tradition, and Change* (Albany, N.Y., 1986).

Recently initiated is the Henry A. Wallace Series on Agricultural History and Rural Studies with Richard Kirkendall serving as general editor. Two recent books in this series are Harold Lee, *Roswell Garst: A Biography* (Ames, 1984), and Alan I Marcus, *Agricultural Science and the Quest for Legitimacy: Farmers, Agricultural Colleges, and Experiment Stations, 1870–1890* (Ames, 1985).

2

"We Dance in Opposite Directions": Mesquakie (Fox) Separatism from the Sac and Fox Tribe*

MICHAEL D. GREEN

> Much confusion has long surrounded the identity of the groups of native peoples that make up what the federal government has called, since it made a treaty with them in 1804, the "united Sac and Fox tribe." Michael Green's essay is a remarkable clarification of that complicated issue. As he provides a clear, concise history of the Mesquakie tribe from its arrival in the Mississippi Valley in the late eighteenth century to the establishment of their settlement in Tama County in the mid-nineteenth century, he also offers a powerful interpretation of the emergence of "a strong and growing sense of Mesquakie 'nationalism'" that "finally asserted itself in the novel decision to purchase and live upon a separate land base."

AS ETHNOHISTORIANS continue their efforts to interpret Native American history, the issues raised by Robert F. Berkhofer, Jr., in his essay "The Political Context of a New Indian History," will become increasingly important to their analysis. Ethnohistorians will become more responsive to the evidence of political factionalism and they will discover in community political conflict a useful device for reaching a better, fuller and more precise understanding of the social and economic as well as political processes they are trying to explain. This

---

*"Mesquakie" has been used throughout this paper to refer to the Indians known by the United States as "Fox." It is the name they prefer. [In 1996 the preferred spelling is *Meskwaki*. — Ed.] In the hope of avoiding unnecessary confusion, however, the term "Fox" has been retained whenever it appears in government documents, as in "Sac and Fox Agency" or "Sac and Fox Tribe." I am indebted to Donald Wanatee of the Mesquakie Settlement for the title.

Reprinted by permission of Duke University Press from "'We Dance in Opposite Directions': Mesquakie (Fox) Separatism from the Sac and Fox Tribe," *Ethnohistory* 30, no. 2 (Spring 1983), 129–40. Copyright © 1983 by American Society for Ethnohistory.

is no easy task, particularly because among some tribal groups the problem of factional politics is complicated by the presence of several levels of identification and thus several conceptions of factional loyalty.[1]

In considering the Mesquakies, for example, historians have lagged far behind anthropologists and other scholars in their attempts to understand and document their history. Historians have tended to see the Sauks and Mesquakies (Sacs and Foxes) as one people and have assumed that the issues and events of Sauk history also controlled the Mesquakies. Black Hawk and Keokuk, Sauk leaders active in the early nineteenth century, have become well known figures in Sac and Fox history while contemporary Mesquakies such as Poweshiek, Wapello, and others have been forgotten. Were it not for the significant ethnographic work of such scholars as William Jones, Truman Michelson, the University of Chicago Fox Project, directed by Sol Tax, and the recent work by folklorist Fred McTaggart, the Mesquakies might have been overlooked altogether.[2]

Most historians have come late to the realization that the Sauks and Mesquakies had to be understood separately before any real sense could be made of their histories. My own previous studies and publications on "Sac and Fox factionalism" were done without appreciating the existence of what now seems to have been a strong and growing sense of Mesquakie "nationalism" during the nineteenth century. This feeling found expression in many ways, some of which are still being discovered. One of the most striking series of events which shows the determination of the Mesquakies to exercise their Mesquakiehood occurred in the 1840s and 1850s when they separated themselves from the Sauks physically and politically and began to buy land in central Iowa for a permanent Mesquakie settlement.[3]

In the spring of 1857, five Mesquakie men toured the Iowa River valley in central Iowa looking for a site on which to settle their families and friends. They represented eighty people who had wintered in camps on the Iowa and Cedar Rivers, and who eagerly awaited the news that a location had been

---

1. Robert F. Berkhofer, Jr., "The Political Context of a New Indian History," *Pacific Historical Review*, 40 (August 1971), 357–82.

2. William T. Hagan, *The Sac and Fox Indians* (Norman: University of Oklahoma Press, 1958); William Jones, *Fox Texts*, Publications of the American Ethnological Society (1907), vol. I; Jones, *Ethnography of the Fox Indians*, ed. M. W. Fisher, Bureau of American Ethnology Bulletin 125 (1939); Truman Michelson, *Fox Miscellany*, Bureau of American Ethnography Bulletin 114 (1936); Fred Gearing, Robert McC. Netting, and Lisa R. Peattie, eds., *Documentary History of the Fox Project, 1948–1960* (Chicago: University of Chicago Department of Anthropology, 1960); Fred McTaggart, *Wolf That I Am: In Search of the Red Earth People* (Boston: Houghton Mifflin Co., 1976). An excellent recent synthesis of Mesquakie ethnology is Charles Callender, "Fox," in Bruce G. Trigger, ed., *Northeast* (Washington: Smithsonian Institution, 1978), vol. 15 of *Handbook of North American Indians*, William C. Sturtevant, gen. ed.

3. Michael D. Green, "The Sac-Fox Annuity Crisis of 1840 in Iowa Territory," *Arizona and the West*, 16 (Summer 1974), 141–56.

found. The delegates knew the area well, and knew where they wanted to buy. David Butler, a farmer in Tama County, was willing to sell eighty acres of his Iowa River bottom land, and in July the deal was made. For $1,000 the settlers bought a home and a future for themselves, their friends in Kansas, and their children. There seemed to be no further doubt. Mesquakies would remain in Iowa forever.[4]

For generations Iowa had been an important part of the Mesquakies' world. By the end of the seventeenth century they probably were crossing the Mississippi from Wisconsin to hunt. As refugees from massacring French armies (which had reduced the free Mesquakie population to perhaps 100 people) they were offered protection by the Sauks. During the 1730s the two allied tribes sought safety in Iowa on the headwaters of the Wapsipinicon and Des Moines Rivers. By the 1740s they had returned to the Fox-Wisconsin waterway in central Wisconsin, but by the 1780s the two tribes had moved southwest and settled in the Mississippi valley. The Sauks concentrated on the east side, near the mouth of the Rock River. The Mesquakies, their numbers greatly enlarged by the repatriation of many prisoners held by tribes previously allied with the French, occupied townsites primarily west of the Mississippi.[5]

During the years they lived in the Mississippi valley, the Sauks and Mesquakies resided in substantial permanent towns surrounded by large and productive fields of corn, beans, and squash. They lived in these towns from April to October, with a short summer hunt in July, between the planting and harvesting seasons. Then, after the corn was gathered, they dispersed in small family groups for the long winter hunt, living sheltered from the weather in camps in the thick bottom groves along the interior rivers. In early spring they made maple sugar and then returned to their towns to plant, tend, and harvest their crops. This settlement pattern continued, with some relatively minor modifications, until the press of Anglo-American occupation displaced them.[6]

---

4. The 1857 purchase is described in "Council of Old Men at Ta ta pa shi's, 24 August 1905," Indian File, State Historical Society of Iowa, Iowa City [hereafter abbreviated as SHSI]; and Horace M. Rebok, *The Last of the Mus-qua-kies and the Indian Congress, 1898* (Dayton: W. R. Funk, 1900), 33–35.

5. There are many histories of Mesquakies in the seventeenth and eighteenth centuries, especially regarding their relations with the French. The best remains Louise Phelps Kellogg, "The Fox Indians during the French Regime," *Proceedings* of the State Historical Society of Wisconsin (1907), 142–88. A convenient synthesis is Zachary Gussow, "An Ethnological Report on the Historic Habitat of the Sauk, Fox, and Iowa Indians," in *Sac, Fox and Iowa Indians I* (New York: Garland Publishing Co., 1974), 121–84. See also Rebok, *Last Days of the Mus-qua-kies,* 18–20.

6. "Letter to Reverend Dr. Jedidiah Morse, by Major Morrell Marston, U.S.A., commanding at Fort Armstrong, Ill.; November, 1820," in Emma Helen Blair, *The Indian Tribes of the Upper Mississippi Valley and Region of the Great Lakes* (Cleveland: Arthur H. Clark Co., 1912), 2:148–53; "'Account of the Manners and Customs of the Sauk and Fox nations of Indians traditions.' A report on this subject, sent to General William Clark, Superintendent of Indian Affairs, by Thomas Forsyth, Indian agent for the U.S. Government; St. Louis, January 15, 1827," in *ibid.*, 2:233–34.

President Thomas Jefferson's administration vigorously pursued a policy of United States expansion into the Northwest. Between 1803 and 1809, United States commissioners concluded fifteen treaties of land cession with the tribes between the Great Lakes and the Ohio and Mississippi Rivers. William Henry Harrison, governor of Indiana Territory, personally negotiated twelve of them. The sixth negotiation, conducted in St. Louis during the fall of 1804, joined the United States for the first time in a treaty relationship with the Sauks and Mesquakies. Signed by four Sauks and no Mesquakies, the 1804 treaty ceded to the United States a tract of some fifty million acres located mostly between the Illinois and Mississippi and south of the Wisconsin River in present northwestern Illinois. In payment the Sauk signers accepted $2,234.50 down, an annuity of $1,000, $400 of which was to be given to the Mesquakies, and the promise that Sauk residence on the ceded tract could continue until the United States needed the country for its own people.

The significance of the treaty lies in its designation of the native signatories as representatives of the "united Sac and Fox tribe." Harrison, who apparently misunderstood the true character of the Sauk and Mesquakie friendship and alliance, assumed that the two tribes were in fact one. Harrison's mistake ignored the separate existence of Sauk and Mesquakie towns, the separate operation of Sauk and Mesquakie councils, and the separate conceptions of Sauk and Mesquakie identity. A seemingly innocuous error, the nomenclature of the 1804 treaty engraved forever on the official consciousness of the United States the false belief that the "united Sac and Fox tribe" existed.[7]

During the 1820s, Anglo-Americans began to occupy lead mining sites in northwestern Illinois and agricultural sites in the river valleys, including the valley of the Rock, the location of Saukenuk, the major Sauk town. Claiming their rights under the 1804 treaty, these settlers demanded that the United States remove the Sauks and put the country they continued to occupy up for sale. About 1829, many Sauks began to move across the Mississippi onto Mesquakie lands. They had decided not to resist the United States demands to evacuate the 1804 cession. These Sauks followed the advice of Keokuk, a politically ambitious and notoriously eloquent war leader. About 800 residents of Saukenuk refused to abandon their town. These people, mostly Sauks with a small number of Mesquakie and Kickapoo individuals, listened to Black Hawk, an aging Sauk war leader who believed the 1804 cession was invalid and unenforceable. In the spring of 1830, Black Hawk led his people home to Saukenuk from their winter hunt in Iowa. White settlers in the Rock valley resented the presence of these Indians, and during the months before they left to hunt in

---

7. Charles J. Kappler, comp., *Indian Affairs, Laws and Treaties* (Washington: Government Printing Office, 1904), 2:74–76. Mesquakie tradition is unequivocal on the question of their distinctiveness. "The Sacs and Foxes never had any Village together. They never remained together as one people." "Address of Pu Shi To Ne Kwa (1905)," Indian File, SHSI.

SAUK AND MESQUAKIE COUNTRY IN IOWA
Land Cessions Marked by Date

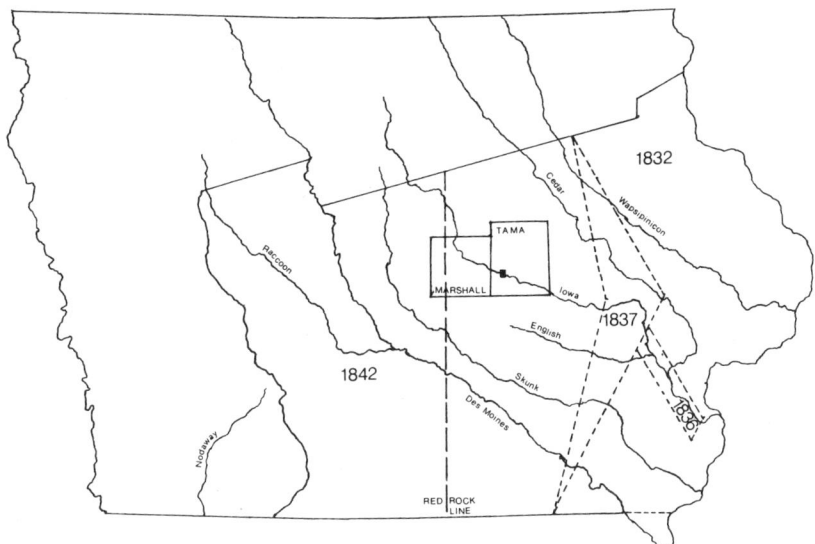

the fall there were several incidents. When the Sauks returned in 1831, the Army forced them to leave. Black Hawk led his people back to the Rock River valley in April 1832. The settlers panicked, Illinois governor John Reynolds mobilized the militia, and before long United States troops from St. Louis and the East Coast were on the scene. The whites called the battles they fought between May and August in Illinois and Wisconsin the Black Hawk War. When it was over the people of Black Hawk's band were dead, captured, or in hiding. Black Hawk, his two sons, and several of his advisors were captured and shipped off to prison.[8]

While the United States knew that the Sauks were divided and the Mesquakies were uninvolved in the Black Hawk War, the governor viewed them all as members of one "united tribe." Because they had failed to stop Black Hawk's band from crossing the Mississippi, they shared with him some responsibility for the war. Acting on this logic, General Winfield Scott dictated

---

8. The best short analysis of the Black Hawk War and its causes is Anthony F. C. Wallace, "Prelude to Disaster: The Course of Indian-White Relations Which Led to the Black Hawk War of 1832," in Ellen M. Whitney, ed., *The Black Hawk War of 1832* (Springfield: Illinois Historical Library, 1970), 1:1–51. For Black Hawk's interpretation of the war, see his *Autobiography*, ed. Donald Jackson (Urbana: University of Illinois Press, 1955). Mesquakie views on the Black Hawk War are in William Jones, "Notes on the Fox Indians," *Iowa Journal of History and Politics*, 10 (January 1912), 108–12; and "Address of Pu Shi To Ne Kwa (1905)," Indian File, SHSI.

a treaty of peace to the "Sac and Fox Tribe" which required them to cover the cost of the war with a cession of land on the west side of the Mississippi. The territory in question included the rich lead deposits known since the 1780s as "Dubuque's Mines" but owned and controlled by the Mesquakies. Whites had wanted the property for many years but the Mesquakie clan leaders had consistently ruled that only Mesquakies could mine and sell the lead. It could be no coincidence, therefore, that Scott forced the Mesquakies to pay for the Sauk war.

To ease the blow of such a heavy demand, Scott rewarded the "neutral" Sauks and Mesquakies by permitting them to keep a tract within the cession. This reserve, an area of ten by forty miles along the Iowa River, included most of the Mesquakie towns and fields as well as the new homes of the refugee "neutral" Sauks.[9]

Perhaps as galling to both tribes as this extorted cession, Scott also appointed Keokuk as head chief of the "Sac and Fox Tribe." Such presumption was shocking to many Sauks because Keokuk, a member of the Fox clan, was not of the proper lineage to be a civil chief. Scott's decision was an outrage to the Mesquakies. They had never considered themselves to be members of any "Sac and Fox Tribe." They were Mesquakies and they governed themselves in their own village councils. Scott's commission to Keokuk made the Mesquakies subject to his control. Never ones to tolerate strong leadership among themselves, the Mesquakies could scarcely accept the rule of a Sauk.[10]

Keokuk's tenure as head chief of the so-called Sac and Fox Tribe was as controversial as his appointment. There were many factors which complicated the politics of the two tribes, both internally and in their relations with each other, but certainly there were few questions as supercharged as the nature of Keokuk's leadership. There was, for example, a rapidly intensifying feeling of animosity among the Mesquakies toward the Sauks. This "jealousy" reflected the Mesquakie concern that their autonomy was threatened by the prominence of their Sauk guests. The continued insistence by the United States that the two tribes were halves of the "Confederated Tribe of the Sacs and Foxes" and the appointment of Keokuk as the head chief of this "tribe" convinced the Mesquakies that their rights as a separate people were being denied.[11]

---

9. Kappler, *Laws and Treaties,* 2:349–51; "Address of Pu Shi To Ne Kwa (1905)," Indian File, SHSI.

10. Winfield Scott and John Reynolds to William Clark, 22 September 1832, Office of Indian Affairs, Documents Relating to Ratified and Unratified Treaties, National Archives, Record Group 75, Microcopy T494, reel 2 [Hereafter cited as OIA:DRT]. For analyses of Mesquakie conceptions of authority and leadership, see Walter B. Miller, "Two Concepts of Authority," *American Anthropologist,* 57 (1955), 271–89; and Alexander Mamak, "The Traditional Authority Systems of the Sac and Fox Indians," *The Mankind Quarterly,* 10 (Jan.–Mar. 1970), 135–47.

11. John Beach to Thomas Harvey, 1 Sept. 1846, Senate Document 1, 29th Congress, 2nd Session (serial 493), 299. [My abbreviated citation for government documents, to be followed throughout, is SD 1, 29/2 (493), 299.]

Mesquakie anxiety reached a climax during the summer of 1841 when they began to hear rumors that the Sauks were bargaining with the United States to sell "a large body of their lands (or rather our lands) without either consulting us or advising us of the contemplated treaty, or giving us any opportunity of being present or having any agency in making said treaty." In an indignant letter of protest, ten Mesquakie leaders demanded an end to such outrageous Sauk behavior. "Previous to the Black Hawk War of 1832," they explained, "we the Foxes resided west of the Mississippi and owned the land in Iowa and the Sauks resided on the east side of the Mississippi. At the conclusion of that war at the treaty at Rock Island we consented that the Sauks should come over and reside among us. It was agreed between us that the Sauks should reside in the lower end of the Territory. . . . We the undersigned live at Poweshiek's village on the Iowa river where all the Foxes reside [and] those bands of Indians residing in the lower end of the Territory on the lower Des Moines do not alone constitute the Fox nation. . . . They have no right to sell any lands on the North East of the Desmoines without our consent." Indeed, they concluded, the Mesquakies held title to all the Iowa land, and they would "protest against the validity of any treaty which may be concluded without our agency."[12]

Village locations in Iowa tend to support this Mesquakie notion that Iowa was divided between themselves and their Sauk guests. Poweshiek's town was the largest in the two tribes, and the vast majority of the Mesquakies lived there. It was located on the Iowa River, moving further up the river with each successive cession. The Sauks, on the other hand, concentrated their towns on the Des Moines River, some 100 miles to the south. Wapello's Mesquakie town, located on the Des Moines after the 1836 cession of the Iowa valley reserve, was the only exception to this geographically separated pattern of settlement. But his was an unusual case because, though recognized as a Mesquakie chief, Wapello was born a Sauk and had only a small Mesquakie following. He had a reputation among the Mesquakies for being corrupt and deceitful, a man with strong supernatural powers who was to be feared.[13]

Simultaneously, a second conflict developed, but one which cut across tribal lines. The political rivalry between the two Sauks, Keokuk and Black Hawk, was as old as the War of 1812, and it precipitated a factional political struggle within the Sauk tribe which became a major concern during the 1830s

---

12. "Copy of a letter to Gov. Chambers, By Fox Indians," 30 Aug. 1841, Doc. 915, Folder 80, Antoine LeClaire Collection, Putnam Museum, Davenport, Iowa. Governor John Chambers tried to blame Mesquakie concern over separate negotiations with the Sauks (which he denied) on their traders whom, he claimed, misled the Mesquakies "for mischievous purposes." Chambers to T. Hartley Crawford, 13 Sept. 1841, Office of Indian Affairs, Letters Received, Sac and Fox Agency, National Archives, Record Group 75, Microcopy 234, roll 730. [Hereafter cited OIA:LR:SF.]

13. Donald Wanatee, Interview, 19 May 1976.

and early 1840s. Moving beyond the animosities of the Black Hawk War, the factions clashed over the payment of the annuities, the large sums of money paid each year by the United States to tribes which had previously sold lands. Government authorities usually preferred to pay the funds to the chiefs, partly because it was more convenient and partly because control of the tribal treasury frequently enhanced the power of the chiefs; and agents found dealing with a few powerful leaders easier than working with tribal councils. So, four "money chiefs" received the annual cash payment—Keokuk and Appanoose (Sauks) and Poweshiek and Wapello (Mesquakies).

There was great dissatisfaction within both tribes over the ways these chiefs spent the money. Among the Sauks, the nucleus of the "disaffected party" was composed of those loyal to the old Black Hawk faction, and augmented by others who resented General Scott's unnatural appointment of Keokuk to the leadership of the Sauks. Wishecomaque, or Hardfish, led the anti-Keokuk party. He was a member of the proper clan for civil leadership, the Sturgeon or Fish clan, and his father had been civil chief in the years before 1830 when Keokuk was just another Sauk warrior, distinguished only by his oratorical skills and a driving ambition. In a heated confrontation early in 1840, Hardfish charged that Keokuk had "been the Servant of my father you have received by his bounty the rank of Brave and Counsellor. But since his Death you have usurped my seat or at least you Pass for the head Chief of our Nation among the White people."[14]

Among the Mesquakies, opposition to the "money chiefs" was fed by the belief of the Black Bears that Poweshiek, a Brown Bear, had usurped the office of head chief back in 1830 when a Menominee and Sioux war party had massacred most of the Mesquakie council. At that time, the surviving councilors had appointed Poweshiek, on the recommendation of his sister, as a kind of temporary regent to act as civil chief until the proper Black Bear grew up. Poweshiek later refused to step aside, and he used his control over the annuity money to create a following. Indeed, all the "money chiefs" distributed the tribal wealth with an eye toward political advantage. Known friends of theirs enjoyed a higher credit limit at the traders' stores. Only the chiefs had unlimited charge accounts, of which they took full advantage, meaning that a disproportionate share of the tribal funds supported the lavish tastes of a few. Keokuk rode a $1,000 horse.

Finding that they could unite against their "money chiefs," dissatisfied Mesquakies and Sauks joined in complaints that they did not receive a fair share of the money and demanded that the entire sum be distributed on a per capita basis. The intensity of their anger disrupted the federal administrative

---

14. "A Memorial of an Indian Council Held at the Trading (Post) of W. Phelps the 19th of February 1840," OIA:LR:SF, roll 731.

apparatus in Iowa, caused bitter confrontations within the tribal councils, and in 1841 forced a change in government policy which temporarily removed the "money chiefs" from control over the payment.[15] Negotiations over additional land cessions in the 1830s and early 1840s occurred within the context of these bitter internal conflicts.

The Sauks and Mesquakies enjoyed less than fifteen years of legal residence in Iowa following the Black Hawk War. The economic promise of the lush agricultural land, ideal mill and town sites, and rich lead deposits proved enormously attractive, and settlers soon swarmed across the Mississippi. In the early years the white population grew geometrically, from 10,531 in 1836 to 23,242 in 1838 to 43,112 in 1840. Though far from filling up the Black Hawk Purchase, as the tract ceded by the Mesquakies in 1832 was called, these settlers pressed against its boundaries and demanded additional purchases of Indian land. Four times between 1835 and 1841 the two tribes met with government agents to discuss such sales. In 1836 they gladly parted with the 400 square mile "Keokuk's Reserve" on the eastern reaches of the Iowa River. That tract was already overrun with squatters. In 1837, a delegation of chiefs from both tribes, while visiting in Washington, agreed to cede the "Second Purchase," a 1.25 million acre tract west of the Black Hawk Purchase. Then, in 1840, the government began seriously to consider the complete removal of the two tribes from Iowa.[16]

There were talks during the fall of 1841, but they were broken off because the Indians were unwilling to part with all their Iowa lands and move northwest onto a stillborn "Indian Territory North" which the government hoped to develop. For the Sauks and Mesquakies, such a move would have put them in the front yard of their most bitter enemies, the Sioux, and there was no argument strong enough to overcome their unwillingness to do that. In addition, they did not

---

15. For more information on the rivalry between Keokuk and Black Hawk and the subsequent factionalism in the Sauk and Mesquakie tribes, see Alvin M. Josephy, *The Patriot Chiefs* (New York: Viking Press, 1961), ch. VII, "The Rivalry of Black Hawk and Keokuk;" P. Richard Metcalf, "Who Should Rule at Home? Native American Politics and Indian-White Relations," *Journal of American History*, 61 (December 1974), 651–65; Green, "Sac-Fox Annuity Crisis," 141–56; Donald Wanatee, Interview, 19 May 1976; George Davenport to Carey A. Harris, 14 September 1838, OIA:LR:SF, roll 730; "Address of Pu Shi To Ne Kwa (1905)," Indian File, SHSI. In "The Black Hawk–Keokuk Controversy," H. Glenn Jordan and Thomas M. Holm, eds., *Indian Leaders: Oklahoma's First Statesmen* (Oklahoma City: Oklahoma Historical Society, 1979), 64–78, Don Fixico based his erroneous interpretation of the rivalry between Black Hawk and Keokuk on the false belief that Keokuk was a Mesquakie rather than a Sauk.

16. The treaties of 1836 and 1837 are in Kappler, *Laws and Treaties,* 2:474–78 and 2:495–96. The population figures come from William J. Petersen, *The Story of Iowa: The Progress of an American State* (New York: Lewis Historical Publishing Co., 1952), 1:356. For greater detail on the negotiation of the treaties of 1836 and 1837, see Michael D. Green, "Indian Affairs in Iowa Territory, 1838–1846: The Removal of the Sacs and Foxes," unpub. MA thesis, University of Iowa, 1965, 40–63.

need the money; they had just received their first annuity payment in two years, a combined total of nearly $80,000.[17]

The talks in October, 1842, the fifth negotiation in a decade, produced a treaty of cession and removal. In return for a total consideration of over $1 million, the Sauks and Mesquakies ceded all their holdings in Iowa—the "New Purchase" of some 11 million acres. The agreement provided that they evacuate the eastern half of the cession, marked by the "Red Rock" line, by 1 May 1843. By 11 October 1845, three years after the date of signing, the two tribes were to remove entirely from Iowa. Their destination was to be a "permanent and perpetual residence" upon a "tract of land suitable and convenient for Indian purposes," to be assigned by the President "upon the Missouri river, or some of its waters." The site chosen for them was on the Osage River in east-central Kansas.

The government secured this treaty in 1842 only because the pressure on the Sauks and Mesquakies was too strong to be resisted. For several months the traders had been preparing the Indians with demands to pay their debts and with sharply reduced credit limits. Iowa Territory Governor John Chambers, chief United States negotiator at the treaty ground, exploited their poverty by authorizing $10,000 in bribes to be distributed to the Indian delegation, especially to the Mesquakies, who most bitterly opposed the cession. Sauk and Mesquakie leaders signed the document in an atmosphere of political distrust, tribal animosity, and potential economic catastrophe. It should come as no surprise, therefore, that large numbers of people denounced its terms, particularly among the Mesquakies, who considered themselves to be the rightful owners of the land.[18]

Mesquakies began almost immediately to violate the treaty. Most of their towns were east of the "Red Rock" boundary line, and they faced a major uprooting in the spring of 1843 when the eastern half of the cession was supposed to be vacated. They, along with the Sauks, located their new towns near the junction of the Raccoon and Des Moines Rivers. But the Mesquakies missed the good hunting in the English, Iowa, Cedar, and Wapsipinicon River valleys of eastern Iowa, and they visited that country during the winter of 1843–44. In response to complaints brought by settlers, Governor Chambers called on the Dragoons from Fort Des Moines to remove them. Captain James Allen, at the head of twenty-eight mounted troops, spent much of February, 1844, in performing this duty.[19]

---

17. "Minutes of a Treaty Council held at the Sac and Fox Indian Agency in the Territory of Iowa on the 15th day of October 1841," OIA:LR:SF, roll 731.

18. Green, "Sac-Fox Annuity Crisis," 154–56; Chambers to John Spencer, 13 October 1842, OIA:DRT, roll 4; Kappler, *Laws and Treaties*, 2:546–49.

19. Fort Des Moines Returns, February 1844, National Archives, Record Group 94, Microcopy 617, roll 307. Mesquakies also spent the winter of 1844–45 east of the "Red Rock" line. Beach to Chambers, 1 September 1845, SD 1, 29/1 (470), 483.

Eighteen months later, the prospect of another such meeting between Mesquakies and Dragoons seemed imminent. Sac and Fox Agent John Beach reported problems in preparing the Mesquakies for the long trek to eastern Kansas. "The Sauks, under the good management of Keokuk," were nearly ready to move. The Mesquakies, on the other hand, were "less satisfied with the idea of leaving the country . . . which, from long possession, they [love] naturally." While Beach hoped he had convinced them that there was no alternative to their withdrawal, he was far from certain that the emigration would go smoothly. Wetemah (Poweshiek's brother), Kawkawke (Crow), and Wolfskin, all influential Mesquakie leaders, were quite opposed to moving to Kansas with the Sauks. Poweshiek, due to a genuine change of mind or to Wetemah's influence, joined them in their hostility to the 1842 treaty which he had signed. There was talk in government circles that all four of them should be arrested and jailed in order to guarantee Mesquakie removal. Poweshiek tried to keep a foothold in Iowa by asking permission for the old and sick of his people to remain on the Des Moines over the winter. Agent Beach denied the request, however, and hinted that if the Mesquakies were not on the trail by 11 October he would ask the army to move them. When moving day arrived, Beach reported that all the 2200 Sauks and Mesquakies had left the agency and were heading west along the Raccoon.[20]

The Mesquakies did indeed leave the agency on schedule, but Beach erred in reporting that they were all headed west along the Raccoon. At least 200, and perhaps many more, had instead moved north along the Des Moines and the Skunk. On 10 December 1845, Lieutenant R. S. Granger carved a grim inscription in a rock on one of the high timbered bluffs overlooking the Des Moines River in Boone County, about fifty miles north of Fort Des Moines: "Found 200 Indians Hid On and Around This Mound They Cried, No Go! No Go! But We Took Them to Ft. D.[es Moines]." Throughout January and February, 1846, squads of Dragoons and a "four-mule government team" combed the Des Moines and Skunk valleys "hunting Indians, catching them every day and hauling them to Des Moines." The soldiers must have lost their Mesquakie captives nearly as quickly as they found them, however, as there were only 125 under the watchful eye of Lieutenant Patrick Noble when he and his twenty-five troopers set out early in March for Fort Leavenworth. The Mesquakies in Noble's company belonged to Wetemah's band, and when they reached Fort Leavenworth they immediately turned north, away from the newly established "Sac and Fox" Agency on the Osage River,

---

20. Beach to Harvey, 1 May 1946, OIA:LR:SF, roll 732; Chambers to Crawford, 4 June 1845, in "Letters of Governor John Chambers on Indian Affairs, 1845," *Iowa Journal of History and Politics,* 19 (April 1921), 261; Beach to Chambers, 1 Sept. 1845, SD 1, 29/1 (470), 484–86; Beach to Chambers, 18 Sept. 1845, OIA:LR:SF Emigration, roll 744; Beach to Chambers, 11 Oct. 1845, *ibid.*

and moved onto the reservation of the Kickapoos located in the northeastern corner of Kansas.[21]

By mid-1846, Agent Beach had to report that less than 250 of the total 1271 Mesquakies were on the Osage River reservation where they were supposed to be. Wetemah's band was with the Kickapoos and Poweshiek's band, numbering over 500, had never left Iowa. They were camped on the head waters of the Nodaway River, in the southwestern part of the state, in the country of the Potawatomies. Both bands were planting corn and by every sign showing their intention to remain where they were.[22] If the estimated numbers of Wetemah's and Poweshiek's bands were even remotely accurate, nearly 400 additional Mesquakies were eluding the troops. They probably could have been found living in isolated parts of central Iowa.

It would seem that there was little on the Osage River to attract the Mesquakies. In his first annual report following the removal from Iowa, Agent Beach described the relocated "Sac and Fox" agency as "pleasantly situated, moderately well timbered, with timber of excellent quality," and an "agreeably diverse" scenery. But, he went on, "spring water is scarce and stream water is deemed fatal to the health," and the rocky subsoil made digging wells extremely difficult. The place, he concluded, "has the reputation of being decidedly unhealthy."

Its reputation was well deserved. Epidemics of cholera swept through the Osage River reservation twice during the summer of 1849, carrying off a large but undetermined number of victims. During the next two summers, smallpox visited the reservation. Agent John R. Chenault originally estimated that 300 Indians died between May and September, 1851, but by October, 1852, he was "sure that mortality was higher. . . . A large additional number of deaths occurred among them during the past winter from pneumonia and other diseases." But Chenault, no diagnostician, still believed the country was healthy. The Sauks and Mesquakies sickened and died in large numbers, he explained, because they "expose themselves greatly during very inclement weather" while hunting. That, plus liquor, brought on the diseases.

In describing the slow development of farming among the Sauks, Beach reported in 1847 that the "soil is so much worse than in Iowa" that to produce

---

21. J. G. Lucas. "The March of the Dragoons," *Annals of Iowa,* 3rd series, 29 (Oct. 1945), 95; William N. Grier to R. B. Garnett, 13 Feb. 1846, OIA:LR:SF, roll 732; George M. Brooke to R. Jones, 23 Feb. 1846, *ibid.*; Ballinger Aydelotte, "The Great Indian Scare," in James B. Weaver (ed.), *Past and Present of Jasper County Iowa* (Indianapolis: B. F. Bowen and Co., 1912), 1:403; "Fort Des Moines, No. 2," *Annals of Iowa,* 3rd series, 4 (Oct. 1899), 175–76; Louise Barry, *The Beginnings of the West: Annals of the Kansas Gateway to the American West, 1540–1854* (Topeka: Kansas State Historical Society, 1972), 572.

22. Beach to Harvey, 11 May 1846, OIA:LR:SF, roll 732; Harvey to William Medill, 3 Feb. 1846, OIA:LR:SF Emigration, roll 744; Alexander Street to Beach, 30 April 1846, OIA:LR:SF, roll 732; Harvey to Medill, 6 July 1846, *ibid.*; Steven Watts Kearny to Harvey, 6 May 1846, *ibid.*

a comparable corn crop required "working extra hard." Hard work would not bring rain, and the people on the Osage River reservation labored through an "unparalleled drought" in 1850 which produced no corn and threatened the tribesmen with starvation.[23]

It was not only bad water, the threat of sickness, or sterile land that kept the Mesquakies away from the Osage River reservation. They stayed away, except for short visits to see friends and collect their share of the annuity, because it was the "Sac and Fox" reservation, and to live there was to continue to accept Sauk dominance. The Mesquakies had had enough of Keokuk, the Sauks, and the "united Sac and Fox tribe." In the spring of 1846, while his band remained in Potawatomie country, Poweshiek and fifteen Mesquakie headmen went to Fort Leavenworth to meet with Superintendent of Indian Affairs Thomas Harvey. The Indians told Harvey that their people had planted corn and intended to stay where they were, and asked for permission to go to Washington to see the President. Poweshiek said that the Mesquakies wanted to get presidential recognition as a separate tribe, with a separate home, separate annuities, and separate political leadership. They would not cross the Missouri and live with the Sauks. Harvey denied their requests. The Mesquakies could neither go to Washington nor separate themselves from the Sauks. The two tribes had been united by many treaties, he lectured, and it would be impossible to violate them. Also, they could not stay with the Potawatomies, as that tribe would soon have to remove.[24]

Many Mesquakies refused to accept the decision of the Indian Office. For the next ten years they adapted their traditional annual life cycle to fit a new set of needs, spending three, if not four, seasons in the river valleys of central Iowa. They simply transformed what had once been their winter hunting camps into summer farming communities. They spent the spring, summer, and fall on the rivers of Iowa, raising their crops. Some probably stayed in Iowa during the winter. Many, however, commuted to Kansas to wait out the cold and collect their annuity money.[25]

Between 1846 and 1852, there were sometimes as many as 1200 Indians camped along the Iowa River in central Iowa. In addition to Mesquakies, there were Potawatomies and Winnebagoes in fairly substantial numbers. The Mesquakies arrived on the Iowa about March, early enough to make maple sugar,

---

23. Beach to Harvey, 1 Sept. 1846, SD 1, 29/2 (493), 300; Beach to Harvey, 1 Sept. 1847, SD 1, 30/1 (503), 846; Barry, *Beginnings of the West*, 865, 1002; John R. Chenault to Luke Lea, 17 Feb. 1851, SD 1, 32/1 (613), 326; Chenault to Lea, 3 Oct. 1852, SD 1, 32/2 (658), 381; "Young Bear's Notes on Me-Skwa-Ki History, August 1905," Indian File, SHSI.

24. Harvey to Medill, 6 July 1846, OIA:LR:SF, roll 732.

25. Mary Ann (Ferrin) Davidson, "An Autobiography and Reminiscence," Iowa Department of History and Archives, Des Moines, 15 [published in *Annals of Iowa,* 3rd series, 37 (Spring 1964), 241–61]; Kearny to Harvey, 6 May 1846, OIA:LR:SF, roll 732.

and left after the fall harvest to go where "they could get provisions more plentifully." By the end of the 1840s Tama and Marshall Counties were organized and the settler population of the area had grown dense enough to be irritated by a sizeable gathering of Indians. The whites complained that the Indians destroyed timber, pulled up surveyor's stakes, and killed game. They were, in the eyes of the frontier farmers, a nuisance that should be removed. The government agreed. These Mesquakies, Potawatomies, and Winnebagoes were in central Iowa in violation of their treaties, and as "renegades" they should be sent to their reservations. In 1850, 1851, and 1852, mounted troops hunted through the Des Moines, Skunk, Iowa, and Cedar River valleys for the Indians. They captured many Mesquakies and sent them to Kansas. But it was impossible to catch them all, and Mesquakies continued to appear.[26]

Throughout these years of rootless hardship, the Mesquakies persisted in their efforts to win a recognition of separate status from the government. In 1848 Poweshiek requested, and the Kickapoos extended, permission for his band to live on their reservation north of Fort Leavenworth in northeastern Kansas. It was probably there that the Mesquakies who left Iowa during the winter months stayed. But Poweshiek's people still had to collect their annuity money at the "Sac and Fox" agency. This was inconvenient for them, and it kept alive the notion that they belonged there with the Sauks. At least as early as 1851, Poweshiek requested that the government pay the annuities belonging to his band at the Kickapoo reservation. This would have been more convenient for the Mesquakies, but more importantly, it would have forced the government to act on the assertion that they were distinct from the Sauks. Mesquakie identity was never threatened among the Kickapoos—the government had no preformed conception of a "Kickapoo and Mesquakie Tribe." For Poweshiek and his band, well over half the total Mesquakie population, this request was a continuation of the larger effort to force the United States to deal with them as an independent tribe.

The Indian Office refused to accede to the Mesquakies' wishes. Citing a number of reasons, ranging from the fear that by paying Poweshiek's band separately the government would be setting a precedent for other "splintering

---

26. There is an enormous body of evidence to document the presence of Mesquakies in Iowa between 1846 and 1852. Some select items are: Davidson, "Autobiography and Reminiscence;" Harvey to Medill, 5 Oct. 1847; OIA:LR:Council Bluffs Agency, roll 217; Joseph N. Cooper, "Some Early History," in William Battin and F. A. Moscrip, *Past and Present of Marshall County, Iowa* (Indianapolis: B. F. Bowen and Co., 1912), 1:72; J. E. Fletcher to Alexander Ramsey, 22 Sept. 1849, OIA:LR:Minnesota Superintendency, roll 428; Orlando Brown to Thomas Ewing, 30 Nov. 1849, SD 1, 31/1 (550), 949; William Williams, "History of Webster County, Iowa," *Annals of Iowa,* 7 (July 1869), 284–85; "Contract by Bvt. Maj. S. Woods, U.S.A. Army to A. D. Stephens," 1 June 1850, Iowa Department of History and Archives, Des Moines; Don Carlos Buell to Woods, 3 March 1851, OIA:LR:SF, roll 732; Lewis A. Armistead to Irvin McDowell, 20 Feb. 1852, and Endorsement by Bvt. Brig. Gen. N. S. Clarke, 11 March 1852, *ibid.,* roll 733.

of tribes" to the assertion that there was no good reason for the Mesquakies to be dissatisfied with the Osage River reservation, the government concluded that it would "violate the letter and the spirit of the treaties to presume the Sacs and Foxes are Split."[27] But split they were—separated by the Mesquakies self-image and the distance between Kansas and Iowa.

In early 1852 two citizen groups petitioned the state government of Iowa to permit the Mesquakies to remain within the state and purchase land for a permanent settlement. It is unclear just what motivated these settlers. Perhaps they felt sorry for the Mesquakies; perhaps they knew the Indians would do them no harm; and perhaps they wanted access to the Mesquakies' annuity money. There does seem to have been a deliberate policy on the part of the Mesquakie council to create a positive public image in the state, thereby to "prevent a recurrence of Federal interference. Friendly relations were at once established with every settlement within their reach and the most rigid discipline enforced to prevent depredations or disturbances by reckless members of the band. Prominent citizens were waited on and their good offices sought."[28]

Perhaps in partial response to this publicity blitz, the Iowa legislature enacted a law on 15 July 1856 which authorized the Mesquakies to purchase land in the state and requested the United States to pay their portion of the "Sac and Fox" annuity in Iowa.[29] The exact origins of this legislation are uncertain. Clearly, pro-Mesquakie public opinion was a factor. The newly forming Iowa Republican party, strongly anti-slavery, also seems to have taken a hand in the matter. Josiah Grinnell, Republican legislator and candidate for the United States Senate, wrote that the Mesquakies came to his attention during his 1856 campaign in the form of a charge that "he who would shelter black runaway slaves would favor the Indians, petitioning the state to remain here on their old hunting grounds." Alerted to the wishes of the Mesquakies, Grinnell recalled, "on investigation [I] became their friend." When some of his constituents brought him a petition calling upon the law makers to grant the Mesquakies the right to buy land, Grinnell supported it. Governor James

---

27. Ewing to David D. Mitchell, 11 Feb. 1852, OIA:LR:SF, roll 733; Chenault to Mitchell, 5 May 1852, *ibid.*; Mitchell to Lea, 8 May 1852, *ibid.*

28. Rebok, *Last Days of the Mus-Qua-Kies*, 33; "Marion Resolution," 5 Feb. 1852, and "Linn County Citizens' Petition," 1852, Indian File, SHSI. See also the "Safe Conduct" issued to "Maumewaleka and Waukemo" by James M. Berry, Judge of Linn County, Iowa, apparently in 1852 (Indian File, SHSI). Berry attests that these two Mesquakies are "honest and good disposed Indians" and gives them "permission with their band to pass through the country unmolested so long as they disturb no one — and also hope that the citizens generally will help them on the way by giving them provisions and all assistance possible to assist them on their way."

29. *Laws of Iowa*, 1856 (Extra Session), Ch. 30.

Grimes, the first Republican to hold that office in Iowa and an ardent enemy of slavery, also supported the Mesquakies.[30]

When the law passed, the Mesquakies found and bought the first parcel of their Tama County settlement. With the governors of Iowa serving as trustees, they ultimately purchased over 3000 acres of Iowa River bottom land. The United States refused to pay the annuity in Iowa, however, and for the next decade the Mesquakies went without. In increasingly desperate poverty the Mesquakies lived by hunting and begging, two occupations that annoyed their white neighbors. Tama and Marshall County citizens bombarded Washington with petitions begging relief; the Iowa legislature demanded action, Congressman Grinnell joined the struggle, and in 1866 Congress ordered the Indian Office to establish an agency at the Tama County settlement of the Mesquakies, appoint an agent, and pay their annuity money.[31] While this authorization did not explicitly recognize the Mesquakies, it did quite obviously recognize the existence of a distinct band of the "Sacs and Foxes" who were separated physically from the rest of the "united tribe."

For well over a century, the Sauk alliance was a major factor in Mesquakie affairs. Indeed, the Mesquakies probably owed their national existence to the willingness of the Sauks in the 1730s to take them in. But they never intended to trade their identity for survival. When, after the French defeat of 1760, Mesquakie numbers rebounded to the point where they could once again defend themselves, the Alliance became an equal partnership. The Mesquakies, at least, never thought of it as anything else. Thus they were unperturbed by the nomenclature of the 1804 treaty. Only in 1832, when General Scott anointed Keokuk as head chief, did the Mesquakies realize the true significance of the "united Sac and Fox tribe" and their position within it. Once discovered, they

---

30. Josiah Bushnell Grinnell, *Men and Events of Forty Years: Autobiographical Reminiscences of an Active Career from 1850 to 1890* (Boston: D. Lothrop Co., 1891), 275. The possibility that there is a connection between abolitionism and the Mesquakie settlement in Iowa gets additional support from the 1856 annual report of Commissioner of Indian Affairs George W. Manypenny. He devoted considerable attention to the "general disorder . . . in Kansas Territory." The "din and strife between the anti-slavery and pro-slavery parties . . . have united upon the soil of Kansas in wrong doing toward the Indians!" It had been impossible properly to settle and provide security for the tribes removed to Kansas, "and the pledges of this government that it should be to them and their posterity a permanent home forever" have not been fulfilled. "Their condition is critical, simply because their rights and interests seem thus far to have been entirely lost sight of and disregarded by their new neighbors." Manypenny to Robert McClelland, 22 Nov. 1856, SD 5, 35/3 (875), 572–73. It is conceivable that abolitionist leaders in Iowa, like Grimes and Grinnell, wanted to rescue the Mesquakies (Iowa's Indians) from the dangers of "Bleeding Kansas." I am indebted to L. Edward Purcell of Lexington, Kentucky, formerly Historical Editor, State Historical Society of Iowa, for suggesting such a connection.

31. Grinnell, *Men and Events of Forty Years,* 276; Rebok, *Last Days of the Mus-qua-kies,* 33–36; "Young Bear's Notes on Me-Skwa-Ki History, August 1905," Indian File, SHSI; "Council of Old Men at Ta ta pa shi's, 24 August 1905," Indian File, SHSI; Duren J. H. Ward, "Mesquakia," *Iowa Journal of History and Politics,* 4 (April 1906), 179–89.

spent fifteen years learning what to do about it. It was a period of great political conflict, of economic innovation, of dispossession, and of cultural and social confusion. But despite the reluctance of the United States to rectify Harrison's mistake, Mesquakie nationalism endured Sauk domination and finally asserted itself in the novel decision to purchase and live upon a separate land base. Thus the Mesquakies proclaimed their identity, and preserved it.

BIBLIOGRAPHICAL NOTE

With no Indian reservations within the boundaries of the state and few dramatic confrontations between the native peoples and European-American settlers, few professional historians in the past three decades have been attracted to the study of Iowa's native peoples other than Black Hawk, whose famous conflict with settlers and the federal government actually took place in Illinois. One book contains a pretty balanced variety of perspectives on Iowa's Indian tribes: Gretchen M. Bataille, David M. Gradwohl, and Charles L. P. Silet, eds. *The Worlds between Two Rivers: Perspectives on American Indians in Iowa* (Ames, 1978). An article drawing on recent literature that recognizes native peoples as active participants in the dynamics involved in the fur trade focused on several tribes who lived in the area that was to become Iowa: Thomas F. Schilz and Jodye L. D. Schilz, "Beads, Bangles, and Buffalo Robes: The Rise and Fall of the Indian Fur Trade along the Missouri and Des Moines Rivers, 1700–1820," *Annals of Iowa* 49 (1987), 5–25.

The so-called Black Hawk War is the subject of a popular, fictionalized account in Allan W. Eckert's The Winning of America series, *Twilight of Empire: A Narrative* (Boston, 1988). John E. Hallwas, "Black Hawk: A Reassessment," *Annals of Iowa* 45 (1981), 599–619, briefly reviews previous assessments of Black Hawk before adding his own. The most recent biography of Black Hawk is Roger L. Nichols, *Black Hawk and the Warrior's Path* (Arlington Heights, IL, 1992).

Not surprisingly, the Sauk and Mesquakie Indians have received the most attention. William Hagan's valuable tribal history, *The Sac and Fox Indians* (Norman, OK, 1958), is now nearly forty years old. A more recent, more narrowly focused account is Royce Delbert Kurtz, "Economic and Political History of the Sauk and Mesquakie: 1780s–1845" (Ph.D. diss., University of Iowa, 1986); see also his "Timber and Treaties: The Sauk and Mesquakie Decision to Sell Iowa Territory," *Forest and Conservation History* 35 (1991), 56–64. A unique and very interesting literary account of efforts to collect Mesquakie stories is Fred McTaggart, *Wolf That I Am: In Search of the Red Earth People* (Boston, 1976). Ronald A. Rayman wrote a brief account of the establishment of the Sac and Fox Indian Agency, "Joseph Montfort Street: Establishing the Sac and Fox Indian Agency in Iowa Territory, 1838–1840," *Annals of Iowa* 43 (1976), 261–74. For a fascinating account drawing on material culture evidence, see Ruth B. Phillips, "Clothed in Blessing: Meaning in Mesquakie Costume," *Annals of Iowa* 51 (1991), 1–25. See also Ginalie Swaim, "'Clothe Yourself in Fine Apparel': Mesquakie Costume in Word, Image, and Artifact," *Palimpsest* 72 (Summer 1991), 70–82; Gaylord Torrence, "A Mesquakie Drawing," *Palimpsest* 69 (Summer 1988), 64–68; and Gaylord Torrence and Robert Hobbs, *Art of the Red Earth People: The Mesquakie of Iowa* (Iowa City, 1989).

R. David Edmunds, *The Potawatomis: Keepers of the Fire* (Norman, OK, 1978), and James A. Clifton, *The Prairie People: Continuity and Change in Potawatomi Indian Culture, 1666–1965* (Lawrence, KS, 1977), are good accounts of a tribe with some Iowa experience. Ronald A. Rayman describes "The Winnebago Indian School Experiment in Iowa Territory, 1834–1848," *Annals of Iowa* 44 (1978), 359–87. The larger Winnebago experience in Iowa Territory in the 1830s and 1840s deserves more attention.

3

The Frontier in Process: Iowa's Trail Women as a Paradigm

GLENDA RILEY

European-American settlers began to arrive in Iowa even before the Mesquakie purchased their settlement in the 1850s, and the pioneer experience continued in northwestern Iowa into the 1890s. Unlike some other frontiers, the settlement of the Iowa frontier was a family experience, involving women and children as well as the much vaunted old settlers (primarily male) who were the focus of most traditional frontier history. In recent years scholars in women's history have been debating the extent to which frontier and later rural women were unwilling participants in this story—that is, oppressed victims of a patriarchal society—or heroic challengers of oppressive mores and standards. (Similar debates have occurred in Native American studies, labor history, and other areas of racial, ethnic, and class studies.) Before such debates could occur, women first had to make their appearance in historical narratives as active participants in the frontier experience. Glenda Riley was herself a pioneer in making that happen.

DURING THE NINETEENTH CENTURY the western portion of America exploded into an unbelievable multitude and variety of frontier regions. Some sprang up overnight while others disappeared overnight; most, however, were created gradually and peopled incrementally. In time, they usually prospered and became the stuff from which dreams were being shaped not only in the rest of the United States but throughout much of the world.

There was no neat line or pattern to these developments. Frontiers did not march across the western portion of the continent from the Ohio Valley to the Pacific Ocean. They appeared wherever there was land, gold, lumber, or some other asset that was attractive enough to draw people from their homes like a magnet. Neither was there any line where any particular frontier began.

Originally published as Glenda Riley, "The Frontier in Process: Iowa's Trail Women as a Paradigm," *Annals of Iowa* 46 (1982), 167–97. Copyright © 1982 by the State Historical Society of Iowa. Reprinted by permission of the publisher.

Signing a deed or pounding in a claim stake might mark a settler's arrival, but it did not mark the beginning of a settler's frontier. On the contrary, the pioneer's frontier experience actually began sometime during the transitional phase between the old and the new, the settled and the frontier, the East and the West.

That transitional link was the trail — the time spent and the space crossed by settlers in order to reach their chosen frontier. As they were traversing this link the pioneers were not living in suspended animation. They did not board their wagons in Vermont and descend a few hours later on the edge of a verdant prairie or a raw gold field as a modern jet traveler might. Rather, they invested many weeks or months as well as untold amounts of physical and psychic energy to get to the frontier region which promised them so much. The trail was not a pleasure trip, a joyride, or a vacation. It was difficult work for people to transport themselves from the known to the unknown. It was even more difficult for them to create the necessary metamorphosis in themselves which changed them from the settled into the settlers. In short, the trail was not just a prelude to a frontier which suddenly began when a river was crossed or an artificially drawn boundary line was reached. The trail was a kind of frontier in itself; a temporary frontier of a community in movement. The trail was a frontier in transit, a frontier in motion, a frontier in the process of becoming.[1] As a result, the trail experience was serious business because it was the first chapter of frontier life. What the migrants did, said, thought, and learned on this moving frontier helped shape the outcome of their own personal dramas.

Migrants had to apply their energies to four basic areas of endeavor while on the trail: 1) performing the chores connected with daily living, now with the duress of the trail environment added; 2) physically moving themselves to their promised land; 3) learning, practicing, and honing the skills that would spell survival in their new homes; and 4) reshaping their psychological mind-set from looking back to the East to looking forward to the West. Some were successful in these areas, others were less so. Some were enthusiastic about the venture, others were not. But for good or ill, once on the trail they were already part of the surging and demanding American frontier.

What did the rigors of this frontier in transit mean to women in particular? As casual observers and serious scholars tried to fathom the ways the trail affected the women who tackled it, a predominant generalization emerged. This image pictured a forlorn, beleaguered trail woman forced to leave her comfortable home by a dominant husband blind with wanderlust. Due to her supposedly inherent weakness and domestic nature she begged her husband at every opportunity to turn back east, she choked in the dust, she became weathered in the sun, and she continuously bemoaned her fate and that of her poor

---

1. Allan G. Bogue, "Social Theory and the Pioneer," *Agricultural History* 34 (January 1960): 24.

children in a primitive land.² Somehow this portrait, although widely accepted and certainly supported by actual cases of women who did suffer, does not ring quite true. Its generality, the inclusiveness of its terms, are themselves cause for suspicion. But how can it be tested when there were so many trails during so many eras heading for so many destinations? Clearly, it can only be tested, in a sense, trail by trail. If it is found wanting on even one trail then the mandate is evident: other trails during other times to other places must be examined more thoroughly and objectively as well.

In many ways, the Iowa-bound trail was typical of other frontier trails, especially those to family-farm frontiers. As such, the Iowa trail is a useful case study. It was an episode which began with early white squatters in Iowa's Half-Breed Tract in 1828 and had more or less vanished by 1870, the United States Census Bureau's official closing date for the Iowa frontier. Its travelers originated primarily in the farm areas of the Ohio Valley, then in the southern states, the middle states, the New England states, and other countries. Many came seeking a better climate, improved health, richer land, or a more promising future for their children. Others set out to escape inordinate taxation, the system of black slavery, or personal financial problems. Most migrated in extended family units which often included or were supplemented by both single men and women. And although there were no census-takers on the trail, later territorial and state census data indicated that most migrated to take up land and become farmers.³

From these factors several additional characteristics of the Iowa trail can be intuited. The abundance of families indicates a high proportion of women and children on the trail. The capital needed to make the trek, purchase seed and tools, and invest in land suggests that, despite popular belief, the very poor were not common among the migrants. And the fact that most migrants were

---

2. See for example John Faragher and Christine Stansell, "Women and Their Families on the Overland Trail to California and Oregon, 1842–1867," *Feminist Studies* 2 (1975): 150–166; John Faragher, *Women and Men on the Overland Trail* (New Haven: Yale University Press, 1979); Dorys C. Grover, "The Pioneer Women in Fact and Fiction," *Heritage of Kansas: A Journal of the Great Plains* 10 (Spring 1977): 35–44; Emerson Hough, *The Passing of the Frontier* (New Haven: Yale University Press, 1921), especially 93–94; Georgia Willis Read, "Women and Children on the Oregon-California Trail in the Gold Rush Years," *Missouri Historical Review* 34 (October 1944): 1–23; Lillian Schissel, "Women's Diaries on the Western Frontier," *American Studies* 18 (Spring 1977): 87–100; Page Smith, *Daughters of the Promised Land* (Boston: Little, Brown and Company, 1970), especially 223; Christine Stansell, "Women on the Great Plains, 1865–1890," *Women's Studies* 4 (1976): 87–98. For a discussion of images and their development see Glenda Riley, "Images of the Frontierswomen: Iowa as a Case Study," *Western Historical Quarterly* 3 (April 1977): 189–202; "Women in the West," *Journal of American Culture* 3 (Summer 1980): 311–329; and Beverly J. Stoeltje, "'A Helpmate for Man Indeed': The Image of the Frontier Woman," *Journal of American Folklore* 88 (January–March 1975): 25–41.

3. Allan G. Bogue, *From Prairie to Corn Belt: Farming on the Illinois and Iowa Prairies in the Nineteenth Century* (Chicago: Quadrangle Books, 1968), 22–33; Martin Ridge, "Why They Went West," *The American West* 1 (Summer 1964): 40–57; Iowa Census of 1880, 57, 168–170.

agrarian in background means that they already had some training in the skills they needed to make the westward move.

In other ways, the Iowa trail was less representative, particularly of overland routes to the Far West. Most Iowa-bound settlers were traveling over parts of the country which were comparatively well-settled, a situation which created a certain amount of ease for them in that they could occasionally buy supplies along the way and could sometimes stay at inns or campgrounds. References to fresh produce, friendly shopkeepers, and campgrounds established specifically for the covered wagon people abound in the diaries and letters of Iowa pioneers. This is not to argue that their time on the trail was easy, but there is little in their history or mythology to compare with the tragedy of those trapped for a winter at Donner Pass.

Because of the settled nature of the countryside through which they traveled, Iowa-bound migrants had relatively little to fear in the way of confrontations with Native Americans. Land treaties, President Andrew Jackson's removal policy, and outright genocide had essentially cleared the portion of the United States lying northeast of the Mississippi River of native populations. Indians valiantly resisting white encroachments did not play a notable role in the recounting of the Iowa trail saga.

Moreover, besides moving through populous countryside, these settlers were moving westward in a time period marked by increasing industrialization and technology which supplied them with a variety of modes of transportation. Legend to the contrary, the covered wagon was not the only alternative in existence in mid-nineteenth-century America. Given the media image of pioneers, it is rather startling to learn that many of them actually opted for other means of conveyance to the Iowa frontier.

Riverboats, for example, were one widely-used type of transportation. When the Harris family came to Iowa from Pennsylvania they chose to go virtually the entire way by river. A daughter wrote that the boats carried them "first down the Allegheny to Pittsburgh; thence down the Ohio River on the steamboat, 'the Diadem,' to Cairo; thence on the 'New England' up the Mississippi to Keokuk." She commented that although they traveled in deck passage to economize, they remembered it as a speedy and enjoyable trip, often made pleasurable by the company and song of other passengers.[4]

Rail routes were another possibility. Leaving New Hampshire in 1855, the Motts chose a rail route all the way to the Iowa line. They began their journey going by railroad first to Boston then on to Niagara Falls where they crossed the suspension bridge into Canada. They continued on the railway until the end of the line on the Mississippi River across from Dubuque. On the last lap of the trip they took a steamboat to Lansing in northeastern Iowa and

---

4. Joanna Harris Haines, "Seventy Years in Iowa," ed. Frank Herriott, *Annals of Iowa* 27 (October 1945): 98.

finally engaged stage passage to Decorah, their final destination.⁵ In 1858, the Newtons tried a slightly different combination. They began their trip with a stagecoach ride from their Connecticut home to Fair Haven where they boarded a steamboat to New York. There they boarded "the cars" for Chicago and after visiting the city for a few days, they again boarded the cars for Davenport. They then rode to the end of the rail line in Louisa County, Iowa, where they hired a driver and team to transport them to their new home in Keokuk County.⁶

As the various steamboat and railroad companies increased their services, improved their facilities, and multiplied their routes, more settlers selected them as a quick and easy means of moving to Iowa. But despite these attractions, both the boats and "cars" had some serious disadvantages. Space limitations curtailed the settler's needs and desires to move household goods, farm implements, seed, stock, and even clothing. Because such goods were more in demand and thus more expensive in Iowa than back East, the unequipped settler could expect some difficulty in obtaining goods as well as some expense in paying for them. In addition, boat and rail fares were expensive and were often prohibitive if more than two or three members of the family were making the trip.

In the face of these drawbacks, the overwhelming majority of Iowa's pioneers elected to use covered wagons. Although they had the deserved reputation of being slow and awkward, their unwieldy bulk accommodated family members, goods, equipment, and animals. The journey would take considerably longer than it would by boat or rail, but the migrants would enjoy the initial advantage of having their belongings, seed, and stock with them in a territory with little surplus. And, if necessary, the prairie schooner, as it was known, could even become a temporary home for the settlers when the trail finally came to a welcome end.

ALTHOUGH they did not express it overtly, most pioneers recognized the trail as the beginning of the frontier. Realizing the magnitude of their undertaking they focused their mental and physical efforts on each minute detail of the trip ahead. They already knew from emigrants' guides, word-of-mouth, and personal accounts that any small oversight or lack of attention to a petty detail could make the difference between success and failure, between survival and destruction. So family members worked on the necessary preparations as a team, but like any effective team they divided the labor according to the skills of the individuals involved. This of course meant a traditional division of labor. Because of their long experience with machinery and stock the men took responsibility for the wagon and its team. The women, on the other hand, worked

---

5. Abbie Mott Benedict, "My Early Days in Iowa," *Annals of Iowa* 17 (July 1930): 331.

6. Edith H. Hurlbutt, "Pioneer Experiences in Keokuk County, 1858–1874," *Iowa Journal of History* 52 (October 1954): 327–328.

long and hard to prepare the needed clothing, bedding, kitchenware, and foodstuffs for the trip.

In practice, however, the division was not this clear. Men and women helped each other whenever possible, overlapped duties, and shared tasks. In the case of the wagon the men usually made the final selection. They chose from two basic types: the large Conestoga wagon which was approximately fifteen feet long, five feet wide, and five feet deep or the smaller, lighter Emigrant wagon which measured about ten feet in length, four feet in width, and two feet in depth.[7] Their choice was based on how much they wanted to carry and how fast they wanted to travel. In either style they looked for a sturdy, well-constructed box which would not shake apart on some desolate stretch of trail. Once the wagon was selected, the men were expected to equip it with running gear as well as to find and train suitable animals to haul it and its contents hundreds of miles through sun, dust, rain, mud, and snow.

At this point the women took over for the final segment of the wagon consisted of the cloth top, the production of which was assigned to the women of the family due to their familiarity with fabrics and their sewing skills. This was a long-term and difficult job since the top was frequently stitched by hand. In planning a wagon cover for one of their journeys, Kitturah Belknap explained that she would "make a muslin cover for the wagon as we will have a double cover so we can keep warm and dry; put the muslin on first and then the heavy linen one for strength. They both have to be sewed real good and strong and I have to spin the thread and sew all those long seams with my fingers." According to Belknap, time and expertise by the woman or women were the two essential ingredients needed to produce a roof which would successfully shelter the travelers from inclement weather during their long westward journey.[8]

While the production of the cover was progressing, women, aided by the men and children, were also giving much thought to the equipping of the wagon box. The degree of thoughtfulness and efficiency expended on this task could also spell disaster or success for the migrants. A family's entire future had to be assembled and packed in that limited space. This meant that every item they owned or purchased had to be critically examined in terms of its potential usefulness on the Iowa frontier. Equipment had to include all the clothing, food, cooking utensils, bedding, medicines, and tools that might be necessary to sustain family and animals along the trail as well as seed, farm implements, and furniture to carry them through the beginning phases of establishing a homestead.

---

7. B. J. Zenor, "By Covered Wagon to the Promised Land," *The American West* 11 (July 1974): 32–33.

8. Kitturah Penton Belknap, "Reminiscences," Iowa State Historical Department, Division of the State Historical Society, Iowa City, Iowa.

Although equipping the box was a chore involving both men and women, there was still something of a division of labor along customary lines. The men usually readied items such as firearms, tools, and furniture. They also utilized every possible space on the outside of the wagon box to hang buckets of grease to be used for the axles, barrels of water for the stock, and spare parts for the wagon. Then they busied themselves training the team that was to pull the wagon as well as preparing the family's other stock for the long journey ahead. At the same time women took the primary responsibility for items of food, clothing, and medicine which they began to prepare well in advance of the day of departure. Kitturah Belknap left a detailed account of her preparations which consumed all her spare moments during an entire winter.

> I have to make a feather tick for my bed . . . the linen is ready to go to work on, and six two bushel bags all ready to sew up . . . have cut out two pair of pants for George . . . I have worked almost day and night this winter, having the sewing about all done but a coat and vest for George. Will wash and begin to pack and start with some old clothes on and when we can't wear them any longer will leave them on the road.[9]

With the experience of one other migration behind her, Belknap knew what would be needed so despite her exhaustion and ill health she also dipped enough candles to last a year; prepared a complete medicine chest; packed home-sewn sacks with flour, corn meal, dried fruits, and other foodstuffs; assembled dishes and cooking pots; and cooked enough food to last the first week. Her final preparation was to put together a work-basket of sewing so that she wouldn't have to spend any idle moments during the trip. Meanwhile her husband, George, built an ingenious camp table, practiced with the oxen he had selected to draw their wagon, and readied the other stock for travel.

Belknap was delighted with the camp table since it perfectly complemented the ambience she was determined to maintain on the trail. She had already decided to start off with "good earthen dishes" although she was realistic enough to bring tin dishes as a back-up in case the earthen ones were broken. She also had made "four nice little table cloths." With these accoutrements, she declared that she was "going to live just like I was at home."[10]

This cooperative venture between men and women in readying themselves, their families, and their goods for the trail resulted in a fully loaded prairie schooner which must have been an impressive sight. It has been estimated that they ranged from 1500 to 2000 pounds, not counting the additional weight of their human passengers.[11] Many had an assortment of farm animals tied to the back end or dangling in crates tied to the sides.

---

9. Ibid.
10. Ibid.
11. Zenor, "By Covered Wagon," 37.

Moreover, many men and women worked together to incorporate individualized refinements depending on their own needs and inventiveness. The Belknaps prepared a secure spot for Kitturah's rocking chair so that she could ride comfortably while sewing. They also arranged a miniscule play corner for their young son and devised a clever folding bed which would allow them to sleep in the relative comfort of their wagon. The Shuteses arranged their wagon to accommodate Ann Shutes and her infant at night. A common practice, which soon became an accepted part of trail lore, was sewing canvas pouches to the inside of the wagon cover. Catherine Haun found their "pockets" invaluable for small items which needed to be kept in easy reach such as cooking knives, firearms, and toilet articles.[12]

Those people who chose a smaller wagon usually had a shorter distance to cover, but they too were experts at utilizing every possible inch of space. Mary Moore McLaughlin described her family's wagon as "a low, long-coupled, straight-box, two-horse wagon, made roomy and comfortable by an extension of the wagon bed over the wheels." Although it was relatively limited in size, it was crammed with many items, including some things that were apparently family treasures. McLaughlin especially remembered "mother's little cane seated rocker, our family pictures and books, one bureau, and a jar of honey." Like most other families, the Moores made every effort to create additional space. They hooked a small table upside down on top of the feed box at the back of the wagon to hold "the cooking utensils, the dinner box, the stove rack used for campfire cooking, and two splint-bottom chairs." When it was unhooked it quickly converted into a convenient and comfortable dining area.[13] These various refinements and additions seem to indicate that some effort was made to provide at least a minimal amount of comfort while on the trail.

Of course, the physical provisions for the journey were only a part of the settlers' total preparations. They also had to begin the process of psychological separation from their families, friends, and neighbors long before they actually began bending the trail grass. The trauma of parting cannot be overemphasized. Unlike modern society where the average person moves many times in his or her life, most nineteenth-century people were accustomed to being part of a region, a town, a neighborhood, and a kinship network. These people shared value systems, social life, customs, and traditions. They shared the joy and the tragedy of births, weddings, and deaths. They called upon each other for help in times of crisis. And they gathered together to pray or to celebrate a holiday.

There is little actual evidence that this emotionally wrenching process was any harder on women than on men. Again, popular myth to the contrary, both men and women seemed to share the pain. Granted, it was more socially ac-

---

12. Belknap, "Reminiscences"; Mary Alice Shutes, Diary, Iowa State Historical Department, Division of Historical Museum and Archives, Des Moines, Iowa; Catherine Margaret Haun, "A Woman's Trip Across the Plains," Huntington Library, San Marino, California.

13. Katharine Horack, "In Quest of a Prairie Home," *The Palimpsest* 5 (July 1924): 252–253.

ceptable for women to show it than for men; so while Hiram Shutes stole away from his family for a secret farewell with his mother, Kitturah Belknap could openly refuse to attend a last church service because of her emotional state.[14]

A family's decision to leave was not only traumatic for them, but also for those who would be left behind. An announcement of impending departure thus initiated a transition period during which both the soon-to-be pioneers and those remaining at home attempted to adjust to the idea of separation. The rituals recognizing the coming separation included dinners, dances, family visits, and special church services, all designed to wrap the migrants in a warm cloak of good wishes and friendship of the people they had known for so many years.

Defying their brave attempts to invest the break with a festive air, the morning of the actual departure usually presented a heartrending scene. In the murky early morning light, people gathered around the migrants to help them load their wagon, to serve them breakfast, to grasp their hands one last time, and to wish them luck in the new country. Sleepy-eyed Mary Alice Shutes peered through the dim light of a predawn bonfire to discover that a great number of relatives and friends had come to see her family off and to cook breakfast as a "final display and effort of friendship." She sensed the strain in the air: "The younger kids know something unusual is going on but don't understand it like the older folks do. . . . Some of the older ones seem to welcome the solitude away from the fire. . . . they have said their goodbyes and are just waiting." Although she sympathized she did not really understand. From her perspective as a thirteen year old, she was thinking more of the excitement of the "good lark ahead of us" than of those to be left behind.[15]

It was a common practice for some friends to ride along with the migrants and their wagons for the first few miles in an extended goodbye ceremony. But as the outskirts were reached, these riders gradually dropped back and returned home, leaving the wayfarers to begin their expedition. As they waved one last farewell to their friends and to the life they had known, the pioneers finally confronted the trail which would transform them into frontierspeople.

SCARY, EXCITING, INTIMIDATING, PROMISING — these and many other words must have flowed through the travelers' minds as they assessed the scene unfolding before them. Their trepidation may have been allayed somewhat by the fact that they did not lack for company in their trek towards Iowa. One observer went so far as to portray Iowa migration as a mass movement. As early as 1836 he claimed:

> The roads were literally lined with the long blue wagons of the emigrants slowly wending their way over the broad prairies — the cattle and hogs, men and dogs, and frequently women and children, forming the rear of the

---

14. Shutes, Diary, and Belknap, "Reminiscences."

15. Shutes, Diary.

van—often ten, twenty, and thirty wagons in company. Ask them, when and where you would, their destination was the "Black Hawk Purchase."[16]

The huge, distended wagons forced their iron-covered wheels into the earthen trail leaving tracks that were reinforced by thousands of wearying footsteps of both people and animals. By the time the migrants converged on Iowa, the marks of their passage were clearly etched on the prairie. Recalling her family's move in the 1860s, McLaughlin later wrote, "I can see now the two tracks of the road, cut deep by the wagon wheels and washed out by the rains."[17] These tracks became a kind of map for those who followed as well as a testimonial to those who had already completed the demanding journey.

Whenever they had the opportunity, migrants would join with another group to swap information, to exchange bits of trail lore, or to travel together for as long as their routes coincided. McLaughlin remembered that at times they traveled alone, but when possible they joined with other "movers." She remarked that they "were always glad to have company, especially when fording swollen streams, for then we could double up teams and take turns in making the crossing." Her explanation of gregariousness on the trail was perhaps too simplistic. Joining with others, comparing points of origin as well as destinations, and making new friends was at once a tie with a past filled with friends, an attempt to maintain identity in a world which reduced everyone to a common denominator, and practice for a future which would demand the establishment of many new contacts. Hiram Shutes, as a case in point, was enthusiastic as well as touched when he met someone from his home region or someone who planned to settle in the same area of Iowa as his family.[18]

Some migrants, perhaps anticipating the anonymity and anomy of the trail, traveled in groups. When the Willises announced their intention to relocate in Iowa they were surprised and pleased to learn that "most of the immediate relatives soon sold their homes, loaded their goods into wagons, and started for Iowa" with them. They traveled as a group helping each other whenever they could by "fording streams, wading through mud, and enduring untold hardships" together. The Harris family put together a very similar kind of caravan. Numbering ten people, they moved along in two huge covered wagons pulled by yokes of oxen as well as in a two-seated buggy pulled by a team of horses.[19]

What neither of these chroniclers articulated was the hedge the family caravan formed against the onset of loneliness, the disintegration of family unity, and the often stark aspects of the moving frontier. Furthermore, neither they nor many other Iowa women writers specifically discussed why they had

---

16. Quoted in Bruce E. Mahan, "The Iowa Pioneers," *The Palimpsest* 49 (July 1968): 247.
17. Horack, "In Quest of a Prairie Home," 254.
18. Ibid.; Shutes, Diary.
19. Bessie L. Lyon, "Grandmother's Story," *The Palimpsest* 5 (January 1924): 4; Haines, "Seventy Years in Iowa," 103–104.

placed themselves in such a threatening, albeit potentially fulfilling, situation. Of the few that even mentioned motivation, Mary Ann Ferrin stated that she "was fond of adventure and preferred to go with my husband." Similarly, McLaughlin said that her mother liked to move: "father always said that whenever he wanted to move he had only to tell mother of his plans and she was ready and willing to go."[20]

According to the traditional image, however, a woman was simply an appendage to the males of the family; her husband, father, or brother made the decision for her and in the proper manner of a "True Woman" of the nineteenth century she accepted that decision. This stereotype of the female migrant as an appendage of the male migrant even clouds attempts to understand the motivation of the unmarried woman, that is, the female migrant who made the decision to move on her own rather than in conjunction with other family members, especially male family members. It has generally been assumed that the unmarried female relocated only to *become* an appendage; in other words, she moved west to marry one of the surplus male settlers already in Iowa.

Such thinking obviously reflected a society in which all women were expected to marry and in which the preponderance of women actually did marry. Despite the emergent feminist movement of the 1840s, marriage was still seen by most Americans as the only appropriate be-all and end-all of a young woman's life. It is not surprising then, that many young women capitalized on the population imbalances in Iowa to further their own marital careers.

Regardless of the stereotyped thinking of the era about women, many ambitious single women did head for the Iowa frontier as laborers, missionaries, and teachers. Catharine Beecher in particular encouraged groups of women teachers to choose western careers, because she saw employment opportunities for them and because she regarded women as civilizing influences necessary to a new society. In addition, some unmarried women moved, as did men, to take up land although the data on them are incomplete at best and impressionistic at worst. Unfortunately, curiosity butts its head against Newhall's 1846 guide to Iowa which listed only the occupation of dairy maid as a possible job for a woman, against gazetteers and almanacs that reflect women primarily as seamstresses and dressmakers, or worse yet, against Iowa census reports that sometimes categorized women as "not gainfully employed."[21]

If assessing the motives of the single woman is difficult, the task of unearthing the motives of married women (or women otherwise part of a family unit) is nearly impossible. Because they were dependent members of these family units, their part in the decision-making process was usually obscured

---

20. Mary Ann Ferrin Davidson, "An Autobiography and a Reminiscence," *Annals of Iowa* 37 (Spring 1964): 245; Horack, "In Quest of a Prairie Home," 250.

21. Kathryn Kish Sklar, *Catharine Beecher: A Study in American Domesticity* (New York: W. W. Norton & Company, Inc., 1976), 97–98, 102; John B. Newhall, *A Glimpse of Iowa in 1846; or, the Emigrant's Guide* (Iowa City: State Historical Society, 1957), 61.

by the aggregate family decision. As a result, some rather tenuous suppositions have been formulated. One of these argues that many women had no motivation beyond obeying or pleasing their husbands. Another holds that since income production was the husband/father's ascribed duty in nineteenth-century society, he made the decision as to how and where that income would be produced and the rest of the family had to acquiesce.[22]

Certainly, nineteenth-century society cast men in the role of breadwinners, initiators, and decision-makers, but Iowa women's manuscript sources do not uphold a theory of repression towards them. Rather, women in family units ran the gamut from acceptance of, identification with, or support of, to initiation of the idea of settling on the Iowa frontier. As these women touched upon their feelings about migrating to Iowa the emotion which most often surfaced was one of optimism rather than bitterness. And like men, they too were sensitive to the pushes and pulls which caused their friends, neighbors, relatives, and ultimately themselves to decide to uproot their ties, their lives, and their families. These pushes and pulls, after all, tended to be oblivious of gender. Women were not dumb and blind; they could see worn out lands, the poor health of a family member, or the richness of the West as well as men could.

WHATEVER THEIR INITIAL MOTIVATIONS, Iowa women tended to respond to the demands of the trail with hard work, generally buoyant spirits, and relatively few complaints. In the four basic areas of enterprise necessitated by the moving frontier they usually made sincere, and often highly successful, attempts to achieve and even excel.

The first area, the performance of all the regular chores connected with daily living, was not only time-consuming for women (whether at home or on the trail), but it was made even more troublesome by the primitive conditions of the trail. To the credit of most trail women, they cared for the needs of their families in as homelike an aura as they could create during the time the wagon was their only home and the trail their only backyard.

One of the easier problems for them to resolve was their families' sleeping arrangements. The wagon presented itself as an obvious "bedroom" and many of the wayfarers took advantage of its minimal protection. The Titus party was delighted to find that its two wagons "were roomy enough for all," but they did not remark on the comfort or the space provided by their accommodations. Most groups found that all members would not fit into the wagons so they turned them over to the most needy members: the aged, the ill, the small children, or the women with infants. The Harrises developed another alternative;

---

22. See for example Faragher and Stansell, "Women and Their Families on the Overland Trail," 153 and Stansell, "Women on the Great Plains," 90. For a different view, see Julie Roy Jeffrey, *Frontier Women: The Trans-Mississippi West, 1840–1880* (New York: Hill and Wang, 1979), 32–34.

whenever they could locate a tavern they boarded the women of the party there while the men slept nearby in the wagons.[23] Others utilized tents, deserted houses, or simply slept outside, using a variety of quilts, feather ticks, or corn husk mattresses to shield them from the chill air and the unrelentingly hard ground.

Most campers combined a night watch with an all-night fire to protect their camp. Shutes mentioned that "the men folks arranged about turns for night watch to watch the stock and keep the fire going as a warning for intruders to keep away." Later in her diary she reported that they had a "nice campfire going to keep wild animals away — mostly the small kind." The eerie shadows created by the flickering fire combined with the noises of a wilderness night must have provided a strange and frightening backdrop for the travelers. Recalling the night she spent in the wagon as a small child, McLaughlin vividly remembered that, "as the twilight settled into darkness, the wolves came slinking around the camp; and while they howled we children snuggled closer together in our beds in the wagon box, begging father to build the fire higher."[24]

Occasionally, some travelers were fortunate enough to be afforded shelter for a night by a friendly family who still remembered its own trek west. For Kitturah Belknap one instance of such hospitality was particularly welcome. The Belknap party crossed an eighteen-mile stretch of prairie in the freezing snow during which Kitturah drove the team so her husband could herd the stock. "I thought my hands and nose would freeze," she related. "When I got to the fire it made me so sick I almost fainted." Luckily, they were taken in by a family of eight people living in a tiny, isolated cabin. Belknap thawed out her frozen provisions for dinner and then, sick with a toothache, she bedded down on the floor with the other five members of her party. They arose at four a.m. in order to eat breakfast without disrupting their hosts and set off for more miles of snow-covered prairie somewhat refreshed by the brief interval spent indoors.[25]

The Shuteses' situation was not nearly so desperate when they met with a hospitable family who had come to Iowa in the 1840s and had been helping migrants ever since. The Shuteses had just been chased out of a deserted log cabin by what the children called "striped kitties," but which were more correctly identified by their father as skunks. After their close escape, they were happy to spend a night in the host family's barn and to be treated to a breakfast of buckwheat cakes, fresh side pork, and coffee. Mary Alice was especially pleased with the meal because "you could eat your fill with no smokey taste."[26]

---

23. Lydia Arnold Titus, "From New York to Iowa," ed. Bruce E. Mahan, *The Palimpsest* 2 (October 1921): 319; Haines, "Seventy Years in Iowa," 104.

24. Shutes, Diary; Horack, "In Quest of a Prairie Home," 254.

25. Belknap, "Reminiscences."

26. Shutes, Diary.

Mary Alice's observation regarding the breakfast highlights the fact that women had a much harder time feeding their families than they did figuring out where they would sleep. Women tackled the arduous job of meal preparation by developing a trail-craft, the ingenuity of which rivaled the woods-craft or plains-craft of their male counterparts. Using reflector ovens, prairie stoves, or just campfires, they concocted meals which ranged from adequate to wonderfully unforgettable.

Lydia Titus was particularly adept at campfire cooking. She "fried home-cured ham or bacon with eggs" while she "boiled potatoes or roasted them in the hot ashes." The Lacey family settled for a cold lunch from a big barrel that Sarah had packed with suitable provisions, but at night she insisted upon cooking them all a hot meal over a campfire. She prided herself on always offering them "meat or eggs and a warm vegetable for all, as well as pie or cake." McLaughlin recalled a homey scene focusing on prairie chicken: ". . . father would bring water, build a fire and take down the little green table and splint-bottom chairs from the back of the wagon, while mother prepared the meal. We were at home on the prairie with prairie chicken for supper!"[27]

Another woman's diary referred to cooking over an open fire, cooking in the rain, and cooking food on Sunday to be eaten during the first part of the following week. One Sunday her project of fixing beans was interrupted by a sudden rain shower. "Wasn't it a shame!" she lamented. "Mine were almost done when a shower came up and drove me into the wagon. The beans taking advantage of my absence burned up. Nothing was left for me but to cook more." Like many trail women, she augmented her cooking facilities with whatever resources came to hand. At one camp spot she made biscuits after obtaining permission to bake them in a nearby house and at another she prepared eggs on a borrowed campstove.[28]

As the migrants neared Iowa, the task of food preparation became more difficult due to decreasing fuel supplies. The prairies did not readily yield wood for their fires so the pioneers often had to purchase wood just as they did food. When wood was totally unavailable, they twisted hay, prairie grass, or slough grass into "cats." This created an extra job for the women and children who had to spend hours in producing fuel by collecting and twisting the hay or grass, but it was perhaps more agreeable than the other widely employed option of collecting dried animal excrement, euphemistically called cow-chips or buffalo-chips, for use as fuel.[29]

---

27. Titus, "From New York to Iowa," 319; E. May Lacey Crowder, "Pioneer Life in Palo Alto County," *Iowa Journal of History and Politics* 46 (April 1948): 162; Horack, "In Quest of a Prairie Home," 254.

28. Jane Augusta Gould, Diary, Iowa State Historical Department, Division of the State Historical Society, Iowa City, Iowa.

29. Robert L. Munkres, "Wives, Mothers, Daughters: Women's Life on the Road West," *Annals of Wyoming* 42 (October 1970): 198.

Another problem of the prairie region, limited water supplies, made it increasingly difficult for the women to effectively wash the clothing and bedding of the party. When the rain barrels were full, when a farmhouse with a well was located, or when a stream was reached, the women and girls seized the opportunity to refresh garments dirtied and worn by traveling in heat and dust. Gould's note regarding clothes washing was typical. "At four p.m. I commenced and did a real large washing—spreading the clothes on the grass at sunset." At a later point in her diary she expressed shock because, while they were "laying over because it was the Sabbath," she discovered that "the women were doing up their week's washing!"[30]

Gould's observation offers a critical insight into women's work on the trail: their tasks were often out of pace with the rhythm of other trail work. Rest periods for the men and younger children, such as meal stops or evenings, were the very times women began their chores. Then, of course, to complicate matters even more there was the ever-present task of childcare. Any attempt to determine the proportion of children on the trail is thwarted once again by the lack of census data regarding the trail experience. Although their actual numbers remain a matter of conjecture, mention of their existence is liberally scattered throughout women's sources.[31] Moreover, there is little indication that anyone thought it unusual for children to make the demanding trip, even at very tender ages.

The story of Lydia Titus is fairly representative. In 1869, when she and her husband resolved to make Iowa their new home, her young sister and her husband announced that they were going along. Both couples sold their farms and stock, "keeping only a wagon apiece and four horses," to transport themselves and their children. Lydia had an eight-year-old daughter, a three-year-old son, and a ten-month-old girl while her sister had a six-week-old baby girl, yet neither woman visualized moving such young children as an extraordinary undertaking. They soon learned that they were not alone in their decision. There were many others, such as the Archers, who with four wagons were moving nineteen people; thirteen were children between the ages of two and the early twenties.[32]

For trail women, the problem of physically protecting the children was in all probability the most distressing aspect of childcare on the trail. Despite their constant vigilance, children often got too far off to the side of the road or lagged too far behind the train, causing their parents more than a few anxious moments. Furthermore, the possibility of accident, illness, and disease

---

30. Gould, Diary.

31. Faragher and Stansell, "Women and Their Families on the Overland Trail," 156; see Read, "Women and Children on the Oregon-California Trail," for a discussion of the number of women and children on the Overland Trail.

32. Titus, "From New York to Iowa," 318–319; Margaret E. Archer Murray, "Memoir of the William Archer Family," *Annals of Iowa* 39 (Fall 1968): 369.

constantly hovered over them. Although they carried some medicines, they knew that the services of a doctor would be virtually unobtainable in case of serious trouble. Elisha Brooks always remembered the starkness of the situation when illness hit him and the other children of his party. "A picture lingers in my memory," he said, "of us children all lying in a row on the ground in our tent, somewhere in Iowa, stricken with the measles, while six inches of snow covered all the ground and the trees were brilliant with icicles." Similarly, Shutes recorded the terror she faced when sleepy young Archie bounced off the wagon and barely escaped having his head crushed by the wagon wheel. "Am sure luck is with us," she sighed with relief upon finding out that Archie was dazed but otherwise uninjured.[33]

Evidently, the migrants themselves did not see these hazards as much greater than those of their former lives for they persisted in undertaking the trip with babies and children. In some cases, optimism offset the threat of adversity. One couple traveling with two infants was described as "young and full of hope and made light of the hardship." In other cases, a spirit of necessity prevailed. As "Grandmother" Brown summed it up, "then I never thought about its being hard. I was used to things being hard."[34]

THESE MANY TASKS, demanding enough in themselves, were aggravated by the fact that women were also expected to help in the second area, that of physically moving the group to the new land area. When the caravan was on the move women were not relieved of duties. Childcare naturally continued, but women also contributed to what were generally male tasks such as driving the team and herding the stock. Haun called it lending "a helping hand." She explained that, "the latter service was expected of us all—men and women alike." Belknap, for instance, frequently took over the lines and drove the team to free her husband to tend the unruly stock. And Lyon's mother routinely drove the wagon part of each day so that her husband could stretch his legs by walking behind it. When their wagon became mired in mud, she even mounted their horse and, with "the baby in her arms" and her small son astride behind her, guided the horse in rescuing the wagon.[35]

Women also engaged in the battle against sun scorched prairies, biting snow storms, mud sloughs, and wide streams and rivers. The latter could often be forded or ferried across with comparative ease, but in some cases their depth or flooded condition due to a recent storm presented a great barrier to settlers, their wagons, and their animals. This resulted in some classic tales of groups

---

33. Quoted in Ruth Barnes Moynihan, "Children and Young People on the Overland Trail," *The Western Historical Quarterly* 6 (July 1975): 292; Shutes, Diary.

34. Crowder, "Pioneer Life in Palo Alto County," 156; Harriet Connor Brown, *Grandmother Brown's Hundred Years, 1827–1927* (Boston: Little, Brown and Company, 1929), 103.

35. Haun, "A Woman's Trip Across the Plains"; Belknap, "Reminiscences"; Lyon, "Grandmother's Story," 4–5.

pushing ahead with the help of their women. In 1832, for example, Caroline Phelps and her husband were stymied by flooded Sugar Creek which they finally crossed by swimming on horseback and floating on driftwood. In the process, Phelps, who already suffered an eye swollen shut by an infection, was knocked down and kicked in the forehead by a frightened horse. She roused herself sufficiently to pick up her baby and get them both across the creek, after which the men of the party brought their wagon across in pieces. Her comment on the affair demonstrated her vigor: "we had a good supper and a good bed . . . the next morning I was quite refreshed."[36]

Even if they escaped these kinds of perils, all of the Iowa-bound migrants had to confront the Mississippi River. Throughout most of the pioneer period, railroads and highways alike ended abruptly on the east bank leaving the settlers to traverse the river by boat or ferry. Bridges across the Mississippi were not constructed until the late 1860s due to the bitter opposition of steamboat companies and ferry operators so, in spite of steadily improving technology, settlers had to deal with this impediment to their progress.

For most people, crossing was a time-consuming but interesting event. When the Shuteses reached the Mississippi, they learned they had just missed a bad flood which had prevented crossings of any kind for several weeks. "Not just too much water," they were informed, "but too much trash and big trees that would smash anything in their way." Fortuitously, Hiram had been advised to arrive ahead of his party and get their name "in the pot" for a place on the ferry so they had to wait less than a day. When they left their camp spot and approached the ferry, they were quickly caught up in the excitement of throngs of people, escalating noise levels, animated talk of high water, and piercing blasts from the whistle of the steam-powered ferry. As they gradually edged up the loading plank, the men took responsibility for the wagons, the children led the blindfolded horses, and the mother shepherded the small children. Once out upon the swirling waters, Shutes felt that her mother had "the real job sitting on a chair holding the baby and Howard."[37]

For some women, the crossing was not this easy. In the mid-1860s a lone woman who had already managed moving herself and four children under age eleven to join her husband in Iowa, was appalled to learn that cracking ice on the Mississippi River prevented teams from transporting any more settlers over it that winter. She was told that she would have to wait until the ice cleared and the ferries began to run again. Faced with four exhausted children and a diminished cash reserve, she decided to join a few others who were walking to Iowa over the groaning ice floes. She picked up the baby, distributed the luggage among the older children, and set out. Her daughter later recounted their perilous crossing:

---

36. Caroline Phelps, Diary, Iowa State Historical Department, Division of the State Historical Society, Iowa City, Iowa.

37. Shutes, Diary.

> I can see yet, as in a dream, that great expanse of gray ice. Even then it was cracking, and as we went on there was a low grinding sound . . . we were constantly warned not to crowd together or we would break through. Mother who, with all her burdens, was clipping along with the rest would call out cheering and encouraging me to come along. I don't think she had realized how wide the river was, how far the distant shore.

When asked what had given her the courage to keep going across the splitting ice, she replied, "I was thinking of your father and all he had been writing about you children growing up in Iowa."[38]

Obviously, time on the trail was far from dull for most women; neither was it uninstructive. As they carried out their chores and helped with the other trail work they were concomitantly developing themselves in the third area—the sharpening of the skills that would serve them so well both on the moving frontier and in their new homes. Since they were predominantly farm women in origin they were not naive about what would be required of them; food processing, cooking, spinning, weaving, and a myriad of other skills were already in most of their repertoires. Yet, on the trail, they demonstrated creativity, and at times pure genius, in the way they adapted them to the conditions at hand.

Kitturah Belknap was a perfect illustration. Using a Dutch oven, a skillet, a teakettle, and a coffeepot, she devised meals which were just like "at home." These regularly featured her salt-rising bread which she worked at in between her other chores.

> When we camped I made rising and set it on the warm ground and it would be up about midnight. I'd get up and put it to sponge and in the morning the first thing I did was to mix the dough and put it in the oven and by the time we had breakfast it would be ready to bake. Then we had nice coals and by the time I got things washed up and packed up and the horses were ready the bread would be done and we would go on our way rejoicing.

Butter for the bread was not a problem for Belknap either. When the cows were milked at night, she strained the milk into little buckets which were covered and set on the ground under the wagon. In the morning she skimmed off the cream, put it in the churn in the wagon, and after riding all day she had "a nice role of butter." Kitturah further supplemented their meals with foodstuffs bought along the way. She would keep her eye out for a farmhouse where she might purchase a head of cabbage, potatoes, eggs, or other fresh foods. She soon became trailwise: "where there were farms old enough to raise anything to spare, they were glad to exchange their produce for a few dimes."[39]

Despite the prevalence of this kind of grit, there were some women who never did make it in the last area—changing their mind-set from eastern in orientation to western. Some of these, regretting their decision or finding

---

38. Francis E. Whitely, "Across the Mississippi," *The Palimpsest* 15 (January 1934): 13–15.
39. Belknap, "Reminiscences."

themselves unable to cope with the demands of migration, voluntarily turned back. Like every society, the trail had a certain number of misfits, but these were not only women for some men also decided to terminate the venture. As one woman pointed out, "some liked the new country, but others . . . returned to their native States."[40]

Some scholars have argued that the work which women performed and the mental anguish they endured on the trail was not repaid by a bond of inclusion in what was essentially a male-directed undertaking. They have claimed that in consequence women soon became alienated and disheartened by the migration experience.[41] If Iowa women experienced these feelings, they generally avoided recording them. Perhaps they realized that any domestic routines they could recreate, any assistance they could offer, and any supportive feelings they could extend were all necessary to the preservation of their families and themselves under the duress of migration. Most seemed to understand that their tasks, whether in material or psychological realms, were absolutely essential in subduing the trail and getting their families to the promised land.

For the most part, they seemed at least to keep open minds toward both the frontier in transit and the frontier in Iowa. More often than complaint, Iowa trail women expressed a sense of equanimity. This was apparent in Gould's remark that it was "decidedly cool camping out and cooking by a campfire, but we must do as we can." It was also reflected in Shutes's statement that "we have a lot of weary miles behind us. Glad to have done it but would not care to do it over again, or very soon anyway." Furthermore, the harshness of the trail environment was often leavened by a spirit of fun. Singing, dancing, and good-natured courting were frequently part of the scene as the settlers moved closer to their new homes. The following diary notation was not uncommon: "I hear the merry notes of a violin. A general cheerfulness prevails."[42]

Had these women been totally hardened and bitter, they could not have been as awed and as pleased as they were by the prairie country which gradually enveloped them. One exulted that "the prairies were just one great flower garden." Another remembered how her family learned to love the open prairie as they traveled across its broad expanse. Another emphasized that she could not adequately describe "the magnificence of the wild flowers that made the prairies for miles in all directions one gorgeous mass of variant beauty." And yet another called it "a perfect garden of Eden."[43]

---

40. Titus, "From New York to Iowa," 315.
41. Faragher and Stansell, "Women and Their Families on the Overland Trail," 160; Stansell, "Women on the Great Plains," 87–90.
42. Gould, Diary; Shutes, Diary; Gould, Diary.
43. Cowles, *Early Algona*, 123; Horack, "In Quest of a Prairie Home," 253; Haines, "Seventy Years in Iowa," 104; Mrs. E. A. Hadley, Journal, Iowa State Historical Department, Division of the State Historical Society, Iowa City, Iowa.

It appears then, that in challenging the trail, many Iowa-bound women also challenged the nineteenth-century stereotype that women were weak, emotionally insecure, and capable of existing only within the confines of a home tucked away from the realities of a harsh world. Although the westward journey broke and embittered some women, so many emerged from it intact or even strengthened that it is unconscionable to generalize any longer. Many trail women were strong because, in reality, life for most nineteenth-century American women was difficult in spite of their location. As one woman put it, her parents survived the crude conditions of the road because "their early lives had been spent amid such surroundings."[44] That their lives were *not* easy, or even satisfactory at home, was the very reason that most people were on the trail. It was tough, but at least it offered the hope of increased rewards for their deprivation and toil.

MANY OF THESE TRAIL WOMEN not only survived the trail, but they went on to settle the Iowa frontier, to live to tell about it, and often to recount many happy times as well. And a great number became trail women again in their life, this time tackling the overland route to the Far West. Kitturah Belknap, Lucy Cooke, E. Allene Dunham, Eliza Ann Egbert, Catherine Haun, and Virginia Ivins were only a few of the Iowa women who eventually went on to cross the Plains in order to pioneer the Far West just as they had pioneered Iowa. And on the overland route, as on the trail to Iowa, they recorded positive impressions of their trek.

As one might expect from previous descriptions of Kitturah Belknap, her mettle and spunk survived the long route to Oregon in 1848. She prided herself on having the only dinner table in the train with a cloth on it, she industriously sewed and mended in her spare moments, and she became an adept trader with farmers, emigrants, and Indians in order to supplement their food supply. Although she noted the fear aroused by the presence of Indians and Mormons, a quarrel in the next wagon caused by a husband's refusal to give in to his wife's demands to turn around, and her son's serious illness, her own spirits remained high. Thus, her description of the journey was sprinkled with comments such as: "the road is good and I am standing the riding fine," "it is a fine spring morning," "have had fine weather, good roads and all have been well," and "I have washed and ironed and cooked up a lot; find our appetites improve the longer we are out."[45]

A similar mood emanates from the trail letters of Lucy Cooke, a young mother with a year-old baby who emigrated to California with her husband and his parents in 1852. Her mother-in-law's lamentations about the trip, frequent outbreaks of cholera, and the rigorous mountain crossings failed to

---

44. Crowder, "Pioneer Life in Palo Alto County," 156.
45. Belknap, "Reminiscences."

intimidate her. She too was able to find "luxuries" along the trail: candy and preserves from Ft. Laramie, a fine dinner in a boarding-house in Salt Lake City, and an impressive collection of furs garnered from trading some of her goods with Native Americans. At Salt Lake she wrote her sister back in Iowa that, "so far as we have come, there's nothing to fear on the road. Two-thirds of the distance has been good as a turnpike road. . . . I wish I were seated in your snug parlor, telling the wonders of travel."[46]

Actually, it was her husband William who was depressed by the trip, rather than Lucy. She told her sister that,

> William often wishes we were back, and says so soon as he gets any more than he started with he'll be with you. If I were very anxious I think William would send me back to you in the spring, and he go on alone to California; but it looks best we journey together.

During their next lap, four months to California, she wrote, "so far enjoy ourselves. . . . We live first rate." And when they finally sighted Lake Tahoe, she rejoiced that "our trials would soon be of the past, whilst the future, oh, where was the limit?"[47]

Because E. Allene Dunham crossed the trail to California as a young girl with her family in 1846 her remembrances are of a slightly different nature. She did, however, mention amenities such as camping at a farm, her mother and the baby staying in a hotel, staying in an emigrant campground, and buying milk from farms along the way. She remembered a few unfriendly Native Americans, but said that the majority acted pleasantly, begged for food, and invited the emigrants to visit their camps. Dunham's other recollections centered around gathering wild flowers, playing on rocks, hiding in the sagebrush, and the highlight of the trip, being taken to mountain peaks by some young women of the train who "took their revolvers and we had a fine time." Her conclusion: "We children knew nothing only to enjoy ourselves, and we surely did."[48]

Like Dunham, Eliza Ann Egbert crossed the Plains in 1852 as a girl. Although she noted accidents, deaths, "impudent" Indians, and loss of stock, she did not dwell upon them. Instead, she noted her appreciation of "a beautiful camp ground near a little stream on the prairie," "fair weather today and good road," "delicious water," and "good grass." Her son was later to say of her,

> No doubt the young emigrants endured many hardships, but if so, they are not stressed in the diary, nor do I remember that they were ever mentioned by my mother in the many times I have heard her speak of the trip. To them it was the big adventure and the hardships were accepted as part of that adventure.[49]

---

46. Lucy Rutledge Cooke, *Covered Wagon Days: Crossing the Plains in 1852* (Modesto, California: Privately published, 1923), 7–37, 41–44.

47. Ibid., 49, 60–70.

48. E. Allene Taylor Dunham, *Across the Plains in a Covered Wagon* (n.p., n.d.), 1–20.

49. Eliza Ann Egbert, Travel Diary, California Historical Society, San Francisco, California.

Catherine Margaret Haun, on the other hand, made the trip as a young bride in 1849 due to family financial trouble and her own poor health. She maintained that the hazards of the trail did not frighten her. "Indeed," she wrote, "as we had been married but a few months, it appealed to us as a romantic wedding tour." Overall, the trail proved therapeutic for her: "In my case, as in that of many others, my health was restored long before the end of the journey." The first few days of the trip, however, she found to be extremely tiresome and she described herself "dazed with dread." She avoided confiding her fears to her husband because she didn't want to add to his burdens for she believed that "he would certainly have turned back for he, as well as the other men of the party, was disheartened and was struggling not to betray it."[50]

From that point on her frame of mind improved and she even surprised herself by offering, despite her lack of experience, to do all the cooking for her party when the hired cook quit. She found her companions to be "a wonderful collection of people," the youngest of whom was a six-week-old baby. Like the other women of the train, she helped drive the wagon, cared for the children, and caught up with her washing and mending on Sundays. Although they were passed by many discouraged emigrants returning east along the trail, she urged her husband onward. She was more than pleased that they were among the dozen or so people out of the original 120 in the train that reached Sacramento as scheduled.[51]

The last tale of the overland trek was written by Virginia Ivins, a Keokuk woman who left for California in 1853 with her husband, one-year-old son, aunt and uncle, five drovers, and a German cook named Carl. Around the time they neared Ft. Laramie she noted that, "On the whole we were having a rather good time; were all well, were becoming inured to privations, and things were moving along quite satisfactorily." She was aware that frequently there were Indians around but said they never bothered the camp. Although only twenty years old, she often cheerfully helped with the heavy cooking chores. And near the end of the journey, when she felt seriously ill, she stated that she "simply endured without complaint" but "made the best of the somewhat difficult situation and was quite cheerful when my husband was with me." When foul weather and broken-down wagons beset them she went to the aid of her husband because he was "altogether discouraged, hardly knowing what to do and seemed to depend on me for advice."[52]

When, near California, he was offered several lucrative jobs they decided to continue on their way since, according to Ivins, "ease had no charms for

---

50. Haun, "A Woman's Trip Across the Plains."
51. Ibid.
52. Virginia Wilcox Ivins, *Pen Pictures of Early Western Days* (Keokuk, Iowa: n.p., c. 1905), 52–69, 96, 101, 111, 114.

us then." She basked in the limelight created for her by the scarcity of women, remarked often on the lovely weather, and congratulated herself for having remained "perfectly cool in every danger we had encountered." When the end was finally sighted she found herself "almost jubilant" to have survived a "most trying and tedious journey" successfully.[53]

Here, then, are the stories of six representative women who crossed the most feared trail of all-the route across the Plains to the Far West. Yet the conditions they recounted and the emotions they expressed were very similar to those of many women on the Iowa trail. There was a hardiness, a creativity, a buoyancy of spirit on the part of all these women that makes one wonder if the frontier in transit was as detrimental to women as myth would have us believe. The similarities were more than coincidental; the goods purchased along the way, the enjoyment of scenery and climate, the lack of serious problems with Native Americans, the shoring up of tired and discouraged men, the determination to reach the intended destination were all recurrent themes which cannot be ignored. The replacement of the image of trail women with a more balanced picture is clearly long overdue.

BIBLIOGRAPHICAL NOTE

Glenda Riley has been the most active scholar defining the experience of Iowa's frontier women. In the 1970s she edited a series of pioneer women's diaries for the *Annals of Iowa,* and she published interpretive articles based on her research in those and other sources in the *Annals of Iowa,* the *Palimpsest,* the *Western Historical Quarterly,* the *Pacific Historical Review,* and *Vitae Scholasticae.* That material all came together in *Frontierswomen: The Iowa Experience* (Ames, 1981). She has since extended her reach and most recently published *The Female Frontier: A Comparative View of Women on the Prairie and Plains* (Lawrence, KS, 1988). Riley's perspective is largely shared by Julie Roy Jeffrey, *Frontier Women: The Trans-Mississippi West, 1840–1880* (New York, 1979); and Sandra L. Myres, *Westering Women and the Frontier Experience, 1800–1915* (Albuquerque, NM, 1982). For contrasting views of frontier women's experience, none focused primarily on Iowa, see John Mack Faragher, *Women and Men on the Overland Trail* (New Haven, CT, 1979); Christine Stansell, "Women on the Great Plains, 1865–1890," *Women's Studies* 4 (1976), 87–98; and Lillian Schlissel, "Women's Diaries on the Western Frontier," *American Studies* 18 (1977), 88–92.

Given the preoccupation with pioneer life in earlier publications of the State Historical Society of Iowa, it is remarkable how little work has been done on this topic in recent years. Much of the work that has been done has, like much of Riley's own early work, focused on women's diaries and journals. For regional examples, see Lillian Schlissel, *Women's Diaries of the Westward Journey* (New York, 1982); and

---

53. Ibid., 116–120.

Elizabeth Hampsten, *Read This Only to Yourself: The Private Writings of Midwestern Women, 1880–1910* (Bloomington, IN, 1982). A particularly noteworthy Iowa example is Judy Nolte Lensink, *"A Secret to Be Burried": The Diary and Life of Emily Hawley Gillespie, 1858–1888* (Iowa City, 1989).

More generally, on frontier and settlement issues, see Roger L. Nichols, ed., *American Frontier and Western Issues: A Historiographical Review* (Westport, CT, 1986), which contains historiographical essays on the environment, economic development, agriculture, urbanization, transportation, mining, social history, Indians, women, ethnic groups, foreign affairs, territorial government, and the army. For an excellent general account of the frontier experience, see Malcolm J. Rohrbough, *The Transappalachian Frontier: People, Societies, and Institutions, 1775–1850* (New York, 1978), especially chapter 13, "The Last Frontier of the Old Northwest: Illinois, Wisconsin, and Iowa." For Iowa, the Summer 1988 issue of the *Palimpsest* offers several perspectives on life in territorial Iowa, focusing particularly on frontier families, material culture, land ownership, and territorial government. Finally, although historians like to point to all the ways the essay errs, Frederick Jackson Turner's seminal essay, "The Significance of the Frontier in American History," still spawns a cottage industry of those who trace its influence and argue with it. To understand many of the debates among historians ever since, students of the Iowa frontier would do well to familiarize themselves with that essay and the ensuing discussion.

4

Farming in the Prairie Peninsula, 1830–1890

ALLAN G. BOGUE

The goal of most Iowa frontiersmen and frontierswomen was to establish farms. That process is traced in a remarkably broad account in the following essay by Allan Bogue. His essay is the oldest one in this collection, but it is one that has stood the test of time particularly well. Bogue's creative use of quantifiable evidence from census materials set the standard for much of the rich work in rural and agricultural history since then. The book from which this essay was drawn, From Prairie to Cornbelt: Farming on the Illinois Prairies in the Nineteenth Century *(Chicago, 1963), was recently reprinted by Iowa State University Press.*

FLARING WESTWARD from the upper valley of the Wabash lies the prairie triangle, embracing most of central and northern Illinois and almost all of Iowa. Much of this region today lies in the heart of the corn belt. Its economic history is a story of practical experimentation, adaptation, and change as its restless settlers endeavored after 1820 to unlock its wealth. To do so, the prairie pioneers had to adapt techniques and crops to the novel environment of an almost treeless grassland at a time when both technology and markets were undergoing revolutionary change. In 1830 the farm-makers had hardly begun their task; by the 1890s the land was tamed, the corn belt a fact, its farmers on the threshold of a golden age.

"THE SOIL is as black as your hat and as mellow as a[n] ash heap . . . ," wrote Oliver Ellsworth to his brother from Bloomington, Illinois, in 1837.

Originally published as Allan G. Bogue, "Farming in the Prairie Peninsula, 1830–1890," *The Journal of Economic History* 23 (1963), 3–29. Copyright © 1963 by Cambridge University Press. Reprinted with the permission of Cambridge University Press.

"If you, John, will come on, we can live like pigs in the clover. . . ."[1] Particularly, the prairie farm-makers were the children of New York, Pennsylvania, the Ohio valley states, the British Isles, the German states, and, to a lesser extent, the Scandinavian countries. A sampling of the manuscript Federal censuses indicates that the typical farm-maker was a man in his thirties, married, and the father of several children who had accompanied him from his previous place of residence. Among the native-born, older residents were found generally farther from their birthplace. For some twenty or thirty years after first settlement, the average age of the farm operators in new communities increased. The frontier population was not a cross section, therefore, of that in older settlements. The typical pioneer was younger and possibly better prepared to cope with farm-making problems than the average operator of the older settlements.[2]

Taken as a group, the farm-makers were mobile. No matter the age of the community, between 50 and 80 per cent of any new group of farmers were gone ten years later. The prosperous were most likely to stay, but some of these too might leave after very short periods of residence. Undoubtedly, ethnic and cultural origins were linked at times to persistence patterns, but

---

1. "Ninety-Eight Years Ago in Bloomington," *Journal of the Illinois State Historical Society* 28 (April 1935–Jan. 1936), 209. Iowa settlement is described in: Cardinal Goodwin, "The American Occupation of Iowa, 1833 to 1860," *Iowa Journal of History and Politics* 17 (Jan. 1919), 83–102; William L. Harter and R. E. Stewart, *The Population of Iowa: Its Composition and Changes. A Brief Sociological Study of Iowa's Human Assets*, Iowa State College of Agriculture and Mechanic Arts, *Bulletin* No. 275 (Ames, 1930). There is a series of excellent population maps based on the township population figures given in the state censuses of 1856, 1867, and 1875 in G. B. Schilz, "Rural Population Trends of Iowa as Affected by Soils" (Ph.D. diss., Clark University, 1948), pp. 67, 68, 69. See also Clare C. Cooper, "The Role of Railroads in the Settlement of Iowa: A Study of Historical Geography" (M.A. thesis, University of Nebraska, 1958). The basic accounts of settlement in Illinois are: Arthur C. Boggess, *The Settlement of Illinois, 1778–1830*, Chicago Historical Society's *Collection*, Vol. 5 (Chicago, 1908); William V. Pooley, *The Settlement of Illinois from 1830 to 1850*, University of Wisconsin, *Bulletin* No. 220, "History Series," Vol. 1 (Madison, 1908). The appropriate volumes of the *Centennial History of Illinois* include useful summaries of the settlement process; see particularly the maps in Solon J. Buck, *Illinois in 1818* (Springfield, 1918), pp. 4, 174, 384; Arthur C. Cole, *The Era of the Civil War, 1848–1870* (Springfield, 1919), pp. 16, 330. The various accounts of the immigrant groups are also helpful, as are the materials of the Federal censuses.

2. The discussion of pioneer demography in this and the following paragraph is based on Harter and Stewart, *Population of Iowa*, pp. 16–17; Mildred Throne, "A Population Study of an Iowa County in 1850," *Iowa Journal of History* 57 (Oct. 1959), 305–30; William Bowers, "Crawford Township, 1850–1870: A Population Study of a Pioneer Community," *ibid.* 58 (Jan. 1960), 1–30; and my own unpublished studies of farmers in Bureau County, Illinois, in 1850 and 1860, and farmer turnover in townships in Bremer, Davis, Hamilton, and Washington Counties, Iowa. The method in these studies stems mainly from James C. Malin's article, "The Turnover of Farm Population in Kansas," *Kansas Historical Quarterly* 4 (Nov. 1935), 339–72. Miss Throne utilized both population and agricultural manuscript censuses, as I did in my township studies. In the Bureau study of farmer households, I made use primarily of the population censuses. The work of Throne, Bowers, and myself revealed patterns of turnover in Illinois and Iowa similar to those discovered by Malin, but to some degree I interpret them differently than did Malin. For similar research, see Merle Curti *et al.*, *The Making of an American Community: A Case Study of Democracy in a Frontier County* (Stanford: Stanford Univ. Press, 1959), pp. 55–83.

TABLE 4.1
FARM OPERATOR TURNOVER IN FOUR IOWA TOWNSHIPS
BY DATE OF ARRIVAL

	1850		1860		1870		1880	
	No.	%	No.	%	No.	%	No.	%
Crawford Twp.[a]								
Group 1	66	100.0	21	31.8	11	16.6	7	10.6
Group 2	–	–	94	100.0	35	37.2	23	24.5
Group 3	–	–	–	–	141	100.0	36	25.5
Union Twp.								
Group 1	81	100.0	35	43.2	22	27.2	11	13.6
Group 2	–	–	84	100.0	41	48.8	25	29.8
Group 3	–	–	–	–	149	100.0	44	29.5
Hamilton Twp.								
Group 1	–	–	50	100.0	28	56.0	14	28.0
Group 2	–	–	–	–	64	100.0	30	46.9
Warren Twp.								
Group 1	–	–	28	100.0	12	42.9	7	25.0
Group 2	–	–	–	–	163	100.0	72	44.2
Group 3[b]	–	–	–	–	102	100.0	47	46.1

[a]The counties were Washington, Davis, Hamilton, and Bremer.
[b]This group was continental-born, consisting mainly of natives of the German states, with a few Frenchmen and Swiss as well. This group was included in Warren Township, Group 2, as well as being placed in a separate category.

facile generalizations on this point cannot yet be made. In Bureau County, Illinois, some 46 per cent of the British-born farmer householders of 1850 remained in 1860; only 28 per cent of the German-born farmers stayed. Of the New England–born farmers of 1850, 45 per cent remained in 1860, but only 24 per cent of those who claimed Kentucky and Tennessee as their birthplaces remained. As Table 4.1 shows, persistence among the members of such groups rose over time, and 10 to 15 per cent of groups that had lost 60 to 70 per cent of their numbers between 1850 and 1860 remained in 1880. These residuals were important; they formed the continuing core of the western communities.

Census-derived turnover patterns suggest a number of conclusions. Original land disposal policies could hardly have been a direct controlling influence on the farming operations of the majority of midwestern pioneers. They bought their land at second, third, or even fourth hand, rather than from the government. The turnover rates suggest also that new communities lost much valuable agricultural experience soon after farmers had accumulated it.[3] They force us to qualify the stage formula of agricultural settlement which appeared in the

---

3. Malin, "Turnover of Farm Population," p. 356.

travel and guide literature of the early national period and ultimately in Frederick Jackson Turner's famous essay.[4]

IF THE AMERICAN PIONEERS had once believed that the prairies were infertile because trees did not grow there, they were rejecting this misconception by the 1820s. The smaller prairies of Ohio and the barrens of Kentucky had already demonstrated that treeless lands could grow abundant crops. As late as the early 1850s, however, some Iowa settlers maintained that the lack of timber on the larger prairies of the state rendered them useless for intensive husbandry.[5] But other farm-makers were already adjusting to this limiting factor.

Adjustments to the timber shortage took various forms. In part, the claim club reflected the unique features of the prairie landscape. Where timber and prairie alternated, locations in or near wooded areas were relatively much more attractive. This set the stage for associations, which the early comers used to engross the best locations in their own hands for resale to later arrivals or large land speculators.[6] If the Midwest had been all prairie or all timber, the clubs would have been less common. More important, as the land passed into private hands, there developed a landholding pattern of which the timber lot was an integral part. Settlers on the prairie purchased five or ten acres along the stream bottoms or in the prairie groves and drove five, ten or fifteen miles to cut building timber or to split rails during the winter months.[7] Broken in surface

---

4. Elias Pym Fordham, *Personal Narrative of Travels in Virginia, Maryland, Pennsylvania, Ohio, Indiana, Kentucky; and of a Residence in the Illinois Territory: 1817–1818*, edited by Frederick Austin Ogg (Cleveland, 1906), pp. 125–27; John Mason Peck, *A New Guide for Emigrants to the West containing sketches of Ohio, Indiana, Illinois, Missouri, Michigan, with the Territories of Wisconsin and Arkansas, and the Adjacent Parts* (Boston, 1836), pp. 114–16. In citing Peck, Turner also called attention to a number of similar analyses. See *The Frontier in American History* (New York: Henry Holt and Co., 1920), p. 21, fn. 36.

5. Western Historical Company, *The History of Cedar County, Iowa containing a History of the County, its Cities, Towns, &c,* ... (Chicago, 1878), pp. 600, 605. A number of accounts of nineteenth-century agriculture give attention to the particular problems of the prairies, but are not cited specifically by the writer in later notes. Percy W. Bidwell and John I. Falconer, *History of Agriculture in the Northern United States, 1620–1860* (Washington: The Carnegie Institution, 1925); Theodore L. Carlson, *The Illinois Military Tract: A Study of Land Occupation, Utilization and Tenure*, Illinois Studies in the Social Sciences, 32, No. 2 (Urbana, 1951); Paul W. Gates, *The Farmer's Age: Agriculture, 1815–1860*, Vol. 3, *The Economic History of the United States* (New York: Holt, Rinehart & Winston, 1960); Earle D. Ross, *Iowa Agriculture: An Historical Survey* (Iowa City: State Historical Society of Iowa, 1951); Fred A. Shannon, *The Farmer's Last Frontier: Agriculture, 1860–1897*, Vol. 5, *The Economic History of the United States* (New York: Farrar & Rinehart, 1945). See also Mildred Throne, "A History of Agriculture in Southern Iowa, 1833–1890" (Ph.D. diss., State University of Iowa, 1946).

6. Allan G. Bogue, "The Iowa Claim Clubs: Symbol and Substance," *Mississippi Valley Historical Review* 45 (Sept. 1958), 231–53.

7. Leslie Hewes,"Some Features of Early Woodland and Prairie Settlement in a Central Iowa County," *Annals of the Association of American Geographers* 40 (March 1950), 51, 53. This pattern first came to my attention while working in the county records of Hamilton and Bremer Counties, Iowa.

and relatively deficient in organic content, the timber soils were often much less productive than the prairie soils, but the price of timber land remained above prairie land prices for thirty or forty years after the arrival of the first settlers.[8]

When he sought to fence his crops against marauding livestock, the prairie farmer faced the timber problem at its most acute.[9] The Virginia worm-rail fence with stakes and riders was an efficient, although somewhat untidy fence. But it demanded timber in large amounts, and the rails might last no more than ten to twenty years. The willow and cottonwood groves of the pioneers were of no immediate help. Some farmers tried to conserve resources by moving the division fences on their cropland as needed and by resorting, where possible, to the Shanghai rail fence in which several of the lower rails were omitted; such solutions were mere stopgaps.

Farmers suggested a variety of substitutes for rail fences. Early settlers had high hopes for ditch and earthen bank fence, capped perhaps by rail or hedge, but the prairie herds had discredited sod fence, on the Illinois prairies at least, by the early 1830s. Smooth iron wire fencing was popular briefly during the 1840s, but the strands stretched and sagged, inspiring only friendly contempt among western livestock. By the 1850s, farmers close to major water routes or to Chicago-based rail lines could use board fencing, although its cost was a deterrent.

By the 1850s, Osage orange had emerged from a host of competing hedge plants as a practicable living hedge. Initially it was inexpensive, but it started slowly and demanded continuing attention. Over time, hedging involved a considerable labor cost. Despite problems in its culture and a shortage of seed during the Civil War, Osage orange hedge gained in popularity and made up a significant percentage of the fencing in prairie counties during the early 1870s. Meanwhile, many prairie farmers had supported an institutional solution to the fencing problem. This was the herd law, which held the owners of livestock responsible for their confinement. In herd-law contests in the 1860s and 1870s, there was sometimes a clear split in sentiment between timbered and prairie regions of the same county. The invention of a practicable and cheap barbed wire

---

8. Adrian H. Lindsey, "The Nature and Cause of the Growth of Iowa Land Values" (Ph.D. diss., Iowa State College, 1929), p. 144.

9. The following account is based mainly on: Clarence H. Danhof, "The Fencing Problem in the Eighteen Fifties," *Agricultural History* 18 (Oct. 1944), 168–86; Earl W. Hayter, "Barbed Wire Fencing — A Prairie Invention: Its Rise and Influence in the Western States," *Agricultural History* 13 (Oct. 1939), 189–207; Mary Louise Rice, "The Role of the Osage Orange Hedge in the Occupation of the Great Plains" (M.A. thesis, University of Illinois, 1937); Margaret Beattie Bogue, *Patterns from the Sod: Land Use and Tenure in the Grand Prairie, 1850–1900* (Springfield: Illinois State Historical Library, 1959), pp. 117–21, 133–36; U.S. Commissioner of Agriculture, *Report*, 1871 (Washington, 1872), pp. 504–5; as well as numerous references in *The Prairie Farmer*, 1841–1889 (began publication as *The Union Agriculturist and Western Prairie Farmer*); *The Iowa Homestead and Western Farm Journal*, 1858–1883; and the annual *Reports* of the Iowa State Agricultural Society, 1856–1890.

TABLE 4.2
AVERAGE FENCING COSTS PER ROD, 1840–1874

	Board	Wire	Picket	Sod	Worm	Post and Rail	Four-Strand Barbed Wire
1840–1860[a]	$1.75	$.83	$.43	$.40	$.55–.75		
1871 Illinois[b]	1.31				.99	$1.27	
1871 Iowa	1.31				.91	.94	
1874 Iowa[c]							$.60

[a]*Prairie Farmer,* March 1846, pp. 90–91; July 1846, pp. 204–5; Feb. 1847, pp. 67–68; April 1848, p. 113; May 1848, p. 144; Oct. 1848, p. 302; July 1848, p. 211; March 1850, p. 76; April 1850, pp. 117–18; April 2, 1864, p. 226; *Union Agriculturist and Western Prairie Farmer,* Oct. 1841, p. 77; Nov. 1841, p. 43; *Northwestern Farmer,* April 1856, p. 104; *Iowa Homestead and Western Farm Journal,* Jan. 3, 1873, p. 1; Frederick Gerhard, *Illinois As It Is:* . . . (Chicago, 1857), pp. 311–12. The estimate for seven-rail worm is mine, based on a rail cost of two cents per rail.
[b]United States Commissioner of Agriculture, *Report,* 1871, p. 509.
[c]Iowa State Agricultural Society, *Report,* 1875, p. 43. By 1885, barbed-wire fencing costs were probably well below thirty cents per rod, depending upon the local cost of labor and posts. The wire for a rod of four-strand fence cost ten cents at that time. *Prairie Farmer,* April 4, 1885, p. 209. Three-strand fencing was probably always much more common than four.

solved the fencing problem. The cost of a four-strand barbed wire fence in the mid-1870s, as shown in Table 4.2, was less than half that of a board fence and a third less than the cost of rail fencing, where rails were available.

Prairie farm-makers argued both about the method of breaking prairie sod and about the nature and capabilities of the soils which lay beneath it.[10] Over time, the breakers learned that the proper time for breaking prairie extended from early May to late July. They also changed the approved technique of breaking from one in which the furrows were as deep as five inches and the overturned furrow slices lay in neatly flat, tight rows to one in which the plow pared off a thin rind of grass and roots, leaving the furrow slice broken and riffled. The pioneers of northwestern Iowa believed that they hastened the decomposition process by planting a sod crop of flax.[11]

The farm-makers assumed that there were important differences in the soils of the prairie regions. A writer in the *Prairie Farmer* of 1851 presented an analysis of western soils based on their suitability for wheat culture. On the uplands where the white oaks grew was a pure wheat soil; that supporting yellow and red oaks differed somewhat; and where the burr oaks and hazels grew was "perhaps the richest soil." Least adapted to wheat culture, he maintained, was the soil of the open prairie.[12] Others suggested that wheat grew

---

10. *Prairie Farmer,* May 1843, p. 118.
11. L. S. Coffin, "Breaking Prairie," *Annals of Iowa* 5 (July 1902), 447–52; *Prairie Farmer,* May 1841, pp. 34–35; Oct. 1841, p. 76; April 1842, p. 34; Iowa State Agricultural Society, *Report,* 1879 (Des Moines, 1880), p. 35. Hereafter the latter series will be cited as I.S.A.S.R.
12. "W" in *Prairie Farmer,* April 1851, pp. 166–67.

best on the soil of the timbered tracts or on the soil of the barrens, those stretches of alternating timber, hazel brush and prairie. Some believed that newly broken prairie was superior for wheat-growing to old prairie fields.[13] By the mid-1840s there had emerged the idea that much of northern Illinois constituted an "infected district," in which tame grasses and clovers would not grow.[14] As late as 1866, the editor of the *Prairie Farmer* mentioned that "the generally conceived ideas that prairie land is not well adapted to the production of tame grasses" were being disproved.[15]

If the prairie environment perplexed the pioneer on occasion, it also rewarded his efforts. Whatever their regional variations, the prairie soils were usually highly productive, with considerable staying power. Nor was there need here for the farmer to invest a generation of family labor in removing a heavy mantle of forest. It is hard to exaggerate the importance of this fact in explaining the rapid development of mechanized agriculture in Illinois and Iowa after 1850.

A VARIETY OF FACTORS may have influenced the pioneer farmer of the prairie triangle when he made his production plans. Markets, transportation facilities, the general price level, changes in the prices of farm products relative to each other, his cultural heritage, and his understanding of prairie soils all probably affected the farmer's calculations. On the other hand, it is sometimes suggested that pioneer agriculture was essentially subsistence agriculture or that there were typical frontier cropping sequences through which the farmers moved as their communities developed. The data of the Federal agricultural censuses from 1850 to 1890 give us considerable information about such matters. Maps based upon average county production per improved acre of the field crops, and upon numbers of farm animals per farm, show areas of high and low production on a subregional basis in Illinois and Iowa as early as 1850.[16]

Had the farmers in newly settled areas been subsistence farmers, their counties would not ordinarily have appeared among the leading producers of wheat or corn per improved acre in Iowa or Illinois in a particular census year. Yet this was the case. Nor apparently was there any one crop-production or

---

13. *Prairie Farmer*, Feb. 1854, p. 56; June 1854, p. 205; *Northwestern Farmer*, Jan. 1857, p. 7; I.S.A.S.R., 1857, pp. 256, 434; 1863, p. 481; 1866, p. 186.

14. *Prairie Farmer*, Oct. 1848, p. 324.

15. *Ibid.*, Nov. 3, 1866, p. 281.

16. Prior to 1880, the Federal census does not show acreages planted to the various field crops, giving only total yield per county and improved acreages. Maps based on production figures, of course, must be used with caution. Unusual seasons and regional differences in soil productivity could both distort production maps in comparison to maps based on acreage. However, comparison of maps based on acreages in 1880 with those based on production in the same year does reveal very similar patterns. Some of the Iowa state censuses do give acreages planted to specific crops, and maps based on these figures suggest that the maps based on Federal production figures give a fairly accurate picture of production patterns.

farm-management sequence through which most pioneer farmers of Illinois and Iowa moved. The farm-makers of northern Illinois and Iowa placed considerable emphasis upon wheat production in early years and later moved to heavier dependence on other combinations of crops and livestock; the farmers of central Illinois and southern Iowa gave a much more important place in their plans to corn and livestock from the very beginning. If one must have a yardstick for measuring the basic difference between the agriculture of older and more recently settled communities, most satisfactory would be the relative amounts of improved land. Better still, but impossible to calculate, would be the percentage of labor used in farm-making tasks in contrast to that used directly in the production of food, feed and fiber.

The farmers of the prairie triangle were never monoculturists. Even when they described themselves as wheat farmers or corn-hog farmers, their farming operations were really combinations of wheat, corn, oats, barley, hay, cattle, sheep, hogs, and other minor enterprises. Enough farmers in any particular area reacted similarly to the economic and physical environments to produce subregional production patterns. Many of these patterns, however, were unstable. Between 1849 and 1879 the area of high wheat production in Illinois shifted from northern Illinois to the southwestern region of the state. The area of highest hog production per farm unit moved northward from its position in southern Illinois in 1850 to lie particularly in the Military Tract in 1880. In 1850 central Illinois below the Sangamon reported the largest numbers of other cattle per farm unit, reflecting the stocker and feeder operations of that region. By the 1880s the upper Military Tract and adjacent counties to the north had become the major feeding area in Illinois. On the other hand, there were elements of stability in the production patterns of these prairie states. The counties of southeastern Iowa, for instance, were always the leading sheep producers in that state. Hay was always much more important to the farmers of northern Iowa than to those farther to the south.

By the 1870s and 1880s, the subregional patterns of crop and livestock production in Illinois and Iowa were beginning to resemble those which prevailed in the early twentieth century. The increasing concentration of milk cows in extreme northern Illinois during this period stamped the agriculture of that region as closer to the agriculture of southern Wisconsin than to the corn and livestock farming of central Illinois. During the 1880s the milk cow was coming to dominate the agriculture of northeastern Iowa. In the same decade oats assumed a more significant role in the agriculture of central and northern Illinois and Iowa. Barley emerged as a crop of considerable importance in northwestern Iowa. By 1880 the farmers of the Grand Prairie had concluded that it was to their advantage to concentrate on cash grain production; the farmers of the northern Military Tract had already linked their destinies to the feeder steer and the hog. Although the outlines of the eastern livestock area of Iowa were becoming clear by 1880 and a western livestock area was present, the cash grain section ultimately found in north central Iowa was still in flux.

Some of the counties there, of course, were still raw frontier. Wheat production was still important in northwestern Iowa, and farmers there were experiencing difficulty in finding strains of corn which would ripen early enough for their needs.

Comparison of the production maps based on the censuses from 1850 to 1890 does in general reveal that the farmers of the various subregions in Illinois and Iowa specialized increasingly in particular crops or farm enterprises. If the census statistics of 1850 are to be trusted, however—and there are grounds for skepticism—one must qualify the generalization somewhat. The average production of corn per improved acre and the holdings of hogs and other cattle per farm unit in the leading counties of both Iowa and Illinois during the census year 1850 were actually greater than those reported from the leading counties in some subsequent censuses. The farmers of McLean County, Illinois, for instance, reported seventeen other cattle per farm unit in 1850; not until 1890 did Warren County farmers surpass this with a figure of eighteen other cattle per farm unit.

Crop and livestock enterprises were related to each other in a variety of ways. Not surprisingly, corn and hogs were strikingly complementary. Frequency tables based on the production returns of ninety-eight Illinois counties in the agricultural census of 1850 show, for instance, that forty-eight counties appeared in the same quintile as corn producers which they occupied as hog producers. Tables illustrating the relationship between corn production and other cattle and corn production and milk cows show much weaker relationships. Only twenty-seven counties ranked in the same quintiles as producers of both corn and other cattle; in the case of corn and milk cows the number was only sixteen. The census returns of 1890 showed the same rank order of correlation, but the relationship between corn production and hog raising had weakened, while that between other cattle and corn raising had strengthened somewhat; with 102 counties reporting, the quintile correlation of corn to hogs was thirty-nine and that of corn to other cattle was thirty-four. On the other hand, some farm enterprises in the prairie triangle were notably antipathetic to each other. High wheat-producing counties were almost never high corn-producing counties, for instance.

THE AGRICULTURAL PRODUCTION MAPS reflect a variety of geographic factors. As early as 1849, some of the Shelbyville Moraine counties of Illinois seemed to mark a transition in farming patterns. In the crop-production maps of 1869, if not earlier, one can see reflected the contrasting topography and soil conditions of the northern and southern portions of the Illinois Military Tract. During the 1880s the farmers of northwestern Iowa turned to barley, in part because the loessial soils and relatively lower humidity of that area were highly congenial to the crop.

Transportation facilities played their part in shaping subregional production patterns. Every one of the Mississippi River counties of Iowa fell in the top quartile of wheat producers in the state during 1849. As soon as the Illinois and Michigan canal was completed, farmers of north central Illinois discovered that they could now sell part of their corn production as a cash crop for shipment to other regions. The railroads which girded Illinois and Iowa after 1850 produced comparable changes on a broader scale. In interior areas where herds had formerly been driven to feed on surplus corn, the farmers had now the option of letting their corn be shipped to feed cattle and hogs elsewhere. If the farmers of northwestern Iowa found barley a profitable crop during the 1880s, it was in part because railroad construction in that section guaranteed a market for a small-grain specialty.

Underlying the production responses of prairie farmers, of course, was the fact that they were producing for an expanding domestic and foreign market. We cannot here recount the developments, innovations and inventions which allowed midwestern producers to enter these markets on competitive terms: lard oil, dressed beef, refrigeration, and futures trading, to mention a few of them. The meaning of some of these developments was unclear to most prairie farmers. What many of them did understand, however, was that the relationship between corn and hog prices made it almost always profitable to feed hogs. In Iowa, one hundred pounds of pork was worth less than ten bushels of corn in only three years between 1861 and 1900. Iowa price indices show also that beef prices were relatively stable through the whole period from 1864 to 1896. On the other hand, the declining significance of wheat in the economy of many districts in Illinois and Iowa undoubtedly reflected the very striking decline in the index of wheat prices between 1866 and 1896, relative to the indices of other major farm products.[17]

Students of agricultural development in the Midwest of the nineteenth century have often suggested that cultural or ethnic influences affected the decisions of farmers. With the contention that particular cultural or ethnic groups drew upon their unique heritages to help in solving the problems of adaptation to the midwestern environment, there can be little quarrel. Quite possibly, English settlers did bring improved drainage techniques to the Illinois prairies.[18] Englishmen may well also have solved a major problem in the development of Osage orange hedging by introducing the plashing technique.[19] Hungarian refugees evidently did introduce Hungarian grass or millet in Iowa, although the experiment was of little long-range significance.[20] Undoubtedly the Yankees, those "shrewd, selfish, enterprising, cow-milking" men

---

17. The price indices referred to here are based on data presented by Norman V. Strand in *Prices of Farm Products in Iowa, 1851–1940*. Iowa State College of Agriculture and Mechanic Arts, Research Bulletin No. 303 (Ames, 1942), pp. 934, 938–42.

18. George Flower, *History of the English Settlement in Edwards County, Illinois, Founded in 1817 and 1818 by Morris Birkbeck and George Flower* (Chicago, 1882), pp. 165–66.

19. *Prairie Farmer*, August 12, 1862, p. 111.

20. *Northwestern Farmer*, Dec. 1857, p. 457; June 1858, p. 191.

spread the skills of dairying in many western communities.[21] And John M. Peck argued that even the southerners most wedded to dog and gun better appreciated the need of keeping a clean cornfield in the crucial June weeks than did some of their tidier Yankee neighbors.[22] It would have been strange had western farm-makers not brought their fund of previous experience to bear on the unique problems of midwestern agriculture.

Writers on occasion, however, have suggested that the members of particular cultural groups consistently followed farming practices which were significantly different from those of neighbors who drew upon other cultural heritages. The Norwegians and Danes, one writer hints, may have had a particular affinity for the wet prairie in central Iowa.[23] Contemporaries wrote that the Yankees were more apt to be orchardists than were farmers of other backgrounds.[24] Both contemporaries and later writers have suggested that the Germans, and to a lesser extent the Scandinavians, farmed differently from their neighbors. The Germans were pre-eminently wheat growers in southwestern Illinois. In Iowa, they grew more barley than did their neighbors and preferred mules for draft stock.[25] Two eminent agricultural historians wrote:

> ... what pulled most of the debt-ridden out of the red was the combination of pluck, perspicacity, and pigs. This was particularly so in the case of the German and Swedish immigrants. Less skilled in the management of horses, sheep, and beef cattle than the English and native Americans, they concentrated with dogged tenacity on their hogs. ... The chief economy practiced by the German farmer that made him competitively efficient was fattening his hogs behind beef steers.[26]

Where there is so much smoke there certainly ought to be fire. But it is quite possible that the Norwegians and Danes of Story County, Iowa, moved to the wet prairie because that was the only land which they believed they could afford. The area of Illinois which became pre-eminently a fruit region was settled for the most part by southerners, not Yankees. I selected 10 per

---

21. H. C. M. Case and K. H. Myers, *Types of Farming in Illinois: An Analysis of Differences by Areas,* University of Illinois Agricultural Experiment Station, *Bulletin* No. 403 (Urbana, 1934), p. 123. The quotation is from Pooley, *The Settlement of Illinois from 1830 to 1850* [99], p. 385, quoting *Chicago Weekly American,* Feb. 4, 1837.

22. John M. Peck, *A Guide for Emigrants, Containing Sketches of Illinois, Missouri, and the Adjacent Parts* (Boston, 1831), pp. 153–54.

23. Leslie Hewes and Philip E. Frandson, "Occupying the Wet Prairie: The Role of Artificial Drainage in Story County, Iowa," *Annals of the Association of American Geographers* 42 (March 1952), 33.

24. I.S.A.S.R., 1859, p. 246.

25. John C. Weaver, "Changing Patterns of Cropland Use in the Middle West," *Economic Geography* 30 (Jan. 1954), 19; Herbert Quick, *One Man's Life* (Indianapolis, 1925), p. 194; U.S. Commissioner of Patents, *Report,* 1850 (Washington, 1851), p. 242; I.S.A.S.R. 1863, p. 378; 1865, p. 400; 1870, pp. 483, 490, 527.

26. Charles W. Towne and Edward N. Wentworth, *Pigs: From Cave to Corn Belt* (Norman: Univ. of Oklahoma Press, 1950), pp. 208–9, 210–11.

cent samples of the continental-born farmers, mostly Germans and Scandinavians, in Bremer and Hamilton Counties, Iowa, from the manuscript census of 1880 and compared their farming operations with those of like samples of the native-born. One of the few common patterns in the agriculture of the former group in the two counties was that these farmers kept fewer hogs than the native-born. Obviously, we must make many more detailed comparisons of this sort before we can put cultural influences in their proper perspective. When local conditions reinforced cultural bias, the members of a particular cultural group may have farmed somewhat differently for a time. Greater difficulty in obtaining access to capital may have accounted for differences also. Perhaps, however, cultural differences were more clearly apparent in diet, minor farm practices, and socio-economic behavior such as the use of wives in the fields, than in significantly different combinations of enterprises, maintained over a considerable period of time.

None of the foregoing means, of course, that all farmers in an agricultural subregion of Illinois or Iowa farmed in exactly the same way. It is true that there were considerable numbers of so-called general farmers in most western communities. They kept up to six or seven cows and young stock of varying ages.[27] Through the 1840s they might own a yoke or two of oxen. By the 1850s they usually owned at least one horse and perhaps two or three. If one of these was a brood mare, such farmers raised the occasional colt. They ordinarily tended several sows and their litters. In their fields the general farmers grew corn and the small grains. They derived their cash income each year from the sale of a few steers or perhaps a fat cow; they might sell a horse or a colt. Fat hogs, however, frequently brought them their largest increment of cash income. Generally they sold some grain, wheat or oats, and corn on occasion. Depending on the time and location, they might also have some barley, buckwheat, or even timothy seed for sale. They, or more likely their wives, made butter and traded the excess, along with a few eggs perhaps, at the local store. But even the general farmers differed in the scale of their operations, and other differences stemmed from the varying speeds with which they adapted to new developments in crop and livestock management and in agricultural technology.

If the general farmers provided a kind of matrix of farm operators in the western community, there were also specialists living side by side with them. Usually operating larger farms than average, such men might concentrate on growing cash grain or raising hogs or on cattle feeding. Occasionally, and more commonly by the 1870s, one finds the fine stock man who sought to sell breeding stock to his neighbors, or by the late 1870s looked also to the western ranges for his market. In a sense, the operations of these specialists were

---

27. Here I generalize on my examination of the agricultural census rolls of some ten counties scattered through Iowa and Illinois for the years 1850 and 1880 as well as a study of the rolls of all Iowa counties in the latter year.

complementary to those of the general farmer. This was particularly true in the case of the cattle feeder. Cattle feeders never constituted a majority of the farmers in any particular community. In Clarion Township, Bureau County, lying in the heaviest feeding area of Illinois for instance, only 21 per cent of the farmers bought or sold as many as twenty cattle during the year 1879.[28] But from the general farmer the cattle feeder might purchase surplus corn, two or three steers, weanling pigs or stocker hogs.[29] He might rent the stalk fields after the general farmer had picked his corn crop in order to provide a month or so of forage for stocker steers.[30] He might even work out a feeding contract with the general farmer so that the latter could in effect sell a portion of his labor along with surplus corn and hay. The unique characteristics of a particular agricultural subregion perhaps derived particularly from the activities of the specialists plus minor differences in emphasis in the farming operations of the general farmers as compared with those in other areas.

WHILE CHANGES in production patterns went on, the prairie farmers worked a considerable change in the fundamental elements of production — plant strains, breed, and techniques. In so far as they grew wheat, they changed from heavy emphasis on winter wheat in the 1840s to considerable dependence on spring wheat and by the late 1870s back, in many cases, to winter wheat. Within the broader pattern, the popularity of specific strains or varieties rose and fell with great suddenness. In the corn field, the northern flints, supposedly dominant in much of Illinois during the 1840s, yielded to the dent corns, so that one writer could use "western" as a synonym for "dent" in 1866.[31] But the dents that came to rule the fields of the prairie triangle were themselves the products of hybridization with the northern flints — some of it accidental, some of it purposeful. Some western farmers understood simple hybridization techniques by the early 1840s.[32] Delay in

---

28. This figure is derived from a farm-by-farm count in the Illinois manuscript agricultural census of 1880, in the possession of the Illinois State Archives, Springfield. The columns showing cattle bought and sold in the previous year were evidently not totaled for publication in the printed census of 1880. Comparable county percentages in Iowa ranged from 15.1 per cent to 1.4 per cent. Manuscript copies of the Federal agricultural census for Iowa are available at both the State Historical Society, Iowa City, and the Department of History and Archives, Des Moines.

29. The diaries of George F. Green of Miles, Jackson County, Iowa, present a particularly fine picture of the operation of a cattle feeder and dealer during the early 1870s. These were made available to me through the kindness of Mrs. Curtis Frymoyer of Wilton Junction, Iowa, a great-granddaughter of Mr. Green.

30. A common price in Putnam County, Illinois, about 1850 for wintering two- and three-year-old cattle was $2.00 to $2.50 per head. U.S. Commissioner of Patents, *Report*, 1850 (Washington, 1851), p. 404.

31. *Prairie Farmer*, June 23, 1866, p. 429.

32. Edgar Anderson and William L. Brown, "The History of the Common Maize Varieties of the United States Corn Belt," *Agricultural History* 26 (Jan. 1952), 2.

the development of varieties suited to the growing season of north central Iowa, however, did slow down the development of corn-belt patterns of farming in that area.[33]

Under the ministrations of midwestern farmers, the American lard hog emerged in its most impressive form. For the lean, stump-sucking, mast-fed rangers of the 1830s and early 1840s, swine-raisers by the early 1870s had substituted fat hogs of gargantuan size.[34] The farmers of the Neponset area in Illinois particularly prided themselves on their hogs, and one of them reported that in a month and a half of the winter of 1870–1871, nineteen farmers there shipped 932 hogs weighing well above four hundred pounds each.[35] Typifying the development, in a sense, was the rise of the Poland China, an Ohio contribution originally, but so popular and known by so many names in the Midwest of the early 1870s that the editor of the *Western Live Stock Journal* tried to resolve the conflict by suggesting the name "Great Western," only to withdraw it in favor of "Polyonomous."[36] By the end of this decade, however, changes in consumer demand were making themselves felt and packers and butchers were turning increasingly to hogs sold at earlier ages and at weights in the vicinity of two hundred pounds.

The nondescript prairie steer of the 1830s that might attain a top weight of 850 pounds at the age of five or six years had yielded place to animals that could reach weights in excess of 1,300 pounds in their third or fourth years by the late 1860s and early 1870s.[37] Some zealots or publicity-conscious feeders indeed, brought the midwestern steers of this era to weights of a ton or more. Exhibited before the Chicago Board of Trade in 1867, "Bob Burns," "Abe Lincoln," and "John Williams" averaged almost 3,200 pounds in weight.[38] John Dean Gillett's mammoth steers of the next decade gained international fame.[39] Undoubtedly there were still many very scrubby native steers in prairie feed lots during the 1870s, but shorthorn blood had worked a marvelous improvement.

---

33. See the conclusions in Clare C. Cooper, "The Role of Railroads in the Settlement of Iowa: A Study in Historical Geography," pp. 136–38.

34. For early descriptions of western hogs see: John Woods, *Two Years' Residence in the Settlement on the English Prairie, in the Illinois Country, United States . . .* (London, 1822, reprinted in Vol. 8 of Reuben Gold Thwaites, ed., *Early Western Travels, 1748–1846* [Cleveland, 1906]), p. 285; William Oliver, *Eight Months in Illinois, with Information to Emigrants* (Newcastle upon Tyne, 1843, reprinted Chicago, 1924), pp. 80–81; John M. Peck, *New Guide for Emigrants to the West*, p. 284.

35. *Prairie Farmer*, June 4, 1870, p. 169.

36. *National Live Stock Journal*, March 1871, p. 223.

37. For early descriptions of Illinois cattle see: Oliver, *Eight Months in Illinois*, p. 104; Peck, *New Guide for Emigrants*, p. 168.

38. *Prairie Farmer*, Jan. 4, 1868, p. 9.

39. Paul W. Gates has described Gillett's stock interests in "Cattle Kings in the Prairies," *Mississippi Valley Historical Review* 35 (Dec. 1948), 391–96.

At first glance the invasion of midwestern pastures and feed lots by Texas steers during the late 1860s and early 1870s may seem to represent a retreat from the rising standards of quality found among the domestic steers. In reality the Texas interlude emphasized the fact that the stockmen of Illinois and Iowa were businessmen, alert for profit. Although critics stigmatized the invaders as mere "vitalized rawhide," the prices of the lean rangers were low enough so that they repaid a period of fattening on prairie corn or blue grass as generously as did local steers, despite the superior fattening qualities and choicer meat of most domestic animals.[40] One Illinois stock firm estimated that to feed the Texans required only half the capital necessary to handle prairie steers.[41] To the stockmen of central Illinois the Texas era drove home the lesson that local agricultural resources were most profitably used for feeding rather than rearing cattle. Other regions could supply the stocker and feeder beasts.

Although Illinois stockmen continued to obtain considerable numbers of steers from local general farmers, particularly in the more broken areas of the state, such cattle represented a declining percentage of those fed. Similar developments took place in Iowa, although at a somewhat slower pace.[42] The farmers who raised young cattle for sale as breeding stock provided an exception to the rule that, relatively speaking, it did not pay to maintain breeding herds in the prairie states. But the fine stockmen of Sangamon County, Illinois, or the West Liberty area in Iowa found the ranchers of the plains country to be increasingly important among their customers.

In the thirty years between 1850 and 1880 there occurred a veritable revolution in agricultural technology. In part the prairie farmer was simply the beneficiary of industrial achievements which were being applied to agriculture throughout the country. A portion of the new agricultural technology, however, bore directly on the peculiar problems of prairie agriculture. The stories of the steel plow, barbed wire and harvesting machinery are well known. Less emphasized, however, are the changes in the technology of corn culture. Here the important developments of the period were the horse-drawn corn planter and the riding and walking straddle row cultivators. A variety of practicable models of both were available by the early 1860s.[43] Together with the steel plow, these implements increased by at least twice and perhaps three times the twenty

---

40. *Iowa Homestead*, Feb. 23, 1877, p. 60.

41. James N. Brown's Sons in *National Live Stock Journal*, April 1874, pp. 123–24.

42. John A. Hopkins, Jr., *Economic History of the Production of Beef Cattle in Iowa* (Iowa City: The State Historical Society of Iowa, 1928), is a standard and very useful account of the development of the cattle industry in Iowa.

43. R. L. Ardrey, *American Agricultural Implements: A Review of Invention and Development in the Agricultural Implement Industry of the United States* (Chicago, 1894), pp. 30–35, 36–39. George W. Brown's two-row planter was the first to win a considerable reputation, but there were at least three other two-horse corn planters on exhibit at the Illinois State Fair in 1854. *Prairie Farmer*, Nov. 1854, pp. 405–6.

acres of corn which a single worker could bring through satisfactorily to harvest in earlier years.[44]

Superficially at least, the agricultural-machinery inventors failed the prairie farmer most flagrantly in the corn harvest. Although a corn harvester useful for cutting and bundling fodder or ensilage corn had appeared by the end of the century, no satisfactory corn picker was available. But there was little of the urgency in corn-picking time that characterized the harvest of the small grains. Although October and November were the most pleasant months for corn picking, the ears could remain on the stalk until the following April or March with little damage to the grain. The prairie farmer had almost six months available for the task, when other farm duties were not of an urgent nature. Even so, the character of the corn harvest changed drastically between the 1830s and the 1880s. At the earlier date, western farmers cut great quantities of corn fodder and piled or cribbed the ears in shuck to wait the husking frolic. Farmers still cut some corn fodder in the 1880s, but as Herbert Quick so ably pictured in *The Hawkeye*, they more commonly exploited the fact that one man armed with husking peg and aided by a driverless team pulling a wagon equipped with a throw board could pick as much as one hundred bushels of corn per day from the stalk.[45] No doubt this was several times the average product of the laborer of the 1830s and doubtless too, the work was much less fun than a husking frolic. In the meantime the Virginia or Kentucky system of feeding cattle their corn on the cured stalk had yielded generally to a regime of ear corn and hay fed in bunkers, although under certain conditions farmers might resort to the so-called Illinois system of turning cattle or hogs into the corn fields to pick their own feed.[46]

In part mechanization accounted for the changes which occurred in the draft animals of the prairie triangle between the 1840s and 1880s. As long as plowing was the major machine task in grain culture, oxen held an honored place on many farms. Although horses admittedly, under good conditions, could plow two acres per day to the one and one half expected of oxen, the greater strength of mature oxen and the smaller investment involved in them appealed to farmers.[47] Mechanical harvesting equipment, however, changed the picture drastically. If the reciprocating cutting bars were to operate effectively, the machines must

---

44. Peck, *Guide* (1831), p. 150; *Prairie Farmer*, Jan. 6, 1866, p. 2. In *ibid.*, March 14, 1863, p. 163, "Small Farmer" struck a more conservative note, arguing for thirty to thirty-five acres. Estimates of 1885 give forty to fifty acres, *Prairie Farmer*, Feb. 7, 1885, p. 82; Feb. 28, 1885, p. 130.

45. Herbert Quick, *The Hawkeye* (Indianapolis, 1923), pp. 263–64. The one hundred-bushel-per-day man was never common. Two wagonloads or seventy bushels per day was a day's work. A good team, a heavy crop, a strong youthful back, a short haul to the granary and an immediate change of wagons were all essential for a one hundred-bushel day. I am indebted to my colleague John Clifford on this point.

46. For use of these terms in primary source material see: U.S. Commissioner of Patents, *Report*, 1845 (Washington, 1846), p. 384; *Prairie Farmer*, March 14, 1868, p. 163; April 11, 1868, p. 236; among secondary works, Hopkins, *Beef Production*, has a particularly useful section on feeding methods, pp. 122–42.

47. John Savage Diary, May 6, 1862, Department of History and Archives, Des Moines, Iowa.

move at a faster clip than oxen displayed. At the same time, however, the weight of such machinery emphasized the need of larger and stronger horses than the Morgan or other roadster strains that farmers had preferred until this time. The light horses, also, as one journalist put it, "were too weak in the poop" for farm-to-market hauling over heavy prairie roads or to fill the needs of the prairie towns and cities for heavy dray horses.[48] The importation of Norman or Percheron breeding stock was a response to this situation.[49]

Between the 1830s and the late 1870s, machinery increased the productivity of the worker in the small-grain fields by perhaps four to six times, in the hay meadow by certainly as much, and in the corn field by perhaps twice.[50] Farmers, of course, did not spend all of their time in work on those crops or tasks which had yielded to machinery. Yet it would not be too rash probably to suggest that, over-all, the potential productivity of the individual agricultural laborer doubled during this period, most of the increase coming after 1855. Wage data are both difficult to find and hard to interpret. Apparently, however, the increased productivity of agricultural labor was not reflected in agricultural wages.[51] At the same time, the percentage of nonfamily labor was increasing in farm family households. Table 4.3 suggests that it probably rose by some 5 per cent between 1850 and 1880 in central Illinois and eastern Iowa. Evidently some farmers by the 1870s were either farming more intensively or increasing the size of their farm units. The latter suggestion is not confirmed by state averages until the next decade.

---

48. *Prairie Farmer,* July 27, 1872, p. 237.

49. The standard work on the Percheron is Alvin H. Sanders, *History of the Percheron Horse* (Chicago, 1917).

50. Despite its importance, we lack satisfactory work on the subject of labor productivity in nineteenth-century agriculture, although at least one scholar is now working on it. The most frequently used secondary works are: Fred A. Shannon, *The Farmer's Last Frontier Agriculture, 1860–1897,* pp. 140–46, and Leo Rogin, *The Introduction of Farm Machinery in its Relation to the Productivity of Labor in the Agriculture of the United States during the Nineteenth Century* (Berkeley: Univ. of California Press, 1931). The tendency has been to give too much emphasis to the relatively few examples given in U.S. Commissioner of Labor, *Report,* 1898, *Hand and Machine Labor* (2 vols.; Washington, 1899). Rogin pointed out (pp. 227–29) that in the case of wheat-growing these examples suggested labor input requirements under machine methods which were considerably less than those prevailing in many parts of the country in the 1920s as given by C. D. Kinsman in an *Appraisal of Power Used on Farms in the United States,* U.S. Department of Agriculture, *Bulletin* No. 1348 (Washington, 1925), p. 59. It seems clear that wheat culture under hand methods required more than sixty hours of human labor per acre, although seeding in standing corn might reduce the amount; the Kinsman estimate under machine methods in the mid-1920s was fifteen hours in both Indiana and Illinois. Students have been less interested in the labor savings effected in the hay meadows, but see U.S. Commissioner of Agriculture, *Report,* 1872 (Washington, 1873), pp. 289–90. See my references for corn culture in note 44.

51. U.S. Department of Agriculture, *Wages of Farm Labor in the United States,* Division of Statistics, Misc. Series 4 (Washington, 1892), pp. 16–17, 65–66; U.S. Commissioner of Patents, *Report,* 1845 (Washington, 1846), p. 1152; John Goodell, ed., *Diary of William Sewall, 1797–1846, formerly of Augusta Maine, Maryland, Virginia and Pioneer in Illinois* (Beardstown, 1930); Benjamin F. Harris, Ledger and Day Book, First National Bank, Champaign, Illinois. See also U.S. Industrial Commission, *Report,* XI (Washington, 1901), pp. 140–41.

TABLE 4.3
MALE WORK FORCE SAMPLE, FOUR CORN-BELT COUNTIES, 1850–1880[a]

	300 Farm Households Iowa and Illinois				240 Farm Households Jones County, Iowa			
	1850		1880		1850		1880	
	No.	%	No.	%	No.	%	No.	%
Owner-Operator	242	45.1	226	36.8	198	51.8	193	43.3
Tenant Householders	14	2.6	42	6.8	45	11.8	34	7.6
Laborer Householders	36	6.7	33	5.4			17	3.8
Additional Males 15 Years and Over (family)	187	34.9	200	32.5	98	25.7	134	30.1
Additional Males 15 Years and Over (nonfamily)	57	10.7	115	18.5	41	10.7	68	15.2
Total	536	100.0	616	100.0	382	100.0	446	100.0

[a]This table is based on data from the manuscript agricultural and population censuses of 1850 and 1880. The three hundred households include one hundred in Clarion Township, Bureau County, one hundred in Center Township, Cedar County, Iowa, and one hundred in Dutch Creek Township, Washington County, taken in order from the census enumerator's rolls. In Washington County in 1850, it was actually necessary to follow the enumerator through several townships to obtain one hundred families. I made no effort to obtain the same households in 1880; because of turnover this would have been a hopeless task. These selections of "neighbors" of course were not random samples. To check the work a 10 per cent random sample was taken from Jones County, Iowa, in 1880 and the same number of households, 240, was taken at random from the 1850 Jones County census, amounting in that year to almost half of the rural households. I used a standard set of random number tables in this process. I did not exclude households which were headed by women, but I did not include the ladies in my final table. Among the 240 farm households of Jones County there were seven women householders in 1850 and six in 1880; among the three hundred households there were eight in 1850 and nine in 1880. Census enumerators did not list tenants in 1850, but by comparing the property returns in the population census with the farm returns of the same year, it was possible to designate men who listed no real property, but reported a farm business as tenants. Since farm returns were in part based on the previous year's production, some new tenants may have been missed. Evidently a number of the Jones County enumerator's return sheets were not included in the final agricultural census compilation of 1850; I did not, therefore, attempt to separate tenants and householders who were simply farm laborers in that year. The number of householders designated as laborers may be too large. I placed them in this category if they designated themselves as farmers or farm laborers, and reported neither real property nor farm production. Some farmers who had just arrived in the community but had not yet purchased a farm may therefore have fallen into this group, as well as the occasional tenant farmer.

THE CHANGES sketched above in prairie agriculture did not take place with equal speed or thoroughness on every farm. In general, the operators of the larger units first adopted the cropping patterns and combinations of enterprises best adapted to the peculiar economic and physical environments of the agricultural subregions in Illinois and Iowa or led in the introduction of improved livestock.[52] A few owners of average-sized or small farms, however, were as

---

52. For a discussion of these matters and a case study see Allan G. Bogue, "Pioneer Farmers and Innovation," *Iowa Journal of History* 56 (Jan. 1958), 1–36.

innovation-minded as the larger operators and gentlemen farmers were notorious experimenters. Occasionally, no doubt, landlords also assisted in the innovation process either through specific leasing terms or by retaining a larger share in management decisions than ordinary. There is reason to suspect that the innovators were somewhat better educated than the average farmer and certainly no older than the average age of farm operators in their communities. Almost certainly, too, the innovator was found among those who provided leadership in farm clubs, Grange chapters and agricultural societies. He was also apt to be a community leader in the broader sense, a township or county officeholder.

Although the Illinois Industrial University was conducting cattle-feeding experiments in the 1870s and 1880s and testing varieties of corn in the 1880s, the agricultural colleges of Illinois and Iowa made only minor contributions to the agricultural adjustments of the farmers in those states prior to 1890. The adjustments stemmed rather from the ideas, successes and failures of the farmers themselves and of the mechanics and businessmen who served them. Few, if any, inventions or adaptations were the work of isolated geniuses who sensed an important need and met it by the application of principles hitherto unapplied to the problem. The early files of the *Prairie Farmer* confirm Jonathan B. Turner's role as the most articulate of the promoters of Osage orange hedge, but he was certainly not the first midwesterner to suggest the possibilities of Bois d'Arc in print.[53] John Deere received no mention in an article on the development of the steel plow in northern Illinois which appeared during the mid-1840s.[54]

"The power of capital in this newly settled or *settling* region," wrote Morris Birkbeck in 1818, "is not thoroughly understood...."[55] A shortage of capital and credit retarded economic change in the prairie triangle through much of the period of our interest. Historians generally agree that farm-making on the prairies called for more capital than had been the case in older timbered regions. Scarcity of capital, of course, was a relative matter and generally typi-

---

53. *Prairie Farmer*, Sept. 1841, p. 65; March 1842, p. 26; Sept. 1844, p. 217.

54. *Ibid.*, Feb. 1846, p. 42.

55. Morris Birkbeck, *Notes on a Journey in America, from the Coast of Virginia to the Territory of Illinois* (London, 1818), p. 144. We need more studies of farm credit in the nineteenth-century Midwest, particularly of lending at the local level. At this point the major dependence must be on William G. Murray, *An Economic Analysis of Farm Mortgages in Story County, Iowa, 1854–1931*, Iowa State College of Agriculture and Mechanic Arts, Agricultural Experiment Station, *Research Bulletin* No. 156 (Ames, 1933); David Rozman, "Land Credit in Walnut Grove Township, Knox County, Illinois," *Journal of Land and Public Utility Economics* 4 (Aug. 1928), 305–12; Margaret Beattie Bogue, *Patterns from the Sod,* pp. 156–75; Allan G. Bogue, *Money at Interest: The Farm Mortgage on the Middle Border* (Ithaca: Cornell Univ. Press, 1955), pp. 1–43. For interest rates in other lines of enterprise in the same period, see Frederick R. Macaulay, *Some Theoretical Problems Suggested by the Movements of Interest Rates, Bond Yields and Stock Prices in the United States Since 1856* (New York: National Bureau of Economic Research, 1938), A3–A176, and Lance E. Davis, "The New England Textile Mills and the Capital Markets: A Study of Industrial Borrowing 1840–1860," *The Journal of Economic History* 20, No. 1 (March 1960), 1–30.

cal of new settlements. The rate of return on loans backed by farm property in Illinois and Iowa rode above 10 per cent for the most part during the 1850s, 1860s, and early 1870s, a more handsome yield than that from funds invested in a variety of enterprises elsewhere. During the 1840s the rate may have been still higher, and certainly was in areas where Federal land sales were scheduled to take place shortly.

Easier access to credit would no doubt have speeded changes in farm practices and affected the combination of enterprises on many prairie farms. Complaints of plows that would not scour long after the development of the steel plow reflected the reluctance of western farmers to pay the added cost of the steel implement—almost double that of iron plows. Horses no doubt would have replaced oxen much more rapidly than they did if credit had been easier. Although available markets and transportation facilities modified the pattern, the pioneer farmer was under economic pressure to find the farming system which required the smallest capital outlay. This in many cases was cash grain farming. No doubt easier credit would have allowed some farmers to introduce livestock into their production programs to a greater extent at an earlier period than they were able to do. It would doubtless also have more rapidly eliminated from the prairie scene the Sucker and Iowa barns, those hay-topped draughty stables which sheltered many of the prairie farm animals in the early years of farm-making.

Western interest rates were related to the age of the community as well as to broader factors in the American economy as a whole. But, if rates tended to fall during the settling-in process, the farmer of our period discovered that he must increase his investment in farm machinery and add to the size of his farm if he were to use his labor most effectively in the new era of horsepower technology. And from the time that the first settler ran his claim lines in most prairie settlements, the direction of land values was steadily upward, except in years of acute depression. Although there are other ways of viewing them both, land speculation and tenancy are properly considered in the perspective of capital deficiency.[56]

The land speculator was prepared to sell land on credit, a service which the Federal Government refused to offer after 1820. Speculation was a mechanism, in other words, which allowed the impecunious settler to capitalize his sweat and muscle. The taxes which speculators paid on their lands prior to sale to resident farmers assisted pioneer communities, hard up for public revenues, in providing community services for the early settlers.[57] Perhaps the fees which they exacted for their service were greater than need be. But given the insti-

---

56. Of American agricultural historians, Paul W. Gates has devoted the most attention to land speculation and tenancy in the Midwest. Typical of his work is "The Role of the Land Speculator in Western Development," *The Pennsylvania Magazine of History and Biography* 56 (July 1942), 314–33; and *Frontier Landlords and Pioneer Tenants* (Ithaca: Cornell Univ. Press, 1945).

57. Margaret B. Bogue and Allan G. Bogue, "Profits and the Frontier Land Speculator," *The Journal of Economic History* 17, No. 1 (March 1957), 2–3, fn. 7.

tutional framework and the capital resources of the settler class in general, the speculators may actually have speeded the development of some areas, instead of retarding it as is often suggested.

The Federal census takers did not collect data on tenancy prior to the enumeration of 1880, and part of the literature on prairie tenancy is devoted simply to proving that it existed at an early date. The manuscript censuses of 1850, 1860, and 1870 do provide information from which we can calculate fairly precise maximum and minimum estimates of tenancy. Thus between 7 and 11 per cent of the farm operators in Clarion Township, Bureau County, Illinois were tenants in 1850, as were between 10 and 22 per cent in Union Township, Davis County, Iowa.[58] In those sections of Illinois and Iowa which settlers occupied between 1830 and 1890, probably between 5 and 15 per cent of the farm operators were tenants at a very early stage of settlement. They became so because they did not have the funds with which to purchase a farm for themselves, or in some cases the means to develop their own small holdings rapidly enough to insure an income in their first years' residence in a new community.

We can never know the exact composition of the landlord class. Some lessors were land speculators or large holders who rented land in order to improve it or to defray the cost of taxes and supervision prior to sale. Some few planned long-term tenant operations. Others were moneylenders who met the costs of upkeep on foreclosed land by renting. The greatest number of prairie landlords, however, was probably made up of the owners of only one farm or at the most several—farm widows, local businessmen, county officers and especially farmers, both active and retired.[59] These latter types of landlords became more common as communities aged, but they were present in numbers soon after the first settlers had arrived.

By 1900, just under 50 per cent of the farmers in one Iowa county were tenants; the maximum in Illinois was over 60 per cent. The rates of tenancy were much higher in some districts of the two states than in others. Why so? The areas of highest tenancy lay mainly on highly productive soils. The wet prairies of east central Illinois and central and northwestern Iowa supported

---

58. The procedure here is to extract from the manuscript population census the names of all those heads of households listing themselves as farmers, but owning no real estate. This group comprises the maximum number of possible tenants. By checking these names against the agricultural census rolls, one can find those who reported a farm business. This group represents the minimum number of possible tenants, and probably all of those who were farming on any considerable scale. Since, however, the agricultural census in part involved reports on the crops harvested in the previous year, some new tenants may not have given a farm return. This method of course disregards bachelor tenants who did not maintain their own households, but the number of these was probably quite small. The Federal Census of 1880 did, of course, show tenancy present in the frontier region of northwestern Iowa.

59. I hazard this suggestion on the basis of much reading in the biographical sketches in the county histories. Such information defies quantification for various reasons, but certainly does show a wide distribution of the ownership of tenant farms.

a high percentage of tenant operators.[60] Drainage was necessary to make the wet prairies fully tillable, in effect raising the price of the land for the farmer. On the other hand, the high productivity of these soils, once brought to tilth, encouraged businessmen to buy farms as investments. Prosperous farmers invested their savings in tenant farms as well. Some owner-operators of these areas amassed competencies rapidly and retired to live on their savings and rents. Instead of liquidating estates by cash sale, nonresident heirs preferred to retain or divide the family holdings in the belief that they could find no safer investment. In limited districts long-term tenant estates which dated from the settlement period may have increased the rate of tenancy. Finally, topography and marketing facilities encouraged cash grain farming in the wet prairie region, a type of farming operation which was somewhat more adapted to tenancy than those in which greater emphasis is placed on livestock. But, in 1900, there was a high rate of tenancy in eight of the nine westernmost counties of Iowa, which lie on the well-drained Missouri loess of the western slope. Here drainage was no great problem, but most of the other factors inducing high tenancy rates were apparently present.

It is clear that the farmers of the prairie triangle in Illinois and Iowa experienced their greatest difficulties during the mid- and late 1870s. Depressed prices, bad seasons, and, in Iowa, even grasshoppers bedeviled them. We need to know much more abut the behavior of taxes at the community level in the nineteenth century, but local commitments for railroad building especially may have made tax rates relatively high and sticky in many counties during the 1870s.[61] In many cases, too, farm units were too small to allow the operator and his family to utilize the enhanced labor productivity which machinery had given them — they were underemployed. In three widely scattered Iowa townships the percentage of real estate mortgages which went to foreclosure proceedings between 1852 and 1896 was 3.2.[62] But of the mortgages filed between 1870 and 1874, inclusive, and between 1875 and 1879, inclusive, the average number going to court was 5.2 per cent in both cases. By contrast the failure rate in the years 1885–1889 and 1890–1896 was 1.7 and 1.8 per cent. Some-

---

60. For a discussion of the northern wet prairie with maps see Leslie Hewes, "The Northern Wet Prairie of the United States: Nature, Sources of Information, and Extent," *Annals of the Association of American Geographers* 41 (Dec. 1951), 307–23.

61. The works bearing most particularly on this subject are Kathleen Bessie Jacklin, "Local Aid to Railroads in Illinois, 1848–1870" (M.A. thesis, Cornell University, 1958); Earl S. Beard, "Railroads in Iowa, 1865–1875: A Study of Attitudes" (M.A. thesis, State University of Iowa, 1950); Robert M. Haig, *A History of the General Property Tax in Illinois,* University of Illinois *Studies in the Social Sciences,* III. (Urbana, 1914), p. 1; John E. Brindley, *History of Taxation in Iowa* (Iowa City, 1911). My own research on the taxation of agricultural land in Muscatine County, Iowa, showed that taxes there were probably higher relative to the value of agricultural land during the 1870s than in the later years of the century.

62. These were Warren Township, Bremer County, Union Township, Davis County, and Hamilton Township, Hamilton County, data taken from the Mortgage Indexes and Registers and analyzed by me. The findings are in accord with the works cited in note 55.

what less precise evidence reveals a similar picture in Illinois. Contrast these percentages with the failure rates of 40 and 50 per cent which occurred in parts of Kansas during the late 1880s and early 1890s. Here, no doubt, is one reason why the farmers of Illinois and Iowa had little interest in Populism. Perhaps, too, the time-hallowed notion of a thirty-year agricultural depression following the Civil War does not fit the facts for all parts of the Middle West.

The more progressive farmers of the prairie triangle evidently entered the 1880s aware that their best future lay in increasing the size of their farm units to take advantage of the new technology. They had learned, too, that profit lay in judicious combinations of corn, hogs, and cattle while not discarding the small grains, particularly oats, nor ignoring tame grasses and clovers — a necessity as the prairie-grass commons disappeared. Corn-root worms and smut convinced farmers who cast their lot unreservedly with the corn crop that some rotation paid. The need to utilize labor supplies effectively worked to the same end. Prairie farmers now found that tiling rewarded the investment. The farmers of the black-earth counties in Illinois took up this task seriously in the 1880s, although there had of course been much ditch drainage earlier. The farmers of the wet prairies in Iowa followed suit in a few years. Cheap labor and falling interest rates helped speed the tasks of adjustment. Ten per cent was the usual rate on farm mortgages in 1878 in central Illinois and much of Iowa; it had fallen to 6 per cent by 1896.

If owner-operators were apparently solving their problems with considerable success during the 1880s and 1890s, the same was hardly true of the tenants or farm laborers who aspired to ownership. During the last half of the nineteenth century, the increased productivity of agricultural labor benefited the farm operator considerably more than it did the laborer. At the same time, the land equivalent of the monthly agricultural wage fell drastically. Land obtained for $1.25 per acre in central Illinois or eastern Iowa in the 1830s or 1840s now commanded prices of $40 to $60 and, in many cases, even more. The cost of drainage alone could add from $5 to $20 to the farmer's investment in his acres. The cost of necessary machinery had also increased during the same period, but in the face of rising land values it had become proportionately less important in the total investment of the owner-operator. According to the Federal censuses, land and buildings accounted for 76 per cent ($1,261) of total investment in land, machinery, and livestock on the "average farm" of 1850 in Illinois and 77 per cent ($1,125) in Iowa; the corresponding 1900 figures were 89 per cent ($7,586) and 84 per cent ($8,023) in these two states. Tenancy rates, therefore, edged upward in Illinois and Iowa during the last years of the nineteenth century. We should remember, however, that no agricultural area in the national history of this country has been able to absorb all of its would-be farmers.

SO THE VIRGIN LAND of central Illinois and Iowa gave way to farms, to feed lots and above all, to corn fields. A recent writer has maintained:

"By 1879 there existed a well defined, although unnamed corn belt. . . ."[63] At his date the northwestern and western boundaries of the corn belt as we know it were, of course, still quite fluid. But in Illinois and the older areas of Iowa, regional allegiance to the corn plant had been pledged somewhat earlier. In 1870 the *National Live Stock Journal* used the phrase "corn belt" in its columns.[64] It would be years yet before it became a part of national or official parlance. But out in Illinois and Iowa the farmers already knew that productive soils and the recurring miracle of broad-leafed fields of green, growing in rain and summer heat, had set their land apart.

BIBLIOGRAPHICAL NOTE

Nineteenth-century agricultural history seems to be especially rich in contested topics, especially for the number of historians engaged in the subdiscipline: claim clubs, tenancy (the "agricultural ladder"), land speculation, the capitalist transformation, crop diversification, and other topics have yielded starkly contrasting interpretations, even though they rely heavily on more "scientific," quantifiable evidence. Much of the recent work in the field of agricultural history continues to take as its point of departure the pioneering quantification work done at the University of Iowa by Allan Bogue and his students, especially Robert Swierenga, and much of it relies heavily on evidence from Iowa. On quantification at the University of Iowa from the late 1950s through the 1970s, see chap. 1, "Inside the 'Iowa School,'" in Bogue's *Clio and the Bitch Goddess: Quantification in American Political History* (Beverly Hills, CA: Sage Publications, 1983), 19–50; and William Silag, "Pioneers in Quantitative History at the University of Iowa," *Annals of Iowa* 46 (1981), 121–34.

The literature in the new rural and agricultural history is too vast, even on Iowa, for a brief bibliographical note. The essays and their bibliographies in Lou Ferleger, ed., *Agriculture and National Development* (Ames, 1990), especially those by R. Douglas Hurt, Donald L. Winters, Dorothy Schwieder, Elizabeth Fox-Genovese, and Kathleen Conzen, provide a good guide to the literature. For an early definition of and agenda for the new rural history, see Robert P. Swierenga, "Theoretical Perspectives on the New Rural History: From Environmentalism to Modernism," *Agricultural History* 56 (1982), 495–502. On the use of census materials by historians, see Robert P. Swierenga, "Historians and the Census: The Historiography of Census Research," *Annals of Iowa* 50 (1990), 650–73. On tenancy, see Donald L. Winters, "Agricultural Tenancy in the Nineteenth-Century Middle West: The Historiographical Debate," *Indiana Magazine of History* 29 (1982), 128–53; and idem, *Farmers without Farms: Agricultural Tenancy in Nineteenth-Century Iowa* (Westport, CT,

---

63. William Warntz, "An Historical Consideration of the Terms 'Corn' and 'Corn Belt' in the United States," *Agricultural History* 31 (Jan. 1957), 40.

64. *National Live Stock Journal*, Nov. 1870, p. 78.

1978). On claim clubs, see the frequently reprinted essay by Allan G. Bogue, "The Iowa Claim Clubs: Symbol and Substance," *Mississippi Valley Historical Review* 45 (1958), 231–53. On land speculation, see Robert P. Swierenga, *Pioneers and Profits: Land Speculation on the Iowa Frontier* (Ames, 1968); and idem, "Land Speculator 'Profits' Reconsidered: Central Iowa as a Test Case," *Journal of Economic History* 26 (1966), 1–28. On "the capitalist transformation," see Steven Hahn and Jonathan Prude, eds., *The Countryside in the Age of Capitalist Transformation* (Chapel Hill, NC, 1985).

Although much of the new rural history focuses on the social experience of rural dwellers, that focus appears primarily in works dealing with the twentieth century, which will be treated in the note to Deborah Fink's essay below. Most nineteenth-century rural and agricultural history still focuses largely on agriculture's economic aspects. Among the most recent work, the most widely cited is probably Jeremy Atack and Fred Bateman, *To Their Own Soil: Agriculture in the Antebellum North* (Ames, 1987). On Iowa specifically, see David W. Galenson and Clayne L. Pope, "Economic and Geographic Mobility on the Farming Frontier: Evidence from Appanoose County, Iowa, 1850–1870," *Journal of Economic History* 49 (1989), 635–55. A notable exception to the economic focus is Fred W. Peterson, *Homes in the Heartland: Balloon Frame Farmhouses of the Upper Midwest, 1850–1920* (Lawrence, KS, 1992); and idem, "Tradition and Change in Nineteenth-Century Farmhouses," *Annals of Iowa* 52 (1993), 251–81. The standard history of Iowa agriculture remains Earle D. Ross, *Iowa Agriculture: An Historical Survey* (Iowa City, 1951).

5

The Political Culture of Antebellum Iowa: An Overview

ROBERT COOK

Along with their farms, Iowa's early settlers established political institutions. Like frontier and settlement issues, early Iowa politics, especially the formation of the Republican Party, was long a staple of Iowa history. As historians in recent decades have become increasingly interested in the social fabric of life, the nature of their research and writing about politics has changed, but the quantity has not diminished. They focus more on political and ideological issues and on the makeup of various constituencies rather than on narratives of elections and individual accomplishments. Iowa was a key player in the demise of what historians call the second party system and the rise of the third. The story has been told many times, but in this essay Robert Cook retells it using the terms historians have developed in recent years. This essay engages in historiographical conversation more explicitly and more extensively than any other in this volume, a fitting approach for such a well-worn topic.

THE POLITICAL CULTURE of the antebellum United States has been exercising historians ever since the professionalization of their discipline in the late nineteenth century. During the first half of the twentieth century most historians used traditional paradigms to explain the volatile politics of the 1840s and 1850s. Focusing primarily on the activities of political elites, they explained support for the Whig, Democratic, and Republican parties in terms of the great national issues of the day—tariffs, banking, and the expansion of slavery, to name just three.[1] After the Second World War, however, a growing interest

---

1. Eric Foner, *Free Soil, Free Labor, Free Men: The Ideology of the Republican Party Before the Civil War* (New York, 1970), 1–10, is a useful brief introduction to the literature on the causes of the Civil War.

Originally published as Robert Cook, "The Political Culture of Antebellum Iowa: An Overview," *Annals of Iowa* 52 (1993), 225–50. Copyright © 1993 by the State Historical Society of Iowa. Reprinted by permission of the publisher.

in the social fabric of American politics spawned research into the dynamics of party affiliation at the grass roots. Much of that research focused on developments at the state or regional level.²

In 1961 Lee Benson's pathbreaking study of New York during the Jacksonian period stimulated a wide-ranging debate over the bases of popular participation in American politics during the formative years of the republic. Benson argued that partisanship in New York was largely a product of ethnicity and denominational attachment. Political organizations attracted voters not primarily because they adopted attractive policies but because their rhetoric, choice of candidates, and overall worldview meshed with a voter's experience and values.³

Benson's "ethnocultural" interpretation of New York politics challenged the traditional notion that antebellum voters cast their ballots as issue-oriented individuals. The cultural identity of groups, not support for antislavery or Henry Clay's American system, explained party affiliation. Although later works by Ronald Formisano, Paul Kleppner, and others confirmed the ethnocultural interpretation, it did not go unchallenged. Eric Foner's influential *Free Soil, Free Labor, Free Men* and Michael Holt's provocative analysis of politics in the 1850s, for example, cast doubt upon it by suggesting that voters were more issue-conscious than Benson and other ethnocultural historians claimed.⁴

By the early 1990s a new synthesis was beginning to emerge. That synthesis took into account the findings of the ethnoculturalists, but highlighted the links between party affiliation and economic change. Fusing the new cultural history (grounded in the writings of anthropologist Clifford Geertz and the British Marxist historian, E. P. Thompson), the emerging "republican synthesis," modernization theory, and the insights of the Benson school, historians such as Harry Watson, Charles Sellers, and Bruce Levine posited that while political affiliation in the antebellum period had diverse social, ideological, and economic roots, the key to understanding the era lay in a phenomenon called the market revolution.⁵ This helpful term—more comprehensive than

---

2. V. O. Key, *Southern Politics in State and Nation* (New York, 1949) was a pioneering study of voting behavior in a single region.

3. Lee Benson, *The Concept of Jacksonian Democracy: New York as a Test Case* (Princeton, 1961).

4. Ronald P. Formisano, *The Birth of Mass Political Parties: Michigan, 1827–1861* (Princeton, 1971); Paul Kleppner, *The Cross of Culture: A Social Analysis of Midwestern Politics, 1850–1900* (New York, 1970); Foner, *Free Soil, Free Labor, Free Men;* Michael Holt, *The Political Crisis of the 1850s* (New York, 1978).

5. Clifford Geertz's contribution to the synthesis is encapsulated in "Ideology as a Cultural System," in David Apter, ed., *Ideology and Discontent* (New York, 1964), 47–76. Edward P. Thompson, *The Making of the English Working Class* (London, 1963), provided the model for several sparkling studies of early American labor, most notably Sean Wilentz, *Chants Democratic: New York City and the Rise of the American Working Class, 1788–1850* (New York, 1984); and Bruce Laurie, *Working People of Philadelphia, 1800–1850* (Philadelphia, 1980). For an introduction to the growing corpus of work on republican ideology in the United States,

George R. Taylor's "transportation revolution," coined in the 1950s—denotes the transformation of the United States in the space of roughly seventy years (1790–1860) from a relatively simple, preindustrial society to an increasingly complex, modern economy.[6]

The agency of this transformation, commercial-industrial capitalism, had a critical impact on the institutions and social fabric of the nation, prompting seismic shifts in the loci of political and economic power, and forcing a rearrangement of the traditional bonds among individuals and groups alike. Master craftsmen became capitalist entrepreneurs; journeymen found themselves subsumed within the ranks of an incipient proletariat; and middle-class women were relegated to the domestic sphere.[7] Joint stock corporations rose and fell with the economic cycles; increasing numbers of black slaves toiled on southern plantations to fuel the consumer boom in North America and Europe; and thousands of eastern farm families migrated westward to capitalize on the growing demand for foodstuffs. The nation's spatial and qualitative economic growth undermined the old certainties such as status and kinship networks by promoting occupational and geographical mobility. The inevitable search for security, order, and control led people to turn to new institutions or to try to revitalize old ones. Churches, trade unions, masonic lodges, and political parties were swept by the winds of change as reformers and conservatives sought new agendas, notably, sabbatarianism, temperance, and land reform. A wave of Catholic immigration from Europe after 1830 added to the confusion. So too did the birth of the abolitionist movement in the same decade. In short, the latest historical research has revealed the market revolution to have been an agent of unparalleled social ferment, and one with important consequences for our understanding of antebellum politics.

Iowa, of course, participated fully in this transformation. In fact, its period of greatest demographic, economic, and institutional expansion coincided exactly with its encounter with the market revolution. Strangely, however, the state's antebellum political culture has been sadly neglected. Important monographs on individual politicians and the early Republican party do exist, but they do not answer the questions that historians of American

---

see Robert E. Shalhope, "Toward a Republican Synthesis: The Emergence of an Understanding of Republicanism in American Historiography," *William and Mary Quarterly* 29 (1972), 49–80; and Daniel T. Rodgers, "Republicanism: The Career of a Concept," *Journal of American History* 79 (1992), 11–38. The best attempt to analyze American development in terms of the modernization process is Richard Brown, *Modernization: The Transformation of American Life, 1600–1865* (New York, 1976). The concept of the market revolution has been developed by, among others, Harry L. Watson, *Liberty and Power: The Politics of Jacksonian America* (New York, 1990); Charles G. Sellers, *The Market Revolution and Jacksonian America, 1815–1846* (New York, 1991); and Bruce Levine, *Half Slave and Half Free: The Roots of Civil War* (New York, 1992).

6. George R. Taylor, *The Transportation Revolution, 1815–1860* (New York, 1951).

7. On the evolution of the American working class, see Bruce Laurie, *Artisans into Workers: Labor in Nineteenth-Century America* (New York, 1989).

party politics are now asking.[8] The old debates over whether the state's Republican party was ideologically sound on the issue of race or whether its leaders were hand in glove with the railroads need recontextualizing in the wake of the new scholarship.

That is the task of this essay. Fortunately, in the past three decades scholars have produced a number of sophisticated studies of the early Iowa economy.[9] By synthesizing this literature with recent work on party politics in the antebellum United States, one can sketch the political culture of antebellum Iowa in a way that offers a fresh perspective for students of Iowa politics while adding Iowa's experience to the record of the national experience. The overview begins by investigating the impact of the market revolution on the trans-Mississippi West. Debates generated by the adaptation to new market conditions reveal the fundamental dynamics of interparty competition during a period when expanding population and economic growth were transforming the face of the prairies. Jacksonian Democracy claimed the allegiance of a majority of Iowa voters in the 1840s, but material and ethnocultural divisions arising from the processes of change played a key role in promoting a relatively healthy two-party system on the west bank of the Mississippi River. This second party system broke down in the late 1840s and 1850s, however, undermined by escalating ethnocultural and sectional divisions. The third party system emerged in the late 1850s and 1860s out of the ruins of the second.

THE MARKET REVOLUTION came quickly to the wooded river valleys and open prairies of Iowa. The United States was barely a trans-Appalachian power when it emerged from the Revolution, and the Mississippi valley was

---

8. Morton Rosenberg, *Iowa on the Eve of the Civil War: A Decade of Frontier Politics* (Norman, OK, 1972), is the most reliable account of antebellum Iowa politics. Important, if old-fashioned, biographies include William Salter, *The Life of James W. Grimes* (New York, 1876), and Dan Elbert Clark, *Samuel Jordan Kirkwood* (Iowa City, 1917). Other states have been better served, and Iowa itself has been the focus of important ethnocultural studies of the late nineteenth century. Significant studies of other states include Stephen L. Hansen, *The Making of the Third Party System: Voters and Parties in Illinois, 1850–1876* (Ann Arbor, MI, 1980); Stephen E. Maizlish, *The Triumph of Sectionalism: The Transformation of Ohio Politics, 1844–1856* (Kent, OH, 1983); Dale Baum, *The Civil War Party System: The Case of Massachusetts, 1848–1876* (Chapel Hill, NC, 1984). Ethnocultural studies of politics in the late nineteenth century in which Iowa figures prominently include Richard J. Jensen, *The Winning of the Midwest: Social and Political Conflict, 1888–1896* (Chicago, 1971); and Ballard C. Campbell, *Representative Democracy: Public Policy and Midwestern Legislatures in the Late Nineteenth Century* (Cambridge, MA, 1980).

9. Insightful modern studies of the early Iowa and midwestern economies include Allan G. Bogue, *From Prairie to Corn Belt: Farming on the Illinois and Iowa Prairies in the Nineteenth Century* (Chicago, 1963); Robert P. Swierenga, *Pioneers and Profits: Land Speculation on the Iowa Frontier* (Ames, 1968); idem, *Acres for Cents: Delinquent Tax Auctions in Frontier Iowa* (Westport, CT, 1976); Erling A. Erickson, *Banking in Frontier Iowa, 1836–1865* (Ames, 1971); Donald L. Winters, *Farmers Without Farms: Agricultural Tenancy in Nineteenth Century Iowa* (Westport, CT, 1978); Jeremy Atack and Fred Bateman, *To Their Own Soil: Agriculture in the Antebellum North* (Ames, 1987); Timothy Mahoney, *River Towns in the Great West: The Structure of Provincial Urbanization in the American Midwest, 1820–1870* (Cambridge, 1990).

a thinly populated region under the nominal control of France. Jefferson's purchase of Louisiana gave the new republic sovereignty over the country, but it remained thinly settled until population growth in the East, burgeoning European and domestic demand for foodstuffs (principally grain), and technological advances such as the steamboat and the cotton gin opened up the area to white settlement on a massive scale. Although whites had long been interested in the lead mines centered around Galena and Dubuque, colonization of the future territory of Iowa did not begin in earnest until after the Black Hawk Purchase of 1832. By 1844, the white male citizens of Iowa were ready to write their own constitution and apply for admission to the American Union. Granted generous borders by Congress in 1846, they prepared to make a garden of what, from their perspective, had hitherto been an unproductive wilderness.[10]

The market revolution had an immediate impact on Iowa, bringing about the rapid destruction of the indigenous civilizations. Tribes such as the Sauk and Mesquakie, the Winnebago and the Potawatomi found their self-sufficient, communal societies swept aside by the tide of white settlers who crossed the Mississippi after 1832. Within twenty years these tribes had been banished from Iowa. The few natives who remained were forced to make concessions to Euro-American mores. Even the fierce resistance of the Sioux had been broken by the time the Civil War began in 1861.[11] The tragedy of these peoples was not unlike that of other hunter-gatherers in other parts of the globe: the San in Cape Colony, the aborigines of Australia and Tasmania, the indigenous peoples of the Brazilian interior. All discovered that technology, demography, and disease were usually on the side of the white intruders and that the spirits of their ancestors were no match for crusading Christianity (Protestant or Catholic).

Replacing the hunting and gathering economies of the indigenous tribes was a dynamic form of commercial capitalism that had already begun to transform white communities back east. All of Iowa's early settlers had felt the effects of this new force: some, such as the agricultural migrants from New England and the South, may have been casualties; others, particularly farsighted merchants and eastern farmers with capital, had benefitted from it. The economy the early settlers helped to construct was a complex and changing one, but its initial vitality lay in the export of foodstuffs.[12] Farm prices were buoyant for much of the 1830s and 1840s, providing incentives for grain

---

10. For a reliable account of the political and socioeconomic development of prestatehood Iowa, see Leland L. Sage, *A History of Iowa* (Ames, 1974), 52–79.

11. Ibid., 45–51, 58–59, 70–72, 107–8.

12. The growth of commercial farming in Iowa is the subject of several studies, but see especially Mildred Throne, "Southern Iowa Agriculture, 1833–1890: The Progress from Subsistence to Commercial Corn-Belt Farming," *Agricultural History* 23 (1949), 124–30; Earle D. Ross, *Iowa Agriculture: An Historical Survey* (Iowa City, 1951), 12–50. Mahoney, *River Towns*, places early Iowa's economic development firmly in a regional context. For details of one of antebellum Iowa's most significant food-processing industries, see Margaret Walsh, *The Rise of the Midwestern Meat Packing Industry* (Lexington, KY, 1982).

producers to purchase and improve fertile land in the West. With the federal government keen to dispose of public lands at relatively cheap prices, speculators with access to credit had no difficulty gaining control of vast acreages and selling them off to migrant farmers for a profit. At the same time that land sales were taking place, villages and towns began to spring up, first along the major river courses, then on the open prairies themselves. These urban centers competed vigorously for the export trade of the region, serviced the consumer demands of their hinterlands, and, in the case of the largest of them on the Mississippi, dispatched the foodstuffs to St. Louis or Chicago. By the late 1840s, small cities such as Dubuque, Davenport, Keokuk, and Burlington were processing significant quantities of local meat and grain themselves.

THE SOCIAL STRUCTURE of the young state was determined largely by the expanding commercial economy of the upper Mississippi valley. At the top of the scale were, unsurprisingly, those with money and land: prosperous farmers in the countryside, wealthy merchants and lawyers in the towns. Each of these groups speculated heavily in real estate during the 1840s, capitalizing on rising prices to build up and entrench their dominant position in society.[13] A thriving middle class consisting of millers, commercial farmers, grocers, professionals, and skilled workers developed quickly as the fluid frontier gave way to more mature (if by no means rigid) patterns of settlement. Poorer squatters, itinerants, and unskilled farm and urban workers made up the lower sorts. Many of this latter group were European migrants. Irish Catholics were particularly conspicuous as manual laborers in the river cities; a few were free blacks from the Old Northwest and the upper South.[14]

Iowa's antebellum political leadership was composed largely of white males drawn from the upper and middle ranks of society. This too was hardly surprising. Wealth gave people access to education, connections, leisure time, and power. In geographical terms it made them more persistent — more committed to one particular location, less inclined to keep moving on in pursuit of the American Dream.[15] Even though early Iowa was a rhetorically egalitarian and (in relative terms) politically democratic society, poor men seldom found

---

13. Swierenga, *Pioneers and Profits,* 101–2; Allan G. Bogue, "The Iowa Claim Clubs: Symbol and Substance," *Mississippi Valley Historical Review* 45 (1958), 231–53.

14. No one has systematically analyzed class formation in antebellum Iowa. My comments here are derived principally from my own trawls through the 1850 and 1860 federal manuscript censuses. Relevant local studies include George A. Boeck, "An Early Iowa Community: Aspects of Economic, Social, and Political Development in Burlington, Iowa, 1833–1866" (Ph.D. diss. University of Iowa, 1961), chaps. 2, 4, 7, 10; and David W. Galenson and Clayne L. Pope, "Economic and Geographic Mobility on the Farming Frontier: Evidence from Appanoose County, Iowa, 1850–1870," *Journal of Economic History* 49 (1989), 635–55. On Iowa blacks before the Civil War, see James L. Hill, "Migration of Blacks to Iowa, 1820–1960," *Journal of Negro History* 66 (1966), 289–303.

15. Galenson and Pope, "Economic and Geographic Mobility," 644.

their way into the state legislature, let alone the United States Congress. Notwithstanding Frederick Jackson Turner's frontier thesis, substantial settlers (be they self-made men or the beneficiaries of inherited wealth) dominated political life in Iowa during the antebellum years.

How did members of the state's socioeconomic elite manage to maintain their hold on power in an age when aristocratic notions and ostentatious shows of wealth were hardly de rigueur for aspiring officeholders? What, to rephrase the question in more scientific terms, were the key elements of linkage between elites and masses in early Iowa? To answer this question properly we need to probe the political culture of the day, for this complex phenomenon conferred legitimacy upon government and thereby provided one of the most important social gels of the age.

THE STATE'S POLITICAL CULTURE was a dynamic one, forged out of a constant dialogue among the voters, their representatives, and, increasingly, the partisan press. One might even go so far as to say that the dialogue was as fertile as the soil on which it took place. Put simply, it consisted of a set of primary and secondary values. The primary values were shared in common by white Iowans and provided rich fiber for the growth of what was one of the most democratic societies in the western world in the middle of the nineteenth century. The secondary values were the roots of a highly competitive two-party system whose seeds had been blown across the Mississippi from the East.

The primary values need not detain us long. They were ones held by nearly all native-born white Americans in this period: a deep commitment to republican government, the sovereignty of the people, and the developing concept of meritocracy. The sources of these values were American nationalism and the Bible. All native-born Iowans had been reared on the myths of the Revolution — they knew from what their schoolteachers and parents had told them that the nation had been founded by heroes, that republican governments were superior to monarchies, and that the United States was a haven from the corruptions of the Old World. The vast majority of Iowans had no doubt, too, that there was a God — an inscrutable and capricious one, perhaps, but a God nonetheless. They knew this because they had been listening to stories from the Old and New Testaments since their birth. Denominational allegiance complicated matters, but every Iowan knew the worth of individual responsibility and self-discipline, even if they did not always practice what they had been taught. Republican and Christian values were reinforced by the growth of the new commercial economy: free labor capitalism meant that one had to sink or swim on one's own merits. Perhaps this had always been the case, even in preindustrial societies. But at least in the old days communities and kinship networks had provided some kind of safety net. Nineteenth-century economic development continued to erode traditional society, forcing Americans — Iowans included — increasingly to fall back on their own devices.

Local politics would have been a dull affair had they been shaped solely by these fundamental cultural values. What gave political conflict its edge on the prairies were the debates occasioned by commitment to these values. Everyone agreed that republicanism was a good thing, but how was republicanism to be defined? How was it to be protected in a rapidly changing world? Who was to protect it: government or the people themselves? Religion did much to shape Iowans' worldview, but what sort of Christian country was America, was Iowa, supposed to be? A Protestant one presumably, but which variant of Protestantism was to hold sway: evangelical or liturgical, Methodist or Baptist? Most people accepted that the influence of the market economy was healthy (it did after all lead to progress), but what role should the people and their representatives take in controlling and nurturing it? Should they, indeed, make any attempt to interfere with forces that many economists claimed had their own irrepressible dynamic? And what of the institutions thrown up by the market: banks, railroad corporations, and textile mills? Should they be left to their own devices, or should they be reined in as threats to the public good?

THE FIERCE INTERPARTY COMPETITION of the 1840s and 1850s emerged from the debates over such broad questions and the secondary values they spawned. The parties themselves, some more influential and long-lived than others, exercised a remarkable influence over the lives of most Iowans from the territorial period onwards. They did so because most people—even women who could not vote—perceived them as legitimate governing entities and effective media of public opinion.

Political parties did not gain legitimacy automatically, however. The only way the major organizations—Democrats, Whigs, and Republicans—secured it was by convincing substantial sections of the electorate that they were representing the interests of the people and the republic. Each did this in rather different ways, but all tailored their appeals from the ideological cloth outlined above—specifically by identifying credible threats to Protestant-Republican values and institutions.

Jacksonian Democrats (regnant at first the territorial and then the state level until 1854) captured a majority of the electorate largely by pursuing a policy of negative government and free market economics. Government meddling in the affairs of the people, they argued, portended the kinds of tyranny perpetrated by the British before the Revolution. Democrats pointed to institutions such as the Second Bank of the United States and (closer to home) the Miners' Bank of Dubuque as evidence of corrupt power sources created by legislative fiat.[16] Although by no means opposed to the commercial economy,

---

16. See Erickson, *Banking in Frontier Iowa*, 16–35, for an account of the Jacksonians' successful assault on the Miners' Bank.

they held that government should not immerse itself unduly in matters best left to market forces. In practical terms that meant that Democrats objected to granting special favors to individual transportation companies and were generally suspicious of banking corporations. The 1846 Iowa Constitution, a largely Jacksonian creation, prohibited Iowans from setting up banks within the confines of the state.[17] The legal code of 1851 was another product of Democratic rule. It included a general incorporation law that ended the cumbersome practice of chartering joint-stock companies one by one.[18]

Iowa Democrats, like their copartisans in other regions of the United States, fought against governmental intervention in all walks of life, not just the economic sphere. In particular, they opposed efforts by evangelical Protestants to use governmental power to reform antebellum America's turbulent society in their own image.[19] Campaigns to prohibit liquor sales, abolish slavery, and maintain the sanctity of the sabbath were anathema to many Democrats because they smacked of interference in the lives of a free people. Far from promoting order and discipline, contended Jacksonians, such campaigns caused social unrest and, in the case of the abolition movement, threatened the very fabric of the Union. Expressing complete confidence in the people, these standard-bearers of laissez-faire explicitly rejected the notion that economic growth and moral reform required the heavy hand of government.

Whigs were not convinced by such reasoning. In their view Iowa could not hope to take full advantage of eastern demand for western grain without federal and local government aid. The Whigs' central contention was that notwithstanding the fertility of the prairies, the land was valueless until it was first improved—tilled, fenced, and well-stocked with animals—and then linked to the market by an efficient financial and transport infrastructure. Iowans needed plank roads, navigable rivers, railroads, banks, and credit. Without these accoutrements of a modern economy, they would surely lose out in market competition with the inhabitants of other western states. The prairies would remain a wilderness unless they were integrated properly into America's expanding commercial nexus by public-spirited legislators and judges.[20]

---

17. Ibid., 47; *Journal of the Convention for the Formation of a Constitution of the State of Iowa* (Iowa City, 1846), 85–86.

18. *Iowa Code* §43.10 (1851).

19. Democratic resistance to evangelical interference in government was highlighted at the 1844 constitutional convention when Jacksonian delegates resisted a Whig motion to open the daily proceedings with prayer. Benjamin F. Shambaugh, *Fragments of the Debates of the Iowa Constitutional Conventions of 1844 and 1846* . . . (Iowa City, 1900), 21–22.

20. The best introduction to Iowa Whiggery remains Louis Pelzer, "The History and Principles of the Whigs of the Territory of Iowa," *Iowa Journal of History and Politics* 5 (1907), 46–90. On the ideology of the national Whig party, see Daniel W. Howe, *The Political Culture of the American Whigs* (Chicago, 1979). For a representative summary of Whig economic policy in the 1840s, see William Penn Clarke's critique of the 1846 constitution in Howe, *Political Culture*, 349–52.

Throughout their party's short-lived existence (1840–c. 1855), Iowa Whigs campaigned relentlessly for public assistance to be given to fledgling corporations (banks, railroads, and milling companies). They fought to obstruct the Democrats' assault on the Miners' Bank of Dubuque and unreservedly welcomed the railroad as the harbinger of modern civilization.[21] Like the Jacksonians, they too extended their philosophy of government into the private sphere. Having rather less confidence in the masses than their opponents, however, Whigs tended to favor using the legislature and courts to enforce basic standards of Protestant morality. Much (though by no means all) of the support for the so-called blue laws against gambling, desecration of the sabbath, and drinking came from Whigs.[22] So too did the modicum of legislative opposition to the state's virulently racist stance on black in-migration.[23]

Race, in fact, was an integral element in the political culture of the day.[24] Both major parties in the 1840s were racist, but while the Democrats were virulently Negrophobic, Whigs tended to be more paternalistic in their attitude towards blacks. This was partly a consequence of their different constituencies, but also a result of their divergent views of society. The Democrats' broad definition of political society (all adult white male citizens of the republic) was only possible because they excluded a wide range of groups from it.[25] Positing the inferiority of African-Americans (as well as American Indians) made it easier for them to claim that all white men were equal under the law. The more conservative Whigs possessed a hierarchical, but in some ways more inclusive, worldview that encompassed "inferior" races, although the former

---

21. Whig support for the Miners' Bank was evident in the 1844 Iowa House when James Grimes of Burlington fought to introduce a substitute bill designed to stave off repeal of the bank's charter. 1844 *Iowa Territorial House Journal*, 76. Whig strength in the Council (the upper house) gave the bank a temporary stay of execution, but a Democrat-controlled legislature killed off the institution the following year.

22. Iowa House Whigs voted 10–1 to support an act to punish gaming in 1843. 1843 *Iowa Territorial House Journal*, 190. In the same session of the Iowa legislature, Whig support for a sabbatarian bill was consistently stronger than that of their opponents. Ibid., 129, 134–35; and 1843 *Iowa Territorial Council Journal*, 104, 117. Iowa Whigs publicly endorsed temperance at their state convention in February 1854. Herbert S. Fairall, *The Iowa City Republican Manual of Iowa Politics* (Iowa City, 1881), 38. They gave almost full support to a prohibitory liquor law at the ensuing session of the General Assembly. 1855 *Iowa Senate Journal*, 201; and 1855 *Iowa House Journal*, 229–30. Although these measures would not have passed without Democratic support, Jacksonian members provided the bulk of opposition to each of them.

23. The Iowa legislature restricted the entry of blacks into the territory in 1839. Whig opposition to the law is noted in Robert R. Dykstra, "White Men, Black Laws: Territorial Iowans and Civil Rights, 1838–1843," *Annals of Iowa* 46 (1982), 422.

24. See Robert R. Dykstra, *Bright Radical Star: Black Freedom and White Supremacy on the Hawkeye Frontier* (Cambridge, MA, 1993).

25. John Ashworth, *"Agrarians" and "Aristocrats": Party Political Ideology in the United States, 1837–1846* (London, 1983), 221–23. Ashworth concedes that Jacksonian theory was unable to encompass African-Americans, but he deemphasizes racism as a component of the Democrats' worldview. Jean Baker, *Affairs of Party: The Political Culture of Northern Democrats in the Mid-Nineteenth Century* (Ithaca, NY, 1983), 212–58, redresses the balance.

were in no doubt that the vast majority of such peoples were destined to occupy a position at the foot of the social scale (perhaps with a few lower-class whites who had failed to better themselves). The Democrats' preoccupation with race, however, made them much more tolerant of poverty-stricken European immigrants than the Whigs, whose suspicion of the lower sorts frequently rendered them xenophobic.[26] Religious divisions exacerbated racial and ethnic differences between the two parties in Iowa. Many evangelical Whigs advocated the use of government to create a truly Protestant republic — by preventing liquor sales, for example, or (in rather fewer cases) by opposing the state's official endorsement of white supremacy. They were therefore inclined to oppose the rising political influence of Irish Catholics, for the latter were renowned for their drinking and reluctance to support the crusade against slavery.[27] Democrats, on the other hand, endorsed cultural pluralism as a vital component of republican ideology and rejected Whig criticisms of foreign immigrants.

More township-level research needs to be done on the precise nature of the two major parties' constituencies in Iowa.[28] We know enough, however, to sketch the social and ethnic composition of both the leadership and their partisan supporters. Whig and Democratic leaders were generally wealthy men — mostly attorneys from the eastern and southern states who speculated heavily in real estate or at the very least found the law a remunerative profession in a frontier region beset by rival land claims and horse thieving. Most of them had been born in the United States, had received an above average education, and resided in the larger urban centers of the state.[29] These factors gave them enormous advantages over the vast majority of their constituents; town-dwelling, for example, made them more cosmopolitan, more aware of what was happening in the world around them, and placed them closer to the main concentrations of capital in both the state and the nation. As boosters, they were frequently at the center of the intense interurban competition for the trade of the backcountry that took place in Iowa before the Civil War. Prominent lawyers such as Charles Mason and James Grimes, for example, endeavored to place their home town of Burlington ahead of Keokuk in the race for railroad connections to the East.[30] The fact that Mason was a committed Demo-

---

26. Bruce Collins, "The Ideology of the Ante-bellum Northern Democrats," *Journal of American Studies* 11 (1977), 103–21, stresses the Democrats' emphasis on cultural pluralism.

27. The links between temperance and nativism are explored in Ronald F. Matthias, "The Know Nothing Movement in Iowa" (Ph.D. diss., University of Chicago, 1965), chap. 1.

28. The importance of applying multivariate techniques to random township data in order to determine grass-roots voting behavior is stressed by J. Morgan Kousser, "The 'New Political History': A Methodological Critique," *Reviews in American History* 4 (1976), 1–14. Township statistics figure prominently in Dykstra, *Bright Radical Star*.

29. See the sketches in Edward H. Stiles, *Recollections and Sketches of Notable Lawyers and Public Men of Early Iowa* (Des Moines, 1916).

30. See, for example, James Grimes to Charles Mason, 13 February 1852, Charles Mason Papers, State Historical Society of Iowa, Des Moines.

crat and Grimes a rising star in the local Whig party indicates the prevalence of intraelite cooperation behind the scenes. All Iowans shared a commitment to economic growth (not to mention personal profit), but politically active lawyers and their mercantile allies were better placed than most settlers to benefit from the processes of change.

The parties' constituents were a polyglot bunch.[31] In ethnoreligious terms, the Democrats fared better among European immigrants than the Whigs: Catholic Irish and Germans were particularly devoted to the Jacksonian cause, partly because the Democrats appeared to be less ethnocentric than the Whigs, and partly because the Whig party was perceived as a vehicle for bigoted evangelical Protestantism. Many of the upcountry southerners who migrated to Iowa in the late 1830s and 1840s were also Democrats, principally because they had opposed the dominance of large Whig slaveholders in states such as Tennessee and Virginia. Many of these people were Baptists and Methodists, and were naturally suspicious of the more Yankeefied denominations that were at the forefront of moral reform in the antebellum period, principally Congregationalists and Presbyterians. In Iowa, hard-pressed Whigs drew a good deal of support from members of these latter churches, as well as from areas of Quaker settlement, such as Henry County in the southeast. New Englanders and British immigrants appear to have favored the Whig party, too, not only because of its moral concerns but also due to its generally Anglophile ethos.

Class, too, may have played an important role in Iowa politics before the mid-1850s. Although we know that the leaders of both parties came from the middling and upper ranks of society, there is no hard evidence to show that wealth and status seriously affected partisan attachments among ordinary voters. However, work on political affiliation in other American communities during the antebellum period does indicate that Whigs performed better in urban areas and attracted a disproportionate amount of support from relatively prosperous individuals integrated into the market economy.[32] Without township-level data it is impossible to say whether a similar pattern was evident in early Iowa. The best one can do is note that Whig and Democratic rhetoric was redolent of class divisions. Democrats attacked their opponents as aristocrats and tools of eastern capital; they poured flattery on ordinary settlers, courting the votes

---

31. There is no ethnocultural analysis of voting behavior in antebellum Iowa. My speculative remarks in this paragraph are therefore based on various studies of Jacksonian politics, especially Watson, *Liberty and Power*, 194, 222–23; Richard Carwardine, "Evangelicals, Whigs and the Election of William Henry Harrison," *Journal of American Studies* 17 (1983), 47–75; and Kleppner, *Cross of Culture*, chap. 3. William E. Gienapp, *The Origins of the Republican Party, 1852–1856* (New York, 1987), 423–39; George H. Daniels, "Immigrant Vote in the 1860 Election in the Case of Iowa," in Frederick C. Luebke, ed., *Ethnic Voters and the Election of Lincoln* (Lincoln, NE, 1971), 110–28; and Robert P. Swierenga, "The Ethnic Voter and the First Lincoln Election," ibid., 129–50, support the view that there was a strong ethnic and religious basis to popular voting behavior in antebellum Iowa.

32. Watson, *Liberty and Power,* 236; Paul Goodman, "The Social Basis of New England Politics in Jacksonian America," *Journal of the Early Republic* 6 (1986), 36–37.

of workingmen and independent-minded farmers.[33] Whigs, on the other hand, spoke of a harmony of interests among classes, and publicly identified themselves with banks and manufacturers.[34] Such rhetoric clearly hinted at differences of status and wealth between the parties' constituencies, although ethnocultural divisions almost certainly cut across class lines.

The main elements of interparty competition in Iowa during the years of the second party system were thus economic and ethnoreligious in origin. Arguably, however, it was the system's primary focus on economic concerns that kept the Democrats in power for so long. Specifically, their advocacy of liberal land policies for western settlers (explicit in their vocal support for a generous preemption law and implicit in their vision of a republic of self-reliant yeomen farmers) proved exceptionally popular with the electorate.[35] Even though the Whigs recognized the need to appeal to the people in the same obsequious terms as the Democrats, they never quite succeeded in casting off their image as social conservatives. Whig strategists clearly hoped that their endorsement of economic growth and the institutions necessary to promote it would capture the imagination of the public. Would not everyone benefit, they reasoned, if the economic pie got bigger thanks to the banks, the transportation companies, and, of course, the hard work of those who tilled the soil? The answer may well have been yes, but in an age when the Money Power was regarded as a serious threat to republican liberties, such an argument was destined to fall on stony ground.

Part of the problem was that the national Whig party was manifestly unsympathetic to a generous policy of land distribution in the West, but Iowa Whigs were also hindered by the fact that the local economy was still immature enough to permit their opponents to lambast banks and other corporations as monopolistic and predatory.[36] When, in the late 1840s, population did expand beyond the immediate confines of Iowa's navigable rivers and eastern railroads began to approach the Mississippi, Whig party leaders found their materialistic appeals undercut by the readiness of many Democrats to tone down their agrarian rhetoric and welcome the advent of the iron horse.[37] For the truth was

---

33. For example, the 1841 Democratic platform attacked the Whigs as blue-stockinged "Federalists," supported the passage of a preemption law to safeguard the rights of "the hardy pioneer," and called for the destruction of the Bank of the United States. Fairall, *Manual of Iowa Politics*, 12–13.

34. Iowa Whig platforms in the 1840s consistently expressed support for high tariffs (to boost domestic industry), government aid for internal improvements, and banks of issue. Ibid., 14, 16–17, 22–23.

35. Democratic support for preemption was a key feature of the party's 1841 election platform. Ibid., 12–13.

36. For Jacksonian attacks on banking in the 1844 constitutional convention, see Shambaugh, *Debates*, 69–70.

37. Democratic support for railroads is detailed more fully in Robert Cook, *Baptism of Fire: The Republican Party in Iowa, 1838–1878* (Ames, 1993), chap. 2.

that at first all Iowans, regardless of their partisan allegiance, regarded the railroads as a godsend. The new technology promised to reduce the costs of transporting their foodstuffs to market (most likely to Chicago, the emerging hub of the midwestern economy, rather than to St. Louis) as well as to increase the value of their property. Small wonder enthusiastic Iowa farmers began voting local tax aid to railroads as soon as they were given the opportunity in the early 1850s.[38]

It is not easy to determine the role of issues in the political culture of the day, but the careful thought that went into drawing up election platforms suggests that the politicians themselves were in no doubt that the voters responded to more than just the sign-ridden language of their speeches. Iowans rejected the constitution of 1844 because they wanted larger borders for their state and (in some cases) a continuation of low territorial property taxes.[39] Nor was it only local issues to which they responded. When voters dumped the Democrats in 1854, their decision was linked to their anger at that party's congressional support for the despised Kansas-Nebraska Act.[40] Of course, issues were often related to value systems—evangelical Protestantism, Roman Catholicism, working-class republicanism—but early Iowans were a practical people who wanted something more than symbolic gestures from their representatives at Iowa City and Washington. If those representatives did not respond to their wishes, then they could always be ousted at the polls.

All this should not be taken to mean that a perfectly democratic relationship existed between the leaders and the led. Early Iowa was clearly not some kind of Turnerian frontier utopia. Most antebellum political parties sought power not only to formulate policy but also to capture the spoils of office. The United States at midcentury possessed no real bureaucracy at the state or federal levels. The day-to-day operation of government was carried out by political appointees aided by a few clerks who owed their position to the workings of the patronage system. Loyal party workers in townships across the state expected to gain some reward if their organization triumphed at the biennial elections for governor and legislature. Having attached themselves to, say, a member or prospective member of the General Assembly, they would then require the successful individual to promote their efforts to become a federal postmaster at home or (in the case of newspaper editors) win a contract to print public documents. Officeholders further up the party hierarchy could use their positions to establish profitable connections with merchant capitalists (politicians in office were always useful to eastern railroad magnates and local merchants) and, by dispensing patronage as judiciously as possible, build up durable power bases in Iowa. Factionalism was an obvious

---

38. John Lauritz Larson, *Bonds of Enterprise: John Murray Forbes and Western Development in America's Railway Age* (Cambridge, MA, 1984), 59.
39. Sage, *History of Iowa*, 84–88.
40. Cook, *Baptism of Fire*, chap. 2; Rosenberg, *Iowa on the Eve of the Civil War*, chap. 4.

consequence of the spoils system, for disappointed office seekers were often swift to join alternative power networks in an effort to feed at the public trough. The Dubuque Democratic party, for example, was riven by a dispute between rival politicos during the late 1850s.[41]

The struggle for spoils was fierce throughout the antebellum years and makes it harder to pinpoint the motivation behind all the speeches and platform-making of the day. Was the rhetoric of conspiracy, reform, and economic growth genuinely policy-oriented, or was it really a smokescreen behind which ambitious politicians could advance their own selfish projects? There is no easy answer to this question. Some individual Iowa politicians did regard politics as little more than a game; "it's like ratting-fun," remarked one of them.[42] Such men may have had little commitment to the ideal of representative democracy or to the stated policies and values of their party. That was probably not the case with most antebellum politicians, however. All Iowa politicians were ambitious — either for themselves, their cause, or most probably both. That is hardly surprising, for they were, on balance, no more nor less altruistic than their constituents. What is striking is the degree of their loyalty to party; surprisingly few Whigs, for example, regarded their organization's persistently poor electoral performances as an excuse to jump ship and run as Democrats. That was not simply because they feared being exposed as traitors or "soreheads," but rather because they had a strong sense of party allegiance. Values as well as office motivated the majority of Iowa politicians before the Civil War.

SUSTAINED AS IT WAS by such a diverse political culture, why did the second party system begin to disintegrate in Iowa in the late 1840s? Two major factors were to blame: the increasing seriousness of the sectional conflict between North and South; and a rise in prominence of ethnocultural issues which began to undermine popular faith in the existing political structure.

Iowa politics — even in the 1840s, when communications with the rest of the United States were relatively primitive — was by no means isolated from national affairs. Western voters were perfectly capable of responding to developments occurring beyond the boundaries of the state: local papers were full of national news and editorials telling them what to think about the great issues of the day — the Mexican War, the crisis with Britain over Oregon, the debates in Congress preceding the Compromise of 1850. Party platforms bristled with planks about such faraway happenings, for party strategists were well aware that it took more than the Miners' Bank of Dubuque or the Scott County Hydraulic Company to mobilize the voters.[43] As Michael Holt has

---

41. Rosenberg, *Iowa on the Eve of the Civil War*, 172.

42. James Thorington to William Penn Clarke, 3 January 1857, William Penn Clarke Papers, State Historical Society of Iowa, Des Moines.

43. See Fairall, *Manual of Iowa Politics*, 11–28, for Whig and Democratic platforms in the 1840s.

rightly pointed out, issue generation was what antebellum politics was all about.[44] Without issues, voters could become dissatisfied and lose interest in politics and politicians.

On balance, the Democrats got the best of the national debate in the 1840s. Their emphasis on spatial rather than qualitative economic expansion, confident assertions of American nationalism, and glorification of the white republic appealed more to pioneering folk than the Whigs' constant harping on the need for government-aided economic growth. What weakened the Democrats' grip on power in Iowa was (a) their reliance on the southern wing of the party at a time when northerners were growing fearful of proslavery efforts to undermine their liberties and (b) the destruction of the minority Whig party and its replacement by a much more formidable opposition.

Although both of these developments were connected, the second was not wholly a product of the first. The Whig party collapsed because its political leaders could not turn changes within the political culture of the state to their own advantage — at least not within the straitjacket imposed by the existing party system. Growing population in the counties west of the Mississippi and the inevitable maturation of what had once been a rather crude frontier society prompted increased support for the machinery of a modern economy. The Whigs should have been able to make something of this, but they found their efforts blocked by the readiness of the Democrats to welcome the advent of the railroads from the East and, in some cases, to support the removal of the constitutional prohibition of banking.[45] At the same time, Whig leaders were confronted with insistent calls from their evangelical wing to legislate against liquor sales, put an end to the desecration of the sabbath, and provide a stronger bulwark against the dictates of the South. These demands drove a wedge between National Whigs (supporters of the 1850 Compromise who generally abhorred agitation over "moral" questions because of their divisive impact on the Union and the party) and Free Soil Whigs, who believed not only that the time had come to stand up to the blustering of southern slaveholders, but also that an alliance with Iowa's small band of political antislavery men could make the difference between electoral success and failure.

At first it seemed that the fusionist strategy of the Free Soil Whigs might liberate the state from the thraldom of the Democrats. Adverse public reaction to Stephen Douglas's attempts to abrogate the sacred Missouri Compromise early in 1854 resulted in a Whig–Free Soil alliance prior to the gubernatorial contest of that year.[46] The antislavery Whig, James Grimes, won a narrow majority on the basis of his opposition to the Kansas-Nebraska Act and an unashamedly Whiggish campaign address extolling the virtues

---

44. Holt, *Political Crisis*, 102–3 and *passim*.
45. Erickson, *Banking in Frontier Iowa*, 96.
46. Sage, *History of Iowa*, 127–28.

of positive government.⁴⁷ No sooner had the Whigs finished celebrating this dramatic victory, however, than their dreams of political hegemony were shattered by an upsurge of political nativism directed against Roman Catholic immigrants.

The Know Nothing party's reign in Iowa was brief but eventful.⁴⁸ Drawing impressive support during 1855 from American-born artisans in the river towns, anti-Catholic evangelicals, and southern migrants, the new party called for curbs on the political and social influence of Catholic immigrants. Although Whig leaders had always evinced some sympathy for nativism (not least because so many of the foreigners voted Democrat), their desire to win over Protestant Germans tended to mitigate their xenophobia. Thus, with the Democrats generally sympathetic to the immigrants, frustrated Iowans had only the Know Nothings to turn to when they found Catholic immigrants threatening both their jobs and their cultural hegemony. Politicians from the major parties were quick to jump on board the nativist bandwagon, for it seemed that the latter would carry all before it. Remarkably, however, the Know Nothings vanished as quickly as they had appeared. They did so because a much more durable and powerful force came into its own during the winter of 1855–56. That force was political antislavery.

The Republican party of Iowa was founded in February 1856.⁴⁹ Its central tenet was simple: opposition to the spread of slavery in the United States. Slavery had not bothered most white Iowans during the 1840s and early 1850s. Few of them liked it, but hardly anyone save a few abolitionists and Free Soilers wanted to endanger the Union by campaigning against it. What changed this reluctance to upset the apple cart was the growing perception among all northerners, not just Iowans, that the South was attempting to impose its immoral and backward institution on the rest of the country. Northerners thought that such an attempt, evidenced by the passage of the new Fugitive Slave Law and the Kansas-Nebraska Act, amounted to a perversion of the ideals on which the republic had been founded and threatened the livelihood of free, independent citizens.⁵⁰

The once preposterous notion that a tiny group of wealthy planters — the "slave power" in contemporary parlance — was plotting to destroy the rights of northerners took on added significance in late 1855 when a fierce guerrilla

---

47. The most recent and most sophisticated account of Grimes's gubernatorial victory is in Gienapp, *Origins of the Republican Party*, 121–22.

48. The only full-length account of political nativism in Iowa is Matthias, "Know-Nothing Movement in Iowa."

49. The best accounts of the formation of the Republican party in Iowa are Louis Pelzer, "The Origins and Organization of the Republican Party in Iowa," *Iowa Journal of History and Politics* 4 (1906), 487–525; and David S. Sparkes, "The Birth of the Republican Party in Iowa, 1848–1860" (Ph.D. diss., University of Chicago, 1951), chaps. 4–5.

50. James Grimes capitalized on these themes in his address "To the People of Iowa," issued in the early stage of his 1854 gubernatorial campaign. See Salter, *Life*, 39–50.

war involving free state and proslavery forces erupted in neighboring Kansas.[51] That conflict presented leaders of the embryonic Republican coalition with the proof they had been looking for—proof that southern planters and their northern Democrat allies were engaged in a vast conspiracy to spread slavery across the United States. To a large extent, then, Iowa's Republican strategists (most of whom had been Free Soil Whigs) were able to capitalize on popular fears and expectations that hitherto had helped keep the Democrats in office for so long: antipathy toward "aristocrats," concerns for the welfare of free white labor, and a profound suspicion of unrestrained power.

Opposition to the extension of slavery did not constitute the only string to the Republican bow, however. Land reform, a protective tariff, support for banking and railroads, tighter voting restrictions on immigrants, qualified endorsement of temperance, and even a popular referendum on black suffrage were all designed to add to the party's electoral appeal between 1854 and 1860.[52] Such policies were carefully crafted to win over different sections of the electorate except voters who made up the Democrats' core constituency. Protectionism and watered-down nativism, for example, appealed to artisans in the river towns; endorsements of prohibition and other moral reforms attracted mainstream evangelical Protestants; and banking reform (backed by Republican delegates at the 1857 constitutional convention in Iowa City) must have been music to the ears of commercial farmers desperate for reliable credit and currency facilities.[53] But in the final analysis it was the Republicans' careful use (their opponents would have said "manipulation") of the slave power argument that enabled coalition builders to overcome the Know Nothing challenge, broaden the base of the old Whig constituency, and finally convert the new organization into the majoritarian force in local politics.[54]

Iowa Democrats struggled hard in the late 1850s to regain their lost ascendancy. They sought to convince voters that the Republicans were abolitionists, disunionists, and advocates of miscegenation and to reactivate the former Jacksonian coalition by attacking banks and Yankee moralists.[55] Time and events, however, were against them. Commercial farmers wanted an economic infrastructure fit for the middle of the nineteenth century. The Republicans' Whig-

---

51. The role played by Kansas in Republican electoral successes during the mid-1850s can be traced in Rosenberg, *Iowa on the Eve of the Civil War,* chaps. 9–10; Sparkes, "Birth of the Republican Party," 146; and Cook, *Baptism of Fire,* chap. 3.

52. For Republican platforms, 1856–1860, see Fairall, *Manual of Iowa Politics,* 40–41, 42–44, 46–51, 54.

53. Erickson, *Banking in Frontier Iowa,* 90–91; Sage, *History of Iowa,* 133–49. Counties specializing in wheat production for the market were among those switching from the Democrats to the anti-Nebraska coalition in the 1854 gubernatorial election.

54. On the Republicans' use of slave power rhetoric, see William E. Gienapp, "The Republican Party and the Slave Power," in Robert H. Abzug and Stephen H. Maizlish, eds., *New Perspectives on Race and Slavery: Essays in Honor of Kenneth M. Stampp* (Lexington, KY, 1986).

55. Cook, *Baptism of Fire,* chaps. 4–6; Rosenberg, *Iowa on the Eve of the Civil War,* chaps. 9–10.

gish emphasis on positive government was thus much more conducive to their aims than the seemingly outmoded laissez-faire policies of the Jacksonians. More significant than this, however, was the fact that the South appeared to grow even more hostile in the second half of the 1850s. The caning of Charles Sumner, the national Democratic administration's ill-judged attempts to impose a proslavery settlement on Kansas, the Dred Scott decision, and aggressive southern calls for a federal slave code for the territories did nothing to convince Iowans that popular sovereignty — the Douglas Democrats' local solution to the slavery question — was a solid enough bulwark of northern rights. When war came in April 1861, Iowa Democrats had little choice but to support the newly elected Republican government of Abraham Lincoln. Their world had turned upside down.

Antebellum Iowa's political culture was thus as vibrant as the times. Economic change and ethnic variety, sectionalism and nationalism, republicanism and racism all combined to promote fierce interparty competition in the region by providing political elites with a roster of concrete issues and value-laden totems which they employed to mobilize the people. Hindsight, however, reveals that a high price had to be paid for such richness. After thirteen thousand patriotic Iowans perished in the ensuing struggle to prevent southern slaveholders from destroying the American Union, a sterile political culture grew up rapidly around Iowa's Grand Old Party. Relying heavily on past glories, Republicans went on to dominate state politics for nearly three-quarters of a century. Aside from a brief flirtation with power between 1889 and 1893, local Democrats would not taste lasting political success again until the advent of the New Deal.

BIBLIOGRAPHICAL NOTE

Because this essay is so recent and so historiographical, readers are simply referred back to the essay and its footnotes for bibliographical suggestions. I add only the subsequently published Winter 1994 issue of the *Annals of Iowa* with essays by Robert Dykstra, Ronald Matthias, and Tyler Anbinder devoted to the Know Nothings of Iowa.

6

"Men Did Not Take to the Musket More Commonly than Women to the Needle": Annie Wittenmyer and Soldiers' Aid

Elizabeth D. Leonard

Iowans are proud of their contributions to the Civil War. They responded fully to every call for troops for the Union cause; ultimately, one-half of the male population of the state took some part in the war, the highest proportion of any state in the Union, and nearly one-third of those were killed, died of disease, or were wounded. Because of the tremendous price paid by those who fought on the battlefields, when Iowa historians have focused on the Civil War, they have usually offered accounts of battles in which Iowa soldiers were involved. Recently, however, historians have begun to pay attention to the social impact of the war. Women's contributions, in particular, have received new attention. Because of her prominence in Civil War relief efforts, Iowa historians have long noted with pride the contributions of Annie Wittenmyer and the women who worked with her. Generally, though, that contribution has been seen as one of "support," an implicitly subservient role. In her recent work, Elizabeth Leonard calls attention to the "gender battles" that Wittenmyer's work engendered. Those battles, Leonard concludes, opened up new opportunities for women in the professions and in public life after the war, much as historians have shown happened in the wake of women's actions in the two world wars of the twentieth century.

Iowa had two armies serving the nation—the great column, 78,000 strong, of boys in blue at the front, and that other army of men and women who furnished the muscles of war here at home. . . . Nations are not saved by muskets alone, but by the great, strong hearts that beat in one impulse, and whose sacrifices are not in the smoke of battle, but in the loyal duty that lies nearest, and without visible reward.
—S. H. M. Byers, *Iowa in War Times*

Reprinted by permission of W. W. Norton & Company from *Yankee Women: Gender Battles in the Civil War*, by Elizabeth D. Leonard (New York: W. W. Norton & Company, 1994), 51–82, 102–3. Copyright © 1994 by Elizabeth D. Leonard.

BITS AND PIECES of information about Annie Wittenmyer's life prior to the outbreak of the Civil War in 1861 combine to present the impression of an energetic, well-to-do merchant's widow in the town of Keokuk, Iowa, long dedicated to local benevolent activities. Perhaps it is to be expected, then, that thirty years after the war ended, in her preface to *Under the Guns: A Woman's Reminiscences of the Civil War*, Wittenmyer addressed the commencement of her wartime activities in soldier relief in a rather mundane tone, as if to suggest that the war itself brought to this longtime philanthropist not so much a break with her normal life as a shift into a new field of labor. "Camps and hospitals," she wrote, "were established near my home in Keokuk, Iowa, early in April, 1861. I began at once my ministrations to the sick in these newly established hospitals, and, during my daily visits, closed the eyes of the first Iowa soldier who died in the war. From that time on till the close of the war I was actively engaged all along the lines."[1] For Wittenmyer, service to Iowa's soldiers constituted nothing more than an extension of the benevolent work in which she had been engaged for years. Such was a woman's Christian duty, to care for those in need. In the war, for Wittenmyer as for countless other middle-class women whose patriotic roots ran deep, responsibility to country merged with responsibility to God. And so, with women across the Union, she moved quickly into action after the firing on Fort Sumter.[2]

In comparison with other women who sought to commit themselves in various ways to the Union's cause, Wittenmyer had distinct advantages. For one thing, her late husband, William Wittenmyer, had left her wealthy enough to pursue her work voluntarily, as she did for many months. In addition, the presence in her two-story brick home of her parents and her married sister (whose husband had enlisted) made it possible for her to leave her son behind with a clear conscience.[3] Moreover, Wittenmyer's widowhood itself limited the challenges she might anticipate as she moved into an ever wider scope of activity. No one accused her of licentious behavior or of abandoning her proper role in her family. The combined influence of these advantages by no means guaranteed Wittenmyer absolute freedom of movement, nor did it dictate her future prominence, for certainly many women relief workers of similar background and condition remained in the shadows. Her personal and financial

---

1. Annie Wittenmyer, *Under the Guns: A Woman's Reminiscences of the Civil War* (Boston, 1897), i–ii. See also Ruth A. Gallaher, "Annie Turner Wittenmyer," *Iowa Journal of History and Politics* 29 (1931), 520; "Mrs. Annie Wittenmyer," *Annals of Iowa* 4 (1900), 277–79; and Tom Sillanpa, *Annie Wittenmyer: God's Angel* (Evanston, IL, 1972), 11. For a full study of middle-class women and benevolent work before, during, and after the war, see Lori Ginzberg, *Women and the Work of Benevolence: Morality, Politics, and Class in the Nineteenth-Century United States* (New Haven, CT, 1990).

2. Wittenmyer had three brothers in the military service: William (a surgeon in the Second Iowa Infantry), James (First Iowa Cavalry), and sixteen-year-old Davis, who followed James into the First Iowa Cavalry and mustered in by claiming to be nineteen. A fourth brother was unable to enter the service "because of a physical disability." See Gallaher, "Annie Turner Wittenmyer," 519–20.

3. Sillanpa, *Annie Wittenmyer*, 1–12.

independence, however, minimized for Wittenmyer specific obstacles to wartime service that others encountered full force.

On the 31st of May, 1861, the following news item appeared in Keokuk's daily newspaper, *The Gate City*:

> *Volunteer Aid Society*: The Ladies of the city are requested to meet on Saturday afternoon at 3 o'clock in the Medical College Hall, for the purpose of forming a Volunteer Aid Society.[4]

This formal summons masked the range of relief activities in which many of the town's women had already been engaged for troops passing through and stationed in Keokuk, strategically located at the southeastern corner of the state on the Mississippi River. Indeed, as soon as Iowa's soldiers had begun to gather in Keokuk, in response to President Lincoln's call to arms, townswomen had dedicated themselves to their support, supplying beds, bedding, clothing, food, and other essential items, regularly visiting soldiers' encampments and hospital bedsides, and gathering material of all sorts, including "200 needle-books, filled with the necessary appliances for repairing the wardrobe," to forward to regiments in the field.[5] But, in the six weeks between the attack on Fort Sumter and the end of May, it became clear that a systematization of women's individual and frequently disparate efforts could only serve the troops better. The result was the establishment of the Keokuk Ladies' Soldiers' Aid Society. The Society immediately named Wittenmyer its "Corresponding Secretary," assigning her responsibility for establishing and maintaining contact with sister societies throughout the state of Iowa.

Once organized, the Keokuk Society began in earnest to live up to its initial proposal "to furnish . . . the Hospital stores needed for the comfort and recovery of our sick and wounded soldiers from Iowa," as a supplement to the inadequate supplies being furnished by a Federal Government unprepared for the massive mobilization a Union victory would require.[6] From the start, the Society's members did not stint on the attention they gave to the local military hospital. As a published report later explained, women of the Keokuk Society considered the support of the hospital and its patients — already numerous, due to outbreaks of camp illness, even before any real fighting began — their unique responsibility, and they took to the task with vigor, detailing individuals to visit the wards and determine what needs existed, in order to supply them as quickly and efficiently as possible. On one occasion, when sick soldiers far exceeded the number of beds available at the hospital, on the request of the surgeon in attendance, Society members produced overnight twenty-five "ticks" — straw-filled mattresses common wherever soldiers were quartered. Moreover, relief workers connected with the hospital regularly found themselves involved in

---

4. *The Gate City*, 31 May 1861.
5. "Report of the Ladies' Soldiers' Aid Society," *The Gate City*, 15 April 1862.
6. Ibid.

matters beyond those of strict material demand and supply, as they "stood over the beds of those very low, administering cordials and stimulants; . . . bathed fevered brows; and when all nursing was in vain . . . procured, made up, and sent in the burial shroud for many, that the friends of the deceased might feel that all respect has been paid to the honored dead."[7] For most of the Society's women, Keokuk's military hospital was as close as they would get to the battle front, although attendance at the death of soldiers from around their state undoubtedly seemed to bring the front very close indeed.

The horizon of the Society's activity, however, lay far beyond this one local military hospital. Although the Society's explicit purpose—to supply the needs of Iowa's regiments—seems to reflect a relatively narrow orientation toward the state rather than the nation, from a different perspective the Keokuk Society's goals appear quite broad. For Wittenmyer and her colleagues aimed at coordinating not only one town's relief activities, but the relief activities of women across Iowa. In fact, with Keokuk as the hub of Iowa's military activity —the point from which the state's regiments not only embarked for the war, but also the point to which they returned for medical care[8]—it was logical that the townswomen envisioned their Society as the state's central organization for soldier relief. It made sense in their minds to encourage Iowa's women to organize their efforts and funnel their supplies through Keokuk.

And so, in September, the state's newspapers widely circulated the following notice "To the Ladies of Iowa":

> We address you in behalf of the "Soldiers' Aid Society" of this city, and invite you to organize in your respective districts and cooperate with us in providing the Iowa volunteers, and especially in furnishing their hospitals with such comforts and conveniences as the Government does not provide.
>
> As our society will be in direct communication with the troops, they will, through their Secretary [Wittenmyer], transmit to you from time to time such items of intelligence as will advance the interests of your associations. . . .
>
> All packages sent to the "Soldiers' Aid Society," Keokuk, express prepaid, will be forwarded to their destination free of charge.[9]

Even before the September notice, women's societies had been springing up around the state of Iowa, and many had already begun to channel their supplies through Keokuk as a result of Wittenmyer's effective fulfillment of her job as corresponding secretary, and of Iowa women's recognition of Keokuk's geographic centrality.[10] Immediately, the Society began keeping

---

7. Ibid.
8. Gallaher, "Annie Turner Wittenmyer," 521; Sillanpa, *Annie Wittenmyer*, 14.
9. *The Gate City*, 16 September 1861.
10. In June, Mrs. C. D. Allen of Iowa City wrote to Mrs. Chittenden of the Keokuk Society requesting "further information, about the sending of boxes, to the care of Mrs. Whittenmyer [*sic*]." Mrs. C. D. Allen to Mrs. Chittenden, 20 June 1861, in the War Correspondence of Annie Wittenmyer, 1861–1865, State Historical Society of Iowa, Des Moines (hereafter cited as "War Correspondence").

track of its dispersals of goods, at one early date some $35 worth to the Second, $8.20 to the Fifth, and $22.40 to the Seventh Iowa Regiments.[11] More than a desperate cry into a vacuum of inactivity, the September notice constituted an affirmation of the Keokuk Society's willingness to control a system of statewide soldier relief efforts that was rapidly falling in place.

The Society's September notice had another meaning, however, in light of the establishment of the United States Sanitary Commission (USSC) in New York City three months earlier, in mid-June 1861. The USSC—formed as a national umbrella organization for the coordination of soldier relief—attempted, from its inception, to guarantee its own preeminence in the field, as well as the preeminence of a national rather than a state-by-state outlook on war relief, by convincing or compelling local associations to direct all of their supplies through its offices in the various theaters of war, for general dispensation. As one historian has argued, for some women engaged in soldiers' aid, "the idea of a large-scale plan and a relationship with a prestigious national center may have offered special appeal," but for others, the program of the USSC represented a clear threat to local control, as well as a challenge to the sovereignty of a given region, and to a more community oriented understanding of women's role in the crisis. Consequently, the "practice of ignoring Sanitary circulars and sending contributions where it was believed they could do the most good was widespread."[12] Such was certainly the case in Keokuk. In its September circular, the Keokuk Society demonstrated its resistance to USSC control and its determination to retain jurisdiction over sanitary affairs in Iowa by publicly soliciting supplies from other local organizations to be distributed at the Society's discretion.

Throughout the fall of 1861, Wittenmyer and the Society proceeded to ignore notices from the USSC and instead busied themselves with the work of coordinating state relief efforts, and with beginning the process of distributing supplies to the increasingly scattered Iowa troops.[13] In August, Wittenmyer had followed the Second Iowa south along the Mississippi through Missouri to ascertain the regiment's needs.[14] In September, she took her first official trip to bring bandages, medicines, clothing, and food to the field.[15] The trip took about ten days; she returned briefly to provide information and collect more supplies, and then left again, for another three weeks, establishing a pattern that would continue long into the war.

---

11. "Report of the Ladies' Soldiers' Aid Society," *The Gate City*, 15 April 1862.

12. Rejean Attie, "'A Swindling Concern': The United States Sanitary Commission and the Northern Female Public, 1861–1865," (Ph.D. diss., Columbia University, 1987), 126, 131.

13. The 1862 "Report" indicated that, by the end of September, some forty local relief associations in Iowa had come under the Keokuk Society's authority. "Report of the Ladies' Soldiers' Aid Society," *The Gate City*, 15 April 1862.

14. *The Gate City*, 5 August 1861.

15. "Report of the Ladies' Soldiers' Aid Society," *The Gate City*, 15 April 1862.

Some months after Wittenmyer first headed south, the Society explained the key reason behind its decision to send the female corresponding secretary rather than a male representative on such "missions of mercy": "[W]e concurred in the judgment," stated an 1862 "Report of the Ladies' Soldiers' Aid Society" printed in the *Gate City*, "that a woman, by her wide and quick sympathies and by her life-long experience as nurse in the sick room, was far better qualified to discover at a glance the wants and necessities of the sick; and with means at her disposal, to supply them with delicate tact and discriminating judgment."[16] The "Report" thus explicitly indicated the Society's opinion that a woman would perform the required tasks more competently than a man, given her nature and her "life-long experience" as a caretaker. The "Report" thereby addressed potential critics of Wittenmyer's abandonment of Victorian gender conventions, suggesting that even though it demanded that some individuals travel far from home and community, war relief work—just another form of charity—was still women's work. The "Report" did not explain the Society's specific choice of Wittenmyer, but undoubtedly her financial and personal independence constituted critical factors, along with her efficiency and her willingness to go.

In the wake of the September 1861 trip, forerunner of countless trips to follow, Wittenmyer expanded her title within the Society from "corresponding secretary" to "general agent." As Wittenmyer became more influential within her own organization, she also developed a broader base of recognition and support throughout the state. Wittenmyer sent home informative and emotionally stirring reports about the troops as she travelled, which state newspapers gladly published. "Mr. Editor," she wrote in October 1861 from the camp of the Second Iowa, "We are glad to know that our Iowa troops are the best officered and best drilled men in the field; they make a good impression wherever they go."[17] Wittenmyer's published letters provided welcome news about the soldiers, stimulated interest in relief activities, and enhanced her reputation.

Even as Wittenmyer and the Keokuk Society were actively and successfully cultivating their stature in the field of relief to the Iowa troops, forces closer to home than the USSC prepared to undercut them. On October 13, 1861, over four months after the first meeting of the Keokuk Society, Iowa Governor Samuel J. Kirkwood created the Iowa State Army Sanitary Commission as a direct auxiliary of the USSC. There is some evidence to suggest that the Governor simply hoped thereby to "strengthen" the work of the Keokuk Society.[18] More likely, the State Sanitary Commission represented his response to pressure from the USSC to bring his state's relief efforts into line with the national organization's plan. In any case, Governor Kirkwood immediately

---

16. Ibid.

17. *The Gate City*, 21 October 1861.

18. Earl S. Fullbrook, "Relief Work in Iowa during the Civil War," *Iowa Journal of History and Politics* 16 (1918), 198.

named thirteen distinguished male citizens of the state to the Commission's leadership. He appointed the Reverend A. J. Kynett of Lyons, Iowa, to a position parallel to Wittenmyer's: "corresponding secretary and general agent."[19]

Two weeks later, on October 28, the Governor compounded what quickly came to be perceived as a direct insult to the Keokuk Society, with a brief notice in the *Gate City* describing the new Commission. As if to deny the women's effective inroads into the very public context of wartime sanitary affairs, this official notice of the Commission's establishment failed entirely to mention the relief work already in progress by the Keokuk Society or any other women's organizations throughout the state. Instead, it outlined the tasks that lay ahead of the new commissioners, which substantially overlapped with the work Wittenmyer and her colleagues had already undertaken: visiting the various Iowa regiments and reporting on the sanitary and medical conditions of their encampments, determining regimental needs, and arranging for their supply.[20]

The women's disgust with the Governor's actions, and his failure to acknowledge their organization and their months of loyal service to Iowa's soldiers poured forth in a scathing unsigned article published three weeks later, probably written by a group of women in the Society and almost certainly resonant with the opinion held by Wittenmyer, who was nevertheless far too busy—and probably too savvy—to compose it herself. (After all, an overt individual attack on the State Sanitary Commission could potentially threaten her own reputation.) This remarkably bold and lengthy complaint demonstrated the women's unwillingness to retreat from the position they had assumed in Iowa's sanitary affairs, and raised several important issues relating to the right of the Governor's men to supplant them.

In the first place, the article addressed the fact that the women's commitment to soldier relief predated by "three or four months" that of the Governor's organization, granting them an obvious seniority in the field. The article then pointed to the successes the Keokuk Society had thus far achieved in multiplying the commitment of women around the state, in forwarding needed supplies to the front, and in getting the various Iowa associations into "very fair working order," such that they "gave promise and assurance of being equal to the work they had taken in hand."[21] The women's associations in general, and the Keokuk Society in particular, the article argued, not only predated the men's Commission but also made the Commission superfluous. In short, the women were doing fine on their own.

---

19. Fullbrook, "Relief Work in Iowa during the Civil War," 198–99. As the secretary of the Keokuk Society would later describe them, the other key members of the State Sanitary Commission consisted of "two Bishops, two or three Reverends, three or four Honorables and three or four Bankers." "Report of the Ladies' Soldiers' Aid Society," *The Gate City*, 15 April 1862.

20. *The Gate City*, 28 October 1861.

21. *The Gate City*, 18 November 1861.

In addition to expressing the Society's anger over the establishment of the State Sanitary Commission, the article also contained a revealing comment concerning the women's perception of the difference between their own style of working and the style they anticipated from the men. Up to now, the article asserted, "The women were all earnestly interested and were doing matters in their own way, without sounding a trumpet before them or magnifying their efforts by eliciting the services of the Honorables of our State in order to blazon them abroad." Now, however, a number of Iowa's prominent male figures, the "honorables," had come to realize that "there is a great deal of glory running to waste in this matter," that "there is a chance for salaries and fees in carrying out this benevolent measure which may be parcelled out to the wealthy men of the State."[22] These "honorables" clearly intended to avail themselves of such advantages, at the expense not only of the women who had preceded them into sanitary work, but also of the soldiers about whom the men undoubtedly cared little. The women of the Keokuk Ladies' Soldiers' Aid Society, who for months had given their time and energy voluntarily and with great success to the cause of soldier relief, defiantly expressed their frustration that a new commission composed entirely of prestigious male figures was about to supersede them, capture whatever accolades were associated with war relief, and undermine the work itself.

The mocking tone taken in the article with regard to "salaries," "fees," and "glory" suggested that, in contrast to the "honorables," these good, Victorian, Protestant women did not expect financial rewards so much as they sought the more basic reward of simply being allowed to continue their work unimpeded. By leaving the women alone, the article seemed to say, the men would acknowledge the propriety of what the Keokuk Society and other local women's organizations were doing, and would legitimize the wartime role that women across the state of Iowa had assumed. The article thus soundly rejected the constraints of a prewar gender system, which characterized the more public, administrative aspects of war relief as inappropriate for women, and asked that Iowa's women in general, and the Keokuk Society in particular, be allowed to continue doing what they had already been doing, without interference. "We trust," the article commented sarcastically, that those who "constitute the Sanitary Commission, will 'post up,' roll up their sleeves and 'pitch in,' and show the women how matters ought to be done. We should be right glad to see them take a personal interest in the matter and make a personal effort, or else get out of the way and not stand as an obstruction in the way of the women of Iowa, who would do this thing up much better without them."[23]

Simply but heatedly the women demanded the right to continue doing the patriotic work they had undertaken, in the style they deemed most appropriate, without outside intervention. By seeking not only to gather the supplies needed

---

22. Ibid.
23. Ibid.

by the soldiers, but to manage and control their distribution and to receive credit for doing so, Keokuk's women demonstrated two key things: their aversion to perceived male pork-barrel "politics as usual," and their full determination to protect the territory they had staked out for themselves in the war effort, even if that territory exceeded the gender boundaries the Governor and his men considered appropriate.

Governor Kirkwood displayed his early anticipation of friction between the Keokuk Society and the Commission, and specifically between the organizations' leaders, by writing to Wittenmyer two weeks before the women's angry *Gate City* article appeared, praising her work and requesting her cooperation with the Commission and with her counterpart, the Reverend Kynett. "You have set an example to the women of your state," wrote Governor Kirkwood placatingly, "which I hope will be followed. . . . Rev. Kynett . . . is corresponding secretary of our organization formed to systematize the efforts . . . in this good cause. May I request you will communicate with him and endeavor to have all efforts to this end concentrated?"[24] If he hoped to appease Wittenmyer with this letter and convince her to relinquish control over Iowa sanitary affairs and resume a more acceptable role scraping lint and rolling bandages at home, Kirkwood should have considered his sentences more carefully. His use of the phrase "our organization," in referring to the Commission, implied a contrast between "ours" (the Commission) and "yours" (the Keokuk Society), giving the former legitimate status while denying it to the latter. It was a nuance that Wittenmyer would not have missed. The Governor further insulted Wittenmyer and the Keokuk Society by suggesting that, in his mind, the new Commission now officially constituted "Iowa's organization," whereas the Keokuk Society did not. Kirkwood then compounded the offense by stating explicitly that the Commission was designed to "systematize" the presumably "unsystematic" efforts already underway by women across the state, a characterization that the Society's members certainly would not have shared.

As the women's *Gate City* article indicated, the submission of the Keokuk Society to the direction of the Iowa State Army Sanitary Commission, and even just the harmonious coordination of the two organizations' activities, required far more than a poorly worded request from the Governor. The establishment of the Iowa Commission rapidly created confusion in the broad field of the state's relief work, and aid societies across Iowa now found themselves having to choose between loyalty to the Commission, with its impressive affiliation to the USSC, and loyalty to the Society, with its prior record of efficiency and its familiar faces and ways. A substantial proportion of women's aid organizations reiterated their support of the Keokuk Society. A typical letter from A. S. Marsh of Mt. Pleasant, Iowa, reached Wittenmyer at the end of November 1861: "Our corrisponding [sic] secretary has been in corrispondence [sic] with the Secretary of this state's Sanitary Commission [Kynett] who strongly urged

---

24. Samuel Kirkwood to Annie Wittenmyer, 6 November 1861, War Correspondence.

all hospital goods to be sent to their care. The society however, seems favourable as far as they have expressed themselves, to sending them subject to your direction."²⁵ In December, Mrs. J. B. Howell, president of the Keokuk Society, wrote to Wittenmyer in the field about the receipt of more letters of support. "I have read several letters from ladies of our state," she wrote, "and from the interest they manifest I should think the zeal of our ladies is on the increase and that there is also decided preference for our organization to that of the state San. Com."²⁶

Early in 1862, the Commission, finding the task of absorbing the Keokuk Society's numerous allies more difficult than anticipated, attempted to assert its dominance over state sanitary affairs by calling for the financial records of all Iowa aid associations, as if its own hegemony was a given. Secretary of the Keokuk Society Mary Strong wrote defiantly to Wittenmyer, "We have resolved not to notice it [the Commission's mandate] at all."²⁷ Accustomed to ignoring the demands of the USSC, the women of the Keokuk Society decided to ignore the Commission's demands as well and to continue the work of gathering and distributing relief supplies—through Wittenmyer—just as before. Still, the Commission's order provoked concern among leaders of the Society regarding the continuing confidence and loyalty of the Society's affiliates. Would the Society's failure to comply with the Commission cast a shadow over their own operations? Even as they refused to provide the Commission with financial information, Society leaders like Lucretia Knowles wrote to Wittenmyer in the hope of developing a formal account of her expenditures. "People are beginning to ask what we have done with the money we received," she wrote, and requested that Wittenmyer begin keeping more detailed records to be forwarded to the Society's treasurer.²⁸ As Mary Strong explained later, "our friends through the State do not know what to do, whether to send to us as heretofore or whether we have united with the Commission."²⁹ It was not so much that other aid associations questioned the integrity of Wittenmyer and the Keokuk Society, as that the existence of the Commission and its insistence on "systematization" under its authority made necessary a rethinking of the Society's practices. That rethinking included a formalization of procedures, suggesting that in order for the women to retain the position they had carved out for themselves in Iowa's sanitary affairs, they would have to conform, at least somewhat, to the dictates of male organizational style, at least in terms of their record-keeping standards, which had hitherto been less rigid and grounded in a simple but absolute trust in Wittenmyer's uprightness. As Strong would later publicly insist, "We are satisfied that we could not have

---

25. A. S. Marsh to Annie Wittenmyer, 21 November 1861, War Correspondence.
26. Mrs. J. B. Howell to Annie Wittenmyer, 9 December 1861, War Correspondence.
27. Mary Strong to Annie Wittenmyer, 18 March 1862, War Correspondence.
28. Lucretia Knowles to Annie Wittenmyer, 4 February 1862, War Correspondence.
29. Mary Strong to Annie Wittenmyer, 18 March 1862, War Correspondence.

a more economical, efficient, untiring and prudent agent to distribute our stores. Not a single box or bundle of articles has been lost that has been sent through this Society for distribution by our Agent."[30] But the need to convey and sustain this trust in public against the suspicions aroused by the Commission's demands required certain structural changes, particularly as quantities of supplies grew and systems of allotment and delivery became more complex with the war's intensification.

Like the issue of salaries and titles, the bookkeeping issue highlighted differences in style in the two organizations, differences rooted in gender. At the same time, it pinpointed stresses the Victorian gender system was undergoing on the home front as a result of the war. As long as men and women functioned within their own theoretical "spheres" of activity (men in public and women in private), questions of style did not arise. In other words, no man challenged a woman's caretaking and management techniques when she exercised them within the context of her own household or even her immediate community. By crossing over into men's "sphere," however, by taking her skills out into the larger public realm — specifically the realm of war — a woman automatically elicited criticism. The women of the Keokuk Society, and Wittenmyer in particular, had undertaken a massive project of organized caretaking in the indisputably public, traditionally male domain of war. To many observers, the undertaking was entirely inappropriate. In order to continue operating and to relieve some of the pressure their activities exerted on a stubborn Victorian gender system, the Keokuk Society's leaders increasingly felt compelled to adopt male standards of professionalism, including the keeping of much more careful, detailed accounts of the receipt and distribution of supplies than had previously been the case. Soon they would discover the benefits of salaries and titles as well.

Needless to say, the adjustment was not an altogether smooth one, and it is not surprising that Wittenmyer seems at first to have taken offense at Knowles's request for accounts. Was someone questioning her integrity? At this early stage in the war, Wittenmyer was still learning the many-faceted art of political maneuvering, in this case the art of responding tactically to one "squeaky wheel" in order to protect the operation as a whole. In a March 1862 letter to Wittenmyer, Knowles reflected Wittenmyer's irritation when she exclaimed,

> [W]hat in the world are you exercising your mind so much about your expenses for? Who suspects your honesty madam? I don[']t know of a soul under the sun that does, & if you do I wish you would name the person. . . . [T]he Society does not wish you to feel disturbed or distressed in mind on account of your expenses; & I can assure you that nobody imagines that you spend our money for oysters & mint-juleps, or Theater tickets.[31]

---

30. "Report of the Ladies' Soldiers' Aid Society," *The Gate City*, 15 April 1862.
31. Lucretia Knowles to Annie Wittenmyer, 4 March 1862, War Correspondence.

Knowles sought to reassure the sensitive Wittenmyer that, within her Society, she had earned complete trust, and that the attempt to systematize accounts represented only a precautionary measure in light of the Commission's anticipated and real challenges. With some grumbling, Wittenmyer complied.

Although she resented the suspicion she thought implicit in the inquiries about her handling of sanitary supplies and funds, Wittenmyer had early on recognized that the Society would need to act carefully and with political shrewdness to ensure its future. In the field, therefore, she consistently matched home front attempts by Society leaders to preempt the Commission with her own efforts to monopolize the support of the military and the army medical establishment. By December 1861, Wittenmyer was writing home from St. Louis: "I have made several important arrangements, that will secure the interests of our society here after. One is that every box of supplies sent from our state, to reg[i]ments surgeons &c &c are to be turned over to our society, that is to me, or any other agent we may have out, to be used as our society may direct. All of the surgeons and many of the officers are pledged to this."[32] In another letter, she confided to Mrs. Howell that shortly, "I shall have seen and arranged with *every surgeon* [and] then the bogus San'y Com'n of Iowa is *as dead as a door nail,* for all that they send out will be turned over to us."[33] Wittenmyer's "arrangements" in St. Louis and elsewhere aimed to ensure that control of (and also credit for) the state's relief supplies would remain with the Keokuk Society as a whole, and with Wittenmyer herself in particular.

In addition, Wittenmyer continued to press the military and the federal government for free transportation for herself and countless boxes of supplies.[34] By the spring of 1862, she had achieved her goal of a free federal government pass, presented by Secretary of War Edwin Stanton and signed by President Abraham Lincoln, allowing her to travel without restriction on all rivers and railroads across the theater of war. As the 1862 *Gate City* "Report" proudly stated, "From Generals in Departments and Divisions, besides from officers and Surgeons in Regiments and Hospitals, our Agent has met with every courtesy and necessary aid and co-operation."[35] Wittenmyer's ability to muster so much support from important men in the field represented a real coup. Her efforts to elicit public acknowledgment and endorsement of the women's organization and its dominance in Iowa's relief work had met with an important victory.

Still, a decided frustration lingered among the Society's leaders with regard to their inability to command exclusive control and loyalty at home in Iowa, and

---

32. Annie Wittenmyer to Mrs. Chittenden, 2 December 1861, War Correspondence.
33. Annie Wittenmyer to Mrs. J. B. Howell, 3 December 1861, War Correspondence.
34. Annie Wittenmyer to Captain Parsons, 28 February 1862, War Correspondence.
35. "Report of the Ladies' Soldiers' Aid Society," *The Gate City*, 15 April 1862. In *Under the Guns,* Wittenmyer quite proudly displayed her intimacy with General and Mrs. Ulysses S. Grant, providing numerous anecdotes in which the three figured together. Indeed, Julia Dent Grant composed the book's introduction.

to press their claim to superior form, style, and success in providing relief to Iowa's troops. Wittenmyer wrote privately to the Governor in March 1862, expressing her annoyance: "The State San'y Commission are accomplishing nothing, they have received but few goods, and those goods have gone into the hands of the Western Commission and are now lying in the St. Louis Depots. Not one dollar[']s worth of goods committed to their care have reached our Iowa troops." Expecting that Kirkwood might question her motives, Wittenmyer insisted, "I am well posted with regard to these matters and will make no statement that I can not substantiate." She went on to emphasize the Society's (and her own) competence, adding, that should Kirkwood have any doubts, "all of our Iowa officers and surgeons will bear me out in this statement."[36]

Because the women had been so quick to commit themselves to the soldiers' relief, because they had for months actively, efficiently, and voluntarily discharged their perceived duties in the war, and because they so firmly believed that the work of war relief belonged in the hands of women, they seethed over their continuing struggle to obliterate the Commission's power and influence. Appointed by the Governor and affiliated directly with the USSC, the Commission seemed to have received its legitimacy on a platter, obviating the need for it to prove its worth by actually providing sanitary relief to the soldiers as the Society, through Wittenmyer, had so diligently done for months. Even worse, not only could the Commissioners automatically pose as "legitimate" in a way that the women could not; in addition, the Commissioners received state-funded salaries, despite the uncertainty of their real contribution to the work of relief. An army chaplain loyal to the Society complained to Wittenmyer in January 1862 about the paid male commissioners' emphasis on image. He wrote, "Men coming down here and looking around a little, gathering information from Surgeons, chaplains and others, amounts to a pleasure excursion and a nice one if their expenses are paid, and they are fattened with a salary."[37]

Ironically, as much as the Society's leaders initially understood their work as an extension of women's nature and Christian responsibility and thereby necessarily an unsalaried endeavor, in truth, not all women's personal finances permitted full-time voluntary devotion to such "labors of love." Around the state of Iowa, as across the nation, individual women could only give of their time, energy, and material goods in relative proportion to their resources. At the beginning of the war, women such as Wittenmyer and the other leaders of the Keokuk Society were generally able to give a great deal, expecting little more in return than gratitude, recognition, and the satisfaction of having obeyed a "higher call." Ultimately, however, the length and brutality of the war would try both the ability and the willingness of even the wealthiest women of Iowa to

---

36. Annie Wittenmyer to Samuel J. Kirkwood, 20 March 1862, Correspondence of the Adjutant General, Civil War Years, State Historical Society of Iowa, Des Moines (hereafter cited as "Adjutant General's Correspondence").

37. Chaplain Ingalls to Annie Wittenmyer, 11 January 1862, War Correspondence.

continue freely committing themselves and their assets to sanitary work. Wittenmyer's determination to get the federal government to underwrite the Society's activities indicated that she knew the women could not continue indefinitely to provide relief to the soldiers without some external financial support.

Along with the women's awareness that the salaries received by the "honorable" men functioned in some way publicly to legitimize the Iowa Commission (regardless of individual need or the Commission's actual effectiveness), over time, this realization that some measure of government subsidy would be necessary simply in order for their own work to continue, accelerated the Society's revision of its originally "purely benevolent" ideals. In other words, as time passed and their control of sanitary affairs remained tenuous, the women began to appreciate the benefits of salaried status, official recognition, and professional acknowledgment, coming to realize that, in the public sphere, the granting of professional titles and the exchange of money for labor somehow served to validate, in a fashion previously unfamiliar to them, the work that a person performed. In April 1862, the Society's *Gate City* "Report" revealed this change of heart, brought on by the competition with the Commission. Mary Strong wrote pointedly that the Society—unlike the Commission— having as yet received no subsidy from the State Government (in contrast with the generosity of the Federal Government), "we cannot but think it will soon see the justice of granting us some appropriation from the public Funds to assist us in carrying out our designs; when it considers how long we have been engaged in this work, how much we have labored, and how much we have accomplished by self-sustained exertions."[38] Even more important, when Governor Kirkwood soon after sponsored a bill to appoint Wittenmyer one of two Iowa State Sanitary Agents (the other one being Kynett) and to appropriate to her $100 per month for salary and expenses, she did not refuse.[39]

It is difficult to determine precisely the reasons behind Kirkwood's decision to push the appointment of Wittenmyer through the state legislature. Possibly he believed that by formally elevating her status and the status of the Keokuk Society, he could reduce the tension between the women's organization and the Commission and elicit greater cooperation between the two. Since creating the Commission, as his November 1861 letter to Wittenmyer indicated, Kirkwood had ventured to bring the Society, and through it other Iowa women's aid organizations, under its supervision. At least initially, Kirkwood, like so many others, could not accept the independence of the Keokuk Society, either because he could not believe that the women were capable of managing their own affairs, or because he felt that to allow them to do so was somehow improper.

---

38. "Report of the Ladies' Soldiers' Aid Society," *The Gate City*, 15 April 1862.

39. "*Be it enacted by the General Assembly of the State of Iowa*," read the bill, "That the Governor be and he is hereby authorized and required to appoint two or more agents (one of whom shall be Mrs. Annie Wittenmyer) as Sanitary Agents for the State of Iowa" ("Mrs. Annie Wittenmyer," *Annals of Iowa*, 280).

Correspondence between Wittenmyer and the Governor at the beginning of 1862 suggests that she made at least some superficial efforts to accede to his request that she cooperate with the Commission. "[W]e have favorably considered the proposition made by the San'y Com'n to unite with them," she wrote in January,

> and I have just communicated the [Society's] terms [for union] to Rev. Kynett. ... We deprecate [sic] the existence of *two* associations for the same purpose, as rivalry, faultfinding, and feelings of animosity are apt to follow, and we desire to sustain amicable relations with all. ... I am exceedingly anxious for a union of the two associations, and have urged it with great zeal, as I would then be relieved of a great deal of the labor and responsibility that now necesarily [sic] falls upon me.[40]

Whatever one believes about Wittenmyer's sincerity, or about the nature of the undefined "terms" that she offered to Kynett and the Commission, the negotiations ended in acrimony. Mary Strong wrote to Wittenmyer in March, "You have probably heard of the failure in regard to our uniting on honorable terms with the Sanitary Commission."[41] In the April 1862 *Gate City* "Report" Strong characterized this failure as the Society's refusal to yield its independence to an organization "whose plans had not yet been carried out with any success, whose agents had not been proved for fidelity or experience, whose executive policy was so different from that which we had found so advantageous."[42] The Governor's authorization of Wittenmyer as a State Sanitary Agent represented in part his acknowledgment that a union between the two organizations was far outside his grasp, and that his best hope for a solution to the problem lay in fostering their acceptance of parity.

There was, however, an element of even greater capitulation in the Governor's promotion of Wittenmyer. In her own March 1862 letter to Kirkwood addressing the organizations' failure to unite, Wittenmyer concluded with a request that the Governor and the state legislature now honor "our claims to public patronage," i.e., provide the Keokuk Society with some portion of the financial support that it had already extended to the Commission. She further threatened that a refusal of these claims would "oblige" the Society to expose the Commission's ineffectiveness "before the *people* of the state and *appeal to them for help.*"[43] Wittenmyer was not the only Society member to hint at the possibility of publicly challenging the Commission's competence. Other

---

40. Annie Wittenmyer to Samuel J. Kirkwood, 10 January 1862, Adjutant General's Correspondence. Wittenmyer may well have lacked sincerity when she asserted that she was "exceedingly anxious for a union of the two organizations," but she certainly knew that open conflict was counterproductive for the Society. Her attempt, sincere or not, to assuage the concerns of the Governor could only reflect well upon herself and the Society.

41. Mary Strong to Annie Wittenmyer, 18 March 1862, War Correspondence.

42. "Report of the Ladies' Soldiers' Aid Society," *The Gate City*, 15 April 1862.

43. Annie Wittenmyer to Samuel J. Kirkwood, 30 March 1862, Adjutant General's Correspondence.

members of the Society considered discrediting the Commission in order to reinforce the Society's position. "The [Iowa] Sanitary Commission is in very bad odor here," wrote Mrs. C. D. Allen of Iowa City to Mary Strong in February 1862.[44] In March, Lucretia Knowles wrote to Wittenmyer: "If they are doing *nothing* why can *we not make it public?*"[45]

In April, the Society did attack the Commission in its *Gate City* "Report." "We have . . . learned," wrote Secretary Mary Strong, "that great quantities of stores from the Iowa State Sanitary Commission . . . were lying unused and uncalled for [in St. Louis], for a great length of time, when our troops at distant Posts were in daily need of them. . . . This detention of supplies has been noticed repeatedly." Moreover, she continued, goods that did get distributed seemed to have random destinations, a situation that Strong described as "depriving our women of Iowa of the satisfaction of providing for the comfort of those brave men who have won honor for their State."[46] Through Strong, the Society formally addressed the Commission's ineptitude, but also reemphasized the women's own understanding of wartime sanitary work—a highly organized and public form of caretaking—as a logical extension of the "natural" association of women with the home into the community writ large. From the women's perspective, it was organizations of *men* such as the Iowa Army Sanitary Commission, and implicitly, perhaps, the USSC as well, that undermined sacred notions of caretaking by distributing supplies randomly and carelessly, without women's deliberate purpose and sensitivity to need. The debate over competence and control unmasked the enormous tension in the gender system that women's intrusion into the public context of war had produced. Exerting pressure on antebellum Victorian gender constraints, Wittenmyer and her female colleagues claimed only to be doing what was proper, and what they knew best how to do.

Regardless of how he felt about Wittenmyer personally, Kirkwood knew that she commanded the loyalty of a great number of women throughout the state, without whose allegiance Iowa's relief work would come to a halt. Because he could not ignore the Society's increasingly loud and deliberate claims for official support, nor the widespread criticism of the Commission, Kirkwood sought a new solution to the conflict in his "war at home" by elevating Wittenmyer's status, making the two associations relatively equivalent, and thereby promoting, he hoped, their merger. This attempted compromise, too, failed however, as neither organization proved willing to surrender, and Wittenmyer's achievement of official stature only served her as another lesson in political tactics. She and the Keokuk Society continued for over a year to function independently of the Commission, competing vigorously with it for the state's available relief supplies.

---

44. Mrs. C. D. Allen to Mary Strong, 29 February 1862, War Correspondence.
45. Lucretia Knowles to Annie Wittenmyer, 21 March 1862, War Correspondence.
46. "Report of the Ladies' Soldiers' Aid Society," *The Gate City*, 15 April 1862.

Under the leadership of Kynett, the State Commission put up a good fight, drawing on its allegiance to the USSC and its leaders' greater experience in political maneuvering to continue rallying — or coercing — support from local women's aid associations. In March 1863, Amelia Bloomer described to Wittenmyer how the confusion produced by the existence of two major relief organizations in the state, and skillful exploitation of this confusion by the Commission, had affected the Council Bluffs Soldiers' Aid Society of which she had at one time been president and which, in its early stages, "was independent in its action," funnelling supplies largely through the Keokuk Society. "This arrangement," she wrote, "had my full sanction and approval, and for a time the other ladies interested concurred." But then, she proceeded, "the State Sanitary Commission commenced sending its circulars to us . . . [and] urged that it was best for Societies to opperate [sic] through the commission [as] their aid was more sure of being judiciously applied." For a while the Council Bluffs Society ignored the Commission's recommendations. Over time, however, the presence in the town of an "honorary member of the Commission" who "felt that the commission would look for him to do something here" made it difficult for the local women's group to maintain their distance. The final blow to the original women's organization came when the Commission's "honorary member" called a meeting "of ladies" explicitly for the purpose of their forming "a branch of the State Commission."

> The meeting was not very large — many did not understand the matter — those who did had in caucus fixed it all to suit themselves. . . . [T]he ladies kept still and voted as directed, by ballot. . . . I found after the meeting adjourned that many of the ladies supposed it all the same as the other society, and considered the funds &c in the Soldiers['] Aid Society as belonging to the new society. I soon set them right in the matter.

In any case, the women's organization of Council Bluffs quickly dissolved into the new, adroitly orchestrated auxiliary of the Commission, leaving leaders like Bloomer hurt and bitter. "I have never since taken an active part in labors for the soldiers," she wrote to Wittenmyer.[47] No doubt, the Council Bluffs story was not unique.

The Commission and the Keokuk Society continued to battle throughout 1863. In addition, that year saw the levelling of scandalous charges against Wittenmyer that simultaneously highlighted and threatened to erode her growing prominence. The accuser, a Reverend Emonds from Iowa City, publicly charged Wittenmyer with selling rather than simply distributing supplies, specifically eggs, butter, and sauerkraut. In response, Wittenmyer published a vehement statement of denial in the *Iowa City State Press*, in which she angrily pointed out the financial and other sacrifices she had consistently made since the start of the war in order to pursue relief work, including neglecting her "own property and business involving thousands of dollars." Emphasizing

---

47. Amelia Bloomer to Annie Wittenmyer, 2 March 1862, War Correspondence.

the "Christian obligation" that underlay her devotion to sanitary work, Wittenmyer recalled all the good that she had done, and the little she had requested in return. "[S]o far from ever having betrayed such a spirit of littleness and meanness" as selling supplies would imply, she wrote, "my hands have ever been open to feed the hungry and clothe the naked; and the lowist [sic] and most degraded of Earth's fallen children who came to me for aid and sympathy have been in no wise turned away empty. Is it then probable that I would turn aside from my high mission to *peddle butter and eggs* . . . ? Such statements are not only *untrue* but *ridiculous*."[48]

The scandal never took a legal turn, remaining instead in the realm of charges and countercharges. There is also no evidence to suggest that Emonds's accusations had any foundation in fact. Rather, he seems to have twisted the details of a temporary emergency arrangement between Wittenmyer and the Governor, in which the state furnished Wittenmyer with money to purchase some essential supplies in the north, and ship and resell them at cost to Iowa regiments in the south.[49]

Emonds's attack on Wittenmyer implied a desire to reduce her undeniable status in the state's sanitary affairs by undermining her reputation for fair and honest dealing. The Governor's assistant, N. H. Brainerd, wrote several letters of support to Wittenmyer as the scandal unfolded, revealing his own and the Governor's frustration with the whole affair and displaying anger at the upheaval that further jeopardized the establishment of harmony in Iowa sanitary affairs.

Much like the earlier questions raised about her bookkeeping procedures, Emonds's unproven charges outraged Wittenmyer's sense of herself as both a charitable and increasingly public figure, and her sharp response demonstrated the strength of her determination to protect her growing reputation. In April 1861, Wittenmyer had already been locally prominent in benevolent activities, but her public stature two years later dwarfed her earlier image. Gone by this time should have been any lingering impressions of her simply as a good Protestant woman temporarily devoted to the work of supplying the troops. Wittenmyer had not only survived the threat posed by the establishment of the Iowa State Army Sanitary Commission some eighteen months before, but had also maintained her position in state sanitary affairs with such tenacity and resolve that even official support had begun to shift increasingly in her direction. Governor's Assistant Brainerd wrote to her in May 1863: "You are becoming more widely known and appreciated in your efforts than heretofore & will soon be able to treat with silent contempt all who may oppose [you.]

---

48. Copy of a statement sent to the *Iowa City State Press* by Annie Wittenmyer, 3 March 1863, War Correspondence.

49. Note by Wittenmyer attached to a letter from C. D. Allen to Annie Wittenmyer, 13 April 1863, War Correspondence. Wittenmyer noted also that the arrangement had proved impracticable, "as the men had not been payed [sic]," and that she had ended up giving away the supplies she had purchased. She requested in the future "to be excused from any further duty on that line."

I think Brother Kynett has found it very u[n]profitable to fight you and will let you alone hereafter."[50] Clearly, by mid-1863, Wittenmyer had made a place for herself in Iowa sanitary affairs from which she refused to be forcibly removed. In the broad scheme of things, over the course of more than two years of relief activity, Wittenmyer had challenged prevailing expectations about the professional abilities of women such as herself, and she had held her ground until others found themselves compelled, at least temporarily, to yield and adjust their views.

Twice during the fall of 1863, representatives of various local Iowa relief organizations convened with the goal of resolving once and for all the conflict in state sanitary affairs. According to one historian, the debate revolved around the question of which organization best represented the interests of Iowa relief work, not only in its structure, philosophy, and basic practices, but in its external relationship to institutions such as the USSC. Representatives expressed concerns about the negative effect that the ongoing existence of two competing organizations and two prominent and mutually uncooperative leaders was having on the whole enterprise of sanitary relief in the state. In the end, the two conventions produced a new association, called the Iowa Sanitary Commission, which essentially became an amalgam of the two earlier associations without the formal leadership of either Kynett or Wittenmyer — although her influence remained far stronger than his — and which went on to continue Iowa's relief work until the end of the war.[51]

In December 1863, as the new organization was getting underway, Kynett officially resigned his position as "Corresponding Secretary and Gen'l Ag't of the Iowa [Army] Sanitary Commission."[52] It is tempting to interpret Kynett's resignation as a simple concession of defeat and to assume that the new Iowa Sanitary Commission abruptly yielded all loyalty to an entirely female Wittenmyer faction. Such was not, however, the case. Rather, the leadership of the new organization reflected a measure of compromise between the two previous associations — with their distinct approaches to war relief — made possible, perhaps even necessary, by Wittenmyer's refusal to crumble. Although the president of the new Commission was Justice John F. Dillon of Davenport, the leadership as a whole consisted of both men and women from around the state.[53]

Wittenmyer retained her official position as an Iowa State Sanitary Agent for some six months after Kynett's resignation, by which point her successes at home launched her into new projects in the field of war relief, this time at the national level. In her last months as an Agent, Wittenmyer faced renewed

---

50. N. H. Brainerd to Annie Wittenmyer, 19 May 1863, War Correspondence.
51. Fullbrook, "Relief Work in Iowa during the Civil War," 212–35.
52. A. J. Kynett to Samuel J. Kirkwood, 1 December 1863, General Correspondence of Governor Samuel J. Kirkwood, State Historical Society of Iowa, Des Moines.
53. Fullbrook, "Relief Work in Iowa during the Civil War," 225.

attempts to dislodge her and to limit the power she exerted over state sanitary affairs. Early in 1864, for example, opponents tried unsuccessfully to revoke the 1862 legislation that had made her an Agent in the first place, but Wittenmyer's evermore numerous defenders easily stymied this final challenge.[54] By not surrendering to defeat and by outlasting the man who symbolized opposition to her dominance of Iowa sanitary affairs, Wittenmyer ultimately won her war at home, setting the stage for her involvement in sanitary efforts on the grander, national scale. She emerged from the Civil War a nationally known figure, even as Kynett's name quickly faded from memory.

In November 1863, Nettie Sanford had written to Wittenmyer expressing her support. "I think you have too many friends to allow Mr Kynett or any other Reverend to take the Commission from your hands," she wrote. And she continued,

> It is strange, passing strange, that the charities of women must pass through the censorship of all the *pantaloons* in this state. . . . The heart that has the warm impulses of kindness and love for the soldier that woman has, generally has the head to . . . plan for concentration of action with others. . . . Believe me the whole movement against you and woman's right to dispense alms will fall to the ground. The idea is too absurd to be entertained by the intelligent people of the country.[55]

In retrospect, Sanford's comments appear prescient. They also revive the discussion of the women's particular aims in the work of war relief, and of the way in which the women's determination to pursue their goals fostered tension in the midcentury, middle-class gender system. According to Sanford, war relief belonged in the hands of women, whose very nature qualified and even favored them for the work. She also addressed the issue of competence, by claiming that women had sufficient "head" to order the impulses of their hearts, thus refuting the notion that women engaged in soldier relief required some external (male) influence to systematize and control their efforts. Women, she wrote, were both emotionally and intellectually constituted for the labor of sanitary aid, and it was "absurd" for anyone to believe otherwise.

Whether Sanford would have formulated her thoughts on the subject so clearly and so adamantly without the stimulus of the struggle for command of Iowa's sanitary affairs, is a question that cannot be answered. The conflict between the two organizations certainly pushed women like Sanford to try and define a position from which to argue for the right to pursue the war work they had chosen. In any case, Sanford articulated with striking brevity the

---

54. Ibid., 230–31. Mrs. N. H. Brainerd's March 1864 letter to Annie Wittenmyer included a list of resolutions passed by the Iowa City Ladies' Aid Society in her favor, and forwarded to the Iowa Senate and House of Representatives. Among other things, the Iowa City organization threatened to reject all connection with the "official State Agencies for the relief of our suffering heroes and seek those who do not discard merit but who honor patriotic devotion to the work in which we are engaged." Mrs. N. H. Brainerd to Annie Wittenmyer, 11 March 1864, War Correspondence.

55. Nettie Sanford to Annie Wittenmyer, 12 November 1863, War Correspondence.

fundamentals of two years of conflict between Wittenmyer and Kynett; between the Keokuk Ladies' Soldiers' Aid Society and the Iowa State Army Sanitary Commission; between the women who believed themselves quite capable of carrying out the administrative and managerial aspects of a task for which their female hearts equipped them, and those, mostly men, who disagreed. In the end, it seemed, the women had won.[56]

After resigning her position as Iowa State Sanitary Agent in May 1864, Annie Wittenmyer moved on to a variety of other projects, none of which embroiled her again in the kind of controversy that she had experienced for the first three years of the war. In all her later work, Wittenmyer encountered far less resistance to her undertakings than she had in the early years. One explanation for this change lies in the fact that, by late 1863, she had proven her administrative skills, her fierce tenacity, and the futility of trying to thwart her. Equally important, however, Wittenmyer manifested a growing awareness of the art of the shrewd political maneuver. The Civil War saw Wittenmyer's transformation from a wealthy widow busily engaged in the benevolent affairs of her hometown, into a nationally known, politically astute leader of a broad range of war relief work. And although she displayed no explicit desire to advance the larger cause of women's rights, Wittenmyer's own personal transformation and her employment of women to assist her in her later projects foreshadowed changes in the field of professional benevolence as a whole.

After the war, Reverend Henry Bellows offered accolades to Union women on the home front who had contributed significantly and efficiently to the war effort through their local aid societies. "Men did not take to the musket," he wrote, "more commonly than women took to the needle."[57] Women, having surrendered to the military "their husbands and sons, their brothers and lovers," had devoted themselves to the business of soldier relief, and they had done so, "not in the spasmodic and sentimental way, which has been common elsewhere, but with a self-controlled and rational consideration of the wisest and best means of accomplishing their purpose." Women had acted systematically, with "business-like thoroughness in details," "sturdy persistency," and, most importantly, in "thorough cooperativeness with the other sex." Bellows proffered his supreme compliment to the women of the ten thousand soldiers' aid societies across the Union, when he wrote that they had "proved by their own experience that men can devise nothing too precise, too systematic or too complicated for women to understand, apply and improve upon, where there is any sufficient motive for it."[58]

---

56. In February 1864, before resigning her official position, Wittenmyer filed a formal account of her fifteen months as a State Sanitary Agent, and a summary of her suggestions for improving the relief work already underway and for developing new avenues of labor for the duration of the war. The state subsequently published her report. See Annie Wittenmyer, *Reports of Mrs. Annie Wittenmyer, State Sanitary Agent* (Des Moines, 1864).

57. Linus P. Brockett and Mary C. Vaughan, *Woman's Work in the Civil War: A Record of Heroism, Patriotism, and Patience* (Philadelphia, 1867), 56.

58. Ibid., 56, 58.

Bellows enthusiastically celebrated women's wartime efforts in soldiers' aid. By characterizing war relief as a field of endeavor in which men led the way and women—as men's subordinates—cheerfully followed their example, however, he glossed over the possibility that women in Civil War relief work had created their own systems and developed their own tactics in contrast and often in conflict with those of men, and in so doing had displayed qualities and behaviors that betrayed the Victorian stereotypes of woman's "nature." In fact, Wittenmyer, the women who worked with her, and other women across the Union, had challenged prevailing notions about the propriety of middle-class women serving in public caretaking roles, and about the idea of such women's incapacity for professional work and public leadership, by becoming leaders and administrators of work they initiated on their own, in ways they themselves devised, and with vigor, determination, and efficiency that caught off guard men who considered themselves the masters of such endeavors. In so doing, Wittenmyer and women like her provoked concern among some observers about possible long-term postwar changes in Victorian gender arrangements. By laying this emphasis on the harmony, no doubt also experienced, among women and between women and men in aid society work, Bellows left little room for the consideration of the sort of struggles in war relief that Wittenmyer's story reveals.

BIBLIOGRAPHICAL NOTE

Patricia Dawson and David Hudson identified more than 150 items published about the Civil War between 1952 and 1991. Particularly in the 1960s, as Americans celebrated the war's centennial, regimental histories and accounts of Iowa soldiers' roles in particular battles proliferated. Perhaps the most notable of these were by Edwin Bearss, a research historian for the National Park Service and a prolific author of Civil War military history. Several of his multi-part articles appeared in the *Annals of Iowa* in the 1960s. More recent military history about battles in which Iowans were involved includes *"Seeing the Elephant": Raw Recruits at the Battle of Shiloh* (Westport, CT, 1989); and William L. Shea and Earl J. Hess, *Pea Ridge: Civil War Campaign in the West* (Chapel Hill, NC, 1992). A useful summary of Iowans' participation in Civil War battles is Mildred Throne, "Iowans and the Civil War," *Palimpsest* 40 (1959), 369–448; for a more concise summary, see Julie E. Nelson and Alan M. Schroder, "Iowa and the Civil War: A Military Review," *Palimpsest* 63 (1982), 98–105. A powerful account of the personal wartime experiences of nine young men from a rural community near the border between Linn and Buchanan Counties is Sharon Ham, "End of Innocence," *Palimpsest* 60 (1979), 76–97. Steve Meyer has collected, without scholarly analysis, a set of valuable primary sources related to the Civil War experiences of Iowans in *Iowa Valor* (Garrison, IA, 1994).

Kenneth L. Lyftogt, *From Blue Mills to Columbia: Cedar Falls and the Civil War* (Ames, 1993), combines an account of local soldiers' participation in the war with an account of activities in the local community during the war. Other than that and the work on Annie Wittenmyer, the new emphasis on the social history of the Civil War has not yet made it into print, although a few Ph.D. dissertations recently completed or in progress may soon find their way into print; watch for work by David Ferch, Russell Johnson, and Lori Lisowski. For non-Iowa examples of this new Civil War history, see Maris A. Vinovskis, ed., *Toward a Social History of the American Civil War: Exploratory Essays* (New York, 1990); Catherine Clinton and Nina Silber, ed., *Divided Houses: Gender and the Civil War* (New York, 1992), which contains an essay by Reid Mitchell about "becoming a man" for the Civil War generation, based largely on the experiences of a soldier from Palmyra, Iowa; and Anne C. Rose, *Victorian America and the Civil War* (New York, 1992).

Opposition to the war in Iowa has received its due. See, for example, Frank L. Klement, "Rumors of Golden Circle Activity in Iowa during the Civil War Years," *Annals of Iowa* 37 (1965), 523–36; David L. Lendt, "Iowa and the Copperhead Movement," *Annals of Iowa* 40 (1970), 412–27; and Hubert H. Wubben, *Civil War Iowa and the Copperhead Movement* (Ames, 1980).

7

Iowans and the Politics of Race in America, 1857–1880

ROBERT R. DYKSTRA

Iowa's African-American population has never exceeded 2 percent of the total population of the state (and did not exceed 1 percent until after 1960). Yet race was a key factor in the timing of Iowa's entry into statehood, and it remained an important issue in the state through the 1870s. It has periodically reemerged as an issue at various times and places in Iowa's subsequent history. Robert Dykstra has been, like Allan Bogue, a strong advocate of quantification. As this essay shows, however, he also has an exceptional ability to successfully integrate narrative and quantification into an invaluable account of the politics of race in Iowa in the nineteenth century.

THIS STUDY is about "life at the extremity of a culture," as V. S. Naipaul so skillfully characterizes the American frontier.[1] It examines white racism on the notoriously racist Middle Border in the era of the Civil War.

In those years every state and territory in the Union, whether initially free or slave, whether embracing large or small numbers of African-Americans, whether located in the North or the West or the South itself, had to confront the ultimate likelihood of black civil equality, of African-American equality before the law. A pioneering people, advancing westward for nearly half a century, their long southern flank originally exposed to slavery, Iowans persistently responded to that egalitarian prospect—the central issue imposed upon them by the nation's great sectional controversy, by the Civil War, and by the aftermath of the war.

---

1. V. S. Naipaul, *A Turn in the South* (New York, 1989), 165.

"Iowans and the Politics of Race in America, 1857–1880" includes ideas and text developed further in Robert R. Dykstra, *Bright Radical Star: Black Freedom and White Supremacy on the Hawkeye Frontier* (Cambridge: Harvard University Press, 1993), Copyright © 1993 by the President and Fellows of Harvard College; portions reprinted by permission of the author and Harvard University Press. This essay provides source notes only for direct quotations and for material not fully referenced in the book.

These women and men were not Iowans in the twentieth-century sense. They were New Englanders and New Yorkers, Pennsylvanians and Ohioans, southerners from Maryland and Virginia and North Carolina, immigrant Irish, Britons and Scots, Germans, Scandinavians. Their racial attitudes, we may suppose, had been shaped by the various cultural dispositions they brought with them. But once west of the Mississippi River the white adult males among them—that is, the politically empowered—had to devise a *common* polity that, however initially abstract the reality of a black presence, arranged the terms for interracial association. These terms themselves became increasingly salient political questions as small gatherings of black and white activists, occasionally prodded by abolitionist emissaries from the East, provoked debates over such tangible issues as integrated public schooling, equal access to welfare benefits and to the courts, interracial marriage, fugitive slave rendition, and—most extraordinarily—black voting and office-holding.

Iowa's early African-American community never grew as large as many continued to predict. In 1840, seven years after the territory had been legally opened to settlement, there were only 188 black Iowans—a mere .4 percent of its pioneers. By 1850 the number had risen to 333. On the eve of the Civil War it stood at 1,069. In 1870 black Iowans totaled 5,762, and in 1880 they were 9,516 in number—still just .6 percent of all residents of the Hawkeye State.[2]

How, one might ask, could they have been an issue? The answer is that the rights and privileges of blacks—like slavery itself—prove to have been issues in every "free" jurisdiction in America by the Civil War era, even though the black presence everywhere outside the South was almost nil. In no northern state save New Jersey, for example, did nonwhites make up so much as 3 percent of the population in either 1860 or 1870.[3] Yet white racial bigotry often has nothing much to do with first-hand interaction with blacks.

Frontier Iowans, like midwesterners in general, reacted not to the *fact* of a black presence but to the *prospect* of it. By the late 1850s white Iowans disturbed by the likelihood need only look across their southern border, where lived some 115,000 slaves. The largest concentrations of these African-Americans —in about the same proportion to whites as in western Kentucky or on Maryland's Eastern Shore—lay scattered the width of Missouri within thirty to fifty miles of the Hawkeye line.[4] A ceaseless theme of Iowa's conservative editors and politicians, both before and after emancipation, was that the immediate

---

2. Calculated from Leola Nelson Bergmann, *The Negro in Iowa* (Iowa City, 1969), 34; Bureau of the Census, *Historical Statistics of the United States: Colonial Times to 1970,* 2 vols. (Washington, DC, 1975), 1:27.

3. Calculated from Bureau of the Census, *Historical Statistics,* 1:25–35.

4. J. G. Randall and David Donald, *The Civil War and Reconstruction,* 2d ed. rev. (Lexington, 1969), 4–5, 66; James M. McPherson, *Ordeal by Fire: The Civil War and Reconstruction* (New York, 1982), 29.

consequence of legislating racial equality in any form would be an overwhelming inrush from Missouri's nearby "black belt." That it never happened is almost beside the point.

Partly in consequence, no doubt, Iowa's original black code proves to have been as harsh as that of any antebellum free state. Its statutory law banned interracial marriage, excluded blacks from public welfare benefits, excluded black children from public schools, disallowed black testimony in litigation involving whites, did not allow blacks to practice law, and required all black residents to register with the local authorities and to post bond for good behavior — later replaced by an outright exclusion law entirely banning nonwhite migration into the Hawkeye State. And Iowa's early constitutions excluded blacks from being counted in state censuses, from being considered in legislative apportionment, from serving in the militia, from voting, and from sitting in the legislature.

It can be argued, in fact, that Iowa was the most racist free state in the antebellum Union. In the 1840s it was the only free state whose legislators refused to instruct its congressional delegation to vote in favor of the Wilmot Proviso, which would have banned slavery from the nation's newly acquired western territories. It was also the only free state whose U.S. senators both voted for the notorious Fugitive Slave Law of 1850. And in 1851 its legislature (preceded only by that of Oregon Territory) passed the first black exclusion law enacted in a free jurisdiction in the nineteenth century. Finally, its first equal suffrage initiative, that of 1857, came within one-half of a percentage point of being the most crushing defeat on record for an equal-rights referendum.

Constructing this black code took twenty years, from 1838 to 1858. Its dismantling took the next twenty-two years, until 1880. Two important aspects of the building and dismantling process are worthy of note.

First is the matter of periodization. The years of the code's enactment for the most part coincided with a reactionary Democratic hegemony in Iowa. In contrast, the period of its destruction mainly coincided with the ascendancy of Iowa's Republican party — which, beginning in 1854 as an Anti-Nebraska coalition of Free Soilers and Whigs, dominated Iowa as thoroughly as the Democrats had ruled it before that date. The significance of this is that the most important policy battles over black equality occurred *within* the Whig, Anti-Nebraska, and Republican parties, the Democrats always serving as ideological caretakers of the most rigidly conservative policy alternatives at any given time.

Second, destruction of Iowa's black code was accomplished in various formats: some components expired in the law codification of 1851. Others vanished in the 1857 constitutional convention, still others in the General Assembly during the Civil War and in the state supreme court.

But the main challenge presented by the Iowa case is to explain how a voting population numbering some 340,000 adult males by 1880 could twice have given popular referendum majorities *in favor of* equal rights. Such successes are absolutely unprecedented in the annals of race relations in America, and unless they can be explained Iowa must remain, quite mysteriously, what historian Jean H. Baker has termed "the exception."[5]

FIRST, the facts. In 1857 Iowans went to the polls and made their preferences known about equal suffrage—that is, about allowing adult African-American males to vote. Among the two dozen or so such referendums held in the North in the mid-nineteenth century, Iowans' miniscule 11 percent approval was one of the nation's lowest levels of support ever.

In 1868 Iowans again went to the polls and made their preferences known on equal suffrage. This time their Yes vote soared to 57 percent of the ballots cast—reflecting the first civil rights proposition in American history to gain a majority in any state where voters knew unequivocally what they were casting ballots for and against.

In 1880 Iowans made their preferences known on opening the General Assembly to blacks. Equal rights won by a landslide—63 percent of the ballots cast. Thus, in a matter of just twenty-three years, a large population's positive attitude in a matter of racial equality before the law rose by a phenomenal 52 percentage points—a truly remarkable political achievement.

Interpreting these facts is of course a more complicated task. Note table 7.1. The data of this and subsequent tabulations derive from "ecological regression" procedures that, in this case, provide estimates of how Republicans and Democrats behaved in the three referendums. Who was a Republican and who a Democrat is determined by how Iowans voted in an immediately adjacent partisan election. (The 1857 Republicans, for example, are those who voted for John C. Frémont for president in 1856; the 1868 Republicans are those who supported the Republican gubernatorial candidate in 1867; those of 1880 voted for the Republican gubernatorial nominee in 1879.) Columns represent the three referendums. The top panel indicates how Republicans voted, the bottom panel how Democrats behaved.

Each qualified voter had four options on each referendum question: (a) voting Yes (in favor of equal rights); (b) voting No; (c) "rolling off"—that is, voting for party candidates or other referendum issues, but then refusing to cast a ballot either way on equal rights; or (d) not voting—that is, staying home on election day. Among Republicans the most notable change between 1857 and 1868 was a dramatic enlargement of the Yes vote. But the Yes percentage then slumped in 1880, a downturn reciprocated not by an increased No vote or in more Republicans failing to turn out at the polls, but rather in a swollen roll-off. Among Democrats, virtually none of whom *ever* voted Yes on equal rights, the most dramatic change was a huge drop in No ballots between 1868 and 1880, a shift that corresponds to an identical rise in roll-off.

---

5. Jean H. Baker, *Affairs of Party: The Political Culture of Northern Democrats in the Mid-Nineteenth Century* (Ithaca, 1983), 244n.

TABLE 7.1
MAJOR-PARTY VOTER POSITIONS ON EQUAL RIGHTS, 1857–1880[a]

	1857	1868	1880
Republicans			
Voting Yes	25	87	58
Voting No	11	4	7
Rolling off	37	7	35
Not voting	27	2	0[b]
	100	100	100
Democrats			
Voting Yes	0[b]	0	0[b]
Voting No	85	100[c]	25
Rolling off	0[b]	0	75
Not voting	15	0	0[b]
	100	100	100

[a]Percentages estimated. Regressions: 1856 presidential returns x 1857 Proposition 2 returns (county N = 70); 1867 gubernatorial returns x 1868 Proposition 1 returns (county N = 97); 1879 gubernatorial returns x 1880 Proposition 2 returns (county N = 98).
[b]Percentage set at minimum value and others adjusted.
[c]Percentage set at maximum value and others adjusted.

These changes suggest that the specific context of each referendum was different, as indeed it was.

Back in 1857 Iowa's Republican party was running scared. Its leaders were primarily concerned with obtaining popular ratification—against formidable Democratic opposition—of a new state constitution that, most importantly, would permit banking to be carried on within the state. "Proposition 1" being their first priority, Republican leaders had tried to stop equal suffrage from being paired with the forthcoming constitutional referendum, fearing that it would provoke a negative vote on the new organic instrument. But a few racially progressive Republicans of minor stature within the party, but nevertheless representing a strongly committed voting bloc, forced its inclusion on the ballot as "Proposition 2." In response, Iowa's Democrats seized the occasion to argue (falsely) that the triumph of *either* measure would mean the imposition of equal suffrage, integrated public schools, and all the other horrors dear to Democratic party propagandists throughout the nation.

As Jacksonian rhetoric became ever more shrill, Republican newspaper editors and other party spokesmen increasingly assured readers and auditors that black suffrage was *not* a Republican-sponsored or -endorsed initiative. Only two Republican editors suggested that voters ought to approve equal suffrage—and they said so with great circumspection. The combination of Democratic hostility and Republican avoidance yielded predictable results.

Only 8,479 hard-core, ideologically egalitarian Republicans voted in favor of Proposition 2. It was, in short, an equal rights disaster.

But by 1868, the year of the second referendum, the situation had changed considerably. Once again a progressive Republican minority had forced the party to confront the equal rights issue — in part as a response to effective lobbying by the state's small but politically resolute black community. But this time the radicals made up what might be thought of as a "critical mass" within the state's higher Republican circles. In 1865 they included practically the entire echelon of elected state officials (governor, lieutenant governor, secretary of state, auditor, and superintendent of public instruction) and virtually all of the Republicans nominated to succeed them. Judge C. C. Cole of the Iowa Supreme Court, a Harvard Law School graduate, took pride in having been "probably the first man of influence in the state to put himself publicly on record" in favor of equal rights.[6] Congressman Hiram Price, perhaps the state's leading banker and railroad capitalist, almost single-handedly pushed an equal suffrage plank — the controversial "Resolution 4" — through the June 1865 Republican state convention. And that measure was subsequently championed by a small host of prestigious Civil War military officers. By 1868 even such racial conservatives as U.S. Senators James Harlan and Samuel J. Kirkwood had clambered aboard the bandwagon. To Iowa's Republican rank and file the egalitarian promptings of such respected leaders reverberated with the preemptive authority of Higher Law.

Within two months of Appomattox, then, Iowa's Republican party supported black rights both as an expression of simple equity and as a response to the duty laid on all Iowans by congressional Republicans, who were at that moment urging equal suffrage in the South as the only means of consolidating the Confederacy's demise. But national Democrats (and Republican conservatives everywhere) were making much of the fact that few *northern* states allowed black suffrage — and therefore it would hardly be fair to force it on the South. For reasons both of immediate principle and of larger national policy, therefore, Iowa's Republican rank and file were in 1868 implored — by their politicos, by their newspaper editors, and by presidential candidate Ulysses S. Grant himself — to vote Yes on equal suffrage.

Grant's message was that he "hoped the people of Iowa, whose soldiers achieved such immortal renown in the field, would be the first state to carry impartial suffrage unfalteringly." It had gone down in other states, as an interviewer paraphrased his words, "but he trusted that Iowa, the bright Radical star, would proclaim by its action in November that the North is consistent with itself, and willing to voluntarily accept what its Congress has made a necessity in the South."[7]

---

6. A. T. Andreas, *Illustrated Historical Atlas of the State of Iowa* (1875; reprint, Iowa City, n.d.), 363.

7. Quoted in *Des Moines Weekly Register,* 4 November 1868.

A technical point of nineteenth-century voting procedure is relevant here. Before the advent in America of the Australian ballot, the printing of election tickets fell to local political parties: at polling places on election day, each voter accepted from his own party's men on the scene a unitary ballot — a long, narrow "slip ticket" — and he then cast that ballot as printed (unless he had the temerity to "scratch" a printed name and substitute another, a practice frowned on by partisan poll watchers).

Referendum issues normally appeared at the end of the long list of candidates on the ticket. In 1868, as a prosuffrage strategy, Iowa's Republican county organizations had the rights proposition included on the GOP ballot with only the Yes alternative printed. This meant that if one wanted to cast a Republican ballot and then vote *against* black suffrage one had to scratch the printed Yes and pencil in No. Several thousand voters did just that; it was not easy to qualify as a conservative Republican in 1868, but not impossible. About an equal number rolled off — supporting Grant but then apparently ripping the end from the ballot before depositing it in the ballot box. Taken together, about 10 percent of the general's supporters revealed themselves as deep-seated racists by casting write-in No votes or by rolling off. But equal suffrage won handily.

By contrast, 1880's referendum proved to be a complicated affair. The 1868 plebiscite had not only ratified black suffrage, but also had removed from Iowa's constitution all other discriminatory provisions but one — a clause asserting that only "free white" males could serve in the legislature. (This was not an oversight: maneuvering by a small racist block in the 1866 assembly had exempted this provision from the repeal initiative.) In the 1870s the state's reformers moved on to other issues, their energies coopted by the bitter antimonopoly and prohibition wars of Iowa's Gilded Age. By 1880, most Iowans — racists and egalitarians alike, even the state's black community — had forgotten that a vestige of the antebellum black code was still alive and well and living in the Iowa constitution.

One legislator had not forgot, and his actions remind us again of the surprising importance of individual political heroes to this story. Elden J. Hartshorn, a young Civil War veteran, was still reading law in Vermont during Iowa's 1868 referendum. But he soon headed west, settling on the frontier in northwest Iowa and beginning a lengthy career representing his area in the General Assembly. Virtually single-handedly Hartshorn kept the issue alive session after session, but with very little fanfare — in part, no doubt, because his immediate constituency was an enclave of immigrant Irish. Today the statue on the Palo Alto County courthouse lawn is not that of a Union soldier but of the immortal Irish patriot Robert Emmet. Hartshorn's friends and neighbors, who had rejected black suffrage in 1868 by the largest county margin in the state, would love him not for his stand on equal rights but for his having legislatively forced a railroad to build through Emmetsburg.

Ultimately, due to Hartshorn's quiet persistence, a proposition to repeal the "free white" clause got onto the 1880 ballot—but so quietly that the Republican leadership was caught flat-footed. Neither party, in fact, had thought to devise an official position on "free white" repeal. Less than two weeks before the referendum a hasty attempt was finally made to rally a Republican majority for repeal. But it was a botched job. The confusion was not all bad: not one editor—Republican, Democrat, or Greenbacker—urged a No vote on repeal, and since there were no formal party positions two Democratic editors even recommended voting Yes. Significantly, however, only about a third of Iowa's GOP editors urged a Yes vote, the rest being neutral or taking no notice at all of the upcoming proposal.

In 1880 the repeal proposition passed with an enormous majority. But less than half of those who came to the polls that day cast ballots one way or another on the "free white" clause. A majority of Iowa's electorate, in other words, did not vote at all on the question. We may guess that a great many of them—perhaps most—did not vote because (unlike in 1857 and 1868) they had not been *told* which way to vote.

The conclusion to be drawn from the impartial suffrage disaster of 1857 is that rank-and-file Republicans acted as expected of them: if their leaders saw no virtue in black equality, then neither would they. In 1868 just the opposite—both the idealistic and pragmatic value of black equality was impressed on Republicans and they accordingly expressed egalitarian choices. Finally, the 1880 referendum shows what could happen when *no* very coherent election messages came across from leadership to rank and file in any of the three political parties.

ONE ASSUMES, in all this, that many Iowans actually changed their minds about equal rights. But, given the rapid growth typical of a frontier population, Iowa's 1868 electorate was necessarily very different from what it had been in the fifties. It is within the range of statistical possibility, in fact, that 1868's triumphant Yes vote could have been cast solely by new voters (men who had arrived in the state after 1857 or who had come of voting age during the intervening years) without a single Iowan having reversed his 1857 position in 1868.

For two influential leaders, at least, change can be documented. General Grenville M. Dodge had been reared in a Democratic household in New England. His diary reveals him to have been a youthful racist: he provoked a dustup with a black waiter in a Boston restaurant, and he helped heckle a black abolitionist lecturer. But twelve years later, after removing to Iowa and becoming a Republican, he wrote from his wartime base command in Mississippi that "I have some very fine negro troops, well drilled and doing the same [combat] duty as the white troops."[8] And later he reminisced of his close work as one of

---

8. Grenville M. Dodge to brother, 27 June 1863, in "Dodge Records," typescript, 23 vols., State Historical Society of Iowa, Des Moines, 3:379.

General Grant's intelligence chiefs with black informants and line-crossers; they were, he testified, both invaluable and extraordinarily trustworthy. Apparently in consequence, by 1865 Dodge was a Reconstruction hard-liner and a firm advocate of Iowa's Resolution 4. "You know we have got to meet this question," he privately lectured a colleague about impartial suffrage, "and I of course have but one view on it, that is . . . fight for it on the ground of right, justice &c. and educate the people up to it."[9] And the general, it should be added, was a man to be reckoned with: in the 1870s and 1880s he was considered to be one of the three most powerful political figures in the state.

Meanwhile, the person at the head of the 1865 Republican state ticket also had defined his position on black equality. Although born of old Yankee stock in New York's radical Burned-Over District and coming of age in the equally abolitionist Western Reserve, Col. William M. Stone had been reared, like Dodge, a Democrat. In Iowa, after briefly flirting with Know Nothingism, he became a Republican. As a regimental commander home recuperating from wounds, he was elected governor in 1863 and was now standing for a second term.

Self-confident, uncommonly gregarious and uninhibited for a public man, Stone early in his reelection campaign adeptly began to defuse Democratic baiting about the racially progressive Resolution 4 by laying out the history of his personal feelings on black freedom and white supremacy. Regarding Iowa's first suffrage proposition he recalled, "In 1857 . . . I voted against it, not because I was opposed to it as a question of abstract right, but simply on the ground of expediency. I doubted whether we were ready for it." (Which is to say that he did no more than internalize the prevailing Republican party line.) And when the war came Stone was at first willing that it be won without dislodging slavery. A newspaper reporter paraphrased his explanation: "He had been rather slow upon this subject, and had never been regarded as a strong advocate of emancipation. He had been conservative on this question. He had been raised a Democrat, and shared the views of that party." "I was so conservative," added Stone, "[that] I did not endorse Lincoln's preparatory proclamation of emancipation as heartily as many did. I questioned its expediency at the time; although by the time when he issued the final proclamation . . . I was fully prepared to sustain it." (Note the rapid adjustment being described here: in three and one-half months Stone's attitude toward emancipation had shifted 180 degrees.)

Stone also felt initially uneasy about the idea of enlisting African-Americans as servicemen: "He was not, for some reason, very much in favor of the organization of colored regiments." But it had been ordered. "And [now] he believed if they would take out of the war what the black men had done, in various ways, as guides, teamsters, mechanics, laborers, and soldiers, the war

---

9. Grenville M. Dodge to Samuel J. Kirkwood, dated 7 January 1866 (but actually 1867), Kirkwood Papers, State Historical Society of Iowa, Des Moines.

would still be raging." Without the black military contribution "he seriously doubted whether we ever could have conquered the South." About suffrage reform in postwar Iowa, finally, Stone admitted in July 1865 that he had been hesitant about Resolution 4 only two weeks earlier. "It is true he was not in favor of putting that plank in the platform, because he did not think there was any practical necessity for it. He was not a member of the convention, but if he had been he should probably not have favored its adoption." Yet it was now a *fait accompli,* and he willingly accepted the challenge it posed. He declined to say how he would personally vote on equal suffrage when the time came, "but with his present feelings and convictions he was in favor of it."[10]

What one discerns in Stone's attitudinal odyssey is not some deep conversion experience, but simply that the governor read the newspapers, listened to his peers, and reflected on what he had read and heard. And he, in turn, powerfully conveyed his changed views to others. ("Upon the hustings," says a colleague, "he was one of the most effective political orators that the State has ever had.")[11] In later speeches, for example, Stone elaborated, if a bit vaguely, on the contributions of Iowa's own 60th U.S. Colored Infantry Regiment, and folksily emphasized how those of its members credited to Iowa's wartime manpower quota had exempted over two thousand white Iowans from the 1864 draft.

Governor Stone deftly transposed the logic of suffrage reform, as expounded by Judge C. C. Cole and other political intellectuals, into a vernacular appropriate for a listening electorate. In doing so he discovered how effectively the fight for equal rights could be linked to America's cherished egalitarian ideals. In a remarkable platform confrontation between himself and his openly racist opponent, Colonel Thomas Hart Benton, Jr., Stone cornered the colonel into answering a series of questions, during which Benton laconically admitted his objection to the phrase "all men are equal before the law." "Well," said Stone, delighted to portray Benton's confession as far to the right of the accepted range of attitudes, "this is the first time I ever heard an American citizen state that he did not believe in the equality of all men before the law!" The audience exploded in applause.[12]

Twenty years earlier, only the most extreme antislavery constitutionalists dared argue that the Founding Fathers and the nation's first state documents had been deliberately abolitionist. Now that notion became the common currency of Stone's discourse. "I say that we [Republicans] carried out the spirit of the Declaration of Independence," Stone insisted, "in that resolution, when

---

10. "Address of Gov. Wm. M. Stone, Delivered at Keokuk, July 1st, 1865," *Des Moines Daily State Register,* 12 July 1865.

11. Edward H. Stiles, *Recollections and Sketches of Notable Lawyers and Public Men of Early Iowa* (Des Moines, 1916), 73.

12. "Speech of Gov. W. M. Stone, Delivered at the Court House in Des Moines, on Monday evening, October 2, 1865," *Des Moines Daily State Register,* 5 October 1865.

we said that 'all men were equal before the law.' (Applause.) We stand where Madison and Franklin and Jefferson stood, when we asserted that 'all men are equal before the law.' We stand where stood the framers of the federal Constitution and where the men stood who fought the battles of the Revolution. (Applause.) I tell you this principle that all men are equal, comes from the Almighty God Himself, and it must and will prevail. (Applause.)"[13]

THE AUDIENCE RESPONSE to Stone is as charged with meaning as the governor's words. The measure of its significance, of course, is whether or not important numbers of Iowans modified, if not their underlying racial attitudes, then at least their conceptions of how they should *behave* with respect to equal rights. How many who had voted No in 1857 then voted Yes in 1868?

Analysis credibly suggests that a great many Iowans did in fact change their minds on suffrage reform in the sixties and seventies. In the following table, in order to augment comparability, each set of voting returns sandwiched between parallel lines equals 100 percent. And in the last four tables each group's Republican percentage — that is, its proportion of all Republican voters, including those not voting at all — stands alone as a quick measure of the upper limits of any group's potential for referendum support.

The topmost row of table 7.2 shows that only about 25 percent of Frémont supporters voted Yes in 1857, but that some 78 percent of them voted Yes eleven years later. Assuming it to be true that virtually no Democrats voted Yes in 1857, and in addition that all those who voted Yes in 1857 also voted Yes in 1868, we can conclude that many Republicans did, like Governor Stone, change their minds. In numerical terms, something like 25,000 antebellum Republicans who had not supported equal suffrage before the war — by voting No, by rolling off, or by not turning out to vote at all — switched to approving impartial suffrage in 1868.

The rest of table 7.2 compares later Republican electorates. All of them favored equal suffrage in 1868 even more enthusiastically. The 1880 vote, however, was a different story. Every GOP electorate later supported "free white" repeal at a lower frequency than it had supported equal suffrage in 1868, although the depth of the declension varied between polar extremes. The 1864 and 1865 electorates favored Proposition 2 by 70 and 77 percent; the electorate of 1866, as well as every postwar presidential electorate, gave the proposition only about 50 percent of their ballots; and the 1867 electorate's 62 percent looks much like a transition vote.

Turnout data suggest a possible reason for this pattern. Eighteen sixty-five and 1867 were years of low Republican turnout at the polls, while in 1866 and in presidential elections from 1868 through 1880 Republican turnouts surged to new heights. Only the more determinedly ideological Republicans — and

---

13. Ibid.

TABLE 7.2
HOW SELECTED REPUBLICAN ELECTORATES VOTED ON EQUAL RIGHTS, 1857–1880[a]

	1857			1868				1880			
	Yes	No	Rolled off	Not voting	Yes	No	Rolled off	Not voting	Yes	No	Rolled off	Not voting
Frémont voters (1856)	25	11	37	27	78	0[b]	4	18				
Lincoln voters (1860)					87	0[b]	1	12				
Lincoln voters (1864)					95	0	1	4	70	12	10	8
Stone voters (1865)					93	0[b]	6	1	77	23	0	0[b]
Wright voters (1866)					80	3	8	9	47	19	28	6
Merrill voters (1867)					87	4	7	2	62	22	16	0[b]
Grant voters (1868)					91	4	5	0	52	9	39	0
Grant voters (1872)									50	12	38	0[b]
Hayes voters (1876)									51	8	41	0[b]
Garfield voters (1880)									54	3	43	0

[a]Percentages estimated. Regressions: see table 7.1.
[b]Percentage set at minimum value and others adjusted.

therefore the more egalitarian—may have felt compelled to attend the polls in 1865 and 1867. By contrast, we may guess, the high-turnout elections attracted hosts of the less reflective and less issue-oriented Republicans, accounting for those electorates' more conservative behavior in 1880.

The Republicans of 1865, 1866, and 1867 also voted No in 1880 by comparatively large proportions—around 20 percent. One may hypothesize a reason. The members of this important Republican minority, intensely patriotic but also socially conservative, had been persuaded in 1868 that black voting and office-holding were necessary adjuncts to consolidating Union victory over an unrepentant South, a strategy requiring the enfranchisement of Iowa's own blacks. They voted Yes in 1868 despite their misgivings. Like conservative Republicans elsewhere in America, however, in the early 1870s they grew increasingly uncomfortable with their national party's formal support of southern Republican organizations whose biracial composition and outspoken radicalism so deeply offended the South's "better class" of whites. Elsewhere such dissatisfaction moved Republican conservatives into the Liberal Republican cause of 1872, with its rejection of President Grant and its ill-fated alliance with the Democrats behind Horace Greeley's presidential hopes. But few Iowa Republicans —so the relevant voting analyses suggest—could bring themselves to repudiate Grant, the great personification of national triumph in the Civil War. Iowa's Liberal movement, in consequence, is most appropriately seen as just another fusion by which the state's Democrats sought to overcome their numerical handicap. And not until the opportunity to reject "free white" repeal in 1880 did the lingering racism of Iowa's conservative Republicans find specific political expression.

An important minority of the Republican electorates of 1868 through 1880 rolled off on "free white" repeal. They did so at frequencies of about 40 percent—or 25 to 30 points lower than their Democratic counterparts. But it can be assumed that they did so from much the same impulse that caused the Democratic roll-off. The advent in 1877 of a conservative Republican administration in Washington, headed by a president pledged to ring down the curtain on Reconstruction, was for masses of Republican loyalists the practical equivalent of the Democrats' famous New Departure policy of the 1870s, which called for an end to issues connected to the late war. Those Iowa Republicans who rolled off, like their Democratic opposite numbers, were doing more than silently confessing their need of party guidance. By refusing to vote at all on Proposition 2 they, too, testified that the American political universe no longer defined the civil equality of blacks as pertinent.

It seems reasonable to suppose, the importance of party loyalties and precise political contexts notwithstanding, that some voter groups shifted position on equal rights more readily than others. Postwar Republican efforts to generate support for black civil equality presumably had less influence among some types of Republicans, in other words, than among others.

Iowa's work force of 1856 provides the first set of such groups (table 7.3). Men of all categories shifted position on equal suffrage between 1857 and 1868, their Yes percentages reflecting increases of from 32 to 40 percentage points. But what is again emphasized is the overriding salience of party: each group's improved behavior on suffrage closely parallels its increased Republican vote. Among the farmers of prosperous counties, for example, an approximately 11-point rise in percentage Republican is matched by something like a 37-point rise in percentage Yes, a behavior pattern replicated by each of the other three occupation groups, holding as true for the more Democratic farmers from counties of middling prosperity as for the others. This of course does not prove that a heightened Republicanism *caused* each group's dramatically enlarged Yes vote, but—given the Iowa Republican party's campaign aims in the late 1860s—that is a fully justifiable inference. Unfortunately, there are no comparable occupation data with which to extend the analysis forward to 1868 and 1880.

Antebellum churchgoers form yet another set of Iowans whose changing behavior toward equal rights can be usefully disaggregated, in this instance by major denomination—those religious bodies whose members hypothetically constituted at least 2 percent of all churchgoing Iowans, as extrapolated from the 1860 federal census of "church accommodations." In table 7.4 denominations are listed in descending order of size, with the state's largest group, its Methodists, divided into their original northern and southern Iowa conferences.

In 1856 Iowa's downstate Methodists, its Catholics, its Disciples, and its Episcopalians registered as predominantly Democratic. By 1868, however, all but the Catholics had grown decisively Republican, while the Disciples and Lutherans each proved to be closely divided in political preference. The Lutherans formed Iowa's only major denomination whose early Republican proclivities declined somewhat after the Civil War, a behavior no doubt induced by the revivified liquor issue and the Republican party's inescapable identification among German voters with prohibition reform.

In any event, the members of all church groups dramatically elevated their support for equal suffrage between 1857 and 1868. Iowa's Quakers provided the steepest rise, some 70 percentage points. In 1857 Quakers had been the most Republican of all churchgoers, the only denomination casting virtually no ballots against equal rights, and the religious group yielding the highest voter roll-off. Only tepidly egalitarian, rank-and-file Quakers were at least sufficiently embarrassed by Proposition 2 that they refused to act like Democrats by straightforwardly opposing it. In 1868 Quakers still formed the most Republican denomination, but now virtually all who turned out at the polls—including the great majority of those who had rolled off in such numbers in 1857—cast unflinching Yes ballots.

Other voter position changes proved almost as dramatic. The Yes vote among Presbyterians and Episcopalians rose by over 50 points, while among

TABLE 7.3
How the 1856 Work Force Voted on Equal Rights, 1856–1868[a]

	1856				1857			1868				1868		
	Republican	Yes	No	Rolled off	Not voting	Yes	No	Rolled off	Not voting	Republican	Yes	No	Rolled off	Not voting
Farmers:														
Prosperous counties	42	9	71	8	12					53	46	52	2	0[b]
Middling counties	40	9	67	10	14					46	41	59	0	0[b]
Poorer counties	50	15	57	23	5					60	55	41	0	4
Nonfarmers	40	3	16	27	54					47	39	38	5	18

[a]Percentages estimated. Regressions: 1856 occupations × 1856 presidential, 1857 Proposition 2, 1868 presidential, and 1868 Proposition 1 returns (county N = 68).
[b]Percentage set at minimum value and others adjusted.

TABLE 7.4
How Prewar Churchgoers Voted on Equal Rights, 1856–1868[a]

	1856	1857				1868				
	Republican	Yes	No	Rolled off	Not voting	Republican	Yes	No	Rolled off	Not voting
Methodists (downstate)	28	1	65	17	17	54	47	45	3	5
Presbyterians	54	9	4	30	57	70	63	26	4	7
Methodists (upstate)	52	19	46	13	22	69	64	27	4	5
Roman Catholics	18	0[b]	45	0[b]	55	38	33	67	0	0
Baptists	49	8	49	35	8	59	47	37	8	8
Congregationalists	68	24	29	15	32	75	71	19	4	6
Disciples of Christ	6	0	100[c]	0	0	48	46	54	0	0[b]
Quakers	80	18	0[b]	51	31	90	90	0[b]	0	10
Lutherans	61	33	19	35	13	54	52	48	0	0
Episcopalians	17	0[b]	48	45	7	59	56	0	7	37

[a] Percentages estimated. Regressions: 1860 church seats × 1856 presidential, 1857 Proposition 2, 1868 presidential, and 1868 Proposition 1 returns (county N = 42), with groups listed in descending order of size in 1860.
[b] Percentage set at minimum value and others adjusted.
[c] Percentage set at maximum value and others adjusted.

TABLE 7.5
HOW PREWAR ETHNOCULTURAL GROUPS VOTED ON EQUAL RIGHTS, 1856–1868[a]

	1856	1857				1868			
	Republican	Yes	No	Rolled off	Not voting	Republican	Yes	No	Rolled off	Not voting
New Englanders	82	8	0[b]	31	61	100[c]	100[c]	0	0	0
New Yorkers	67	18	63	21	0[b]	70	58	36	6	0[b]
Pennsylvanians	19	0[b]	72	0[b]	28	59	56	38	1	5
Ohioans	94	32	2	12	54	62	54	0[b]	8	38
Southerners	0[b]	0[b]	71	29	0[b]	21	14	86	0[b]	0[b]
Irishmen	5	0[b]	31	0[b]	69	0	0	100[c]	0	0
Germans	35	0[b]	70	30	0[b]	10	5	95	0	0[b]

[a]Percentages estimated. Regressions: 1856 voter nativities × 1856 presidential returns (township N = 150); 1856 voter nativities × 1857 Proposition 2, 1868 presidential, and 1868 Proposition 1 returns (township N = 127).
[b]Percentage set at minimum value and others adjusted.
[c]Percentage set at maximum value and others adjusted.

TABLE 7.6
How Postwar Ethnocultural Groups Voted on Equal Rights, 1868–1880[a]

	1868				1880				
	Republican	Yes	No	Rolled off	Not voting	Republican	Yes	No	Rolled off	Not voting
New Yorkers	86	86	0[b]	0	14	49	19	19	41	21
Pennsylvanians	71	64	34	2	0[b]	61	23	0[b]	56	21
Ohioans	65	63	0[b]	2	35	42	32	23	35	10
Southerners	38	22	65	13	0[b]	37	37	39	10	14
Irishmen	0[b]	0[b]	89	0[b]	11	0[b]	0[b]	57	10	33
Germans:										
Mainly Lutheran	39	38	53	5	4	44	33	0[b]	45	22
Mainly Catholic	14	0[b]	84	0[b]	16	23	0[b]	84	1	15

[a]Percentages estimated. Regressions: 1870 voter nativities x 1868 presidential, 1868 Proposition 1, 1868 presidential x 1868 Proposition 2 returns (township N = 127); German religious division from German States subfile (township N = 101).
[b]Percentage set at minimum value and others adjusted.

Methodists of both Iowa conferences, among Congregationalists, and among Disciples it rose by over 40. Baptists and Catholics improved by at least 30 points, Lutherans by almost 20. Lutherans and downstate Methodists behaved similarly in expressing only precarious Republican majorities in 1868, and in being the only Republican-oriented denominations splitting their referendum votes fairly evenly between Yes and No options. Lutherans aside, the most obvious central tendency is that each religious body increased both its Republicanism and its support for equal rights, the first increase presumably prompting the second.

The behaviors of Iowa's major prewar ethnocultural groups, each such voter classified by his birthplace as given in the 1856 Iowa manuscript census, is portrayed in table 7.5. (States lying outside New England and the South are treated, simply by default, as individual "ethnocultural" divisions.) Statistically projecting the distributions of smaller groups forward in time from 1868 to 1880, however, necessarily reduces their sizes to the point that plausible results are not forthcoming. The analyses employ only nativity groups making up at least 6 percent of all enumerated birthplaces.

Vast numbers of the prewar cohort changed their politics between the 1850s and the late 1860s. The Republican proclivities of Iowa's Pennsylvanians, who had been strong for the Pennsylvania Democrat James Buchanan in 1856, rose a startling 40 points in switching decisively to Grant in 1868. That of the Ohioans, however, inexplicably plummeted almost as precipitously. The perambulations of the other major birthplace groups fell between these behavioral extremes. The Republicanism of New Englanders and southerners rose by about 20 points each, although those two voter groups were sharply at odds in their majority attitudes toward Grant. Again, due no doubt to the reemergent liquor issue, the Germans' Republicanism declined by about 25 points. Only among two extreme groups—the solidly Republican New Yorkers and the overwhelmingly Democratic Irish—did the presidential support levels of 1856 merely duplicate themselves in 1868.

Neither Irishmen nor Germans gave support of any substance to equal suffrage in 1857 or in 1868, but the Yes percentages among all other groups rose sharply. Like the Quakers, the New Englanders had been overwhelmingly Republican in 1856; they had shied from heartily embracing suffrage reform in 1857, rolling off rather than voting No. But, like the Quakers, the Yankees proved themselves roaring egalitarians in 1868, their Yes vote rocketing upward by some 90 points. The Yes percentages of other voters rose more modestly: the Pennsylvanians' by some 50 points, the New Yorkers' by 40, the Ohioans' by 22, the southerners' by 14. New Yorkers alone increased their support of equal suffrage without any commensurate rise in their Republican percentage between 1856 and 1868.

Between the 1868 and 1880 referendums these upward trends for the most part reversed themselves. Table 7.6 depicts the behavior of the post–Civil War generation of ethnocultural groups, each voter classified by place of birth as given in the 1870 federal manuscript census. The comparatively small size of the New England contingent dictated its exclusion from the analyses, which with only one exception include groups comprising at least 6 percent of the whole.[14]

The minority Republicanism of voters within Iowa's predominantly Democratic ethnocultural groups — southerners, Irishmen, and Germans of both religious persuasions — proved as strong in 1880 as in 1868. But that of the firmly pro-Grant groups of 1868 — New Yorkers, Pennsylvanians, and Ohioans — had declined a good deal as the politics of the 1870s shifted to new concerns. But these three groups' Yes percentages on equal rights fell much more drastically than their enthusiasm for GOP presidential candidates. Support declined nearly 70 points among New Yorkers, over 40 points among Pennsylvanians, over 30 points among Ohioans. In contrast, the Yes percentage among the mainly Democratic southerners and German Lutherans held steady between 1868 and 1880, that of the former even rising a bit — by about the same frequency it had risen from 1857 to 1868. But when it came to equal rights for blacks, Iowa's Irishmen and German Catholics proved wholly immune to improvement: virtually no voter of either immigrant group cast a Yes ballot in 1868 or 1880. Ballot majorities for "free white" repeal carried only the Pennsylvanians, Ohioans, and German Lutherans, while the New Yorkers and the southerners divided their ballots fairly equally on 1880's Proposition 2. Great numbers of the postwar voter cohort, like the prewar generation before it, changed position on equal rights, but in a negative rather than a positive direction.

A LONG LIFETIME LATER, amid the political excitement and intellectual ferment of the 1960s, a fresh generation of American historians — paralleling the rise of similar schools of thought within several academic disciplines — began framing what became known as the "ironic" approach to the history of American race relations. The term rose from historian C. Vann Woodward's influential shift in perspective, as reflected in the fading optimism of successive editions of *The Strange Career of Jim Crow* (1955). This enormously important book, by arguing that southern segregation was neither primordial nor immutable, originally had implied the impermanence of racist attitudes in the South. But Woodward's revised viewpoint only reflected a general historiographical change that stemmed from historians' abruptly elevated social consciousness and their tendency to defer to the escalating cynicism and anger that distinguished the black movement culture of the sixties. Simultaneously, a circle of prominent black Afro-Americanists innovated what

---

14. The exception are voters of German nativity who had been born in German states containing Roman Catholic majorities in the nineteenth century. These states are identified in Gerald Shaughnessy, *Has the Immigrant Kept the Faith? A Study of Immigration and Catholic Growth in the United States, 1790–1920* (New York, 1925), 276–77.

historian August Meier has termed "the new paradigm of black history," an extreme form of which embraced the deeply held conviction that white America is—and always has been—hopelessly and unredeemably racist.

It now seemed pedagogically imperative that the historical failures of America's democratic ideals be fully and frankly exposed. In consequence, the scholarship of the past twenty-five years has stressed the perceived attitudinal shortcomings of abolitionism and the early Republican party, of Emancipation and Reconstruction, and of such pivotal figures as Abraham Lincoln, the congressional Radicals, and Ulysses S. Grant. And to some extent America's failed egalitarianism came to resemble a thematic orthodoxy. As such, it proved implicitly more sympathetic than otherwise to the view that true progress toward racial equality in America had been, for all practical purposes, nil.

How frontier Iowans' encounter with equal rights is to be brought into a proper relation with this scholarship is clearly problematic: its literature suggests no plausible explanation for the black suffrage victory of 1865–1868. But more fully than expected, perhaps, enlightenment is to be found in the classic behavioral literature on racial attitudes and attitude change, the intellectual product for the most part of the 1940s and 1950s.

From the perspective of today's bitter frustration over persistent residential segregation, continued hostility to busing and affirmative action, and the perplexing role of race in the seeming intractability of black poverty, much of that earlier literature seems quaintly dated. But it had been of critical relevance in the post–World War II years, when America confronted its last powerful vestiges of what sociologist Joe R. Feagin usefully terms "direct institutionalized discrimination," an ample substantiality of law and precedent of which Iowa's black code had once been an unmistakable part.[15] The experience of nineteenth-century Iowans achieves an affinity less with the more recent writing on race relations than with this behavioral literature of an earlier era, a few highlights of which merit review.

Gunnar Myrdal's magisterial survey of racial discrimination in the United States, *An American Dilemma* (1944), conveyed a number of important messages. One of them may be characterized as procedural, and as August Meier and Elliott Rudwick perceptively observe, it "elevated to the level of a scientific theory the strategy that black Americans throughout their history had employed in their struggle for social change."[16] Movement toward racial equality in the United States, argued Myrdal, could be achieved by straightforwardly addressing the collective conscience of its white majority, specifically emphasizing the dissonance between America's universalistic egalitarian values ("all men are created equal") and the widespread denial of those values by black subjugation, segregation, and exclusion.

---

15. Joe R. Feagin, *Racial and Ethnic Relations*, 3d ed. (Englewood Cliffs, 1989), 15.

16. August Meier and Elliott Rudwick, *Black History and the Historical Profession, 1915–1980* (Urbana, IL, 1986), 122.

Myrdal, in short, viewed the incongruities between the nation's elevated, fervently cherished ideals and its pervasive racial discrimination—the "American dilemma" of the title—not as an occasion for despair but as a splendid opportunity. Millions of white Americans were troubled, he said, by the internalized conflict of values and behavior, to the repression or rationalization of which they were forced to devote so much psychological energy and from which (consciously or unconsciously) they yearned to be freed. Overcoming discrimination, he reasoned, was therefore to a greater degree than generally realized a matter of deliberate social engineering, the outcome having been biased in favor of equality. Racial progress mainly required a properly enlightened leadership brave enough to make the appropriate argument from scientific fact and official national principle. The rank and file would fall into line much more readily than imagined.

In 1949 Robert K. Merton modified the Myrdal hypothesis by suggesting that any strategy to reduce racial discrimination needed to distinguish among different personality types. White Americans, he noted, consisted not just of outspoken egalitarians and implacable racists, but also of "unprejudiced discriminators" and "prejudiced nondiscriminators." The former happened to be those who, despite their own lack of prejudice, supported color discrimination out of deference to the prejudice of others (to hire a black receptionist, for instance, might be bad for business). The latter, in contrast, were bigots whose inclination to discriminate was held in check in deference to others (to *refuse* to hire a black receptionist might be bad for business). While both types were persons of expediency, the timid egalitarian suffered some degree of guilt for violating his or her conscience and thus was vulnerable to induced behavioral change à la Myrdal. But the inhibited bigot was under strain when he or she *conformed* to America's egalitarian values, so that legal controls, strictly administered, probably would be required to keep such discriminatory impulses suppressed over the long run.

A year later T. W. Adorno and his associates published their monumental study of the "authoritarian personality," mandating further refinement of the Myrdal hypothesis. The authors demonstrated that among deeply prejudiced persons—a category including hard-core white racists—bigotry rises from the neurotic needs of the bigoted, a psychological plight usually attributable to emotional deprivation in childhood. Healing any such person, they suggested, would require some form of psychotherapy.

Gordon W. Allport's pioneering theoretical work, *The Nature of Prejudice* (1954), acknowledged the value of Adorno's psychodynamic theory in reaching the neurotically bigoted, but its author skillfully reasoned that *most* white prejudice was not deep-seated. It was probable, said Allport, "that about a half of all prejudiced attitudes are based only on the need to conform to custom, to let well enough alone, to maintain the [prevailing] cultural pattern."[17] Later

---

17. Gordon W. Allport, *The Nature of Prejudice*, 25th anniversary ed. (Reading, 1979), 286.

research by Thomas Fraser Pettigrew, one of Allport's most respected students, established this with some precision. Only about 15 percent of white adult Americans are uncompromising racial bigots whose extreme antiblack prejudices rise from authoritarian personality needs, noted Pettigrew. At the other extreme "roughly 25 percent of white adults in the United States consistently support full rights for Blacks, and in most situations will not exhibit antiblack attitudes or behavior."[18] But the large majority, something like 60 percent, hold *no* deeply motivated opinions about African-Americans, and this majority could be expected to exhibit whatever racist—or racially tolerant—behavior their society's institutions and leaders appeared to expect of them. It was this "conforming three-fifths," as Pettigrew called them, who were susceptible to pressure and persuasion, and therefore capable of changing their behavior from discriminatory to egalitarian in fairly short order.

Allport and Pettigrew emphasized the importance of organic and statute law. Just as discriminatory legal codes had served to increase race prejudice, so laws that require egalitarian behavior tend to decrease prejudice. "Legislation aims not at controlling prejudice, but only its open expression," wrote Allport. "But when expression changes, thoughts too, in the long run, are likely to fall into line. . . . What we are here speaking of is the basic habit of democratic society. After free, and often fierce, debate, citizens bow to the majority will. *They do so with a special kind of willingness if the legislation is in line with their own private consciences.* On this point civil rights legislation has a marked advantage. . . . People need and want their consciences bolstered by law, and this is nowhere more true than in the area of group relations." But the effects are most striking when the legalities come by way of sudden imposition—court decisions, executive orders, administrative rulings. "Strong and forthright action from 'higher up' . . . is, after an initial flurry of excitement, generally accepted," said Allport. "The *fait accompli* is often welcomed if it is in line with one's conscience."[19]

These and numerous ancillary formulations touch the Iowa experience at a number of points. One encounters Merton's nonprejudiced discriminator in the figure of Josiah B. Grinnell, a militant abolitionist who, as an expedient, supported school segregation in the 1858 legislature and opposed equal suffrage on the floor of the 1865 Republican convention. There was also William Patterson, an apt illustration of Merton's prejudiced nondiscriminator. A legislator who supported equal rights in 1842 and 1846, most likely in deference to his Congregational and Quaker constituents, he later, while representing racially divided Keokuk in the 1857 constitutional convention, revealed himself as an ultraconservative on matters of race.

---

18. Thomas F. Pettigrew, "The Mental Health Impact," in *Impacts of Racism on White Americans,* ed. Benjamin P. Bowser and Raymond G. Hunt (Beverly Hills, 1981), 116.
19. Allport, *Nature of Prejudice,* 276, 470–71.

Allport's *fait accompli* principle greatly illuminates Governor William M. Stone's own series of timely psychological adjustments to the Emancipation Proclamation, to the Lincoln administration's approval of black troop enlistments, and to the Iowa Republican convention's surprise passage of Resolution 4 in 1865. And nothing more eloquent than the Myrdal hypothesis explains the applause accorded Stone's bold appeal to the traditional American sense of equity, justice, and fair play, as well as to the alleged egalitarian intentions of the Declaration of Independence, of James Madison and Benjamin Franklin and Thomas Jefferson, of the framers of the United States Constitution, of the soldiers of the Revolution, and of Almighty God.

Indeed, America's most cherished state paper, the Declaration of Independence, that "inexhaustible arsenal" of egalitarianism as historian Benjamin Quarles has called it,[20] was drawn upon repeatedly by progressively disposed delegates to the 1857 constitutional convention and the 1865 Republican caucus, as well as by innumerable Republican editors and campaigners of the latter 1860s. But it was not Myrdalian rhetoric alone that made the difference in the mass conversion of Iowa's Republicans to equal rights. It was also the Allportian civic stature of those who spoke out: as noted earlier, they included an impressive solid front of the state's Republican leadership.

Allport's discussion of "status aspects of contact" decodes an ostensible paradox relating to white Iowans' wartime responses to African-Americans. On the one hand, Iowans soldiering through the South earned a harsh reputation for race prejudice, supposedly generated through their being thrown into close association with freshly liberated masses of black refugees. It was a racist image plausible enough to tempt postwar Democrats and conservative Republicans into making it the basis for a political movement—the "Union Anti-Negro Suffrage" and "Conservative Republican" coalition parties of 1865 and 1866. On the other hand, Iowans in General Sherman's army grew so enraged by news of the Confederate massacre of nearly two hundred surrendered black artillerymen at Fort Pillow, Kentucky, that they unceremoniously executed a score of rebels captured in a fire fight in Georgia. The difference, as Allport would explain it, is that the masses of southern blacks were a destitute peasantry of bottom-of-the-barrel socioeconomic status, casual contact with whom predictably increased race prejudice among fascinated midwestern farm boys and artisans. But the African-Americans slaughtered at Fort Pillow had been fellow soldiers, colleagues in the transcendent endeavor that was the war to preserve the Union. For the same reason, it appears, the power of Iowa's own 60th U.S. Colored Infantry to draw rank-and-file Republicans toward equal suffrage in 1865 embodies much the same quality: the Republicans of the Hawkeye State could not conceive of their soldiery, no matter what their color, as anything but their civic equals.

---

20. Benjamin Quarles, *Black Mosaic: Essays in Afro-American History and Historiography* (Amherst, 1988), 107.

No behavioral configuration is more satisfactory than the Merton-Allport-Pettigrew concept of the conforming majority in accounting for the outcome of the June 14, 1865, GOP convention: 663 Republicans, most of whose attitudes toward African-Americans no doubt ranged from neutral or mildly negative to hostile on the morning of that day, had by evening voted overwhelmingly to bestow the elective franchise on blacks — despite the hotly predicted political costs. Such had been the transforming effect of sheer eloquence upon the conforming majority. And how little the opposition to equal rights among rank-and-file Republicans stemmed from irredeemable racism was detected a few weeks later by an inquisitive Democratic loyalist. "Some of them (say, one third) declare that they never can vote for Negro suffrage," he confided to his state chairman about the Republicans in his area, "[but] my own opinion in regard to this matter is that they dont have so much objection to the *principal* involved as they have to running the risque of coming before the people upon that rather touchy question."[21] Not true prejudice, incredibly enough, but merely politics, he said, underlay lukewarm Republican attitudes toward suffrage reform.

Something like Pettigrewian proportions can be roughly calculated for the division of Iowa's Republican electorate of 1865 into Adornovian racists (perhaps 13 percent), racial egalitarians (another 13 percent), and the superficially racist majority (74 percent) for whom the party's progressive messages would prove decisive by 1868. And neither Allport nor Pettigrew would have been surprised, had they learned of it, by pioneer Iowans' accomplishment: these midwesterners' behavior, although a remarkably early example of successful antidiscriminatory mobilization, lay well within the range of American group behaviors deemed psychologically credible. But neither Iowans' rejection of equal rights in 1857 nor their decidedly equivocal approval in 1880 would be judged peculiar. Each such expression of public choice, to Allport and Pettigrew, would have been determined by the success or failure of the psychological strategy with which each proposal had been placed before the voters. And the soundness of any such strategy would have depended on how artfully it engaged the well-defined sociocultural imperatives and opportunities available.

Allport wrote in the year of the famous *Brown* v. *Board of Education* decision by the U.S. Supreme Court that began the process of dismantling formal school segregation in America — a decision that would, in his opinion, have been "psychologically sounder" had the court insisted on an immediate, rather than gradual, acquiescence with its ruling. By 1958 he was already deploring the failure of national leadership and "the sorrowful results that have come from indecisiveness and delay."[22] He would be dead by the time his own Boston exploded in violence over the issue of school busing, an experience some behavioralists interpret as a failure of the Allportian approach.

---

21. Robert Robinson to Laurel Summers, 17 July 1865, Summers Papers, State Historical Society of Iowa, Des Moines (italics added).

22. Allport, *Nature of Prejudice,* xxii.

Thus Howard Schuman and his colleagues warn that "it is too extreme
... to claim that attitudes can be treated as epiphenomena and that determined leadership (as in [Harry Truman's] desegregation of the military) is all that is needed to bring about behavioral change, with attitudes likely to follow thereafter. This point of view tacitly assumes situations in which leaders have their authority protected from serious challenge."[23] Schuman and associates are impeccable sociologists but in this case bad historians: it can hardly be said that President Truman was invulnerable to racist voters in 1948 when—in the midst of a presidential campaign crippled by the revolt of the segregationist "Dixiecrats"—he issued his famous executive order integrating the armed forces. He was far more politically vulnerable, certainly, than was Governor Stone in 1865, given the strength of Iowa's Republican hegemony. But the civil rights successes of the post–World War II era, in which both Truman and the Myrdal hypothesis played such prominent roles, do invite comparison with the Hawkeye State in the years immediately following Appomattox.

In several respects the situations seem remarkably similar, with Iowa in the late 1860s being asked to play a role vis-à-vis the militarily defeated but politically rebellious South that the South itself in the early Cold War years would be asked to play vis-à-vis Japan and the third world. In 1868 presidential candidate Ulysses S. Grant hoped that Iowans would willingly enact equal suffrage as a means of helping legitimize its congressional imposition on the ex-Confederate states, a statement anticipating in its geopolitics President Truman's comment, inelegantly summarizing a point made by Myrdal, on the need for racial equality in the American South. "The top dog in a world which is over half-colored," said Truman, "ought to clean his own house."[24] Perhaps the juxtaposition of the two postwar eras is of use in highlighting the role of political necessity—the need of the national government to achieve high moral purpose for its exertion of power—in generating racial progress. The successes of the years 1865–70 and 1945–65 in eliminating direct institutionalized discrimination obviously owe much to larger national agenda.

That fact also illuminates the failure of Iowa's egalitarian majority of 1868 to hold firm in 1880. As Pettigrew has warned, the relapse of the conforming majority may be expected to occur whenever it receives retrogressive signals from its government and opinion leaders. That, of course, is precisely what occurred in the United States from the 1890s through World War I, with devastating effects on the limited racial equality achieved in the Civil War era. The 1880 referendum outcome suggests that Iowans anticipated this national declension.

---

23. Howard Schuman, Charlotte Steeh, and Lawrence Bobo, *Racial Attitudes in America: Trends and Interpretations* (Cambridge, 1985), 207.

24. Quoted in David W. Southern, *Gunnar Myrdal and Black-White Relations: The Use and Abuse of* An American Dilemma, *1944–1969* (Baton Rouge, 1987), 123.

"THE STORY of our inferiority is an old dodge," Frederick Douglass once remarked, "for wherever men oppress their fellows, wherever they enslave them, they will endeavor to find the needed apology for such enslavement and oppression in the character of the people oppressed and enslaved."[25] Blaming the victims, the victimizers establish their moral innocence. This cause and effect emphasizes an extremely important historical truth: white racism was politically essential to black slavery.

Historians may continue to disagree over which came first to colonial America, race prejudice or black bondage. But much of the original significance of that debate has been diminished by the impressive arguments of such scholars as Frank M. Snowden and St. Clair Drake that systematic antiblack discrimination was not present in the ancient Mediterranean civilizations, and by the evidence presented by Bernard Lewis and others that racism was an innovation by certain Muslim writers at the very moment Muslim kingdoms were busily expanding a monopoly of the sub-Saharan slave trade. Within medieval Europe slavery remained as color-blind as it had been in the ancient world, the word "slave" (and its equivalent in Arabic, French, Spanish, Portuguese, Italian, and German) originally denoting a person of Slavic origin. Not until the 1450s, when Turkish capture of Constantinople severed Europe's connection with the great Black Sea slave markets, and Portuguese trading ships reached the Cape Verde coast of Africa, did slavery in the West begin its long association exclusively with blacks. And with this shift came the assemblage of racist folk-myths and fantasies to which the American experience would give such copious expression.

It seems plausible that white racism was (and is) inherent or innate in neither Western Civilization nor Christianity, in neither capitalism nor any other particular economic system, in neither the Euro-American collective unconsciousness nor its sociobiological genes. And one might further infer that prejudicial behavior and attitudes can indeed be changed—most inclusively by destroying whatever oppressive labor system they had been summoned to protect in the first place. What separated nineteenth-century Iowa from the South in this regard was that in the Hawkeye State there was no *economic* investment in the theory of black inferiority; black Iowans could become equal under law without disturbing the prevailing system of labor. It is perhaps no accident that black southerners would not be truly emancipated until passage and enforcement of the Civil Rights Act of 1964 and the Voting Rights Act of 1965—by which point southern agribusiness was well on its way, through mechanization, to overcoming its traditional need for cheap labor.

For those who would know the history of American racism there are compelling reasons to ponder such an exceptional instance as Iowa's. Such examples, writes historian J. Morgan Kousser, "refute or at least greatly com-

---

25. Frederick Douglass, "What the Black Man Wants," in *The Equality of All Men before the Law Claimed and Defended,* ed. George L. Stearns (Boston, 1865), 38.

plicate the pessimistic view . . . that white racial opinion in nineteenth century America was uniformly and deeply racist."[26] That unnecessarily grim perspective obscures or discounts the real gains made. More importantly, it implicitly demeans the courageous idealism of those, both black and white, who fought for racial justice. And it trivializes the nineteenth century's moral capacity for yielding more substantive equality than it did in fact yield.

Far too much of the inequity to which the idealistic addressed themselves so long ago has survived, in one form or another, the years of incredible change from their day to ours. Yet when so many seem unchallenged by what clearly remains America's most important unresolved agendum, when new initiatives seem desperately needed, when the complacent suggest that there is no longer a problem and the angry believe that the problem is unresolvable, it is good to have positive examples to prompt us. The circumstances, processes, and strategies that won frontier Iowans to the civil equality of blacks remind us that there are egalitarian precedents as well as a racist tradition in America's past.

BIBLIOGRAPHICAL NOTE

Robert Dykstra's long-awaited book, *Bright Radical Star: Black Freedom and White Supremacy on the Hawkeye Frontier* (Cambridge, MA, 1993), is a marvelous account of the politics of race in Iowa from the 1830s to 1880. In 1984 Dykstra engaged in a fascinating exchange of views over the politics of race with Hubert Wubben. See Hubert H. Wubben, "The Uncertain Trumpet: Iowa Republicans on the Iowa Black Suffrage Victory," *Annals of Iowa* 47 (1984), 409–29; Robert R. Dykstra, "The Issue Squarely Met: Toward an Explanation of Iowans' Racial Attitudes, 1865–1868," ibid., 430–50; and Hubert H. Wubben, "Further Reflections on the Iowa Black Suffrage Victory," ibid., 544–46. Other studies focusing on race in this early period include Arnie Cooper, "A Stony Road: Black Education in Iowa, 1838–1860," *Annals of Iowa* 48 (1986), 113–34; and Richard Acton, "To Go Free," *Palimpsest* 70 (1989), 50–61, which recounts the case of Ralph, a former slave who, unlike Dred Scott, was ruled free to remain in Dubuque rather than returned to his former owner.

The standard account of African Americans in Iowa is Leola Nelson Bergmann, "The Negro in Iowa," *Iowa Journal of History and Politics* 46 (1948), 3–90; reprinted in 1969 in booklet form by the State Historical Society of Iowa, with an editorial addendum by William J. Petersen. See also James L. Hill, "Migration of Blacks to Iowa, 1820–1960," *Journal of Negro History* 66 (1981–82), 289–303. African-American newspapers, most notably *The Iowa Bystander,* one of the nation's longest-

---

26. J. Morgan Kousser, "Before *Plessy*, before *Brown*: The Development of the Law of Racial Integration in Louisiana and Kansas," in *Toward a Usable Past: Liberty under State Constitutions,* ed. Paul Finkelman and Stephen E. Gottlieb (Athens, 1991), 218.

running black newspapers, published in Des Moines, are among the best sources on the African-American experience. See Allen W. Jones, "The Black Press in Iowa, 1882–1987," in *The Black Press in the Midwest* (Westport, CT, 1995).

Except for an outstanding essay that drew heavily on correspondence to Iowa's congressional delegation—James F. Findlay, "Religion and Politics in the Sixties: The Churches and the Civil Rights Act of 1964," *Journal of American History* 77 (1990), 66–92—most of the other work on race in Iowa has focused on African Americans' experiences in local communities. Valuable studies include Robert Neymeyer, "May Harmony Prevail: The Early History of Black Waterloo," *Palimpsest* 61 (1980), 80–91; William L. Hewitt, "So Few Undesirables: Race, Residence, and Occupation in Sioux City, 1890–1925," *Annals of Iowa* 50 (1989/90), 158–80; Jack Lufkin, "The Founding and Early Years of the National Association for the Advancement of Colored People in Des Moines, 1915–1930," *Annals of Iowa* 45 (1980), 439–61; Bruce Fehn, "'The Only Hope We Had': United Packinghouse Workers Local 46 and the Struggle for Racial Equality in Waterloo, Iowa, 1948–1960," *Annals of Iowa* 54 (1995), 185–216; and Hal S. Chase, "Struggle for Racial Equality: Fort Des Moines Training Camp for Colored Officers," *Phylon* 39 (1978), 297–310. Two books focused on the coal-mining community of Buxton, which had a large African-American population: David Mayer Gradwohl and Nancy M. Osborn, *Exploring Buried Buxton: Archaeology of an Abandoned Iowa Coal Mining Town With a Large Black Population* (Ames, 1984); and Dorothy Schwieder, Joseph Hraba, and Elmer Schwieder, *Buxton: Work and Racial Equality in a Coal Mining Community* (Ames, 1987).

8

Town Development, Social Structure, and Industrial Conflict

SHELTON STROMQUIST

Historians have increasingly come to understand that communities were not simply the products of their founders and prominent citizens; their character was shaped both by outside forces and by those who made their livings in everyday occupations as well. At the same time, history has become an increasingly specialized, balkanized field. Thus it is a challenge to take all of the forces that shape a community into account in an integrated essay. Shelton Stromquist's essay addresses significant issues at the intersection of labor, railroad, and community history. And, as community history, it is a rare comparative look at how the structure of two different communities affected the way they responded to the same development—in this case a strike by railroad workers.

> *Omaha Capitalist*: Do you call that a survey for a new Railroad? Why it looks like a pumpkin vine.
> *Kansas Speculator*: Well, you see, we had to twist it around a good deal, so as to take in all the points at which we could buy land cheap.
> *Omaha Capitalist*: A road like that will never pay. It doesn't start anywhere or go anywhere.
> *Kansas Speculator*: Oh! We can keep it running awhile on the profits of our town lots; that's easy enough.
> *Omaha Capitalist*: But what will you do after all the lots are sold?
> *Kansas Speculator*: Straighten it out.
>
> —*Switchmen's Journal* (May 1887)

Aside from the principle involved, we deem it of vast interest to us and to every citizen of Creston and every town along the Q. line and every businessman, especially, that the boys win the present struggle. They are part of us, they are our best citizens.... Some have their all invested in a home, others

---

Reprinted from *A Generation of Boomers: The Pattern of Railroad Labor Conflict in Nineteenth-Century America*, by Shelton Stromquist (Urbana and Chicago: University of Illinois Press, 1987), 142–49, 158–87. Copyright © 1987 by the Board of Trustees of the University of Illinois. Used with the permission of the author and of the University of Illinois Press.

have homes part paid for, and others have obligations contracted which if the strikers lose and were compelled to look elsewhere for employment, would be such a blow to the financial condition of our city that she would not recover for years to come.

—Creston, Iowa *Daily Advertiser*, March 4, 1888

RAILROAD EXPANSION in late nineteenth-century America accelerated the settlement process and extended it continentwide. Within twenty-five years, from 1865 to 1890, a dense fabric of railroad lines was woven across the lands west of the Mississippi. This expansion created a profound demand for labor to construct, operate, and maintain these new roads. It opened new territories to settlement, provided a transportation mode for the massive relocation of population, and created truly national markets for manufactured goods. This growth, grafted onto existing commercial and transportation networks, also generated profound instability. Frontier conditions were transitory; the scarcity of labor and the plentifulness of land did not persist; and the benefits of an immediate national market for agricultural products were offset by the flood of cheap manufactured goods that stifled local industrial growth in many communities.

Railroads decisively altered the urban landscape of nineteenth-century America. For older market cities that had been sheltered from outside competition by a "tariff barrier" of isolation, commercial growth unlocked opportunities and unprecedented perils. Some towns limited to waterborne commerce saw their fortunes decline by comparison with "backcountry upstarts" that happened to be located on the new rail lines. Many towns competed frantically in the tribute they offered the iron horse and its corporate masters. Others that were heavily committed to servicing the wagon or canal trade turned their backs on the unsightly intruder. Not only did the railroads promise spectacular growth to some existing settlements, they also created "magic cities" (a common nickname for railroad towns) to service their operations. Blessed by the arrival of a substantial railroad labor force with its considerable payroll, a retinue of tradesmen, land speculators, and dealers in "liquid hardware," these towns exploded at regular intervals on the vacant prairie. The redirection of land settlement, townbuilding, and the flow of commerce and immigration along new rail lines restructured the pattern of urban growth.[1]

Railroad development stimulated two overlapping networks of urban economic activity. First, it extended an existing marketing network that had been

---

1. The literature on the urbanizing effects of railroad development is substantial. See, for instance, Paul W. Gates, *The Illinois Central and Its Colonization Work* (Cambridge, Mass.: 1934); Albert Fishlow, *American Railroads and the Transformation of the Ante-Bellum Economy* (Cambridge, Mass.: 1965); Richard C. Overton, *Burlington West: A Colonization History of the Burlington* (Cambridge, Mass.: 1941); Richard Wade, *The Urban Frontier: The Rise of Western Cities, 1790–1830* (Cambridge, Mass.: 1959); Julius Rubin, "Urban Growth and Regional Development," in David T. Gilchrist, *The Growth of Seaport Cities, 1790–1825* (Charlottesville, Va.: 1967), 1–21 provides a useful framework for understanding pre-railroad urban economic development.

built on prerailroad commercial activity, quickening the flow of goods and population and stimulating diversification in manufacturing. Second, it generated a service network of divisional operating and repair facilities.[2] The locational requirements of the marketing network were different from those of the service network. Some established marketing centers built on their initial advantages by acquiring railroad connections to a wider market and became regional centers for the wholesale trade, for manufacturing, and for processing agricultural products. Some also acquired the added economic stimulus that came with servicing railroad operations. Urban settlements in the service network were blessed with the direct economic stimulus of railroad-related spending and construction.

Beyond the existing market cities, the railroads, with a relentless logic, platted and brought into existence division towns at intervals of 200 to 300 miles to provide repair facilities and the changeover of train and engine crews. The economic growth and diversification of these towns beyond their divisional functions was initially incidental to their primary function. A few division towns happened to be located in areas where a substantial demand already existed for marketing agricultural or mineral resources. The diversion of that trade from water to railroad transportation meant rapid urban growth. A more common pattern was that new railroad division towns experienced an initial period of spectacular growth fueled by the construction and development of railroad operations, followed by a period of very slow growth or even stagnation as they fought to overcome the advantages of more established urban marketing centers and waited for their hinterlands to fill up. For many such railroad towns that aspired to grow beyond their service function, the perceived critical ingredient for future growth was the acquisition of a competing railroad line and the competitive rates that this would bring.

The combination of marketing and service functions varied from one railroad division town to another, as did the specific patterns of their growth. However, two basic types of communities stand out from the welter of towns

---

2. Historical geographers have shown some interest in the railroad's impact on settlement patterns. See Chauncey D. Harris and Edward L. Ullman, "The Nature of Cities," *Annals of the American Academy of Political and Social Science* 242 (1945): 7–17; Edward L. Ullman, "The Railroad Pattern of the United States," *Geographical Review* 39 (1949): 242–56; John Hart Fraser, "The Middle West," *Annals of the Association of American Geographers* 62 (June 1972): 258–82; Howard J. Nelson, "Town Founding and the American Frontier," *Association of Pacific Coast Geographers Yearbook* 36 (1974): 7–23; D. W. Meinig, "American Wests: Preface to a Geographical Interpretation," *Annals of American Geography* 62 (June 1972): 159–84; Michael P. Conzen, "A Transport Interpretation of the Growth of Urban Regions: An American Example," *Journal of Historical Geography* 1 (1975): 361–82. For the most part these studies examine the impact of the railroad on urban location and economic growth in relation to marketing functions. The service functions of railroad division towns are only sporadically mentioned in the literature and nowhere systematically classified. Gunnar Alexandersson, *The Industrial Structure of American Cities: A Geographic Study of Urban Economy in the United States* (Lincoln, Neb.: 1956), mentions these service functions, as does Robert L. Wrigley, Jr., "Pocatello, Idaho, as a Railroad Center," *Economic Geography* 21 (1943): 325–36.

within the railroad service network: market cities and railroad towns. Market cities were communities, generally settled before the entry of railroads, that enjoyed initial advantages based on favorable location within the prerailroad commercial networks. The river towns of the Ohio, Mississippi, and Missouri river valleys are good examples. The railroads extended the commercial domination of these towns, enabled them to diversify in manufacturing and processing, and sustained if not spurred their spectacular growth. Many of these towns also were deemed appropriate sites for the location of railroad shop and switching facilities. Most acquired in time multiple railroad connections to larger urban centers.

Railroad towns, in the way the term is used here, were communities whose very existence was predicated on the location of railroad shop and service facilities. Generally created through the direct or indirect agency of the railroads themselves, they enjoyed no initial commercial or industrial advantages. Their location was strictly determined by the logic of railroad construction. Their initially spectacular growth was commonly limited by the slower pace of agricultural settlement and the absence of a flourishing commerce that could provide the basis for diversification and growth. Lying within the commercial hinterlands of more developed cities and generally lacking competitive railroad connections, they found it difficult to grow beyond the direct services they provided to their patron railroad.

Both types of towns had a full complement of workers to repair and operate their railroads. Whether small or large, diversified or limited to railroad operations, each town had a force of railroad shopmen, enginemen, trainmen, and track repairmen. The size of the division town did not directly affect the size of the railroad labor force. Only in the case of switchmen and freight handlers did a community's nodality in a regional market and its interconnections with other roads significantly affect the number of men that would be required.

The position of railroad workers within the social structure of a railroad division town varied with the size and composition of its working class and with the extent of its commercial and industrial diversification. In larger market cities the proportion of railroad workers in the total labor force of the community might be as low as 1 percent. In outlying railroad towns, they comprised as much as 35 percent and effectively dominated the labor force.[3] Market cities commonly possessed a self-conscious and well-organized elite that promoted,

---

3. The distribution of railroad workers as a proportion of the local labor force is based on an analysis of all towns in Iowa with over 100 employees in 1895 (see below). The 2 percent figure is for Dubuque with 685 railroad men, and the 35 percent is for Creston with 596 railroad men. Secretary of State, *Census of Iowa for the Year 1895* (Des Moines: 1896). A few other studies using twentieth-century data have identified "transportation and communication" towns that have from 6 percent to 14 percent of their workers in that industrial class. J. F. Hart, "Functions and Occupational Structure of Cities in the American South," *Annals of the Association of American Geographers* 45 (1955): 269–86; C. D. Harris, "A Functional Classification of Cities in the United States," *The Geographical Review* 33 (1943): 86–99.

with notable success, a series of transportation improvements and other measures to strengthen and diversify the local economy. Railroad towns had a smaller, more locally oriented elite whose aspirations were frustrated by their inadequate means and their inability to grow beyond the limits imposed by a single transportation route.

AS CONFLICT between railroad workers and their employers spread from one region to another, communities in the railroad service network found themselves in the middle, pulled in one direction by the roads that held out the promise of economic growth and in the other by some of their own citizen-strikers whose very livelihoods and protective organizations were in jeopardy. Numerous commentators on the strikes of railroad workers discerned differences in the community support workers enjoyed. For instance, during the engineers' strike of 1888 on the Chicago, Burlington & Quincy Railroad (C. B. & Q.), company officials cited the "disloyalty" of division towns from Creston, Iowa, west through Nebraska as being particularly nettlesome.[4] During the Pullman boycott, officials of the Northern Pacific identified the Missouri River as a rough dividing line between the communities that were in outright rebellion and those that manifested a more conciliatory attitude toward the road.[5] At the same time that citizens in Spokane, Washington, organized in strong support of the company, those in Sprague demonstrated "a very bitter attitude" toward the company.[6] A historian of the Great Northern strike of 1894 found Saint Cloud, Minnesota, to be a similar dividing line on that road.[7] Citizens in Kansas railroad towns responded in diverse ways to the railroad strikes of 1877 and 1878—from active support of strikers to adamant hostility.[8]

Even in communities where workers at one time enjoyed vigorous community support, conditions could change and support be withdrawn. An analysis of strikes on the Erie Railroad in Hornellsville, New York, demonstrates that the strike of 1877 was a turning point. Under increased pressure from the company and fearful for the economic future of the town, community leaders pressured the railroad workers to return to work. When the workers struck

---

4. R. W. Colville to G. W. Rhodes, August 25, 1885, Engineers' Grievance Committee Papers, 1885–86 (33 1880 3.1), Burlington Archives.

5. J. W. Kendrick to T. F. Oakes, July 13, 1894, General Manager's Correspondence (unprocessed), Box 2266, Northern Pacific Archives.

6. *Ibid.*

7. Amos Flaherty, "The Great Northern Strike of 1894: When Gene Debs Beat Jim Hill," in *The People Together*, ed. Meridel LeSueur et al. (Minneapolis: 1958), 21–23.

8. See Joseph F. Tripp, "Kansas Communities and the Birth of the Labor Problem, 1877–1883," *Kansas History* 4, no. 2 (Summer 1981): 114–29, and James H. Ducker, "Workers, Townsmen and the Governor: The Santa Fe Enginemen's Strike, 1878," *Kansas History* 5, no. 1 (Spring 1982): 23–32.

again in 1881, the community leaders directly opposed them.[9] Economic development could alter the class relations of local businessmen and railroad workers; changes in the racial and ethnic composition of the labor force could shatter the social solidarity that townsmen and workingmen formerly enjoyed.[10]

The importance of community support and its fragility is testified to by workers and by company officials throughout this period. During the strike on the Great Northern in the spring of 1894, American Railway Union Director W. P. C. Adams urgently telegraphed a stern warning to his men on the Northern Pacific, who were anxious to strike in sympathy. "Popular sentiment must be our weapon. It is the millstone of the scriptures; fall upon it and it will break you; fall under it, it will crush you. Jim is rolling down Hill with his stone; let him go. It is the silent force, irresistible in the affairs of men. Do not forget this, nor the people who set it in motion. The strikers of the Great Northern have a monopoly of its use now, but it is only loaned to us. Let us not lose it. It is a weapon we must win often before it is ours to keep."[11] Early in the Burlington strike, company officials felt that community attitudes were so important to the outcome of the strike that one railroad official carefully monitored and tabulated editorial comment in the region.[12] Public relations campaigns were mounted by both the Burlington and the Northern Pacific to plant favorable editorials in the local press.[13]

The question of how communities responded to industrial conflict in the late nineteenth century has received its most extensive treatment in the work of Herbert Gutman. In a series of case studies of industrial strikes in the 1870s, Gutman sketched a remarkable pattern of community support for working-class townsmen who struck against "outside" corporations. Citing the peculiarities

---

9. *New York Tribune*, July 26, 1877; *New York World*, July 28, 1877; *Hornell Daily Times*, May 11, 1881. See also Shelton Stromquist, "Class and Community in a Nineteenth Century Railroad Town: Hornellsville, New York, 1860–1880" (Master's essay, University of Pittsburgh, 1973), 125–27, 177–79; Michael J. Cassity, "Modernization and Social Crisis: The Knights of Labor and a Midwest Community, 1885–1886," *Journal of American History* 66, no. 2 (February 1979): 41–61, argues that a similar change in community support occurred in Sedalia, Missouri.

10. Nick Salvatore, *Eugene V. Debs, Citizen and Socialist* (Urbana, Ill.: 1982), 85–87, 181–82, is particularly sensitive to the changing relationships between local business leaders and an emerging militant leader of the working class in the context of a developing midwestern industrial city; also, Nick Salvatore, "Railroad Workers and the Great Strike of 1877: The View from a Small Midwestern City," *Labor History* 21 (Fall 1980): 522–45. On the impact of racial and ethnic changes in the railroad towns of the Northwest, see W. Thomas White, "From Class to Community: Varieties of Radical Protest in the Railroad Industry of the Pacific Northwest, 1894–1917" (Paper presented at the Annual Meeting of the American Historical Association, Washington, D.C., 1982), and W. Thomas White, "A History of Railroad Workers in the Pacific Northwest, 1883–1934" (Ph.D. dissertation, University of Washington, 1981).

11. W. P. C. Adams to Employees of the Northern Pacific, April 22, 1894, General Manager's Correspondence Files, Box 2265, Northern Pacific Archives.

12. "Lists of Newspapers . . . for and against Strike," Strike Papers, 1888 (33 1880 9.11), Burlington Archives.

13. W. G. Pierce to [unnamed], Bozeman, Montana, December 12, 1893, General Manager's Correspondence Files, Box 2264, Northern Pacific Archives.

of small-town life that permitted face-to-face relationships even during rapid industrialization, Gutman attributed the support to an "organic" sense of community and to a distrust of the new, impersonal forces of economic life embodied in the corporations. This support for workingmen in smaller industrial towns and cities he contrasted to the repression and isolation that workers faced in larger metropolises such as New York and Chicago.[14]

Gutman's analysis does not account for the differences in response among smaller industrial communities. That such differences existed is apparent from even a cursory examination of the descriptions of western railroad strikes. Of equal importance, his analysis does not explain why popular sentiment might change from support of striking workers to neutrality or opposition.[15]

Railroad towns, like other industrial communities, were changing entities whose class relations reflected their economic growth and whose elites imbibed deeply the elixir of community progress. In their pragmatic pursuit of progress, community leaders bristled under their competitive disadvantages, attributing their misfortunes to unfair rates and land engrossment of "monopolistic" railroads. Under such conditions the trials of striking railroad workers who owned homes and bought from local merchants seemed clearly allied with their own. However, in the face of the enormous power of the railroads to consign certain communities to oblivion and others to future dominance, business and professional leaders were often more than willing to accept the railroad's modest promises of future benefits and to turn their backs on the shattered remnants of worker organizations and community solidarity. These changes in the class relations of railroad division towns occurred as railroad workers experienced the effects of a growing labor surplus. This wider crisis deepened local antagonisms.

The scattered and sometimes conflicting evidence of differences in the ways communities responded to railroad strikes invites systematic analysis.[16]

THE STATE OF IOWA offers a remarkable setting in which to examine more closely the effects of railroad development on urban growth and the so-

---

14. The best theoretical statement of Gutman's views on the response of nineteenth-century communities to industrial struggles appears in Herbert Gutman, "Workers Search for Power: Labor in the Gilded Age," in *The Gilded Age: A Reappraisal*, ed. H. Wayne Morgan (Syracuse, N.Y.: 1963). See also his other essays in *Work, Culture, and Society in Industrializing America* (New York: 1977).

15. Gutman stresses the need for further study of this problem in relation to the changing structure and economy of smaller industrial cities in his essay "Class, Status, and Community Power in Nineteenth-Century American Cities: Paterson, New Jersey: A Case Study," in Gutman, *Work, Culture, and Society in Industrializing America*, 259–60.

16. See Jeremy W. Kilar, "Community and Authority: Response to the Saginaw Valley Lumber Strike of 1885," *Journal of Forest History* 20 (April 1976): 67–79, for an analysis of absentee ownership and industrial concentration as factors in community support of strikes. Another useful analysis of community class differences and behavior in strikes is John Foster, *Class Struggle and the Industrial Revolution: Early Industrial Capitalism in Three English Towns* (London: 1974).

cial structure of communities. Its comparatively uniform topography and its agricultural specialization have attracted historical geographers looking for an "ideal" setting for the identification of central place hierarchies.[17] The history of railroad expansion in the state is strikingly symmetrical. Within a period of four years (1854–1857) three trunk lines radiating from Chicago reached Iowa's eastern border on the Mississippi—the Chicago, Rock Island & Pacific at Davenport in 1854, the Chicago, Burlington & Quincy at Burlington in 1856, and the Chicago & Northwestern at Clinton in 1857. Each of these roads connected with Iowa-initiated roads, and though construction was interrupted by the depression of 1857 and by the Civil War, all three reached Council Bluffs, their Missouri River terminus, between 1867 and 1869. By that time they had been joined by a fourth line, from Dubuque to Sioux City (the Dubuque & Pacific Railroad). All of these roads received substantial financial assistance from local communities in the eastern part of the state and, most critically, federal land grants totaling more than 4.5 million acres, under legislation enacted in May 1856. According to Governor William Larrabee, these swaths of railroad land represented nearly one-eighth of Iowa's total land area.[18]

The Iowa trunk lines created and maintained one of the first and most persistent "pools," stabilizing rates and regulating the flow of freight over their lines to and from the Union Pacific in Nebraska. Iowa shippers and farmers were likewise pioneer agitators against exorbitant and discriminatory freight rates. Under legislation passed in 1874, Iowa railroad commissioners regulated freight rates on a strictly mileage basis, crystallizing an era of warfare between the railroad corporations and what they perceived to be "the granger element" in Iowa politics. After a lapse of nearly ten years, and supported by different political interests, Iowa legislators in 1888 again sought to impose some order on the rates through a revitalized board of railroad commissioners.[19]

Iowa's extensive and parallel railroad development created a network of division towns that serviced railroad operations. The presence of older commercial towns on the Mississippi and Missouri rivers, which antedated but promoted railroad development, and newer settlements in the interior of the state which were created to service trunk-line operations, offers an opportunity to test the utility of our typology as a basis for differentiating the responses

---

17. Brian J. L. Berry, *Geography of Market Centers and Retail Distribution*, (Englewood Cliffs, N.J.: 1967), 5–9.

18. On the development of Iowa railroads, see Julius Grodinsky, *The Iowa Pool* (Chicago: 1950); Iowa Board of Immigrants, *Iowa: The Home for Immigrants* (Des Moines: 1870), 40–46; Sidney Halma, "Railroad Promotion and Economic Expansion at Council Bluffs, Iowa, 1857–1869," *Annals of Iowa* 42 (Summer 1974): 371–89; Herman C. Nixon, "The Economic Basis of the Populist Movement in Iowa," *Iowa Journal of History and Politics* 21, no. 3 (July 1923): 381–83; William Larrabee, *The Railway Question: A Historical and Practical Treatise on Railroads, and Remedies for Their Abuses* (Chicago: 1898).

19. George H. Miller, *Railroads and the Granger Laws* (Madison, Wis.: 1971), 97–116; Frank H. Dixon, *State Railroad Control with a History of Its Development in Iowa* (New York: 1896).

MAP
MAJOR IOWA RAILROAD TOWNS, CA. 1879/80

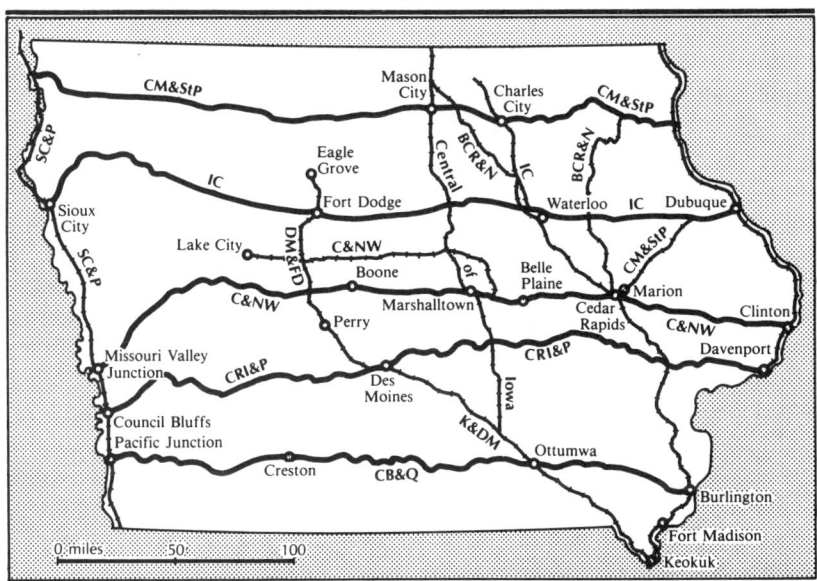

of communities to industrial conflict.[20]

For the purpose of identifying Iowa towns that had significant divisional functions within the railroad network, we have selected all towns that had more than 100 railroad employees in 1895. The designation of 100 or more railroad employees as the criterion for a town having significant divisional functions is to some extent arbitrary. A division headquarters required the residence of both operating and shop employees. While the size of the required labor force varied a good deal, from towns having only a small roundhouse and light branch traffic to those having major repair shops and heavy mainline traffic, some minimum number of railroad workers is a prerequisite for a town's designation as the headquarters of an operating division. We are interested in those towns in which substantial numbers of railroad workers resided and whose divisional functions within the railroad network were more major. A town with 100 or more railroad men in a predominantly agricultural state would

---

20. Iowa's exceptional record of census-taking during the nineteenth century makes it possible to compare the growth patterns of a large number of cities. From as early as 1850 — biennially until 1875, and thereafter at five-year intervals — Iowa recorded village, town, and hamlet populations over one hundred persons. The 1895 state census published not only aggregated populations but, for all towns of one thousand or more, provided a detailed occupational breakdown. On the basis of these census data, it is possible to identify with certainty all towns having large concentrations of railroad employees and to sketch the occupational and industrial structure of these towns.

TABLE 8.1
CLASSIFICATION OF SELECTED IOWA URBAN PLACES

Regional City (50,000–200,000)	Market City (10,000–50,000)	Railroad Town (under 10,000)
Des Moines	Burlington	Belle Plaine
	Cedar Rapids	Boone
	Clinton	Charles City
	Council Bluffs	Creston
	Davenport	Fort Dodge
	Dubuque	Lake City
	Fort Madison	Marion
	Keokuk	Mason City
	Marshalltown	Missouri Valley
	Ottumwa	Perry
	Sioux City	Eagle Grove
	Waterloo	

SOURCE: Secretary of State, *Census of Iowa for the Year 1895* (Des Moines: 1896).

seem to meet both the test of a sufficiently large work force to perform divisional functions and to reflect a significant level of industrial concentration. Twenty-four towns meet that criterion, with numbers of railroad workers ranging from 100 to 685. (Thirty-five towns had 9 to 50 railroaders, and twelve had from 51 to 99.) These twenty-four towns had 93.6 percent of all railroad employees in the state, while the remaining forty-seven towns had only 6.4 percent of the state's railroad employees.

One attribute separating market cities from railroad towns was size. If we use size as a working basis for classification, Iowa towns with railroad service functions can provisionally but very clearly be divided between market cities and railroad towns (see table 8.1).[21]

Within every region a few cities grew beyond the size and functional limits of a market city. Although they may have continued to function as railroad division headquarters, their exceptional growth led to the diminished importance of the railroad service function. While they shared many characteristics with market cities, the dimensions of their growth and the extent of their diversification ultimately set them apart. Des Moines is such a city in Iowa.

Not surprisingly the larger towns in the railroad network generally had experienced some settlement prior to the railroad. The larger of the market cities were all prerailroad river entrepôts on the Mississippi or Missouri Rivers. With few exceptions the cities that were settled by the railroad remained the smaller towns in 1895, located generally in the western interior of the state.

---

21. Secretary of State, *Census of Iowa for the Year 1895* (Des Moines: 1896).

Although the larger river cities grew noticeably with the acquisition of rail lines, the railroad labor force declined as a proportion of the total labor force as the towns grew further. By 1895 railroad men were as few as .6 percent of the labor force in Davenport and as much as 10.2 percent in neighboring Clinton. By contrast, in smaller, interior towns rail employees were a much higher proportion of the working population. In very small towns such as Lake City nearly 16 percent of those gainfully employed worked on the railroad, and in Creston fully 35 percent of all employed people were railroad men.

Market cities and railroad towns differed not only in the proportion of railroad workers in the local labor force, but also in their growth patterns and economic diversification. Market cities in Iowa were generally settled before 1860 and before they had acquired railroad service. From the Mississippi River westward in the eastern half of the state, rail lines were built during the 1850s. Council Bluffs and Sioux City did not acquire rail lines until the end of the 1860s. The railroad towns in the interior of the state were settled in the late 1860s and early 1870s, during the same years in which they acquired railroad lines. If we compare the growth rates of market cities and railroad towns at intervals from the time their populations were first recorded in the Iowa state census, significant differences are apparent (see figure). Population data for Iowa cities are first available for 1850. With the exception of the Missouri

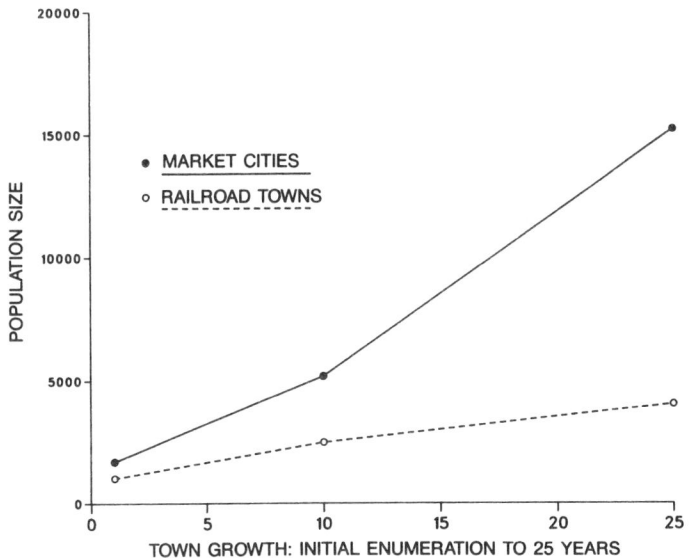

AVERAGE SIZE OF SELECTED IOWA URBAN PLACES, 1850–1900

Note: Because Des Moines' growth did not exceed that of "market cities" during its first twenty-five years, it has been put in that class for the purposes of this figure.

Source: Secretary of State, *Census of Iowa for the Year 1895* (Des Moines: 1896).

River towns, population data for the first five-year period of all division towns being analyzed reflect at least the anticipatory growth effects of railroad expansion.

When Iowa market cities first appeared in the state census, they were on the average 40 percent larger than railroad towns. During the first decade for which population data are available, the growth of market cities was significantly greater than for railroad towns. The initial impact of railroad development is reflected in the population growth of market cities during this first decade. For most railroad towns, their initial size as first recorded in the census reflects the presence of railroad operations. It is during the second and third decades of growth that the character of market cities fully blossomed. Building on their initial advantages, they enjoyed more sustained economic growth than the railroad towns. The average initial size of railroad towns was 60 percent of the more established market cities. After twenty-five years of growth the average size of railroad towns had fallen to 27 percent of that of the market cities. While railroad towns grew an average of 297 percent during their first twenty-five years, market cities grew by 800 percent. Servicing railroad operations was still an important economic function for market cities, but during this period of growth they also acquired major manufacturing and wholesaling enterprises.

Manufacturing and wholesaling activity were overrepresented in market cities as compared with railroad towns. Manufacturing was conducted on a larger scale in market cities—firms were on the average three times larger and nine times more numerous. The contrast in terms of wholesale marketing was even greater. Fully two-thirds of the railroad towns had no wholesalers at all, whereas market cities averaged fifteen. The three railroad towns with some wholesale business had fewer than three firms each.[22]

Only with respect to railroad employment itself did railroad towns outstrip market cities. Together, market cities and railroad towns possessed 93.6 percent of all railroad employment in the state. Although railroad towns had only 15.8 percent of all employed persons in the two types of cities, their share of railroad employment was nearly double that figure, 35 percent.

---

22. Iowa Bureau of Labor Statistics, *Seventh Biennial Report, 1895–96* (Des Moines: 1897), 19–55. The Iowa Bureau of Labor Statistics conducted annual surveys of businesses (manufacturing, wholesale, and retail) for a number of years in the 1890s. The figures for 1895 were used in order to complement the data on population growth and occupational distribution from the 1895 census. Because of the focus on the distribution of manufacturing and wholesaling between towns rather than counties, and because the Bureau of Labor Statistics data were tabulated by county, two railroad towns (Marion and Belle Plaine) and four market cities (Cedar Rapids, Clinton, Fort Madison, and Keokuk) were dropped from consideration because they were in counties with multiple urban centers of more than 2,000 population. As one consequence of the elimination of these towns, the relative share of manufacturing and wholesaling of the market cities is understated, which only strengthens the conclusions being drawn here. Those towns that remained under consideration were the only towns with more than 2,000 people in their respective counties. It was assumed that all manufacturing and wholesaling enterprises in those counties were in those towns.

The impact of railroads on urban development in Iowa produced a configuration of cities that is explicable in part by distinguishing the growth performance and social structure of market cities from that of railroad towns. Market cities were urban settlements that had enjoyed some notable economic development prior to the entrance of the railroad. Their growth was enhanced, and their dominance over a significant area of wholesale trade was secured by the railroad. By contrast, railroad towns were smaller, newer settlements that generally originated with railroad expansion itself. Their growth though initially spectacular was subsequently more sluggish. Their share of the state's manufacturing and wholesale trade was disproportionately low, though their share of railroad employment by comparison to market cities was disproportionately high. An analysis of two representative communities will provide a detailed comparison of the formation of their social structure and their response to industrial conflict.

BETWEEN 1855 AND 1869 southern Iowa acquired a major trunk line with direct connections to Chicago and thence to the East. This brought the promise of a place in the transcontinental system pioneered by the Union Pacific and the Central Pacific. Urban growth followed close on the heels of the Burlington & Missouri River Railroad's construction, which connected the intrepid Mississippi River entrepôt of Burlington with an impatient and ambitious Council Bluffs on the Missouri. In so doing, it vitalized the growth of numerous agricultural villages in the eastern part of the state that were fortunate enough to be located on the new road, and it planted settlements in the central and western parts of the state whose ambitions, if not their growth, quickly caught up with the older towns on the state's borders.

Two towns are particularly noteworthy. In addition to the different functions they performed in the commercial and manufacturing network of southern Iowa, each was an important service center for railroad operations. Burlington maintained a large complex of machine shops and roundhouses, whose importance within the Chicago, Burlington & Quincy system grew over time.[23] More than three hundred men in the running trades alone made their homes in the city. The city's switching yards offered interconnections with four other roads.[24] Creston, approximately two hundred miles farther west, was also a major divisional headquarters with large machine shops and a sixty-stall roundhouse. More than three hundred railroad men operated trains east and west from that point.

---

23. *Portrait and Biographical Album of Des Moines County* (Chicago: 1880), 713–14.

24. Department of the Interior, Census Office, *Statistics of Population of the United States at the Tenth Census,* June 1, 1880 (Washington, D.C.: 1883). Interconnecting roads were the Burlington, Cedar Rapids & Northern, the Burlington & Western, the Burlington & Northwestern, and the Keokuk & Northern. The last three were subsidiaries of the Chicago, Burlington & Quincy.

Burlington and Creston provided similar railroad services. They differed enormously, however, in the ways they developed and in their size, economic diversity, and class structure. One was a market city; the other a railroad town. Although each was an important center of strike activity in 1877 and 1888, their responses to industrial conflict were widely divergent.

IN 1850, with just less than two decades of development under its belt, Burlington had a population of over four thousand. Its "flint hills" and river frontage were already thickly settled. A generation of cabin stores that supplied the needs of settlers and river travelers had already given way to a panoply of small retailers, who specialized in dry goods, groceries, hardware, and drugs. Even by 1840, Burlington exported significant quantities of pork, grain, and cattle. Small-scale manufacturing started early. In 1833, R. S. Adams began producing shoes and boots (fifty years later his grandson employed one hundred men who turned out four hundred pairs a day); the manufacture of carriages and buggies began in 1844; and by 1850 two "seven by nine" foundries were doing an annual business of about $10,000.[25]

Also by 1850 a small but cohesive group of merchants and lawyers had begun a campaign to improve the poor transportation that was an obstacle to Burlington's further development. Twelve miles of rapids on the Mississippi just north of Keokuk at the southeastern tip of Iowa made river navigation impossible during low water. Estimates of Burlington's losses in business due to the rapids varied from $50,000 to $160,000 annually. Her leading citizens organized and reorganized between 1845 and 1855 in pursuit of the latest internal improvements.[26] Men from Burlington initiated regional conventions at which river dredging, plank roads, and finally railroads were discussed and where political support and financial commitments were sought from a broad constituency of Iowa and Illinois residents. "Plank fever" did produce a road that traversed the thirty-five miles inland to Mount Pleasant, but even as it was completed in 1851, stronger interests coalesced around the prospects for railroad development.[27]

In 1852 the Burlington & Missouri River Railroad was incorporated by forty-six Burlington promoters. More significantly, as early as April 1851, Burlington voters overwhelmingly approved a loan of $75,000 to secure a branch of the Peoria & Oquawka Railroad. This promised a connection to the Chicago market, which would permanently eliminate the problem of the Keokuk rapids. Because of the enthusiasm of the Burlington promoters and the

---

25. H. H. Hartley and L. G. Jeffers, *Business Directory and Review of the Trade, Commerce, and Manufactures of the City of Burlington, Iowa* (Burlington: 1856), 6, 14–15; *Portrait and Biographical Album of Des Moines County*, 762.

26. George A. Boeck, "A Decade of Transportation Fever in Burlington, Iowa, 1845–1855," in *Patterns and Perspectives in Iowa History*, ed. Dorothy Schweider (Ames, Iowa: 1973), 135–52.

27. *Ibid.*, 146.

financial commitment from the city and from numerous private stock subscribers, Burlington ultimately beat out Oquawka, Illinois, for the position of western terminus. Simultaneously, promoters in Galesburg, Illinois, fought to be included by forging an alliance of separate railroad lines that connected the Chicago and Aurora Railroad with Mendota, Galesburg, and (via the Peoria & Oquawka) Burlington. Local promoters won financial backing for these linkages from the Michigan Central Railroad, which was searching for a western outlet, and from the citizens of Aurora, Galesburg, and Burlington. Each town ultimately became the headquarters of an operating division of the Chicago, Burlington & Quincy Railroad.[28]

Burlington's ambition to build a road linking the Mississippi and Missouri rivers was actively pursued between 1852 and 1855. After a desperate fight in the state legislature, a charter for still another parallel road across Iowa was finally secured. (Two lines had been designated to receive land grants, but four finally did so.) Burlington's coterie of tireless promoters, frustrated by Congress's slowness to act on the federal land grant, turned once again to the hustings for financial support. A "railroad convention" in Fairfield, Iowa, in 1853 saw representatives of six counties along the projected route to the Des Moines River resolve for the road's construction and for legislative authority that would allow counties to subscribe stock. Michigan Central and Chicago, Burlington & Quincy officials, moving quickly to consolidate control over their western extension, acquired a controlling interest in the Burlington & Missouri and specified the conditions for the road's extension to the Des Moines River. The counties between Burlington and Ottumwa had to subscribe $450,000, with an additional $150,000 in individual subscriptions. In response to a direct appeal from James F. Joy of the Chicago, Burlington & Quincy, the city of Burlington contributed an additional $75,000 and a long-term lease to the riverfront land that was needed for shops and a depot.[29]

Even before the first C. B. & Q. train entered town Burlington's economy had taken a leap forward. Its population grew by 79 percent in the four years after 1850. "Nearly every branch of mercantile and mechanical enterprise has tripled or quadrupled," a local business directory boasted in 1856. "Some of our enterprising merchants have given up the retail business entirely and have turned their attention to the jobbing of Dry Goods, and their arrangements have been so perfected as to guarantee to western and country merchants that they will not only *save* but will make money by getting their supplies here."[30] Even during the first year of the railroad's operation, Burlington lumber dealers sold almost as much on a wholesale basis outside the city as they did within it. Of the 10 million feet of lumber brought into the city, 1.25 million was "sold into the country east of the river," 3.5 million in the country west of the river, and

---

28. Overton, *Burlington West*, 15–24, 39–52; Boeck, "A Decade of Transportation Fever," 148–52.
29. *Ibid.*, 153–56; Overton, *Burlington West*, 57–60.
30. *Census of Iowa, 1895*; *Business Directory* (Burlington: 1856), 8, 13.

5.25 million was consumed in the city itself. "Manufactories" multiplied rapidly. By 1856 there were three breweries, two plow manufacturers (one employing 20 hands), a planing mill, a sash factory (10 hands), and three iron foundries (140 hands).[31] The first private bank, owned by F. J. C. Peasley, was founded in 1851 and was intimately connected (through its offspring, the National State Bank) to the B. & M. Railroad.[32]

Although Burlington's place among the metropolises of the upper Midwest seemed assured, the city's relationship with the B. & M. and with the C. B. & Q. Railroad was occasionally frayed, as control of the road passed farther and farther from the hands of local citizens. On May 11, 1858, a letter from "Justice," which appeared in the *Burlington Hawkeye*, questioned the city's financial contribution to the construction of the road. "Why," he asked, "should the city donate accretions and city credit for the purpose of filling the pockets of a few individuals who make it a practice (warrior-like) of demanding tribute money every time they visit us, and threaten us, if we do not comply with their request, with total annihilation."[33]

The next year John G. Foote, former treasurer of the B. & M. Railroad, who had been displaced as corporate control shifted to Boston, expressed concern over the impact of absentee ownership on the community. In his account of this period, Richard C. Overton refers to an open letter to the *Burlington Hawkeye*, in which Foote insisted that the B. & M. be managed so as to "promote . . . the interests of the State and of the City and not entirely the interests of a few nonresident stockholders and directors."[34] Foote was further concerned over the personal interest of the railroad directors in land adjacent to the road and the letting of construction contracts.

When Mayor Corse signed over conveyance of the land leased by the B. & M. Railroad in December 1866, it contained certain stipulations designed to assure a "continuing identity of interest between the city and the company." Specifically, it required that the B. & M. shops be located in perpetuity within the city limits and that the conveyed land be used for railroad purposes only.[35]

Differences between citizens of Burlington and the railroad erupted again in the early 1870s, shortly after the consolidation of the Burlington & Missouri with the Chicago, Burlington & Quincy. The *Hawkeye* pronounced the consolidation a benefit to Burlington, in spite of the anxiety of some that it might suffer in the freight rate-making process. C. E. Perkins, a Burlington resident of nearly fifteen years and a C. B. & Q. vice-president, wrote to his mentor, John Murray Forbes, a Boston director of the road. Perkins indicated "that

---

31. *Ibid.*, 8, 13.
32. *Portrait and Biographical Album of Des Moines County*, 769.
33. *Burlington Weekly Hawkeye*, May 11, 1858, quoted in Overton, *Burlington West*, 101.
34. *Burlington Weekly Hawkeye*, April 13, 1857, quoted in Overton, *Burlington West*, 115.
35. Overton, *Burlington West*, 218.

consolidation did not please the Burlington people but he did not see how it could 'set the town back any.'"[36]

As a result of a successful suit by Burlington businessman Elisha Chamberlain and a number of other citizens, which restrained the city from levying a tax of .25 percent on real and personal property to pay the interest on bonds issued to the B. & M. in the 1850s, the City Council and the County Board of Supervisors repudiated their bonded indebtedness to the railroad. The citizens claimed that the city "had no authority . . . to create an indebtedness for a private purpose."[37]

Controversy between Mississippi River towns and the Iowa pool railroads over freight rates reached fever pitch in the 1870s. But this conflict was resolved during the course of the decade, when numbers of individual wholesalers and jobbers in the river towns reached understandings with the roads over rates that would grant them control of their "natural" markets. Freight rate agitation and anti-railroad sentiment shifted westward in the next decade as new towns sought to carve out their own tributary areas in the face of discriminatory rates that favored eastern Iowa interests.[38]

A final point of irritation between the city of Burlington and the railroad involved the relocation of the C. B. & Q.'s shops to land annexed by the city in 1881 (thereby permitting the railroad to fulfill the terms of the lease conveyed in 1866). The road then proceeded to lay out a new town, West Burlington, outside the city on company-owned land to house the shop work force. The Chicago, Burlington & Quincy organized this new "company town" without the encumbrances of an established municipality, selling building lots to its employees on an installment plan and offering building sites to churches, businesses, and manufacturers.[39]

Such "abuse" at the hands of an outside corporation served to complicate the relationship between the city and its railroad, but Burlington's continued growth constantly buttressed recognition of the underlying common interests of the city's business leaders and their railroad benefactors. In 1891 local historian Clara Rouse noted that "Burlington never has a 'boom.' She marches quietly to success and is steadily advancing, reaching out a little further all the time, cautious, but growing richer and richer in her advantages."[40] Local Burlington railroad officials, most notably Charles E. Perkins, maintained a close and proprietary relationship with the city, promoting its newspapers and politi-

---

36. *Ibid.*, 275.
37. Augustus M. Antrobus, *History of Des Moines County, Iowa, and Its People* (Chicago: 1915), 455.
38. Miller, *Railroads and the Granger Laws*, 97–116; Ripley, *Railroads, Rates and Regulations*, 163, 242–43.
39. Antrobus, *History of Des Moines County*, 148; Federal Writers' Project, *Iowa: A Guide to the Hawkeye State* (New York: 1949), 522.
40. Clara B. Rouse, *Iowa Leaves: Six Chapters* (Chicago: 1891), 238.

cal leaders for wider recognition, participating actively in its Board of Trade, and occasionally holding political offices. The National State Bank, Burlington's largest bank and a descendant of F. J. C. Peasley's private bank, gave up its president, J. C. Peasley, to serve with the Burlington as a financial officer and ultimately first vice-president. Both Peasley and Perkins continued to serve on the bank's board of directors through the 1880s.[41] The city's largest lumber dealers were closely related through stock ownership and interlocking directorates; the largest, the Burlington Lumber Company, did business almost exclusively with the railroad and its subsidiaries, providing bridge timber and "large dimension stuff."[42]

Burlington's wholesale dealers and manufacturers dominated the councils of the Board of Trade, comprising 64 percent of the membership. Retail merchants, though much more numerous in the population, made up only 10 percent of the membership of the Board of Trade. An informal survey conducted by the *Hawkeye* during the early days of the 1888 Burlington strike testifies to the interlocking interests between wholesalers, manufacturers, and the railroad. The survey indicates that wholesalers "doing business with the smaller towns along the Burlington system" had their business reduced by 50 to 75 percent. Manufacturers found their operations "greatly limited," though not as much as wholesalers because their markets were more widespread and they could thus to some extent use other routes. All were unanimous in their condemnation of the men on strike.[43]

CRESTON'S DEVELOPMENT and its relationship to the railroad followed a different route. Its origins lay in the maneuverings of town-site promoters for a profit-maximizing location of the western Iowa division headquarters. An 1889 history of the town noted that "the site for the town was purchased by inside officials of the railroad company who organized themselves into a town company. Their individual names are never used, the property being managed by a trustee. About 250 acres were included in the town as first laid out."[44] Indeed, when the road reached Union County in the fall of 1868, Afton, the county seat, enjoyed a minor boom as the temporary terminus of the road. Some local investors, believing that the division headquarters would be located in the existing village of Cromwell in Union County, made substantial investments in land there, which resulted "unprofitably to them by reason of the changes in plans."[45]

---

41. David L. Lightner, *Labor on the Illinois Central, 1850–1900* (New York: 1977); *Portrait and Biographical Album of Des Moines County*, 769.

42. *Portrait and Biographical Album*, 771.

43. James Maitland, *Historical Sketches of Burlington, Iowa* (Burlington: n.d.), 18–19.

44. *Biographical and Historical Record of Ringgold and Union Counties, Iowa* (Chicago: 1887), 722.

45. C. J. Colby, *Illustrated Centennial Sketches, Map, and Directory of Union County* (Creston: 1876), 17.

Creston rose dramatically in the manner of new railroad towns from the soil of the unsettled prairie in central Union County. By early 1870 the town boasted "the largest engine house in the West," with attendant machine shops employing several hundred men. Only a few months before, the community had consisted of two frame houses, twelve cabins, and five tents.[46] In 1875 the visiting editor of the *Prairie Farmer* was impressed by the bustling air of this little prairie city. From fifty to eighty trains were made up daily, and the Burlington & Missouri employed 650 local men, with a payroll of nearly $40,000 per month. "Business in Creston," he noted, "is conducted nearer on a cash basis than any other point along the line in Iowa." Railroad men had built and occupied "some of the finest residences in the town."[47] The city directory in the next year pointed out that the railroad workmen "contribute largely to the support of its businesses and municipal interests."[48]

During its first decade Creston's population rose no less spectacularly than its railroad facilities. A population of 416 in 1870 had risen to 4,081 in 1880. That growth, however, was based largely on servicing railroad operations and employees. In 1876 approximately 33 percent of the labor force worked directly for the railroad, and by 1895, 35 percent of the labor force was employed by the C. B. & Q. Railroad. The 1880 U.S. Census of Manufactures lists only a handful of small firms in "blacksmithing, clothing and saddlery," averaging three employees apiece. Two building contractors employed ten workers apiece, making them the largest employers in town, outside of the C. B. & Q. Two flour mills employed seven and nine men, respectively. The town had no wholesale dealers.[49] Even in 1892, Creston had only a few small manufacturing firms—a sash factory, a cigar factory, a soap works, and a small foundry and machine shop.[50]

By the early 1880s, Creston's growth slowed considerably, and local community leaders were haunted by the possibility of stagnation. In a January 1885 editorial, the editor of the city's largest newspaper, the *Creston Daily Advertiser*, raised the question, "What Is Creston's Future?"

> Many times, within the past few years, in the *Advertiser*'s "cranky" efforts to awake the citizens, businessmen and taxpayers of Creston to a realization of the necessities of our young city, have we stated that Creston was far ahead of herself; that every branch of business in the city was overdone, and that unless a new railroad, manufactories or some enterprise besides what she possessed were soon added, she must step down from the proud position she

---

46. J. L. Tracey, *Guide to the Great West* (Saint Louis: 1870), 197.

47. *The Prairie Farmer*, December 14, 1875, quoted in Colby, *Illustrated Centennial Sketches*, 20–21.

48. Colby, *Illustrated Centennial Sketches*, 20.

49. U.S. Department of the Interior, Census Office, *Manufacturing Schedules*, Des Moines County, Iowa, 1880.

50. *Iowa State Gazetteer, Business Directory, and Farmers' List* (Dubuque, Iowa: 1892).

has occupied as the boss city of the slope, the metropolis of Southwestern Iowa, and degenerate into a small inland town with limited prospects for her future.[51]

As previously noted, Burlington's difficulties with the C. B. & Q. Railroad irked a portion of the city's population, but they did not fundamentally affect the prospects for the city's continued growth. The economic benefits of Burlington's relationship to the railroad were readily apparent. In contrast, leading citizens of Creston in the mid-1880s persistently identified the city's inability to sustain economic growth with the "iron grip of the mighty and avaricious Q. still on its throat." Without "railroad competition" cities like Creston saw themselves victimized by inherently discriminatory freight rate-making practices. As the *Advertiser* pointed out, manufactories, wholesale and jobbing firms "are what build up and make a place substantial" by adding to the producing and consuming population of a town. But plainly, "such institutions cannot exist where there is no railroad competition."[52]

Committees of leading businessmen, and indeed the newly instituted Board of Trade, organized, just as Burlington businessmen in the early 1850s, to secure a competing railroad line through the city. Like their Burlington counterparts, they sought to secure Creston's economic future through improved transportation. But unlike the Burlington experience, their campaign was infused with an explicit opposition to the "monopolistic" C. B. & Q., and unlike their Burlington counterparts, they were ultimately unsuccessful.[53]

Creston's Board of Trade, organized in 1886, was dominated by retail merchants, who comprised 60 percent of the membership and dominated the committees that sought competing railroad lines.[54] (Only one manufacturer and two aspiring wholesalers were members.) Storekeepers were tied directly to the interests of their customers, so that in towns like Creston, where railroad men dominated the labor force and generated a substantial amount of the town's income, the interests of railroad workers were likely to find support among the retail merchants they patronized.

Retail merchants in both Burlington and Creston found their interests directly affected by the railroad strike of 1888. Their problem, unlike that of wholesale merchants, was not the absence of transportation and the interruption of business, but rather "many of their best customers were among the striking men," and those men had significantly less disposable income to buy goods or to go toward "paying old bills."[55] What differentiated the two communities, among other things, was that in Burlington retail merchants had significantly

---

51. *Creston Daily Advertiser*, January 7, 1885.
52. *Ibid.*
53. *Biographical and Historical Record of Ringgold and Union Counties, Iowa* (Chicago: 1887), 725.
54. *Ibid.; Creston City Directory* (Creston: 1889).
55. *Burlington Hawkeye*, March 1, 1888.

less influence in the business councils of the city than had wholesalers and manufacturers, whereas in Creston they were community leaders and their views dominated in the Board of Trade and the press.

Speaking for Creston's leading merchants during the 1888 strike, the *Daily Advertiser* urged the support of "every citizen of Creston, . . . that the boys win the present struggle." It warned that because of the investments in homes and "obligations contracted," if the railroad men were to lose the strike and have to leave the community, it "would be such a blow to the financial condition of our city that she would not recover for years to come."[56] Such a position was consistent not only with the basis of Creston's economy as it existed in the 1880s but with the "anti-monopoly" framework within which Creston boosters fought to unlock the city's potential for economic growth. The initial advantages of older market cities that secured early railroad connections and more favorable treatment in the making of freight rates continued to operate in a manner that was perceived by the newer railroad boom towns as systematically inhibiting their own development.

DURING MUCH OF THE FIRST DECADE of Creston's existence, a small coalition of railroad officials and men with sizeable real estate interests dominated political and social life. Men like R. P. Smith and J. B. Harsh settled in Creston early and built considerable wealth on their "judicious investments" in land. In 1887 it was said of Harsh that "but few tracts of land within a radius of twenty miles of Creston . . . have not at one time or another passed through his hands."[57] Five of the fourteen men whose biographies appeared in the city directory of 1876 listed their primary occupation as real estate dealer.[58]

Less than ten years after the town's settlement, with the population of the community nearly doubled, a much more diverse pattern of economic and social influence was apparent. Of the ninety-six individuals whose subscription biographies are included in the 1887 county history, 65 percent had arrived within the previous ten years.[59] Nearly 20 percent had worked at one time

---

56. *Creston Daily Advertiser*, March 2, 1888.
57. *Biographical and Historical Record of Ringgold and Union Counties*, 468.
58. Colby, *Illustrated Centennial Sketches*, 60–66.
59. The use of subscription biographies as a means of identifying community elites is not without its potential problems. As the product, at least in part, of self-selection, they are open to the bias of those who would promote their social position beyond their real stature in the community. Likewise, some substantial men in the community might have disdained contributing their biographies. The value of the biographies is in the richness of the information conveyed about individuals, including in most cases very specific accounts of their migrations, their education, their various business ventures, their associational and political affiliations. We have checked the membership list of the Burlington Board of Trade against the biographies and found that, with the exception of those who died or left the community, the coverage is nearly universal. On the other hand, there were a few obvious cases of individuals whose biographies were very brief and whose occupational and associational affiliations were very humble, who appeared to be using the biographies as a

for the Chicago, Burlington & Quincy, many of them in the shops and running trades. No railroad workers had been elected to public office during the first half of the 1870s, but by the early 1880s, railroad workers were regularly elected to local offices. The Knights of Labor was highly visible in local affairs, members being elected at various times to justice of the peace, the city council, and the state legislature. The town was among the stronger centers of support for Greenback and Union Labor politics in the state. Chicago, Burlington & Quincy estimated that 35 percent of Creston's shopmen belonged to the Knights of Labor.[60]

Burlington's business and political elite stands in sharp contrast to Creston's. Manufacturers and wholesalers dominated the city's affairs with considerable continuity throughout the railroad era of the nineteenth century. Wholesalers were prominent among the incorporators of the Board of Trade in 1872, and they were a dominant bloc on the board in 1881 (when they comprised 31 percent of the membership and 39 percent of the officers and members of standing committees).[61] In contrast to Creston's elite, where an overwhelming majority of the members were very recent arrivals even by "new town" standards, Burlington's upper crust were older and sank deep roots in the economic and social structure of the city. An examination of the subscription biographies of 252 Burlington residents that were included in a history of Des Moines County published in 1888 reveals that 68 percent had been in the community at least eighteen years, longer than Creston had even existed as a community.[62] Forty-three percent had been in the community for more than twenty-eight years. The greatest number who arrived in any decade (seventy-four) were either born in or entered the community during the decade of the 1850s, in the midst of the economic transformation wrought by the railroad. Their business careers reveal remarkable patterns of interaction in the formation of partnerships and the purchase and inheritance of businesses. An identical proportion of Burlington's and Creston's elite (20 percent) evidenced some background in railroad work. The noteworthy difference is that while 57 percent of the Creston men with railroad backgrounds were identifiable primarily as operating employees (running trades) or shopmen, only 25 percent of Burlington's railroad elite came from such working-class occupations. Upper-class Burlington,

---

vehicle for social mobility. These cases were few and readily identifiable. The richness of the source and its accessibility have persuaded us to use it for the limited purpose of identification of elites, taking into account the exceptions noted above.

60. Colby, *Illustrated Centennial Sketches*, 93–96; *Biographical and Historical Record of Ringgold and Union Counties*; C. W. Eckerson to G. W. Rhodes, July 23, 1885, Engineers' Grievance Committee Papers (33 1880 3.1), Burlington Archives; Fred Haynes, *Third Party Movements Since the Civil War, with Special Reference to Iowa* (Iowa City: 1916); Nixon, "The Economic Basis of the Populist Movement," 3–107.

61. *The History of Des Moines County, Iowa* (Chicago: 1879); Maitland, *Historical Sketches of Burlington*, 18.

62. *Portrait and Biographical Album of Des Moines County, Iowa*.

however, had a much larger proportion of men with railroad backgrounds who had been supervisors or officers. In Burlington, 33 percent of the men had been supervisors (shop foremen, roadmasters, and so forth), and 25 percent were officers (presidents, solicitors, superintendents); in Creston, the proportions were 10 percent and 5 percent.

Creston and Burlington were a study in contrasts as they entered the era of the "Great Upheaval" in the late 1870s. Burlington's elite, based in manufacturing and wholesaling, was comparatively stable and well organized. Its leadership of the community, secured in the agitation for "internal improvements," was not fundamentally challenged. In Creston, members of the business elite, many of whom were new to the community, rode uneasily at the head of a broad coalition of small merchants, railroad men, and dealers who serviced the agricultural trade. In Burlington, railroad workers were one segment of a heterogeneous labor force; in Creston, their numbers dominated. In Burlington, a diversified local economy had been built on the foundation of prerailroad economic growth; the railroads enabled the city to extend these initial advantages into regional dominance of wholesaling and jobbing and into the development of diversified manufacturing. Creston's economy was created and limited by the railroad. Local capital generated from land sales or from the railroad payroll, though substantial when compared with the cash flow of neighboring (and envious) farm villages, was not the stuff of which great manufacturing centers are built. Dependence on a single rail line, it was perceived, discouraged further economic development.

Differences in the economic structure and growth performance of a market city and a railroad town led to differences in the composition, turnover, and solidarity of local elites. The eruption of industrial conflict elicited divergent responses that were consistent with the structure of class relations in these communities.

MANY FACTORS shaped the way communities responded to industrial conflict. On one level, as Herbert Gutman suggested, personal relationships and loyalties within smaller communities were a more compelling basis for action than the impersonal influences of outside corporations. But on another level, as the foregoing analysis has suggested, even industrial cities like Burlington had experienced a level of economic development and market growth that created the basis for significant class differences and for the mobilization of public opinion by elites whose loyalties to their railroad benefactors were stronger than their sense of community with local railroad workers. The antimonopoly perspective of Creston's local boosters provided the basis for a more sympathetic response to the plight of railroad workers striking against the "avaricious Q." And that response was secured by the power that Creston's railroad workers wielded as the primary consumers of the goods that the town's leading businessmen retailed. But even in Creston, this community support was more transitory and the sense of community solidarity more fragile than might have been predicted.

An examination of how Burlington and Creston responded to the railroad strikes of 1877 and 1888 provides an opportunity to test for one market city and one railroad town the way in which differences in their development, their social structure, and the composition of their elites help to explain community responses to strikes. By implication, such comparisons could be undertaken for other sets of railroad towns and other types of industrial communities.

Wage cuts during the depression of the 1870s ushered in an era of tumultuous labor relations on the railroads. The Chicago, Burlington & Quincy Railroad was not immune. Between 1876 and 1888 men in the running trades and switchmen and shopmen agitated over wage rates and work rules. The road experienced major strikes in 1877 and in 1888. Even after the epochal "Great Strike" of engineers, firemen, and switchmen in 1888, isolated pockets of shopmen managed to assert their sympathy with the Pullman strikers in 1894. The purpose in this section is to compare the extent of community support in two very different division towns in Iowa.

THE RAILROAD STRIKE OF 1877 spread westward and reached Iowa on July 24, more than a week after it had begun in the East. All classes of employees on the Chicago, Burlington & Quincy had experienced recent wage cuts. Further, in September 1876, engineers found themselves with a new "apprenticeship" system imposed by the company that reduced the wages of first- and second-year engineers. "Classification," as the system was called, stirred resentment from the beginning and continued to be a source of unrest until the Great Strike of 1888.

Large meetings of railroad men were held in Creston, Ottumwa, and Burlington on July 23. The Creston men acted first, resolving to strike the next day and sending a committee east. The men in Burlington waited for results from the other divisions. They met again on the evening of July 24, admitted only railroad men, and heard speakers from Galesburg and Creston exhort them to join the work stoppage. They drew up a list of demands representing the sentiments of dozens of different trades and on July 25 joined the strike.[63]

Charles E. Perkins, still a vice-president of the C. B. & Q. and stationed in Burlington, immediately recognized his helplessness in the face of the strikers' numbers and the support they enjoyed from the state's "pastoral" government and populace. A lumber dealer from rural Afton had indicated in a telegram to Perkins on July 25 that "the railroad enemies here are confined to the 'granger element' with a few exceptions." Perkins already appreciated that public sympathy ran against the railroads and "rather to the rebels." His remedy, for which he argued vociferously within Chicago, Burlington &

---

63. *Burlington Daily Gazette*, July 23, 25, 1877; Charles E. Perkins to Robert Harris, July 23, 1877, Strike Papers, 1877 (33 1870 3.1), Burlington Archives.

Quincy management circles, was a suspension of all traffic, and to "say to the mob and the public, 'until our property is protected by the constitutional authorities we will go out of business.'"[64] Within his realm of authority he stopped all passenger trains out of Burlington, hoping thereby to exert pressure on the community, and he was instrumental in activating the Burlington Board of Trade to use its good offices to end the strike. By the next day, July 26, Perkins telegraphed President Robert Harris that public opinion was "beginning to come around." The initial solidarity of the strikers was shattered on July 26 when conductors in Burlington voted to return to work, taking with them a significant number of brakemen.[65]

Most revealing about the quality of community support for the strikers in Burlington were the activities of the Board of Trade and results of two "citizens' meetings." The striking railroad men called a meeting at the Opera House on the evening of July 27 to "consult" with citizens. The well-attended meeting heard brief opening remarks by two attorneys, a minister, and the land commissioner of the railroad, which were cautious and noncommittal. They were followed by three engineers and a shopman who vigorously defended the strike. At this point, "adjournment was hastily procured" by the striker who chaired the meeting, amid much shouting and confusion. There was a call for a meeting the following night and a resolution urging "the appointment of a committee of businessmen to act with us in endeavoring to procure what we think we are entitled to."

The next afternoon, invited members of the Board of Trade met in their offices without consulting the railroad men and drafted a series of resolutions stating that: "On behalf of the businessmen of this city we deprecate and have no sympathy with strikers among employees in any calling . . . and recommend to the workingmen immediate resumption of work so that trade may be restored to its proper channels." They went on to offer their assistance in presenting the grievances of railroad employees to the company and in procuring assurances against the discharge of the strikers. They also appointed a Committee of Ten, who represented the wholesale interests of the city, with one railroad official and a minister added for good measure.

It was already apparent that the men on strike and many citizens viewed the second "citizens' meeting" from very different perspectives. In urging a large turnout for the meeting, the *Burlington Gazette* reported, "the workingmen have called the meeting. They claim their grievances are not understood by the citizens generally and they want to explain them." The paper also noted that the Committee of Ten from the Board of Trade proposed to meet with the

---

64. G. W. Beymer to C. E. Perkins, July 25, 1877, *Ibid.*; C. E. Perkins to Mr. Walker, July 22, 1877, *Ibid.*

65. C. E. Perkins to Robert Harris, July 26, 27, 28, 1877, *Ibid.*; *Burlington Daily Gazette*, July 27, 1877.

Strikers' committee *while* the meeting was going on, to negotiate an end to the difficulties — not at all what the men on strike had in mind.⁶⁶

George Price, a striking engineer, was chosen permanent chairman of the meeting. He called on Robert Donahue, a member of the Board of Trade's Committee of Ten and a wholesale dealer in iron and steel. Donahue argued to the large assemblage that the strike was unwarranted and ill-advised, declaring that labor and capital were not inherently antagonistic. His remarks were drowned in hisses and shouts. Chairman Price took the podium and "spoke excitedly" and with much anger. "I propose to counsel with men who are directly interested and not with outside parties. If they cannot discriminate between actual want and capital, the sooner the crash comes the better [loud applause].... We don't want to advise with outside parties; we haven't asked anybody here to advise us." Other businessmen who were called upon refused to speak, citing "the ungentlemanly way Mr. Donahue had been treated." The meeting was temporarily patched together with a new chairman but finally broke up, with the underlying divisions in the community visible to all.

The next day, July 29, the *Burlington Gazette* declared the meeting "a pronounced failure" that had "rather the effect of widening the breach between the men and the company than of helping to close it." The *Gazette* also noted that those few businessmen who did speak up in sympathy with the striking railroad men "have been attacked in private ... and attempts made to injure them in their business...."⁶⁷

The strikers' solidarity continued to dissolve as divisions widened in their own ranks. Shopmen voted in the late afternoon of July 29 to return to work. Perkins noted to President Harris that "public opinion here in Burlington has finally reached the point where it would not only give us moral but physical support if necessary."⁶⁸ The *Gazette* also took note of the changed mood in the community. There were more "harsh words and angry altercations" on the street. "The citizens are becoming irritated with the interruption of service." By the next day, the strike in Burlington was over.⁶⁹

In Creston the strike began earlier and ended later. The strikers' meeting on July 23 was "quiet and orderly." Resolutions were passed outlining their demands, including a restoration of shopmen's pay to the level of 1873 and of engineers' and firemen's pay to the 1876 levels. A committee was appointed and instructed to meet with strikers in towns on the eastern divisions of the road and to present the demands to management. Crowds in excess of fifty were constantly on hand at the depot to stop incoming trains. A local official

---

66. *Burlington Daily Gazette*, July 27, 1877; *Burlington Hawkeye*, July 27, 1877; Robert Harris to C. E. Perkins, July 28, 1877 (33 1870 3.1), Burlington Archives.

67. *Burlington Daily Gazette*, July 31, 1877.

68. C. E. Perkins to Robert Harris, July 28, 1877, Strike Papers, 1877 (33 1870 3.1) Burlington Archives.

69. *Burlington Daily Gazette*, July 28, 29, 30, 1877; *Burlington Hawkeye*, July 28, 29, 30, 1877.

warned vice-president T. J. Potter that "it would probably be best not to excite them" by sending any further trains, and a roadmaster advised Perkins to send state troops, as "the law and order element is intimidated there." Perkins grew restive with Creston's intransigence on July 30 as the strike moved to a conclusion on the eastern end of the road. He telegraphed threateningly to a handful of Chicago, Burlington & Quincy friends in the town that Creston might find itself "left out, if they wait a little longer." Warning that the town would experience greater harm than the railroad, he added sternly, "I mean just what I say." And later in the day he again telegraphed R. P. Smith, a land dealer, A. D. Temple, a banker, and William Scott, a grain dealer, to say that his patience was nearly exhausted and that "I shall be sorry to see many mechanics owning property in Creston give up their permanent occupations, and I suppose you will." Urging them once more to "make the men see the situation as it is," he warned that "the interest of the community is at stake in this matter." Even as Perkins noted to his Creston confidants that the men in Burlington were returning to work on the assurances offered to them, T. J. Potter warned him that a committee from Creston was proceeding to Burlington with the intention of getting the shopmen and engineers to go out again.

With the strike movement collapsing nationally, Creston strikers from all departments met on July 31 and resolved to end their strike in the same orderly fashion they had begun it and to return to work "in a body." A relieved R. P. Smith telegraphed Perkins that night, "Thank God, Creston breathes again." The strike in Creston ended the next day, August 1, with no visible lines of division among strikers or between the men and the community.[70]

ALTHOUGH THE CHICAGO, BURLINGTON & QUINCY experienced no major labor unrest for the next eleven years, its workers, led particularly by engineers and firemen from western Iowa and from Nebraska, continued to push for equalization of pay and the abolition of classification.[71] Creston entered a period of stagnation and even lost population, while Burlington began another cycle of vigorous growth.

As the Mississippi River towns of Iowa consolidated their grip on the state's jobbing and wholesale trade, agitation for railroad regulation was renewed in the western section of the state. Assertions against the dire effects of railroad monopolies found a ready constituency among owners of small businesses in isolated towns served by a single road, among the "granger

---

70. T. J. Potter to C. E. Perkins, July 24, 1877, Strike Papers, 1877 (33 1870 3.1), Burlington Archives; W. A. Chatterton to T. J. Potter, July 30, 1877, *Ibid.*; J. W. Chapman to C. E. Perkins, July 31, 1877, *Ibid.*; C. E. Perkins to R. P. Smith, A. D. Temple, and William Scott, July 30, 1877, *Ibid.*; R. P. Smith to C. E. Perkins, July 31, 1877, *Ibid.*; T. J. Potter to W. B. Strong, August 1, 1877, *Ibid.*

71. C. H. Salmons, *The Burlington Strike* (Aurora, Ill.: 1889), 29–100, and Donald L. McMurry, *The Great Burlington Strike of 1888: A Case History in Labor Relations* (New York: 1956).

element" of western farmers who felt victimized by both railroad rates and land policies, and increasingly among railroad workers themselves, though their participation in this predominantly agrarian coalition was always more tenuous. As political support for a renewal of mandatory state regulation of railroad rates mounted in early 1888, a Knights of Labor assembly of railroad workers came out vigorously for state regulation, protesting the coercive methods of railroads in forcing employees to sign petitions opposing the legislation and objecting to the habitual threats by railroad corporations to withhold benefits to towns that failed to support the railroads on this issue.[72]

The economic and political solidarity that crossed class lines in communities like Creston and was buttressed by ties of small community life — proximity of residence, property ownership, and participation in social and fraternal organizations — found its most common manifestation during the mid-1880s in the Noble and Holy Order of the Knights of Labor. The Knights articulated an antimonopoly ideology around which a broad class of self-styled "producers" could rally.

Chicago, Burlington & Quincy officials manifested considerable concern over the rapid growth of the Knights in the ranks of their employees. One official from Galesburg indicated that he had heard that the Knights had a "heavy" membership in Creston. "I would not be surprised if such were the case," he went on, "as the farther west we go, the stronger the rolls of these 'Communist' societies seem to be." A local newspaper published by the Republican banker J. B. Harsh estimated that the Knights had 125 members in Creston by the spring of 1885. Master Mechanic C. W. Eckerson believed that one-third of the Q. shopmen were members of the Knights as well. He also reported that the Knights were led by the mayor, an alderman, two justices, a newspaper editor, and "quite a number of the same stripe." Superintendent of Motive Power G. W. Rhodes, in his summary of the investigation of the Knights, noted that politicians, merchants, and petty officials seemed to join the organization for political reasons. He found that laboring men reaped some benefit from such alliances within the Knights; "in the case of any mandates [strikes] they are bolstered by the sympathy of those they aid in politics."[73]

When members of Typographical Union No. 131 struck the *Creston Advertiser* in 1885 because it had employed a scab printer from Kansas City, the Knights of Labor as well as the Railroad Brotherhoods, the Cigarmakers, and the Farmers' Alliance from neighboring townships rallied to their support. The local divisions of the brotherhoods of engineers and firemen proclaimed that "being laboring organizations" they would support the striking printers by boycotting the *Advertiser*. When the striking printers started up their own local

---

72. *Creston Daily Advertiser*, February 11, 1888.

73. *Creston Gazette*, March 30, 1885; R. W. Colville to G. W. Rhodes, August 25, 1885, "Engineers' Grievance Committee Papers, 1885–86" (33 1880 3.1), Burlington Archives; G. W. Rhodes to H. B. Stone, August 25, 1885, *Ibid.*; C. W. Eckerson to G. W. Rhodes, July 23, 1885, *Ibid.*

weekly, *The Workingmen's Advocate*, which rapidly became recognized as the largest "Knights of Labor" newspaper in the state, the railroad brotherhoods declared it their official organ as well.[74]

The publisher of the *Advertiser*, S. A. Brewster, was the object of the strike. He was also the loudest voice in the community decrying the effects of the Chicago, Burlington & Quincy "monopoly" on the city's growth. While vowing to beat the printers—theirs was not a strike of labor against capital, but of labor against labor, he claimed—he argued for labor organizations which would strike for "elevating the laboring classes and for mutual aid and protection and for insurance." He insisted that all citizens would benefit from a restoration of the railroad competition for which he so assiduously worked, but "especially the laboring people as a class."[75]

Brewster poured unflagging energy into his campaign to build an "antimonopoly" coalition that might secure the city's future prosperity. The city was not marked by fundamental class divisions, he asserted with some exaggeration in the midst of his own printers' strike. "All people in this city with but very few exceptions are working people. We have but two or three capitalists. Some of this latter class today class themselves with the laboring people, belong to labor organizations."[76] This apparent classlessness only thinly disguised serious schisms within the community. Not only did the action of the printers alienate Brewster from many laboring men, whom he patronizingly referred to as some of his "best friends," but the boycott of the *Advertiser*, which they initiated and enforced along with their trade union and business allies, polarized the community.

Brewster found unity sadly lacking even among Creston's businessmen and property owners. When a party of Chicago, Burlington & Quincy officials visited the city on a tour of the line in August 1885, the beleaguered publisher bemoaned their cool reception. He quoted the *Ottumwa Democrat* approvingly when it described a meeting of local businessmen that had resolved "to take action relative to the meeting with the officials of the Burlington." By contrast, in Creston, the visiting officials of the railroad encountered no organized committee of businessmen prepared to lay their grievances before them and "ask for redress." In fact, Brewster reported, "the officials were obliged to walk over the city, hunt up the businessmen and talk with them."

Brewster noted that there were at least three groups among Creston's "leading citizens." Some were under obligations to the C. B. & Q. and feared incurring its wrath. Others believed that the proper remedy for their freight rate grievances was through legislation. And, in Brewster's words, those in another group "feel that the proper thing is for us to stand up like men and ask for our rights." Brewster's views were apparently confirmed by a reporter

---

74. *Creston Daily Advertiser*, March 12, 1885; *Creston Daily Gazette*, April 23, 1885.
75. *Creston Daily Advertiser*, March 30, April 21, 1885.
76. *Ibid.*, December 14, 1885.

for the Chicago Inter-Ocean who had been commissioned to "write up" the city in a half-column and reportedly left in disgust after a few days, declaring that he had never seen a city of Creston's size whose businessmen and property owners were so sharply divided.[77]

If the business stagnation and the high freight rates suffered by Creston in the mid-1880s left her business leaders demoralized and divided, expediency required that they defend the interest of the railroad workers whose incomes underpinned the city's economy. In defense of his record of support for the interests of the "laboring class" S. A. Brewster recalled that he and other businessmen had actively supported the "railroad boys" in their strike against the C. B. & Q. in 1877. He wrote, "Their interests and our own are identical. And at any time in the future as we would have done in the past should the employees on the Q. either in the shop, yard, offices or on the road strike for better wages, which we believe would be nothing more than they deserve, so long as they made a square and honorable stand for their request, they would find the *Advertiser* to their back and doing all it could to advance their interest."[78]

ON FEBRUARY 26, 1888, engineers and firemen on the entire length of the Burlington system walked off the job to enforce their demand for equalization of pay and for an end to classification of engineers. Although the strike was remarkably solid from one end of the line to the other, there were important differences in the patterns of strike participation and in the community support the strikers generated in various division towns.

In Creston a large and vocal segment of the Creston community rallied to the support of the strikers, as it had in the previous strike. All five of the city's newspapers supported the men on strike (none of the newspapers in Burlington did).[79] At the urging of the men on strike, two committees of Creston citizens complained, in a petition to the State Railroad Commission, that the Chicago, Burlington & Quincy was operating its trains with incompetent men. The first petition was from seven local physicians; the second, from thirty-nine citizens, almost all in the retail trade. The commission held two days of hearings in the community and sustained the citizens' charge.[80]

At the end of the first week of the strike, Mayor F. J. Taylor, who was under intense pressure from the railroad, hired special police to assist in "maintaining the peace," in spite of the absence of disorder of any kind. On March 26, thirty-six of the special police struck, prompting the company to augment its own force of Pinkerton detectives. At a special session of the city council,

---

77. *Ibid.*, August 12, 21, 1885.

78. *Ibid.*, March 30, 1885.

79. "Lists of Newspapers," Strike Papers, 1888 (33 1880 9.11), Burlington Archives.

80. "Testimony Regarding the Strike before the Iowa Board of Railway Commissioners," Strike Papers, 1888 (33 1880 9.11), Burlington Archives.

Alderman John McCaffery, who was a leading member of the Knights of Labor and the Union Labor party, "arraigned the railroad company severely for inciting violence by the importation of Pinkerton toughs." Superintendent Brown of the railroad's Iowa lines was present for the special council session and warned that he was authorized by President Perkins to notify the city that if it failed to protect the road's loyal employees, the company would close its shops in Creston and move its workers to Burlington. "These men," he asserted, "are going to run engines and fire engines on the C. B. & Q. and it is for the city and council of Creston to say whether they will drive out forty, fifty or possibly a hundred families or whether they will extend to them proper protection." The superintendent's warning notwithstanding, the Creston City Council voted, with but one dissent, to instruct the mayor to notify Division Superintendent Duggan that he must keep his police force strictly on company grounds.[81]

The next day, the *Advertiser*'s editorial page boiled with indignation "at again having this emaciated old skeleton drawn from the corporation closet and flaunted in their faces because they dare to have independent ideas which are not in sympathy with the great Q. monopoly." The editor recounted the number of times since 1877 that Creston had been threatened with the removal of its shops because it supported strikers, or appointed committees to investigate competing lines, or demanded lower freight or passenger rates.

> Now because some citizens dared to petition the governor for an investigation of the competency of the men running the engines, they are threatened by these Q. bulldozers, and lastly because our citizens sympathize with our *resident, property-owning, taxpaying, striking* brotherhood men and because some of the toughs the Q. has picked up to take the places of the strikers have been thumped for their insolence upon the street, by some of the strikers, the Q. cries that the city is not protecting its new men and property and threatens to close its shops here and remove the workmen to Burlington.
>
> Bah on such Balderdash. We are tired of it. It has retarded permanent investments and improvements in our city long enough. Our citizens owe the C. B. & Q. nothing.[82]

For several months the prospect of the Chicago, Burlington & Quincy removing its shops from the city was a lively source of controversy. Numbers of towns in western and central Iowa petitioned the C. B. & Q. affirming their unshakeable loyalty to the road (in contrast to Creston) and requesting to be the beneficiaries of the threatened relocation. In spite of the threat, there were continuing manifestations of community support for the strikers, including boycotts against merchants who opposed the strike.[83]

---

81. *Creston Daily Advertiser*, April 3, 1888.

82. *Ibid.*, April 4, 1888; some evidence of a similar antimonopoly basis for community support for striking railroad workers in Sedalia, Missouri, in 1885 is offered by Michael J. Cassity, "Modernization and Social Crisis," 47.

83. *Creston Daily Advertiser*, August 21, September 4, December 20, 1888.

Burlington, however, showed virtually no evidence of popular sympathy for the men on strike. The striking railroad men kept largely to themselves. Adequately supplied with willing conductors, brakemen, and shopmen to guard company property, the local division superintendent, O. E. Stewart, did not have to rely on the city force for protection. The majority of the new men were recruited locally.[84]

Shortly after the inauguration of the strike, Superintendent Brown informed the *Burlington Hawkeye* that if the other divisions of the road "were as well off as the Eastern Iowa Division, all passenger trains and some freights would be running."[85] Throughout the first month of the strike the *Hawkeye* published a barrage of editorials and letters condemning the strikers. They reserved particular venom for the switchmen's sympathy strike in late March and the "insane demand" that the men should "assume the right to dictate to the owners whom they should employ."[86] The bitterness engendered by the strike was expressed in an exchange of letters between "A Businessman" and "A Lady Reader of all the Papers." Replying to his accusations that the striking men were trying to "cripple the road" and place a tax on the public, the lady reader challenged the businessman to have the moral courage to reveal his identity, and alluding to the possibility of a boycott, she suggested that "we would like to form his acquaintance; we would like to know whether he wears brass buttons or flour dust on his coat, or threads and ravelings from a dry goods store." She closed her letter with the wish that he and his business might "rest in peace."[87]

The editor of the *Hawkeye* waded into the fray by reminding readers of Martin Irons, the "dictator" of the Southwest strikes, "who is now tending a peanut stand in St. Louis." The newspaper saved its harshest reprimands for Burlington's sister city, Creston, which "has been conducting itself in a disgraceful manner from the first."[88] Echoing the words of President Perkins, the *Hawkeye* urged communities to welcome the new Chicago, Burlington & Quincy employees "who have come into our family. . . . It should be understood by all that these men are here to stay with us and become part of us." Along with Pinkerton detectives, strikebreakers brought into Burlington from outside the community were housed temporarily in the company hospital, which was dubbed by the strikers the "Casino." Its inmates were visited by a welcoming committee of prominent businessmen and loyal trainmen.[89]

---

84. O. E. Stewart, "Strike Notes" (33 1880 9.83), Burlington Archives; "Clippings from Burlington Papers" (+ 33 1880 9.22), *Ibid.*

85. *Burlington Hawkeye*, February 28, 1888.

86. *Ibid.*, March 30, 1888.

87. *Ibid.*, March 29, 30, April 1, 1888.

88. *Ibid.*, April 3, 14, 1888.

89. *Ibid.*, April 6, 18, 1888.

As the strike wore on through the summer months and into the fall, Creston opinion leaders feared for the "moral and social scars" of the strike. The editor of the *Advertiser* renewed his agitation for making Creston a major manufacturing and wholesaling center. He reported a reassuring conversation with General Manager Stone during the latter's tour of the Chicago, Burlington & Quincy system in late June 1888. Stone had expressed the company's continued interest in Creston, despite concern for the manifest lack of protection for loyal railroad men. "So long as things move on in Creston as they are now moving there is no cause for any such removal."[90]

Early in January 1889 a special committee of the Brotherhood of Locomotive Engineers negotiated an unsatisfactory end to the strike. The terms of the settlement were bitterly denounced by a number of Creston engineers as an outrageous sellout. The company declared itself willing to accept but did not feel obliged to honor applications for work from the old engineers and firemen. One hundred men on the Western Iowa Division at Creston reapplied; only fifty-three in Burlington did so. None were rehired in either town.[91]

With the strike settled, leading citizens turned to the task of healing the wounds opened during the conflict. The *Creston Daily Advertiser* had already argued that those who had taken the places of the strikers must be accepted as residents of the community, "to mingle as such in our social and business life." Looking ahead, the newspaper urged citizens to accept the results of the strike. "Let the scars made in the heat of the conflict be healed, let the hatchet be buried." The crucial matter was Creston's future welfare and prosperity, which should occupy all its citizens' attention "to the exclusion of personal bickerings or unavailing discussion of past events." And discussion did turn to other topics — the possibility of another railroad through Creston, the prospect that the C. B. & Q. would expand its shops in the city to construct locomotives, and the general "building up" of the city as the "future metropolis of southwestern Iowa."[92]

By the early months of 1889, the Chicago, Burlington & Quincy Railroad was well on its way to creating a tractable work force. The men who had struck in Burlington and Creston were barred from future employment on the road and with few exceptions left the communities to search for other work. With them went the economic and social force of brotherhood organization in the communities. Most of the new men joined the Burlington Voluntary Relief Association, a company-sponsored insurance scheme designed to replace the shattered brotherhoods. This was but one of several organizations in Creston that formed in the wake of the strike to harmonize class interests.

Industrial peace revived Creston's urban ambitions. Community solidarity was as much the basis for the realization of those ambitions as it had ever

---

90. *Creston Daily Advertiser*, July 3, 1888.
91. "Lists of Enginemen who struck," Strike Papers, 1888 (33 1880 9.51), Burlington Archives.
92. *Creston Daily Advertiser*, March 2, 1888, January 7, 16, 1889.

been. Railroad men and their purchasing power still provided the economic foundations of the city's commercial trade. But now this community solidarity led to accommodation rather than resistance to the C. B. & Q. In spite of lingering antimonopoly sentiment, Creston's leading citizens and her railroad men identified their interests more with those of the railroad than in the days before the strike. The "recent unpleasantness," as it was referred to, and Creston's heritage of insolence to the railroad monopoly were put aside for the time being. Illusory though Creston's ambitions may have been, the town pursued them with a diehard pragmatism that sought to emulate the social and economic development bequeathed by historical and geographical forces to her rival, Burlington. Such pragmatism could again conceivably lead to sympathy for her workers in another confrontation with the distant railroad corporation. But it would come only when an organized and assertive local labor movement demanded it. In the absence of an effective labor movement, the community pursued other alliances in behalf of its own development.

RAILROAD DIVISION TOWNS were a particular species of the genus of industrial communities. They had common characteristics because of their role within the railroad service network. Differences among them were a function of the differences in the timing and pattern of their settlement, the extent of prerailroad economic development and their ability to transcend the economic limitations of servicing railroad operations. These differences produced differences in class structure and contrasting community behavior in response to the conflicts between railroad labor and capital.

Railroad division towns have been classed as either market cities or railroad towns. The analysis of Burlington and Creston suggests how structural differences help to explain differences in the way these communities responded to industrial conflict. In general, market cities, which were older and more economically diversified and which enjoyed comparatively steady growth and a more unified elite, supported railroad capital. Railroad towns, which were newer communities whose economies were more concentrated in servicing railroad operations, whose growth was less stable, and whose elites were smaller and more divided, more often supported their fellow citizens who were railroad men.

Even in communities that provided substantial support for striking railroad men there was an underlying ambivalence which surfaced in the face of the strikers' defeat. Long-term economic growth inevitably meant alliances with railroad corporations, even though, in the short run, communities might find it necessary to support the class interests of politically and economically powerful railroad workers.

"Producers' consciousness" and agitation against the railroad's "monopoly" power over rates and land allowed residents of these railroad towns to see the world divided into two classes—producers and monopolists. But the distinction between class and community interest was blurred. Producerism masked sharpening class divisions. To the extent that communities supported the more narrowly defined "class interest" of railroad men against their corporate managers, that support was lent in the name of "community interest." But when railroad men lost their power to enforce their class interest as community interest (because of lost strikes, the blacklist, elimination of the brotherhoods, and migration out of the community), that community interest resurfaced in another form. Producers' consciousness could also applaud the initiatives of *productive* capital when it promised to benefit the community through the construction of new facilities, timely donations to public institutions, and a reduction of freight rates.

The instincts of economic self-preservation dictated different responses to railroad strikes in different situations. Smaller railroad towns were no less "modern" or market-oriented than their larger and more diversified competitors. The structure of their economies and the barriers to further growth shaped their perception of their interests. The plight of victimized railroad men was readily fused with the frustrated ambitions of town promoters in an antimonopoly coalition that promoted progress, independence, and community solidarity.

The defeat of the C. B. & Q. strikers in 1888 and the introduction of a labor force loyal to the railroad corporation were important elements in the disintegration of that antimonopoly coalition in towns such as Creston. In again welcoming the proffered patronage of the railroad and in reaffirming their own urban ambitions, the people of Creston found that their differences with the railroad, which had been so manifest during the recent strike, seemed to dissolve. Just as citizens of Burlington welcomed their new "scab" neighbors, the people of Creston came around to "burying the hatchet" with theirs. In so doing they inaugurated a new era in railroad-community relations, which was quickened by their metropolitan ambitions.

BIBLIOGRAPHICAL NOTE

The literature on railroads will be included in the note following the next essay. The topic of town development has seen some of the best work in Iowa history. Particularly noteworthy is the work of Timothy Mahoney on Mississippi River towns: *River Towns in the Great West: The Structure of Provincial Urbanization in the Midwest, 1820–1870* (New York, 1990); "Urban History in a Regional Context: River Towns on the Upper Mississippi, 1840–1860," *Journal of American History* 72 (1985), 318–39; "Down in Davenport: A Regional Perspective on Antebellum Town Economic Development," *Annals of Iowa* 50 (1990), 451–74; and "Down in Davenport: The Social Response of Antebellum Elites to Regional Urbanization," *Annals of Iowa* 50 (1990), 593–622. On Mississippi River towns, one should not overlook the beautiful and insightful work of John W. Reps; his most recent book is *Cities of the Mississippi: Nineteenth-Century Images of Urban Development* (Columbia, MO, 1994). In addition, although I have generally not cited unpublished material, I cannot resist citing here Loren Nelson Horton, "Town Planning, Growth, and Architecture in Selected Mississippi River Towns of Iowa, 1833–1860" (Ph.D. diss., University of Iowa, 1978).

In the same two issues of the *Annals of Iowa* in which Timothy Mahoney's work on Davenport appears, William Silag analyzes the effects of railroad development on town development in three counties in northwestern Iowa and assesses the degree of economic opportunity available to individuals in Sioux City: "The Conquest of the Hinterland: Railroads and Capitalists in Northwest Iowa after the Civil War," *Annals of Iowa* 50 (1990), 475–506; "Opportunity and Achievement in Northwest Iowa, 1860–1900," *Annals of Iowa* 50 (1990), 623–49. See also Silag's "Citizens and Strangers: Geographic Mobility in the Sioux City Region, 1860–1900," *Great Plains Quarterly* 2 (1982), 168–83; and "Gateway to the Grasslands: Sioux City and the Missouri River Frontier," *Western Historical Quarterly* 14 (1983), 397–414. See also H. Roger Grant, "Iowa's New Communities: Townsite Promotion along the Chicago Great Western Railway's Omaha Extension," *Upper Midwest History* 2 (1982), 53–63. Historical geographers have much to teach historians about town development. See, for example, the various works of John C. Hudson, such as "A Location Theory for Rural Settlement," *Annals of the Association of American Geographers* 59 (1969), 365–81; and *Plains Country Towns* (Minneapolis, 1985); and Michael P. Conzen, "Local Migration Systems in Nineteenth-Century Iowa," *Geographical Review* 64 (1974), 339–61.

For subsequent urban development, Lawrence H. Larsen, "Urban Iowa One Hundred Years Ago," *Annals of Iowa* 49 (1988), 445–61, used census data to provide an interesting portrait of urban life in Iowa's seven largest cities in 1880. Maureen Ogle, in two outstanding essays, offered a comparative perspective on three smaller Iowa cities — Boone, Iowa City, and Marshalltown — to explain why such cities developed municipal services: "Redefining 'Public' Water Supplies, 1870–1890: A Study of Three Iowa Cities," *Annals of Iowa* 50 (1990), 507–30; and "Efficiency and System in Municipal Services: Fire Departments in Iowa, 1870–1890," *Annals of Iowa* 50 (1991), 841–60.

The history of Iowa's working class and labor unions has been slighted until recently, when a spate of work has emerged, especially on meatpacking workers. The most comprehensive work available, based on the monumental collection of oral histories from the Iowa Labor History Oral Project of the Iowa Federation of Labor, AFL-CIO, housed at the State Historical Society of Iowa, Iowa City, is Shelton Stromquist, *Solidarity and Survival: An Oral History of Iowa Labor in the Twentieth Century* (Iowa City, 1993). Ralph Scharnau offered a fascinating narrative of the impact of one of Iowa's earliest labor organizations on one Iowa community in "Workers and Politics: The Knights of Labor in Dubuque, Iowa, 1885–1890," *Annals of Iowa* 48 (1987), 353–77; then he extended his reach across the state in "The Knights of Labor in Iowa," *Annals of Iowa* 50 (1991), 861–91, and across time in "Workers, Unions, and Workplaces in Dubuque, 1830–1990," *Annals of Iowa* 52 (1993), 50–78.

On meatpacking, Wilson Warren has, over time, provided a nearly complete history of workers at Morrell's Ottumwa plant; see *Annals of*

Iowa issues for Fall 1984, Spring 1992, and Summer 1995. Warren also offered a valuable account of a rare period of cooperation between farm and labor organizations in "The 'People's Century' in Iowa: Coalition-Building among Farm and Labor Organizations, 1945–1950," *Annals of Iowa* 49 (1988), 371–93. For other important work on Iowa meatpacking workers, see Roger Horowitz, "'It Wasn't a Time to Compromise': The Unionization of Sioux City's Packinghouses, 1937–1942," *Annals of Iowa* 50 (1990), 241–68; Dennis Deslippe, "'We Had an Awful Time with Our Women': Iowa's United Packinghouse Workers of America, 1945–1975," *Journal of Women's History* 5 (1993), 10–32; Bruce Fehn, "'Chickens Come Home to Roost': Industrial Organization, Seniority, and Gender Conflict in the United Packinghouse Workers of America, 1956–1966," *Labor History* 34 (1993), 324–41; idem, "'The Only Hope We Had': United Packinghouse Workers Local 46 and the Struggle for Racial Equality in Waterloo, Iowa, 1948–1960," *Annals of Iowa* 54 (1995), 185–201; and the forthcoming collection of essays by Dennis Deslippe, Bruce Fehn, Deborah Fink, Mark Grey, Rick Halpern, Roger Horowitz, Peter Rachleff, Paul Street, and Wilson Warren, edited by Shelton Stromquist and Marvin Bergman.

The attention to Iowa's meatpacking workers is gratifying, but it would be good to see some attention to other Iowa workers as well; they are pretty much overlooked. There are good narrative accounts of several working-class events. On Kelly's Army's trek across Iowa in 1894, see the two-part article by Carlos Schwantes in the *Annals of Iowa* 46 (1982/83), 487–509, 567–92. On coal miners, see Dorothy Schwieder, *Black Diamonds: Life and Work in Iowa's Coal Mining Communities* (Ames, 1983); Dorothy Schwieder, Joseph Hraba, and Elmer Schwieder, *Buxton: Work and Racial Equality in a Coal Mining Community* (Ames, 1987); and Merle Davis, "Horror at Lost Creek: A 1902 Coal Mine Disaster," *Palimpsest* 71 (1990), 98–117. On migrant workers, see Terry Ofner, "The 19th-Century Harvest Hand," *Palimpsest* 70 (1989), 76–92; and Merle Davis, "'You Were Just One of the Unfortunate Ones,'" *Palimpsest* 70 (1989), 96–102.

9

Iowa's Struggle for State Railroad Control

JOHN LAURITZ LARSON

Whereas Shelton Stromquist investigated the relationship between railroads and the development and social structure of Iowa communities, John Larson's essay addresses the struggle between railroads and the state itself over railroad regulation. The importance of railroads for Iowa's development has long been recognized. But historians have traditionally seen railroad companies as prime representatives of the worst of Gilded Age America, with their "robber barons" depriving farmers of their livelihoods as those heroic farmers fought back valiantly against the superior power and wealth of the corporate villains to restore justice to economic relationships. Recently some business historians, led by Maury Klein, have tried to rehabilitate the reputation of at least some of those railroad companies and their leaders. John Larson, drawing on that work as well as that of social and cultural historians, such as Robert Wiebe, who have assessed the responses made by rural and small-town people to the threats to local control posed by the growth of large bureaucratic institutions after the Civil War, here presents a balanced view of the expansion of rail networks and the struggle to regulate them in Iowa.

THE ORDEAL OF RAILROAD REGULATION grew out of hundreds of clashes between local commercial and political interests and the advancing national railroad systems. A recurrent problem from before the Great Rebellion to the First World War, the American railroad question produced a swamp of economic confusion and popular hostility apparently without bottom. First the pro rata movements of the East, then the Granger outbreak in the Middle West reflected local outrage at the introduction of new competition that was favored by long-distance railroad rates. Unfortunately, local efforts such as the mid-

---

Excerpts reprinted, with some editing by the author for continuity, by permission of Harvard Business School Press from *Bonds of Enterprise: John Murray Forbes and Western Development in America's Railway Age,* by John Lauritz Larson (Boston: Division of Research, Harvard Business School, 1984), 111–207. Copyright © 1984 by the President and Fellows of Harvard College.

western Granger laws usually failed to produce the desired results because the problem derived from a multitude of technical complaints that varied from town to town throughout the railroad network. The sum of these complaints was an incoherent tangle that had to be adjudicated either by the marketplace (however clumsy) or by legislative fiat. Neither option appealed unequivocally to a free, ambitious, democratic, and capitalistic people.[1]

By the last third of the nineteenth century the railroads had outgrown the structures of local government and all traditions of local economic control. As corporations combined into large interstate systems, frustrated reformers turned to the federal government for instruments of protection. Such an exercise of federal power was condemned by railroad managers as dangerous innovation, but the business structures themselves were just as new. In 1887 Congress opened a new era by passing the Interstate Commerce Act, but federal regulation did not supplant state and local control. Local tempers continued to flare. State legislatures such as Iowa's struggled to perfect a system of railroad regulation that guaranteed the public interest. Each time the agitation necessarily focused on corporate power, not the technical complaints of one shipper against the next. Not surprisingly, the resulting regulations often failed to improve the transport market, and they sometimes made it worse. Nevertheless, the ordeal of regulation was a necessary step in the passage of Americans through the railway age. It set aside forever the unchallenged liberalism of the middle decades of the nineteenth century and ushered in a new age of business, philosophy, and social science.[2]

The complexity of the struggle of Gilded Age Iowans against the power of the railroad corporations can be seen most clearly by personalizing the story — as nineteenth-century participants were wont to do. In general terms, the blessings of modern transportation were clear, even to hot-tempered Iowa farmers; but each individual consumer, voter, taxpayer sought his fortune in a particular place, usually served by a single railroad, with a history in that location for fair (or shady) dealing. That specificity of experience informed the kind of popular agitation that fueled campaigns for railroad control. One such particular railroad was the Chicago, Burlington & Quincy, which built and operated the Burlington and Missouri River Rail Road across southern Iowa. The B&MR itself had a brief history independent of the CB&Q, and that history had brought local promoters and politicians into connection with

---

1. On the localism behind regulation and federal agitation, see Lee Benson, *Merchants, Farmers, and Railroads: Railroad Regulation and New York Politics, 1850–1887* (Cambridge, Mass., 1955); and George H. Miller, *Railroads and the Granger Laws* (Madison, Wis., 1971).

2. See Alfred D. Chandler, Jr., *The Visible Hand: The Managerial Revolution in American Business* (Cambridge, Mass., 1977); Glen Porter, *The Rise of Big Business, 1860–1910* (New York, 1973); Samuel P. Hays, *The Response to Industrialism, 1885–1914* (Chicago, 1957); and Robert H. Wiebe, *The Search for Order, 1877–1912* (New York, 1967). James Willard Hurst, *Law and the Conditions of Freedom in the Nineteenth-Century United States* (Madison, Wis., 1956), details this trend in government-business relations. See also James A. Ward, "Image and Reality: The Railway–Corporate State Metaphor," *Business History Review* 55 (1981), 491–516.

John Murray Forbes, a Boston railroad developer, his investors, lawyers, and managers, who "rescued" the faltering line just before the Civil War, built it across frontier Iowa in the late 1860s, and directed its (sometimes abusive) relations with local farmers and merchants throughout the era of state regulation. Their particular story illustrates not just the structural outlines of clashing interests and market forces but also the intensity of frustration and the depth of feeling that accompanied the struggle for railroad regulation.[3]

IN MAY 1865, barely a month after the end of the Civil War, Major General Quincy A. Gilmore asked John Murray Forbes if he would build a railroad on the sea islands off South Carolina. Forbes responded with a firm negative: "I hope my labors in the way of railroad building are done," he explained, "having been one of the pioneers in such enterprises, and being now entitled to a rest." But he urged the general to press forward his scheme before the government of South Carolina could be reinstated and the army's jurisdiction curtailed. Reconstruction for Forbes was the act of forcibly bringing the South into harmony with the industrial integration and progressive outlook now favored in the North, and no procedural stumbling blocks, like the resurgence of stubborn local democracy, should be allowed to bar the way. Throughout the Reconstruction era Forbes begged his wartime friends not to split the Republican party by intrigue and plotting, because "upon the unity and cohesion" of that party depended the "successful restoration of industry and order for years to come."[4]

In May 1866, a little over a year after the signing of the peace, Senator James W. Grimes rose in the U.S. Senate to denounce the continued proliferation of federal agencies. "During the war," he lectured, "we drew to ourselves here, as the Federal Government, authority which had been considered doubtful by all, and denied by many of the statesmen of this country." Grimes reminded his colleagues that the extraordinary powers exercised in war were justified only by the state of emergency: "That time," he thundered, "has ceased and ought to cease." The only honorable course for the victors, according to Grimes, was to go back to "the original condition of things, and allow the States to take care of themselves." For Senator Grimes, Reconstruction was an act of restoration. He did not acknowledge what men like John Murray Forbes believed was the primary truth in the Civil War: that the consolidation of power to and the administration of progress from the center was the meaning of the victory. Between Forbes and Grimes lay the great unsettled issues of the American Civil War.[5]

---

3. See *Bonds of Enterprise*, chapters 3–4.

4. John Murray Forbes (hereafter cited as JMF) to Quincy A. Gilmore, 21 May 1865; JMF to William Pitt Fessenden, 13 April 1868; in *Letters of John Murray Forbes (Supplementary)*, ed. Sarah Forbes Hughes, 3 vols. (Boston, 1905), 3:17, 113.

5. James W. Grimes, Speech in the U.S. Senate, 8 May 1866, in William Salter, *The Life of James W. Grimes* (New York, 1876), 292–93.

For more than three decades Forbes had tried to bring order to his changing world, first in a small commission house at Canton, then in ever expanding railroad lines, and finally in the government of the nation. Despite his addiction to conservative, paternalistic postures, Forbes's successes depended on emerging liberal systems of business and government. His personal interpretation of the war left him a thorough nationalist, and he feared any return to antebellum ways. Unrepentant Southerners naturally would seek to reverse the outcome of the war by a return to states' rights heresies; and if loyal Republicans like James W. Grimes could relapse so completely, there was much to be feared in the West as well. The Republican party's work was unfinished. Forbes envisioned his party as an army of occupation not only in the South but in the house of government itself. "We owe it to the living and the dead," he wrote in 1868, "to keep together until we have absolutely secured the fruits of our dearly bought victories."[6]

It was to watch and assist in this continuing revolution that John Murray Forbes "retired" once more from active business. Ironically it was business, not politics, that brought the great questions back into focus in the postwar years. The hegemony of the Republicans stifled debate and turned the electoral process into a factional exercise that corrupted partisans and in time repulsed men like Forbes. At the same time, ideological issues gave way to bread-and-butter complaints emanating from the economic distortions of the war and its aftermath. Outside the South, two issues transcended partisan quarreling: currency deflation and railroad regulation. On the money question there was no simple, clear division among men, but the railroad question resolved itself into a challenge by the advocates of localism to the encroachments of national interests.[7]

The public vehicle of protest in the postwar struggle for railroad control was a farmers' movement called the Grange. Men like Forbes called it agrarian reaction, but the Grangers often were inspired and led by local merchants who were threatened by emerging national markets. Remembering with James W. Grimes the reservations they had about the party of Lincoln, western farmers and local moguls rose up in the early 1870s to defend the ideals of the early American republic. By now the story of Forbes, the Iowans, and the Burlington Route was but a single example of a larger phenomenon that was regional in scope and so complex in nature that no contemporary understood the problem well. Forbes could not fathom the West's devotion to antiquated theories of business and government while the Iowans only dimly perceived that they had too great a stake in the new age to go back to "original conditions."

---

6. JMF to William Pitt Fessenden, 23 May 1868, in *Letters and Recollections of John Murray Forbes,* ed. Sarah Forbes Hughes, 2 vols. (Boston, 1899), 2:165.

7. For economic issues, see Robert P. Sharkey, *Money, Class, and Party* (Baltimore, 1959); Irwin Unger, *The Greenback Era* (Princeton, 1964); and Walter T. K. Nugent, *Money and American Society, 1865–1877* (New York, 1968). For politics, see Richard Jensen, *The Winning of the Midwest* (Chicago, 1971); and Paul Kleppner, *The Cross of Culture* (New York, 1970).

THE PROBLEM with "original conditions" was that they belonged to a preindustrial, prerailroad world. By the end of the Civil War the shape of American business and society had been irreversibly altered by three decades of railroad development, and the return of peace brought an explosion of new construction in the West that would reach the Pacific Ocean before the decade's end. Adam Smith's eighteenth-century model of merchant capitalism still supplied the language of political economy for most practical-minded Americans, but the conditions of trade scarcely resembled the markets of England ninety years before. Railroads had brought isolated markets into competition with each other in ways that local entrepreneurs were powerless to address. At the same time, competition between carriers in the railroad network was governed, not by commodities markets, but by the capacity of the system and the demand for transportation. Competition—the "invisible hand" that supposedly regulated Smithian markets—now threatened local enterprise all across the railroad system while it seemed to encourage the railroad's assumption of monopoly powers. Railroads were a centralizing force in the American economy, and by the end of the war it was clear that something was "wrong" with the laws of trade.

The evolution of economic language itself made it hard to respond to the changing situation. For example, back in the 1840s railroad transportation universally was seen as an "artificial" advantage in the commercial environment. Western boosters like the editor of the *Burlington Hawk-Eye* confidently claimed that these "artificial means of prosperity" would complement and preserve the natural advantages of their own commercial centers. But progressive entrepreneurs like Forbes dedicated their energies to eliminating just those barriers of time, space, and physical geography that defined the "natural" commercial network. By 1865 this sense of conscious intervention in economic geography had been lost among railroad men. They saw the railroad system as a natural environment in its own right, obeying natural laws of trade. Those who sought to defend the priority of accidental geographical location or the old river routes now were charged with "artificially" obstructing progress. This adaptation of old language by the forces of change rendered traditional economic rights incoherent in the postwar world.[8]

As a merchant, John Murray Forbes had been raised to believe in the natural laws of trade. He easily transferred his theories from foreign commerce to his new railroad enterprises. However, few merchants and farmers at the

---

8. *Burlington Daily Telegraph*, 5 Jan. and 2 Feb. 1852, quoted in Richard C. Overton, *Burlington West: A Colonization History of the Burlington Railroad* (Cambridge, Mass., 1941), 52, 57; Minutes of Directors Meeting, 2 Feb. 1852, Burlington & Missouri River Rail Road Records, Chicago, Burlington & Quincy Railroad Archives, Newberry Library, Chicago (hereafter cited as CB&Q-Newberry); G. D. R. Boyd, "Sketches of History and Incidents Connected with the Settlement of Wapello County," *Annals of Iowa*, first ser., no. 6 (1868), 186. For a careful analysis of this intellectual reversal in its economic and legal contexts, see Morton J. Horowitz, *The Transformation of American Law, 1780–1860* (Cambridge, Mass., 1977); and Hurst, *Law and the Conditions of Freedom*.

local level in the West were prepared to embrace all the changes wrought by the transportation revolution. For Forbes, new developments were inevitable and resistance was futile. Local western interests saw the same developments as corrupt and threatening to their economic independence. It was this contrast of perspective that caused B&MR Treasurer John N. Denison to defend rate discrimination at Burlington as the "fate of all western cities and towns." To the towns this fate was a "return to serfdom."[9]

During the 1850s, the trunk lines of eastern railroads had met at Chicago, then feeders radiated into the rich farming districts to the north, west, and south of that city. Although the first rails to the Mississippi fed produce into the downstream trade, the superior facilities at Chicago were already reversing that flow by 1861. To capture the bulk agricultural business, the railroads built grain elevators at convenient collection points, often creating new towns for the purpose. Chicago grain merchants pioneered the bulk elevator, ran rail spurs directly to the docks, devised automatic systems for loading freight cars and steamships, and implemented uniform systems of grading, pricing, and warehouse receipts.[10]

For a host of smaller towns in the Mississippi Valley the success of Chicago was a mixed blessing. Prairie towns in Illinois and Iowa river ports like Dubuque, Clinton, Davenport, and Burlington all entertained visions of their growing importance in the railroad network. Unprepared for the streamlined integration of the Chicago market, most of these centers found their own growth quickly stunted by rates and services that made Chicago more attractive to interior shippers. By offering more attractive rates than the hometown buyers, Chicago railroad agents were soon in a position to dictate terms to the interior as well. The legitimate advantages of the commercial system through Chicago brought powerful examples of centralization and integration with eastern markets to the heart of the agricultural Midwest. The outlines of the new system were evident when the war closed the Mississippi River in 1861; the absence of meaningful river competition during the war allowed the rapid consolidation of this power and opened the door to monopolistic abuses.[11]

---

9. John N. Denison to Henry Coffin, 31 Jan. 1862, in Box 5D4.1, CB&Q-Newberry. For the first appearance of such dislocations, see Benson, *Merchants, Farmers, and Railroads.*

10. Miller, *Railroads,* 9 (and chap. 1 generally); John F. Stover, *History of the Illinois Central Railroad* (New York, 1975), 71–79; Belcher, *Rivalry,* 102–3, 150, 171; Albert Fishlow, *American Railroads and the Transformation of the Ante-Bellum Economy* (Cambridge, Mass., 1965), 275–98. Miller points out that the *diversion* of established trade was not significant, but that almost all of the *new* commerce in the fast-growing valley was carried through Chicago. See Wyatt W. Belcher, *The Economic Rivalry between St. Louis and Chicago* (New York, 1947), 23–24; George Rogers Taylor, *The Transportation Revolution, 1815–1860* (New York, 1951), 389; and John G. Clark, *The Grain Trade in the Old Northwest* (Urbana, Ill., 1966), 264–78.

11. According to Miller, *Railroads,* 12, the process of "refinement and rationalization almost always meant loss of local control." For restrictions on the wartime river trade, see Belcher, *Rivalry,* chaps. 8 and 9.

The central element in the railroads' power to manipulate the flow of trade was the rate-making process, yet the "science" of rate making was makeshift at best. Overall levels and average rates meant nothing to particular shippers; it was the relative structure of rates that mattered. Dozens of variables influenced the rate on any class of freight at each station on the line, and freight agents were expected to adjust the published schedule of tariffs whenever necessary to maximize revenues at their stations. High fixed costs called for increased volume to spread these costs more widely. Because terminal and handling charges did not vary with the length of trip, short hauls were substantially more expensive per mile. Interregional "through traffic" passed at far lower rates than local freight in order to compete at distant markets. Seasonal fluctuations and a chronic imbalance between bulk agricultural exports and compact manufactured imports resulted in periodic car shortages followed by underemployment of equipment throughout the system. Finally, the presence of rail or water competition at any terminal pressed rates downward, while single-service "way points" were charged all that "the traffic would bear." Given the circumstances, railroad freight agents quoted charges that varied wildly.[12]

Even a perfect rate structure would have seemed unfair to the western shippers because the objectives of the railroad network were different from those of local producers. Rationalization of a national market necessarily discriminated between primary and secondary centers of trade. Furthermore, the laws of supply and demand, as they bore on the transportation business itself, often contradicted the behavior of commodities markets. High demand for transportation resulting from a good harvest, for example, made transportation dear just when the price of grain was lowest. On the other hand, crop shortages that raised grain prices also raised the price of transportation, except at the most competitive points, because carriers had to recover fixed costs on the reduced volume. At such times more expensive corn would bear the higher charge. If this was unfair to certain captive shippers, it was the price to be paid for large regional advantages in the new transport system. Unable to store their services or withdraw from the market, railroad managers followed shifting rules of competition that baffled the shipping public—and many railroad men as well.

These serious problems were aggravated by ignorance of the real cost of transportation by rail for any given service. In their struggle to show an overall profit most railroad men disregarded questions of equity in the rate structure. Citing the time-honored principle, "what the traffic will bear," they constantly intervened to manipulate the supply of traffic and the rate it would bear through monopolistic agreements with grain merchants, wholesalers, manufacturers, and steamboat companies. Collusive agreements among the railroads to divide

---

12. For a brilliant treatment of the rate-making process and its historical development, see Miller, *Railroads,* 16–41.

the business further curtailed competition. By the late 1860s these practices resulted in wild distortions of the competitive environment and "unjust" discrimination against individuals and localities. Large shippers depended on the favor of their railroad friends. Intermediate cities rose or fell in response to the structure of local rates. Certain shippers and towns made unprecedented gains while the majority of small merchants and farmers in the Mississippi Valley lost all control over where and how and at what price they sold their crops. If railroad rates were often fair and equitable, they were always arbitrary. The threat of destruction, even more than actual abuses, focused public hostility on the arrogance and power of the railroad managers. While the best of these managers proclaimed the virtues of the "natural laws" of supply and demand, they constantly defied those laws from necessity or from habit.[13]

Ironically, free competition had created the problem both for the midwestern shippers and their railroad rivals. Rate discrimination grew out of competitive pressures, from consumers and railroad promoters, to build developmental lines faster than the territory could support them. For two decades John Murray Forbes had been preaching the gospel of patient development, but his argument fell on deaf ears. Neither railroad builders nor anxious pioneer patrons would be stayed in their frantic rush to the West. As a result, conflict was built into the original bargain and proved almost impossible to overcome. Distortions in the rate structure reflected the railroad managers' understandable need to raise immediate income while building a revenue base for future defense against competition. Techniques of operating efficiency that made possible reductions in interregional freight rates favored long- over short-haul business. Furthermore, aggressive merchants in those local markets blessed with competing rail service encouraged the rate wars that so heavily taxed their less fortunate neighbors. Railroad defenses against ruinous competition were indistinguishable in character from monopolistic abuses. Western interests therefore unfailingly pressed for *more* competition to recover their independence. At the same time that eastern capitalists like John Murray Forbes were condemned for dominating the western economy, they were forced to expand their investments in response to the demands of western people. If Forbes refused, others would invade the territory he already controlled.

CHARLES E. PERKINS sat uncomfortably at the center of all these contradictory pressures. Perkins had come to Burlington in 1859 as a clerk on the B&MR. As the war drew off his immediate superiors, he took on the duties of land agent, assistant treasurer, and assistant secretary. Forced to sit out the war in Iowa, and finding little employment as yet in selling railroad lands, Perkins became the principal liaison between cousin John Murray Forbes, the Burlington company, and the people of Iowa. His considerable talents as a manager together with the circumstances of his confinement in the Burlington

---

13. Ibid.

office cast young Perkins in the mold of a company man, a role that in time would make him an invaluable resource to the Forbes group and the Burlington railroad.[14]

Perkins believed that the Iowa line was the key to the postwar success of Forbes's whole railroad network. Forbes was inclined to agree; but still preoccupied with the Union victory, he paid too little attention to Iowa's development. As competitive construction extended new lines all around him, Perkins's situation grew desperate. A traffic contract with CB&Q helped finance construction from Iowa earnings, which by the end of summer 1865 were "very large," and throughout 1866 he pressed for bonuses to speed construction. Slowly the work progressed. By June 1867 the line had advanced only forty-seven miles, while the Chicago & North Western (C&NW) had completed its line to Council Bluffs, complete with bridges at the Mississippi and Missouri rivers. Still, the Burlington line had earned nearly half a million dollars in the past fiscal year, and less than half had gone for operating expenses, but Perkins knew that completed lines soon would draw off his traffic and drive down prevailing rates. When the Burlington line finally reached the Missouri River its profit margin was sure to be slim. Construction from current earnings must be done very soon or not at all.[15]

Perkins's efforts to finish the line were hindered at every turn by public impatience with the B&MR. Since the Boston men had seized control in 1857, local support had been melting away. Now, with Granger agitation breaking out across the region, Perkins quietly tried to cultivate new friends in Iowa circles. Whenever he could, Perkins reminded his western Iowa "friends" that rate regulations favored only those eastern Iowa interests, "who having the road care nothing for the interests of the State at Large." When it seemed prudent, he issued a friendly line expressing his "interest" in some local election. At one point he asked Forbes to send out a man with money and doctrine enough to buy out the *Burlington Hawk-Eye,* whose current editor was hostile. Perkins's politics, however, were not entirely insincere. He made positive efforts to secure the city of Burlington against commercial losses resulting from the new Mississippi River bridge. Even as the superintendent of a "foreign" railroad, Charles Perkins was deeply attached to Burlington and worked conscientiously to develop his adopted community.[16]

---

14. See Richard C. Overton, "Charles Elliott Perkins," *Business History Review* 31 (1957), 292–309; Overton, *Burlington West,* 112.

15. See John N. Denison to Perkins, 15 May 1865, in General Material, 2, CB&Q-Newberry; Perkins to JMF, 17 and 20 June, 27 Aug., and 10 Nov. 1865; Perkins to James F. Joy, 16 and 21 Dec. 1865; in C-O5, Letterbook D, CB&Q-Newberry. The contract for aid from the CB&Q was recorded on 20 June 1865 in B&MR Records, CB&Q-Newberry; Minutes of Directors Meeting, 27 April 1866, in B&MR Records, CB&Q-Newberry; Perkins to James F. Joy, 2 Nov. 1866; Perkins to JMF, 9 Jan., 8 Feb., and 18 March 1867; in C-O5, Letterbook E, CB&Q-Newberry; CB&Q, *Annual Report, 1867,* 53, 56–57.

16. Perkins to John F. Tracy, 6 Feb. 1866, in C-O5, Letterbook E; Perkins to JMF, 30 Aug. and 10 Sept. 1867, in C-O5, Letterbook F, CB&Q-Newberry.

Progress in Iowa suffered from disinterest back east as well. Because of his growing commitment to the Iowa road, Perkins was the first to recognize weakness among his eastern supporters. James F. Joy, a longtime Forbes associate now closely involved with Kansas City railroads, was the chief doubter. Without coal and timber, Joy reasoned, Iowa could not be settled. Perkins thought this a mistake in judgment, but in time he came to suspect that Joy had "so much else on foot that he pays no attention to us." Naturally the Burlington's lands would not be settled, he argued, "till the road is built." As Joy turned against him, Perkins warned Forbes that endless delay "not only makes the heart sick, it sometimes makes men mad!!" However foreign he looked to later reformers, Perkins had faith in the Iowa line, and in the last years of the 1860s he risked his career in its dogged promotion. In November 1869, after sixteen years of war, delay, and frustration, the B&MR finally was opened to the Missouri River. In the next twelve months its earnings exceeded Perkins's wildest predictions — over $200 million.[17]

CUTTHROAT COMPETITION and uncontrolled railway expansion on the Middle Border produced exactly the price distortions and ruthless practices Forbes had worked all his life to avoid. Yet western people saw the "loose era" of railroad construction that followed the Civil War in exactly the opposite light. Tradition taught them that *too little* competition, not too much, was the great evil. Their experience during the Civil War only reinforced that principle. Postwar prosperity was unevenly distributed. If interregional freight rates had fallen dramatically, the vast majority of producers and merchants continued to pay high local rates at noncompeting points. From their perspective only monopolistic middlemen enjoyed cheap transportation. Railroad owners like Forbes might complain about costs, but as company revenues soared the public refused to believe that the margin of profit was falling. Citing dramatic examples of profiteering, like the Crédit Mobilier of the Union Pacific, people easily condemned large capitalists for fattening their purses at the expense of the commonwealth. In September 1873 the failure of Jay Cooke & Co. and the subsequent collapse of American finance seemed to verify that the swindlers and stock jobbers had struck once more.

At the core of this unrest lay enough real injury to western business that the charges of hardship could not be denied. What was not so evident was the degree to which injured merchants represented their own interests or those of the whole Iowa community. As early as 1860 the mayor and aldermen of Burlington, Iowa, for example, had petitioned the legislature to set maximum rates for freight and passengers in the interest of "Iowa commerce." During

---

17. Perkins to JMF, 4, 11, and 15 Sept. 1867, in C-O5, Letterbook F, CB&Q-Newberry; See Perkins to JMF, 9 and 24 Aug. and 2 Nov. 1868, in C-O5, Letterbook F; Perkins to JMF, 31 Jan. 1869, in C.E.P. Transcripts, Set C, CB&Q-Newberry. See also Overton, *Burlington Route*, 95–96; and CB&Q, *Annual Report, 1869*, 13.

the Civil War there were new demands for canals to the Great Lakes to compete with Chicago railroads. After 1865 meetings of river town merchants repeatedly memorialized Congress and the state legislature for water competition and railroad rate regulation. Dubuque, Davenport, Clinton, Muscatine, and Keokuk joined Burlington in a campaign for statutory rates that would reestablish their role as the marketing centers for Iowa produce. These towns demanded, not pro rata equity, but legal maximum tariffs fixed at or below prevailing Chicago rates.[18]

Interior communities rightly saw these demands as special pleading: "The time has passed," argued one state senator, "when the river towns can hold the enviable position of commercial agents for all the counties lying back of them." In 1870 most interior interests still agreed that the railroad had "brought a better market to every man's door than the river towns could possibly have afforded." Schemes to protect these local centers were undoubtedly selfish, but they sounded an important warning against the loss of local marketing power. Burlington, for example, was already in serious trouble by 1869. Less than half the city's commodity exports still passed through the hands of Burlington dealers. Over 90 percent of southern Iowa livestock moved directly into the Union Stock Yards over the Chicago railroads. Burlington's merchants still handled much of the iron and coal and manufactures coming in from Chicago, but almost three-quarters of the lumber and salt business rolled through town in bulk. A short three years later, in 1872, nearly 80 percent of all CB&Q shipments to and from Iowa passed through the Burlington market without pause. The following year, the consolidation of the B&MR with the CB&Q reduced the city's commerce to strictly local proportions.[19]

The cause of Burlington's problem was rate discrimination. Short-haul rates to Burlington were nearly twice as high as the long rates to Chicago; in 1873 the differential reached a high of two-and-one-half times the through tariff. One hundred pounds of first class freight could be shipped the twenty-eight miles from Mount Pleasant to Burlington for twenty-five cents (18¢ per ton-mile) or it could go through 248 miles to Chicago for eighty-five cents (7¢ per ton-mile). Long-awaited improvements, like the bridge over the Mississippi in 1868 and the completion of the B&MR in 1869, simply accelerated Burlington's decline. Interior cities like Ottumwa, which had lured competing lines during the decade of railroad promotions, received the lowest rates. Burlington's loyalty to the B&MR was proving the ruin of its commerce. Thus, in late 1872, the announcement of impending consolidation with the CB&Q sent shockwaves of concern through the community.[20]

---

18. *Burlington Weekly Hawk-Eye,* 13, 20, and 27 Jan. 1866. See also Miller, *Railroads,* 100–109.

19. *Proceedings of the Fourth Annual Meeting of the Iowa State Grange* (Des Moines, 1873). Shipping statistics from Iowa State Agricultural Society *Reports,* 1869, 1870, 1871, 1872, 1873, 1874.

20. Ibid., 33; *Burlington Daily Hawk-Eye,* 9, 16, 17, and 24 Oct. 1872.

A year later Burlington had had enough. An angry committee of citizens accused the company of "absorbing everything and contributing nothing" to the Iowa town. CB&Q President James M. Walker insisted that his policies were "dictated solely on account of economical reasons." Strict economy of operations alone would reduce charges, he argued, so these measures were ultimately in Burlington's interest. Burlington was not impressed. Local stockholders pushed a hostile resolution through the annual meeting in February 1874 charging violation of contract by the CB&Q. The community was outraged: One citizen renamed the company "Cursed, Bursted & Quarrelsome." Even the supportive *Burlington Hawk-Eye* warned the railroad that Burlington was the "natural and geographic" center of their territory. Sooner or later the owners would "regret the loss of her help and good feeling, which will then be gone to rival railroads."[21]

These harmful effects of consolidation and integration in the railroad network were not long restricted to river towns like Burlington. After 1870 farm prices began falling faster than interior freight rates, and the hardships of local discrimination spread to noncompeting "way points" across the state. More and more voters identified with the complaints of the river town merchants against the railroads. Iowa's Republican leadership, having opposed rate regulation since before 1860, now endorsed antidiscrimination measures in the face of diminishing trade. By 1872 the General Assembly was overwhelmingly in favor of some form of regulation, but the deadlock between river town supporters of maximum rates and more moderate proponents of an advisory commission prevented action that year. The economic impetus for railroad regulation had reached full proportions well before the panic of 1873, but the motive was not well focused. It remained for a second source of western temper to unite the victims of injustice in a campaign against "railroad abuses."[22]

So it was that the Patrons of Husbandry — the Grange — became the reluctant vehicle for a massive regional protest against railroad and industrial power. Oliver Hudson Kelly, founder of the Grange, intended an agrarian fraternity dedicated to education, social intercourse, and the improvement of the farmer's life. But the Grange touched a raw nerve in thousands of frustrated producers in the upper Mississippi Valley. In Iowa, the Grange reflected exactly those values of political economy that had carried James W. Grimes and the infant Republican party to power two decades before. Progressive local development within the "natural order" was supposed to be the goal of the people and their government. During the Civil War Iowa's State Agricultural Society had denounced every attempt to "violate and set at nought the laws of trade and

---

21. James M. Walker to E. D. Rand, et al., 31 Dec. 1873, in Box 3W3.1, CB&Q-Newberry; Minutes of the Annual Stockholders Meeting, 25 Feb. 1874, in B&MR Records, CB&Q-Newberry; *Burlington Daily Hawk-Eye,* 8 Jan. 1874.

22. See farm price series quoted in Mildred Throne, "The Grange in Iowa, 1868–1875," *Iowa Journal of History* 47 (1949), 291. See also Miller, *Railroads,* 104–11.

exchange which God impressed on this continent when He created it." By the end of the war Grimes himself was criticizing government aid to monopolistic railroads. The "true" objective of Republican government, he declared, was to insure that every man was "the owner of his own soil, the owner of his own tools, the owner of his own labor, and his own machinery."[23] Another spokesman accepted the railroads as the "revealers" of American greatness; but as the country was "revolutionized" by the "annihilation" of space and time, Iowans feared being kept "merely as an agricultural population." With a cry of betrayal, the Iowa farmers were called to organize:

> We are furnished with the theoretical elements of agriculture, and the dignity of our calling has so bewildered our ideas that we have allowed huge monopolies and fat corporations to form around us un-noticed, and now they go strutting about carrying State Legislatures [sic] around in their breeches pocket, with their extortionate rates and unjust discriminating power between places and individuals, while hundreds of honest practical farmers in the State of Iowa stand today on the verge of financial ruin.[24]

The response in Iowa was electric. The number of local granges increased from forty in early 1871 to three hundred one year later and eighteen hundred by November 1873. The order peaked ten months later just one unit short of two thousand. The Grange program of cooperative buying and selling was an important attraction, but antimonopoly and antirailroad rhetoric was the symbolic and emotional core of the appeal. On the morning of January 8, 1873, for example, Agricultural Society President John Scott warned his audience that urban interests—merchants, carriers, and laboring mechanics—had learned to suppress competition to insure their profits, while the farmer, in his "so called market," was "but the sport of bulls that toss and bears that squeeze," while everything he bought "from the cradle to the coffin" came to him "priced by a board of trade."[25]

Scott's address proved to be but an introduction for a stunning oration that evening by Governor Cyrus Clay Carpenter. Convinced that rebellion was brewing, this surveyor and land-trader-turned-politician was determined to "take the lead . . . on this question of transportation." He opened with this dramatic blast:

> If . . . today, there is a shadow resting upon the prosperity of the Great West, which it is no exaggeration to compare with the fleshless fingers, the rattling joints, the eyeless sockets, and the grinning teeth of a skeleton, it is found

---

23. See Oliver Hudson Kelly, *Origin and Progress of the Order of the Patrons of Husbandry . . .* (Philadelphia, 1875); Solon J. Buck, *The Granger Movement* (Cambridge, Mass., 1933); and D. Sven Nordin, *Rich Harvest: A History of the Grange, 1867–1900* (Jackson, Miss., 1974). The best single account on Iowa is Throne, "Grange." See also Iowa State Agricultural Society, *Report, 1862*, 126–27; James W. Grimes, Speech in the Senate, 1866, quoted in Fred B. Lewellen, "Political Ideas of James W. Grimes," *Iowa Journal of History and Politics* 42 (1944), 350.

24. Iowa State Agricultural Society, *Report, 1869*, 77; *Iowa Homestead*, 15 March 1872.

25. Iowa State Agricultural Society, *Report, 1872*, 168–76.

in the cost of exchanging commodities over long lines of communication, by expensive agencies, and at exorbitant charges for transportation. *This is the skeleton in every Western farmer's corncrib.*

Carpenter urged farmers to feed more livestock, compressing exports to ten times their value per pound of freight. Diversification of crops and the development of home markets might help as well, but real justice depended on government regulation.[26]

Ordinarily Carpenter would have rejected government "interference" with individual freedom and enterprise, but the new transport system bore such an "intimate relationship to the very existence of organized society," that it now presented a "towering" monopoly. The government "which proves unequal to its control," he reasoned, "abdicates a power for which it will be held responsible at the bar of an enlightened and aroused public opinion." Carpenter denounced efforts to stimulate competition, which only distorted the marketplace. "What the people want is *stability, certainty.*" Rate ceilings must be established. Discrimination against individuals and locations must be stopped. Federally owned and operated trunk lines should be built to set standards of service and tariffs that private interstate lines would have to meet. Carpenter denied the assertions of men like Forbes that public enterprise would fail. Pointing to the number of railroad failures since the panic of 1837, he insisted that private capitalists with decades of experience had no better record than the experimental public works of the 1830s. Finally, Carpenter predicted that radical reductions in freight rates would so boost the volume of business that the railroads would increase their revenues.[27]

The governor's plan was comprehensive, yet believable; his tone, determined. Even James S. Clarkson, editor of the *Iowa State Register,* railroad favorite and boss of the state Republican party, put his seal of approval on Carpenter's words. Three weeks later the Iowa State Grange held its convention in Des Moines, with a turnout that astounded editor Clarkson. Nearly one thousand delegates convened in the capital city despite the heavy snows of an Iowa winter. Astonished themselves at the growth of their order, the Grangers found little to add to Governor Carpenter's address. They petitioned their legislature and begged Congress to restore the farmers' "God-given rights." The presence in Des Moines of a thousand angry Grangers did stir the special session of the General Assembly to take up the railroad question, but reform was still a year off.[28]

---

26. Ibid., 194–95; Mildred Throne, *Cyrus Clay Carpenter and Iowa Politics, 1854–1898* (Iowa City, 1974), 159.

27. Iowa State Agricultural Society, *Report, 1872,* 194–213.

28. Throne, *Carpenter,* 160; Jonathon Periam, *The Groundswell: A History of the Origins, Aims, and Progress of the Farmers' Movement* (Cincinnati, 1874), 264; *Iowa State Daily Register,* 28 and 31 Jan. 1873; *Fourth Iowa State Grange, 1873,* 23–24, 29.

BY 1873 the midwestern agitation for rate law reform had received national attention, and the protest was destined to intensify. Illinois and Minnesota had already enacted rate regulations, and the legislatures of Wisconsin and Iowa repeatedly debated the issue. CB&Q General Manager Robert Harris readily conceded that "wild and unreasonable and unnecessary [rate] cuttings and discriminations" were "at the bottom of all this noise." Had railway managers taken a sincere interest in an equitable solution, one might have emerged, but the image of farmer-legislators dictating policy to private corporations so offended men like John Murray Forbes and Charles E. Perkins that they made little effort to reconcile. Forbes blamed the Grangers' rebellion on the persistent failure of the "slow agricultural mind" to comprehend the postwar world. The farmers "don't mean to do wrong," he conceded, but they failed to understand the cause of differential rates. With "time and patience and with such timely concessions as steel rails and close management will warrant," Forbes thought he could show the farmer that "good economical management aided by such competition as he can get up will give him his best and only chance of getting his local transportation cheapened."[29]

Forbes saw the Grangers in the light of the unfinished revolution that was begun during the Civil War, and he was fully confident that the emerging systems of industry and commerce would eventually benefit these misguided farmers. Charles Perkins agreed that it was time to start "educating the popular mind" on the question of railroad regulation, and he admitted that the railroads had a credibility problem. "It wont [sic] do," he argued, "to try to prove that all RRd men are saints." Still, the principles of corporate freedom had to be defended by the roads to keep the farmers from "going on the wrong track." It was E. L. Godkin of *The Nation,* a New York weekly that John Murray Forbes had financed just after the war, who finally put into words the larger issue presented by the Grangers' complaints: "The locomotive is coming in contact with the framework of our institutions. In this country of simple government, the most powerful centralizing force which civilization has yet produced has, within the next score years, yet to assume its relations to that political machinery which is to control and regulate it."[30] For Godkin the question was rhetorical: Like Forbes he assumed that the framework of political nationalism and corporate economy already taking shape in the United States was the true and proper response to the locomotive's challenge. For western men, however, that was the whole question.

The midwestern railroad protest quickly broadened into a contest of regions and cultural values that added more heat than light to the questions.

---

29. Robert Harris to T. J. Carter, 24 March 1873, quoted in Miller, *Railroads,* 22. See also Miller, *Railroads,* chap. 4, on Illinois legislation; JMF to a stockholder, [c. 16 June 1873], in Box 8C6.5, CB&Q-Newberry.

30. Perkins to John W. Brooks, 2 March 1873, in C.E.P. Transcripts, Set A, CB&Q-Newberry; *The Nation,* 10 April 1873.

Grangers linked the farmers' problems to corruption among businessmen and politicians in the Grant administration in Washington. Stung by the charge, easterners blamed western demagogues for all the special pleading in Congress that was demoralizing public life. Godkin even condemned the farmers for losing their "rugged" virtues: Clinging to the railroads, the "modern frontiersmen" demanded all the conveniences of church, school, newspapers, and magazines; his wife and daughters "must have a piano and silk dresses . . . and their minds, instead of being intent on the homely joys of the forest and the prairie, are vexed by the social and religious discussions of the East." The western press replied in kind; with each exchange the chasm widened. By association with rich and powerful speculators all railroad men were turned into scoundrels. Charles Perkins struggled vainly to produce a comprehensive, balanced discussion of the railroad question which "*everybody* would read"; but such a short course in complicated economics was not forthcoming. Out of the East came more invective, culminating in the insufferable charge that without "'railroad speculators,' there would not be any West at all."[31]

Gross insensitivity to regional culture simply hardened the Grangers' animosity toward the new commercial systems. The Chicago Farmer's Convention in October 1873 called on its brethren to withdraw wherever possible from interdependent markets, avoid debt, buy home manufactures, oppose tariff protection, and organize farmers everywhere. The bitterness in Granger rhetoric was unmistakable. One correspondent in the *Iowa Homestead* complained sadly that the farmer considered himself "but a beast of burden." With the "whole load upon his back he has neither profit nor honor. Those who ride despise him." Shifting from the language of economy to political liberty, Iowa Grange Master A. B. Smedley rallied his brothers to the defense of "free Republican" institutions: "If that eternal vigilance which has been called the price of liberty is not exercised, if this aggressive power is not boldly met and restrained by wise and reasonable legislation, all the industrial interests of our country must languish."[32]

In April 1873 local Iowa granges launched an antimonopoly third party movement that was quickly captured by cynical leaders in Iowa's old Democracy. Holding its nominating convention at the height of the August harvest, the new Anti-Monopoly party offered a slate of familiar Iowa Democrats and drew up a platform that was little more than the antebellum program of the party of Jackson. Thoroughly co-opted by party professionals, the Grangers' efforts nevertheless forced the Grand Old Party to take a vigorous antirailroad stand. Forced to break with his railroad friends, party boss James S. Clarkson agreed to redeem the pledge on railroad regulation. Governor Carpenter introduced a plan com-

---

31. *The Nation*, 12 and 19 June, 17 and 31 July 1873; Perkins to JMF, 9 Sept. 1873, in General Material, 2, CB&Q-Newberry; *The Nation*, 2 Oct. 1873. For reprinted editorial clips from around the country, see *Iowa State Daily Register*, 27 Sept. 1873.

32. Edward Winslow Martin, *History of the Grange Movement; or, The Farmer's War against Monopolies . . .* (Philadelphia, 1873), 509; "A Letter to Farmers from Jones Co.," *Iowa Homestead*, 12 Dec. 1873; *Fourth Iowa State Grange, 1873,* 28.

bining the maximum rate bill of the river town merchants with a classification of roads by earnings that protected small or weak lines. Experienced commercial spokesmen had little trouble steering the river town plan, with Carpenter's classification, through a legislature overwhelmingly controlled by farmers.[33]

Just at the height of the Iowa debates, CB&Q President James M. Walker proudly announced record earnings for the company. Charles Perkins bitterly thanked the directors for conferring "a favor upon the long suffering public which it will not [soon?] forget!" The Iowa tariff bill passed on March 8, 1874, and was signed by the governor on March 23. Essentially protective of the river town merchants, the new law indirectly promised stable rates and relief from discrimination in the interior as well. Having finally struck at the railroads, Iowa's mood turned sober. Carpenter himself had grave doubts that the benefits would meet popular expectations. The Iowa Grange, which had backed a rival system of advisory commissioners, insisted that the wrong bill had been passed, but they hoped for the best. All that was left was to wait and see. Editor James S. Clarkson put it best: "Our Iowa people are now nearing the real railroad crossing, and Gov. Carpenter, even before he hears the bell ring, may as well be looking out for the cars."[34]

By 1874, Illinois, Iowa, Wisconsin, and Minnesota had each passed restrictive railroad legislation. The term "Granger Laws" was fixed almost immediately, but these measures were neither radical nor agrarian. The important rights claimed by western legislators were entirely customary. Eastern capitalists such as John Murray Forbes saw the movement as a personal affront, and this contributed to the misinterpretation of the Granger Laws in the centers of eastern commerce. Furthermore, because Forbes and his class of entrepreneurs assumed that the new corporate order was already triumphant, they could not understand these resurgent defenders of local autonomy. When western tempers flared, eastern capitalists attributed the anger to agrarian reaction or alien communism—thereby concealing their own assault on local democracy and traditional American values.[35]

Caught in the middle, reflecting the ambiguity of the moment, was the Grange. By 1874 the farmers' movement had acquired its final, awkward position as an instrument of protest in modernizing America. In its celebration of the soil, moral economy, and divine social order, the Grange was romantic,

---

33. See Nordin, *Rich Harvest,* 182. Mildred Throne, "The Anti-Monopoly Party in Iowa, 1873–1874," *Iowa Journal of History* 52 (1954), 289–326, narrates the rise and fall of this political party. The Des Moines Anti-Monopoly platform is reprinted in Martin, *Grange Movement,* 513; for James S. Clarkson's commentary, see *Iowa State Daily Register,* 24 Aug. 1873. For additional detail on the legislative process, see Throne, *Carpenter,* 177–83; Miller, *Railroads,* 114–16; and the Des Moines and Burlington newspapers for Jan. through March 1874.

34. Perkins to J. N. A. Griswold, 7 March 1874, in C-O1, P4.1, CB&Q-Newberry; James M. Walker to John N. Denison, 28 Feb. 1874, in Box 3W3.1, CB&Q-Newberry; *Iowa State Daily Register,* 8 May 1874, quoted in Throne, *Carpenter,* 181.

35. See Miller, *Railroads,* 29, 161–71; Horowitz, *American Law,* 255; Hurst, *Law and the Conditions of Freedom,* chap. 3.

backward looking, and nostalgic. At the same time the Patrons' program of cooperation, combination, and class solidarity showed a realistic willingness to "fight fire with fire." Only a deep resistance to the alien principle of combination in the end stood between Granger rhetoric and effective Grange action. Brought up as independent producers—free enterprise capitalists—few Iowa farmers could embrace either the organic unity of a former age or the class solidarity of a modern trade union. Allowing for all the confusion, it was the very liberalism of the farmers' demands that forced their eastern critics to sketch them in caricature.[36]

Beneath the agrarian rhetoric of the midwestern Grange there lay two demands to be met before the farmers would join in the new national economy. First, they wanted their fair share of the profits. They would not go back, as E. L. Godkin advised, to simpler ways just to enrich urban America. Secondly, even if they abandoned the "original conditions" of James Grimes's early Republicanism, farmers and merchants alike refused to be governed by undemocratic combinations of capital. The arrogance of railroads like the CB&Q, which openly ignored the new Iowa tariffs, was a "direct insult to the sovereignty of the state." In the Middle West, the passage of the Granger Laws marked the end of traditional economic order and the beginning of a struggle for recognition within the new industrial systems.[37]

THE GRANGER LAW took effect in July 1874, fixing schedules of maximum rates for freight and passengers across the state. Forbes expected "a long fight" against those political "rascals" and "fools" he thought were responsible for regulation. The task, as Forbes saw it, was to rescue the true principles of political economy from the grasp of licentious democracy. Iowa had gone "about as far as it can go in hostile legislation," concluded CB&Q President James M. Walker in 1874, and there was little to be gained "from any attempt to conciliate voters and politicians in this regard." Walker recommended proceeding "as though no such law had been passed."[38]

No corporate response was more arrogant or inflammatory than this refusal to acknowledge the rule of law. When the new law took effect in July, the company ignored it. The opposition cried out against this insult to the sovereignty of the people. Even the usually supportive *Burlington Hawk-Eye*

---

36. See, for example, the "Declaration of Purposes" drawn up at the National Grange Meeting in St. Louis, 11 Feb. 1874, reprinted in Martin, *Grange Movement,* 535–39.
37. *Fifth Iowa State Grange, 1874,* 34–35.
38. JMF to James M. Walker, 14 March 1874, in Box 3W3.5, CB&Q-Newberry. Forbes was active in the National Republican Committee from 1876 until his break with the bosses in 1884. Unwilling to join the Liberal Republicans, he remained loosely independent ever after. See *Reminiscences of John Murray Forbes,* ed. Sarah Forbes Hughes, 3 vols. (Boston, 1902), 3:159–79; Walker to Perkins, 16 May 1874, in Box 3W3.1, CB&Q-Newberry; Walker to John N. Denison, 11 June 1874, in Thomas C. Cochran, *Railroad Leaders, 1845–1890: The Business Mind in Action* (Cambridge, Mass., 1953), 489.

called for the "strong arm of public will" to reduce the railroad "to serfdom, if necessary." The company remained undaunted. Stubborn Iowans began boarding trains without tickets and then offering the legally prescribed three cents per mile. Walker ordered conductors to accept no payments aboard the cars, forcing passengers to pay higher company fares at the stations. The confrontation created more ill will than real hardship. By autumn, CB&Q revenues had reached record proportions, but the lawsuits were piling up. Should the Iowa attorney general ever move against the Burlington, the defense might go badly. On January 5, 1875, to forestall that possibility, the company sought an injunction in United States court, barring prosecutions under the Iowa tariff law.[39]

The managers of all the Iowa roads were shocked and disappointed in May 1875 when the federal courts rejected the Burlington's plea. Reporting the decision to Forbes, Charles Perkins expressed his fear that the lower court's opinion might be shared by some Supreme Court Justices as well. Furthermore the ruling stirred up the people again. President Walker met the circuit court's ruling with carefully guarded concessions. He outlined a strategy that would minimize public conflict without jeopardizing the company's legal position as long as appeals were pending. Passenger fares quietly fell to the legal limit "to avoid personal collisions and difficulties on the trains and at stations." Freight rates were left in place, however, until such time as "action of the state authorities" or "trouble along the line" should force them down. Considering the $500 penalties for each violation, payable to the state school fund, Walker stressed to his directors the risk in their position. As the legal battles continued he hoped to avoid confrontations and continue the present rates through the year. Next winter the company might better influence "the repeal of this most disastrous legislation."[40]

Furious at Walker's reduction of passenger fares, Perkins poured out his anger to John Murray Forbes. "We made a mistake," he complained, "in not paying $10,000 to defeat the law originally." Reducing passenger fares was another blunder; Perkins thought it indefensible to reduce fares and not freights, and he warned of more trouble with angry shippers than had been seen as yet. In a long essay in June Perkins explained his general theory of regulation more fully. "Communism in any form" was "dishonest and unwise and utterly inconsistent with civilized progress." Because the "regulation of Railroad rates by

---

39. *Burlington Daily Hawk-Eye,* 11 July 1874; Walker to J. D. Wright, 7 Oct. 1874, in Box 3W3.1, CB&Q-Newberry. The application for an injunction, 5 Jan. 1875, is in Box 33-1870-4.1, CB&Q-Newberry. For an account of the legal questions, see George H. Miller, "Chicago, Burlington and Quincy Railroad Company v. Iowa," *Iowa Journal of History* 54 (1956), 289–312.

40. Perkins to JMF, 15 May 1875, in C.E.P. Transcripts, Set C, CB&Q-Newberry. See also Miller, "CB&Q v. Iowa," 304–5. Perkins had gained control of the *Burlington Hawk-Eye* through loans totaling $5,000 of Forbes's money. Perkins to JMF, 11 Jan. 1875, in C.E.P. Transcripts, Set C, CB&Q-Newberry; James M. Walker to J. N. A. Griswold, 19 May 1875, in Box 3W3.1, CB&Q-Newberry.

the public" amounted to confiscation of property — communism — there were but two ways to solve the railroad question: "Either the Government must buy[,] own & operate the Railroads or the laws of competition, of supply and demand, must solve the problem." Perkins warned Iowans that their railroad laws were not only ill-advised, but "bad." Capitalists would shun their state. "The right of property," he lectured, "is at the bottom of all stable Government."[41]

John Murray Forbes agreed with Perkins's arguments but he knew the matter was not so simple. The right of property claimed by Perkins was not unusual; the novelty lay in allowing chartered corporations to pursue their rights to the injury of individual private interests. In the popular mind, corporations enjoyed a legal, but not a moral, identity as individuals. Therefore justice must somehow work in favor of the "true" individuals against these legal fictions. Public regulation of railroad rates tended to skew the conflict of rights in favor of the individual shipper, which Perkins saw as an assault on the rights of the corporations. The occasions for conflict and injury were legion. There were literally millions of transactions in which freight rates were quoted, and the sheer volume of trade insured that extraordinary examples of discrimination would occur.

One such case of discrimination on the Burlington line reached E. L. Godkin's desk at *The Nation,* illustrating the root of hostility between the carriers and the shippers. A merchant in Glenwood, Iowa, reported "great hardships" that were caused by a rate structure that favored Chicago and New York. Local freights near Glenwood moved cheaper on wagons, and coal from nearby Iowa mines cost no less than Pennsylvania fuel on the retail market. The Burlington's rates rendered competition "between the great marts of the country impossible." Even Perkins was surprised to learn that the facts of the case were true, but he agreed with General Superintendent Robert Harris's explanation: "It is not the business of Railroads to open up 'competition between the great marts of the country.'" The people expected their railroads to be neutral servants in the contest between individual buyers and sellers, but the railroads had become contestants themselves in a national market that scarcely felt Glenwood's pain.[42]

Here was the basic ambiguity that plagued the railroad question for a generation: Railroads could not erase distance for Iowa corn without erasing distance for Pennsylvania coal. The hopes of the first generation of Iowa railroad promoters, to preserve their natural advantages while removing geographic barriers, had been vain from the start. Charles Francis Adams, Jr., a Massachusetts railroad commissioner and an early student of rate regulation, was among

---

41. Perkins to JMF, 26 June 1875, in C.E.P. Transcripts, Set C, CB&Q-Newberry; Perkins memorandum (draft of an essay), [c. June 1875], in C-O1, P4.1, CB&Q-Newberry.

42. C. E. Sherman to "Editor," *The Nation,* 30 June 1875, transcribed in Perkins's hand, in Box 3P4.2, CB&Q-Newberry; Perkins to Robert Harris, 6 Aug. 1875; Harris to Perkins, 9 Aug. 1875, in Box 3P4.2, CB&Q-Newberry.

the first to articulate the connection between economic aspirations and cultural attitudes in a "history" of the recent Granger Movement. The people, Adams explained, had assumed that railroad transportation was "subject to a law of supply and demand exactly in the same degree as factories and mills in the production of cotton cloth or flour." Adams was convinced that such competition was "simply impossible." Frustrated by the imperfect results of railway competition, western people were then infuriated by the arrogance and bad manners of railway officials from directors to baggage handlers. It came as no surprise to Adams that these farmers applied their exaggerated faith in popular legislation to the elimination of injustice at the hands of rude servants of these foreign masters.[43]

The solution, thought Adams, lay in getting farmers and railroad managers alike to forget about free competition. His critique of the Granger Movement brought into focus the structural novelties of railway economics and the cultural assumptions that obscured the vision of all parties concerned. This highborn Bostonian could hardly approve the tantrums of western democracy, but he did recognize that the axioms of political economy so dear to his own class of businessmen did not square with reality. Railroads could not compete at every shipping point, nor could they withdraw from the market once built. Discrimination, combination, and monopoly were the natural consequences of competition under those conditions. Men like Forbes and Perkins and the western shippers all failed to understand that, and their grievances could be traced to this interpretive failure. Adams hoped to steer debates toward the practical issues of railroad policy, but neither the railroad men nor the shippers were prepared to abandon the language of free competition.

Theoretical arguments, especially if they contradicted treasured notions about the laws of trade, could not easily replace experience as the source of truth about railways. John Murray Forbes admitted that young Adams was "smart, but he is totally inexperienced." Charles Perkins, who was something of a theorizer himself, reprimanded Adams for handing the Grangers "more ammunition" with which to attack business interests. Neither man could agree with Adams that there was something wrong with the commercial system. Forbes suspected instead that there were "dishonest politicians working upon" the people. When Adams criticized the railroads for subverting the regulatory force of public opinion, Forbes could not even see that this was possible.[44]

It may have been impossible for business to ignore public opinion, as John Murray Forbes believed, but it was very much within the power of business to affect public opinion and materially improve the climate of politics. In the case of the Iowa Granger Law, it was clear that the people must be shown the

---

43. Charles Francis Adams, Jr., "The Granger Movement," *North American Review* 120 (1875), 399.
44. Perkins to E. L. Godkin, 6 Nov. 1875, in General Material, CB&Q-Newberry; JMF to W. P. Garrison, 18 March 1870, in *Letters of JMF (suppl.)*, 3:115.

error of their legislation and brought back into sympathy with their railroads. Burlington strategy was drawn accordingly. In mock compliance with the Iowa law the Burlington raised all through rates to the level of local tariffs. Then the company terminated all special concessions to favored shippers. This application of the antidiscrimination guidelines of the law, without the overall reductions in charges, worked an immediate hardship on those shippers most eager for relief. Exploiting the uproar, the railroads blamed every increased cost, each curtailment of services, or individual hardship on the "hostile" statute. Emphasizing the radical image of antirailroad agrarianism, the companies launched a propaganda campaign against the Grange itself to discredit the regulatory movement. "The howling has been as hideous as it has been untruthful," wrote Coker F. Clarkson, leading Granger and farm editor of the *Iowa State Register.* The rate law that the Grange had actually opposed in 1874 was now being used to ruin their order, while the merchants who had drafted the bill pledged their timeless allegiance to "free capital, free competition, and free commerce."[45]

Charles Perkins was in charge of Iowa politics for the CB&Q, and he pinned his hopes on repealing the rate law in the General Assembly. As the Iowa lawmakers gathered in February 1876, Perkins tried again to explain the railroads' discomfort with the ironclad tariff in 1874. It was true that some roads earned record profits in 1875, but this was entirely the result of unusually *high* rates mandated by the law. Why then were the railroads seeking repeal? Because "the rates which they are charging to Chicago are higher than the products can bear and at the same time bring in enough return to the producer to encourage & stimulate industry to its utmost." Perkins's sudden interest in producer welfare was perfectly "logical" and should be evident to "every farmer in Iowa": The railroads were fixtures that could not be moved, so they were "directly interested in developing the country" they occupied. In short, the railroad managers were concerned that dangerously high rates would stifle the enterprise of Iowa. Perkins overlooked the fact that his entire schedule of rates violated Iowa law.[46]

Heroic arguments notwithstanding, the Iowa lawmakers were not ready to repeal their statute. Instead they adopted an amnesty measure forgiving past violations in return for immediate compliance. Perkins feared that the session had done nothing more than "call attention to the fact that we are not obeying the law." With the benefit of hindsight he now believed that the Burlington "ought to have complied" with the law from the start, and then "in combination with the other Roads" it should have put up through rates "even higher than they have been — but that is a vain regret." Discussing the problem with Robert Harris,

---

45. Mildred Throne, "Repeal of the Iowa Granger Law, 1878," *Iowa Journal of History* 51 (1953), 107, 110.

46. Perkins memorandum (draft of article), [c. Feb. 1876], in Box 33-1880-4.65, CB&Q-Newberry. A number of additional documents trace Perkins's thoughts and activities regarding repeal of the Iowa law. The public misrepresentation of the Burlington's rate structure was exposed late in the campaign for repeal, but by then petitions begging for relief had done their harm.

now president of the CB&Q, Perkins acknowledged that acceptance of the amnesty was the best course. Only a Supreme Court ruling against the Granger Laws would materially alter the situation, and he did not expect one that spring. The Burlington directors stalled and studied as long as possible, then on May 10, 1876, they accepted the terms of the amnesty. The Iowa rates were law.[47]

IN MARCH 1877 the United States Supreme Court upheld the so-called Granger Laws. This affirmation of local prerogative struck a blow to the railroads, to be sure; but recovery from the long depression was well under way and most Iowa railroad leaders were now focusing on extensions more than rates. Renewed competition promised to soften up the political opposition as poorly served communities clamored for rails. For a majority of Iowans the threat of being left behind now outweighed the benefits of rate regulation. Other Granger states had already revised their regulations, and most Iowans agreed that the time had come for modification of the original tariff law.

The repeal effort centered this time on the establishment of an advisory commission with investigatory powers. Of the various proposals introduced in the 1878 session, the most popular called for railroad commissioners, appointed by the governor, who were authorized to investigate complaints and to examine the books of the companies, reporting their findings to the legislature each year. If the circumstances warranted, the commissioners might recommend prosecution in the civil courts. Substantially the same bill that the Grangers had favored four years before, this commission system was now the more popular alternative to ironclad tariffs.[48]

With a patience born of desperate self-interest, the river town wholesalers, especially in Dubuque, Davenport, and Clinton, tried once more to defend the 1874 tariff law. The hardships endured by Iowa shippers were due to railroad retaliation, not to Granger tariffs. The roads had prospered and continued to build in Iowa in spite of themselves. The merchants of Clinton ended their memorial with an impassioned plea for increased, not diminished, protection:

> It is the same spirit of extortion, discrimination, defiance of public opinion, and disregard of the interests of the State, which forced the people of Iowa to the adoption of the Iowa Tariff Law as a measure of protection against its rapacity, and which should be checked and bridled not alone by State but by National control. The Tariff Law is in no wise responsible for these extortions — it had cured the evil within the borders of the State, and it should be the effort of the people of Iowa . . . to secure Congressional regulation of railroad traffic between the States.[49]

---

47. Perkins to Robert Harris, 25 March 1876, in Box 33-1880-4.65, CB&Q-Newberry. For details of legislative actions, see Throne, "Repeal," 110–16.

48. Boxes 33-1870-4.2, 4.33, and 4.41, CB&Q-Newberry, contain miscellaneous documents relating to the repeal of the Granger Law and the establishment of the Iowa Railroad Commission, including a draft of Walker's proposal for such a bill (in 4.33).

49. Memorial of the Citizens of Clinton, Iowa, [c. Feb. 1878], in Box 33-1870-4.3, CB&Q-Newberry.

Time and again the river towns had promised to forward the surplus of Iowa to the markets of the world, but their consistent failure to perform told the tale. Unwilling to enthrone the river merchants as permanent masters of their trade, most Iowans in 1878 sought a solution that could grow with the territory. The advisory commission was their answer.[50]

Charles Perkins and other railroad managers welcomed the appointment of Iowa's new railroad commissioners: Peter A. Dey, a civil engineer with railroad experience; James W. McDill, a lawyer, former district judge, and congressman; and former governor Cyrus Clay Carpenter. Moderation seemed to mark their collective understanding of the job ahead, and CB&Q President Robert Harris was confident that these men would "seek to consider the general interest of the State rather than that of particular localities or particular interests." Harris greeted their appointment with this word of advice: Seek a resolution to the complex "Railroad problem" through "patient and disinterested study."[51]

Harris's injunction was laudable, but the new Iowa commissioners lacked both the tools of analysis and the disinterested perspective that were needed to assess the railroad question. Adequate series of statistics, on which quantitative studies might have been based, did not exist. The best figures—those compiled by the railroads—hardly were credible in the public's eye. Neither was their charge simply to lower rates. Arbitrariness and inconsistency received equal condemnation from shippers, yet nobody wished to see pro rata pricing reintroduce the tyranny of distance. Finally, in light of the four years just past, the Iowa commissioners were expected to harmonize relations between shippers and carriers—an objective that brought them inexorably back to politics. In the coming 1880s the railroad commissioners would be hard put to serve the "general interest of the state" while being fair to the owners of invested capital, regardless of the principles applied.

Popular faith in the doctrine of economic progress had carried a revolution in trade and commerce for nearly two generations in America, yet at the bottom of the postwar regulation question lay a nagging fear in the popular mind that this progress was illusory. Rhetoricians like E. L. Godkin might easily attribute the whole progress of the nation to the blessings of organized capital and railroads, but most Iowa farmers had worked too hard to believe that. They piled up record harvests, yet they watched friends and neighbors brought to despair. They borrowed money and reinvested earnings in more land and equipment just to keep even with falling prices. Good harvests and profitable

---

50. Ibid. See also *Iowa State Daily Register,* 7 and 12 March 1878; *Burlington Daily Hawk-Eye,* 8, 9, and 10 March 1878; and Throne, "Repeal," 117–30. Throne places a good deal of emphasis on the interference by railroad lobbyists in the legislative process; however, it is not necessary to prove "corruption" to explain the general support for repeal.

51. Perkins to Thomas J. Potter (telegram), 12 March 1878, in Box 33-1870-4.41, CB&Q-Newberry; Robert Harris to W. C. Sipple, to J. W. McDill, to Peter A. Dey, and to Cyrus C. Carpenter, 28 March 1878, in Box 3H4.2, CB&Q-Newberry.

years understandably slipped from memory when crop failures—or worse, record yields—ruined farm incomes and jeopardized mortgaged homesteads. Aggregates meant little as each man approached reality in person. In the final decades of the nineteenth century, the popular resentment of railroad corporations and the continuing struggle for state railroad control fed on hundreds of thousands of private views.

COMPETITIVE CONSTRUCTION and endless cycles of competition and combination were the chronic causes of rate discrimination in Gilded Age America. Discrimination in turn was by now the prime cause of agitation for railroad control. Struggling like Sisyphus against the "monopolies," shippers encouraged the construction of parallel lines while the carriers tried vainly to police themselves with pools and promises. Long-distance rates fell to the margin and below, while local freights staggered under recuperative charges. Public demands for regulation seemed to alternate with the outbreak of warfare among the roads themselves. That is why, as Charles Perkins explained to John Murray Forbes, a new boom would surely follow the period of recovery from the panic of 1873. By the time Perkins assumed the presidency of the CB&Q in 1881, that boom was under way.

The accession of Charles Perkins brought aggressiveness once more to the head of the Burlington railroad. Shy, reflective, and totally sincere, Perkins nevertheless had a way of achieving his objectives that appeared to others belligerent. He was a big, barrel-shaped man with a small face and a great mustache that concealed his mouth altogether. Dressed for business in his suit, waistcoat, gold chain, hat, and walking stick, he cut a commanding figure. Charles Francis Adams, Jr., a longtime friend and professional adversary of Perkins, found him no less exasperating than the "typical head of a small independent state." According to Adams, Perkins jealously guarded his "petty independence," always begging for "peace and two-thirds of the traffic."[52]

John Murray Forbes was sure that his younger cousin was the right man to lead the Burlington railroad into the coming age. Perkins was family, which still counted heavily with the older man. More importantly, Perkins was a company man whose loyalty could not be doubted. He passed his whole career on the Burlington Route. Finally, Charles Perkins was a systematic manager, which Forbes was not, and this is what made him modern. Even before taking command Perkins had restructured the internal operations of the Burlington. In the two decades of his own administration, Perkins wrote hundreds of pages in letters and memoranda detailing his theories of organization, administration, and human relations—some passages of which are classic statements of management science. Ironically for Forbes, Perkins despised paternalism as

---

52. Edward C. Kirkland, *Charles Francis Adams, Jr., 1835–1915: The Patrician at Bay* (Cambridge, Mass., 1965), 114.

a dangerous intrusion in a scientific world. He established lines of authority and communication and enforced them strictly. His hierarchy was both elegant and symmetrical. Atop the whole structure sat John Murray Forbes, chairman of the board, elder statesman, and founder of the firm. Perkins could not describe Forbes's actual duties, but "in our case," he concluded, "he is the head man."[53]

Public relations and corporate image played important new roles in Perkins's science of railroad management. Early in his administration he launched an advertising campaign to divert public attention from the problem of rates. Calendars, maps, and even playing cards emblazoned with the Burlington name were kept constantly before the traveler's eye, emphasizing service and convenience. Ignorance and misinformation, according to Perkins, were the chief causes of public hostility, and he strove tirelessly to enlighten the people on the principles of political economy. Even when the tone of the local press was enough "to discourage almost anybody," he refused to be demoralized. "[W]e must keep at it," he wrote in 1885, "and do the best we can to educate honest people, who are greatly in the majority." The remainder were "dishonest" and could not be reached "except through their pockets."[54]

Perkins also was a skilled influence broker. He and his lieutenants maintained powerful political connections in Iowa and Nebraska. Often calling on Forbes to feed money or doctrine into local campaigns, Perkins manipulated candidates and officials from either party with no concern for impropriety. He paid $1,900, for example, "nominally for advertising," to the *Burlington Gazette* because it was "for our own interest . . . that the Democratic paper here shd [sic] not be run as a Communistic sheet." This was only one of many "investments" made by Perkins and his staff to further the interests of the company. Should a "friend" thus won subsequently desert him, Perkins thought nothing of having him exposed as a paid lackey of business corporations.[55]

More confident than Forbes in this fast-changing world, Perkins stepped in just as another wave of railroad expansion was cresting. In seven years he doubled the size of the Burlington system. His ideal goal was inherited from Forbes: A "theoretically perfect Railroad system would be long and not very wide," holding to itself "a belt of country perhaps 50 miles wide — with arms

---

53. Perkins to Frederick Billings, 10 Nov. 1884, in Cochran, *Railroad Leaders*, 437. Perkins deserves a full-length biography, but none exists. Richard C. Overton alone has read a significant portion of Perkins's voluminous writings; his "Charles Elliott Perkins," *Business History Review* 31 (1957), 292–309, introduces Perkins's character, and *Perkins/Budd* (Westport, Conn., 1982), analyzes a good sample of his writings. Alfred D. Chandler, Jr., *The Railroads: The Nation's First Big Business* (New York, 1965), 97–128, sets Perkins in context with his fellow railroad managers.

54. Perkins to Thomas J. Potter, 22 Dec. 1884, and Perkins to William W. Baldwin, 18 March 1885, in Cochran, *Railroad Leaders*, 185, 440; Overton, *Burlington Route*, 202.

55. Perkins to JMF, 29 May 1879, in Box 3F3.2, CB&Q-Newberry; Perkins to James M. Walker, 23 April 1880, in C.E.P. Transcripts, Set A, CB&Q-Newberry. See also Cyrenus Cole, *A History of the People of Iowa* (Cedar Rapids, 1921), 449–50.

here & there reaching to great centers not within the system." But the ability of any man to impress order upon the structure of railroad markets was being destroyed by easy money and cutthroat competition. Consolidations were now taking place on a scale never imagined, and the resulting giant systems seemed ever more vulnerable. Strategies were determined by the growth of the systems themselves. Equilibrium proved elusive.[56]

Agitation for railroad regulation in the 1880s shifted focus to the federal level, a natural outgrowth of frustrations at lower levels of government. Local efforts to restrain the carriers always had been blunted by the limits of state jurisdiction. The railroad network ignored state boundaries, and most corporations now operated interstate roads as single units of enterprise. The rate structures devised by these roads conformed to the interstate market for transportation, and this frequently compromised local ambitions. Furthermore, interstate roads could flout state regulations or exploit the local application of laws to their systemwide advantage—the Burlington had tried both recently in Iowa. If there was to be effective regulation of these emerging railroad systems, it would have to come from an authority more comprehensive than the state.[57]

It was rate discrimination rather than high rates per se that continued to irritate most consumers. Railroad charges had fallen steadily and dramatically since the Civil War, but the benefits had not come evenly. Waves of competitive construction, like the one under way in the West in the 1880s, exacerbated the problem. Excess capacity yielded cutthroat competition that drove down through rates and exaggerated the high freights paid by captive shippers. Of course, discrimination was inherent in any national transport system that overcame the barrier of distance. Most shippers and carriers now knew that this was true. Still, "unfair" discrimination sparked their persistant complaint, and here the emotional component took hold once more. One veteran of the Iowa struggle concluded that the railroads "assumed greater powers than those of Deity": "They abrogated time and space; they changed the geography of the country. If rates were a guide, Omaha was situated between Chicago and Iowa, Denver was on the Mississippi, and San Francisco on the Missouri, while the interior towns of Iowa and Nebraska were located on Behring Strait."[58] The fact that railroads had been built for the express purpose of abrogating time and space did not make the complaint less bitter.

---

56. Perkins to JMF, 29 June 1879, in Cochran, *Railroad Leaders,* 432. See also Overton, *Burlington Route,* 197–98.

57. Albro Martin, "The Troubled Subject of Railroad Regulation in the Gilded Age: A Reappraisal," *Journal of American History* 61 (1974–75), 339–71, brilliantly summarizes the whole problem and its bearing on the passage of the Interstate Commerce Act.

58. N. B. Ashby, *Riddle of the Sphinx* (Des Moines, 1890), quoted in Throne, "Grange," 311; see Higgs, "Railroad Rates," 293–96; Aldrich, "Note," 428–32; Martin, "Troubled Subject," 343–44. No single statement on rates in the period can escape attack from another point of view. These authorities disagree on details, timing, and emphasis. Suffice it to say that it would have been hard for contemporaries to argue against high or rising rates by the late 1870s.

For Charles Perkins the problem of regulation was an intellectual challenge that transcended the expedient matters of company policy and business practice. He thought of rate making as a "contest" between the agent and the shipper, and the shipper "usually" got the "benefit of any doubt." Perkins believed that the "evil" of oppression by railroad pricing was "theoretical and imaginary, not real." To remedy the trouble "you *may* make" state or federal tariffs, but they would have to be "fixed and inelastic." Given such a fixed price, no businessman could undersell his neighbor; "you take out of business the 'root hog or die' principle." He worried about the vitality of the competitive system as a whole, and he could not imagine the survival of free enterprise with a transportation system that was neutral to all. Railroad transportation was "commerce," he argued, "not a tax or a toll." The ordinary laws of wholesale and retail trade therefore governed transport services as well, and if commercial practices worked occasional hardships on individuals, they were on the whole "beneficial to mankind."[59]

Of this benefit the public was not persuaded. Individual cases of abuse seemed to outweigh the evidence of overall gain, and by the middle of the 1880s a popular clamor for federal regulation no longer could be ignored. In 1885 the United States Senate established a select committee to investigate the whole problem of interstate commerce. Headed by Shelby M. Cullom of Illinois, this agency collected testimony from shippers and railroad officials across the nation. Its first act was to circulate a questionnaire among railroad executives, asking for their views on the nature of the problem and the various alternatives. Perkins responded for the Burlington, and once more he took the high road of theory. He dismissed as "trifling" those instances of inequality that inevitably occurred in a free market. No country so prosperous as the United States could possibly be suffering from burdensome railroad rates. If certain centers of trade enjoyed better service and cheaper rates, this was hardly the fault of the railroads. With this last assertion Perkins shed the whole weight of historical reality in American railroad development. From that point forward his argument flowed with clarity and force. He was correct, of course, that arbitrary discriminations and ruthless competition did not *necessarily* accompany railroad development. Unfortunately, in this country they did.[60]

Perkins was especially eager to shift attention away from the moral emphasis of public rhetoric, toward the cooler logic of abstract market systems. "Justice" played no part in the laws of trade, he argued, and it should not be interjected by force. In context, the railroad question was incredibly complex and riddled with traditional notions and conventions. Perkins wished to rise

---

59. Perkins to JMF, 24 Sept. 1879, in Box 3F3.2, CB&Q-Newberry; JMF to Perkins, 25 March 1881, in Box 3F3.1, CB&Q-Newberry; Perkins to JMF, 11 June 1885, in Cochran, *Railroad Leaders,* 441; Perkins memorandum, 20 Dec. 1883, quoted in Overton, *Burlington Route,* 182.

60. Charles E. Perkins, *Letter to Hon. S. M. Cullom* (Cambridge, Mass., 1885), 3–8. This is the pamphlet edition of the original letter, dated 21 Sept. 1885 at Burlington, Iowa.

above the history. The bare "right to regulate the charges of railroads" was "no longer disputed," he admitted. At issue now was the wisdom of public interference. Society might take hold of the business either by regulating rates or by limiting the construction of new lines. He warned against both:

> If you limit construction, it will be more or less necessary for society to interfere directly with the price of transportation, which, on the whole, it is not best to attempt, because reasonable prices can only he produced by natural adjustment; while, on the other hand, if you attempt to fix prices by law, without limiting construction, it will not be regarded as reasonable by private investors; and the tendency will be to drive railroad property into the hands of speculators, and to impair its efficiency and usefulness. Let competition and the fear of competition, direct and indirect, regulate the prices.

In sum, the transportation problem "was working itself out more rapidly than could have been thought possible twenty years ago." For Perkins, the "real Railroad Question" was no longer how to secure cheap transportation, but how to preserve free enterprise in America.[61]

Perkins's essay was well crafted and powerful, but he had missed the point. Even John Murray Forbes found his analysis naive in places. Free trade in railroad construction, Forbes sputtered, only loaded up the "solid Roads with cats (something as the early surveyors boots used to be weighted with rattlesnakes hanging on to them . . .)." When Perkins tried to deny that watered stock influenced the price of transportation, Forbes balked again. "Fraudulent value," Forbes reminded his cousin, was "often interjected in order to deceive" the public. It might be "inexpedient" to legislate against watered stocks, "but it is not unjust." Forbes knew that Perkins's argument was abstract, his analysis out of context; still he found the whole compelling. He was ready to endorse it "even if you don't care to alter a word of it." Unnerved by the starkness of Perkins's warnings, Forbes recoiled at the prospect of government control as "a step backwards toward the dark ages."[62]

By the summer of 1885 both Perkins and Forbes had begun to see federal railroad regulation as a form of civil disintegration. Sweeping away the record of failures in private enterprise in the last several decades, Forbes traced the industry back to his early days when the country was "*strewed* with the wrecks of State Rail Roads from Michigan to Pennsylvania." What the states had failed to do "would be ten times worse under U.S. management involving an enormous patronage & in short almost a revolution." Forbes could not overstate the danger from such "*centralization*" — the "Sum of all folly not to say wickedness." Once an avid proponent of central control, the old nationalist Forbes now cringed at the prospect of using government power to restrain the systems he had created. Why? Because politicians, not entrepreneurs, had gained control of government after the Civil War. Forbes had welcomed politics when it

---

61. Ibid., 8, 21–22, 26–27.
62. JMF to Perkins, 25 Aug. 1885, in Box 3F3.1, CB&Q-Newberry.

fostered his image of national unity and enterprise, but now he withdrew. He feared the national party machinery, even more than the old state democracies. In Europe, nationalism was leading to socialism by "pampering the unwashed classes." Such a drift was apparent at home as well, where Forbes thought it could run *"right up to* communism." It was Perkins who put the finest point on the matter: "In a republic where every man votes you are lost if you don't insist upon and rigidly adhere to the principle that Government is merely to protect life and property."[63]

FOR JOHN MURRAY FORBES the passage of the Interstate Commerce Act in February 1887 marked the end of true liberalism in America. But for people like the Iowa shippers along the CB&Q it was a sign of new hope. The country's first effort at federal railroad regulation laid down broad antidiscrimination principles and established a permanent board of commissioners to administer its provisions. The new law prohibited pooling, by which the railroads had hoped to achieve a measure of stability through self-regulation. On the more difficult question of long- and short-haul discrimination, the lawmakers hedged: Greater charges for the shorter haul were prohibited only if the services were performed under "substantially similar circumstances." The mandate was vague, the implied challenge broad. However, the mere passage of a national law, embodying tough antirailroad language and establishing continuous oversight of the railroad industry, made a favorable popular impression. Here was proof after all that the railroads were not beyond the reach of popular government. With renewed zeal, the Iowans turned their attention once more to the problem of state railroad control.[64]

Since 1878, when the Iowa General Assembly had repealed the maximum rate law, the Board of Railroad Commissioners had been responsible for supervising Iowa's railroads. Their role was strictly advisory, and the commissioners enjoyed limited powers. They could only investigate complaints that were brought to them by an injured party, and their recommendations were unenforceable. Their first purpose was to reduce the hostility between the people and the carriers; "adjustment and harmony" were their primary goals. Measured against these modest objectives, the advisory commission succeeded reasonably well. The commissioners maintained communication with the railroad companies, securing their cooperation in some rate adjustments and mollifying the shippers in other cases. Some members of the board were perhaps too intimate with railroad executives, like Judge J. W. McDill with Charles Perkins, but on the whole the Iowa board had established its integrity. The commission

---

63. JMF to Perkins, 12 Sept. 1885, in Forbes–Perkins Letters, CB&Q-Newberry; Perkins to Edith Forbes Perkins, 7 April 1886, in C-O1, P4.6, vol. 6, CB&Q-Newberry.

64. See Benson, *Merchants, Farmers, and Railroads,* 242–45; Gabriel Kolko, *Railroads and Regulation* (Princeton, 1965), 42–63; Martin, "Troubled Subject," 361–64.

had not wrestled the railroads into submission, but that was never its stated goal.[65]

The Iowa commissioner law of 1878 was the product of chastened optimism that followed the depression of the 1870s and the ill-fated Granger Law. Its limited objectives reflected the mood of a people whose anger had been vented and whose future looked momentarily bright. The illusion of harmony, however, peaked with the farm price index in the early 1880s, and the popular mood turned angry once more. By 1884 overproduction was forcing down farm prices, and rural communities felt the familiar squeeze of reduced income and steady, high local charges for transportation. Even Perkins admitted that some reductions probably were in order, but he would not act for fear that the regulatory commission would hold him to the lower rate forever. Six years of "harmony and adjustment" had gained little real compromise from the railroads serving Iowa.[66]

The inadequacy of the Iowa system in the face of changing popular feelings came to light in June 1885 at the interstate commerce hearings in Des Moines. Senator Shelby M. Cullom's committee listened intently to the commissioners' accounts of the general progress they felt had been made toward lasting harmony between carrier and shipper. Then countless merchants, farmers, and wholesalers paraded through the hearings telling tales of hardship, injury, and ruin which the embarrassed commissioners were powerless to address. Many shippers proved by their testimony that they only wanted lower rates for themselves, or higher rates for their competition, but the overall pattern of arbitrariness and inequity could not be dismissed. Animosities spread across the state as farm prices and local business continued to slide. By early 1886 Iowans had grown tired of "charming" theories about natural laws and railroad charges. Even Perkins's confidant on the Iowa board, Commissioner J. W. McDill, had reached his limit: "The man who goes down under the doctrine of the survival of the fittest can never be satisfied with his downfall because it is the result of a law which may be shown to serve the universe so well."[67]

McDill's defection came too late to alter the moods of Forbes and Perkins. By March 1886 neither man was receptive to the "ominous warnings" passed on to them by the Iowa railroad commissioners. The "misunderstanding and jealousy" that prevailed between shippers and carriers was truly deplorable, the situation dangerous. The merchants were especially restless, and the commissioners feared that without relief, the "wholesale and manufacturing interests" of Iowa would be "more or less crippled." Perkins replied with a stone.

---

65. Iowa Railroad Commissioners, *Report, 1886,* 33. For a careful examination of the first Iowa commissioner law and its workings, see Frank H. Dixon, *State Railroad Control: With a History of Its Development in Iowa* (New York, 1896), chaps. 1 and 2.

66. J. W. McDill to Perkins, 24 Dec. 1884, in Box 33-1880-4.65, CB&Q-Newberry.

67. J. W. McDill to Perkins, 2 Feb. 1886, in Box 33-1880-4.65, CB&Q-Newberry.

"I have never known of a single case," he wrote, "of failure because of rates charged by a Railroad." More often it was the corporations who were "preyed upon by interested and designing persons, who misrepresented or distorted the facts in order to benefit themselves." State regulation had reached a stalemate just at the time that Congress was debating a federal bill. Both shippers and carriers watched in suspense for an interstate railroad law.[68]

When the new law came, early in 1887, it was hailed in Iowa as a triumph of popular government at the highest level. The Iowa railroad commissioners were personally excited by the prospects of bringing state regulation into "perfect harmony" with the federal Interstate Commerce Act. These professional servants of a troubled industry saw a chance to approach the problem with unity and system.[69] In the popular mind, however, a power struggle had been renewed. Now totally dependent on railroads for their business, but encouraged at last by the promise of federal control, Iowa's shippers struck back at the carriers to recover some of the power that their condition of economic dependency had cost them. This new outburst of local temper was brought into focus by a businessman-turned-reformer, Governor William Larrabee.

WILLIAM LARRABEE was a Connecticut Yankee who had come to Iowa in 1853 — the same year John Murray Forbes took an interest in the Burlington railroad. Larrabee eventually settled in the village of Clermont, in northeastern Iowa, where he prospered as a flour miller, farmer, banker, and land speculator. In 1867, after a brief experiment in railroad construction, he was elected to the Iowa Senate. Nearly twenty years' loyal service to the state and the Republican party placed Larrabee in the running for governor in 1885. Endorsed by the leading papers, he won easily. A stately, prosperous-looking man, the new governor's visage was overwhelmed by a mustache more luxuriant than even Charles Perkins's. Vigorous and energetic at the age of fifty-four, he took office in January 1886, pledging to stop the flow of whiskey and to reform the public finances in the state of Iowa.[70]

What brought Larrabee into conflict with Forbes, Perkins, and the Burlington railroad was a little incidence of economic injustice that perfectly illustrates the escalation of tempers in the railroad question. Nothing in Larrabee's past record suggested radical views on railroad reform; also, there had been no general outcry in the state campaign that year. Prohibition and fiscal responsibility — both solid Republican issues — had given the governor his majority, and it was during a subsequent audit of the public books that a problem arose concerning the CB&Q. The issue sparked an attack on the

---

68. Iowa Railroad Commissioners to Perkins, 18 March 1886, and Perkins to Iowa Railroad Commissioners, 14 April 1886, in Box 33-1880-4.65, CB&Q-Newberry.

69. Iowa Railroad Commissioners, *Report, 1887*, 31–46.

70. See J. Brooke Workman, "Governor William Larrabee and Railroad Reform," *Iowa Journal of History* 57 (1959), 231–34; *Iowa State Daily Register*, 20 May 1885.

railroads that astonished Larrabee's friends and his party. It seems that the CB&Q was charging the state more to transport coal to the Feeble Minded Institution at Glenwood than to transport the same commodity to a site in Council Bluffs. Since the same train serviced both towns, and since Glenwood was nearer the mines, Larrabee thought that the charge was unfair. He asked the railroad commissioners to investigate.

In December 1886, the Iowa board asked the Burlington for an explanation of the Glenwood rate. Perkins responded that competition at Council Bluffs forced a low rate there, but that it should not be construed as a paying rate for a local point like Glenwood. This seemed reasonable to the commissioners, who were familiar with the distortions caused by competition, but Larrabee was not satisfied. He demanded a thorough investigation. While the board was reviewing the case the Interstate Commerce Act was passed, outlawing such discriminations in interstate service and strengthening Larrabee's argument. On February 10, 1887, the commissioners asked the Burlington to end discrimination at Glenwood. Perkins chose not to lower the Glenwood tariff, but to raise Council Bluffs to the higher rate. Larrabee's response was explosive. He refiled the case on March 7, damning railroad company and railroad commissioners alike for ignoring the law and violating the public trust.[71]

Discrimination like that at Glenwood typified differential pricing throughout the railroad system. With the practice now banned in interstate commerce, the whole burden of noncompeting charges was likely to fall on intrastate traffic. This gave Larrabee the opening he needed to introduce new, aggressive principles of regulation. With all the fervor of the newly converted, he swept away fine arguments and demanded that the railroads *prove* that they had not injured the complaining shipper. When the CB&Q argued that their competing rate at Council Bluffs was ruinously low, Larrabee dismissed their plea as nonsense: Rational businessmen did not voluntarily set rates below the cost of service! Perkins's agents then replied that the rate-making process was too complicated for nonspecialists such as the governor to understand. Larrabee denounced this as obfuscation: "It is no use in permitting ourselves to be mystified by having the idea prevail that this is so complex a matter that a reasonable man cannot comprehend it."[72]

Larrabee's attack was novel and broad. It struck at the heart of a cherished conviction of Forbes and Perkins: that the layman just couldn't understand. Iowa's governor abandoned the intricate points of economic theory for the democratic values of utility and equity; he would stop the flow of power to

---

71. Larrabee to Iowa Railroad Commissioners, 6 Dec. 1886; Larrabee to E. C. Morgan, 4 Jan. 1887; and Larrabee to Iowa Railroad Commissioners, 7 March 1887, in William Larrabee Papers, State Historical Society of Iowa, Montauk, Clermont, Iowa (hereafter cited as Larrabee-Montauk). See also "State of Iowa v. C.B.&Q." (filed 7 Dec. 1886, decided 10 Feb. 1887) and other material in Box 33-1880-4.65, CB&Q-Newberry.

72. Iowa Railroad Commissioners, *Report, 1887,* 650; see pp. 634–70 for notes on the hearings, 9 April 1887.

the technicians. With a populism worthy of the original Jacksonians, he set about debunking railroad managers and commissioners alike. Larrabee thought the commission had become dependent on railroad favor (McDill, he believed, was employed by the Burlington). He denounced their delicate procedures and the "trifling character" of their work. Despite the clear limitations of their powers, Larrabee condemned their inaction. "You should know," he thundered, when railroads break the law. "You should not wait to have the complaints brought before you." Before he was through, the governor had outlined nothing less than an advocate's role for the advisory commission that it never would have dared to fulfill.[73]

Embarrassed and resentful, the Iowa Board of Railroad Commissioners finally ruled that the Glenwood rate should be lowered. Their orders came too late. For Governor Larrabee, the issue had outgrown the case at hand. He was dedicated to vigorous railroad control. Reporting to Perkins from the Des Moines hearings, CB&Q Vice President Thomas J. Potter recognized the seriousness of the matter. "We have got to decide whether we will fight or surrender," he concluded, "and I am afraid we will be beaten in either course we may pursue."[74]

Why had Larrabee taken so fierce a stand over the cost of shipping coal? Perkins believed it was demagoguery—partisan madness. But Larrabee was not a demagogue, and he would lose, not gain, a party. What bothered Larrabee was the willful subordination of what he considered to be true republicanism to the demands of "grasping" corporations. Like James W. Grimes, Iowa's original Republican, Larrabee conceived his government to be the protector of the community, the handmaiden of Iowa enterprise and welfare. Institutions of local government were under attack from businessmen and clerks who behaved as if they were above the law; it was the obligation of government to resist. The regulation campaign that followed was not an effort to refine the principles of railroad economics but a war against the arrogance of "experts" who scorned the authority of popular government.

Characteristically, Charles Perkins met Larrabee's challenge with direct correspondence aimed at educating this heretic in the science of trade. The extent of the heresy was made clear in August 1887, when Larrabee proclaimed the railroads to be public highways subject to the same restrictions imposed on banks, hacks, and ferries. The corporation, he argued, was a "mere agency" of society and should never be free to set rates primarily for private profits and stock dividends. Perkins was horrified. Railroads were clearly and undeniably private corporations, as much entitled to their profits as any merchant, farmer, or manufacturer. If the governor desired reasonable railroad rates,

---

73. "Governor William Larrabee v. C.B.&Q." (Rehearing, filed 7 March 1887, decided 7 May 1887), in Box 33-1880-4.65, CB&Q-Newberry. See also J. W. McDill to Perkins, 15 Feb. 1887, in Box 33-1880-4.65, CB&Q-Newberry.

74. Thomas J. Potter to Perkins, 10 April 1887, in Box 33-1880-4.65, CB&Q-Newberry.

Perkins knew but one way to achieve them: "Leave the commercial, as distinguished from the police, management of railroads wholly in the hands of their owners." Iowa's future development would surely be retarded if Larrabee's views prevailed. The governor retorted that the people of Iowa had been fair and generous with the roads: "Do not fear but more railroads will be built." If, as Perkins insisted, the railroads were strictly private businesses, then they were not gifts bestowed upon the people and they deserved no special gratitude. As instruments of private profit, railroads yielded discrimination and injustice; the perpetuation of their freedoms must bring more of the same. It would be folly to leave them alone. "[W]hat do you think of any business man," scolded Larrabee, "who adopts your rule of charging what you can get, one price to one and another to another?" In ordinary trade such a merchant could only hold his patrons "by cunning divisions or some underhanded methods." Nothing but "public sentiment against it" would correct these abuses. Perkins could only deny that such customs existed. Larrabee laughed: Railroad managers always denied these charges.[75]

Perkins's educational efforts were intended to prove the logic of nature's laws of trade, but instead they fueled Larrabee's fire. For a generation Perkins's theories had been promoted as prerequisites to growth and riches. Regulation had always failed because interested parties were persuaded that it was unwise for them. Larrabee challenged the voters of Iowa to compare that wisdom with their own experience. He leveled his criticism at the whole rate-making mechanism, and the people responded. Iowa's Republican party regulars, led by United States Senator William Boyd Allison, whose presidential aspirations hung in the balance, tried to silence the governor. Nothing worked. Perkins's political manager, Joseph W. Blythe, reported that Iowa was "determined upon some anti-RR regulation." He frankly concluded: "I don't believe Clarkson & Allison can stop it." The politicians could only hope that, once elected, Larrabee would settle down.[76]

That hope went unrewarded. Larrabee opened his second term with an antirailroad blast that shocked the party regulars. On January 10, 1888, he outlined for the General Assembly a program of railroad reform that was thorough and stern. Destroy the pass system "root and branch," he began, and reduce the pernicious influence of the railroads upon public officials. Set a maximum two cents per mile passenger fare to minimize discrimination in personal travel between cities and the countryside. Reinstitute maximum rates of freight "on the principal commodities transported by rail," and authorize the railroad commissioners "to reduce said rates at any time when, in their

---

75. Larrabee to Perkins, 9 Aug. 1887; Perkins to Larrabee, 16 Aug. and 31 Oct. 1887; Larrabee to Perkins, 18 Nov. 1887; Perkins to Larrabee, 2 Dec. 1887; Larrabee to Perkins, 19 Dec. 1887, in Box 3P4.13, CB&Q-Newberry. The entire correspondence from June through December 1887 is in this box.

76. Joseph W. Blythe to Perkins, 25 July 1887, in Box 3P4.5, ser. 1, no. 4, CB&Q-Newberry. See also Perkins to JMF, 1 Sept. 1887, in Box C-O, F3.1, CB&Q-Newberry

judgment, they are too high." If the delegation of rate-making powers to an administrative board was deemed unlawful, let the commissioners' rates stand as *prima facie* evidence of reasonable rates. Such a rule would throw the burden of proof onto the offending railroad, which could well afford to defend itself. Larrabee encouraged a bill making railroad commissioners elective, and he urged that they be paid from the state treasury, not from railroad assessments as was then being done.[77]

The governor's program rested on angry assumptions. The corporations had proved unwilling to serve the community fairly. Now they should be prepared to defend their practices against shippers armed with the legal advantage. This was a simplistic, dangerous view that overlooked the mischief that shippers worked in the railroad market. Still, it was no more than John Murray Forbes had predicted back in 1881, when he had called for a better justification for discriminatory rates. The railroads had failed to make their case with the people, and now Larrabee saw them as "public corporations" whose officers should be "required to take an oath to obey the constitution and laws" of the state and the nation. For the good of the commonwealth, "stringent means should be applied to strong corporations, [while] the weak ones should be protected, especially the new roads making efforts to do business at lower rates." The railroad commission should become "a committee of the people obligated to advocate their rights." Railroad commissioners should "exercise full and complete supervision over the railroads . . . compelling them to comply with the laws. . . . With less than this the people of Iowa will not and should not be satisfied."[78]

From this position there was no retreat. Larrabee's party deserted him; James S. Clarkson, Des Moines editor and party boss, declared war on the governor in the morning edition of the *Iowa State Register*:

> It is plain that the Governor intended to make it the most extreme official utterance which has ever been made as to railways, and it is equally plain that he has succeeded in his purpose. The whole color and tone of the message on this subject is intense and exceedingly radical, . . . and suggests a sense of personal animosity, based on fancied personal grievances.

The most "extraordinary" of Larrabee's positions was the "declaration that the Railroad Commission was not made to help establish and maintain justice alike to people and railways, but to deal with the railways without justice and let them take care of themselves as best they can." Clarkson doubted that he could find "a dozen fair-minded people in Iowa" who would endorse "this astounding utterance." In addition to his public attack, Clarkson sent Larrabee eight pages of scorching criticism in a private letter, demanding that the governor rescind

---

77. *Iowa Senate Journal, 1888,* 36–38.
78. Ibid., 64. See JMF to Perkins, 25 March 1881, in Box 3F3.1, CB&Q-Newberry.

his views. Larrabee would not repent; his railroad reforms would be won or lost on the floor of the General Assembly.[79]

To combat the reforms Charles Perkins approved "any plan" that his political agents might adopt. He hoped that the governor had "rather overshot his mark"; but CB&Q Solicitor J. W. Blythe in Iowa prepared for the worst, calling in favors and lining up support for a major legislative battle. No source of pressure was overlooked. The CB&Q and other companies even circulated petitions in their yards and shops, and out along the line of their roads, shipping pleas by the dozen to Des Moines begging the General Assembly to be fair with the roads. Using time-honored techniques, the railroads labored to divide the electorate along lines of conflicting business interests.[80]

The railroads' campaign was met by astute opposition. Governor Larrabee was a veteran of Iowa legislative politics, and he prepared his ground well. Wherever editor Clarkson turned with a word of advice he found the governor ahead of him, "interviewing members of both houses, urging immediate & radical action and saying that the arguments advanced by [Railroad Commissioner] McDill and others are based on fabricated & lying statements of fact." Larrabee controlled the leadership of both houses, and the inertia of his movement left members cautious about taking the railroads' bait. The governor treated senators to dinner in pairs (one solid and one wavering), where, according to Blythe, he set out his case and lay "down on his man." Gradually support coalesced both inside and outside the legislature. The two-cent fare and the abolition of passes were lost in committee, but the essential bill for a strong commission empowered to fix reasonable rates and enforce their application passed both houses and emerged from a conference committee by April 2, 1888. Signed by a triumphant Larrabee on April 10, the new law took effect in just thirty days.[81]

Chapter Twenty-Eight of the Acts of the Twenty-Second General Assembly of Iowa imposed new rules on local transportation. To fix tariffs that were reasonable and just was the stated goal; rebates, drawbacks, pools, and discrimination between persons and places were all prohibited. Differential pricing, to be legal, must be justified by a real difference in the cost or character of service. No greater charge was allowed for short over long hauls whenever the short was contained within the long. Volume discriminations *were* allowed on carload and hundred-pound lots, but no further distinctions were granted between one unit and many. Tariffs must be posted where all eligible shippers might read them. Finally, the board of railroad commissioners was instructed to prepare a schedule

---

79. *Iowa State Daily Register,* 13 Jan. 1888. See also Clarkson to Larrabee, 17 Jan. 1888, in Larrabee-Montauk.

80. Perkins to J. W. Blythe, 17 Dec. 1887, in Cochran, *Railroad Leaders,* 446. See also Blythe's letters to Perkins, Jan. through March 1888, in Box 3P4.5, ser. 1, no. 5, CB&Q-Newberry.

81. J. W. Blythe to Perkins, 5, 8, and 29 Feb. 1888, in Box 3P4.5, ser. 1, no. 5, CB&Q-Newberry. Legislative details and final passage appear in *Iowa Senate Journal, 1888,* 822–28; and *Iowa House Journal, 1888,* 826.

of maximum rates that would serve in a court of law as *prima facie* evidence of reasonable charges. The true radicalism of the act lay in its aggressive mandate: Larrabee's commissioners must advocate the people's cause.[82]

Despite its punitive rhetoric, Larrabee's campaign produced a law that was legally defensible. Of course implementation would be difficult and court challenges were sure to follow. The existing commissioners began at once carefully assembling a schedule of rates, choosing in most cases a published tariff somewhere between the highest and lowest freight currently charged for each class of service. In May, after being reviewed by the railroad freight agents, the commissioners' rates were published, to be effective in thirty days. The Chicago roads immediately cancelled all Iowa tariffs except the highest distance rate; they even broke interstate shipments at the borders, charging high local rates across Iowa. Joined together in a secret pact for mutual defense, the CB&Q and three other lines finally secured an order from the U.S. District Court, on June 27, 1888, restraining the Iowa Board of Railroad Commissioners from enforcing their schedule of rates.[83]

The essential complaint of the railroads was simple: The Iowa rates were "ruinously" low. But this was hard for the railroads to prove. Reflecting the narrowest of views, Judge David J. Brewer continued his injunction one month later, carefully focusing on the level of the rates alone. Brewer thought that the Iowa rates were probably confiscatory, but only time would tell. He exacted a $50,000 bond from the railroad companies for damages in case this injunction were found to be wrongfully issued. Suddenly the high distance rates being charged in Iowa were a liability, and the CB&Q made its first reductions in August. Political negotiations were opened to arrange a compromise between commissioners and railroads, but despite efforts to "put a ring in" the governor's nose, Larrabee proved immovable. In November a newly elected board of commissioners issued another revised schedule, and the railroads returned to Judge Brewer. Both sides idled away the Christmas season waiting for the court's reply.[84]

The prospect of a defeat at the hands of a clamorous democracy depressed Charles Perkins. He complained to Forbes that the Republican party had "gone

---

82. *Laws of Iowa, 1888,* chaps. 28 and 29 (chap. 29 called for the election of railroad commissioners). Ivan L. Pollock, *History of Economic Legislation in Iowa* (Iowa City, 1918), chap. 2, gives a brief survey of railroad and transportation legislation that helps establish the legal context of the 1888 Commissioner Law.

83. See Iowa Railroad Commissioners, *Report, 1888,* 31–41; Perkins to JMF, 19 and 22 June 1888, in Box 33-1880-4.65, CB&Q-Newberry; Henry B. Stone to Perkins, 8 June 1888, in Box 3S7.1, CB&Q-Newberry. The complaint filed with U.S. Circuit Court, Southern District of Iowa, on 27 June 1888 is in Box 33-1880-4.65.

84. See Box 33-1880-4.65, CB&Q-Newberry, for documents relating to legal proceedings. Judge Brewer's decision of 28 July 1888 was clipped from the *Iowa State Daily Register* of that date. See also renewed investigations in Iowa Railroad Commissioners, *Report, 1888,* 805ff. For compromise, see James C. Peasley to Perkins, 19 Oct. 1888, in Box 33-1880-4.5, CB&Q-Newberry; and Perkins to Jacob Rich, 30 Oct. 1888, in C.E.P. Transcripts, Set A, CB&Q-Newberry.

clear over to the Devil," and he agonized over the possible judicial sanction of more state interference in rate making. Perkins was beginning to think that his case was lost. Brewer believed "confiscation" resulted only when the state took "the LAST dollar" of railroad profit, but Perkins thought any compulsory rate "below what the owner of the Railroad might otherwise reasonably charge" was confiscation as well. If the public could claim *any* corporate profits, this was "just as true of the first and every other dollar" as it was of the last. Perkins's lawyers agreed, but they advised him that his position was a legal novelty. Strict vindication of laissez-faire principles might be logically preferable, but a clear victory was unlikely. Throughout January Forbes waited and Perkins fretted. On February 2, 1889, Judge Brewer lifted his original injunction, giving force at last to the Iowa rates. This time Brewer would not condemn the schedule in advance. Only experience would show if the rates were too low. Clearly beaten, Perkins notified the Iowa board that the CB&Q would comply with their ruling immediately.[85]

Charles Perkins was bitterly disappointed in the outcome of the Iowa fight. Despite the effects of a massive strike that had crippled the Burlington most of the year, Perkins blamed the company's losses in 1888 on the effects of hostile rate regulation.[86] Several Burlington directors shared Perkins's gloom, but John Murray Forbes was undaunted. He was sorry his friends took "so blue a view." Judge Brewer's injunction, Forbes always thought, "was a little too good to last." The matter was now securely in the hands of the federal courts, where the railroads would get their best hearing. Patience would be rewarded. Forbes had survived these struggles before—even the passage of federal railroad restraints—and he was not expecting to settle the issue once and for all. Now seventy-six years old and "twice that age if you measure by the strain," the old entrepreneur refused to become demoralized.[87]

FORBES WAS PARTLY RIGHT; the federal courts did prove to be the railroads' surest refuge into the 1890s (the Iowa joint-rate law of 1890 and a similar Nebraska law were struck down by judicial review). Yet William Larrabee, whose local perspective and strident moral quality represented a voice from the past, ultimately foretold a new wave of indignant, popular reform. His attack on the power of chartered corporations was an early example of

---

85. Perkins to JMF, 19 Oct. 1888, in Box C-O, F3.1, CB&Q-Newberry; Perkins memorandum, 25 Dec. 1889; Edward C. Perkins to Charles E. Perkins, 23 Jan. 1889; Wirt Dexter to Perkins, 2 Jan. 1889, in Box 33-1880-4.65, CB&Q-Newberry. Judge Brewer's final decision of 2 Feb. 1889 was clipped from the *Iowa State Daily Register* of that date. On 4 Feb. 1889 Perkins notified the Iowa Railroad Commissioners that the Burlington would comply. Iowa Railroad Commissioners, *Report, 1889,* 29.

86. Overton, *Burlington Route,* 212–14; Donald L. McMurray, *The Great Burlington Strike of 1888* (Cambridge, Mass., 1956).

87. JMF to Peter Geddes, 8 Feb. 1889, in Box 3F3.1, CB&Q-Newberry; JMF to [deleted by editor], [c. Jan. 1889], in C-O1, P4.6, vol. 8, CB&Q-Newberry.

emotional outbursts that would rock city bosses, utility companies, and eventually the great trusts in the decades to come. If his moral view was naive, it nevertheless touched a popular nerve. America was still a democratic republic, where the people supposedly ruled and where the beneficiaries of government were expected to serve the common welfare. Corporations were created by legislators, who were elected by a people whose will they should reflect. It was inconceivable to Larrabee, as it had been to James W. Grimes thirty years before, that a chartered corporation could be forever above the power of the assembly that gave it life. Therefore, it was no crime for the people to reclaim what they had granted. Larrabee's radicalism was part of that populism that was central to the American political tradition. His "novelty" was merely a reflection of the changes that had ravaged the nineteenth-century world. Even railroad men like Charles Perkins, for all their raging against the "populists," were coming to realize that politics and government would never leave an open field for corporate enterprise. "When Adam Smith wrote his book," wrote a resigned Perkins in 1891, "the masses did not rule—now they do; and we are governed, in this country at least, not by the highest but by the average intelligence."[88]

This inevitable role for popular government was the heart of the regulation question. When William Larrabee left Iowa politics in 1890, he retired to his country home to write a definitive treatise on *The Railroad Question*. Larrabee focused his attention almost exclusively on power. In an early chapter on monopoly he found his target: "From time immemorial efforts have been made by designing men to control either commerce or its avenues, the highways on the land and on the sea, by a power which law, custom, ingenuity, artifice or some other agency had placed in their hands."[89] No one doubted the prevalence of such oppressions in former times and under European forms of government, but Larrabee feared that Americans naively believed that their system of government prevented monopoly. Their very faith left them defenseless! Larrabee recited example after example of railroad companies exercising monopolistic powers with impunity, and he assured his readers that only those who received special favors were unaware of the power in this "iron hand." Finally, the railway company was portrayed as "a closely organized body of shrewd, active men" against which unorganized citizens were powerless. Three hundred pages of detailed charges and remedies followed, but every turn of the argument flowed from the assumption that railroad corporations, like medieval bandits, inevitably sought to tyrannize the shipping public.[90]

If Governor Larrabee's argument fell short of comprehending the actual problems of the railroad network, it was an excellent expression of popular sentiment. It is not surprising, given these assumptions, that legislators and

---

88. Perkins to T. M. Marquette, 3 Jan. 1891, in R.C.O. no. 9, CB&Q-Newberry.
89. William Larrabee, *The Railroad Question* (Chicago, 1893), 90.
90. Ibid., 91–123.

reformers rejected pooling and self-regulation by the railroads as absurd. Arguments that exploitation by shippers was the real cause of discrimination, even when true, could not gain credibility with the public. Restraints of cutthroat competition earned no popular sanction in the Gilded Age unless they carried with them a sense of victory over the perpetrators of railroad injustices. Calls for legal minimum rates, however sophisticated, were laughable. Larrabee's warning, not to let the appearance of popular government lull men out of their vigilance, struck a responsive chord in individuals whose local institutions had been snubbed one way or another by a railroad official. Corporation lobbyists were unavoidably recognized as corrupters of republican government. The fact that railroad managers were often arrogant, that their agents were arbitrary and their lobbyists corrupting, brought this moral interpretation fully to life.

Even at the federal level, where corporations had sought protection from irresponsible localism, the vigor of regulatory injunctions continued to grow. After 1887, the Interstate Commerce Commission quickly found the limits of its effectiveness. Like any party at law, the commission could not address inequities in the rate structure as a whole or satisfy more than the individual whose complaint was before it. Further legislation was likely as long as the public complained of injury and abuse, and the popularity of reform was increasing dramatically by 1900. The Elkins Act of 1903 prohibited railroads from abandoning in any case their published schedule of rates. In 1906, the Hepburn Act finally granted the Interstate Commerce Commission the power to fix reasonable maximum rates with the force of law. The Mann-Elkins Act of 1910 forbade long- and short-haul discriminations *under any circumstances;* and like the Iowa law of 1888, it placed the burden of proof for any rate on the railroad company itself. Theoretically, the designs of evil men had just about been proscribed at either the state or federal level by 1910. Unfortunately the causes of distress in the railroad market lay elsewhere, and this regulatory approach missed its mark.[91]

The generation of Iowans that erected the framework for state railroad regulation in the late nineteenth and early twentieth centuries failed to understand all that was behind the hardships they suffered and the benefits they sought. Most reformers did not intend to destroy corporate enterprise as a part of some vengeful attack on progress. On the contrary, the reformers' scrambled for their share of the fruits of booming American capitalism. Many joined the national "Progressive Movement," and like the Grangers and Alliance before them, many so-called Progressives were victimized by opportunistic politicians among their ranks. Still, their movement was not totally cynical. What reformers sought in every case was to establish—or reestablish—popular authority

---

91. Kolko, *Railroads and Regulation,* chaps. 5–9, treats this development as steady progress, but compare the argument with Albro Martin, *Enterprise Denied: Origins of the Decline of American Railroads, 1897–1917* (New York, 1971).

wherever an individual's right to strive and gain seemed threatened by corporate power. At times their anger led them to punish enterprise excessively, but their attacks on industry no more than matched the abuses they had suffered in the past. Unfortunately, by the time the regulatory structure was in place in the United States, the time for guiding the development of railroads was past. The transformation of the national marketplace, and the integration of states within that national system, largely was complete. As a result, the objectives of localism so often found behind the struggle for state railroad control seemed out of place by the time they had been fairly won.

BIBLIOGRAPHICAL NOTE

The history of railroads in Iowa is one of the most significant stories in Iowa history, and there is certainly no shortage of materials on this topic. Patricia Dawson and David Hudson found about 175 items devoted to railroads published between 1952 and 1991. It is unfortunate, then, that no one in recent decades has attempted to synthesize recent scholarship to present a comprehensive view of the impact of railroads on Iowa's economic and social development. The closest I have seen to that is Rebecca Conard's unpublished context statement prepared to document a survey of historic sites related to Iowa railroads. See "Historic Patterns of Railroad Organization and Development in Iowa," National Register of Historic Places Multiple Property Documentation Form, on file in the Historic Preservation offices of the State Historical Society of Iowa in Des Moines; a copy is at the State Historical Society of Iowa, Iowa City.

Actually, much of the best railroad scholarship comes from the early part of the past four decades. See, for example, David S. Sparks, "Iowa Republicans and the Railroads, 1867–1860," *Iowa Journal of History* 53 (1955), 273–86; George Miller, "Origins of the Iowa Granger Law," *Mississippi Valley Historical Review* 40 (1954), 657–80; George A. Boeck, "A Decade of Transportation Fever in Burlington, Iowa, 1845–1855," *Iowa Journal of History* 56 (1958), 129–52; George W. Sieber, "Railroads and Lumber Marketing, 1858–1878: The Relationship between an Iowa Sawmill Firm and the Chicago and North Western Railroad," *Annals of Iowa* 39 (1967), 33–46; and the series of articles on individual rail lines by Frank Donovan, Jr., in the *Palimpsest* in the 1950s and 1960s.

Although much of this older work represents good scholarship, it is often rather narrow in scope and application. Recently, however, historians have begun viewing railroad development along with other topics. Bill Silag shows how railroads contributed to the settlement and development of Sioux City and northwestern Iowa. Timothy Mahoney treats railroads as an integral part of his analysis of regional urban economic systems. (See the citations of Silag's and Mahoney's work in the bibliographical note to Shelton Stromquist's essay.)

The leaders in the movement to rehabilitate the reputation of railroad companies and their leaders are Thomas C. Cochran, *Railroad Leaders,*

1845–1890: The Business Mind in Action (Cambridge, MA, 1953); Albro Martin, *Enterprise Denied: Origins of the Decline of American Railroads, 1897–1917* (New York, 1971); and Maury Klein, *The Life and Legend of Jay Gould* (Baltimore, 1986). The most articulate (and prolific) spokesperson for the rehabilitation of the reputation of Iowa railroad companies is H. Roger Grant; see, for example, "Railroaders and Reformers: The Chicago & North Western Encounters Grangers and Progressives," *Annals of Iowa* 50 (1991), 772–86. The traditional view continues to receive support from good scholarship. See, for example, Philip J. Nelson, "The Rockwell Co-operative Society and the Iowa Farmers' Elevator Movement, 1870–1920," *Annals of Iowa* 54 (1995), 1–24.

On the Patrons of Husbandry, or Grange, the primary mobilizers of opposition to the railroads, the standard account is Solon Justus Buck, *The Granger Movement: A Study of Agricultural Organization and Its Political, Economic, and Social Manifestations, 1870–1880* (Cambridge, MA, 1913). More recent accounts include D. Sven Nordin, *Rich Harvest: A History of the Grange, 1867–1900* (Jackson, MS, 1974); Thomas A. Woods, *Knights of the Plow: Oliver H. Kelley and the Origins of the Grange in Republican Ideology* (Ames, 1991); and Donald B. Marti, *Women of the Grange: Mutuality and Sisterhood in Rural America, 1866–1920* (Westport, CT, 1991). On the Grange in Iowa, see Myrtle Beinhauer, "Development of the Grange in Iowa, 1868–1930," *Annals of Iowa* 34 (1959), 597–618.

Besides railroads, the history of Iowa transportation and its effects on the development of the state has been slighted. William H. Thompson, *Transportation in Iowa: A Historical Summary* (Ames, 1989), provides an overview of limited depth and analysis. A recent nod to bus transportation is in Margaret Walsh, "Iowa's Bus Queen: Helen M. Schultz and the Red Ball Transportation Company," *Annals of Iowa* 53 (1994), 329–55. Most seriously in need of solid interpretive work is the impact of automobiles and roads on Iowa's development. The obvious place to begin is with the Good Roads movement. An early work on that topic is George S. May, "The Good Roads Movement in Iowa," *Palimpsest* 36 (1955), 1–64. Another early (and related) critical development was the Lincoln Highway. Offering different approaches to that topic are Drake Hokanson, *The Lincoln Highway: Main Street across America* (Iowa City, 1988); and Rebecca Conard, "The Lincoln Highway in Greene County: Highway Politics, Local Initiative, and the Emerging Federal Highway System," *Annals of Iowa* 52 (1993), 351–84. Particularly noteworthy, too, is chapter four of Thomas J. Morain, *Prairie Grass Roots: An Iowa Small Town in the Early Twentieth Century* (Ames, 1988); more than half of that chapter, devoted to new technologies in the first third of the twentieth century, assesses the impact of automobiles on the lives of the residents of Jefferson, Iowa. It is not too early to begin assessing the impact of interstate highways on the development of the state and on particular communities, much as Conard and Morain have done for early automobiles and roads.

Changes in communication technology were probably as significant as changes in transportation technology, although they have received far less attention. We need more work that follows the lead of Roy Alden

Atwood, in "Interlocking Newspaper and Telephone Company Directorates in Southeastern Iowa, 1900–1917," *Annals of Iowa* 47 (1984), 255–69; idem, "The Rural Press and the Electronic Mythos: Images and Interlocking Interests in Southeastern Iowa, 1900–1917," *Journalism History* 10 (1983), 1–18; idem, "Routes of Rural Discontent: Cultural Contradictions of Rural Free Delivery in Southeastern Iowa, 1899–1917," *Annals of Iowa* 48 (1986), 264–73; Wayne E. Fuller, *RFD: The Changing Face of Rural America* (Bloomington, IN, 1964); and William B. Friedricks, "The Newspaper that Captured a State: A History of the *Des Moines Register,* 1849–1985," *Annals of Iowa* 54 (1995), 303–37.

10

Why the Populist Party Was Strong in Kansas and Nebraska but Weak in Iowa

JEFFREY OSTLER

Because the Populists' presidential candidate in 1892 was Iowan James Baird Weaver, the Populist movement in Iowa has always received what is probably more than its fair share of attention. In fact, Weaver's People's Party was not very successful in Iowa. Historians have traditionally explained that failure by noting that Iowa farmers were not suffering economically as much as the farmers of Kansas and Nebraska, where the party did better. In this essay, Jeffrey Ostler counters that argument. In the process, he also suggests that an exclusively economic or ethnocultural analysis of quantifiable data is not sufficient; historians must also understand the distinctive political cultures that develop in different states. His comparative perspective is extremely valuable and may serve as a model for other historians.

The influence of factious leaders may kindle a flame within their particular States but will be unable to spread a general conflagration through the other States. . . . A rage for paper money, for an abolition of debts, for an equal division of property, or for any other improper and wicked project, will be less apt to pervade the whole body of the Union than a particular member of it, in the same proportion as such a malady is more likely to taint a particular county or district than an entire State.

In the extent and proper structure of the Union, therefore, we behold a republican remedy for the diseases most incident to republican government.
— James Madison[1]

AS THEY APPROACHED THE ELECTION OF 1892, leaders of the newly-formed People's party professed optimism. James B. Weaver, the party's

---

1. Alexander Hamilton, James Madison, and John Jay, *The Federalist Papers* (New York, Mentor edition, 1961), 84.

Copyright © 1992 by Western History Association. Reprinted by permission. The article first appeared as "Why the Populist Party Was Strong in Kansas and Nebraska but Weak in Iowa," *Western Historical Quarterly* 23 (November 1992), 451–74.

presidential candidate, proclaimed in late August, "The whole group of States west of the Missouri is with us and the tide is sweeping eastward." Another prominent Populist predicted that the new party would carry more states than Cleveland or Harrison.² The results of the November balloting, however, proved that these hopes had been too sanguine. The Populist party was strong in the Rocky Mountain and Plains states, but it was unable to gain more than a foothold in the "Solid South" and failed entirely to achieve any meaningful level of support east of the Missouri River (see fig. 10.1). In crucial farm states — Michigan, Illinois, Indiana, Wisconsin, and Missouri — the Populists fared poorly, receiving at most eight percent of the total vote. Even in Weaver's home state of Iowa, voters spurned the native son, giving him only five ballots in every hundred. It was as if a prairie fire originating in the Great Plains had somehow burned out, or had been extinguished, at the border between those states and the states to the east.

What accounts for the success of the People's party in the states of the Great Plains and its lack of support in Iowa and other states of the Midwest? Historians who have addressed the regional and national pattern of support for the People's party have answered this question in economic terms: the People's party flourished in those areas where farmers suffered severe and unique economic hardships. The People's party gained little support in places where farmers prospered and thus had no reason to embrace a third party.³ I contend that economic conditions alone do not explain why People's parties developed in some states but not in others. To understand the pattern of support for the People's party, I will take into account economic and political variables through a comparison of two Populist states (Kansas and Nebraska) and one non-Populist state (Iowa). The first part of the essay compares economic conditions circa 1890 between Populist Kansas and Nebraska and non-Populist Iowa; it concludes that differences in economic conditions do not explain why farmers

---

2. *National Economist*, 27 August 1892, p. 369; 13 August 1892, p. 346.

3. Frederick Jackson Turner, *The Frontier in American History* (New York, 1920), 32; John Donald Hicks, *The Populist Revolt: A History of the Farmers' Alliance and the People's Party* (Minneapolis, 1931), 1–35, 268–69. Although historians engaged in heated debate about the nature of Populism from the mid-1950s to the mid-1960s, they continued to accept the view that Populism had little potential to attract farmers outside of those few areas with severe and unique conditions of economic hardship. See Richard Hofstadter, *The Age of Reform: From Bryan to F.D.R.* (New York, 1955), 99–100; Robert H. Wiebe, *The Search for Order, 1877–1920* (New York, 1967), 85; Samuel P. Hays, *The Response to Industrialism, 1885–1914* (Chicago, 1957), 27–28; Michael Paul Rogin, *The Intellectuals and McCarthy: The Radical Specter* (Cambridge, 1967), 188–89; Walter T. K. Nugent, *The Tolerant Populists: Kansas Populism and Nativism* (Chicago, 1963), 54–58. With the exception of Lawrence Goodwyn, *Democratic Promise: The Populist Moment in America* (New York, 1976), studies of Populism since 1965 have generally focused on a particular state or locale, and although scholars have qualified the economic determinism in the earlier literature, the extent to which economic conditions explain the pattern of support for the Populist party across the Midwest or the nation remains unclear. For a comprehensive overview of this extensive literature see Gene Clanton, *Populism: The Humane Preference in America, 1890–1900* (Boston, 1991), 186–91.

FIGURE 10.1
POPULIST VOTING, 1892

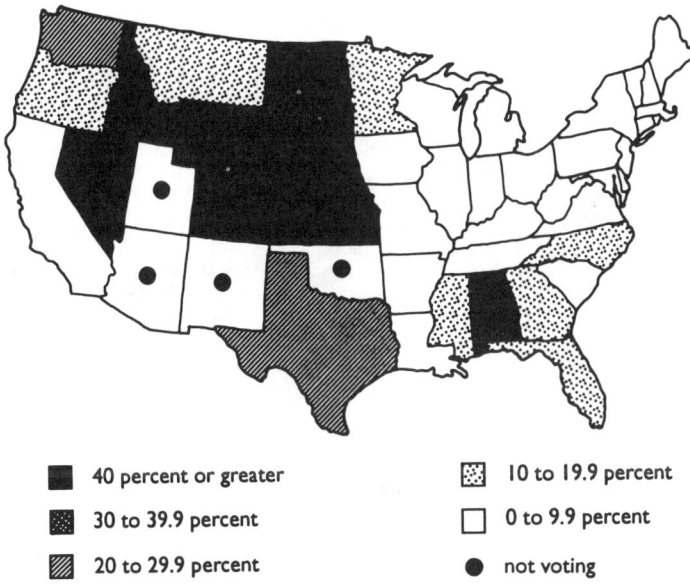

- ■ 40 percent or greater
- ▨ 30 to 39.9 percent
- ▨ 20 to 29.9 percent
- ▨ 10 to 19.9 percent
- ☐ 0 to 9.9 percent
- ● not voting

SOURCE: *Congressional Quarterly's Guide to U.S. Elections,* 2d ed. (Washington, DC, 1985), 343.

launched an independent political movement in Kansas and Nebraska, but not in Iowa. The second part focuses on state party systems as the critical matrix for the political development of the agrarian protest movement in Kansas, Nebraska, and Iowa, and shows how a competitive party system in Iowa encouraged the farmers' movement to seek reform from within the two-party system, while non-competitive party systems in Kansas and Nebraska encouraged farmers to form an independent political party.

Lawrence Goodwyn's observation that most American farmers were "potential Populists" underscores the reality that all farmers in the late nineteenth century, regardless of geographical location, planted and harvested under the harsh terms of a deflationary economy.[4] These conditions debilitated those carrying long-term debt obligations. Although foreclosures were uncommon in most of the Midwest in the 1880s, many farmers felt the squeeze of falling prices and feared they might lose their independence.[5] Economic conditions

---

4. Goodwyn, *Democratic Promise,* 314.
5. From 1864 to 1896 the price of farm products fell by over sixty percent. See George F. Warren and Frank A. Pearson, *Prices* (New York, 1933), 26–27. Economic historians like Douglass C. North argue that farmers did not suffer from deflation since prices for non-agricultural products, transportation rates, and interest rates also fell. See Douglass C. North, *Growth and Welfare in*

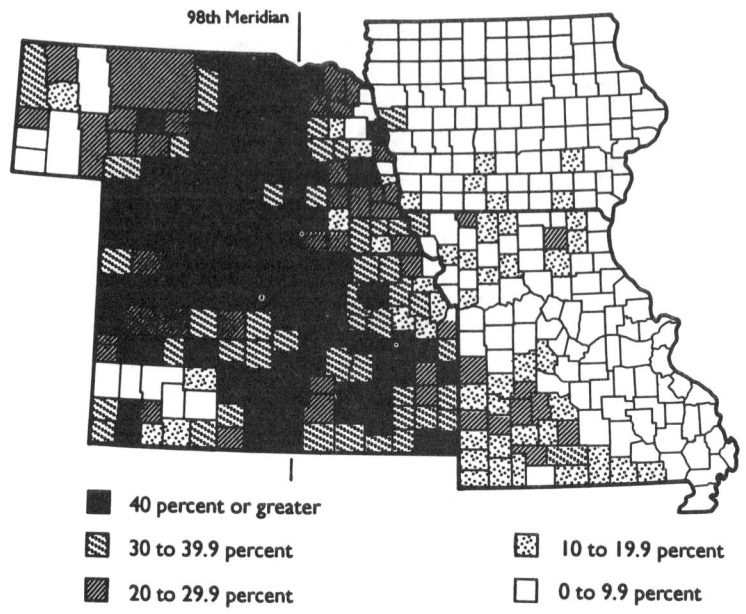

FIGURE 10.2
LEVEL OF SUPPORT FOR POPULISM:
KANSAS, NEBRASKA, IOWA, AND MISSOURI

SOURCE: See note 6.

were not as severe in Iowa as they were in central and western Kansas and Nebraska; still, farmers in the Hawkeye state were poor and had economic rationale to join a third party.

Look at the patterns of Populist voting across Kansas, Nebraska, and Iowa in figure 10.2. (Missouri is included on the map, although it is not central to the analysis of this essay.)[6] What is noteworthy in the pattern is the decisive break

---

the American Past: A New Economic History (Englewood Cliffs, NJ, 1974), 131–37. While correct on the first two counts, interest rates did not drop as rapidly as prices. See Jeffrey Ostler, "The Fate of Populism: Agrarian Radicalism and State Populism in Kansas, Nebraska, and Iowa, 1880–1892" (Ph.D. diss., University of Iowa, 1990), 37–43.

6. In Kansas and Nebraska voting for the Independent gubernatorial candidates in the election of 1890 is the best index of Populist strength, because this election was a genuine three-way contest. In subsequent elections Populist-Democrat fusion obscured the core Populist vote. For Iowa and Missouri, the Populist vote shown is for the presidential election of 1892, as there was not yet an independent party in those states in 1890. Election returns are found in Kansas Secretary of State, *Biennial Report, 1888–90* (Topeka, 1890), 85–86; Nebraska Legislative Reference Council, *Nebraska Blue Book and Historical Register, 1918* (Lincoln, 1918), 451–52; Iowa Secretary of State, *Iowa Official Register, 1893* (Des Moines, 1893), 119–92; Missouri State Department, *Official Manual of the State of Missouri, 1893–94* (Jefferson City, 1893), 19.

in Populist voting at the political boundary between the two Populist and non-Populist states. Although there were numerous counties in eastern Nebraska showing strong Populist support, no significant level of Populist voting occurred across the Missouri River in Iowa. The break in Populist voting at the Kansas-Missouri border is also striking. It is doubtful that farmers in western Iowa or Missouri could be prosperous, while their neighbors in eastern Nebraska or Kansas were indigent. The definition of the geography of Populism by a political boundary indicates that state-specific political factors shaped the voting behavior of farmers.

It is important to note that support for the People's party was strong in eastern Kansas and Nebraska (see fig. 10.2).[7] The relatively strong support for Populism in eastern Kansas challenges the usual association of Populism with severe conditions of economic hardship, since by several measures, conditions in eastern Kansas and Nebraska differed little from those in Iowa. Consider precipitation: a 1948 study concluded that the normal rainfall in the wet months from April through September was twenty-five inches in eastern Kansas, twenty-one inches in eastern Nebraska, and twenty-three inches in Iowa.[8] Or, take population density. Farmers first settled in eastern Kansas and Nebraska in the 1850s, and after the Civil War, agriculture developed in the eastern counties. By the 1880s, with population densities above twenty persons per square mile, eastern Kansas and Nebraska had clearly passed the frontier stage. Agricultural practices were similar on both sides of the Missouri River. "Corn is king," was the common saying in all three states. There was little wheat grown either in Iowa or in Kansas and Nebraska during the eighties, and the dairy industry of northeastern Iowa remained undeveloped. Not until after the Populist revolt did farmers on the Plains begin to plant winter wheat.[9]

Having made these general observations, we can consider economic factors. One of the basic factors affecting the economic condition of farmers is transportation costs. In early 1890, the Interstate Commerce Commission reported that the average rate on corn to New York was 35 cents per 100 pounds from Iowa and 40.5 cents from Kansas and Nebraska. Although rates were slightly lower in Iowa than in Kansas and Nebraska, the difference meant little in terms of prices. In December 1889, the average price of a bushel of corn was

---

7. The average Populist percentage for the thirty-three eastern Kansas counties was 33.1 percent, which in a three-way election was at virtual parity with the other parties. In the twenty-six eastern Nebraska counties the average Populist percentage was a substantial 23.3 percent.

8. Snowden D. Flora, "Climate of Kansas," in Kansas State Board of Agriculture, *Report of the Kansas State Board of Agriculture, June 1948* (Topeka, 1948), 10.

9. Clarence L. Petrowsky, "Kansas Agriculture before 1900" (Ph.D. diss., University of Oklahoma, 1968), 139, 149; James C. Olson, *History of Nebraska* (Lincoln, 1955), 205–6; Earle D. Ross, *Iowa Agriculture: An Historical Survey* (Iowa City, 1951), 72–75, 82; Keach Johnson, "Iowa Dairying at the Turn of the Century: The New Agriculture and Progressivism," *Agriculture History* 45 (April 1971): 95–110; James C. Malin, *Winter Wheat in the Golden Belt of Kansas: A Study in the Adaptation to Subhumid Geographical Environment* (Lawrence, 1944), 157.

19 cents in Iowa, 18 cents in Kansas, and 17 cents in Nebraska. Iowa prices were at such ruinous levels that the *Iowa State Register* urged farmers to burn corn as fuel rather than sell it at a loss.[10]

Table 10.1 summarizes other factors. Two indicators bearing upon the relative profitability (or unprofitability) of agriculture are the value of livestock and farm products. As shown in table 10.1, these two measures were higher in Iowa than in Kansas and Nebraska. However, a third factor, property value, is clearly a superior measure of the relative degree of hardship, as it indicates conditions over a long period of time and reflects an aggregate of conditions. Because the price of land embodies judgments about past levels of profitability, it reflects influences such as drought, transportation rates, and the productivity of the land.[11] The average farm value was higher in Iowa than in central and western Kansas or Nebraska (see table 10.1). But the average farm value in eastern Kansas and Nebraska was identical to the value in Iowa, which is a strong indication that there was no substantial difference in economic conditions between non-Populist Iowa and Populist eastern Kansas and Nebraska.

Three further variables, all related to the level of indebtedness, reinforce this conclusion (table 10.1). The first is the ratio of the value of mortgages to the value of mortgaged property. Although the ratio was much higher in central and western Kansas and Nebraska, it was actually lower in eastern Kansas and Nebraska than in Iowa, indicating that Iowa farmers were in about the same economic condition as farmers in eastern Kansas and Nebraska. However, the second variable, the interest rate on mortgage loans, was lower in Iowa than anywhere in Kansas and Nebraska, suggesting that the burden of indebtedness may have been less for Iowa farmers. The third variable brings together the first two, as a ratio of the annual debt obligation to the value of mortgaged farms.[12] This ratio, the debt-to-property-value ratio, indicates the relative levels of hardship across the three states, as it encompasses factors such as transportation costs, drought, productivity, costs of borrowing, interest rates, and the level of indebtedness. That this ratio was lower in eastern Kansas and Nebraska (8.88) than in Iowa (9.11) strongly indicates that the level of hardship in Populist eastern Kansas and Nebraska was no greater than in Iowa.

---

10. Interstate Commerce Commission, *Interstate Commerce Reports*, vol. 3 (Rochester, 1893), 95; Department of Agriculture, Bureau of Statistics, *Corn Crops of the United States, 1866–1906*, Bulletin 56 (Washington, DC, 1907), 15–20; *Iowa State Register* (Des Moines), 18 January 1890, p. 4.

11. Robert William Fogel, *Railroads and American Economic Growth: Essays in Econometric History* (Baltimore, 1964), 53.

12. The total annual debt obligation is determined by adding one-fifth of the value of the mortgage (this assumes a five-year term for loans) and the per annum interest on the value of the mortgage. For example, on a mortgage of $2,000 with an interest rate of eight percent on a farm valued at $5,000, the annual debt obligation would be $400 (one-fifth of $2,000) added to $160 (eight percent of $2,000) for a total of $560. The ratio of the annual debt obligation to the value of mortgaged property would be 11.2 percent.

TABLE 10.1
SELECTED INDICATORS OF ECONOMIC CONDITIONS, 1890 CENSUS

	Ks.	Neb.	Iowa	eastern Ks./Neb.	central Ks./Neb.	western Ks./Neb.
value livestock per farm	$ 769	$ 818	$1025	$ 889	$ 796	$ 536
value farm products per farm	$ 571	$ 588	$ 789	$ 659	$ 626	$ 265
value average farm	$3359	$3542	$4247	$4207	$3426	$1678
mortgage/value mortgaged property	36.00	32.40	33.30	31.90	36.20	41.10
interest rate*	8.15	8.22	7.36	7.89	8.46	9.33
annual debt/value mortgaged property	10.13	9.14	9.11	8.88	10.22	12.03

*arithmetic mean of county averages.
SOURCE: U.S. Census Office, *Report on the Statistics of Agriculture in the United States at the Eleventh Census: 1890* (Washington, DC, 1895), table 6; U.S. Census Office, *Report on Farms and Homes: Proprietorship and Indebtedness in the United States at the Eleventh Census: 1890* (Washington, DC, 1896), tables 103, 108.

This conclusion is reinforced by looking at figure 10.3, which maps the pattern of debt-to-property-value ratio across Kansas, Nebraska, and Iowa (again, Missouri is included as a contiguous state). As would be expected, those counties with the highest ratio were concentrated in the western and central regions of Kansas and Nebraska. There were, however, some counties in Iowa and Missouri with a debt-to-property-value ratio above ten percent, which was comparable to the ratio in some Great Plains counties. Most significantly and, unlike the voting patterns examined earlier (fig. 10.2), state boun-daries did not define the overall pattern of the debt-to-property-value ratio. Counties with low and moderate ratios were scattered throughout eastern Kansas and Nebraska, Iowa, and Missouri, making it clear that conditions in much of non-Populist Iowa and Missouri were similar to those in many parts of Populist Kansas and Nebraska.

The patterns here demonstrate the inadequacy of a strictly economic interpretation of Populist voting. Had the appeal of Populism been limited to exceptional areas of extreme hardship, the level of support for Populism would have declined sharply at the eastern boundary of the Great Plains in central Kansas and Nebraska. Populism would have been as weak in eastern Kansas and Nebraska as it was in Iowa. But the strong manifestation of support for Populism in eastern Kansas and Nebraska, under conditions similar to those in Iowa, demonstrates that Populism was capable of developing in the conditions of moderate economic hardship common to much of the Midwest.

The results of an assessment of the economic condition of Iowa's farmers undertaken by the state Bureau of Labor Statistics confirm that farmers in Iowa faced significant economic hardship in the late 1880s and early 1890s.

FIGURE 10.3
RATIO OF ANNUAL DEBT OBLIGATION TO VALUE OF MORTGAGED PROPERTY, 1890: KANSAS, NEBRASKA, IOWA, AND MISSOURI

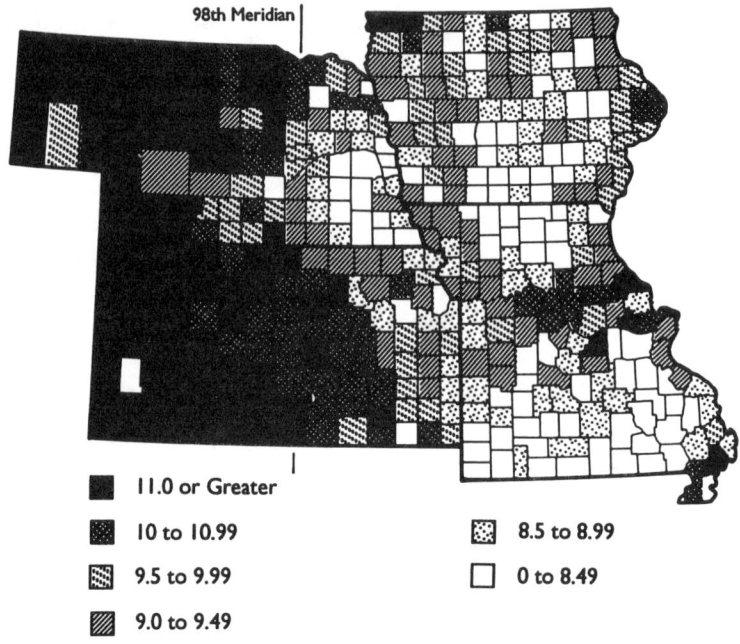

■ 11.0 or Greater
▨ 10 to 10.99
▦ 9.5 to 9.99
▧ 9.0 to 9.49
▨ 8.5 to 8.99
☐ 0 to 8.49

SOURCE: Calculated from data in U.S. Census Office, *Report on Farms and Homes: Proprietorship and Indebtedness in the United States at the Eleventh Census: 1890* (Washington, DC, 1896), tables 103, 108.

By far, the majority of the 1,015 respondents to the bureau's questionnaire reported that Iowa's primary agricultural products, with one exception, had not been profitable from 1885 through 1890. Over ninety percent of the farmers judged that they had raised cattle, wheat, oats, and barley at a loss, and eighty-five percent reported the same about growing corn. A consensus of unprofitability was absent only for hogs. A majority (fifty-seven percent) agreed that only hog-raising made money.[13] Since few farmers depended entirely on hogs and most relied on selling some surplus corn and other grains or specialized in cattle raising, the findings indicate that farming in Iowa was a marginal proposition at best.[14]

---

13. Iowa Commissioner of Labor Statistics, *Fourth Biennial Report, 1890–91* (Des Moines, 1891), 55–57.

14. It is doubtful that any but a few highly capitalized farming operations relied entirely on hog production. Although most corn was fed to livestock, a significant percentage of the corn crop in Iowa was shipped out of the county in which it was grown. Department of Agriculture, *Report of the Statistician* 60 (March 1889): 55; Department of Agriculture, *Report of the Statistician* 71 (March 1890): 71; Department of Agriculture, *Report of the Statistician* 82 (March 1891): 62.

The bureau appended to its report the written observations of several hundred farmers that debts weighed heavily on farm households in Iowa. Farmers stressed that, although few farms in their area had actually been foreclosed, many of their neighbors had been forced to sell their farms or to deed their property to the mortgagee in lieu of actual foreclosure. In a typical response, one farmer reported that only five percent of farms in his county had been lost through foreclosure since 1880, but forty percent of farms had undergone "forced sales to avoid foreclosure." Another farmer warned that "scores of others are hanging on with a death grip, trusting that better times will come."[15] Other farmers stressed the difficulty of making interest payments. Because most money lenders wanted interest rather than land, they preferred to grant extensions rather than foreclose when farmers were delinquent with interest payments or could not repay the principal. Had it not been for exten-sions, claimed one farmer, eighty percent of those in his area, since 1880, would have lost their farms. While this was perhaps an exaggerated figure, it does emphasize that a large number of farmers had difficulty freeing themselves from debt.[16]

The agricultural economy had not collapsed, nor were Iowa farmers destitute, but clearly they were burdened by debt because of low prices, and they felt that if conditions did not improve, hundreds or thousands would fail. "Two years' [crop] failure," one farmer judged, "would close out ninety per cent and less than ten years of present prices will bring the same result."[17]

It requires a comparative analysis of politics to understand why hard-pressed farmers in Kansas and Nebraska turned to a third party, while those in Iowa did not. For almost two decades following the Civil War the G.O.P. dominated politics in all three states. In the early eighties the idea of a Democratic resurgence seemed as remote as the revocation of divine law. One Iowa Republican boasted that his state "will go Democratic when Hell goes Methodist."[18] Yet, in the mid-1880s the political situation in Iowa began to diverge from the states to the west.

Trouble for the Iowa G.O.P. began in 1884 when the Democratic and Greenback parties fused and attempted to capitalize on agrarian discontent by campaigning on economic issues. Democratic orators linked Republican tariff policy to low agricultural prices, while their Greenback partners, led by James B. Weaver, contributed a well-developed critique of the railroads and the national banking system. "[O]ur railway corporations have control of the government," Weaver told farmers,

---

15. Iowa Commissioner of Labor Statistics, *Fourth Biennial Report*, 69, 89.
16. Ibid., 61.
17. Ibid., 84.
18. Thomas Richard Ross, *Jonathan Prentiss Dolliver: A Study in Political Integrity and Independence* (Iowa City, 1958), 65.

The banker has hold of one end of the grain sack, the railway magnate the other, and the farmer has what he can scoop up with his hands. The only way to get out of the servitude to monopolies, is to take the reins of government out of republican hands.[19]

The results of the election proved the viability of the Democratic/Greenback antimonopoly coalition. Weaver and three Democrats were elected to Congress, and with Greenback support, the Democrats won forty-seven percent of the presidential vote, a substantial improvement over their meager thirty-eight percent four years earlier.[20]

In 1885, Iowa's antimonopoly coalition chose Charles E. Whiting, a well-to-do farmer and life-long Democrat, to head the ticket. Republicans sought to avoid economic issues by furiously waving the "bloody shirt." In an editorial titled "Mr. Whiting of Alabama," the *Iowa State Register*, managed by the powerful James S. "Ret" Clarkson, attacked the Democratic nominee as a Copperhead who had never relinquished his "hatred of the Union and the Union soldier."[21] Whiting and his Greenback allies assailed the record of the Iowa G.O.P. on state economic issues, focusing on the 1878 repeal of the state's "Granger Law" of 1874. The opposition's antimonopoly campaign fell only 7,000 ballots short of proving that Hell really could go Methodist.[22]

The Republican-dominated legislature, which met in early 1886, did little to reverse the perception that the Iowa G.O.P. was subservient to corporate interests. The general assembly killed two bills sponsored by the Knights of Labor and defeated another measure, popular with the farmers, for the direct election of railroad commissioners. These actions worried the chairman of the Republican state central committee; he suggested to Iowa Senator William B. Allison the wisdom of organizing his fall campaign on "national issues," to appeal to voters dissatisfied with the party's record on state reform.[23]

---

19. *Iowa State Leader* (Des Moines), 8 October 1884, p. 6.

20. These and subsequent election figures, except as noted, are from Congressional Quarterly, *Congressional Quarterly's Guide to U.S. Elections* (Washington, DC, 1985).

21. *Iowa State Register* (Des Moines), 9 September 1885, p. 4.

22. *Iowa State Leader* (Des Moines), 11 October 1885, p. 4; 30 October 1885, p. 4. For an account of the emergence of party competition in Iowa that stresses the importance of ethnocultural issues see Richard Jensen, *The Winning of the Midwest: Social and Political Conflict, 1888–1896* (Chicago, 1971), 89–121.

23. Ralph Scharnau, "Workers and Politics: The Knights of Labor in Dubuque, Iowa, 1885–1890," *Annals of Iowa* 48 (Winter/Spring 1987): 353–77, especially 362–63; Iowa Senate, *Journal, 1886* (Des Moines, 1886), 343–44, 442–43, 491, 507; Iowa House, *Journal, 1886* (Des Moines, 1886), 421–22, 534, 656, 755; Charles Beardsley to William Boyd Allison, 17 April 1886 and 15 July 1886, William Boyd Allison Papers, State Historical Society of Iowa, Clermont, Iowa (hereafter Allison Papers). Although it is impossible to determine the validity of charges of corporate domination of politics in these particular instances, there is little question that business interests frequently dictated the Iowa G.O.P.'s position on economic issues. For a fuller discussion of this issue, see Ostler, "Fate of Populism," 103–12.

But Iowa Republicans found it difficult to focus the electorate's attention on the dying embers of sectional strife or the nebulous promise of prosperity through the tariff. The 1886 campaign centered on the Eighth congressional district, where a fusion candidate, Albert R. Anderson, challenged the Republican incumbent William Hepburn on a platform that denounced corporate control of the Republican party, condemned the "extortionate freight rates evidenced by costing two bushels of grain to get one to market," and advocated state and national regulation to prevent the abuses of railroad pooling, stock-watering, and discrimination.[24] Throughout the campaign, Anderson arraigned Hepburn for supporting the Cullom interstate commerce bill, a position which proved the incumbent was "the tool of corporations who [has] not served the people of this district one single hour since he was first elected to Congress." Anderson endorsed the more stringent Reagan bill to outlaw railroad pools and discriminatory rates. Stunned by Anderson's frontal assault, Hepburn dismissed the challenger as a "disgruntled officer seeker" and falsely characterized the Reagan bill as a "pro-railroad" measure.[25]

The issues raised by Anderson stimulated fervent discussion among ordinary citizens in the Eighth District. A reporter for the *Iowa State Register* was astonished to find that interest in this local campaign "overshadows that of [a] Presidential campaign," while another reported that "Reagan and Cullom have become household words."[26] The clash in the Eighth District reverberated throughout the state. The *Iowa State Register* (located in the Seventh District) broadcast blow-by-blow accounts of the campaign, and the state's foremost agricultural journal, the *Homestead,* edited by Henry "Uncle Henry" Wallace, regarded the Anderson-Hepburn contest as more important than "any election held in Iowa for twenty years." Because Anderson focused on interstate commerce, his campaign brought to the state's attention related questions, such as the election of state railroad commissioners. The Democratic *Iowa State Leader* identified this as an important issue, contending that a Democratic vote was a vote for a state railroad commission "elected by the people, on the only fair plan."[27]

The election-day verdict sent Republicans reeling. Anderson soundly defeated Hepburn by a margin of over six percent. A notorious gerrymander allowed the Republicans to win eight of the remaining ten seats, but the combined opposition of Democratic/Greenback fusion tickets, Anderson's "Independent" ticket, and a Knights of Labor ticket in the Second District, actually exceeded the Republican total by six hundred votes. Hepburn attributed his demise to "a revival of the granger craze," and conservative Republicans feared

---

24. *Iowa State Leader* (Des Moines), 13 July 1886, p. 1.

25. *Iowa State Register* (Des Moines), 10 October 1886, pp. 1–2, quotation on p. 2; 19 September 1886, p. 2; 3 October 1886, p. 1.

26. Ibid., 20 October 1886, p. 1; 10 October 1886, p. 1.

27. Ibid., September and October 1886; *Homestead* (Des Moines), 29 October 1886, p. 3; *Iowa State Leader* (Des Moines), 14 October 1886, p. 2; 2 November 1886, p. 2.

their party would go down to defeat the next year. A shaken Republican leader wrote Senator Allison, "I am just getting my breath from our terrible defeat in the Eighth District," and he attributed the disaster to Farmers' Alliances. Unless Congress passed interstate commerce legislation, he warned, "Iowa will not go Republican next year."[28]

Threatened by the antimonopoly opposition, a growing number of Republicans looked more carefully at the farmers' grievances and worried that ignoring demands for reform would cost the party its mandate to govern. During the 1886 campaign, Governor William Larrabee, obviously defensive about the G.O.P.'s failure to make the railroad commission elective in the previous legislature, had pledged that the party would enact this reform if, after "mature consideration," it was deemed in the "best interests of the people."[29] In December 1886, Larrabee brought a case before the state railroad commission against the C.B. & Q. for discrimination in carrying coal to a state institution. When the railroad managers responded by arrogantly asserting the rights of property, the governor broadened his criticisms of railroad practices. By mid-1887, Larrabee avowed that unless the railroad commission reversed its past course of kowtowing to the wishes of the corporations, "I am sorry to say this commission will have to go."[30]

It was in this context of party competition and escalating demands for reform that the Iowa Farmers' Alliance emerged as a force in state politics. After three years of inactivity, the I.F.A. had been reorganized in September 1886.[31] During the summer and fall of 1887, suballiances demanded that legislative candidates of both parties support railroad reform and threatened to vote against any candidate who refused to comply. Given the recent erosion of party strength, many local Republican politicians responded by embracing the antimonopoly cause. Republicans in Page county, for example, nominated "Farmer" S. E. Field on a platform that demanded significant reductions in state and interstate railroad rates. In Montgomery county, the G.O.P. denounced those "traitors to the Republican Party" who had voted against the election of railroad commissioners in the previous legislature and demanded an elective commission "clothed with full power to fix maximum rates of freight charges."[32]

---

28. William P. Hepburn to James S. Clarkson, 5 November 1886, James S. Clarkson Papers, Library of Congress, Washington, DC; James W. McDill to Allison, 22 November 1886, Allison Papers.

29. *Iowa State Register* (Des Moines), 24 September 1886, p. 3.

30. Iowa Board of Railroad Commissioners, *Annual Report, 1887* (Des Moines, 1887), 663–75, quotation on 671.

31. *Western Rural and American Stockman* (Chicago), 4 September 1886, p. 565. The I.F.A. was originally organized in 1881 as an affiliate of the National Farmers' Alliance (later known popularly as the Northern Alliance). See Roy V. Scott, "Milton George and the Farmers' Alliance Movement," *Mississippi Valley Historical Review* 45 (June 1958): 90–109.

32. *Homestead* (Des Moines), 29 July 1887, p. 5; *Clarinda (IA) Herald*, 19 October 1887, p. 4; 2 November 1887, p. 2; *Iowa State Register* (Des Moines), 23 August 1887, p. 2.

By the fall, many legislative candidates had pledged themselves to support railroad reform, although others remained noncommittal. To ensure the election of an antimonopoly legislature, Wallace targeted thirteen incumbents (seven Republicans and six Democrats) and flooded their districts with thousands of copies of the *Homestead*, which assailed their voting records.[33] The G.O.P.'s conservative state leaders, who feared that an outbreak of hostility against corporations would discourage investment in the state and damage Allison's chances for the presidency in 1888, responded with near-hysterical attacks on Wallace, calling him the "Premium Demagogue" and the "Arnold and Davis of the Republican party."[34] The results of the 1887 campaign vindicated the I.F.A.'s nonpartisan strategy. The number of farmers in the House increased from thirty-one to fifty-one, and the legislature had a decidedly antimonopoly complexion. Clarkson predicted that the general assembly, "elected on a campaign of distrust[,] . . . will enact the most radical and sweeping railroad legislation."[35]

As the newly-elected legislators gathered in Des Moines in January 1888, Larrabee, utilizing the prestige of his office, denounced railroad abuses and advocated controls. Suballiances flooded the legislature with petitions demanding reform. A "legion of corporate hirelings" descended on the Capitol, but to one beleaguered lobbyist it was clear that the farmers would have their way. "I am here trying to stay the storm of madness against the railroads," James W. McDill reported to Allison in late February, "but it is a hopeless task. One might as well try to stop a cyclone." From the eye of the storm, J. H. Sweeney, chairman of the state senate committee on railroads, wrote to apprise Allison of the situation. "Our political parties have been improvident in promises, and members of the Legislature are held responsible for their fulfillment," he explained. "They are elected upon the platform of their parties and are placed between two very hot fires." Although Sweeney professed his belief in "conservatism," the heat from his constituents was evidently greater than the heat from a U.S. Senator. With reluctance, he informed Allison, he would support reform.[36]

The 1888 legislature established an elective board of commissioners with power to set maximum rates and passed legislation requiring the present board to reduce intrastate rates.[37] Although this legislation promised only modest economic returns, Iowa farmers saw the law, in symbolic terms, as a monument to the efficacy of their nonpartisan strategy and felt vindicated for their faith in participatory democracy. The legislation of 1888 proved that farmer-citizens,

---

33. Russell Lord, *The Wallaces of Iowa* (Boston, 1947), 103.

34. *Iowa State Register* (Des Moines), 17 September 1887, p. 4.

35. Frank J. Stork and Cynthia A. Clingan, *The Iowa General Assembly: Our Legislative Heritage, 1846–1980* (Des Moines, 1980), 11; Clarkson to William Larrabee, 17 January 1888, William Larrabee Papers, State Historical Society of Iowa.

36. William Larrabee, *The Railroad Question* (Chicago, 1893), 340; McDill to Allison, 22 February 1888; J. H. Sweeney to Allison, 24 February 1888, Allison Papers.

37. Iowa Board of Railroad Commissioners, *Annual Report, 1888* (Des Moines, 1888), 31–33.

acting through their representatives, could prevail over powerful monopolies and secure laws for the benefit of all. The secretary of the I.F.A. characterized the legislature's enactment of most of the Alliance platform as "a matter of profound satisfaction. It proves conclusively that in an agricultural state like Iowa when the farmers stand together in demanding right and just things, these demands will become laws." The farmers were proud that political leaders had listened to them. During the fight for reform, one farmer reported that the members of his suballiance had been "watching the Iowa Legislature" and had found a renewed faith in representative government: "The Alliance organization can 'speak out in meeting' on these questions and issues which concern them and make themselves heard."[38]

The dynamic underlying the passage of the legislation of 1888 was party competition. By exploiting antimonopoly sentiment, the Democratic/Greenback coalition had defined railroad regulation as an important issue in state politics and had demonstrated Republican vulnerability on the issue. Facing this political challenge, a number of Republican politicians supported reform. These supporters ranged from Governor Larrabee to ordinary legislators and from those who pledged support as a matter of political survival to those who did so out of moral conviction, to those who supported reform because of a mixture of both.

After its success in the 1888 legislature, the I.F.A. demanded further state reforms — such as joint rates on shipments across two or more railways, reduced passenger fares, equal tax obligations, reduced legal rates of interest, and antitrust legislation. The organization also endorsed government-owned railroads and the free coinage of silver, two reforms advocated by the People's party. The I.F.A. opposed, however, the controversial proposal known as the sub-treasury plan, which provided government credit on the security of crop deposits.[39]

It would be mistaken to conclude, as Lawrence Goodwyn does, that the I.F.A.'s rejection of the sub-treasury and the People's party were proof of inherent conservatism or of unfamiliarity with economic cooperation, which, in Goodwyn's view, was the basis of Populism. Even if one accepts Goodwyn's contention that a program of economic cooperation led to radicalization and third-party formation in Kansas, a doubtful proposition, the Iowa Alliance's nonpartisanship can hardly be explained by unfamiliarity with cooperation, because the Iowa Alliance developed in advance of the Kansas Alliance a program of economic cooperation.[40] The I.F.A.'s relatively moderate agenda

---

38. *Homestead* (Des Moines), 21 September 1888, p. 8; 29 June 1888, p. 8.

39. Ibid., 13 September 1889, p. 12; *Proceedings of the Iowa Farmers' Alliance, October 29–31, 1890* (Des Moines, 1890), 33; *Homestead* (Des Moines), 10 April 1891, p. 8.

40. Goodwyn, *Democratic Promise,* 260–62. As Goodwyn points out on page 105, there were already several local cooperatives operating in Iowa prior to late 1888 and early 1889 when the first Kansas cooperatives were formed. *Homestead* (Des Moines), 15 July 1887, p. 12; 31 August 1888, p. 8. For further discussion of cooperatives in Iowa, see Ostler, "Fate of Populism," 322–34.

and its nonpartisan tactics are better understood as a response to the opportunities presented by Iowa's competitive party system for exploiting state-level political action.

From 1888 through 1892, party competition continued to reinforce the I.F.A.'s nonpartisan position. Following the collapse of the Democratic/Greenback coalition in the fall of 1887, Democrats capitalized on the mounting criticism of the state's ineffective prohibition law.[41] For governor in 1889, the Democrats nominated Horace Boies, a former Republican who believed in temperance, but viewed prohibition as an infringement on personal liberty. Contending that prohibition did not prohibit, Boies advocated local option, with a minimum license of $500. Boies's candidacy was designed to retain the Democrats' traditional supporters, while attracting anti-prohibition Republicans who would find a Bourbon candidate unacceptable. While the saloon was the centerpiece of the campaign, Democrats also sought to attract farmers by arguing that free trade would remove agricultural surpluses and by affirming Democratic support for railroad regulation.[42]

The G.O.P. nominated Joseph G. Hutchison over "Farmer" Hiram C. Wheeler for governor. Hutchison, an attorney and former state senator with a mixed record on railroad reform, provided the Democrats with an opportunity to exploit state-level antimonopoly issues. In the closing days of a bitterly contested campaign, the Democratic press, recognizing that the farmer vote might be the key to victory, publicized an exposé of Hutchison's record compiled by Newton B. Ashby, the I.F.A. state lecturer.[43] Republicans responded to this eleventh-hour attack by securing statements from Alliance President J. B. Furrow and Secretary August Post, finding Hutchison's pledge to support the 1888 railroad law satisfactory, despite his poor record. Furrow emphatically added that he would vote Republican because "I cannot endure the Democratic position on the saloon question."[44]

Drawing both on the votes of discontented farmers and those opposed to Republican prohibition policy, Boies was elected Iowa's first Democratic governor since the 1850s by the narrow margin of just under 7,000 votes.[45] The 1889 election had also reduced the customary Republican majority in the general assembly to a precarious margin. In both houses, there were seventy-

---

41. The antimonopoly coalition split over persistent disagreements among Democrats between "wets," who favored a low license law and were suspicious of the generally prohibition-minded Greenbackers, and Democrats whose main concern was economic issues and who supported a high license, which was acceptable to Greenbackers. *Iowa State Register* (Des Moines), 2 September 1887, p. 4.

42. *Iowa State Leader* (Des Moines), 29 September 1889, p. 5; 6 October 1889, pp. 2–3.

43. *Iowa State Register* (Des Moines), 14 August 1889, p. 4; *Iowa State Leader* (Des Moines), 13 October 1889, p. 2.

44. *Iowa State Register* (Des Moines), 29 October 1889, p. 1; 27 October 1889, p. 1.

45. For a discussion of the relative weight of ethnocultural and economic issues see Ostler, "Fate of Populism," 338–39.

eight Republicans, sixty-five Democrats, and seven Independents.[46] Under these circumstances, the conservative leadership of the Iowa G.O.P. was immediately forced to contend with the political power of the I.F.A., when the legislature convened in January 1890. There was a possibility that a coalition of antimonopoly Republicans, Democrats, and Independents would support Larrabee against Allison in his bid for a fourth term in the Senate. Larrabee revealed his ambition to unseat the incumbent when he stated publicly that Allison's lack of sympathy with the movement for railroad reform revealed that the senator "hasn't the courage of a mouse."[47]

The Allison machine's efforts to neutralize the Larrabee movement illustrates both the extent to which the I.F.A. was taken seriously as a force in state politics and the process by which it was drawn more securely into the state's political structure. While suballiances were petitioning the legislature for Larrabee, Allison's men were at work behind the scenes to line up support for the incumbent. James "Tama Jim" Wilson, a professor at the Iowa State College of Agriculture and Mechanical Arts, with strong ties to the Alliance, used his contacts on Allison's behalf, in one instance tempting a county Alliance official with a patronage position. Another of Wilson's friends, A. L. Stuntz, the I.F.A.'s lobbyist at the Capitol, pledged to use his influence for the senator. Other Allison lieutenants moved to bury the hatchet with George Finn, the foremost antimonopolist in the state senate, whom conservative Republicans had, for years, scorned as a demagogue of the first rank. Nathaniel M. Hubbard, attorney for the Chicago and Northwestern, informed Allison that he and Joseph W. Blythe of the C.B. & Q. had met with Finn on separate occasions. In a veiled reference to a quid pro quo, Hubbard related that Finn "has agreed positively, and we have accepted all his suggestions."[48]

Although Allison's victory over Larrabee conflicted with the wishes of most members of the Alliance, the defeat did not cause a revolt against the G.O.P.[49] The Alliance had lost one battle, but it had won others before and could expect to secure future demands. Alliance leaders, who had in many cases been won over through patronage, were now closely linked to the Republican party and would be even more reluctant in the future to sponsor a third party.

Following the strong showing of the People's party in Kansas and Nebraska in 1890, third-party advocates in Iowa hoped to make a similar revolution in

---

46. Iowa Secretary of State, *Iowa Official Register, 1890* (Des Moines, 1890), 72–76.

47. *Iowa State Register* (Des Moines), 18 January 1890, p. 4; Leland L. Sage, *William Boyd Allison: A Study in Practical Politics* (Iowa City, 1956), 240–41.

48. *Iowa State Register* (Des Moines), 7 February 1890, p. 4; 18 February 1890, p. 4; 19 February 1890, p. 1; James Wilson to Allison, 11 December 1889, Allison Papers; A. L. Stuntz to Allison, 6 March 1890, Allison Papers; Nathaniel M. Hubbard to Allison, 9 December 1889, Allison Papers.

49. The final vote in the legislature was seventy-eight for Allison, sixty-one for S. L. Bestow, a Democrat, and eight for Larrabee. Larrabee's poor showing was not indicative of his earlier strength. *Iowa State Register* (Des Moines), 5 March 1890, p. 5.

the Hawkeye state. In March 1891, Weaver organized an Iowa branch of the Farmers' Alliance and Industrial Union (known as the Southern Alliance) to recruit farmers to the Iowa People's Party.[50] I.F.A. leaders responded with a vigorous attack on the Southern Alliance, alleging, among other things, that the Alliance's purpose was to form "a gigantic cotton trust."[51] At the annual I.F.A. convention in October, Weaver tried to effect a merger of the two orders, but the I.F.A.'s leadership was unreceptive to such a scheme, since a new, combined Alliance would undoubtedly pursue third-party politics.

Two considerations guided the I.F.A.'s resistance to a third party. The first was the successful history of its nonpartisan tactics. Although the Alliance had encountered setbacks, it had obtained reforms. As the state lecturer pointed out at the October meeting, the list began with the 1888 railroad legislation, but it also included a reduction of the legal rate of interest, a uniform system of school textbooks, and a state anti-trust law.[52] Although these measures were modest, they demonstrated to farmers that farmers could influence policy, obviating the need for a new party.

The second factor in the I.F.A.'s rejection of a third party was its absorption by the state political system. Iowa politicians had learned to appeal to Alliance concerns through friendly contacts with local Alliance leaders, platform-making, campaign oratory, and modest legislative concessions. Politicians had courted the I.F.A. leadership at crucial moments, such as the 1889 election and the 1890 senatorial contest. For their investments within the party system Alliance leaders sought and received rewards. Post, the Alliance state secretary who supported Hutchison in 1889, was sergeant-at-arms at the 1896 Republican National Convention. Furrow, the state president, sought a position as state commissioner of labor statistics, his supporters citing his efforts to keep the Alliance out of the People's party. "Tama Jim" Wilson became secretary of agriculture in the McKinley administration. The Democrats rewarded Ashby for his assistance in the 1889 campaign by appointing him to a position in the Dublin consulate.[53]

The decision of the I.F.A. to remain nonpartisan was crucial for the fate of the Populist party in Iowa. In the absence of an organization to mobilize support for the new party, few farmers would be likely to vote Populist. Iowa farmers experienced economic hardship and organized to protest perceived injustices. They demanded state intervention to remove abuses, and they en-

---

50. *Iowa Tribune* (Des Moines), 25 March 1891, p. 1. The Iowa People's Party was organized, at Weaver's initiative, in June. See the *Iowa Tribune*, 10 June 1891, p. 1.

51. *Homestead* (Des Moines), 10 April 1891, p. 8.

52. Ibid., 6 November 1891, p. 8.

53. Biography of A. M. Post in *Past and Present of Appanoose County, Iowa* (Chicago, 1913), 33–36; H. J. Stevens to Governor Francis M. Drake, 25 January 1896, Records of the Governor, "Appointments," file # GII.338, Iowa Department of History and Archives, Des Moines; Earley Vernon Wilcox, *Tama Jim* (Boston, 1930), 17; Newton B. Ashby, *The Ashbys in Iowa* (Tucson, 1925), 45–46.

dorsed much of the Populist platform. But the modest success of nonpartisanship meant that Alliance leaders and members never experienced the political alienation necessary to turn them towards a new party.

The farmers in Kansas and Nebraska faced a different political situation. While a resurgent democracy challenged the Iowa Republicans, the Democrats in Kansas and Nebraska remained weak and irrelevant, routinely losing elections by a plurality of ten to twenty percent in the mid- and late eighties. The significant battles took place within the G.O.P. between antimonopoly and regular Republicans. From 1886 to 1889, reformers successfully pressured the party to adopt platforms calling for reforms. In 1888, Kansas Republicans, hoping to "disarm the men who preach that republican rule is the rule of the rich and the strong," adopted a platform calling for a reduction in the legal maximum rate of interest to ten percent. The Nebraska Republican party platform of the same year pledged the party to enact laws "to prevent unjust discrimination and extortion in transportation rates."[54]

The failure of the G.O.P. to honor these promises proved to be a crucial determinant of third-party formation in Kansas and Nebraska. As Peter H. Argersinger observes of Kansas, third-party formation was not simply the result of economic distress, but was also a consequence of the Republican party's lack of response to agrarian demands.[55] As will be seen below, the same was true for Nebraska.

The Kansas and Nebraska legislative sessions of 1889 proved to be decisive tests of the Republican party's commitment to reform. As the Kansas legislative session opened in January 1889, there appeared to be overwhelming sentiment for reform. The Topeka *Capital-Commonwealth*, representing the broadest segment of Republican opinion, urged the heavily Republican legislature to honor Republican campaign promises by reducing the legal maximum rate of interest from twelve to ten percent and further advised the legislature to enact a law allowing farmers two to three years to redeem foreclosed farms. Many Republican leaders also urged the legislature to honor the Republican platform and reduce the legal rate of interest.[56] Within a matter of weeks, however, as virtually every Kansas banker explained his views on the folly of such legislation, the *Capital-Commonwealth* reversed itself. Financiers convinced the paper that the proposed legislation would injure those it intended

---

54. *Daily Capital* (Topeka), 25 July 1888, p. 2; 27 July 1888, p. 1; *Omaha Weekly Bee*, 12 October 1887, p. 3.

55. Peter H. Argersinger, *Populism and Politics: William Alfred Peffer and the People's Party* (Lexington, KY, 1974), 20–21, 34. Goodwyn, *Democratic Promise*, 182–85, 194–97, contends that third-party formation was related to the Kansas Alliance's prior experience with economic cooperation. However, as Scott G. McNall points out, Kansas Alliance cooperatives can hardly be considered a catalyst for politicization, since the development of cooperatives and third-party action took place simultaneously. See Scott G. McNall, *The Road to Rebellion: Class Formation and Kansas Populism, 1865–1900* (Chicago, 1988), 245.

56. *Capital-Commonwealth* (Topeka), 6 January 1889, p. 2; 9 January 1889, p. 3.

to help by driving eastern capital out of the state, resulting in even more foreclosures, as farmers would be unable to renew their loans.[57]

Debate on reform dominated the legislative session, but it became evident that the conservatives held the upper hand. The senate defeated a redemption bill. A joint conference of the house and senate eventually agreed on a bill that reduced the legal rate of interest, but all efforts to enforce the provisions failed. Antimonopolists were disillusioned. The *Kansas Farmer* predicted disappointed farmers would refuse to reelect those legislators who had broken party pledges.[58]

The fate of reform in the 1889 Nebraska legislature was the same. Antimonopolists presented evidence showing that rates in Nebraska were thirty percent higher than in Iowa, and they introduced a bill to establish "Iowa rates." This measure passed the house by a margin of fifty-four to thirty-three, but it was smothered in the senate, failing even to reach the floor.[59]

The failure to enact meaningful reform legislation in Kansas and Nebraska was related to the lack of party competition in those states. In the absence of a political threat by the Democrats to steal reform issues, Republican antimonopolists were unable to expand their base. In Iowa, where legislators and many party leaders feared losing elections, a critical mass for reform developed. In Kansas and Nebraska, the Republican party was willing to favor reform in party platforms, but when it became a matter of writing laws, the scales failed to tip in the direction of the antimonopolists. A sufficient number of politicians perceived little political risk in ignoring demands for reform and ultimately accepted the arguments of powerful bankers and railroad magnates.

Political developments in late 1889 and early 1890 confirmed the lethargy of the one-party systems in Kansas and Nebraska, and the inability of these systems to meet the urgent demands of the Farmers' Alliance movement. In Nebraska, with farm prices falling to a historic low during the winter of 1889–90, farmers petitioned Governor John M. Thayer and the state's board of transportation to force railroads to lower their rate on transportation of grain to Chicago by as much as fifty percent.[60] Instead of ordering reductions, the board requested the railroads to voluntarily reduce rates by five cents (about twenty-five percent). The railroads responded with a reduction of 1.125 cents. Alliances condemned this meager gesture as "a bait to catch the farmer's vote" and demanded a special legislative session to secure lower rates.[61]

---

57. Ibid., 18 January 1889, p. 4; 19 January 1889, pp. 2–3.
58. *Kansas Farmer* (Topeka), 28 February 1889, p. 10.
59. *Omaha Weekly Bee*, 16 January 1889, p. 2; 30 January 1889, p. 2; 6 February 1889, p. 2; 20 February 1889, p. 2; 3 April 1889, p. 4.
60. Petition of the Palestine Alliance # 826, 15 February 1890, to Governor John M. Thayer, and Thayer to Central Traffic Association of Missouri, 14 March 1890, John M. Thayer Papers, Nebraska State Historical Society, Lincoln.
61. *Alliance* (Lincoln), 1 March 1890; 5 April 1890.

In late May 1890, Thayer responded to the farmers and called for a special session. But after hasty conferences with railroad officials, Nebraska's chief executive cancelled his call. To the farmers, Thayer's actions demonstrated, once again, that the railroads, not the people, controlled the Republican party and ruled the state. While there had been third-party advocates all along within the Nebraska Alliance, Jay Burrows, president of the National Farmers' Alliance and editor of the state Alliance organ, had counselled against transforming the officially nonpartisan Alliance into a political party.[62] But mounting evidence of Republican intransigence, culminating in Thayer's reversal, forced Burrows to reconsider his position. Disgusted at the unprecedented display of "railroad influence . . . in the circus of the past few months, coupled with the recall of the Governor's proclamation," Burrows endorsed independent state and county conventions as the only way to "SMASH THESE MACHINES." Having experienced a similar process of conversion, nine hundred delegates representing tens of thousands of Nebraska farmers organized the state People's party on 29 July.[63]

In Kansas, politicization centered on the issue of debt relief. In early 1890, Kansas suballiances flooded the governor's office with petitions for an extra session of the legislature to enact a stay of execution law or, at least, a two-year redemption law. Governor Lyman U. Humphrey vowed to give these requests his "earnest consideration," but he eventually heeded investors, who warned that such a move "would result in a great injury to the state . . . in making every lender call his funds in as fast as due." Humphrey informed petitioners that laws impeding foreclosure were unconstitutional, a response that reminded farmers of the ineffectiveness of the previous Republican legislature.[64]

It was the defiant posture of the state's senior senator, John J. Ingalls, who would stand for election to a fourth term in the U.S. Senate in 1891, that clinched the case against the Grand Old Party. In February, William Peffer, the editor of the *Kansas Farmer*, who had hoped for reform from within the Republican party, requested Ingalls to state his recommendations for relieving the depressed condition of agriculture. Ingalls did not give Peffer the courtesy of a response. Instead, the senator mocked the ideals of political reformers, the Alliance included, in an interview with the *New York World*. He characterized the "purification of politics" as "an iridescent dream" and lectured naive reformers that "[g]overnment is force [and] politics is a battle for supremacy."[65]

---

62. Ibid., 12 June 1889; 30 November 1889; 28 December 1889; 8 March 1890.

63. Ibid., 7 June 1890; 2 August 1890.

64. *Kansas Farmer* (Topeka), 12 February 1890, p. 6; R. J. Wadell to Lyman U. Humphrey, 6 February 1890; Humphrey to J. Crans, 14 February 1890; Alliance petitions, Lyman U. Humphrey Papers, Kansas State Historical Society, Topeka.

65. *Kansas Farmer* (Topeka), 26 February 1890, p. 11; Ingalls's interview with the *New York World* on 30 April 1890 is quoted in the *Kansas Farmer*, 21 May 1890, p. 8.

For Peffer and thousands of Kansas farmers, Ingalls's cynical defense of political corruption solidified their growing alienation from the dominant party. Singing "Good-bye, Old Party, Good-bye," thousands of formerly loyal party members turned from the G.O.P. and raised the banner of the People's party.

It is beyond the scope of this essay to discuss the extent to which the situation in Iowa was similar to that in other states in the Midwest where the Populist party also failed to develop. It should be noted, however, that strong agrarian movements emerged in the late 1880s in Missouri, Illinois, and Indiana. Like Iowa these states were characterized by a competitive party system, and the farmers' movements generally remained nonpartisan.[66] Whether party competition was crucial to the nonpartisan course of the farmers' movement in these three states, or whether other factors, related to state politics or otherwise, explain the fact that agrarian radicalism did not take a third-party turn, is an open question and would require further study. However, in identifying the importance of state party systems in the political development of the agrarian protest movement in Kansas, Nebraska, and Iowa, this essay does indicate the necessity of considering state politics in future studies of the agrarian revolt elsewhere in the Midwest and in other regions.

The Populists justified a third party through two arguments. They began from the premise of substantial economic distress, as the Omaha Platform stated: "business [is] prostrated; our homes [are] covered with mortgages; labor [is] impoverished; and the land [is] concentrating in the hands of the capitalists." Farmers everywhere, from Kansas and Nebraska to Iowa and Indiana, could accept this proposition.

The second Populist contention was that the existing parties were incapable of remedying this situation: "We charge that the controlling influence[s] dominating both these parties have permitted the existing dreadful conditions to develop without serious effort to prevent or restrain them. Neither do they now promise us any substantial reform."[67] This rationale for a third party made sense in some states, but not in many others.

In Iowa, where both parties responded to farmers' demands, the Alliance remained nonpartisan and its primary focus remained on state-level reform. Had the political system in Iowa failed to respond at all to the Alliance movement, farmers would have been more likely to form a third party. While the level of support for the Populist party probably would not have been as high as it was in central Kansas and Nebraska, the Populist party in Iowa might well have achieved substantial strength. That Populism did not become, in

---

66. Roy V. Scott, *The Agrarian Movement in Illinois, 1880–1896* (Urbana, 1962), 49; Melvyn Hammarberg, *The Indiana Voter: The Historical Dynamics of Party Allegiance During the 1870s* (Chicago, 1977); Homer Clevenger, "The Farmers' Alliance in Missouri," *Missouri Historical Review* 39 (October 1944): 24–44; Homer Clevenger, "Missouri Becomes a Doubtful State," *Mississippi Valley Historical Review* 29 (March 1943): 541–56.

67. Kirk H. Porter and Donald Bruce Johnson, eds., *National Party Platforms, 1840–1964* (Urbana, 1966), 89–90.

Madisonian terms, a "general conflagration" does not mean there was no fuel for such a fire; rather, it illustrates the effectiveness of the American federal system in containing initial flames.

BIBLIOGRAPHICAL NOTE

The standard authority on Iowa Populism is Frederick E. Haynes; see his *Third Party Movements since the Civil War, with Special Reference to Iowa: A Study in Social Politics* (1916; reprint, New York, 1966), and *James Baird Weaver* (1919; reprint, New York, 1975). More recently, Thomas Burnell Colbert has established himself as an authority on Weaver; see "Political Fusion in Iowa: The Election of James B. Weaver to Congress in 1878," *Arizona and the West* 20 (1978), 25–40; and "Disgruntled 'Chronic Office Seeker' or Man of Political Integrity: James Baird Weaver and the Republican Party in Iowa, 1857–1877," *Annals of Iowa* 49 (1988), 187–207. A provocative interpretation of the origins of Weaver's agrarian populism is in Mark A. Lause, "Voting Yourself a Farm in Antebellum Iowa: Towards an Urban, Working-Class Prehistory of the Post–Civil War Agrarian Insurgency," *Annals of Iowa* 49 (1988), 169–86. A rare treatment of Iowa Populism (besides Ostler's) *not* focusing on Weaver is Peter H. Argersinger, "To Disfranchise the People: The Iowa Ballot Law and Election of 1897," *Mid-America* 63 (1981), 18–35, reprinted in Argersinger's *The Limits of Agrarian Radicalism: Western Populism and American Politics* (Lawrence, KS, 1995).

The national historiography on Populism is vast, with new books coming out every year. One of the most recent and most sweeping interpretive treatments of the whole populist phenomenon is Michael Kazin, *The Populist Persuasion: An American History* (New York, 1995). For a guide to the earlier literature, see note 2 of the preceding essay; note especially the reference to the guide to the literature in Gene Clanton, *Populism: The Humane Preference in America, 1890–1900* (Boston, 1991); and see also William C. Pratt, "Radicals, Farmers, and Historians: Some Recent Scholarship about Agrarian Radicalism in the Upper Midwest," *North Dakota History* 52 (1985), 12–25. Jeffrey Ostler's argument in this essay is expanded in *Prairie Populism: The Fate of Agrarian Radicalism in Kansas, Nebraska, and Iowa, 1880–1892* (Lawrence, KS, 1993).

11

Iowa, Wet or Dry?
Prohibition and the Fall of the GOP

RICHARD JENSEN

While railroad regulation and the struggle to divert the populist insurgency preoccupied Iowa politicians for a couple of decades, the most persistent issue in Iowa politics has been liquor regulation. In the late 1880s the battle over that issue led to the election of Iowa's only Democratic governor between 1854 and 1933. In this essay Richard Jensen supplements traditional political history, which emphasizes biography and election strategy, with an ethnocultural analysis, of which Jensen was a pioneer. He carefully correlates tabulations of election results with variables identified in census data to determine who voted for whom and why. Key to Jensen's analysis is his assumption that "the dominant forces that animated the electorate were party loyalty and, more fundamentally, religion, . . . in conjunction with racial and ethnic loyalties" (xii). Jensen's typology, subsequently borrowed frequently, divided midwestern religious denominations into "pietists," such as Methodists, Congregationalists, and Quakers, and "liturgicals," such as Episcopalians, Lutherans, and Catholics. Religious affiliation, Jensen argues, "shaped the issues and rhetoric of politics, and played the critical role in determining the party alignments of the voters" (58).

> Iowa will go Democratic when hell goes Methodist.
> —J. P. Dolliver, 1883[1]

IN 1888 the Midwest remained a Republican stronghold. The GOP controlled all six governorships and five of the congressional delegations; only Indiana was at all doubtful. Imminent success for the Democrats in any of the states

---

1. Thomas R. Ross, *Jonathan Prentiss Dolliver* (Iowa City, 1958), p. 65.

Reprinted by permission of University of Chicago Press from *The Winning of the Midwest: Social and Political Conflict, 1888–1896*, by Richard Jensen (Chicago: University of Chicago Press, 1971), 89–121. Copyright © 1971 by The University of Chicago.

would have seemed absurd. Yet all of the governors and congressional delegations elected in 1889 and 1890 would be Democratic—it would be one of the most spectacular, and short-lived, political reversals in American history. For many years there had been lurking an issue capable of shaking the loyalty of enough Republicans to defeat that party, and in 1889 it came to a head, defeating overconfident Republicans in four midwestern states and pointing the way to the Democratic landslide of 1890.

The issue was the tension between the pietistic and liturgical world views, and in 1889 it emerged in the guise of the prohibition of the liquor traffic. Indeed, for most of the last third of the century, the liquor question, throughout the Midwest, was the major factor activating the latent tensions and leading to changes in voting patterns. Other issues blazed into prominence from time to time, subsiding as quickly as they ignited, and leaving little impress on voting patterns. But cultural tension was important year in and year out, thanks to a large, articulate, dedicated band of pietistic temperance advocates, and an equally determined body of liturgical opponents. A review of the role of the prohibition question in Iowa from 1855 through 1891 will suggest the contours of the issue, while detailed discussion of the elections of 1889 in Iowa, Ohio, Chicago, and Indianapolis will show its critical importance.

In 1888 Iowa carried high the banner of midwestern Republicanism. Not since the organization of their party had the Republicans lost control of Iowa's electoral votes, its statehouse, its congressional delegation, or its legislature. Leading the GOP were three men of national stature. Senator William Boyd Allison, a serious aspirant to the White House and a power in Congress, enjoyed the deference due the outstanding citizen of Iowa. James Clarkson, editor of the Des Moines *Iowa State Register,* the voice of Iowa Republicanism, was a power in the GOP national committee and directed the national campaigns against Cleveland in 1888 and 1892. The other triumvir, Colonel David Henderson, represented the Dubuque district in Congress, and in 1899 became Speaker of the House. Long years of secure power, however, had rusted the fighting gear of the GOP. Overconfident and carelessly organized, the Republicans relied heavily upon party loyalty of the Iowans who cherished the memory of Lincoln and who endorsed the sound, conservative Republican administration of state and national affairs.[2]

The Democratic party, by contrast, was a motley coalition of losers. The Bourbons sat on top. They were old stock businessmen, editors, or wealthy farmers with an emotional and intellectual attachment to the principles of the Democrats: tariff for revenue only, strong presidents (Cleveland was their hero) and weak congresses, deep fear of corruption, conciliation toward the white South, frugal government, and opposition to radical crusaders, whether abolitionist, socialist, or prohibitionist. In a Republican stronghold, the Bourbons

---

2. Leland Sage, *William Boyd Allison* (Iowa City, 1956), pp. 205–39; Cyrenus Cole, *I Remember, I Remember* (Iowa City, 1936), pp. 138–50, 176.

more often got the prestige of an important nomination than the office itself. Cleveland's entry into the White House stirred their hopes for federal patronage; but the president knew which state parties were important, and in four years gave Iowa only the minor sop of commissioner of patents, and that only after half the term had expired. The Democrats did win local offices in many of the heavily immigrant counties along the Mississippi River, but the Germans and Irish, not the Bourbons, got these plums. Thousands of old Jacksonian Democrats, mostly poor farmers of southern heritage, clung to the party of their fathers without hope or want of patronage. Their aggregate vote was important, but their opinions vague and unheeded.[3]

So bankrupt was the Democratic party after the war that it groped desperately for fusion or submersion into any popular movement that showed even a glimmer of electoral hope. John P. Irish, Iowa Democratic state chairman, in 1873 pronounced his party dead: it was "hopelessly bankrupt," having "outlived its day and its usefulness." He urged Democrats to join the new Anti-Monopoly party. That strategem proved no more successful than had fusion with the Liberal Republicans in 1872, with the Greenbackers sporadically from 1878 to 1886, or with the odd "Union Anti-Negro Suffrage party" in 1865. The Republicans merely flayed the Democrats, even in disguise, as Copperheads, ridiculed their platforms (after extracting any especially popular ideas in them), drew upon their reservoir of party loyalty, and triumphed every time.[4]

In 1889 the Democratic prospects suddenly were not so bleak. Mobilizing its respectable Bourbon candidates and the full voting strength of its rank and file, the party made a new appeal to lukewarm Republicans and independents. Democrats sensed confusion and disarray among the opposition, and vigor and harmony in their own ranks. They had come upon a new stone for their old sling, and now set about to slay Goliath upon the battlefield of the enemy's choosing. The Republican leaders, to their own amazement, found themselves helpless to avoid this deadly conflict, for the battlefield was the cultural and religious values of the people, and the issue was the morality of drinking.

IN 1855 the Whig party of Iowa secured passage of a constitutional amendment to prohibit the manufacture and sale of alcoholic beverages within the state, and then promptly expired. Its successor, the Republican party, concentrating its crusading fervor against slavery, quickly exempted beer and wine, permitted towns the local option of licensing saloons, and neglected to enforce prohibition in counties that did not want it. The beer-drinking liturgical Ger-

---

3. Horace Merrill, *Bourbon Democracy in the Middle West: 1865–1896* (Baton Rouge, 1963); Benjamin F. Gue, *History of Iowa* (New York, 1903), 3:1–4, 14, 61, 96–97, 137. Robert Kelley, *Transatlantic Persuasion* (New York, 1969), without mentioning Iowa, analyzes the Bourbon outlook brilliantly.

4. Mildred Throne, "The Liberal Party in Iowa, 1872," *Iowa Journal of History* (1955) 53:121–52, and "The Anti-Monopoly Party in Iowa, 1873–1874," ibid. (1954) 52:289–326.

mans pouring into Iowa, not to mention the whiskey-guzzling unchurched old Americans, must not be alienated, the ambitious Republicans decided.[5]

The Republicans' refusal to enforce prohibition frustrated both the Democrats, who hungered for a viable issue, and also the reformers, who considered intemperance to be the greatest evil in Iowa. After the Civil War, three distinct positions emerged on the liquor question. Most zealous were the pietistic drys, the total abstainers who considered even moderate drinking to be sinful and properly subject to legislative prohibition. At the other pole the liturgical and unchurched wets, men not adverse to a drink now and then, or perhaps more often, wanted their saloons. Even the liquor dealers among them did not always oppose a little regulation or taxation of the trade — high tavern licenses, after all, might cut down competition. All the wets bitterly denounced any attempt to abolish the saloon as an infringement of personal liberty and constitutional rights. In between came the moderates, who, whatever their own drinking habits, viewed the question not in the stark tones of the wets and drys, but in the gray zone of matters of practical public policy.

The Democrats, their party machinery largely housed and greased by the saloon and powered by its patrons, naturally championed the wet cause. They seldom missed an opportunity to decry "sumptuary laws," as they always called prohibition laws, or to denounce the GOP as "the tool of fanatical preachers," a "Holy Alliance of . . . abolitionists, Whigs, Know Nothings, Sunday and Cold Water Fanatics." Yet no matter how hard they tried, whether they pitched high or low, the Democrats could make little headway on the issue before the Republicans helped them out in the late 1870s and early 1880s.[6]

During the Grant administration, the drys, animated by the good ladies of the Woman's Christian Temperance Union, and muscled by their husbands' votes, formed a Prohibition party. They garnered more scorn than votes, and seemed, at first, ludicrously unimportant and old-fashioned in the Gilded Age. But the shocking excesses of the age — the Whiskey Ring scandals, for example — led many sober drys into the ranks of the crusaders. In Iowa, and across the Midwest, the WCTU prospered and spread, the Sons of Temperance revived, the Order of Good Templars reorganized its teetotaling brothers. Most important, the leading pietistic ministers, headed by Methodists, rekindled their traditional support for prohibition and entered the political fray. Organized into the Iowa State Temperance Alliance, the dry crusaders constituted an unmeasured power of disquieting magnitude to the nervous Republican leaders. Slowly the

---

5. Louis Pelzer, "The History and Principles of the Democratic Party of Iowa: 1846–1857," *Iowa Journal of History* (1908) 6:211, 237; Dan Elbert Clark, "The History of Liquor Legislation in Iowa," ibid. 6:67–68, 80–87; *The Cyclopedia of Temperance and Prohibition* (New York, 1891), pp. 148–49, 587–89; David Sparks, "The Decline of the Democratic Party in Iowa, 1850–60," *Iowa Journal of History* (1955) 53:17–18.

6. Quote from Carl Wittke, *The German Language Press in America* (Lexington, 1957), p. 140. Merrill, *Bourbon Democracy*, pp. 58–60; *Cyclopedia of Temperance*, pp. 148–53, 559–67; *Dubuque Herald*, October 31, 1882.

Republicans edged toward the dry camp. New, more stringent licensing and local option laws in 1868, 1870, 1872, 1873, and 1874 carried Republican endorsement, but failed to satisfy the drys. At the Republican convention of 1875 the drys, in coalition with the soft-money men, almost won the gubernatorial nomination for their champion, General James B. Weaver, only to meet sudden defeat at the hands of desperate moderates and conservatives.[7]

The threatening growth of the dry and inflationist Greenback party after Weaver's defection to it in 1877, coupled with the rising militancy of the dry crusaders, forced the issue. In 1879 the Republicans resolved in favor of submitting to the vote of the people a prohibition amendment to the state constitution that would join Iowa with Kansas and Maine as the driest states in America. The Prohibition party collapsed in 1879, as its adherents rushed to endorse the new Republican pledges. True to the party's platform, the Republican legislatures of 1880 and 1882 passed the necessary legislation for submission, and in anticipation of the outcome curtailed the sale of liquor by druggists.

The special election of June 27, 1882, climaxed the long and bitter struggle for constitutional prohibition in Iowa. In every county of the state, and in nearly every township and school district, the Temperance Alliance mobilized its men and, especially, its women, who could not vote but who had ways of influencing their menfolk. Prohibition of liquor—and this time beer and wine as well—the drys insisted, was merely the natural advance after the legal prohibition of murder, thievery, prostitution, gambling, and political corruption; indeed, they said, it was the best way to banish all those practices from Iowa. The achievement of a higher stage of American civilization and Christian morality, they concluded, rested on the outcome of the vote.[8]

The opposition, mobilized by the Brewers' Association, perforce fought on a narrower field. Funded by a $6000 assessment on beer sales, and with some help from friends in Saint Louis, Chicago, and Milwaukee, the liquor interests worked through local saloons and local Democratic organizations. Denouncing the "puritanical" fanaticism of the drys, the wets hit "sumptuary" laws as alien to the American genius of personal liberty, and the wisdom of the German and Irish liturgical culture. Prohibition, they argued, was not only legally and politically unsound, but was impossible of enforcement, unjust to the honest businessmen of the trade, and a threat to the economic well-being of Iowa.[9]

---

7. Clark, "Liquor Legislation" 6:342–64; Fred Haynes, *James Baird Weaver* (Iowa City, 1919), pp. 80–83; David Brandt, "Political Sketches," *Iowa Journal of History* (1955) 53:341–65; *Cyclopedia of Temperance*, pp. 589–91.

8. Clark, "Liquor Legislation" 6:368–73, 503–19; Brandt, "Sketches" 53: 347–50. The Des Moines *Iowa State Register* (Republican) and the *Dubuque Herald* (Democratic) carried full accounts of the campaign.

9. Clark, "Liquor Legislation" 6:519–24; T. C. Leggett in *Advance* (August 10, 1882), p. 518.

One of Herbert Hoover's most memorable boyhood experiences was that of a hot June day when his mother, a Quaker spiritual leader, brought him along to the polls "where the women were massed in an effort to make the men vote themselves dry." The pietistic Quakers prided themselves on a long record of strong opposition to social evils. The liquor traffic, no less than slavery, appeared to them an abominable curse, which society had to extirpate. Springdale, the prosperous Quaker township in Cedar County that embraced Hoover's village of West Branch, was a Republican stronghold; but even more it was a temperance stronghold—the village Democrat doubled as the village drunk. The townspeople had sheltered John Brown twenty-five years before, and now were equally serious. They endorsed the amendment by a convincing 342 to 29 vote.[10]

A few miles east of West Branch lay another prosperous community of farmers and villagers, Farmington Township. Not less religious than their Quaker neighbors, nor less hard working nor less devoted to the ideals of liberty were the men of Farmington. Yet they were different, for they were German immigrants and liturgical Lutherans. The temperance crusade of the Quakers, the Methodists, and the other pietists struck anxiety into the hearts of the Germans, for they felt they were the target of the new laws; it was their fondness for beer that seemed to call down the wrath of the God-fearing Yankees. The Germans did not appreciate their prospective role as outlaws. Narrowly Republican in 1875, Farmington moved towards the Democrats as the Republicans endorsed more and more dry programs. The amendment failed in the township 25 to 189, and the general elections that fall saw the Democratic share of the vote jump to 78 percent, 21 points higher than in 1881.[11]

The amendment did pass, but not overwhelmingly. The final returns showed 155,436 (55.3 percent) for, and 125,677 against. To a large degree, the vote followed party lines. The Republicans supported the amendment, except for the Germans and scattered other groups. Most of the Democrats voted no, but the efforts of the Temperance Alliance and the churches to woo dry Democrats probably were not entirely futile. The correlation of the vote with party loyalties did not necessarily imply that partisanship *determined* the vote. True, the amendment might have failed had not the Republicans urged moderates and wets in their ranks to support the measure for the good of the

---

10. Quote from Eugene Lyons, *Herbert Hoover* (Garden City, 1964), pp. 4, 16; Herbert Hoover, *Memoirs* (New York, 1951), 1:9; see letter from Laurie Tatum, of Springdale, to *Friends' Review* (July 1, 1882) 35:758–59; *Iowa Census of 1880* (Des Moines, 1883), p. 618, giving township returns for the referendum and for the general elections of 1881 and 1882. *The History of Cedar County, Iowa* (Chicago, 1878), chronicles the stories of West Branch and Farmington.

11. By 1888 the Democrats had consolidated their hold on Farmington and polled 83 percent of its vote for Grover Cleveland. *History of Cedar County*, p. 618; William Harsha, *The Story of Iowa* (Omaha, 1890), p. 155; *Iowa State Register*, October 1, 1889; Frank Hickenlooper, *An Illustrated History of Monroe Co., Iowa* (Albia, Iowa, 1896), pp. 188–89.

party. But for most of the people, support or opposition to prohibition rested on the same pietistic-liturgical basis as support or opposition for the Republican party itself.[12]

Many Republican state leaders, including Allison, Clarkson, Henderson, former Governor Samuel Kirkwood, and State Senator William Larrabee, grew worried when the amendment campaign stirred beliefs and prejudices stronger and more basic than party loyalty. Devoted liturgical Republicans might abandon their party on the issue; thousands did. The practical politicians, seeking to keep the Republican party open to men of all religious persuasions, wanted to banish the temperance issue from partisan politics, and hoped that the passage of the amendment would kill the issue. Their premonitions of danger proved to be solidly grounded.[13]

The anger of the liturgical Germans, directed at the Republicans, led to a plunge in the strength of the GOP in German strongholds. The fourteen most German counties in Iowa, with about a third of their voting population German-born (and many others the sons of immigrants), had produced Republican pluralities of 3,500 in 1876 and 6,400 in 1880. They turned in a majority of 9,320 against the amendment, and in the 1884 presidential election gave Cleveland a plurality of 5,200 votes. The German counties before the referendum were two to four percentage points less Republican than the remainder of the state; after the referendum they were eight to thirteen points less Republican. Only in 1896 did the Republicans recapture the German vote, as table 11.1 suggests.[14] Some of the fine points of the movements between parties appeared in the heavily Catholic city of Dubuque, and may be inspected in table 11.2.

The demolition of the gains the Republicans had made among liturgical German farmers and workers, especially in the larger cities like Dubuque, would not, by itself, be sufficient to cost the GOP control of the state. The amendment, after all, had passed by 30,000 votes, the GOP kept above the 50 percent line. But fate took nasty turns in Iowa politics. The prohibition issue was far from dead. In January 1883 the state supreme court stunned the people and the politicians of Iowa by declaring that a trivial error in the enactment procedure rendered the amendment invalid.[15]

The Republicans dared not resubmit the prohibition amendment, for another temperance crusade might spell disaster. Yet they had to mollify the

---

12. Harsha, *Iowa*, pp. 325–34; Truman O. Douglas, *The Pilgrims of Iowa* (Boston, 1911), pp. 230–31; Samuel P. Hays, "History as Human Behavior," *Iowa Journal of History* (1960) 58:196–97.

13. Sage, *Allison*, pp. 188–93; Brandt, "Sketches" 53:351–52; Johnson Brigham, *James Harlan* (Iowa City, 1913), pp. 290–93, tells of the driest Republican politician.

14. The election returns are based on *The Iowa Official Register* (Des Moines, 1889–1897), *The Iowa Census of 1885* (Des Moines, 1885), *The Iowa Census of 1880* (Des Moines, 1883), and the *Iowa Census of 1875* (Des Moines, 1875). The fourteen German counties were Bremer, Butler, Carroll, Clayton, Clinton, Crawford, Dubuque, Grundy, Ida, Lyon, O'Brien, Osceola, Plymouth, and Scott. In each, more than 10 percent of the 1900 population was German-born.

15. Clark, "Liquor Legislation" 6:529–35.

TABLE 11.1
VOTING PATTERNS IN 14 PREDOMINANTLY GERMAN IOWA COUNTIES, 1876–1896

	1876	1880	1882 referendum	1884	1888
Percent Republican	55	56	39 (% dry)	44	44
Plurality and party	3,500 R	6,400 R	9,300 wet	5,200 D	7,000 D

	1889	1890	1891	1892	1893	1896
Percent Republican	36	36	37	41	42	52
Plurality and party	15,100 D	12,800 D	15,700 D	10,600 D	8,300 D	3,500 D

TABLE 11.2
WARD VOTING PATTERNS IN DUBUQUE, 1875–1885

Ward*	1875 % GOP	1881 % GOP	1882 % dry	1882 % GOP	1881–82 % GOP loss	1885 % GOP
1	24	23	12	16	– 7.5	19
2	30	41	14	30	–11.0	37
3	41	51	10	23	–27.8	33
4	60	62	33	51	–10.7	58
5	40	63	6	22	–40.8	36
..	..	..	..	..	..	..
City	41	50	15	28	–21.5	38
Total vote	2,906	3,528	4,003	3,937	—	4,359

*Ward 1 was predominantly Irish; Wards 3 and 5, German; Ward 2, mixed; Ward 4, the silk-stocking home of wealthy Germans, Yankees, and others.

SOURCE: *Dubuque Herald,* and sources cited in note 14.

angry drys and the moderates who recognized that a majority of the population wanted prohibition. The election campaigns of 1883, 1884, and 1885 focused largely on Republican promises to enact prohibitory legislation. The Democrats used the opportunity to solidify their hold on the German vote, but the Republicans won anyway. The Republican drys rammed through one of the three stiffest prohibition laws in America at the 1884 session of the Iowa legislature; its consequences took a decade to unfold.[16]

---

16. Ibid., 538–41; *Cyclopedia of Temperance,* pp. 109, 104–5, 296–302, 307-9, 502–13.

THE BREWERS AND SALOON-KEEPERS, and their patrons and employees, did not explode many firecrackers on July 4, 1884. That day the new prohibition laws took effect. In hundreds of towns, villages, and crossroad hamlets where dry sentiment was strong, the saloons closed, reluctantly, and not without some rioting. In the larger towns and cities the law was often flaunted, even openly, sometimes with the approval of local officials. The new governor, William Larrabee, formerly a foe of prohibition, suddenly found it expedient to become its most ardent champion. Before Larrabee became governor, the liquor laws had been poorly enforced, except in the more pietistic rural townships. Some 1,800 saloons had flourished before prohibition; in 1885, eighteen months after the laws took effect, perhaps 2,200 regular outlets served the drinkers of Iowa. In the two dozen largest cities there had been 865 saloons paying $290,000 annually in license fees. In 1885, however, no license fees were collected, but more than 1,400 holes-in-the-wall flourished. Larrabee was disturbed by this situation, and initiated strict enforcement of the original laws, which were augmented by new statutes in 1886. During his first administration he forced the saloons to retreat from the fifty-nine counties they had served in 1885, into just twenty-two counties in 1887. No town of more than 1,500 nor any German settlement remained wholly without some facilities for the drinking man, but in the Larrabee years liquor became harder and harder to get in ninety of Iowa's ninety-nine counties. Anyone dying of thirst, however, could obtain a "prescription" from a friendly doctor, and fill it at a friendly "pharmacy"—or he could hunt out a rumshop in the nearest large city; some men preferred to cross the state line, or to import cases of liquor (in the original package) by mail. Everywhere in Iowa the people added a new noun to their vocabulary: "bootlegger."[17]

The assassination of a dry leader in 1886 enraged the temperance men, but opposition to the enforcement of the laws rapidly built up. New laws imposed unusually severe restrictions on druggists, many of whom were ex-saloonkeepers, and the legitimate pharmacists of Iowa angrily demanded relief. Their pleas were answered by further restrictive laws in 1888. Eager prosecutors and informers rushed to obtain the bonuses for uncovering illicit liquor sales; they raided the homes of respectable men suspected of harboring illegal bottles of bourbon or champagne. By 1889 all of Iowa was caught up in the furor over prohibition. The Republicans, however, had seemingly mobilized just enough support to frustrate the drinkers and the Democrats.[18]

THERE IS MUCH RUIN in a ruling party. Not content with their radical temperance position, the Republicans devised other programs to enhance the

---

17. Clark, "Liquor Legislation" 6:541–63; Brandt, "Sketches" 53:354, 358; see *New York Voice*, March 12, 26, 1885, and *Ann. Cycl. 1885:* 499 for details of enforcement.

18. Clark, "Liquor Legislation" 6:558–68; Gue, *Iowa*, 3:138–39; *Cyclopedia of Temperance*, pp. 201–2, 517; *New York Times*, July 27, 1889.

progress of Iowa and test the loyalty of the rank and file. With the strong backing of the party organization, Senator Allison led the opposition to President Cleveland's proposals to lower the tariff. Allison's revisions of the House-passed Mills bill stymied all efforts at tariff reform on the eve of the 1888 election. The farmers of Iowa, most of whom were paying off mortgages, had been growing restless under the mounting burden of debt and did not always appreciate the logic of the protectionists; they wanted higher prices for their land and products, not for their purchases. Led by Clarkson, the protectionists sought to build Iowa into an industrial state; a high protective tariff was needed to nurture the infant industries of the state. "The policy of the Republican party," Allison reassured the farmers, "is to diversify employment and industries and thus find a market constant and sure at our own doors and in our own country for farm products." Allison had a grand dream, the farmers agreed, but some wondered if it was not too long-range, too neglectful of the immediate needs of Iowa agriculture.[19]

Next to prohibition and the tariff, the most talked about issue in Iowa was the regulation of railroad freight rates. Iowa's Granger laws, among the first to regulate rates, had proved unsatisfactory, and had been repealed as soon as the momentum of the Granger movement was spent. Difficult times for the farmers, coupled with animosity toward Eastern stockholders, fueled an undercurrent of hostility toward the roads in the 1880s. The adjustment of rates following the Interstate Commerce Act of 1887 hurt the competitive position of Iowa jobbers and wholesalers vis-à-vis Chicago, and added an articulate, although small, force to the antirailroad coalition. Larrabee himself had played an important, cautious role in regulation legislation before he became governor, but no one expected the bombshell contained in his second inaugural address in January, 1888.[20]

"New ideas, born of the spirit of progress," Larrabee told the legislature, "constantly battle with the musty conceptions of conservatism, prejudice and tradition; and gigantic interests, the creation of our inventive age, are constantly striving to usurp illegitimate, as well as to assert legitimate right." It was tempting for him "to make a truce with the enemy," but "solemn obligation makes the conflict an imperative duty." Larrabee thus declared war on the railroads. After sketching the dastardly record of the railroads in Iowa, the crusading governor denounced their high and unfair rates, and their low wages.

---

19. *Iowa State Register*, October 9, 1889; Cole, *I Remember*, p. 145; *Third Annual Report of the [Iowa] Bureau of Labor Statistics* (Des Moines, 1889), pp. 111–23, for the views of farmers.

20. J. Brooke Workman, "Governor William Larrabee and Railroad Reform," *Iowa Journal of History* (1959) 57:239–54; William Larrabee, *The Railroad Question* (Chicago, 1893), p. 337; Frank H. Dixon, *State Railroad Control* (New York, 1896), pp. 135–38; Benjamin F. Shambaugh, ed., *The Messages and Proclamations of the Governors of Iowa* (Iowa City, 1904), 6:17–18, 73–75; Brandt, "Sketches" 53:358–60. In his unsuccessful bid for the GOP gubernatorial nomination in 1881, Larrabee had the support of the railroads and the wets, but failed to crack the opposition of the reformers. Brandt, ibid., 53:176, 353–59.

Comparing the companies with the cruel British landlords in Ireland, and even with Greek pirates who once "ravaged villages and plundered unfortified places," Larrabee demanded an end to their "usurping unlawful powers and invading public rights." The reform-minded Republican legislature quickly and unanimously enacted a strong bill giving extensive powers to control rates and police the companies to the Board of Railroad Commissioners, which was to become an elective body. The board promptly cut rates 20 percent. The railroads fought back vigorously in the courts and at the polls. A compromise eventually resolved the rate dispute, but not before a new issue further enlivened Iowa politics.[21]

Cleveland and Harrison battled vigorously for the doubtful states in 1888, but Iowa was not among them. Disappointment mingled with pride in the summer of 1888 when Senator Allison failed in his bid for the presidential nomination. The ostensible issue in Iowa was the tariff, but the real excitement came from the railroad issue. Both parties endorsed the principles of regulation. The Republicans endorsed the actions of Larrabee, the legislature, and the regulatory board. The Democrats, however, coyly played on both sides of the fence. The Democratic nominees for railroad commissioner included Peter Dey, who was an incumbent appointed by Larrabee, and Herman Wills. Wills was a nationally prominent leader of the Brotherhood of Locomotive Engineers, which had led the fight *against* regulation. Both Dey and Wills received strong labor union support, and Dey's candidacy pleased the jobbers, wholesalers, and other antirailroad groups as well. The shippers, most of them wealthy Republicans, joined with Henry Wallace's influential farm paper, *Iowa Homestead*, the Farmers' Alliance, and the remnants of the Union Labor party to elect Dey. Meanwhile the railroads rallied their employees, most of them Democrats anyway, to defeat Dey's opponent, John Mahin, who favored both stiff rate regulation and absolute prohibition.[22]

The count of the ballots gave Iowa's thirteen electoral votes to Harrison, his reward for a plurality of 31,000 in the state. The rest of the Republican ticket swept into office, save for Mahin, who polled 200,075 votes to 201,265 for Dey. Peter Dey thus became the first Democrat to carry the state in a third of a century. In the fourteen German counties, at least one Republican in six split his ticket to vote for Dey; elsewhere, only one Republican in twenty-four

---

21. Shambaugh, *Messages* 6:91–107; Workman, "Larrabee" 57:254–61; Sage, *Allison*, p. 211; Gue, *Iowa*, 3:142–52; *Ann. Cycl. 1888*: 444–46; *1889*: 448–49.

22. *Ann. Cycl. 1888*: 446–47; *Dubuque Herald*, October 26, 27, November 7, 18, 28, 1888; *Chicago Herald*, September 9, 1888; Merrill, *Bourbon Democracy*, pp. 203–204; Cole, *I Remember*, pp. 166–68; J. Irwin, "Is Iowa A Doubtful State?" *Forum* (April, 1892) 13:259–61; Sage, *Allison*, pp. 223–32. Pietist ministers also seem to have been unhappy that year with Benjamin Harrison's failure to endorse prohibition. A poll of all the Methodist clergy at the annual convention of the northwest Iowa district showed forty-four favored Clinton Fisk, the Prohibition party candidate, thirty-three supported Harrison, ten were undecided, and one intrepid circuit rider admitted favoring Cleveland. The year before, the ministers had nearly all voted Republican. *New York Voice*, October 25, 1888.

cut Mahin's name, mostly Republican businessmen whose defection to Dey was only an affirmation of confidence in the incumbents on the Board of Railroad Commissioners. The Democrats could hardly expect this silk-stocking vote to come their way again. Much more significant was the large defection of German Republicans to Dey. Mahin contended that he was sacrificed because of his radically dry stance on prohibition. Many of those German Republicans who had not defected to the Democrats in 1882, or who had since returned to the GOP, were restless. If the Democrats were to carry Iowa, it could only be with the capture of their votes, and the issue had to be prohibition.[23]

BY 1889 public opinion in Iowa reached a turning point. The enthusiasm of the drys, unchecked for five years, began to flag. The mysterious postponement of the dawn of a new stage in civilization, and the curious interlude of massive disrespect for the law, led the bitter prohibitionists to demand more laws, stricter enforcement, harsher punishment. Calmer men began to question the wisdom of absolute prohibition in a state with such different religious and cultural values as the Yankees and the Germans represented. A large portion of the upright citizenry clearly rejected the harsh laws — but were they not a minority and ought not the majority rule? While moderates debated these points, other worries abounded in Iowa.

The economic health of the state came into question. The commercial growth of Iowa depended upon an adequate railroad network, but the roads claimed that the new regulated rates stifled the development and extension of their lines. Construction of new mileage abruptly halted in mid-1888; several small lines closed; railroad spokesmen warned of further regression. Urban promoters not only found the railroad situation disturbing, but noted a sharp downturn in the rate of construction and population growth. The value of new private and public construction in Des Moines, for example, had grown rapidly up to 1883, when the city collected $1,200 annual license fees from each of fifty-two saloons. Opponents of prohibition pointed out that with the coming of prohibition and the official closing of the city's saloons, the construction industry slumped. The 1883 level of building activity was reached only once in the next fourteen years.

Iowa was uneasy; the questions the people asked were hard ones. Did the regulation of railroads impede economic growth? Had prohibition slowed the influx of hard-working, beer-drinking German mechanics and farmers? Could the financial crises of the larger cities be resolved from revenues from saloon licenses? Would the manufacture of beer and whiskey in Iowa raise the demand for the state's corn and barley crops? Had cranks and radicals taken control of the Republican party? Did prohibition prohibit? The intense resentment of the Germans and Irish against prohibition, the obvious failure of the noble

---

23. *Dubuque Herald*, November 7, 18, 20, 28, 1888.

experiment, the threatening stagnation of commerce, transportation, construction, and agriculture, coupled with the seemingly blind abandon of the ruling party, readied Iowa for a political revolution. The only ingredient still lacking was firm leadership.[24]

Peter Dey's election made the Democrats confident that they could carry Iowa. The spring mayoralty election in Keokuk gave them a blueprint for the 1889 gubernatorial campaign. Keokuk with its large German and Irish population was wet, but still Republican, even though the city had rejected the prohibition amendment 62 percent to 38 percent. The mayor in 1888 was a dry Republican who enlisted the pietistic churches, some of the businessmen, and the police in a crackdown on the city's many saloons. With resentment high, the Democrats nominated John Craig for mayor in late March, 1889. Craig was a distinguished Bourbon legislator, a good Protestant, a teetotaler, and an advocate of high license fees. A brief, bitter campaign, centering on the saloon issue, ended with a Democratic landslide. Democrats across the state watched the Keokuk race with keen interest—did Craig have the secret, they asked, that would carry Iowa?[25]

Horace Boies, although not widely known outside Waterloo, was the perfect candidate for governor. The Republican commitment to prohibition and protective tariffs had forced him to switch to the Democratic party in 1884. Boies, like Dey and Craig, was a man of unblemished character; he was a teetotaler (his only lodge was the Good Templars), and possessed a totally honest "affidavit face." He articulately opposed paternal government, centralized power, radical prohibition, high tariffs, and intrusions against private property. He favored high license fees, ballot reform, moderate regulation of railroads, harmony between capital and labor and between the diverse cultural groups of Iowa. A Bourbon to the quick, Boies was the hope of Iowa Democrats. At the September state convention he outpolled Mayor Craig 502–161 and became the Democratic nominee for governor.[26]

The Republican leaders realized the dangers in 1889, but the party was out of their control. Allison, Henderson, and Clarkson were in Washington, attending to the critical legislation of the Fifty-first Congress, and to important national party problems. The governing body of the Iowa GOP, the state convention, consisted of delegates elected at county conventions, which in turn

---

24. Will Porter, *Annals of Polk County, Iowa* (Des Moines, 1898), pp. 470–97; Cole, *I Remember*, pp. 154–56, 164–65; Irwin, "Iowa," pp. 262–64; Gue, *Iowa*, 3:147; *Iowa State Register*, November, 9, 10, 1889; *Dubuque Herald*, July 12, November 10, 1889; *New York Times*, August 12, 16, 1889; Harsha, *Iowa*, pp. 337–38. For the doubts of Iowa bankers, see *New York Voice*, July 23, 30, August 13, 1888.

25. *Chicago Tribune*, March 30, April 2, 1889; Clark, "Liquor Legislation" 6:562; *Ann. Cycl. 1890*, pp. 133–34; *Cyclopedia of Temperance*, p. 517; *New York Voice*, October 18, 1888.

26. Cole, *I Remember*, pp. 172–74; Jean B. Kern, "The Political Career of Horace Boies," *Iowa Journal of History* (1949) 47:215–19; *Dubuque Herald*, July 12, September 28, 1889; *Chicago Times*, August 24, 1893.

were largely packed by radically dry or antirailroad political amateurs. Only men committed to railroad reform and strict enforcement of the liquor laws could win the nominations of many local conventions. The crusading pietists in some counties even demanded that all candidates be teetotalers — had that policy been adopted generally, the Republican party of Iowa would have sunk without a bubble. The local lieutenants of the moderate top leadership resisted the trend; but the amateurs, thoroughly organized, controlled the state convention in August, and nominated Joseph Hutchison, a wholesale grocer and a dry who was supposedly a strong friend of rate regulation, to oppose Boies.

Prohibition, the convention declared, "has become the settled policy of the State . . . there should be no backward step. We stand for the complete enforcement of the law." In opening his campaign, Hutchison rejected the idea that prohibition was an experiment that ought to be evaluated pragmatically. It was, rather, a "fixed institution of our progressive state." Every recent election, he noted, had affirmed the will of the majority for strict liquor laws. Iowa, dry Iowa, "has made a struggle for morality, for the reduction of corruption, debauchery, and crime, for the true elevation of the human race, for self-respect, for decency, for manhood, for the wife and family, for the sacred virtue and honor of the home." Dry Iowa, he continued, "has triumphed against the saloon and its thousand attendant evils," yet the Democratic party had just "resolved in favor of this cursed barnacle, which modern civilization, as constituted in Iowa, is determined to destroy." "And today," he affirmed, to the thunderous applause of his parched audience, "by the goodness of God and the continued virtue of our people, we proclaim to the civilized world that we shall maintain the stand we have taken."[27]

The Republican orators and workhorses dutifully rallied to the dry crusade. Hutchison himself had a facility for boring a red-hot audience by droning monotonously through a well-written speech. Occasionally he was eloquent, as when he sternly lectured the German voters at Postville for half an hour on the evils of indulgence in beer and on the need to obey the voice of the majority and stop drinking. Fortunately he escaped the auditorium before precipitating a riot.

The temperance forces enthusiastically rallied to Hutchison. The WCTU dropped the nearly forgotten Prohibition party and worked for the GOP. The pietistic churches did their part, too. The Des Moines Methodist Conference a year before had declared "uncompromising hostility to the liquor traffic," and demanded its "unconditional surrender." Now, only a month before the election, the Upper Iowa Conference resolved that "no Methodist voter should permit himself to be controlled by party organizations which are managed in

---

27. Hutchison quotes in *Iowa State Register*, October 1, 1889; platform in *Ann. Cycl. 1889*: 449–50. The turmoil in the GOP was recorded by the *Iowa State Register*, see especially October 2, 6, 12, 13, November 10, 1889; *New York Times*, August 12, 16, 1889; *Chicago Tribune*, July 1, 21, 1889; October 28, 1891; and Brandt, "Sketches" 53:362–64.

the interests of the liquor traffic." For the benefit of any slow-witted Methodist who thought that high licenses and local option might harmonize the interests of church and state, the conference reaffirmed its "uncompromising hostility to license high and low," and for good measure went on to denounce "desecration of the Sabbath" by baseball games, Sunday newspapers and railroad service. The Good Templars ditched their brother Boies and announced for Hutchison on October 17. The next day the state Baptist convention, meeting in Des Moines, protested "against any movement looking toward the repeal of the prohibitory laws of Iowa." The Baptists further demanded new laws that would effectively dry up "the few remaining rebellious cities in the state." Two days later the Iowa Synod of the Presbyterian church advised its members to "resist, by every legitimate means, every effort to restore this saloon iniquity under any license, high or low."[28] The target of the pietistic scorn, of course, was Horace Boies.

The Democrats concentrated their efforts on Boies' campaign. The other state offices were unimportant; control of the legislature seemed impossible. Boies and his Bourbon managers realized that a winning coalition had to consist of the full traditional Democratic vote, supplemented by wet and moderate Republicans, discontented independents, and any other stray votes available. The German Republicans, it was expected, would provide thousands of votes, as they had for Dey a year before. The Union Labor party, the vehicle of the disintegrating Knights of Labor, might yield up its German voters. Moderate nonpietistic Yankees were to get a reasonable compromise on the liquor issue; radical prohibitionists were to be ridiculed and repudiated. Discontented farmers, many of whom were drys, had to be won over, or at least cross-pressured into staying at home, by a frontal attack on the Harrison administration and the protective tariff. Shippers had to be mollified by an endorsement of the principle of railroad regulation, but railroad workers and officials, and their sympathizers, would be wooed by promises of reasonable, profitable rate levels. Other discontented groups would get special treatment too. Horace Boies would be the articulate champion of all the aggrieved classes of Iowa.[29]

The Democrats' most successful strategem was their appeal to opponents of prohibition. "In the interest of true temperance," the platform read, "we demand the passage of a carefully guarded license tax law . . . of $500 [to] be paid into the county treasury." Each township would have the option of permitting or prohibiting saloons, and could keep for itself all license fees above $500. Boies made his opposition to the existing laws clear; his proposals for local option and high saloon licenses were acceptable to the wets, and strongly appealed to most of the moderates.

---

28. For the Methodists, see *The Political Prohibitionist for 1889* (New York, 1889), p. 76 and *Iowa State Register*, October 9, 1889; for the Baptists, ibid., October 25, 1889; Brandt, "Sketches" 53:362–64; for the Presbyterians, see minutes of the *Eighth Annual Meeting of the [Presbyterian] Synod of Iowa*, Oct. 17–21, 1889 (Mt. Pleasant, Iowa, 1889), p. 222.

29. *Iowa State Register*, November 17, 1889 (editorial).

Generally Boies avoided direct appeals to the ethnic loyalties of the German and Irish voters. That task could be left to local spokesmen. Boies, in countercrusading style, did condemn Know-Nothingism and intolerance. He saw "no material difference in the intelligence, morality or respect for ordinary laws [among] our people. There is and always will be," he added, "a wide difference in their social habits, depending largely upon the customs of their fathers, the influence of education and the surroundings in which they live."[30]

Boies' endorsement of a pluralistic society in Iowa differed sharply from the Republican vision, which saw the pietistic old stock, whether Yankee, Southerner, or Pennsylvania Dutch, as the "leaven" that would transform the immigrants into true Americans. "Where the American leaven was not smothered beyond impressing or absorbing capacity all is well," the leading Republican newspaper editorialized. But, it continued, "Here and there it has not had time to accomplish its task and in these spots the Democrats propose to offer the temptation of the saloon."[31]

It was not the return of the saloon, but the repeal of absolute prohibition that Boies sought. He eloquently defended the right of the local community, not the state, to establish local practices. Local option would preserve prohibition in those areas that wanted it. High licenses would curb all the evils of the saloon without infringing personal liberty, and would also restore needed revenues to the hard-pressed cities. The destruction of the state's brewing and distillery business in 1885 had been an unjust confiscation of private property, he asserted, and the reopening of those manufactures would create a welcome new demand for the corn and barley crops.[32]

Boies had to tread cautiously on the liquor issue. To meet the intense criticism of the pietists, he had to assure the people that Iowa would not become another Chicago, clogged with saloons, vice, and corruption. Most of the factory and railroad managers strongly urged temperance for their men. The more secure ranks of mechanics thought prohibition to be a "good thing for the wage-workers," according to a poll taken a few months before the election. Even the unskilled laborers considered prohibition to be desirable; the coal miners approved prohibition three to one. As the additional remarks of these workers made clear, they were endorsing prohibition for *other* wage workers; they did not, furthermore, think that Iowa had prohibition. Everyone could see that the state had plenty of liquor. Probably the workers felt that prohibition would be good for thrift, industry, and virtue; in their own cases, most may have felt a policy of moderation would serve the best of two worlds.[33]

---

30. For the Democratic platform. see *Ann. Cycl. 1889*: 450. For Boies' speeches, see *Dubuque Herald*, October 6, and November 10, 1889.

31. *Iowa State Register*, October 6, 1889 (editorial).

32. *Dubuque Herald*, November 10, 1889, and Kern, "Boies" 47:219–22.

33. Iowa B.L.S. *Third Report* (1889), pp. 25, 47, 62–63, 131–34, 226–31, *Second Report* (1887), pp. 151–52, 204–11.

To keep the Republicans on the defensive, Boies barnstormed the rural areas denouncing the protective tariff. Answering Allison's promise that American industry would provide a home market for American crops, Boies warned that Iowa's farmers "are not going to wait for a home market to grow up around them." The vital international market, he continued, would be closed by a high tariff. Strong support for the Democratic position came from the Farmers' Alliance and former Grangers. The threat of higher prices for manufactured commodities, along with depressed land and commodity prices and ever-present mortgages, weakened the party loyalty of Republican farmers and strengthened the resolve of the Democrats. The virtual bankruptcy of the GOP on the tariff issue became clear when the *Iowa State Register* began to urge farmers to burn their corn in place of coal, thus saving money and forcing up prices. The GOP soon discovered that burning corn-cobs make a very hot and unpleasant fire.[34]

The confusion of the Republican campaign permitted Boies to run away with the railroad issue. Hutchison strongly defended the new railroad laws as beneficial to manufacturers, farmers, wholesalers, and the railroads themselves. The Democrats undermined his stand by demonstrating that he and his running mate had prorailroad records in the legislature. Boies, however, actually won the support of the railroads. He endorsed the principle of regulation, but promised fair administration and fair profits. The managers and their men threw their political resources behind Boies, while the guilt of association with railroad lobbyists clung to Hutchison.[35]

The Democrats picked up discontented groups wherever they could be found. The Des Moines Negro community, usually strongly Republican, found the Democrats seeking their votes on the liquor issue.[36] An agreement with James Sovereign, Iowa Knights of Labor leader, apparently gave Boies hundreds of votes that otherwise would have gone to the Union Labor or Republican tickets.[37] The disgruntled pharmacists of Iowa had been ignored by the Democrats in 1888, but now Boies promised them relief from the $1,000 bonds and humiliating affidavits of rectitude required by the latest prohibition laws. The Linn County druggists formally endorsed the Democratic platform, and

---

34. Kern, "Boies" 47:219–27; *Chicago Tribune*, October 28, 1889; *New York Times*, November 4, 5, 7, 1889; *Iowa State Register*, October 11, November 5, 11, 1889, and January 24, 1890; *Dubuque Herald*, July 12, September 1, 6, 28, October 6, 11, November 2, 10, 12, 1889. On the farmers' price situation, see Herman Nixon, "The Economic Basis of the Populist Movement in Iowa," *Iowa Journal of History* (1923) 21:387–88.

35. *Cedar Rapids Gazette*, October 23, 28, 1889; *Iowa State Register*, October 15, 16, 24, 27, November 9, 10, 16, 1889; Kern, "Boies" 47:220; Brandt, "Sketches" 53:356–65; Shambaugh, *Messages*, 6:277–80; *New York Times*, August 12, 16, October 5, 12, 14, 18, November 4, 5, 1889; *Dubuque Herald*, September 11, 1888, July 12, August 18, September 3, 28, October 6, 29, 1889.

36. *Iowa State Register*, October 17, 1889; *Chicago Tribune*, September 17, 1890.

37. Fred Haynes, *Third Party Movements* (Iowa City, 1916), p. 334; *Dubuque Herald*, October 26, 1888, August 4, September 6, October 5, 26, 29, 1889.

doubtless many of the state's 1,800 pharmacists voted Democratic for the first time in 1889.[38]

The success of a campaign is seen in the vote. The GOP plurality of 32,000 in 1888 withered to 1,600 for lieutenant governor. The Republicans lost eighteen seats in the legislature, but all their statewide candidates squeaked through. All, that is, save Hutchison. Boies ran 5,000 votes ahead of his ticket, and bested his adversary by 6,564 votes out of 360,945 cast. Boies captured 49.9 percent of the vote, Hutchison 48.1 percent, the Union Laborite 1.6 percent, and the Prohibitionist only 0.4 percent. Boies carried five of Iowa's eleven congressional districts, all but one of which had Republican representatives, and lost three other Republican districts by a total of only 562 votes. Only in two predominantly pietistic old-stock congressional districts did Hutchison hold the 1888 GOP share of the vote.

The excitement of the campaign was seemingly belied by the relatively low turnout. About 78 percent of the eligible men voted, the lowest turnout in any year from 1883 through 1897, except in 1887 when 77 percent had voted. In 1888 less than 50,000 eligible citizens did not vote; in 1889 about 100,000 stayed away from the polls. Republicans by the thousands were disappointed with their party. Some — the Germans, especially — voted Democratic; thousands more registered their unhappiness by staying home. Boies' vote actually exceeded Cleveland's the year before by 243, while Hutchison lagged behind Harrison's total by 38,000. In the fourteen German counties, Boies almost exactly matched Cleveland's vote, but the Republican vote fell from 27,200 to 19,200.

The disaster hit the GOP hardest in the large cities. The nine cities in the state with 14,000 or more population had been a close battlefield in 1888. Cleveland carried only the four most German cities, Dubuque, Davenport, Burlington, and Council Bluffs, garnering 51.8 percent of the two-party vote in the nine. Boies swept all nine, with a phenomenal 64.4 percent of the vote. Even Des Moines, the pride of Iowa Republicanism, fell into Boies' column by a bare 85 votes. Harrison had accumulated a Republican plurality of 33,200 outside the nine cities; Boies' reduced that 90 percent to a mere 3,246. It was Boies' plurality of 9,810 votes in the nine cities that put him in the Iowa statehouse, as table 11.3 shows.[39]

The immigrants who were pleased with Boies on the liquor issue, especially those in the cities, decided the outcome. Table 11.4 presents some

---

38. *Dubuque Herald*, September 7, 8, October 6, 1889; cf. October 5, 1888; Shambaugh, *Messages*, 6:30, 55–56, 285. Nearly $10,000 in fines had already been exacted from seventy-five "pharmacists" convicted of selling liquor in 1887 alone.

39. The nine cities, and their 1890 population, were Des Moines (50,000), Sioux City (37,000), Dubuque (30,000), Davenport (27,000), Burlington (23,000), Council Bluffs (22,000), Cedar Rapids (18,000), Keokuk (14,000), and Ottumwa (14,000). As usual, the *Iowa Official Register* provided the election data.

TABLE 11.3
TWO-PARTY VOTE IN IOWA, 1888 (PRESIDENT) AND 1889 (GOVERNOR)

	President 1888		Governor 1889	
	GOP	Dem	GOP	Dem
Nine largest cities	19,114	20,675	12,261	22,071
Rest of state	192,394	159,202	161,295	158,049
Total for state	211,508	179,877	173,556	180,120

TABLE 11.4
REPUBLICAN SHARE OF TOTAL VOTE, 1888 (PRESIDENT) AND 1889 (GOVERNOR), BY ETHNIC GROUPS IN IOWA*

	Predominantly Liturgical Groups				
	Entire state	14 German counties	9 German city wards	9 Irish wards and townships	7 Bohemian wards and townships
GOP 1888	52.4%	44%	28%	20%	20%
GOP 1889	48.1	36	15	15	16
Loss	−4.2	−7.8	−12.8	−5.4	−4.5
	Predominantly Pietistic Groups				
	31 old stock counties	39 old stock small towns	11 rural Norwegian townships	6 rural Swedish townships	
GOP 1888	53%	59%	77%	73%	
GOP 1889	51	57	74	68	
Loss	−1.8	−2.3	−2.6	−5.2	

*All figures represent Republican percentage of total vote cast, including the small minor-party vote.

of the fine detail of culture-group voting patterns.[40]

Even without the liquor issue, the Republicans suffered reverses. As table 11.4 suggests, Hutchison lost 2 to 3 percent of the vote in the dry Republican Yankee and Norwegian strongholds. The campaign involved many issues, and any parcelling out of losses among them would be simplistic. Businessmen, for example, found Boies' candidacy attractive — in Burlington,

---

40. The data represents sample counties, towns, wards, and townships with the most homogenous populations, and only approximates the voting patterns of individual Germans, Irish, and others. Compare Jensen, *Winning of the Midwest,* chapter 8, note 52, and chapter 10, note 56.

Dubuque, Council Bluffs, Davenport, and Sioux City he carried the traditionally Republican upper-class wards. Did the more sophisticated businessmen admire Boies' style more than his free-trade ideology? Perhaps, but one cannot be sure. One can be sure that it could have been worse for the GOP. The Lee County chairman reported that hundreds of staunch Republicans bolted because "they were tired of free saloons on every street" and liked Boies' high license proposals. More than a third of those Republicans who did vote for Hutchison, the chairman continued, strained party loyalty to do so; again they preferred Boies' stand on prohibition. The low Republican turnout did not represent apathy. On the contrary, it represented one solution to the dilemma of the loyal Republican who could not support his party's nominee or platform in 1889.[41]

IF THE SITUATION COULD BE MADE WORSE, the moralists would find a way. The drys still controlled the legislature, though by sharply reduced margins. The laws regulating druggists were relaxed slightly, and provision was made to provide guardians for habitual drunkards. The legislature could not agree on any basic changes in the prohibition laws, although it did pass a stiffer railroad regulation law that stirred up new legal strife. The Republican legislators defiantly refused to accept Boies' proposals; there would be no "backward step" on Iowa's march toward civilization, they proclaimed.[42]

The Democrats entered the 1890 campaign with unaccustomed confidence. Boies had been unable to legalize liquor, but that meant the initiative on the issue still rested with the Democrats. Boies did downplay the enforcement of the existing laws. His pharmacy commissioner, for example, was a lazy soul with little interest in tracking down errant druggists. Unfortunately, the quality of Boies' other appointments to high state positions also tended to be restricted by the demands of his patronage-hungry party. The fall campaign for minor state offices and congressmen was quiet: the Democrats had too little money, the Republicans too little enthusiasm, to generate much excitement. The liquor issue still sparked most of the arguments, but the new McKinley tariff came in for considerable discussion, too. The election saw the Republicans narrowly salvage the state offices, but for the first time since the formation of the GOP the Democrats gained an edge in the congressional delegation, six to five. The new People's party displayed strength only in the wheat counties along the Nebraska border. Everyone agreed, however, that the Democrats had achieved parity with the Republican party in Iowa. Impish Democrats consoled their proud Republican friends with the thought that, after all, Senator Allison's

---

41. *Iowa State Register*, November 23, 28, 1889; *Dubuque Herald*, November 12, 1889; *New York Times*, November 7, 1889.

42. *Ann. Cycl. 1890*: 445–48; Clark, "Liquor Legislation" 6:575–79.

chances for the GOP presidential nomination in 1892 were enhanced, now that he came from a doubtful state.[43]

Prohibition, complained the angry Republican leaders, certainly does not stop drinking, but it does seem to prohibit Republican victories! Professional Republican politicians had sensed the disaster inherent in a party endorsement of absolute prohibition. The leaders themselves generally were moderate drinkers; no GOP presidential candidate had been an abstainer; few of the men of Congress or other high offices were unfamiliar with strong liquor. Only the fervent moral demands of the politically less experienced dry element — or, more likely, their threat of retribution at the conventions and the polls — forced the party leadership to go along with the prohibition planks. Throughout the 1880s the conflict between wets and drys and moderates raged within the Iowa GOP. A dry challenge to Senator Allison's reelection bid failed in early 1890, but the drys had their way at the state convention the next summer.

At the 1891 convention the outnumbered wets urged the Republicans to at least adopt an ambiguous stand on the liquor issue. The drys would hear none of it; they felt the 1889 loss of the governorship was due more to the tariff than to the liquor issue, and shouted down a local-option plank 951 to 107. Two amateur politicians, both prominent farmers, received the top nominations to oppose the Democratic ticket, which Boies again headed. The main issue again was prohibition, but the Democrats, becoming more confident, endorsed free silver, denounced the McKinley tariff, and called for high licenses. The Republican platform charged that "that outlaw" — the saloon — "has the patronage, council and protection of the Democratic party." The real issue, it insisted, "is law against defiance of law, subordination against insubordination, and the State of Iowa against the Democratic party." Obviously the drys were losing their composure. The people let their opinions be known at the polls: the entire Democratic slate swept to victory. Boies' plurality was 8,200 out of 420,000 votes; his running mates secured margins varying from 829 to 7,946. The distribution of votes repeated and reinforced the patterns set in 1889. But this time turnout soared to 88 percent, the highest in any gubernatorial campaign in Iowa history. Those frustrated Republicans who sat home in 1889 came out in 1891, and most of them voted Democratic. If the Republicans hoped to save Iowa's thirteen electoral votes in 1892, some way had to be found to shake the albatross of dry platforms.[44]

---

43. Clark, "Liquor Legislation" 6:581–83; Brandt, "Sketches" 55:353–58; *Dubuque Herald*, September 17, October 4, 5, 18, 19, 23, 28, 30, November 14, 1890.

44. For platform see *Iowa Official Register 1892*: pp. 162–70, *Ann. Cycl. 1891*: 383–84. Brandt, "Sketches" 55:358–61; Clark, "Liquor Legislation" 6:584–87; Cyrenus Cole, *A History of the People of Iowa* (Cedar Rapids, 1921), pp. 477–81; Kern, "Boies" 47:221–26; Haynes, *Third Parties*, pp. 304–20; Sage, *Allison*, pp. 248–49. *New York Times*, January 28, July 9, 13, 27, September 21, November 12, December 11, 1891, August 18, 1893. *Chicago Tribune*, July 2, October 20, 28, 1891. The Democrats estimated that they lost only 2,000 of their pietistic supporters to the dry Republican appeal in 1891. *Chicago Herald*, November 3, 1892.

THE STRUGGLE OVER PROHIBITION in Ohio closely resembled the pattern in Iowa, and suggests that the liquor issue was not an ephemeral affair in one state, but the indication of conflict between massive forces. While it had never been a dry state, doubtless because of the power of the Cincinnati German community, Ohio did experiment with a variety of licensing laws. The drys got the Republicans to submit a constitutional amendment for prohibition in 1883; the amendment got a plurality, but not the necessary majority of all the votes cast for governor. The Republican gubernatorial candidate, Joseph B. Foraker discovered that the temperance agitation cost him even a plurality of the votes in his race. Foraker did win the 1885 election, however, and tried to avoid antagonizing the German Republicans by insisting that the liquor question "is so related to personal habits and private morals as to render it impossible to make it a political question in the ordinary sense." However the drys were able to pass laws levying an annual statewide tax of $250 on liquor dealers and, more radically, requiring that all saloons close on Sundays.[45]

The temperance issue exploded in 1889 over the Sunday closing laws. In the spring local elections, the Democrats scored major gains in cities across the state. In Cincinnati, the Evangelical Association, a group of public-minded pietistic ministers, demanded enforcement of the hitherto neglected Sunday laws. Working through a Committee of Five Hundred, silk-stocking moralists ran a full slate of independent candidates in the city elections. They swept all the offices, except the crucial post of mayor, which went to John Mosby, a lackey in George Cox's corrupt Republican machine. Mosby slipped into office by promising the Germans continued nonenforcement of the closing laws.

Angered by the barrage of abuse hurled by the ministers and the moralists, the saloon-keepers decided to force the issue. They demanded that Mayor Mosby enforce *all* the ordinances prohibiting common labor on Sunday. For two Sundays in July, the non-essential shops of the city remained closed. Tension soared and violence threatened; the city remembered the bloody riots it had experienced a few years before and prepared for the worst. On July 25 the saloon-keepers, organized into the League for the Preservation of Citizens' Rights, called for a showdown. Three hundred German saloon-keepers formally resolved to openly do business all day on Sundays. A defense fund, bonds, and competent defense attorney stood by in readiness.[46]

---

45. *Cyclopedia of Temperance*, pp. 106–8, 143–45, 152, 651, 335; *Ann. Cycl. 1883*: 607–9, *1886*: 731. Joseph Foraker, *Notes of a Busy Life* (Cincinnati, 1917), 1:128.

46. The *Cincinnati-Gazette* and the *Cincinnati Enquirer* provided full coverage. See also *Chicago Tribune*, March 20, 26, April 1–3, 1889. Foraker, *Notes*, 1:412–14; *Cyclopedia of Temperance*, pp. 268–70. In 1884, 54 men died and 200 suffered injuries in five days of rioting against state militia in the backlash of a thwarted lynching. *Ann. Cycl. 1884*: 630–31; Zane L. Miller, *Boss Cox's Cincinnati* (New York, 1968), pp. 59–64, 79–81. For a similar episode in Madison, Wisconsin, in 1884, without the political repercussions, see David Thelen, "LaFollette and the Temperance Crusade," *Wisconsin Magazine of History* (1964) 47:293–99.

Governor Foraker, just renominated for his third term, shot off a letter to Mosby: "Do not tolerate any defiance of law. No man is worthy to enjoy the free institutions of America who rebels against a duly enacted statute and defies the authorities charged with its enforcement. Smite every manifestation of such a spirit with a swift and heavy hand."[47] The beer-loving Germans of Cincinnati were not about to be smitten. Briefly, massive rioting threatened. Quickly, however, the saloon-keepers' League realized that the conflict could best be won at the fall elections. Armed with heavy assessments from saloons, brewers, distributors, and friends of "Personal Liberty," the League attacked Foraker and called for a massive repudiation of him at the polls. The drys defended the governor vigorously, and the attention of the state focused on the gubernatorial contest.

Foraker carried many weaknesses into the campaign of 1889. His dynamic opponent, Congressman James Campbell, attacked the Republicans' support of high tariffs, denounced Foraker's bid for a third consecutive term, and hurled charges of dictatorial control, fiscal waste, and administrative mismanagement at the governor. Seldom had a midwestern campaign descended to the level of personal abuse that marked this one. At the climax, shortly before the election, Foraker revealed the existence of documents implicating Campbell in a scheme to defraud the state. The chief Republican newspaper, the *Cincinnati Commercial-Gazette*, reproduced the documents, but omitted the signatures of John Sherman, William McKinley, and other Republican leaders apparently equally guilty. Campbell, stunned momentarily, proved that the documents were total forgeries. Foraker and Murat Halstead, the editor of the *Commercial-Gazette*, apologized a few days before the election, but their doom was imminent.[48]

Campbell swept into office by a plurality of 11,000 votes out of 280,000 cast. The remainder of his ticket lost by small margins — twenty-two votes, in the case of the lieutenant governor — but the Democratic legislature reversed those margins the next year. Foraker suffered small losses across the state, and massive ones in Hamilton County (Cincinnati), where he ran far behind his ticket. In Hamilton, Campbell picked up 3,100 more votes than Cleveland's total in 1888, while Foraker ran 8,000 behind Harrison. The Republicans, racked by intraparty feuds, starved for patronage by President Harrison, and confused and humiliated by Foraker's actions, were in disarray. The Germans rightly claimed credit for the upset, and exulted in their prowess.[49]

---

47. Foraker, *Notes*, 1:414, cf. *Cyclopedia of Temperance*, pp. 269–70.

48. The *Cincinnati Commercial-Gazette*, blushing, gives the details. Foraker, *Notes*, 1:402–11; Everett Walters, *Joseph Benson Foraker* (Columbus, Ohio, 1948), pp. 91–97; John Sherman, *Recollections of Forty Years* (Chicago, 1895), 2:1053. *Ann. Cycl. 1889*: 674–75.

49. *Cincinnati Commercial-Gazette*, September 8, 10, 16, November 8, 1889; Foraker, *Notes*, 1:416–21.

"Even the faintest concession to the 'muckers' and law-and-order fanatics," the *Cincinnati Freie-Presse* had warned in September, "would be a nail in the coffin of Republican chances of victory." To the German eye, Foraker and his party conceded too much. The *Cincinnati Times-Star*, spokesman for the Committee of Five Hundred, had rallied the moralists with advocacy of $1,000 saloon licenses and effective Sunday laws should the GOP win. "The Germans waxed wroth at this," snorted the *Cincinnati Volksblatt*, "and the Germans, being mad, they knocked the Republican party into smithereens." "The Germans," the *Volksblatt* added, "thought that a Legislature should pass laws for the people and not against the people."[50]

THE YEAR 1889 was an ominous one for the GOP across the Midwest. In Chicago the Democrats waged a vigorous campaign to recapture city hall in the April elections. Pietistic clergymen criticized Mayor John Roche, a Republican, for tolerating widespread violation of the Sunday closing laws; Catholics grew angry when they discovered that Roche belonged to a secret anti-Catholic society. The Democrats won over the numerous trade union members with promises of more municipal ownership, and darkly warned that the Republicans were moving toward prohibition for the city. The latter charge gained credence from the heated campaign in the industrial suburb of Hyde Park. There the Republicans declared for enforcement of Sunday closing laws and talked of $1,000 saloon licenses. The Germans of the township reacted vigorously. The Republican vote plunged from 55 percent in November, 1888, to 44 percent the next April. In Chicago the Democrats reclaimed city hall with 55 percent of the vote, their best showing in six years.[51] The fall elections for Cook County offices saw the Republicans again hurt by the Sunday closing issue. An interdenominational association of pietistic ministers, including several Jansenistic Catholic priests, demanded the enforcement of the laws. That was enough to spark another Democratic sweep.[52]

The unkindest blow to President Harrison, hardly settled in the White House, came in the October city elections in his home, Indianapolis. There a group of reformers, mostly wealthy Republicans and pietistic ministers, had organized the High-License League of Indiana, and determined to raise the city's low $100 license fee. The Republican city council raised the licenses

---

50. *Cincinnati Freie-Presse*, September 16, 1889; *Cincinnati Volksblatt*, November 8, 1889, quoted in *Cincinnati Commercial-Gazette*, September 17, and November 9, 1889.

51. Bessie Pierce, *A History of Chicago* (New York, 1957), 3:364–66; *Chicago Tribune*, March 17, 18, 22, 25, April 5, 1889.

52. *Chicago Tribune*, September 15, 27, 30, October 21, 28, 1889. Aaron Abell, *American Catholicism and Social Action* (Garden City, 1960), p. 91; for the Jansenistic Irish Catholic involvement in the Sunday closing movement, see M. Sevina Pahorezki, *The Social and Political Activities of William James Onahan* (Washington, 1942), pp. 47, 65–68.

to $250, and the Democrats promptly charted their course, as proclaimed by the *Indianapolis Sentinel:*

> Local option . . . contemplates the exercise by the majority of the power to dictate to the minority in matters of personal right. The democratic theory of government is certainly in conflict with this policy. Democrats believe in the largest measure of individual liberty consistent with social order and the public security. They do not believe the state should usurp the function of private conscience.[53]

The Republicans, handicapped by the removal of their ablest leaders to Washington, attempted to mobilize the support of the pietistic reformers. They declared that "the city must control the saloon — not the saloon the city." Indeed, said Charles Fairbanks, later Theodore Roosevelt's vice president, "It is purely and solely a question of whether the honest, conservative, law-abiding elements shall prevail, or whether a premium shall be placed upon law-breaking." The Democrats had the Keokuk example of how to handle such a situation; so they nominated an outstanding reformer, denounced corruption in the city government, and appealed to the Germans to protect their personal rights.[54]

For the first time in a dozen years the Democrats triumphed in Indianapolis. Disappointed patronage-seekers had refused to work for the Republican ticket. Conservative businessmen, liberal Mugwumps, and personal-liberty Germans all moved toward the Democratic camp. The antisaloon crusade of the ministers was "good morals but bad politics," commented the expert *Cincinnati Commercial-Gazette*, "and as is invariably the case when the preachers step from theology into politics they make a mess of it."[55]

THE UNPLEASANT EXPERIENCES of 1889 troubled thoughtful Republican leaders and led to a reorientation of the party. In Iowa the party professionals ousted the amateur drys in 1893, and buried the liquor issue for another decade with an ingenius "mulcting" plan. In Ohio, the ruling coalition of McKinley, Hanna, and Sherman refused to let the GOP become embroiled in further efforts to enforce the Sunday laws; the party relied on its own mulcting scheme to resolve the tension between drys, moderates, and wets. In Chicago, the drys concentrated their fury, with some success, on an effort to close the World's Fair on Sundays. In Washington, the experiences led to new caution. Finding that President Harrison was ready to propose Sunday

---

53. Quote from *Indianapolis Sentinel*, June 29, 1889 (editorial); *Indianapolis Journal*, April 15, June 5, 18, 1889.

54. Quote from *Indianapolis Journal*, September 15; also July 20, September 16, 18, 26, 1889. *Indianapolis Sentinel*, September 30, October 8, 1889.

55. Quote from *Cincinnati Commercial-Gazette*, October 17, 1891. *Nation* (October 22, 1891) 53:306; *New York Times*, October 8, 28, 1889; *Indianapolis Sentinel*, October 9, 11, November 26 (for election returns), 1889. *Minutes of the [Presbyterian] Synod of Indiana* (Indianapolis, 1887), p. 31; ibid. (1888), pp. 27–28.

laws for the District of Columbia, Secretary of State Blaine warned of trouble. If the relaxed "continental Sunday" enjoyed by the Germans were disturbed, he wrote Harrison, it would "widely and severely affect our party by driving the Germans from us." Harrison dropped the proposal.[56]

The Republicans had played with firewater, and were burned. The politicians of the day never fully understood why innocent laws advocated by nearly all their upright constituents had such sweeping and disastrous aftermaths at the polls. Without quite realizing it, they had assumed that the pietistic ethic was unchallenged in their constituencies. Their opposition came not so much from liquor dealers or frequenters of saloons as from thoroughly respectable liturgical voters who saw prohibition as a threat to their own ethic. Thanks to the closely matched, fully mobilized political system of the Midwest, the grievances of a portion of the population were immediately translated into smashing defeats for the offending party.

The temperance question involved not just liquor but also, and more importantly, the basic religious, cultural, and political values of the people. In the half century since the pietists began to crusade for a single standard of American morality, the lines of antagonism had hardened. The same basic pattern of religious, cultural, and political conflict, if exposed suddenly without planning or warning, and if brought to the arena of partisan politics before the professionals had an opportunity to formulate a reasonable compromise, could explode even more forcefully and fearfully than in Iowa in 1889. In Wisconsin in 1890 the tinder was dry and the pietists struck a spark that led to the downfall of the dominant party; seldom in American history, and only once before in midwestern history (in Ohio in 1863) was a political battle so bitterly fought or so decisively won.

BIBLIOGRAPHICAL NOTE

Ethnoculturalists cut their teeth on analyses of midwestern politics. Pioneering works, besides Jensen's *Winning of the Midwest,* include Paul Kleppner, *The Cross of Culture: A Social Analysis of Midwestern Politics, 1850–1900* (New York, 1970); Ronald Formisano, *The Birth of Mass Political Parties: Michigan, 1827–1861* (Princeton, 1971); and Frederick C. Luebke, *Immigrants and Politics: The Germans of Nebraska, 1880–1900* (Lincoln, NE, 1969). An early call for this new kind of political history came from the (at the time) University of Iowa's Samuel Hays, in "History as Human Behavior," *Iowa Journal of History* 58 (1960), 193–206. For overviews of the new political history, see Allan G. Bogue, *Clio and the Bitch Goddess: Quantification in American Political History* (Beverly Hills, 1983); and Richard J. Jensen, "Histori-

---

56. Blaine to Harrison, November 30, 1889, in A. T. Volwiler, ed., *The Correspondence Between Benjamin Harrison and James G. Blaine* (Philadelphia, 1940), pp. 90–91; *Ann. Cycl. 1890*: 178, cf. *Ann. Cycl. 1889*: 193.

ography of American Political History," in *Encyclopedia of American Political History: Studies of the Principal Movements and Ideas,* ed. Jack P. Greene (New York, 1984), 1:20–22. The ethnocultural interpretation has been facing a challenge recently from historians who charge its proponents with determinism and understating the importance of economic factors. Jeffrey Ostler's essay in this volume represents one such (in his case, implicit rather than explicit) challenge.

An analysis similar to Jensen's, but focusing on the state legislature rather than on voters, is Ballard C. Campbell, "Did Democracy Work? Prohibition in Late Nineteenth-Century Iowa: A Test Case," *Journal of Interdisciplinary History* 8 (1977), 87–116. Don S. Kirschner applied a similar analysis to cultural conflict in state legislatures in Iowa and Illinois in the 1920s in *City and Country: Rural Responses to Urbanization in the 1920s* (Westport, CT, 1970). Thomas G. Ryan moves the statistical analysis of voting on prohibition legislation into the twentieth century in "Supporters and Opponents of Prohibition: Iowa in 1917," *Annals of Iowa* 46 (1983), 510–22. A useful overview of the nineteenth-century battles over prohibition is Dan Elbert Clark's three-part article covering the years 1846–1908, "The History of Liquor Legislation in Iowa," *Iowa Journal of History and Politics* 6 (1908), 55–87, 339–74, 501–68.

Prohibition, as a social reform movement rather than an exclusively political issue, has undergone considerable reinterpretation in the past couple of decades, but Iowa historians have yet to engage that work in their study of the issue in this state. A partial exception is Lee Anderson, "A Case of Thwarted Professionalization: Pharmacy and Temperance in Late Nineteenth-Century Iowa," *Annals of Iowa* 50 (1991), 751–71.

Other Progressive-era social reforms are treated in William L. Hewitt, "Wicked Traffic in Girls: Prostitution and Reform in Sioux City, 1885–1910," *Annals of Iowa* 51 (1991), 123–48; and Douglas Wertsch, "Iowa's Daughters: The First Thirty Years of the Girls Reform School of Iowa, 1869–1899," *Annals of Iowa* 49 (1987), 77–100. Perhaps the most important of the Progressive-era social reforms was the triumph of woman suffrage. See Louise Noun, *Strong-Minded Women: The Emergence of the Woman-Suffrage Movement in Iowa* (Ames, 1969); idem, "Amelia Bloomer, A Biography," *Annals of Iowa* 47 (1985), 575–621; and Diana Pounds, "Suffragists, Free Love, and the Woman Question," *Palimpsest* 72 (1991), 2–15. A standard reference for social reform legislation is John Ely Briggs, *History of Social Legislation in Iowa* (Iowa City, 1915). On women, see Ruth Gallaher, *Legal and Political Status of Women in Iowa* (Iowa City, 1918).

Iowa's political history between the Civil War and the New Deal is well served by Leland L. Sage, *A History of Iowa* (Ames, 1974), 171–287; and Sage's biography of William Boyd Allison (Iowa City, 1956), is, along with Mildred Throne, *Cyrus Clay Carpenter and Iowa Politics, 1854–1898* (Iowa City, 1974), one of the treasures of the State Historical Society of Iowa's series of political biographies. A sample of other political history covering that era includes the most recent (after a long hiatus) addition to the Iowa Biographical Series, *Gilbert N. Haugen: Norwegian-American Farm Politician,* by Peter T. Harstad and Bonnie Lindemann (Iowa City, 1992); Robert Cook, *Baptism of Fire:*

The Republican Party in Iowa, 1838–1878 (Ames, 1994); William H. Cumberland, *Wallace M. Short: Iowa Rebel* (Ames, 1983); idem, "The Red Flag Comes to Iowa," *Annals of Iowa* 39 (1968), 441–54; William L. Bowers, "The Fruits of Iowa Progressivism, 1900–1915," *Iowa Journal of History* 57 (1959), 34–60; Leonard Schlup, "Republican Loyalist: James F. Wilson and Party Politics, 1855–1895," *Annals of Iowa* 52 (1993), 123–49; and George William McDaniel, "New Era Agrarian Radicalism: Smith W. Brookhart and the Populist Critique," *Annals of Iowa* 49 (1988), 208–20; and idem, *Smith Wildman Brookhart: Iowa's Renegade Republican* (Ames, 1995).

12

To Whom Much Is Given: The Social Identity of an Iowa Small Town in the Early Twentieth Century

THOMAS J. MORAIN

After the turn of the century, Iowa communities settled into a pattern of life that was far from unchanging, but somehow seemed less dynamic than in earlier periods. The topical organization of Thomas Morain's book about Jefferson, Iowa, indicates that communities could now be described with portraits as easily as they could with stories. Morain's portrait draws on and contributes to some of the most creative work in state and local history in recent decades. Especially in the past two decades, work that applies the methods of what used to be called the new social history to the study of local communities has emphasized race, gender, ethnicity, and class. Iowa historians have done some very good work in those areas, though even the best of it (except for the work on gender, which will be treated separately) has been largely derivative; that is, it has been case studies testing conclusions drawn from studies of other places. Morain's work on Jefferson, Iowa, indirectly suggests the primary reason for the derivative nature of much of Iowa historians' work on race, class, and ethnicity: Iowa—at least rural and small-town Iowa—was largely lacking in the diversity that draws attention to those categories. Nonetheless, as Morain shows, employing those categories can yield rich insights into the social identity of small-town Iowans. Morain's book is, in a way, a case study itself, fleshing out the classic book by Lewis Atherton, *Main Street on the Middle Border,* with the details of life in one small midwestern town, and also applying insights gleaned from the historiography of the years since 1954, when Atherton wrote his book. Quite aside from its historiographical contribution, Morain's work offers a remarkable portrait of social life in Iowa in the first third of the twentieth century, when small towns still dominated Iowa's social and cultural life.

Reprinted by permission of Iowa State University Press from *Prairie Grass Roots: An Iowa Small Town in the Early Twentieth Century* (Ames: Iowa State University Press, 1988), 33–71. Copyright © 1988 by Iowa State University Press.

> For unto whomsoever much is given, of him shall much be required.
> –LUKE 12:48

HISTORIAN JOSEPH WALL writes that "there is a smugness of attitude within the small town that is a constant source of exasperation to the farmer and of bemused wonder to the city dweller."[1] Jefferson residents at the turn of the century would have been startled to hear themselves called smug, or self-satisfied to an unwarranted degree. Of course, if pressed, they would have admitted that it was true that in literate, white, Anglo-Saxon, evangelical Protestants converged the highest evolutionary forms thus far produced by the most progressive political, economic, and intellectual impulses of western civilization. In that they understandably took a certain degree of satisfaction, and they expected even better things in the future. Rev. Josiah Strong, a spokesman for evangelical Protestantism, wrote confidently in 1893: "We have seen that the world is evidently about to enter on a new era, that in this new era mankind is to come more and more under Anglo-Saxon influence, and that Anglo-Saxon civilization is more favorable than any other to the spread of those principles whose universal triumph is necessary to that perfection of the race to which it is destined; the entire realization of which will be the kingdom of heaven fully come on earth."[2]

Yet theirs was not a self-confidence that expressed itself in a complacent acceptance of the status quo. Those at the top of the evolutionary ladder had a duty toward those on the lower rungs. They felt called to be instruments to lift the ignorant and less fortunate, a task that tempered their appreciation of their most favored status. It was no coincidence that they sang of themselves as "Christian soldiers, marching as to war." They were never allowed to forget that they had battles to fight. The price of progress was eternal vigilance against foes both without and within. The cause would succeed, but no individual was immune from falling away or immune to temptations. There were anxieties behind the self-confident facade.

TO UNDERSTAND how Jefferson residents experienced the remarkable changes of the early twentieth century, it is necessary to recreate their vision of the world and how it operated, the setting into which these changes were introduced. Two important concepts helped to explain how things worked and to confirm their conviction that they were in the front rank of the march of progress.

---

1. Joseph F. Wall, *Iowa: A Bicentennial History* (New York: Norton, 1978), 152.

2. Josiah Strong, *The New Era, or the Coming Kingdom* (New York, 1893), 81, quoted in Robert T. Handy, *A History of the Churches in the United States and Canada* (New York: Oxford Univ. Press, 1976), 280. An excellent treatment of this small town confidence at the turn of the century can be found in Richard Lingeman, *Small Town America: A Narrative History, 1620–Present* (New York: Putnam, 1980), especially Chapter 6, 258–320.

The first was a theory of how the human personality is formed that granted far more influence to genetic inheritance than does modern psychology. Intelligence, industriousness, and sometimes even a disposition to morality were thought to be carried to some extent in the same genetic combinations that influence skin color and height.

Nor was this folk wisdom only. Leading scientists and social theorists of the day gave the theory support. For example, Henry A. Wallace, editor of the influential *Wallaces' Farmer* in the early 1920s and an early advocate of hybrid corn, freely adapted genetic theories to explain human differences. He once said "the farmer who is experienced in the breeding of grains and live-stock has come to have a more genuine appreciation of hereditary characteristics than any other class of our nation. Even tho they lose money by it, farmers can see the peril of allowing admission of large numbers of people of low grade intelligence from southern and eastern Europe."[3] Southern and eastern Europeans were of low-grade intelligence in comparison, of course, to the high-grade intelligence of the people of northern Europe, which included most Greene County residents.

Closely related was the theory of progress through social evolution. Those races with the best characteristics from both heredity and environment advanced faster. It was "survival of the fittest" on a group level. Vic Lovejoy, editor of the *Jefferson Bee,* expressed his own understanding of evolution in a 1925 column. "That there is 'evolution' in the world no sane person will deny," he wrote. "Man himself 'evolved' from a primitive state, a period when he was half wild and barbarous, and had little or no education. This can be proved by history of the peoples of northern Europe, from whom most Americans descended. . . . (T)he change of man to his present state of intelligence and civilization was 'evolution.' The Negro and the Indian have 'evoluted' from savagery to a civilized state."[4]

Because evolution proceeds through time, history becomes the test of superiority. Since England, France, Germany, and the United States were world leaders of the day, history thus certified the superiority of the Anglo-Saxon peoples. Protestantism had grown out of Catholicism and, at least in the Midwest, was on the rise. Capitalism and industrialization had replaced feudalism. All were signs of progressive evolution.

Reconstructing how local residents applied these concepts in daily living is difficult, but one woman who was interviewed tossed out a useful starting

---

3. Henry A. Wallace, quoted in Don S. Kirschner, *City and Country: Rural Responses to Urbanization in the 1920s* (Westport, Conn.: Greenwood, 1970), 37. Two of the best-known works expressing the Nordic supremacy theme are (Theodore) Lothrop Stoddard, *Rising Tide of Color Against White World-Supremacy* (New York: Scribner's, 1920) and Madison Grant, *The Passing of the Great Race* (New York: Scribner's, 1916). Kenneth Roberts published numerous shorter works on the subject, including "Shutting the Gates," *Saturday Evening Post,* 28 January 1922, and "Worth of Citizenship," *Saturday Evening Post,* 18 February 1922.

4. *Jefferson Bee,* 22 July 1925.

point during a discussion of high school social life in the 1920s. She joked that her mother would let her date anyone she wanted, as long as he was not black, a Catholic, or a farm kid. She chuckled as she said it. Nevertheless, in one breath she identified three (and with a little stretch, four) of the fundamental factors by which Greene County residents understood who they were: race, religion, occupation, and gender. The four strongly influenced what people did through the day, where they did it, who their friends were, where they lived, and even to which political party they belonged. Change any one of them, and you altered that person's community identity. Understand them, and you comprehend a great deal about how that mechanic, editor, teacher, housewife, lawyer, or clerk perceived the world and his or her own position in it.

THE ISSUE OF RACE was a significant factor in the social order of 1900. This was not because there was a large nonwhite population in Greene County. In fact there was almost none. Of 17,820 residents reported in the 1900 census only eleven were black. Five of these lived in Jefferson. The 1910 census listed only one mulatto, a person of mixed black and white parentage, as the entire nonwhite population for the county. The number increased slightly by the 1920s but remained exceedingly small (Table 12.1).

Ideas about race are informative, nevertheless. They reflect local residents' view of themselves and their place in the natural order of things. Certain notions about blacks necessarily implied notions about whites. Blacks had remained in a primitive state except when they had come under the influence of whites. Therefore, blacks must be inferior. Conversely, whites must be superior.

The conviction that racial differences beyond skin color were inherent created some uneasiness in a community whose formal ideology emphasized that "all men are created equal." As long as the discussion remained at the ideological level, it was easy to condemn the southern white for institutionalized discrimination and frequent brutalities toward southern blacks. Outspoken southern Negrophobes made it easy to sympathize with the blacks' situation. South Carolina's senator "Pitchfork Ben" Tillman spoke at a Jefferson chautauqua in 1907 and drew a spirited denunciation in the local press for his extreme hostility to racial integration.[5]

Indeed, there was evidence of occasional local integration. A 1904 write-up of a football game between Jefferson and Redfield mentions that a black man named Cottam was playing right guard for Jefferson. Integration in athletics was an issue around the state at the time, and high school or town teams in some communities refused to play opponents who suited up blacks. The article, however, noted that Cottam had been "the victim of both verbal and

---

5. Ibid., 8 August 1907.

TABLE 12.1
POPULATION OF GREENE COUNTY BY RACE, 1870–1925

	White	Nonwhite
1870	4,624	3
1875	7,036	1
1880	12,711	16
1885	15,923	0
1890	15,786	11
1895	16,294	5
1900	17,809	11
1905	16,086	3
1910	16,022	1
1915	16,337	2
1920	16,451	16
1925	16,076	18

SOURCE: 1925 Census of Iowa.

physical abuse on the part of some of the Redfield players."[6] The color line had not disappeared.

Most Jefferson residents were not completely comfortable with the idea of racial equality or full integration in either ideology or practice. In 1902 it was with obvious satisfaction that the *Bee*'s Frank Stillman, writing from the nation's capital, reported that Booker T. Washington's Tuskegee Institute was studiously avoiding the issue of social equality.

> The two questions of politics and social equality are entirely cut out of the curriculum of the institute. Politics is never mentioned and the students have no thought of social equality and are not working to that end. On the contrary, they are sensible young people, who have become thoroughly imbued with the spirit of the institution as directed and inspired by Mr. Washington to wit; That the thing for the colored man to do is to work out his own destiny, make the most of himself and pass up the question of society, social equality and politics. Mr. Washington has impressed his students with the fact that the first thing the negro must do is to prove that he has the stuff to take care of himself and be a man among men; a mechanic, a farmer, a lawyer, a doctor or merchant. When he has worked out that problem, it will be time for him to give attention to politics and social questions.[7]

The report claimed that Washington "has unquestionably solved the negro problem so far as the negro is personally concerned" if blacks would follow

---

6. Ibid., 24 November 1904.
7. Frank Stillman, *Jefferson Bee*, 7 July 1904.

his lead. Postpone the decision about the problem of social equality until the Negro has "worked out" the problem of education. In other words, postpone racial equality.

Until that time came, blacks were both Negroes and "niggers." The term "nigger" found its way into the language in a variety of expressions, none of them complimentary to the black. Rough granite boulders in the fields were "nigger heads," and Brazil nuts were "nigger toes." When the city code banned slingshots, it termed them "nigger shooters." A swindler was a "nigger in the woodpile," and children chose up teams by chanting, "Eeny, meeny, miny, moe; catch a nigger by the toe." "Uncle Tom's Cabin" played at the Jefferson Opera House in 1917, accompanied by a jazz band of "seven, singing, dancing pickaninnies."[8]

In 1916 D. W. Griffith's film classic "Birth of a Nation" played in Jefferson and prompted discussion of racial issues. An epic depiction of American history, its most controversial interpretations were the Reconstruction years following the Civil War. In a favorable review of the film, the *Bee* asserted that criticism expressed by national black leaders about the way blacks were depicted was "not well founded." "True," the writer agreed, "the negro is not shown up in a favorable light in most of the pictures, and yet one cannot help applauding the kindly acts and protection afforded by the old family servants who are depicted as remaining so faithful and true to their former owners." Furthermore, the review went so far as to *forgive* blacks for the trouble they created. After all, it said, they were not responsible for their own acts since whites were to blame for "every crime committed by the negro race, either then or since." The Negro should therefore forget the past.

> The negro, after years of slavery and horrible persecution, could not have been expected to be much else than brutal, when power was placed in his hands. He thought only of his own deep wrongs and some way of being revenged. The negro of today should fully appreciate this, and not look upon the pictures as something portraying the character of the present day black man. That period has passed and gone, and with it the misguided and mistaken "carpetbaggers," most of the racial wrongs of the colored people, and no excuse exists for any revival thereof by reason of moving pictures based upon happenings in the reconstruction period.[9]

The concept of race extended beyond differences based on skin color. Sometimes nationality or ethnic groups were considered to be races, such as the "Nordic" or "Slavic" races, though both were white skinned. This dimension expanded the racial issue into questions of foreign policy and domestic issues by creating a hierarchy among nations that was also assumed to be a part of the natural order. Advanced races had a moral obligation to assist

---

8. *Jefferson Bee*, 8 April 1904; 7 February 1912; 24 October 1917.
9. Ibid., 19 November 1916.

primitive ones, whether or not the latter requested it. This was international relations Yankee style.

For example, when the United States in 1916 was faced with an unstable Mexican government on its southern border and Mexican bandits were harassing American citizens, the argument for U.S. intervention was made not only on the basis of American self-interest but on its potential benefit to the Mexican people themselves. The *Jefferson Bee* voiced this sentiment in a 1916 editorial.

> The *Bee* is of the opinion that this country owes the same duty to Mexico from the standpoint of humanity that it has already performed for Cuba, and Haiti, and Nicaragua, and Panama and the Philippines. It is a moral duty. The Mexican nation has destroyed itself. Nobody but the United States can resuscitate it and put it upon its feet. . . . We have done a hundred times as much for each of them as they can ever do for us. We have done it because we are big, and strong, and able; while they are weak and irresolute and unguided. Can anyone doubt that the people of Cuba and the Philippines and Haiti are happier, and more comfortable and more secure than they were before we intervened to help them? No more can we doubt that the imposition of American will upon the affairs of Mexico gives to these wretched people the only possible chance to ultimately redeem and re-establish themselves.[10]

Similarly, the basis for U.S. intervention in the Philippines was not self-interest but something like a parental responsibility toward a childlike race. "The Filipinos are about as capable of self-government as a herd of tomcats and the worst crime this country could commit against them would be to put them on their own resources," one Iowa editor commented.[11]

Neither the "Negro problem" at home nor American intervention abroad upset Jefferson residents unduly. In each case the problem posed no immediate threat to their sense of the proper order of things or to their own sense of security. There was, however, a dimension to the race question that did generate some uneasiness. It began to undermine their confidence that the "best people" were firmly in control at the national level. Beginning in the 1880s, the number of immigrants to the United States from southern and eastern Europe increased dramatically, a shift from earlier immigration sources from northern and western Europe. In the 1870s immigrants from western Europe totaled 2,000,000 and from eastern Europe, 181,000. Between 1901 and 1910 western European immigration remained at 2,000,000 while eastern European figures jumped to 6,100,000. At the turn of the century Italy, Russia, and Austria-Hungary alone were supplying three out of every four immigrants.[12]

---

10. Ibid., 15 March 1916.

11. *Manchester* (Iowa) *Press*, reprinted in *Jefferson Bee*, 13 January 1915.

12. Charles Beard, *A Basic History of the United States* (New York: New Home Library, 1944), 296.

The "new immigrants" increasingly concentrated in ethnic pockets in eastern cities. Historian Charles Beard notes that the rise of these "foreign cities" within American urban centers was an extraordinary characteristic of the period. In 1900 about 14 percent of the total American population was foreign-born, but the immigrant population was increasingly concentrating in the cities. In urban centers of more than twenty-five thousand inhabitants, the foreign-born accounted for 25 percent of the total. Above one hundred thousand the proportion was 35 percent, and in the largest cities of the nation, immigrants actually constituted a majority.[13] Neither blacks at home nor Filipinos were challenging white, Anglo-Saxon, Protestant control of school boards, city halls, and state legislatures, but Jefferson residents were less sanguine about the immigrant blocs of the cities. It was not a local presence of immigrants that was the source of the unrest. Greene County had never had a large immigrant population. Rather, it was the image of the foreign-born crowding into eastern cities that disturbed the rural and small town residents.

Historian Don Kirschner's excellent study of midwestern rural attitudes toward the city explains that urban immigrant blocs posed a threat to the dominance of "American" (white, rural, Protestant) values in three ways.[14] This was especially true in the 1920s when postwar political upheavals rocked eastern Europe, and alarmed Americans were willing to believe that the disruptions were the results of radical scheming.

First, there was an economic challenge represented most clearly by the labor union. In the months immediately following the armistice, the nation underwent a series of labor strikes, some of which directly affected rural Iowa. In the fall of 1919, for example, as Jefferson was heading into a cold winter, a nationwide coal strike so cut production that the town drew up emergency plans for coal distribution. An emergency coal committee set up a rationing plan to spread existing supplies as efficiently as possible. The electric plant reduced its hours of production. Several railroads reduced the number of trains. The strike ended before residents faced real hardship, but the town was made keenly aware of its vulnerability to disputes between far-off unions and their employers.[15]

To the small town the labor union often appeared as the spokesman for the immigrant. It was easy to link the immigrant to the radical demands of some unions at a time when eastern and southern Europe struggled with socialist and communist uprisings. The *Bee* reprinted a *Chicago Tribune* editorial relating immigrants to labor unrest. "It is small wonder that radicalism takes such ready root among non-American speaking residents when we reflect that speech is coined thought. Our newcomers, many of them, have come out of countries that boil with social tumult. They have been born in the midst of revolutionary

---

13. Beard, *Basic History*, 297.
14. Kirschner, *City and Country*, Chapter 2.
15. *Jefferson Bee*, 12 November 1919.

agitation, nourished upon hatred of autocratic institutions, and into their consciousness have been seared the experiences of unjust domination."[16]

On the same editorial page, a reprint from *New York World* denied that labor radicalism "was the work of ignorant foreigners." It was a struggle between radical and conservative labor in the United States, the author claimed, but this strenuous effort to deny its foreign origin implied a substantial public belief to the contrary.[17]

There was a second challenge. In their swelling numbers and urban concentration, the new immigrants also posed a political threat to the countryside. Democracy is a numbers game, and that fact, once a source of comfort to rural residents who made up the majority, was beginning to take on an ominous ring. Their position of power was being challenged. This prompted a *Bee* editorial in 1919 defending the status quo and opposing foreign interlopers.

> This country is a democracy, and a democracy is ruled by majorities. . . . Those who find intolerable our laws, as provided by the majorities, will have to seek other countries where the laws are to their liking. We are beginning to believe, in view of events now transpiring, that we shall be forced into a position where we must declare that America is for Americans, and for those others who are absolutely loyal to American law and American institutions, and for nobody else. We can adjust ourselves to labor conditions in which every foreign malcontent is eliminated and sent back to the place from whence he came, and we are not sure but that we should be infinitely better off if that very thing were done.[18]

But the immigrants did not go home, nor did they meekly assent to rural domination. In 1928 they captured the nomination of the Democratic party for one of their own, Gov. Al Smith of New York, a Catholic son of an immigrant "wet." Through the first third of the twentieth century, the political clout of the city became an unsettling reality to small town residents.

The third challenge, so closely interwoven with the economic and political, was the cultural. Rural Americans saw the immigrant as a real threat to traditional American values. The genetic arguments applied not only to the Negro but to the southern and eastern European as well. The Nordic was superior in intelligence, and it was Nordic (i.e., Anglo-Saxon) civilization that had developed Christianity and democracy more fully than any other people. A 1919 "Seasonable Sermon" in the *Bee* saw the Prohibition issue as a symbol of American superiority.

> We saw an item in the daily papers the other day that thirty foreigners had applied for passports to Europe, giving as their reason, "no work, no booze." Thank God for small favors. The faster prohibition causes the shipping home of citizens of the syphilitic countries of Europe, the better it suits us. They

---

16. *Chicago Tribune*, reprinted in *Jefferson Bee*, 22 October 1919.
17. *New York World*, reprinted in *Jefferson Bee*, 22 October 1919.
18. *Jefferson Bee*, 12 November 1919.

can't be deported any too fast.... The scum of Europe is not going to flow to this country as it has in the past, for the boozer of the old world would much rather put up with the disagreeables of his own syphilitic land, than come here where the flowing cup is barred and stopped. So let the good work go on.[19]

The economic, political, and cultural images of the new immigrants combined to make them appear as a threat to the rural community. By the 1920s local residents had begun to fear that the national achievements of which they were most proud were endangered by immigrants crowding into the cities who did not appreciate American institutions. Whether the cause was genetic or cultural, the rise of the new immigrants in the cities threatened the proper order of things in two ways. There was the long-standing rural suspicion that city life was corrupting and less wholesome than life in small towns and the farm. Added to this now was the fact that the new urban ethnics had no background in, nor even respect for, traditional American values. In earlier times, rural-urban antagonisms were a family feud, differences between farmers and their city "cousins." The rapid growth of the urban immigrant populations changed that, and the cities began to take on an alien image.

Kirschner reconstructs the vicious circle into which cities like Chicago and New York had fallen, according to the rural Midwest. He calls it a "shorthand of interrelated symbols . . . the mention of any . . . of which was likely to evoke hostile feelings toward the others." As he phrased it, "immigrants were dirty and radical and vice-prone opponents of the American way whose drinking supported the criminal and murderous bootleggers who corrupted city officials who fawned before laborers and sold their souls for the votes of dirty and radical and vice-prone immigrants."[20]

Through the small towns and farms ran the unshaken conviction that their kind of people with their kind of values had made America great. The future of American progress and preeminence in world affairs depended on keeping the nation under the control of the right kind of people. The rise of other ethnic groups never suggested to midwestern Anglo-Saxons that their assumptions about themselves were wrong or needed to be revised in light of new evidence. While there was no immediate danger at the local or state level, there were distressing signs that they were losing control of the cities and that the cities were rapidly growing more powerful at the expense of rural areas. Not only did this new pluralism threaten them personally, but it spelled doom for the march of progress in which, until then, Anglo-Saxon America had been so nobly engaged.

A century earlier, New Englanders had viewed the rise of the West as a threat to not only their own preeminence but also to the survival of American institutions. Their fears motivated a massive campaign to convert western

---

19. Ibid., 19 November 1919.
20. Kirschner, *City and Country*, 48.

settlers to New England standards. In the early twentieth century, midwestern small town residents perceived a similar threat, this time, from the rising tide of immigrants in the city. Genetics, however, was the wild card in the new situation. Could the peoples of southern and eastern Europe ever become 100 percent Americans like Anglo-Saxons? The future of the republic hinged on the answer.

Race, as the issue was understood in the early twentieth century, was important in the way Jefferson residents understood who they were. To be a white Anglo-Saxon meant that one was among the most highly advanced people in human history and could share the honors for the highest level of civilization yet achieved. That was no small distinction. It was a heritage worth defending.

RELIGION was another factor by which Jefferson residents organized the world around them. While the population of Greene County was racially homogenous, it divided into numerous Christian denominations whose members took their church affiliations seriously.

The 1905 Iowa census reports a total church membership in Greene County of 5,569, or 35 percent of the total population.[21] These statistics need to be taken cautiously since they do not distinguish formal membership from denominational preference, nor do they adjust for differences among denominations in what constitutes membership. Nevertheless, the data provide a rough measure of the relative strength of the denominations.

In 1905 Catholics were the most numerous single denomination in the county with 1,680 members, located for the most part in Grand Junction and on farms across the northern tier of townships. Infant baptism helped to swell the Catholic membership rolls relative to those of some evangelical Protestant churches in which young children were not counted as members until baptism. The Catholic population in Greene County was primarily Irish, and outside of Grand Junction, Catholics were mostly farmers. Ten years later, a census reported that Catholic membership had fallen off about 20 percent to 1,330.

Methodists were second in 1905 with 1,421 members but first in 1915 with 1,758. They had more congregations than any other denomination, often supporting several rural churches with the same pastor. Presbyterians were third, followed closely by Baptists and Christians (Disciples). There were around 125 German Lutherans in a small congregation southwest of Cooper, and two small rural congregations of Friends, one near Paton and another north of Scranton. Total church membership declined slightly in the ten years following 1905, from 5,569 to 5,260, consistent with a small population decline of that period.

The strength of Protestant denominations relative to each other was not as significant as their united size relative to Catholics. The religious cleavage

---

21. The Iowa census of 1905 gathered data on the number of members of each denomination, Sunday school attendance, the number of congregations per county, and the value of church buildings.

in Jefferson, as elsewhere in Iowa and the Midwest, was between evangelical Protestantism and Catholicism. Historian Richard Jensen has convincingly argued that the major social and political division in the Midwest through the early twentieth century was a reflection of the Protestant-Catholic schism.[22] Differences among the Protestant churches were minor when compared with the long-standing hostility that separated Protestants and Catholics on such matters as repentance, salvation, and the role of the church and clergy. The former placed strong emphasis on the responsibility of the individual not only for his or her own salvation but for the moral environment of the community. The Catholic faith placed the church as a necessary mediator between God and the individual.

In Greene County the four major evangelical Protestant groups—the Methodists, Presbyterians, Christians (Disciples), and Baptists—had a total membership of 3,319 in 1905, almost twice the Catholic population. In Jefferson itself the margin was far greater. A church membership survey in 1904 reported that of 1,998 residents in town, only 129 were Catholics. Jefferson Protestants outnumbered Catholics nine to one.[23]

To understand the denominational environment of the community, however, one must keep in mind that church affiliation was only one dimension of community life. Members of different faiths also related to each other as neighbors, business associates, friends, classmates, and teammates, all of which cut their own lines through the community. Denominations were important, but no church was large enough to insulate its faithful from contacts with members of other denominations. In particular, the small size of the Catholic population in Jefferson prevented it from establishing a parochial school. Grand Junction, a town not half the size of Jefferson, supported both a public and a parochial high school. In 1915 a bishop speaking at Catholic confirmation ceremonies urged the Jefferson parish to build a parochial school as soon as possible, "a necessary auxiliary to the church if they had a regard for the spiritual and moral interests of their children."[24] It never materialized. For better or worse, Protestants and Catholics mixed in public schools and worked out their accommodations.

In part because parochial institutions failed to appear, the distinctions between Protestants and Catholics were expressed more clearly in ideological or symbolic terms than in everyday relations between the two groups. That is, Protestants tended to denounce Catholicism more than they did Catholics. On their part, Catholics distrusted Protestantism but generally lived in harmony with their Protestant neighbors. This is not to say that there were no antago-

---

22. See Richard J. Jensen, *The Winning of the Midwest: Social and Political Conflict, 1888–1896* (Chicago: Univ. of Chicago Press, 1971).

23. The results of the survey of the religious preference of Jefferson residents were printed in the *Bee*, 13 October 1904.

24. *Jefferson Bee*, 6 October 1915.

nisms; there were. But the record also shows that while there were definite social distinctions between the two groups, individual relations generally proceeded amiably.

For example, the McCormicks and the Brunners were both Catholic members of the country club, which met twice a month for supper and recreation and included prominent Jefferson families. Friday night potlucks raised the issue of Catholics not eating meat on that day, but the necessary accommodations were made. Margaret McCormick Baker played violin in the Methodist orchestra. A. J. Finn, a Catholic, had a photography business and was well respected. The Kendalls and their six children lived across the street from the Rev. A. E. Slothower family in the Methodist parsonage. When Mrs. Kendall died, the Slothower family often helped care for the children, and the Methodist minister and his wife frequently were the ones who saw to it that the Kendall children got to catechism on time with their lessons learned.[25]

It was the impression of Roy Mosteller, raised as a Baptist on a farm northwest of Jefferson, that Protestants "had nothing against average Catholics, but they were afraid of the Pope and the higher ups."[26] The more abstract symbols of Catholicism, "the Pope and the higher ups," seemed more threatening than the actual Catholics they knew, "the average Catholics."

Evangelical Protestantism placed much less emphasis on the role of the sacraments than did the liturgical denominations, like the Lutherans and the Catholics, and the authority of the evangelical denominations to refuse the rites to members was correspondingly less critical. For the Catholic the sacraments of baptism, confession, communion, and last rites were critical steps in salvation. The church played a mediating role between the individual and God. Catholic "superstitions" about the sacraments gave the hierarchy an unwarranted hold on the lay member, according to Protestants. In the Protestant view the Catholic lay member was perceived as something of a victim; it was the priest and the higher ups who used their members' credulity to maintain and strengthen the church. Nevertheless, could anyone be a 100 percent loyal American, Protestants asked, who owed spiritual allegiance to a foreign power, the Pope in Rome? There were even rumors that Catholics were storing guns in the basement of the rural St. Patrick's church west of Churdan, "waiting for the order from the Pope to take over the government."[27]

Catholics on their part had their own reasons for distrusting Protestants. A Yankee legacy was the impulse among evangelicals to feel a responsibility for the morality of the entire community, and it was, of course, a Yankee moral standard that served as the measure of righteousness. Whatever their differences on matters of theology or church government, most Jefferson Protestants sub-

---

25. Interviews with Maxine Trumbo and Gene Melson.
26. Interview with Roy Mosteller.
27. My grandfather, P. O. Morain, told us about the rumors about St. Patrick's Church.

scribed to what might be called the Yankee Confession, an unwritten credo in four parts.

Article One maintained that life is a struggle, a test of will. Article Two declared that the individual, not the government or any other social unit, is responsible for his or her own well-being. Democracy and capitalism were the highest political and economic systems yet devised because they gave the fullest exercise of expression to individual decisions.

Article Three said that in most cases, success is a measure of character. Those with the will and the character to succeed will rise in a free-enterprise system. A 1924 editorial in the *Jefferson Herald* intoned the familiar rhetoric: "There is no such thing as failure to the man who refuses to see failure. There is no such thing as quitting to the man who believes a quitter is a failure, and the man who keeps his head up and eyes open can always make the hill in a manner better than the man who is nearly always looking for some reason to quit. There's a good living for anyone who honestly and truly wants to make it, and there's failure for those who are ready to quit fighting."[28]

It was Article Four that gave the creed its reform momentum. The righteous are responsible for the welfare of the community. St. Luke states: "For unto whomsoever much is given, of him shall much be required." While conversion of the sinner to the higher path was the preferable means of reform, it was sometimes necessary to use the legal authority of the state by making immoral activities illegal. Protestants dominated legislatures, city councils, and school boards, and it was a Protestant moral code that was written into the statute books.

While Protestants extolled the virtues of the separation of church and state, theirs was a Protestant interpretation of what that separation meant. Normally, it meant that no single denomination could use public institutions like the school or government offices to promote itself. It did not mean a ban on all religious teaching.

For example, an evangelist who was holding an evening revival series in the Methodist Church for a week in December in 1915 was also allowed to speak each afternoon at the high school on the general topic of Christianity.[29] Since he did not promote distinctly Methodist doctrines, only the great "truths" of the Christian religion, he was not violating the rule demanding the separation of church and state. However, no Catholic priest was ever accorded such an opportunity since the Catholic church was a single denomination. Protestant ministers could thus use the schools while Catholic spokesmen could not.

Yet for the most part, local Catholics made the necessary accommodations and learned to get along with a minimum of friction. For both groups the more distant or ideological the religious issue was made to appear, the greater the

---

28. *Jefferson Herald*, 20 November 1924.
29. *Jefferson Bee*, 5 December 1915.

antagonism, but on most matters—with a few significant exceptions—daily relations between Catholics and Protestants were friendly.

Furthermore, the Protestant community was by no means monolithic in its attitude toward either Catholicism or Catholics. Protestant expressions of hostility frequently generated angry reactions among other Protestants in defense of Catholic friends. Unlike the race issue in which there was almost no sympathy for integration, there were both Catholics and Protestants who strongly objected to efforts to exacerbate religious antagonisms.

For example, several Jefferson Protestants recalled a vicious anti-Catholic newspaper entitled the *Menace*. Judging from the number who remembered it, one must conclude that the newspaper circulated freely. Its themes were predictable: the immorality of the priesthood, the Catholic plan to undermine American democracy by an armed revolution and to replace it with a Catholic theocracy subservient to Rome, and the nearly absolute power of the church over its superstitious members.

Yet by no means did all Protestants approve of such a publication. Jefferson resident Kellogg Thomas recalls that his father certainly did not.

> I'll never forget the time to this day when I picked up a copy of the *Menace*. Well, it was probably the most scurrilous religious propaganda that anybody ever put out and it was a magazine that was widely circulated. . . . And I read it with avid interest because it had things like how the priests were storing Springfield rifles in the basement of the church, having affairs with the nuns. It was vicious. So I took it home to show my father, and I said, "Gosh, these guys are sure carrying on, aren't they?" And he read it, and I remember he tore it into four or five pieces, and he said, "Do you think Mr. Coyne would do that?" Old Michael Coyne was beyond question of a doubt my father's closest friend. . . . And I said, "Well, no not him." . . . "Well, they have certain things they have to do. For instance . . . they don't eat meat on Friday; they eat fish." (I remember this as if it were yesterday.) "When we had your birthday party last week and (Andrew) was over, the reason we had salmon sandwiches was that (he) was not supposed to eat meat on Fridays. That's one of the things his church believes." And then he said, "Don't ever you repeat anything to anybody or bring anything like that home again." And it was on the pain of getting paddled, and it made a vast impression on me.[30]

If Thomas's illustration is representative, the sensationalism of the publication was part of its appeal. While one cannot ignore its popularity, it is also true that it sometimes provoked angry reactions among Protestants in defense of Catholic friends.[31]

One could draw similar conclusions about Jefferson's experience with the Ku Klux Klan in the 1920s, the most glaring example of anti-Catholic sensationalism. After the Civil War the Klan formed in the South as a vigilante

---

30. Interview with Kellogg Thomas.
31. Interviews with Ruth Hensley and Roy Mosteller.

group to intimidate former slaves. After World War I, labor unrest, political radicalism, and the rising tide of immigration from Catholic countries in southern and eastern Europe convinced some that there was an international conspiracy directed against the United States. The Klan expanded its hate list to include Catholics, Jews, immigrants, and any other "un-American" group (i.e., anyone but white Protestants) and recruited a substantial following throughout the Midwest. In Des Moines, where the Klan had its greatest strength in the state, three KKK-sponsored candidates won election to the school board in 1925, but soon after, the power of the Klan faded rapidly.[32]

Greene County had its own Klan chapters. Details are scarce since the group took precautions to protect the identity of its members and to shield its internal organization from public scrutiny. Even its members were not sure who else belonged since they wore sheets and hoods during their gatherings. Sometimes rumors identified certain individuals as Klan leaders. Two pastors of Protestant churches in small towns around the county were reputed to be important Klan figures.[33]

Around 1924 and 1925 the Klan strength was at its peak. There were several meetings around the county, including a march around the courthouse square and several rallies west of Jefferson. Pauline McCormick Russell vividly remembered a near encounter with the Klan when she was a Catholic girl of seven or eight. It frightened her.

> We'd taken a Sunday ride . . . out on old Highway 30 up there at Danger Hill and there were three men dressed in white and they had torches . . . they were having a meeting some place down there in the timber. My dad always protected us, so we got by there in a hurry. . . . And so that's all I can remember. And it was kind of in the fall of the year. I know the car was open and the men were standing out there with their white outfits on, and I can see them yet. Their outfits didn't go clear to the ground, you know. The only one we'd ever seen (in outfits like that) was my dad's sister (who) was a nun, and so, gosh, we just hadn't ever seen anybody in anything like this.[34]

(It would be poetic justice if those three Klansmen could somehow be informed that they were remembered for a half century because they looked so much like nuns.)

Another account described a Klan rally west of town on the hill where the hospital now stands. Around a fiery cross, Klansmen in white robes listened to speakers denounce all un-American groups while a few hooded guards stopped cars along the highway and questioned the drivers. A funeral at the Methodist Church in Cooper was taken over by Klansmen who sat in their robes and hoods during the services and then provided an escort for the casket

---

32. Kirschner, *City and Country*, 125–26.
33. Interviews with Wayne Winey and Roy Mosteller.
34. Interview with Pauline Russell. Margaret Cudahy also remembered having been frightened by the Klan as a Catholic girl.

as it left the church on the way to the cemetery.[35] Nevertheless, despite its sensationalist rhetoric, trappings, and secret oaths, the Klan apparently left no record of any actual violence against any individuals in the local area.

Moreover, while the Klan's hostility was no laughing matter, memories of it did contain some humorous anecdotes. Several residents claim that Mike Brunner, the operator of the local creamery, was the only local Catholic ever to march in a Klan parade. As one version of the story goes (and there are many variations), Brunner had a five-gallon bucket of ice cream in each hand to deliver to a restaurant on the far side of the square. When he reached the near corner, he found his route blocked by a long, single-file Klan march then in progress. Rather than waiting for the parade to pass and his ice cream to melt, Brunner squeezed into line, marched with the Klan around to the other side of the square, and then broke rank when he got to the restaurant.[36]

Roy Mosteller mentioned an anti-Catholic meeting in Churdan, which he recalled as being associated with the Klan in some way. This meeting, however, was open to the public and attracted an audience of forty to fifty, including three or four Catholic men who came to hear the evils of papacy exposed, as the promotions promised. When the speaker described the increases in the Catholic population in the past several decades, "these three or four Catholics all applauded."[37]

Wayne Winey recalled an incident in a nearby town when a Klansman fell and broke his arm during a Klan rally. Taken to the local doctor, the Klansman felt more than a little sheepish when the doctor made him take off the white robe so that he could treat the arm. The doctor was a friend of his—and a Catholic.[38]

An obvious factor that diminished the Klan's appeal locally was that Catholics were already well integrated into the community social structure. They were not theological abstractions; they were friends, neighbors, and business associates. The friendship between the Thomases and the Coynes that prompted the elder Thomas to tear up the *Menace* had its parallels throughout the community. Charles Hird, a Protestant high school student at the time, implied such an integration during an interview. Asked if he remembered the Klan as "scary," he replied:

> I don't think it was tense because I don't think anyone was afraid of (them). I just thought, you know . . . why do we need this in the community, like we were fighting Negroes and we didn't have any Negroes. We were fighting the Jews, and we didn't have that many Jews. Then you start to blame . . . the Catholics, (but) then you got all kinds of people that (didn't) want to

---

35. My grandfather was the driver in the incident. He told us that a hooded man looked in his window and said, "Oh, it's you, Perce." Interview with Dr. Dean Thompson.

36. I heard this story from several people. I have used the Brunner family version.

37. Interview with Roy Mosteller.

38. Interview with Wayne Winey.

offend their Catholic friends by saying they thought the Klan was all right. I never did figure out who were the people that would join the Klan.[39]

On the other hand, though tensions never succeeded in polarizing the community, Jefferson was by no means a hotbed of ecumenism either. There were tensions, and the designation of Catholic or Protestant had very real significance. One of the continuing sources of friction was the problem of "mixed" marriages.[40] The Catholic Church would not approve wedding ceremonies performed for its members by civil authorities or Protestant clergy. Especially irritating to Protestants was the Catholic insistence that any children born to the union would be brought up in the Catholic faith. In 1908 the diocese reemphasized its position and instructed priests to enforce it rigidly. The *Bee* printed the Catholic rules on the issue on the front page.[41] Weddings between members of different Protestant denominations occasioned little comment, but couples thought twice before crossing the Catholic-Protestant boundary.

Of course, even here there were exceptions. The way the "rules" were translated into actual practice was always a little more complicated. It was Margaret Minnihan Cudahy's impression that, while the issue was discussed in her home, her father gave his Catholic children considerable latitude. She recalled being told "if we met a Catholic who was a good person, fine and dandy, but if we didn't, he says, 'Who is to say who is better?'" They were not forbidden to date non-Catholics. Her brother Frank did marry a non-Catholic who later joined the church, "but she didn't at the time they were married."[42]

In the end it was the couple who had to decide whether their affection meant more to them than church canon. If it did, they usually figured out some accommodation on the religious question. Kellogg Thomas cited one extreme example. A Presbyterian uncle of his married a Catholic, "one of the Hill sisters." Because neither wished to join the other's church, they selected a new denomination, "and for the rest of their lives were members of the Baptist Church. That didn't happen very often, but it did happen. That's kind of an odd compromise."[43] Odd or not, it does signify that church affiliation was an important factor. The groom could not bring himself to join the Catholic church, and the bride refused to join his.

As the century progressed, Protestant denominations began to worship together more often. Born in 1903, Thomas could not recall even having been in "any other church except the Presbyterian Church until I was maybe somewhere in high school except for maybe an odd funeral or two" and considered his experience fairly typical for Protestant youth of the era. He went to at least

---

39. Interview with Charles Hird.
40. Interview with Roy Mosteller.
41. *Jefferson Bee*, 26 February 1908.
42. Interview with Margaret Cudahy.
43. Interview with Kellogg Thomas.

one Presbyterian service every week and sometimes two or three. He was not antagonistic toward members of other denominations, but outside school, the Presbyterians were the most significant group of which he was a part. What he did recall about those years, however, was that a "change was coming about," a change from the former strictness. "People would go from church to church a little bit."[44] When pressed, he could not be more specific, but there seemed to be less denominational rigidity, at least among Protestants.

Catholics remained fairly isolated in religious activities. For the most part, Catholics were forbidden to attend services in other churches, a rule that nourished Protestant hostility toward the Catholic hierarchy. Sometimes the prohibition was interpreted to apply even to entering Protestant churches. Roy Mosteller recalled two girls in the same high school class, a Baptist and a Catholic, who were best friends. Neither would even enter the other's church. He explained, "if the Baptist girl would have to go into her church to pick up a song book or something, the Catholic girl would stand on the porch or vice versa."[45]

Yet here again, there were the exceptions. Catholic Pauline Russell often attended Presbyterian and Methodist services with her girl friends. She claimed that Father Peter Murphy was "very easy" on the subject and that the decision was mostly left to Catholic parents. Protestants had no formal restrictions on attending Catholic services although they rarely did except on special occasions. Nevertheless, during the same years that the Klan was holding rallies, the Methodist young people's Epworth League was attending Christmas Eve mass at the Catholic Church. "We didn't feel that they didn't want us there. They were happy that we were there," Gene Melson recalled.[46]

Catholics and Protestants in Jefferson, well aware of the differences between their faiths, had inherited the distrust and suspicions of centuries of antagonism. Yet as they mingled in daily activities, they found it impossible and ludicrous to respond to each other solely in terms of abstract stereotypes. In a small town, one appears simultaneously in a variety of roles, of which the denominational is only one. In Jefferson, with a very small Catholic population and the same school system for all children, the significance of denomination faded as the century progressed.

ANOTHER MAJOR FACTOR in one's identity in the community was occupation. The 1895 census lists the occupations of Jefferson workers. Professionals and merchants had increased substantially from the 1880s, but there continued to be a strong representation of craftsmen. The diversity of vocation indicates that the small town continued to manufacture many items

---

44. Ibid.
45. Interview with Roy Mosteller.
46. Interview with Gene Melson.

TABLE 12.2.
CATEGORIES OF OCCUPATION, GREENE COUNTY, 1905–1925

	1905			1915			1925		
	Male	Female	Total	Male	Female	Total	Male	Female	Total
Agricultural	3,005	478[a]	3,483	2,655	30	2,685	2,666	42	2,708
Professional	178	230	408	123	198	321	148	196	344
Domestic and personal	70	89	159	95	156	251	83	3,326[b]	3,409
Trades and transport	500	48	548	692	74	766	558	55	613
Manufacture, mechanical	386	101	487	455	56	511	239	13	252
Unclassified	692	7	699	467	–	467	797	55	852

[a]The 478 figure for Greene County females in agriculture is so inconsistent with those of neighboring counties that it suggests a difference in census procedures. For example, Guthrie County borders Greene on the south and reported only 35 females. Story, two counties to the east, recorded 26. The 1915 figure for Greene County is much more consistent with comparable counties.
[b]The sharp increase in this figure suggests that the 1925 census included housewives in this category while previous surveys did not.
SOURCES: Census of Iowa, 1905, 1915, 1925.

for itself and the surrounding vicinity and to provide many services.[47] Data from the Iowa census for occupations throughout Greene County are in Table 12.2.

What a man did for a living tended to identify him—and his family—as part of an informal grouping in the community. To a large extent, friendships and socializing patterns followed occupational lines. For example, when the Jefferson Country Club was formed in 1910, it was an organization of the families of merchants and professionals. Its charter roll read like a "who's who in Jefferson." There were thirteen merchants, nine bankers, three lawyers, two judges, four doctors, two dentists, three real estate dealers, two newspaper editors, the owner of the local telephone company, an auto dealer, a druggist, a hotel manager, an insurance agent, a traveling salesman, and two retired farmers.[48]

These were the most likely candidates for the school board and the city council. They took the lead in civic projects and community organizations. They were what Atherton describes as that "inner circle" present in every country town "whose own personal interests were so tightly interwoven with

---

47. There are numerous systems to classify occupational categories. Merle Curti's intensive study of a Wisconsin county in the nineteenth century, *The Making of An American Community: A Case Study of a Democracy in a Frontier County* (Stanford: Stanford Univ. Press, 1959) uses a complex system of categories: agriculture, professional, personal service, semiprofessional, business, transportation and communication, labor, and five subcategories of artisan (building trades; metal, wood, leather trades; food processing; clothing; and miscellaneous). Don Harrison Doyle, in *Social Order of a Frontier Community: Jacksonville, Illinois, 1825–1870* (Urbana: Univ. of Illinois Press, 1979), collapses Curti's scheme into five. I have divided town jobs into three categories and farming into three. The division was suggested by my father as the major groupings of occupations as they would best be understood by Jefferson residents.

48. *Jefferson Bee*, 6 April 1910.

those of the community at large that one cannot determine where self-interest ended and public spirit began."⁴⁹ If community histories tend to dwell on them more than on others, it is because it was they who left the most abundant records. Their activities became news, and their names appeared more frequently in community annals. On a deeper level, however, they were the ones who had invested most heavily in the community. As Atherton notes, self interest and public spirit meshed. Theirs was a proprietary attitude. They took compliments or criticisms about the town from outsiders in much the same way that parents react to comments about their children. The term "city fathers" is an apt metaphor.

A second group in town consisted of salaried employees, such as store clerks or courthouse workers. A clerk often worked for a merchant for so long that the clerk too became closely identified with the store, like Fred Derry in McCully and Osgood's general store, Bert Tucker in Gamble's clothing store, or Cleve Barr in Roy Curtis's grocery. Clerks were paid by the week or month, and they put in long hours by the sides of their employers.

"Cap" Lyon worked for twenty years for E. H. Carter in the general store. His daughter, Berniece Raver, remembered the many hours her father spent at work. He was the first one up in the morning because he had to be at work at 7:00 A.M. when the store opened. He came home to dinner at 11:00 A.M. and was back at work when the kids came home at noon. The family had supper together at 5:00 P.M., after which he returned to the store and often worked until 10:00 P.M. "We didn't see much of our father," she recalled.⁵⁰

That was six days a week. In addition, on Saturday night, the stores stayed open as late as midnight as farm families wandered around the square socializing, doing their weekly shopping, and attending the movie theater. In 1918 Jefferson merchants moved up store closing time from 8:00 P.M. to 6:30 P.M. The change was controversial. Some store owners feared that the earlier hour would anger farmers and discourage them from doing errands in town after evening chores. The majority argued that with automobiles, farmers could shop earlier with fewer problems. The main impetus for the 6:30 P.M. closing was that it would permit merchants, clerks, and their families to attend the Thursday evening band concert in the park. The *Bee* maintained that the farmers, who also liked to hear the concerts, would not want to deny the store personnel that opportunity.⁵¹

A third group were the laborers and mechanics, those who worked with their hands, often out-of-doors. Delivery men, shoe repairmen, auto mechanics,

---

49. Lewis Atherton, *Main Street on the Middle Border* (Chicago: Quadrangle Books, 1954), 48. A useful model for examining the merchant-professional sector of a midwestern town is provided in Richard Alcorn, "Leadership and Stability in Mid-Nineteenth Century America: A Case Study of an Illinois Town," *Journal of American History* 61 (1974): 685–702. Alcorn compares this group with community norms on several scales, including the length of time they remained in the town.

50. Interview with Berniece Raver.

51. *Jefferson Bee*, 3 July 1918.

carpenters — they sometimes were salaried but often worked for themselves in small shops or garages. They mixed more freely with the clerks than with the merchants and professionals.

My grandfather's first job in Jefferson was in the Hutchinson Bicycle Shop around the turn of the century. Fred Hutchinson added car dealerships when automakers began developing their national marketing systems, and Grandpa started working on Maxwells, Hupmobiles, Fords, and EMFs ("Every Morning Fixits" as the latter model came to be known by disgusted owners). With the coming of the Model-T, Hutchinson dropped everything but the Ford franchise. Grandpa worked there until he and Pete McLaughlin opened a small garage of their own. In 1932 the new Ford dealer switched to Chevrolet, a vehicle Grandpa detested until his dying day and a major reason he opened his own shop. However, the respect in which he held his first employer, Frederick Hutchinson, was evident when my father, Frederick Morain, was born in 1913.

Grandpa's closest friends were the men with whom he worked — Pete, Earl Raver, Ned Wilson. In the summer, on family camping trips along the Raccoon River, the Morains often camped with the families of Cleve Barr, the grocery clerk; Roy Finch, a shoe repairman; and Mort Wolf, the Ford garage service manager. The men commuted to work while the women and children relaxed and played in camp.

Beyond the city limits lived the farmers, by far the largest single occupational group in the county and among whom there was also a well-understood hierarchy. Distinctions were not made by the type of work they did because, before farm specialization, their daily routines were substantially similar. Distinctions were based on whose land they were farming. At the top of the rural ladder were those who owned their own farms, the owner/operators. The lure of cheap land had brought the pioneer to the prairie. When a farmer could begin with almost as little as a team of horses, a cow, some pigs, chickens, and a plow, a young couple willing to work and save had a good chance of some day owning their own farm. With careful management, a little luck, and someone willing to lend them some money, they could look forward to buying a farm. Historian Joseph Wall characterized the long-term expectations of the typical Iowa farmer this way:

> Above all, the farmers wanted to be able at the close of their lives to turn over to one or more of their children their old home places, debt free, better equipped, and more productive than those farms had been when they had acquired them. These expectations seemed to the farmers to make neither unreasonable nor aggressive demands upon society. Most farmers did not expect nor want great wealth. The Carnegie, Rockefeller, Gould dreams of an imperium did not goad Iowa farmers during their waking hours nor disturb their sleep at night.[52]

---

52. Joseph F. Wall, "The Iowa Farmer in Crisis, 1920–1936," *Annals of Iowa* 47 (Fall 1983): 119.

Ruth Suckow's novel *Country People* details the lives of a young German couple in Iowa whose frugality and willingness to push themselves hard won them their own farm, a comfortable retirement in town, and the respect of their neighbors.[53] Suckow had countless examples in real life on which to model her fictional characters. Some families in Greene Country, such as the Thompsons, the Montheis, and the Duffs, were so successful and prolific that they established whole neighborhoods of adjoining farms. One stretch of road southeast of Scranton was called "Duff Road."

Until the widespread use of the tractor after the Second World War, the speed of work horses and the amount of physical labor necessary to run a farm limited the size of most operations to around 160 acres. Census figures recorded that in 1900 the average farm in Greene County was 158 acres, and by 1930 it had grown only to 171 acres. Through the 1930s, therefore, there were often four or five farm units per square mile, maintaining a consistent demand for hired farm labor and small-scale operators. Even if a family owned a whole section, it could not farm it by itself.

However, land prices were rising from the turn of the century through 1920. Intensive drainage removed swamps and small ponds from fertile croplands and allowed farmers to put more of their acres under cultivation. Furthermore, land and life insurance were the two major opportunities for investment for those small town and rural families with some extra money. They did not have ready access to stockbrokers, and not many were willing to gamble on the uncertainties of grain futures.[54] As money went into land, the price went up. The number of tenant farmers rose as it become more expensive to buy a farm. According to the 1900 census, 41 percent of county farms were operated by tenants. By 1930 the figure had climbed to 53 percent. Some rented the farms for a fixed rate, but many took a percentage of the crop and raised livestock. Good tenants might live for years on the same farm. Poor tenants often stayed only a year or two. In hard times security for any tenant was uncertain.

By custom, March 1 was moving day on the farms. Standardizing the day made it more convenient for everyone since those moving out could expect their new homes to become vacant on the same day. Carl Hamilton's *In No Time at All* gives a chilly account of the moves his family made.

> Moving was always harder on Mother than anyone else. Frequently it was a case of moving into a house where the other family had "just moved out." It needed a thorough cleaning before moving in but there was not time. Rugs didn't fit; curtains didn't fit; cupboards didn't fit. The floors were bare pine boards with quarter inch cracks and painted around the edges. The rugs seldom matched the unpainted areas.

---

53. Ruth Suckow, *Country People* (New York: Knopf, 1924).
54. Interview with Fred Morain.

There was no hot water until the cook stove was set up and going. Each room echoed with a hollow, unwelcome sound. The chill of March was throughout the house. If there was electricity, its evidence was found in a bare bulb casting its glare from a cord in the center of the ceiling.

As I look back on those times, I think of Mother and Dad picking corn by hand in those years when they couldn't afford to hire help. But ranking next to that scene in my mind is Mother's lot at moving time. Throughout her years, the date March 1 was always the subject of some comment on her part for "those poor people who are having to move."[55]

The amount of physical labor necessary to run a farm created a demand for a third group of workers in the farm community, the hired hands. Hired sometimes for spring planting or fall harvest, sometimes through the whole season or even the whole year, they formed an essential labor pool for midwestern agriculture. If they were single (and most were), they moved in with the family. On occasion a married man could find a small house on the farm or near it for his family. Sometimes, farm boys in their older teens would hire out in the neighborhood, but most of the hands seemed to come up from Missouri or elsewhere in the South in search of work. A few local stores like Oppenheimer's Clothing served as an informal labor clearinghouse. Under a sign "Men for Jobs/Jobs for Men," notices put farmers wanting help and men looking for work in touch, and contracts were sealed with a handshake. As Hamilton recalls,

> For years, the standard rate of pay was $50 per month plus board and room. No fringe benefits, no bonuses, no social security, no insurance came with it. The man came; he worked. Dad wrote him a check; he left. That was it. He may have added to our lore of stories about hired men, but he didn't clutter up our records. Or the government's.
>
> Once I remember Dad stating flatly at the dinner table that he would *never* pay a man more than $50 a month. One hired man looked at him in a rather peculiar way. But that was all.
>
> Being a hired man, at $50 a month, was supposed to be the first step on the road to farm ownership. Hired man; then a renter; then an owner. It didn't work that way too often.[56]

Although their labor was essential, hired hands had little visibility as individuals in the farm community. They rarely left the farm except on Saturday night and maybe on Sunday morning for church. Neighbors knew they were there but rarely had contact with them. Where they came from or where they went, no one seemed to know or care. Collectively, however, they were an important component in the rural community. The farms needed their help.

An often overlooked group, originally from the farm, provided an important link between town and country. By the turn of the century most small

---

55. Carl Hamilton, *In No Time at All* (Ames: Iowa State Univ. Press, 1973), 6.
56. Ibid., 68.

towns had become the home of retired farm couples who had turned over the operation to their children, to tenants, or to new owners. A couple could live comfortably on the landlord's share of the income from 160 acres or could sell the farm outright and live on the interest. Older couples appreciated the comforts and social opportunities of the town. Suckow's fictional *Country People* described how the old men would find excuses to walk downtown in the morning, to pick up the mail or to buy something, and then congregate at the barber shop or implement dealer to complain about the weather and farm prices and to discuss the crops. The women enjoyed their own social outlets and busied themselves with gardens, sewing projects, and cooking. Their children and grandchildren were often either on the home place or somewhere in the area, and retired couples were an important bridge between the farm and town. They gave their family and former neighbors a place to stay when they visited town and helped keep the towns sensitive to rural needs.

When the Jefferson woman joked that her mother would not let her date "farm kids," she was not implying that farming was not a respectable occupation. Good farmers commanded respect in town as well as in the country. Farming, however, was more than just a man's occupation. It was a way of life for the entire family. Before 1920 rural children were likely to attend one-room schools only through eighth grade. Before rural electrification began in the 1930s most farm homes lacked indoor plumbing, running water, and household appliances that town homes had possessed for two or three decades. Farm wives kept flocks of chickens, raised large gardens, and usually did most of their own baking. The social highlight of the week was the Saturday night trip to town. Poets and politicians may have praised the farmer, but town mothers did not want their daughters to marry and leave the amenities of town life.

One final group of people were residents of neither town nor farm. Their occupational distinction was the absence of occupation. They were "just tramps." Tramps, or hoboes, were not really residents, but at any time, a community was likely to have at least one or two passing through. Before Social Security or expanded welfare programs, these were the nomads of the railroad, grabbing rides in boxcars from town to town where they begged a meal or worked an hour or two for some immediate need. They would appear at the back door, rarely at the front, and ask for food. Sometimes they got it, and sometimes they did not.

Rumor had it that they left signs that only other tramps would recognize to mark homes where there was "an easy touch," so it was unwise to be too generous. There was a report on the signs hoboes supposedly used to identify generous or dangerous homes. A circle crossed by two arrows signaled an unfavorable welcome. A circle around an "X" marked an easy meal. An "X" by a triangle meant that one would be asked to work before getting anything to eat.[57]

---

57. *Jefferson Bee*, 23 May 1907.

Hoboes rarely did any harm, but neither were they invited in to eat at the kitchen table. They seemed more a nuisance than a threat. If a law officer met up with one, he might escort him to the city limits and encourage him to widen his horizons in any direction he chose. In Jefferson tramps often camped around the North Western railroad stockyards on the north edge of town. When times got bad in the cities, more tramps appeared, but their numbers fell off sharply with the Second World War. No one asked their names. Individually, they left almost no permanent mark on the community. They were "just tramps."

FOR WOMEN, whether on the farm or in town, career opportunities were curtailed. In a perverse twist of the language, female human beings who cooked three meals a day over a wood-burning stove, cared for children, sewed, mended, cleaned, canned, washed, and ironed were not considered to be "working." Unless you got paid, you were not working. Boys were encouraged in a variety of career ambitions, but all girls were supposed to become wives and mothers. Those who did not were the exceptions.

There were these exceptions, of course, sometimes by accident but sometimes by deliberate choice. (See Table 12.3.) The Harding sisters, Bess and Winifred, remained single and opened a ladies' dress shop on the south side of the square. Bess had taught school for several terms but was happy to give that up to go into business with her sister.

They bargained with salesmen who stopped in the store, and by the 1930s they were traveling regularly to Omaha to order stock from wholesale dealers. Wilma Downes and Grace Wadsworth taught school for years as married women. May Dunham Rydings continued a memorial stone operation after her husband's death, and Bertha Rutter was for years a secretary/bookeeper for the Milligan grain business. Minnie Wilson, a former school principal and a frequent lecturer at teaching institutes, worked with her husband in his law office though she had no formal legal training. Eva Bradley did washing and ironing in her home. Normally, however, a young woman worked outside the home for a few years in her late teens and early twenties, quit her job when she married, and left the work force forever. Those who returned normally did so because of financial necessity.[58]

---

58. An ad for Mrs. Rydings's cemetery markers appears in the 30 June 1915 *Bee*. An excellent study of female employment is Valerie Oppenheimer, *The Female Force in the United States: Demographic and Economic Factors Governing Its Growth and Changing Composition* (Berkeley: Institute of International Studies, Univ. of California, 1970). See also William Chafe, *The American Woman: Her Changing Social, Economic, and Political Roles, 1920–1970* (New York: Oxford Univ. Press, 1972); Lois W. Banner, *Women in Modern America: A Brief History* (Chicago: Harcourt, Brace, Jovanovich, 1974); and Mirra Komarovsky, *Blue-Collar Marriage* (New York: Random House, 1964). National statistics on percentages of working women often did not include farm women if they worked at home, and as late as the 1910 census, half the American population was still classified as rural. The percentage of rural women in Iowa was, of

TABLE 12.3
WOMEN'S EMPLOYMENT IN GREENE COUNTY BY AGE, 1915

Age	Professional and service	Domestic and personal service
14–17	3	8
18–20	27	27
21–44	157	107
45 and over	11	14

SOURCE: Census of Iowa, 1915.

Jefferson had several female physicians. Dr. Gus Grimmell practiced medicine in Jefferson after her graduation from state university medical school. The daughter and granddaughter of doctors, Dr. Gus, as she was called, was a representative of the growing number of female doctors throughout the latter nineteenth century. Dr. Gus married after several years of medical practice and moved with her husband to Minnesota. A local "who's who" published in 1896 described her as a "charming lady, withal popular in the highest social realm" and "a brilliant and interesting conversationalist." According to long-time residents, she could swear like a trooper. As with the Grimmells, medicine was a tradition in the Morden family. Dr. Elizabeth Ann Morden was practicing in 1905 with her son Roy. When her daughter Leone graduated from a Chicago medical school and decided to return to Jefferson to practice, Roy left to open a practice in Des Moines. The census lists 128 female physicians in the state in 1890, 260 in 1900, and 325 by 1910. Most of them, the Jefferson representatives included, had a clientele chiefly of women and children.[59]

The career of Dr. Gus highlights a major deterrent to women's employment in the professions. Many of the legal barriers to education and professional certification had been removed by 1900, but forbidding obstacles still remained. In her 1918 *Legal and Political Status of Women in Iowa,* Ruth Gallaher noted: "Two considerations deter women from preparing themselves for highly specialized professions: the length and difficulty of the training required, and the difficulty of coordinating such work with homemaking and the care of children."[60] Because social custom and household responsibilities required that mothers be at home with their young children, young women considering a

---

course, significantly higher. For an early assessment of women's employment in Iowa, see Ruth A. Gallaher, *The Legal and Political Status of Women in Iowa* (Iowa City: State Historical Society of Iowa, 1918).

59. *Iowa Illustrated* (Jefferson Edition) 1, no. 2 (June 1896); *Bee,* 13 July 1905; Gallaher, *Legal and Political Status,* 52. See also Mary Roth Walsh, *"Doctors Wanted: No Women Need Apply": Sexual Barriers in the Medical Profession, 1835–1975* (New Haven: Yale Univ. Press, 1977). Walsh (p. 186) displays a chart listing women physicians as a percentage of the total number of physicians in the nation. A peak came in 1910 with 6 percent, a figure not reattained until 1950. Most female physicians specialized in medicine for women and children.

60. Gallaher, *Legal and Political Status,* 45.

professional career usually had to weigh their interest against their desire for a home and family. The combination of career and family open to men was very difficult for a woman to achieve.

Therefore, for the young woman seeking work in a small town, the horizons were limited. In most cases the choice in 1900 was among domestic service, teaching school, and clerical positions. According to the 1915 census, seven out of ten working women were employed in either professional service, which included teachers, or domestic and personal service. (See Table 12.3.)

As a domestic servant, one was the "hired girl" who worked in the home. The rambling two- and three-story homes built in Jefferson before World War I frequently contained two staircases, one off the front hall or the living room and one leading up from the kitchen or pantry. The latter permitted the hired girl to go upstairs to her room or to clean without being observed. Before electrical appliances, maintaining a household required long hours of drudgery, and middle-class women considered some household help a near necessity. The hours were long, the work was hard, and the pay was very low. Working as a hired girl was not an attractive job, but those who needed work had few options. They were not called "maids," a term that smacked too much of aristocracy and class distinctions for the small town. They were more often called "hired help" or just "girls."[61]

Teaching school for a few years between graduation and marriage was a popular career choice for young women and had become identified as women's work, although it had not always been that way. Until the Civil War, men filled a majority of the teaching posts in the state, but due to a combination of factors, the profession underwent a sex change. Men could earn more in other jobs, and women had few options. What really clinched the teaching profession for women was the introduction in the 1880s of teacher certification requirements that mandated attendance at annual teacher institutes or the completion of a teacher training course. A young man might teach in a rural school for a season or two, but the salaries were so low that it did not pay him to invest much time or tuition money to get a teaching certificate. With options, he could afford to leave pedagogy. By 1900 women held 83 percent of the teaching positions in Iowa. When the newspaper listed the names of rural schoolteachers in Greene County in 1917, 119 out of 125 were women.[62]

By modern standards it was easy to become a teacher. At one time, candidates needed only to score well on tests administered by the county superintendent of schools to receive a teaching certificate, but gradually the standards required that they complete some teacher training (normal) courses also. In 1916 the state superintendent of public instruction designated the Jef-

---

61. Atherton, *Main Street*, 101–2.

62. For more about the feminization of the teaching profession in Iowa, see Thomas J. Morain, "The Departure of Men from the Teaching Profession in Nineteenth Century Iowa," *Civil War History* 26, no. 2 (June 1980): 161–70.

ferson High School to receive $1,000 in state aid for a normal course to prepare teachers for rural schools.[63] Through this program high school students could take teacher training courses along with the academic subjects and be certified to teach in a rural school upon graduation.

Teacher salaries were low and recognized as such at the time. The Jefferson school board in 1911 raised wages a little so that teachers earned from $50 to $70 a month, or $450 to $630 for the nine-month term. The superintendent, a male at the time although the position was sometimes held by a woman, got the princely sum of $1,500 for a full year, $125 a month.

There were separate pay scales for men and women teachers. Men received more, justified by the theory that they had more expenses and needed to prepare to support their future families. Maxine Morley wrote a letter to the editor in 1908 objecting to separate pay scales and urging the formation of a teachers' union to improve salaries. She claimed that women's expenses were just as high as men's.

Though she did not mention it, Morley might also have complained that teachers were held to higher moral standards than other occupations. Even the whisper of scandal, founded on fact or not, about those entrusted with the education and moral development of the future generation could jeopardize their careers.[64]

Because many teachers had come to Jefferson from the outside and were restricted in evening activities by social conventions, they did not become involved in civic affairs and rarely had visibility outside of the schools. Local bachelors, however, took more than a passing interest in the arrival of new teachers each fall. Many women who came as teachers stayed in town as wives of local men, but not until their marriage did they enter fully into the civic and social life of the community.

Usually, women's teaching careers ended on their wedding day. Many school districts made it either a formal or informal policy to prohibit married women from classroom positions. When my mother came to Jefferson in 1936 to teach music, her contract stated that marriage would terminate her employment. When she and Dad decided to move up their wedding date from June to Easter Sunday in 1939, she had to get special permission from the school board to continue teaching the remainder of the year as a married woman. (They were married on Sunday in her parents' home in Lamoni, Iowa, and she was back in school Monday morning — a deliberate fifteen minutes early!)

Census figures clearly indicate that for most women, employment outside the home was not a lifelong condition. It began when they completed their education and lasted for most until marriage. Reentry into the work force was the exception.

---

63. *Jefferson Bee*, 12 January 1916.
64. Maxine Morley, letter in *Jefferson Bee*, 20 May 1908.

Part of the resistance to married women as teachers stemmed from public inhibitions about pregnancy. Women sharply curtailed their outside activities for as many as five months before a birth so that they would not expose themselves as being "in a family way." Another major factor, however, was simply the prevailing notion of propriety: married women were supposed to be at home. "Normal" married women spent their time taking care of their husbands, their children, and their homes. Women who wanted to do something else were not the role models school boards wished to place in front of their children.

Older women were sometimes hired when the prospect of a new little bundle from heaven had diminished and their children no longer required as much attention. Grace Wadsworth taught many years in rural schools, and Wilma Downes continued to teach high school business courses during her marriage to a Jefferson merchant. Mr. and Mrs. Downes ate their meals at McDuffies' boarding house. Still, the ideology of gender made these women the exceptions. Teaching school for most women who tried it was an interlude between their own classwork and marriage.

In addition to normal training, girls could take business classes, which meant preparation for secretarial positions. They learned typing, bookkeeping, and shorthand. Wilma Downes taught these courses for many years. Like the normal course, secretarial training provided the work skills necessary for a young woman to find employment for a few years before she married. It was rarely presented as a lifetime career. The skills necessary for that she learned in home economics.

There were some occupations that could be pursued on either a full- or part-time basis, and sometimes the work could be done at home. The clothing industry provided work for local women at the turn of the century. The 1895 census listed thirty women as dressmakers, four more as seamstresses, and thirteen as milliners. Sometimes as a year-round occupation but sometimes for only a few months, women tailored garments and hats on order. As the women's ready-made clothing industry expanded, producing fashionable items at prices much below what could be sewn by hand, the self-employed seamstress all but disappeared. What remained was an occasional order for alterations, but clothing construction as a home industry sharply declined. The hat industry suffered from the vagaries of fashion, and the locally produced product gradually disappeared.

IF YOU KNEW THESE THREE THINGS about a local resident—ethnic background, religion, and occupation, you could make a pretty good bet about his (or, after 1920, her) political affiliation. The system was not foolproof, but you would be right more often than not. An Irish Catholic railroad hand was a good bet to be a Democrat, and a Scottish Presbyterian lawyer whose grandfathers were both GAR members was an odds-on favorite to be Republican.

Of the three factors, religion was probably the best single indicator, according to Richard Jensen's *Winning of the Midwest*. Jensen maintains that until the Depression and the New Deal of the 1930s, the major political division in the Midwest was a reflection of the religious differences between evangelical Protestants and what he terms the "liturgical" churches, the Catholics, Episcopalians, and Lutherans. He writes: "That bridge linking theology and politics was the demand by (the evangelicals) that government remove the major obstacle to the purification of society through revivalistic Christianity, institutionalized immorality (particularly the liquor industry)."[65]

Local churches were not political organizations and did not formally endorse candidates, nor did ministers hold office or wield much influence in the political party. Still, when there was a clearly defined difference between candidates on an issue like Prohibition or state aid to parochial schools, clergy of neither camp were above preaching on Scriptural texts that made it clear how God would vote if he could have met local residency requirements.

Jensen lists three ways that religion affected politics. Theology defined morality and outlined the proper course of action; churches organized people into groups where peer pressure strengthened the tendency toward a unified outlook; and denominations were channels of information and sometimes agents of collective action. While Jefferson congregations rarely took formal action, state or district denominational conventions sometimes did. In 1916, for example, when Republican gubernatorial candidate William Harding called for substantial liberalization of liquor laws, several major Protestant denominations passed resolutions against him.[66]

The Prohibition issue was perhaps the most obvious instance in which churches flirted with political activism. The insistence of most evangelical Protestant denominations that drinking was a sin influenced (granted, in varying degrees) the individual member's attitudes on the question. It took courage for a Methodist to publicly support a candidate who favored the sale of alcohol.

But such Methodists existed. On a farm at the edge of town lived the Wilcox family—Methodist, nondrinkers, and Democrats. Lumund Wilcox recalled one Sunday morning when the minister was urging his flock to reelect a Republican senator because his opponent opposed Prohibition. It was widely understood that the senator himself would have been miserable if the laws he supported on the chamber floor had been vigorously enforced; his own drinking habits were not nearly as bone-dry as his voting record. That was hypocrisy from the pulpit, according to Nancy Wilcox, Lumund's mother, who walked out of the sermon to register her protest.[67]

On the other hand, there were some Irish-Catholic Republicans. Billy McCormick and A. J. Finn were staunch Republicans. Both were drys. With

---

65. Jensen, *The Winning*, 49.
66. Jensen, *The Winning*, 58–59; *Jefferson Bee*, 20 September 1916.
67. Interview with Lumund Wilcox.

so few Jefferson Catholics in the first place and some of them Republicans, the proverbial tie between Catholicism and the Democratic party seemed weaker in Jefferson than it was elsewhere around the state.

Whichever party they favored, most people took their political allegiance seriously. J. E. (Pat) Patterson learned the difference between Republicans and Democrats very early. Every year at the family reunion, often right after dinner, Pat's grandfather gathered all the boys and took them behind the barn for a solemn ritual. First, he took off his coat. Then he took off his vest. Finally, he unbuttoned his shirt and pointed to a Civil War wound on his chest. He made it an annual ritual to impress upon their young minds "what those damn Democrats did to your grandfather."[68] The lesson took, and Patterson served several terms as Greene County Republican chairman. Bess Osgood admitted that she had once voted for a Democrat but vowed that she "would never do that again." In her opinion "you aren't voting for just one man, you're voting for a whole regime. When they get in, they bring all their people in with them. Even if I don't like the (Republican) party man, I vote for him."[69]

Party loyalty was a tradition one did not take lightly. The Civil War had firmly planted Iowa in the Republican column, leading Sen. Jonathan Dolliver to quip that "Iowa will go Democratic when hell goes Methodist." The national Democratic party was tagged as a union of white supremacists in the South and immigrant blocs in northern cities. In Iowa, Democrats were concentrated along the Mississippi River and in neighboring Carroll County. The party also contained the remnants of the populist movement of the late nineteenth century, which had peaked with the Bryan campaign in 1896 and, therefore, had a "radical" taint. Democrats tried to tar the Republicans who supported high tariffs as lackeys of eastern financial and manufacturing interests, but they were fighting at a disadvantage. When it was a choice between something as abstract as the tariff or something as real as the scar on your grandfather's chest, Republicans came out on top every time.

Contrary to a popular myth, it was not Iowa farmers who chalked up the highest majorities for the Republicans. It has always been the small town. In Greene County, Democrats often did much better in the rural areas than they did in towns. Irish Catholics in Cedar and Kendrick townships helped to carry those areas for the Democrats though Protestant Grant and Greenbrier townships could often deliver over 70 percent to Republican candidates. The Republican percentage in Jefferson consistently ran higher than the party's percentage countywide. In 1900, for example, Greene County voters favored Republican William McKinley over Democrat William Jennings Bryan by a two to one margin, while in Jefferson alone it was three to one McKinley. In 1904 three out of four voters in the county supported Republican Teddy Roosevelt. In Jefferson it was five out of six.

---

68. The anecdote was related to me by Judge David Harris.
69. Interview with Bess Osgood.

However one analyzes the data, the obvious conclusion is that Greene County was simply not a fertile Democratic field. When the interviews turned to politics, long-time residents often began naming who the Democrats were—the Wilcoxes, the Cudahys, the Brunners, the Whalens, the Mugans. There were not many in town, in fact so few that their party affiliation distinguished them. Until well into the 1930s, the Democratic party could never put together a strong county organization. Lumund Wilcox, returning to Jefferson from law school in 1934, attended a Democratic county convention. He was one of five people who showed up.[70] The weakness of the party made it difficult to recruit good candidates since the election result was almost a foregone conclusion. The party consistently had difficulty raising money.[71]

The Republican party, by contrast, had a strong organization, and the Republican county chairman had considerable influence. In 1907 the state of Iowa instituted a reform designed to curb the power of local political machines. Rather than nominating all candidates at party conventions, the new law required a primary election in which all party members could vote. The primary changed the rules but by no means eliminated the influence of party organization. The chairman was the man with whom the state or national officials checked when it was time for an appointment. He was also a man to whom candidates for state office paid attention. By the time he was elected chairman, he had worked with local party members enough to win their respect and to have established himself as one who could get something done.[72]

The chairman relied heavily on a few influential party leaders who, by virtue of their occupation or personality, had a strong following, like the Stillmans who edited and published the *Bee,* the only newspaper with a strong countywide circulation. Paul Stillman's popularity put him in the legislature where he became speaker of the house in 1911. The county chairman was normally from Jefferson: farmer and clerk of court John Stevenson, editor Vic Lovejoy, or lawyers Orville Harris and Guy Richardson. Neither the Republicans nor Democrats paid their party officers, but that is not to say that they worked without reward. They satisfied their sense of civic duty, and they took pleasure in the political game.

One final note, however, might help put the role of local politics in proper perspective. There was indeed a love of the "game" of politics that many shared. Throughout the community there was a basic underlying consensus on what the broad ends of the political system should be, and although there might be heated disagreements on how to reach those ends, even political adversaries normally kept things in perspective.

My father recalled an anecdote that illustrates the point well. As a young Democratic attorney and an ardent New Dealer, Lumund Wilcox used to en-

---

70. Interview with Lumund Wilcox.
71. Interview with Fred Morain.
72. Interview with Fred Morain.

joy dropping into the newspaper office to bait Vic Lovejoy. It was not hard. Within a few minutes, Lovejoy would be livid, pounding the desk and castigating Franklin Roosevelt and the whole New Deal program. Quick on the uptake, Wilcox knew how to make Lovejoy's blood pressure soar. When Wilcox left, Lovejoy would lean back in his chair, prop his feet up on his desk, sigh, and tell my father working at the next desk, "Gee, I like that boy."[73]

AT THE TURN OF THE TWENTIETH CENTURY, most Jefferson residents looked at the social order with a sense of satisfaction. People very much like themselves dominated the most important aspects of American life. The major American heroes, like Washington, Jefferson, Franklin, and Lincoln, shared an Anglo-Saxon heritage. The greats of American literature—Irving, Poe, Longfellow, Hawthorne, Melville, and Twain—were in the same tradition. State legislatures, the leading pulpits, and the faculties of major universities likewise were filled with men with whom small town residents felt a cultural kinship. At the local, state, and national level, local residents (at least, the men) saw their own reflection when they looked at those who held power.

Iowa at the turn of the century boasted powerful political figures on the national scene. Republican dominance at home allowed the state's congressional delegation to accumulate seniority, which translated into power. Sen. William Boyd Allison was the senior Republican on the powerful Committee on Appropriations, which reviewed every proposal involving financial support, and was regarded as one of the four most powerful senators in Congress. Iowa's junior senator was Jonathan P. Dolliver of Fort Dodge who had been considered for vice president by both McKinley and Taft. He was widely recognized as an outstanding orator—some said the best in the Senate—and an expert on the tariff question. He was a devout Methodist. Congressman David B. Henderson of Dubuque was speaker of the house from 1899 to 1903, the first representative from west of the Mississippi to hold that office. (Granted, coming from Dubuque, he was not very far west of the Mississippi, but west nevertheless.) Several other Iowa congressmen chaired important House committees. "Tama Jim" Wilson, an Iowa State professor, and Leslie Shaw from Denison served in cabinet positions. Historian Leland Sage writes: "All this Republican power inside Iowa and in its delegation to Congress at the turn of the century was neatly meshed with Republican power in the national administration. It was commonly said to those who wanted something from the federal government, 'Ask Iowa!'"[74] These men were no strangers to local residents. They were "hometown" products whose national influence was a source of self-esteem and comfort to those who worked for their election.

---

73. The anecdote was related to me by Fred Morain.

74. Sage, *A History of Iowa* (Ames: Iowa State Univ. Press, 1974), 220–21. For short biographies of the Washington delegation from Iowa, Sage is an excellent source.

In 1900 even the president of the United States was a product of the small town. William McKinley was eighteen years old when the Civil War broke out. He left his studies at Allegheny College, enlisted in the Union Army, and rose to the rank of major by the end of the fighting. He studied law after the war and began practice in Canton, Ohio. In 1869 he was elected county attorney, and from there to Congress in 1876. He was always a sound-money man and an advocate of a high tariff to promote American industry. He was also a devout Presbyterian respected for his piety.

In 1896 he won the Republican nomination for the presidency. Who was his opponent? It was William Jennings Bryan, another product of the midwestern small town. Born in Salem, Illinois, in 1860, Bryan graduated from Illinois College in Jacksonville where he set up a law practice. In 1887 he moved to Lincoln, Nebraska, and became active in Democratic politics. After two terms in Congress and a defeat in a bid for a Senate seat, he became the editor of the Omaha *World Herald* and began his very successful career as a chautauqua speaker. Also a devoted churchman, Bryan became a champion of biblical fundamentalism and a leader against the teaching of evolution in public schools. Though between the economic policies advocated by Bryan and McKinley there was a world of difference, the two themselves represented the same cultural stream. The question was which Anglo-Saxon evangelical Protestant would occupy the White House.

That, of course, to Jefferson Anglo-Saxon Protestants was the way it should be. In every dimension, America represented the highest evolution among nations and served as a model to those less advanced. America had a special mission among nations. It was indeed "as a city upon a hill." Lincoln referred to the United States as "the last best hope of earth." Democracy had evolved from aristocracy, capitalism from feudalism, and Protestantism from Catholicism. Further progress would come from those on the cutting edge of evolutionary advance.

BIBLIOGRAPHICAL NOTE

The standard work on small towns in the Midwest is Lewis Atherton, *Main Street on the Middle Border* (Bloomington, IN, 1954). The emerging field of community studies was defined by Thomas Bender, *Community and Social Change in America* (New Brunswick, NJ, 1978); and Robert V. Hine, *Community on the American Frontier: Separate but Not Alone* (Norman, OK, 1980). Although much of the early work focused on New England communities, some of the best work has focused on the Midwest. The classic study of a midwestern community is Merle Curti, *The Making of an American Community: A Case Study of Democracy in a Frontier Community* (Stanford, CA, 1959). Curti's study was recently updated by Jane Marie Pederson, *Between Memory and Reality: Family and Community in Rural Wisconsin, 1870–1970* (Madison, WI, 1992). Other classic studies of midwestern communities include Robert

Dykstra, *The Cattle Towns* (New York, 1968); Kathleen Neils Conzen, *Immigrant Milwaukee, 1836–1860: Accommodation and Community in a Frontier City* (Cambridge, MA, 1976); Don Harrison Doyle, *The Social Order of a Frontier Community: Jacksonville, Illinois, 1825–1870* (Urbana, IL, 1978); and John Mack Faragher, *Sugar Creek: Life on the Illinois Prairie* (New Haven, CT, 1986). For a guide to this literature, see Kathleen N. Conzen, "Community Studies, Urban History, and American Local History," in *The Past Before Us: Contemporary Historical Writing in the United States,* ed. Michael Kammen (Ithaca, NY, 1989), 298–310.

On Iowa, in addition to the items on town development listed above in the bibliographical note to chapter four, see the Fall 1989/Winter 1990 special issue of the *Annals of Iowa* devoted to Sioux City; and Glenda Riley, *Cities on the Cedar: A Portrait of Cedar Falls, Waterloo, and Black Hawk County* (Parkersburg, IA, 1988). For fascinating journalistic looks at small Iowa towns, see Douglas Bauer, *Prairie City, Iowa: Three Seasons at Home* (New York, 1979); and Drake Hokanson, *Reflecting a Prairie Town: A Year in Peterson* (Iowa City, 1994).

For Iowa's transition at the turn of the century from a frontier, rural, agricultural society to a more urban, industrial society, see Keach Johnson's two-part article, "Iowa's Industrial Roots, 1890–1910," *Annals of Iowa* 44 (1978), 163–90, and "Iowa's Industrial Roots: Some Social and Political Problems," ibid., 247–77. Among the best sources for understanding the experience of small-town Iowans in the first third of the twentieth century are the short stories and novels by Hamlin Garland and Ruth Suckow, the artwork by Grant Wood, and other literature and art by Iowa's regionalists. For an interpretive guide to that work, see E. Bradford Burns, *Kinship with the Land: Regionalist Thought in Iowa, 1894–1942* (Iowa City, 1996).

13

Rural Iowa in the 1920s and 1930s

The 1920s and 1930s were trying, tumultuous times in rural Iowa. As historians have increasingly focused on conflict rather than progress, these decades have received more attention. For a conference in 1983 devoted to Henry A. Wallace's relationship to Iowa agriculture, the three people most identified with Iowa history since 1970—Leland Sage, Dorothy Schwieder, and Joseph F. Wall—established the context by providing very different accounts of the state of rural Iowa in the 1920s and 1930s. In the following brief essays by Schwieder and Wall, it is interesting to compare how differently two historians can approach the same basic task.

DOROTHY SCHWIEDER

IN THE 1920s, Iowa's farm population was of two minds about its rural way of life. On one hand, farm families lived much as their parents and grandparents had before them, carrying on the time honored tradition of the "favored man of God," comfortable with the rural institutions which had served them well for many decades. But on the other hand, increasingly farm families realized the social deficiencies of rural living. By the 1920s, town society had so outdistanced rural society in regard to modern conveniences and social/cultural opportunities that the sharp contrasts between the two could not be ignored. For rural people these changes created discontent and a strong desire for change. The discontent of the farm population was only one part of the rural scene in the 1920s, however. Increasingly rural life was scrutinized by people from all walks of life. The list of critics comprised both rural and urban dwellers. The Country Life Movement, for example, included many urban constituents who strongly criticized the social deficiencies of rural living as well as the economic disorganization of the American farmer. Rural areas provided critics of their own including state extension personnel, farm journal editors, newspaper editors, and farm dwellers themselves, all urging changes to make farm living more profitable and more socially satisfying.

Originally published as Dorothy Schwieder, "Rural Iowa in the 1920s: Conflict and Continuity"; and Joseph Frazier Wall, "The Iowa Farmer in Crisis, 1920–1936," *Annals of Iowa* 47 (1983), 104–27. Copyright © 1983 by the State Historical Society of Iowa. Reprinted by permission of the publisher.

Of all the criticisms of farm life in the 1920s, however, that of the farm population proved to be the most pervasive and the most unsettling. The discontent of Iowa farm families did not lie with farm living *per se*, but rather with the shortcomings of farm life when contrasted with town or city life. At a time when town dwellers enjoyed many physical comforts and a great diversity of social opportunities, farm people often felt their lives deprived and monotonous by comparison. The crux of the discontent was often social in nature. Since 1900, Iowa's rural society had often been judged by its similarities and contrasts to town society. Town and city living were held up as a model and unfortunately, in most ways, rural society was found wanting. Increasingly critics and supporters alike pointed out the drawbacks to rural living. Farm families were isolated, and as a result, farm living was often portrayed as dreary and monotonous. Moreover, farm families had few social and cultural opportunities. Farm children sometimes received inferior educations in rural schools and many did not have the opportunity to attend high school. Most farm families did not share modern conveniences available to town residents, particularly electric lights, central heating, indoor plumbing, and electric appliances. Certainly farm families had made good use of one new invention, the automobile, but the effects were not always positive: While the automobile helped break down rural isolation it also increased the interaction between town and country people, often further emphasizing the discrepancy between the two ways of life. Yet another source of rural discontent was that the 1920s seemingly brought prosperity to every sector of society except agriculture. In the perception of farm people, town and city residents enjoyed a higher level of material well being than ever while prosperity for farm people faded quickly after World War I.

Although the twenties represented the peak of rural discontent with the social side of farm life, that discontent was certainly not new; the problem had roots that reached far back into the previous century. As Gilbert Fite points out in *The American Farmers: The New Minority*, people had been leaving the farm for the city since the mid-1800s because town and city living offered more physical comforts and more social opportunities.[1] By 1900, the social discrepancy between town and country living seemed to widen. Before the turn of the century, social activities of midwesterners, both rural and urban, centered around three institutions: family, church, and school. Although rural and urban social activities differed somewhat in frequency and form, they remained centered on these three basic institutions. Like rural families, town families were often large and family members frequently lived close together. Families assembled for holidays and social occasions. When social activities occurred outside the family circle, they took place at the community level. For example, town residents celebrated the Fourth of July with activities intended for all

---

1. Gilbert Fite, *The American Farmers: The New Minority* (Bloomington, IN, 1981), 10.

community residents. In a similar fashion, school activities involved all parents and children within a particular school district.[2]

Around 1900, however, social fragmentation began to appear. As Lewis Atherton has pointed out in *Main Street on the Middle Border*, in the late nineteenth century small town residents began "to participate in a national trend toward organizational activities." By the first decade of the twentieth century this behavior was so obvious that Atherton describes it as the "twentieth-century cult of joining." Atherton believes that this development took place because townspeople increasingly were unable to identify with the total community. As towns grew in size and as populations became more mobile, people joined countless organizations to give themselves the feeling of belonging. Whereas people had previously identified with the total community, after 1900 they transferred that identification to a myriad of social and business organizations. Altogether, Americans everywhere became a nation of joiners. That is, Americans in cities and towns became a nation of joiners. Rural people did not have the same opportunities.[3]

After 1900, as more and more ruralites moved off the farm, farm living became the object of considerable scrutiny. The Country Life Commission, established by President Theodore Roosevelt, conducted the most well known study. Roosevelt, like many Americans, believed that rural living produced an intelligent, sturdy, self-reliant population that should not be allowed to dwindle. A continuation of the rural exodus, Roosevelt believed, was cause for alarm. The president responded to the situation by appointing five prominent Americans to the Country Life Commission to study rural conditions and to suggest ways to make rural living more profitable and more attractive. In 1909 the Commission issued its report and included many recommendations intended to improve rural social life. The Commission believed that farmers and community officials should work to provide better schools for young people and should develop curricula directly related to the farm youths' lives: Farm boys should study agriculture while farm girls should study homemaking. The Commission also recommended that country roads be improved, that state extension services be expanded, and that more social opportunities be established for farm women. Throughout the report, Commission members expressed concern over the attractions of town living. They pointed out that rural people continually equated town living with better living.[4]

Other notables also recognized that "drift to the cities" as one of the most difficult problems facing the nation. In 1913, Iowa author Herbert Quick wrote an article for *Good Housekeeping* entitled "The Women on the Farm," in which he dealt with the problem of the farm exodus. Quick related that in his study

---

2. Lewis Atherton, *Main Street on the Middle Border* (New York, 1975), especially chapters 2 and 3.
3. Ibid., 245–249.
4. *Report of the Country Life Commission* (Chapel Hill, NC, 1911), 82–83, 103–106, 121–27.

of rural living, as well as from his own experience as a farm child, he had reached the conclusion that the movement to the cities "has been largely a women movement. I have found the men on the farms much more contented and happy than the women." He perceived the discontent of farm women to be a problem of major proportions and one that needed an early solution. Quick acknowledged that most of the progress had benefited the men on the farm, not the women. He noted: "In the mothers, the wives, the daughters of the farm, toil has many slaves . . . of the open as abjectly held as its slaves of factory and mill. Not for herself alone, but for her daughter's sake, her son's future, has the country mother argued the move to town."[5]

Quick's comment accurately described the lives of rural women in Iowa. Observers of Iowa farm life had long insisted that farm women were greatly overworked. Moreover, many believed that farm women led dreary, isolated lives and were in need of more social outlets. In his article, Herbert Quick had correctly pointed out that one of the major difficulties in reducing the work of farm women was that farmers adopted many machines for outside work because they were profitable; unfortunately, few of the machines and labor-saving devices available for the farm home could be justified in the same manner.[6] The result was that farm women in Iowa, like farm women elsewhere, worked exceedingly long hours performing many of their household tasks in the same manner as their mothers, and sometimes even their grandmothers, before them. As a general rule, farm women performed all work inside the farm home as well as raising chickens. On some farms women helped with milking and occasionally assisted with seasonal work like corn picking. Reflecting on his early life in rural Kossuth County in the late teens and twenties, Andrew Risius remembered that even as a young boy he felt "pity" for his mother because she had to work so hard. The Risius farm had no electricity until 1939. Risius did the washing for her family of ten with a hand-powered machine. Charles and Lola Crim, raised on a farm near Stratford in the teens and the twenties, also related that their mother worked excessively long hours. Lola recalled that in the summer, her mother arose at 4 a.m. so that she could churn butter during the cool part of the day. The one task Crim liked best was mending because that "gave her a chance to sit down." The heavy workloads of Iowa farm women often prevented them from taking part in activities outside the home.[7]

The social roles of other farm family members also had undergone little change since the turn of the century. The activities of farm families continued to revolve around the three basic institutions of family, church, and school. Most social life took place within the family itself. Charles Crim recalled that in the teens and early twenties his family was quite isolated from town events.

---

5. Herbert Quick, "The Women on the Farms," *Good Housekeeping* 57 (October 1913), 426–27.

6. Ibid., 427–28.

7. Interview with Andrew Risius, Titonka, Iowa, December 1982 and interviews with Charles Crim, Mildred Crim, and Lola Crim, Ames, Iowa, March 1983.

The family resided in the southeast corner of Webster County which placed them quite a distance from the county seat and definitely reduced the number of trips that they made to town. But at the same time, Crim remembered that he and his brothers and sisters never wanted for entertainment. The nine children often made their own toys and devised their own games. As a youngster, Crim had farm animals to play with, particularly the colts. Many relatives lived nearby and cousins often came to visit. The Crim family's experience underscores the fact that when children married, they frequently settled close to the parental home which allowed family members to maintain close ties. The Crims, like most rural families, gathered for birthdays, holidays, and other social occasions.[8] Curtis Harnack, an Iowa author, dramatically emphasizes this point in his autobiographical account of growing up in northwest Iowa in the 1930s. In his book, *We Have All Gone Away*, Harnack describes the one time each year when neighbors gathered at his farm home to discuss plans for the cooperative threshing operation. At that time his mother and his Aunt Lizzie "felt a trifle uneasy, for this was the only night of the year when our visitors were other than relatives. With so many dozens of kin on both sides of the family, we needed no further friends."[9]

A major consideration of farm living in the 1920s was the matter of roads. While farm families were quick to purchase automobiles in the late teens and twenties and these were a vital factor in reducing rural isolation, bad roads remained a problem. Although state and local officials initiated road improvement programs in the twenties, particularly the use of gravel, in inclement weather country people still found themselves unable to travel to town. To a large extent, weather determined rural families' travel patterns. The diary of a young farm girl growing up in rural Case vividly illustrates that point. Throughout 1921, sixteen-year-old Helen Brainard dutifully recorded the daily events that took place on her parents' farm. Although Helen wrote about many events, the topic of weather dominated her diary. If it rained, muddy roads were inevitable and that brought a whole series of cancellations for the Brainard family. The first casualty was that the mailman could not make his rounds. If family members had planned a trip to town, rain usually forced a change in plans. Sometimes the family could still make the trip by abandoning the automobile for a horse-drawn buggy. More often than not, in the event of rain, the family stayed home. For the Brainard family, like most Iowa farm families, "bad roads" were often the bane of their existence.[10]

Like their parents and grandparents before them, Iowa farm families in the 1920s attended rural churches and most sent their children to rural schools. Mildred Erickson Crim, who grew up in Hamilton County in the 1920s, recalled

---

8. Interviews with Charles Crim, Mildred Crim, and Lola Crim.
9. Curtis Harnack, *We Have All Gone Away* (Garden City, NJ, 1973), 107.
10. Helen Brainard Diary, 1921, Brainard Family Papers, Iowa State Historical Department, Des Moines.

that "rural people were extremely proud of their little schools" and they believed that rural children received a better education than did town children. State law required that rural children pass eighth grade examinations before becoming eligible to graduate and rural parents believed that this system ensured that their children received an adequate education.[11] While some country schools were staffed with excellent teachers and contained good facilities, all country schools did not fit that description. No doubt many Iowa farm children in the twenties attended poorly maintained, over-crowded facilities and listened daily to ill prepared, disinterested teachers. Rural schools underwent little change in the twenties because school consolidation, underway from 1897, was halted temporarily in 1921.[12]

Country churches, however, did undergo some change during the 1920s. With the help of the automobile, farm people began to attend church in town. As one historian explained: "It was not that farm families had quit going to church, but that they had begun to go elsewhere."[13] One churchman believed that some country people had abandoned the rural churches because their children "were no longer 'satisfied in a little country Sunday school while their chums and playmates were gathered in a large school in a nearby city or village. . . .'"[14] In some areas rural churches consolidated so that they could remain open, while others moved their congregations to town. Many rural churches, however, did survive into the twenties and remained open for several more decades.[15]

While participation in rural churches and rural schools often proved to be a positive experience for young people, attendance in town schools frequently had a negative result. Many rural people recalled feeling "discriminated against," particularly when they attended high school. Charles Crim remembered that he deeply resented being called a "dumb farm kid," a standard label for farm children who attended town school. Many rural residents recalled that as high school students, they felt the stigma of "being different," as well as feeling inferior to town people. Mildred Crim recalled that many farm young people started to high school but did not finish because of the name calling and the many negative remarks directed at them by their town counterparts. One rural resident who attended high school in Jefferson in the 1930s commented that town people felt country people "were socially below them." For some farm people, these negative memories lingered for a lifetime.[16]

---

11. Interview with Mildred Crim.

12. Joseph Wall, *Iowa: A Bicentennial History* (New York, 1972), 188. See Jessie Field, *The Corn Lady* (n.p., 1911) for a view of a resourceful, successful country school teacher.

13. Don Kirschner, *City and Country: Rural Responses to Urbanization in the 1920s* (Westport, CT, 1970), 116–18.

14. Quoted in Kirschner, *City and Country*, 117.

15. Ibid.

16. Interviews with Charles Crim and Mildred Crim; quoted from a forthcoming study by Tom Morain, "Prairie Grass Roots: An Iowa Town in the Early Twentieth Century," 149.

By the mid-1920s, Iowa's rural population seemed to have entered a period of deep uncertainty about their particular way of life. On the one hand, they remained staunch supporters of rural life. Farm families continued to believe deeply in the natural superiority of rural living. For so long farmers had been singled out as providing the moral and spiritual backbone of the nation. Terms such as independent, self-reliant, and hard working had long been used to describe the farm population.[17] Farm families had no reason to reject these descriptions in the twenties. Moreover, rural people continued to be proud of their rural institutions. Yet at the same time, rural discontent continued. Everywhere farm people looked they saw their way of life contrasted with town living and subsequently described as deficient, backward, and greatly in need of change. Even farm journals regularly carried ads which insinuated that by comparison with town living, country homes were dull, monotonous places from which young people longed to escape. The ads urged farm families to purchase radios, lighting systems, stoves, and other products that would enable them to bring the city to the farm. Ironically, even food was included in the advertisers' campaign. In almost every issue of *Wallaces' Farmer* for 1921, the Jello Food Company ran an ad which typically announced: "Time for farm women to learn about jello like city women."[18] As the 1920s progressed, it became increasingly evident that Iowa's rural society contained an inherent contradiction: Farm life was good, but it was not good enough.

While rural people had their own perceptions of the strengths and weaknesses of rural living, country observers offered a plethora of advice on ways to revitalize farm society. To individuals like Henry A. Wallace, editor of *Wallaces' Farmer* and the leading farm spokesman in the Middle West, "The mindlessness and artificiality of city ways were beginning to worm their way into the country."[19] Wallace believed deeply in rural values and rural ways of life, but he perceived that rural society must change if it was to resist the encroachment of urban ways. Writing in *Wallaces' Farmer* in May 1925, Wallace asserted that farm people should become socially independent from town society and that they should develop their own rural culture. He noted, "Too often folks in the country seem to think they can maintain no social and intellectual life of their own. They have the notion that the ideal is to dash off to the nearest small town as often as possible and to lose themselves in its activities." Wallace then went on to sketch briefly his own view: "We want a distinctive culture of our own in the country; we want to prevent our countryside being merely a field for the extension of town habits. No one who looks at it sensibly thinks that our urban civilization is anything to pattern after. Not imitation of the town but the creation of a genuine rural civilization is what we need."[20]

---

17. Kirschner, *City and Country*, 61–62.
18. *Wallaces' Farmer*, 11 March 1921, 481.
19. Kirschner, *City and Country*, 48.
20. *Wallaces' Farmer*, 1 May 1925, 643.

During the 1920s other Iowans, like Wallace, perceived that rural society must change to become more attractive and more satisfying. The Home Economics Department at Iowa State College continued to train home demonstration agents throughout the twenties whose major aim was to help farm families improve the quality of rural life. In 1925, seventeen counties employed home demonstration agents.[21] These women were assisted by members of the ISC Home Economics staff at Ames who frequently traveled around the state presenting lectures and holding workshops. The home demonstration agents presented materials designed to improve all aspects of farm living — ranging from preparing more nutritious meals to utilizing better home ventilation methods to improving personal appearances through hat making. A frequent topic of discussion was home management or how the farm wife could do her work more efficiently and thus have more leisure time.

Much of the advice given to farm families in the twenties concerned farm children. Frequently extension personnel viewed the drawbacks of rural living from the perspective of how they affected young people. Throughout the 1920s, extension people and many others urged farm families to improve the quality of rural life if they wished to keep their children on the farm. In 1921, an extension speaker noted that pig clubs and poultry clubs were important, but it also was necessary to see beauty in other things. Sometimes these needs were coupled with a need for physical comfort on the farm. Yet another extension speaker told a group of farm women in 1925: "The reasons given for much unhappiness on the farm are lack of appreciation for the fine and aesthetic things of life and attention to making homes attractive and comfortable."[22]

Anna E. Richardson, dean of the Home Economics Department at Iowa State College, frequently commented on children's needs. She urged farm communities to initiate the selection of a Blue Ribbon girl and a Blue Ribbon boy to call attention to the achievements of farm youth. Dean Richardson often emphasized the need to upgrade education and opportunities for farm children. Speaking to farm women at a meeting at ISC in 1925, Richardson advocated what she called a "Bill of Rights for Iowa Children." She believed that it should accomplish three things: "First, Iowa boys and girls should be intelligently managed and controlled; second, they should have access to the best education there is; and third, they should have the right to play and enjoy themselves."[23]

During the twenties, social opportunities for some farm families increased through the expansion of farm interest groups, particularly the Farm Bureau and the Farmers' Union. Although their major concern was to help farmers economically, these groups also sponsored a variety of social activities. The Farm Bureau in particular offered women the opportunity to come together for neighborhood meetings where they studied a wide variety of domestic

---

21. Ibid., 23 January 1925, 113.
22. Ibid., 14 January 1921, 62; 23 January 1925, 114.
23. Ibid., 22 January 1925, 114; 13 February 1925, 22.

topics. Many times Farm Bureau women carried out their programs jointly with ISC extension personnel. In January 1925, when Farm Bureau members met in Des Moines for their annual meeting, the members had extensive praise for the positive way that the Farm Bureau had improved their lives and the lives of their families. Farm Bureau officials estimated in January 1925, that almost fourteen thousand Iowa farm women were involved in presenting Farm Bureau programs to their rural neighbors.[24]

At the same time, some rural families followed the advice of Wallace and others and formed community clubs. These clubs increased social activities and developed strong, more cohesive rural neighborhoods. One community club, known as the Evergreen Sporting Association, had roots that reached back to 1905 when farmers in western Wright County met to hunt down a wolf that was threatening their livestock. That group became the nucleus of a general neighborhood club that existed through the 1920s. Neighbors held picnics, sponsored a field day, and participated in a literary society known as the Prohibition Club. The club also sponsored short courses in agriculture and domestic science taught by personnel from ISC. Of all their functions, however, members considered "the social side" the most important. Each month the club planned a community party in some member's home. One club member writing about the practice noted, "The only trouble that we encounter is to find a house large enough for the crowd, which often numbers one hundred and more. The people attending range in age from babies to grandparents, but all come expecting to enjoy themselves."[25]

From the viewpoint of Iowa's rural society, the third decade of the twentieth century could be described in a variety of ways. For some, the twenties offered a chance to revitalize rural society and assist it in warding off the assault of the city. For others, the decade offered a chance to improve the quality of rural life in more limited ways. Yet for others, like the farm population itself, the twenties was a time to rethink priorities and values. Certainly these years created great stress for farm people and produced uncertainty and ambivalence about their way of life. Although attempts were made to rebuild and refocus rural life, some quite successfully, overall the effort was too little and too late. Rural Iowans carried their discontent into the 1930s where, because of the severe depression, it was obscured but not eliminated. During the 1930s, Iowans moved closer and closer to the lifestyle enjoyed by town and city dwellers; urbanization of the countryside had begun. After 1930, some rural associations remained, but for the most part these became less and less important. Certainly in the transition, rural Iowans lost some of the old rural values, but by the 1930s, they seemed willing to pay the price.[26]

---

24. Ibid., 23 January 1925, 113.

25. Ibid., 27 February 1925, 291.

26. See James Shideler, "Flappers and Philosophers and Farmers: Rural-Urban Tensions of the Twenties," *Agricultural History* 47 (1973), 298–99. Also see David B. Danbom, *The Resisted Revolution: Urban America and the Industrialization of Agriculture, 1900–1930* (Ames, Iowa, 1979) for a full discussion of agricultural change during this period.

JOSEPH FRAZIER WALL

WHILE CAMPAIGNING at the Clay County Fair in Spencer, Iowa, in the fall of 1928, the Republican vice-presidential candidate, Charles Curtis, was annoyed by a heckler who asked for a second time a question that Curtis believed he had already answered. Annoyed beyond the limit of political discretion, Curtis had shouted back, "You're asking what I just told you a minute ago, but you were too damned dumb to understand it." That unfortunate phrase, "too damed dumb to understand," was not forgotten by the farmers of the Midwest. It was taken out of context and applied as being indicative of the Hoover/Curtis attitude toward all farmers when that ticket sought reelection in the desperate summer of 1932.[27]

Four turbulent years later, in 1936, as the old militant farm leader, Milo Reno, lay on his deathbed in a Missouri resort spa, he granted a final press interview to a reporter from the local newspaper. When asked what above all he regretted in his long struggle to give the farmers their just rewards, Reno replied that the one thing that continued to vex him was "the fact that the farmers, for whom he had given his entire life, would not cooperate to the extent that their problems might be solved."[28]

It would be difficult to imagine two men more diametrically different in personality, beliefs, or operational methods than Vice-President Charles Curtis and Iowa Farmers' Union President Milo Reno, yet curiously enough they had both arrived at the same evaluation of their rural constituents. Iowa farmers were just "too damn dumb" to understand what was good for them. But in making this final condemnatory judgment, the standpat conservative and the agrarian radical in actuality were making a confession of guilt of the very charge they had levelled against their rural friends. They both were too damned dumb to understand why the programs they advocated were not acceptable to the independent farmer. Curtis never understood why the old Republican formulae of high protective tariffs and trickle-down prosperity, or even the new Hoover programs of a national Farm Board and direct aid to farm cooperatives were not acceptable to the farmer. And although Reno was much closer to the soil than Curtis and instinctively sensed the farmers' basic needs and desires, rationally he was unable to comprehend why he and his organization were unable to get the Iowa farmers to organize to protect their way of life, their status in society. Reno never understood that a basic paradox was built into

---

27. This revised opening paragraph corrects an error in the original text of this essay. The author gratefully acknowledges George Mills's comments calling attention to that error. See George Mills, "Comment," *Annals of Iowa* 47 (1983), 128–29.

28. Excelsior Springs (Missouri) *Daily Standard*, 5 May 1936, quoted in John L. Shover, *Cornbelt Rebellion* (Urbana, IL, 1965), 202.

the whole concept of a union to preserve rugged individualism. He was appalled by the necessity to enforce voluntary embargoes on marketing with coercive picketing on the highways, and as he lay dying, he could in his bitterness only blame his own people for having made his life work a failure.

Neither Curtis, who had long been rendered insensitive to the needs of his region within his cushy cocoon of Washington politics, nor Reno, who was blinded by his own idealism, really understood what was happening to the people who had elected them to high office within their respective spheres. Along with the immediate economic crisis of ten-cent corn and foreclosure sales of mortgaged farms, there was the deeper problem of personal identification that had been a long time in the making, but which was now reaching a critical juncture at this moment of Great Depression. Most farmers themselves would have had difficulty articulating this problem in any comprehensible way. They only knew that something terrible and seemingly inexorable was happening to them and their way of life. The yeoman farmer once had been the very symbol of American life—of Jeffersonian Republicanism and Jacksonian Democracy. In the first census taken in the United States in 1790, 96 percent of the population had been farmers. Cincinnatus had been our greatest hero out of the classical past, and the sturdy yeoman, with wife and children heading west in a covered wagon, was our manifest destiny in a seemingly limitless future.

Within a hundred years, however, farmers had become in Gilbert Fite's apt phrase, "the new minority." But even after the census figures of 1910 revealed their new status, the full impact of being in the minority was not immediately realized. The farmers still had political clout beyond their numbers, thanks in part to the failure of state and national legislatures to reapportion themselves, and the decade from 1910 to 1920 had brought greater economic prosperity to farmers than they had ever known before.

Abruptly in 1920, the farmers discovered not only that they were a minority but that they were an oppressed minority. It was easy, of course, to blame their plight on others, and Milo Reno, John Simpson, A. C. Townley, and other farm leaders were to get a lot of mileage out of demagogic speeches against Wall Street bankers, Chicago grain brokers, and Washington politicians. All of this was useful steam-letting, but if farmers were to rectify in any meaningful way their worsening situation, they had to ask themselves who they were, what they wanted, and what price they were willing to pay for that which they desired.

These three questions were of varying degrees of difficulty to answer. It was relatively easy for farmers to give an answer as to what they wanted. The farmers wanted to stay on the land that they loved. Each wanted to produce as much of the particular product suitable to that land and to the individual's skills as nature, modern technology, and the farmer's own industry would allow. The farmer wanted a price for that produce that would be based on the cost of production plus a fair return for the labor and investment involved.

The farmer wanted easy, short-term credit to meet the immediate annual need of purchasing seed and fertilizer and of hiring temporary additional labor for harvesting, and the farmer also wanted long-term credit at a low rate of interest for capital expenditures of durable equipment and the possible purchase or leasing of additional land. Above all, the farmers wanted to be able at the close of their lives to turn over to one or more of their children their old home places, debt free, better equipped, and more productive than those farms had been when they had acquired them. These expectations seemed to the farmers to make neither unreasonable nor aggressive demands upon society. Most farmers did not expect nor want great wealth. The Carnegie, Rockefeller, Gould dreams of an imperium did not goad Iowa farmers during their waking hours nor disturb their sleep at night.

As to the question concerned with their own identity, here the farmers would also have a ready answer. If they ever asked themselves the question at all, each would answer shortly and simply, "I am my own person, beholden to no one." A valiant answer, to be sure, but by the 1920s, a quite unsatisfactory answer. Modern industrial America had reduced the productive classes to but two categories—labor and management, and in this new simplified taxonomy, the farmer had become an anomaly. Were the farmers labor? Of course, they were. No factory worker worked as long hours as did the farmers during the busy season. It was not nine a.m. to five p.m. for them, but rather five a.m. until nine p.m. "All right," said society, "if you are labor, why don't you organize and strike to get your just demands?" "But," the farmers would reply, "We are not factory hands. We are the owners and managers. We would be striking against ourselves."

"All right, then—you belong to management. Form trusts and pools and marketing agreements. In times of economic recession, reduce costs by laying off workers and letting the plant lie idle for a few months. If prices get too low, create scarcity by limiting production." To which the farmers would reply, "You don't understand. Most of our labor in addition to ourselves consists of our own families. We can't lay them off. And as for our plants, as you call them—we can't let the livestock stand idle like a blast furnace or an assembly line. The animals have to be fed, the cows have to be milked, the eggs have to be gathered. We can't take land out of production if we are to meet our mortgage payments. The lower the prices, the more we had better produce to keep the bank or the insurance company from foreclosing." With a shrug, society would then conclude this imagined dialogue by saying, "Well, you will first have to decide who you are, and then determine what price you are willing to pay to get what you want."

There were many different spokesmen from society to tell the farmers who they were, what they needed, and what the cost would be to obtain those needs. There was the American Farm Bureau Federation, whose meteoric rise in membership immediately after World War I made it the largest farm organization in the history of American agriculture. The Farm Bureau spoke to the large, successful farmers of the Midwest, and it told them they were capitalists, who belonged within the aristocracy of management. To survive, farmers needed to be rational in their planning, expansive in their outlook, scientific in their methods. They had an ally in the government, particularly in the Republican party's administration of that government, who would provide them by an extension service conducted through a county agent system with the latest scientific and technological information on how to produce more at less cost. Like any good capitalists, farmers must continually expand, for the status quo meant not status but decline and death. And what were the costs? Well, there was the cost in increased taxes for these services, but that was minimal. There was the higher cost of abandoning old ways and accepting new ideas—of being willing to listen to your twenty-year-old offspring who had had a couple of years of higher education at Iowa State. And the highest cost of all, an acceptance of the fact that there were going to have to be fewer farmers, farming much larger areas of land. Forget that myth of the yeoman farmer. It was as outdated as the myth of the master-apprentice craftsman. The farmer was going to have to become an ever smaller minority, but minority status need not mean oppression, for the elite of any political-economic system is always the smallest minority of all.

Then there was the Farmers' Union, older than the Farm Bureau, but much smaller in numbers, which spoke to a different group of farmers in a quite different language. The Union told the owners of the small family farms that they were neither labor nor management—no need to try to fit into one of only two confining categories designed for an urban, industrial society. It told them they were Iowa farmers, tillers of 160 acres of the world's best land, food suppliers of the world, preservers of a way of life that was still the essence of America. All they needed in monetary return was the cost of production plus a fair profit. To achieve this, they must band together cooperatively and work in union. They must use the ballot box and push politically for their economic and social rights.

And the costs? They would be minimal. The Iowa farmer must forget old party loyalties and prejudices as the North Dakota farmer had done with the Non-Partisan League and the Minnesota farmer was doing with the new Farm-Labor party. Farmers would have to give up some of their precious free time for union organization. Above all, farmers must remember they are their brothers' keepers lest they be branded with the mark of Cain, for the forced departure of a single farm family from its land diminished all farmers.

The politicians from the major parties also came to the farmers with their proposals for reform and relief. And in Congress, these last remnants of Progressivism were amazingly effective in the first years of painful, post-war adjustment in giving the farmers what they wanted. The Farm Bloc was successful in enacting the Packers and Stockyard Act, in providing increased capital to the Federal Farm Loan System, in obtaining exemption from the anti-trust laws for farm cooperatives, and by the Grain Futures Act, in providing effective regulation of the grain exchanges. These were necessary and major accomplishments, but they were ameliorative not fundamental reforms. The McNary-Haugen Bill promised more, and the farmers were quite willing to pay the cost of "an equalization fee" to finance this program if it would indeed guarantee "a fair exchange value" within the domestic market. But effective as this small Farm Bloc was within Congress, it was unable to prevail against an administration of Coolidge, Mellon, and Hoover, and the McNary-Haugen Bill was twice slain by presidential veto.

With the collapse of the financial world in 1929 and the subsequent precipitous decline of industry, the farmers were dragged into an even deeper depression than they had known in the 1920s. And in this moment of crisis, new, more extreme political voices were heard, eager to tell the farmers who they were, what they should want, and what prices they would have to pay. The Communists in 1932 belatedly discovered that the real action seemed to be not with the unemployed industrial workers in the cities, who were docilely lining up before soup kitchens or quietly selling apples on streets, but rather with the angry farmers in, of all places, conservative Iowa, Nebraska, and Minnesota. So "Mother" Ella Bloor, Lem Harris, and Harold Ware hurried out to Madison County, Nebraska, and Sioux City, Iowa, to tell the farmers they were of the proletariat, and what was needed was a genuine revolution to abolish capitalism and all private ownership of production.[29] But few farmers listened. The Communist program was, for them, confiscatory in its cost.

There were voices from the right as well as the left: the priest of Royal Oak, Michigan, Father Coughlin; William Dudley Pelley and his Silver Shirts; and most interesting of all, Lester Barlow and his Seventy-Sixers. Barlow, an engineer and inventor, had been born and educated in Iowa, later had moved to Connecticut and during World War I had made a small fortune from his improved anti-submarine depth charge bomb. In 1931, he wrote a book entitled *What Would Lincoln Do*, in which he spelled out his program for the political and economic regeneration of America. Much of this interesting little book is devoted to Barlow's grandiose scheme for a national four-lane transcontinental highway. Anticipating by some twenty-five years the interstate system as developed under the Eisenhower administration in the 1950s, even down to the exact location of Interstate 80, Barlow argued that for a cost of two billion dollars the federal government could provide jobs for all of America's unemployed as well as stimulate the country's basic industries and provide a safe and economical national transportation system. But Barlow's vision of a new America went far beyond interstate highways. He called for a national Non-Partisan League that would be outside the existing two-party system. Organized like a people's army of voters, with cadres, companies, and regiments and commanded by a national executive committee and a supreme commander-

---

29. For an excellent account of Communist activity in the Midwest in the 1930s, see Shover, *Corn Belt Rebellion*.

in-chief, the League would in effect determine the country's political and economic agenda. The existing institutions of government at both the state and national level would simply enact and enforce the mandates of the League.[30] In 1932, Barlow also appeared on the Iowa scene to gather in what vintage he could in his native state where the grapes of wrath were rapidly ripening. In far northern Iowa, he was to find some measure of success with his secret Modern Seventy-Sixers clubs and his proposal for a constitutional amendment that would limit any one person's total wealth to $500,000. America would be taken out of the hands of the corrupt financiers and politicians and returned to the small farmer, the small businessman, and artisan. Barlow would later claim, with some measure of truth, that Huey Long had borrowed from him the "Share the Wealth" program which the Louisiana senator would make into a national platform for his presidential ambitions.

Iowa farmers were not lacking a wide range of solutions for their distress in these years of crisis, and with the exception of the Communist program, much in each proposal had its appeal. But each solution also presented difficulties, for each demanded more of the farmers than they were willing to pay. There was either too callous a disregard for one's less fortunate neighbor or else too much cooperation was required with that same neighbor. Some involved too much regimentation or were based on an unacceptable foreign ideology. The farmer was not seeking revolution but rather restoration, not an idealized future Utopia but a past reality. The real revolutionaries, the Iowa farmers instinctively felt, were not they but those creators of a modern America who had brought the farmers to their sorry plight.

So in their anger and frustration, the Iowa farmers struck out blindly — at the insurance companies and banks who were taking their land from them, at the big city dairies and produce houses who were paying the farmers a mere pittance for their milk and beef and pork, and at government who enforced this new order of things and told the farmers with sheriff's deputies and courts of law what they had to do. In the eighteen-month period from September 1931 through April 1933 there were three quite separate and discrete instances of violence in Iowa which received national attention: the so-called "Cow War" of September 1931, in which the farmers of Cedar and Muscatine counties refused to comply with the new compulsory testing of cattle for the eradication of bovine tuberculosis; the picketing of highways in August of 1932 to prevent produce from reaching market which led to shooting and the destruction of property; and the use of force to stop foreclosure sales which culminated in the so-called attempted lynching of Judge Charles Bradley near Le Mars in the spring of 1933. Violence always attracts attention, and these incidents were successful in spotlighting the plight of the midwestern farmer above that of any other group in America's depressed economy.

---

30. Lester P. Barlow, *What Would Lincoln Do: A Call for Political Revolution Through the Ballot* (Stamford, CT, 1931).

Much of the credit—or discredit—for these actions was attributed to the Farmers' Holiday Association and its president, Milo Reno, and indirectly, because the leadership was the same, to the Iowa Farmers' Union. Yet as some historians of this period, most notably John Shover and Dale Kramer, have perceptively pointed out, these instances of direct action were far in advance of the organizations that purportedly were sponsoring them.[31] Milo Reno, John Simpson, and John Bosch neither organized, led, nor even countenanced violence as a means of getting reform. These were the spontaneous acts of individuals, acting without benefit of organization or advance planning. Often these acts had a momentum of their own which carried even the participants along willy-nilly with no clear objective in mind. Some twenty-five years later, I went to the Le Mars area of northwest Iowa and talked with many of the participants in these events. The oral history interviews I conducted confirmed this historical judgment. I talked to people who had stood on the picket lines and others who had served as sheriff's deputies to keep the roads open. No one spoke of organization or platforms or goals. They spoke of their fear, their anger, and the kind of exultant joy they found in doing something, anything, no matter how inchoate and purposeless it may have been.[32]

One of the most valuable interviews I had was with Rome Starzl, then editor of the Le Mars *Globe-Post*. Starzl, who had been editorially sympathetic to the farmer's cause, gave me a most graphic account of the most dramatic episode of the whole period, the Judge Bradley "lynching" attempt. The incident began when a group of farmers, sitting in Bradley's court hearing arguments on the constitutionality of Iowa's new moratorium law on foreclosures, were asked to remove their hats. Angered by this command, they surged forward and grabbed the judge. It was as unplanned, as spontaneous, and as consequential as was Rosa Parks's refusal in 1956 to give up her seat to a white man on a bus in Birmingham. Having taken the first step in anger, the farmers were swept along by their own temerity. They carried the judge out to a truck, and then drove him a few miles out of town. They asked Starzl to come along to get a story for his paper. There on that country road, they stripped the judge down to his long winter underwear. Then they began, Starzl said, to act out a kind of parody of the crucifixion. The farmers began to jeer "King Bradley, King Bradley," as one farmer put a noose around the judge's neck and flung the other end of the rope over a cross beam of a telephone pole. Someone yelled, "The King needs a crown," and slapped a hubcap off the truck on his head. Then, Starzl recalled,

---

31. Dale Kramer, *The Wild Jackasses: The American Farmer in Revolt* (New York, 1956) and Shover, *Cornbelt Rebellion*. See also Roland A. White's uncritical biography, *Milo Reno: Farmers' Union Pioneer* (Iowa City, Iowa, 1941) which unintentionally reveals how out of touch Reno was with the activists within his movement.

32. Interviews with Charles Treinen, Gus Alesch, Ed Clafkey, et al. in the Le Mars-Remsen area of Plymouth County, July 1955.

Bradley said he wanted to offer a prayer. He was praying for his life, but he never once asked them to save his life. What he really said, although he didn't use those words was "Forgive them, Father, for they know not what they do." Having finished his prayer, Bradley quite unexpectedly fainted and fell down on the road while the mob just stood there. At that point, I stepped forward and said, "Listen, none of you men intend to kill this old man, but he may die of a heart attack and you'll be guilty of murder just the same." At that point a few of the men began to move back toward their cars and in a matter of minutes they were all gone except the farmer who had brought me out. The judge had come to by that time. We got him into his clothes and took him back into town. The next day the governor declared martial law in Plymouth County. The National Guard arrived and stayed two months. And that brought an end to the Farmers' Holiday movement in Plymouth County.[33]

Starzl was convinced, as am I after examining the available evidence, that the mob never had any intentions of lynching Bradley. It is, of course, possible that they might have been carried to that extreme by the momentum of their own previous actions. But in actuality, they were acting out a kind of medieval allegorical play, a drama to provide catharsis for all their fears and frustration. Or to put it in a more modern context, the Bradley incident is not unlike the guerrilla theatre device used by youthful protesters of the Viet Nam war in the 1970s. It may have been that what saved Bradley's life was the fact that he too entered into the drama and played out his passion role of crucifixion with utter conviction.

The Bradley incident did indeed kill the Holiday movement. Reno and the other farm leaders were appalled and mortified as were nearly all farmers. No serious additional acts of violence erupted in the corn belt. Yet it is an ironic comment on society that these isolated acts of spontaneous and seemingly purposeless protest perhaps did more to place the agricultural relief problem at the top of the New Deal's agenda for action than had all the conferences, programs, and platforms of the various farm and political organizations combined. Within the first hundred days of the New Deal the farmer got the Emergency Farm Mortgage Act, the Farm Credit Act for short term loans, the Agricultural Adjustment Act, and the Frazier-Lemke Bankruptcy Act. With this legislation, the farmers within three months had got from the New Deal all that they had sought for the past thirteen years. And what price did the farmers have to pay for all this? Enforced limitation on their production, the redefinition of agriculture as a free enterprise activity, and bureaucratic conformity were the price tags. Far too high a cost, shrieked old Milo Reno. Embittered by Wallace's rejection of his ill-defined formula of cost of production plus, without any limitation upon production, and by Roosevelt's refusal to accept an unlimited inflation of the currency, Reno tried to lead his farmers out of the New Deal into a new political allegiance. But Reno had only old slogans and worn rhe-

---

33. Interview with Rome Starzl, Le Mars, Iowa, July 1955.

toric to offer the farmers. Wallace had government checks and the assurance of continued land tenure security. The issue was never in doubt.

Along with the checks, the government also provided an answer to the third question that society had asked of the farmers in 1920. The government told the Iowa farmers who they were. In the modern alien world of big business and big labor, farmers of necessity had to be dependents of big government. Only direct government intervention would enable the individual farmer to survive. It was not the answer the yeoman farmer would have liked, but survival in the modern world had become of far greater importance than self identity in a world that was now forever lost. The farmers willingly accepted the government reins along with their United States federal treasury checks.

BIBLIOGRAPHICAL NOTE

For agricultural unrest in Iowa in the 1920s and 1930s, see Lowell Dyson, "Was Agricultural Distress in the 1930s a Result of Land Speculation during World War I? The Case of Iowa," *Annals of Iowa* 40 (1971), 577–84; idem, *Red Harvest: The Communist Party and American Farmers* (Lincoln, NE, 1982); Rodney Karr, "Farmer Rebels in Plymouth County, Iowa, 1932–1933," *Annals of Iowa* 48 (1985), 637–45; Theodore Saloutos and John D. Hicks, *Agricultural Discontent in the Middle West, 1900–1939* (Madison, WI, 1951); and John L. Shover, *Cornbelt Rebellion: The Farmers' Holiday Association* (Urbana, IL, 1965). William C. Pratt assesses the recent literature in "Rethinking the Farm Revolt of the 1930s," *Great Plains Quarterly* 8 (1988), 131–44. For a gendered perspective on the Farmers' Holiday, see Leslie A. Taylor, "Femininity as Strategy: A Gendered Perspective on the Farmers' Holiday," *Annals of Iowa* 51 (1992), 252–77; compare William C. Pratt, "Women and the Farm Revolt of the 1930s," *Agricultural History* 67 (1993), 214–23.

Milo Reno and the Iowa Farmers' Union await their historian. On the National Farmers' Union, see John A. Crampton, *The National Farmers Union: Ideology of a Pressure Group* (Lincoln, NE, 1965); and William P. Tucker, "Populism Up-to-Date: The Story of the Farmers Union," *Agricultural History* 21 (October 1947), 198–208. For an insider's perspective on the Iowa Farm Bureau, see Robert P. Howard, *James R. Howard and the Farm Bureau* (Ames, 1983). For the role of the Iowa State Extension Service, see Dorothy Schwieder, *Seventy-Five Years of Service: Cooperative Extension in Iowa* (Ames, 1993).

An outstanding account of agricultural politics in these decades is David E. Hamilton, *From New Day to New Deal: American Farm Policy from Hoover to Roosevelt, 1928–1933* (Chapel Hill, NC, 1991). See also James Shideler, *Farm Crisis, 1919–1923* (Berkeley, CA, 1957); Donald Winters, *Henry Cantwell Wallace as Secretary of Agriculture, 1921–1924* (Urbana, IL, 1970); Gilbert C. Fite, *George N. Peek and the Fight for Farm Parity* (Norman, OK, 1954); Peter T. Harstad and Bonnie Lindemann, *Gilbert N. Haugen: Norwegian-American Farm Politician* (Iowa City, 1992); Joan Hoff Wilson, "Hoover's Agricultural Policies, 1921–1928," *Agricultural History* 51 (1977), 335–61; Martin L. Fausold,

"President Hoover's Farm Policies, 1929–1933," ibid., 362–77; Gary H. Koerselman, "Secretary Hoover and National Farm Policy: Problems of Leadership," ibid., 378–95; Theodore Saloutos, *The American Farmer and the New Deal* (Ames, 1982); Michael W. Schuyler, *The Dread of Plenty: Agricultural Relief Activities of the Federal Government in the Middle West, 1933–1939* (Manhattan, KS, 1989); and Richard S. Kirkendall, *Social Scientists and Farm Politics in the Age of Roosevelt* (Columbia, MO, 1967). For an interesting account of how New Deal policies played out in one rural community, see D. Jerome Tweton, *The New Deal at the Grass Roots: Programs for the People in Otter Tail County, Minnesota* (St. Paul, MN, 1988); that account might serve as a model for other local historians. For a fascinating contemporary analysis of the impact of New Deal relief programs on residents of Dubuque, see Jessie A. Bloodworth and Elizabeth J. Greenwood, *The Personal Side* (1939; reprint, New York, 1971).

Frank Yoder, "Staying on the Farm: Surviving the Great Depression in an Iowa Township, 1920–1950," *Annals of Iowa* 51 (1991), 53–78, combined statistical analysis of deed transfers with a close look at the lived experiences of three families in one Iowa township to determine farm families' strategies for holding on to their land through the Great Depression. For a personal perspective on the struggle to survive in rural Iowa in the 1930s, see *Years of Struggle: The Farm Diary of Elmer C. Powers, 1931–1936*, ed. H. Roger Grant and L. Edward Purcell (1976; reprint, De Kalb, IL, 1995). For a detailed account of state legislation to provide relief to those in danger of farm mortgage foreclosure, see Patrick B. Bauer, "Farm Mortgagor Relief Legislation in Iowa during the Great Depression," *Annals of Iowa* 50 (1989), 23–62.

Scholars in recent years have practically made a cottage industry out of studying Iowan Henry A. Wallace. Richard S. Kirkendall is working on what promises to be the definitive biography of Wallace. For now, see Russell Lord, *The Wallaces of Iowa* (Boston, 1947); Edward L. Schapsmeier and Frederick H. Schapsmeier, *Henry A. Wallace of Iowa: The Agrarian Years, 1910–1940* (Ames, 1968); idem, *Prophet in Politics: Henry A. Wallace and the War Years, 1940–1965* (Ames, 1973); Norman D. Markowitz, *The Rise and Fall of the People's Century: Henry A. Wallace and American Liberalism, 1941–1948* (New York, 1973); and Graham White and John Maze, *Henry A. Wallace: His Search for a New World Order* (Chapel Hill, NC, 1995). Richard S. Kirkendall has published several significant articles on Wallace; see, for example, "Henry A. Wallace's Turn toward the New Deal, 1921–1924," *Annals of Iowa* 49 (1988), 221–39, and the very interesting gender analysis he coauthored with Glenda Riley, "Henry A. Wallace and the Mystique of the Farm Male, 1921–1933," *Annals of Iowa* 48 (1985), 32–55. In addition, the Fall 1983 issue of the *Annals of Iowa* is devoted entirely to essays—in addition to the two presented here—on Wallace and his relationship to agriculture by Leland L. Sage, Richard S. Kirkendall, William L. Brown, and Lauren Soth; and the Summer 1988 issue of the *Annals of Iowa* is devoted to articles by Mark R. Finlay and William C. Pratt on Wallace's 1948 campaign for the presidency on the Progressive Party ticket and to an account by Wilson J. Warren of efforts by Fred Stover and others to enact in Iowa Wallace's vision of the "People's

Century" by building coalitions among farm and labor organizations. For a fascinating account balancing competing perspectives on Wallace's controversial spiritual explorations, see Mark L. Kleinman, "Searching for the 'Inner Light': The Development of Henry A. Wallace's Experimental Spiritualism," *Annals of Iowa* 53 (1994), 195–218.

14

World War II and Rural Women

Deborah Fink

Historians of women's experience have generally identified wartimes as watersheds in transforming women's roles in American society. Deborah Fink shows in this essay the opportunities that World War II opened up for rural Iowa women, but she also cautions, as Elizabeth Leonard does in her essay on Annie Wittenmyer's Civil War experience, that the lasting benefits of those opportunities and experiences can be overestimated.

> Whoever you talk to, wherever you go, the talk is about the boys.[1]

ELIZABETH WHERRY, a rural Iowa woman with a son in the service during World War II, wrote this line in her "Country Air" column, a weekly feature of *Wallaces' Farmer*. From 1941 to 1945, news of the war appeared on virtually every page of this popular Iowa farm journal, in the form of editorials, letters from readers, articles, or advertisements. In Open Country, support for World War II and especially for the local "boys" in the service was a *sine qua non*; other issues became secondary concerns against this central goal. Just as with the rest of American society at this time, World War II permeated nearly all aspects of Open Country life. In addition to reading war news in *Wallaces' Farmer*, Open Country people read about the war in other magazines and newspapers and heard about it at extension lessons, on the radio, and in church.

Not only did Open Country people hear about the war, but they also had to change long-established routines because of it. Sugar, meat, coffee, and canned goods rationing affected daily shopping, cooking, and eating patterns. Building materials and farm machinery rationing meant that farm profits could not be reinvested automatically. Nearly every family was potentially affected by the draft. Seemingly insignificant actions assumed a real or imagined mean-

---

1. Elizabeth Wherry, "Country Air," *Wallaces' Farmer* 70 (1945), 145.

Reprinted from *Open Country, Iowa: Rural Women, Tradition and Change,* by Deborah Fink by permission of the State University of New York Press. Copyright © 1986 State University of New York. In order to protect the identities of research subjects, pseudonyms, such as Open Country (a rural area in northwestern Iowa), are used, even in the footnotes, for most of the proper names used in the essay.

ing from the war perspective. Loitering in the lobby of the post office was forbidden. The owner of Center's telephone exchange reported that federal agents visited him during the war to ascertain whether there was spying or treason in the telephone conversations of Open Country people.

World War II brought the outside world to the people of Open Country and gave them a sense of participation in a major global event. Henry A. Wallace, President Franklin Roosevelt's Secretary of Agriculture during the Depression, became Vice President in 1941. Being part of the Iowa family which published *Wallaces' Farmer*, his prominence enhanced the connection between Iowa and Washington. Indeed, the war made sense: it connected seemingly disparate events and gave coherence to disjointed elements of rural life. Even something as ordinary and familiar as an egg was suddenly connected to the war: "An egg on an Iowa farm can be turned into a weapon of war when dried and shipped overseas to feed our army, allies, or civilians behind the lines who—in exchange for food—do work."[2] In contrast to the sense of isolation from the rest of the world that farm people felt previously, war conditions made local events significant in the larger picture.

The war was not an unmitigated hardship. Farmers, plagued with surpluses and low prices in the 1930s, increased production and received higher prices for their products during the war years. Prosperity on the farm was good for rural Main Street, as town business grew in spite of rationing. Moreover, with the federal government's concern for wartime farm problems, Open Country people felt that the United States as a whole was on their side and wanted the same things they wanted. The enemy was outside the country, and rural people joined with city people in pursuit of a common goal.

On the farms as in the cities, the war effected a major recovery from the Depression, and this recovery occurred even before the United States was an official participant. Total Iowa farm income increased 12 percent from 1939 to 1940, attaining its highest level in 10 years. The Iowa State Department of Agriculture made the following assessment in 1940:

> Exceptional and widespread expansion of business throughout the United States was recorded during 1940. The wars of the other continents provided the impetus for the upswing of activities and from the beginning of the year the export demand for war materials was a major dynamic factor. Both government and industrial resources were marshalled toward a huge military defense program, which overshadowed all else in the business situation. . . .
>
> The general position of agriculture improved materially in 1940. Increased acreage over that of 1939 and substantially improved yields during 1940 resulted in the best harvests since 1937, and livestock production attained a new record volume. With higher farm prices and larger marketings, the aggregate cash farm income rose nearly half a billion dollars despite smaller government payments than in 1939.[3]

---

2. "Food Wins Battles," *Wallaces' Farmer* 68 (1943), 473.
3. Iowa State Department of Agriculture, *Iowa Year Book of Agriculture* (Des Moines, 1940), 10–11.

TABLE 14.1
VALUE* OF OPEN COUNTRY FARM PRODUCE SOLD OR TRADED, 1939–1949

Year	All Produce	Livestock	Poultry	Dairy	Crops
1939	$ 7.1	$ 3.6	$ .3	$ .5	$2.6
1944	15.5	10.1	1.2	1.1	3.0
1949	22.8	15.0	1.5	1.2	5.1

*Values expressed in millions of dollars.
SOURCE: U.S. agricultural censuses.

In the words of Willard Cochrane, "The miracle for which farm people were waiting took the form of World War II."[4] The war brought record production and the highest levels of income ever experienced on Iowa farms.[5] By virtually any measure, Iowa farmers did well. The total value of Open Country farm produce increased from $7.1 million in 1939 to $15.5 million in 1944 to $22.8 million in 1949 (see Table 14.1). The value of the average Open Country farm increased from $19,358 in 1940 to $43,108 in 1950.[6] The influx of money had a snowballing effect: increased income meant that the majority of farmers now gained access to hybrid seed corn and power machinery that was beyond their reach during the Depression. As new technology came within their grasp it in turn led to higher production and higher incomes.

Farm production was a specific and crucial part of the war machine. While urban industries were producing ships, tanks, and fighter aircraft, farms were producing food and other raw materials, also essential to the war effort. The USDA related most directly to the war effort on the farm, specifically through the extension network, where it had its separate channels and specific mode of relating to farm people. Thus, the war messages that reached the farms were different in substance and style from those given to the urban population. Parallels are found, however, in the gender specificity of these appeals. Just as in cities, women heard appeals to their patriotism, to their loyalty toward servicemen and to their spirit of self-sacrifice. Just as in urban industry, a good woman did her war work, not for wealth or status, but because it was the least she could do in the face of the supreme male investment in the war. So, on the farm as in the city, because men and women were different, their contributions were different, as were their incentives. Concomitantly, due to the different war experiences, men's claims to the fruits of victory were qualitatively different from women's claims.

---

4. Willard W. Cochrane, *The Development of American Agriculture: A Historical Analysis* (Minneapolis, 1979), 124.

5. Iowa State Department of Agriculture, *Iowa Year Book of Agriculture* (Des Moines, 1946), 17.

6. United States Department of Commerce, Bureau of the Census (hereafter cited as Census Bureau), *Sixteenth Census of the United States: 1940. Agriculture* (Washington, DC, 1942), 1:130; Census Bureau, *U.S. Census of Agriculture: 1950. Counties and State Economic Areas. Iowa*, vol. 1, part 9 (Washington, DC, 1952), 43.

ONE LUCAS COUNTY, IOWA, FARM WOMAN summarized the way she met the war demands: "I have done chores, worked in fields, raised bigger gardens, canned more food and helped with Red Cross work ever since the war began."[7]

Home economics extension, the government's voice in rural homes, covered a broad spectrum of topics during the war. In terms of their duties as housewives, women were responsible for producing healthy potential war workers and soldiers while consuming the fewest resources possible in the process. Women had to redouble their efforts to make do with less in order to free as much labor and produce as possible for the war.

Extension home economists taught women nutrition, which helped them prepare balanced meals so that only a minimal amount of food was diverted from the war effort. They pressed women to raise victory gardens, which enabled them to supply even more of their own vegetables. They taught women home safety and home nursing, which enabled them to care for their own households rather than use professional health workers who were needed in the military. They taught women how to manage household accounts, which in turn created a surplus that could be invested in war bonds. They taught women to care for clothing, thereby minimizing the need for production in the civilian sector.

Extension's Food for Freedom program enlisted special cooperators for every four square miles of rural area, through whom extension blanketed the country with a nationwide network, similar to a telephone tree, that relayed special appeals to all rural families. This program elicited a high degree of cooperation. In Floyd County, Iowa, for example, after a drive to encourage people to use enriched flour and bread, the local agent determined that seven out of eight families received the information and one-half of those families changed to enriched or whole wheat flour or bread within three weeks.[8] As incentives, the extension service presented awards and certificates to the most effective neighborhood leaders.

The war ethos crept into every corner of extension work and turned all of its activities into avenues of support for the war. In 1942, the Open Country Home Demonstration Agent planned an Achievement Day with the theme, "Food Will Win the War and Write the Peace." Township exhibits included "Carrots for Victory," "Vitamins for Victory," and "Whole Wheat for Vitamins and Victory." Rural newspapers across the state constantly reported on victory garden projects, and canning and nutrition classes focused on wartime food programs.

For an article entitled "How Farm Women Help," *Wallaces' Farmer* solicited replies to the question of what women were doing for the war effort,

---

7. "War Jobs at Home," *Wallaces' Farmer* 70 (1945), 232.

8. Meredith Wilson, *Progress of the Neighborhood Leader Plan*, Extension Service Circular 393 (Washington, DC, 1942), 6.

following the established pattern of using the word *help* to signify women's work. The journal received letters from women stating that they did more field work, less housework, canned more fruits and vegetables, and took care of older people in their own homes rather than having others do it. They adjusted time spent visiting and meeting in clubs so as not to interfere with farm work, and they sewed sheets and pillow cases from feed sacks.[9] The war gave farm women a new reason to work hard, to take care of their own families, and to be thrifty.

Due to accelerated mechanization and the rural labor surplus during the Depression, the possibility of a labor shortage was not taken seriously at first. Draft boards selected farmers and hired men, and other men left of their own accord either to enlist in the service or to pursue better paying jobs offered in war industries. As the war continued, the combination of military demands on the heavy equipment industry with the increased demands for farm equipment brought rationing of farm machinery. Although a steady increase in the number of tractors and combines was seen during the war, this increase was not enough to meet the demands. Converging conditions of expanded production, machinery shortage, and the outflow of men all helped to change the farm operation drastically. In 1943, for the first time during the war, farm labor was in dangerously short supply. Hired workers' wages soared and these workers were hard to find at any price.[10]

In the face of the impending breakdown of the farm production system, the government sought ways to keep farm men on the farm, and private businesses helped their efforts with advertising. After 1943, local draft boards more frequently opted to give draft deferments to farmers and hired men, thereby keeping more farmers at home and underscoring the importance of farming as a war industry. As an incentive for men to stay on the farms, Food for Freedom awarded "Certificates for War Service" to 200,000 (male) Iowa farmers to help counter any derogatory remarks they received for not enlisting in the armed service.[11] One advertisement in *Wallaces' Farmer* appealed to the farmer as "A Soldier on the Food Production Front." An advertisement for coffee urged farm women to make Folger's coffee for their men to drink because, "They're on the job every day—sometimes eighteen or twenty hours. America appreciates their work."[12] The awards to and recognition of farm men encouraged them to think that their work was as valuable as that of soldiers, even if they never saw actual combat.

The forthcoming draft deferments and the varied forms of economic and moral encouragement for farm men to continue farming notwithstanding, farm labor remained in critically short supply. Planners began to seek other labor

---

9. "How Farm Women Help," *Wallaces' Farmer* 68 (1943), 84.
10. *Cherokee Times*, 22 June 1943.
11. *Des Moines Register*, 26 May 1943; *Cherokee Times*, 22 June 1943.
12. *Wallaces' Farmer* 68 (1943), 177; *Wallaces' Farmer* 70 (1945), 232.

power elsewhere with farm women among the first to be considered a labor reserve. A survey by the extension service discovered that by 1943 80 percent of Iowa's farm women were doing daily farm chores as compared to 60 percent in 1941.[13] In one of her 1943 "Country Air" columns, Elizabeth Wherry estimated that the average Iowa farm had eight hours of work in simply maintaining a diversified livestock operation. Family members shared the work with a hired worker: two men fed the animals and cleaned the stalls, children helped milk and carry wood, and the woman tended the poultry and separated the cream.[14] A *Wallaces' Farmer* survey found that in addition to increased gardening and canning, 13 percent of the farm women drove trucks and tractors and 29 percent did "lots more" with livestock chores.[15] More women were doing farm work and some women who had done farm work before the war were doing more during the war. This pattern was an intensification of the prewar work of farm women; it did not break any new ground. It was similar to that described generally in reports of women's farm work across the country.[16]

In doing field work, operating machinery, and handling large livestock, farm women were indeed doing "men's work." They also increased their "women's work." In 1942, the government called for an increase of 200 million dozen eggs, or about 13 percent more than in 1941. Unlike the jobs women took over from men, poultry work had always been done by women and as such, the women were the recognized poultry experts—at least at the local level. The country now needed this poultry expertise for the war effort. *Wallaces' Farmer* joined the government in disseminating extension service poultry management advice, including labor-saving techniques, plans for feed efficiency, and instructions for makeshift chicken houses. As before, the *Wallaces' Farmer* poultry material was written as if the primary poultry producers were women, although they urged the women to persuade their husbands to help if extra hands were needed.[17] Advertisements and pictures accompanying articles about poultry showed women. A section of the weekly poultry column called "Sarah Jane Says" was written by an anonymous woman who gave a cheerful, optimistic, and amusing, but educational, running account of the practical problems she encountered with her egg operation during the war years.[18] This was women's work and the model for coping was a woman.

---

13. United States Department of Agriculture (hereafter cited as USDA), *National Summary of Inquiry into Changes in the World of Farm Women and Girls Caused by War Labor Shortages*, Extension Service Circular 395 (Washington, DC, 1942), 4.

14. Elizabeth Wherry, "Country Air," *Wallaces' Farmer* 68 (1943), 19.

15. "War Jobs at Home," *Wallaces' Farmer* 70 (1945), 232.

16. USDA, *National Summary of Inquiry*, 4; "How Farm Women Help," 84.

17. Arthur T. Thompson, "Also Let's Keep 'Em A-Laying," *Wallaces' Farmer* 67 (1942), 61.

18. See, for example, "The Farm Flock," *Wallaces' Farmer* 67 (1942), 442.

Chicken and cream enterprises had long been managed by women, but even increased wartime tasks did not qualify them for general farm management. A newspaper story illustrating women's farm work told of a farmer whose son was in the service and who had his work done by his daughter, who was married to a serviceman:

> "Her mother and I would have been in a spot without her," Mr. Martsching declares. "I left all the driving of the tractor to John—I didn't even drive the family car. I worked only on the jobs where horses could be used."
>
> Marie . . . has disked for oats, disked corn stalks, plowed for corn and beans. In addition she is raising 1,000 chickens, a garden and is now milking eight of the 18 cows night and morning.
>
> All winter she drove the farm truck, hauling grain to the elevator and coal and other necessities to the farm.[19]

Here was a woman doing many of the men's and women's tasks that were required on a farm, while her father was not able even to drive a tractor. Yet the father remained the farm manager and the one who served as spokesman to the reporter. The extension service in Iowa developed a program to give women instructions in farm business management so they could run the farms without men,[20] but I found no record of any woman who actually took over management of a farm as a result of the war.

With intensified work both outside and inside the house, farm women naturally felt considerable stress. In 1943, Elizabeth Wherry wrote in "Country Air":

> Apparently, it takes each group a long time to appreciate its own sacrifice and responsibility. It isn't that I can't see farm women doing the work that lies before them. The thing that alarms me is whether they can keep their health and add one single more chore to their full days. The big problem is whether there can be recruited from the towns enough woman-power to take over some of their work.[21]

Yet the planners, slow to consider women as real workers, were also slow to acknowledge that women who worked made real sacrifices and that there was nothing trivial about that work. A 1943 *Wallaces' Farmer* poultry article stated, "The main problem in raising more chickens is not labor—the women and children say they'll supply that—but housing."[22] Only women's and children's labor was taken for granted. Implicit herein was the assumption that men's labor was scarce and valuable but that other sources of labor were plentiful and waiting to be tapped. In spite of Elizabeth Wherry's warning of exhaustion among farm women, women's labor seems to have been treated

---

19. *Des Moines Register*, 12 May 1943.
20. USDA, *Farm Women on the Home Front,* Extension Service Circular 390 (Washington, DC, 1942), 6.
21. Elizabeth Wherry, "Country Air," *Wallaces' Farmer* 68 (1943), 86.
22. "More Chicks This Year," *Wallaces' Farmer* 68 (1943), 118.

as a separate, unquantifiable resource. As before the war, neither men nor women really saw men's and women's work in the same way. A farm woman who picked corn said, "I'm never fully accepted at corn picking. It is 'man work.' Remarks such as 'the All-American Drawback' or 'Handicap' reach my ears."[23]

In spite of the conceptual separation of women's farm work, their increased farm earnings were real. With rising demand, egg prices increased by 140 percent from 1940 to 1943.[24] Income from livestock, dairy, and crops all showed increases, but Open Country's five fold increase in gross income from poultry production from 1939 to 1944 was the most pronounced (see Table 14.1). This increased poultry income went almost entirely to farm women. For the first time, women began to keep written records of egg and cream income. Rose, a farm woman, left an extensive record of her income from poultry and cream sales, coupled with detailed notes about her expenditures during the war years. Not only was she able to purchase the necessary food and other items consumed in her household, but her record also showed a substantial surplus. The following sample month's income and expenditures for October 1943 illustrates a typical wartime farm household economy. Rose's purchases included:

Oct. 2	hired help	$ 5.00
Oct. 2	pills	1.80
Oct. 2	groceries	5.60
Oct. 2	miscellaneous	2.00
Oct. 2	rug and picture	12.00
Oct. 9	telephone	7.94
Oct. 9	groceries	8.00
Oct. 16	groceries	4.50
Oct. 23	groceries, miscellaneous	4.75
Oct. 25	daughter, birthday	10.00
Oct. 30	groceries	10.50
Oct. 30	son, Christmas present	5.00
	Total	$77.09

Her receipts for this month totalled $126.87, from which she paid for her own hired help and any other expenses for her poultry operation that arose. Shopping on Saturdays, she purchased such things as food, medicine, and household furnishings. Throughout the war years she frequently bought things such as furniture and wallpaper for her home; she paid for a daughter's wedding; and she paid for her chicken feed, chicks, fencing, and equipment. She was also paying the telephone bill and buying presents for her children. Her purchases seem to have been aimed at enhancing her social status and in cementing ties with her children, both of which might have represented an

---

23. Margaret Noll, "When I Husk Corn," *Wallaces' Farmer* 70 (1945), 860.

24. USDA, Crop Reporting Board, *Prices Received by Farmers for Chickens, Turkeys, and Eggs*, Statistical Bulletin No. 357 (Washington, DC, 1965), 130.

investment in her long-term security, but no indication is found that she was seeking to accumulate her own farm capital.

In 1943, she earned $1,541.17 and spent $963.54. Her $577.63 surplus was not unusual during the war, and it represented a modest sum which was entirely hers to spend or invest. She bought her children a total of $663.75 in government bonds over the war years. Even with these extras, she still had a surplus of several hundred dollars and her record does not indicate what she did with this money. A woman featured in *Wallaces' Farmer* as having an exceptional egg operation made $1,119 from eggs alone in 1942.[25] This amount afforded her a surplus beyond what she used in the farm home. Such surpluses, if they continued, might have put farm women in a position to make real choices about what they wanted for themselves and their children.

Even though women put a great deal of effort into wartime farm production and, in some cases, reaped modest profits from this effort, the reality was that women and children could not stretch themselves indefinitely. Wartime farm production demanded increasing labor input from outside the farm population. Food for Victory (a program sponsored by the U.S. Employment Service, the Iowa Farm Bureau Federation, and the USDA's War Board) worked to recruit this labor. The program established county farm labor advisory boards, and each local board was responsible for assessing labor needs, advising on labor efficiency, canvassing schools and townspeople for farm labor, and placing workers. The Open Country board publicized appeals, canvassed and eventually secured several hundred additional farm workers. In 1943, it recruited 143 men and 38 women farm workers.[26]

Much farm work could not, however, be done by any willing worker and some farmers were unhappy with the inexperienced recruits, particularly women, who wanted to work for them. Yet women's labor was needed and some women did find farm employment doing what previously had been men's work. As a speaker at a state meeting of the Iowa Federation of Women's Clubs said, "Women offering to go on the farms do face lack of co-operation from the farmers, but I believe that when the need really arises they will be glad to have part-time workers."[27] The exceptions notwithstanding, men remained the preferred workers; the county boards recruited men first and most vigorously.

Still, women could perform some tasks better than the resident male workers. Detasseling seed corn was one. Producing hybrid seed corn requires a short period each summer of hot, uncomfortable, and boring work removing tassels from corn so it will not pollinate itself. In 1943, the seed companies needed 8000 workers for detasseling and no regular male workers were available. Across Iowa, war prisoners, Menomini Indians, Mexicans, Japanese-Americans, Haitians, and conscientious objectors were formed into detasseling crews.

---

25. "They'll Get More Eggs Now," *Wallaces' Farmer* 68 (1943), 219.
26. Open Country Extension, Annual Narrative Report, County Extension Activities, 1943.
27. *Des Moines Register,* 6 May 1943.

Women also did detasseling. One newspaper said: "All a woman needs to do the job . . . is a desire to perform a patriotic service and the willingness to work for good pay (from $4 to $5 a day for a period of two weeks to a month)."[28] In Open Country, 160 boys and girls earned 50 cents per hour plus a bonus for detasseling in 1943.[29]

Jobs as field hands, which most rural people saw as slightly stigmatizing for women before the war, became more fashionable as a war service. Women found general affirmation and support for this work when it was done in the context of patriotism and sacrifice. The USDA modeled a Women's Land Army, consisting mainly of nonfarm women, after a similar body established in England. Universities offered special short courses to teach women farming skills. Not only were nonfarm women willing to do farm work, city women who became farm workers were portrayed as spunky and attractive as they lent their energy to wartime farming. Far from threatening women's feminity, farm work could be healthy, invigorating, and beautifying so that even glamorous women wanted to do it. Emergency women workers received a special insignia and a "highly practical, and at the same time becoming [outfit of] well-fitting dark blue denim overalls."[30] Camp Fire Girls, Girl Scouts, YWCA, and numerous smaller urban organizations similarly recruited women and girls for farm work.

Women also did more "men's work" in town. In spite of shortages and rationing, the farm recovery brought money and jobs to rural towns. The first resource for handling the extra volume of commerce was the labor of women within the family. Elizabeth Wherry, whose husband had taken a town job and moved the family to town for a period, reported on town women's war efforts in "Country Air":

> Mostly, the small-town woman has contributed thru being a two-sided person. In the first place, there is practically no by-the-day help any more, few handy men to be hired for odd jobs, and not enough reliable high school boys for the after-school jobs.
>
> On top of that, most women with husbands in business are busy keeping books and taking orders coming in over the counter. They go home to prepare an occasional meal or go to the restaurant, often coming back downtown at night to unpack goods or restock shelves — if there's any stock.
>
> In our town, the undertaker's wife is on call at all times. The barber's wife runs his beauty parlor. The wife of the druggist and the wives of both hardware merchants are practically full-time clerks and bookkeepers. Both coal yards have housewives in their offices. Two feed-store wives keep books or keep store. The post-master's wife pinch-hits during the busy half of the day.[31]

---

28. *Toledo Chronicle*, 15 July 1943.
29. Open Country Extension, Annual Narrative Report, County Extension Activities, 1943.
30. Florence Hall, "They're Getting in the Crops," *Independent Woman* 22 (1943), 216.
31. Elizabeth Wherry, "Country Air," *Wallaces' Farmer* 70 (1945), 233.

Women's small-scale home industries continued. As in the 1930s, town women did laundry, cared for children and the elderly, kept boarders, and styled hair in their homes to earn small incomes. In addition to writing about the commercial activities of town women, Wherry casually mentioned that two nights a week, and occasionally on Sunday, four teachers boarded at her home, in addition to a regular full-time boarder.

Besides helping their husbands and working at home, town women found that the war brought a number of new and reclaimed paying jobs for them. Married women teachers, dismissed during the Depression, found that with the shortage of men they had a chance to regain their lost jobs. Although their return to teaching was partially thwarted by the ongoing consolidation of rural schools, once again married women became a significant percentage of the teaching force. A small number of war-related jobs were available to women through the local political patronage system. Ardith, who lost her job as principal of Center High School at the outbreak of the Depression, was tapped to work in the rationing office. Another woman was named to a job with the Iowa Board of Control where she placed orphans in northwest Iowa counties. Open Country extension service hired two women to run the office which placed farm workers.

The majority of nonfarm women did volunteer work through a variety of organizations, all of which oriented their agendas toward addressing war conditions. Many women voluntarily sacrificed to meet needs of men who were in positions of hardship because of the war. Women's church groups, which previously focused on such projects as church upkeep, visiting invalids, and mission work, cancelled church suppers because of rationing and focused their attention on the war. The Farmtown Presbyterian Women's Guild replaced its annual Christmas party and gift exchange with an offering taken for a "War Service Fund." Church women packaged boxes of books, cookies, and personal articles for the servicemen of their congregations. The Red Cross distributed wool yarn to women who agreed to knit sweaters and mufflers for soldiers.[32]

The most important result of this volunteer work was in the broadened and diffused sense of purpose it bestowed on the women workers rather than in the practical benefits rendered to servicemen. D'Ann Campbell described the busywork developed by the Red Cross to involve women in its programs:

> The most spectacular waste of volunteer time was the Production Corps, which attracted 4 or 5 million women. Their job was to hand-knit millions of garments for soldiers and to roll billions of surgical dressings. The Red Cross vehemently denied that machines could do the job — arguing first that not enough factories could make dressings, then that the Army had specifically asked for their help, and finally that, though the machinery existed, a labor shortage prevented its utilization.[33]

---

32. *Open Country Bulletin,* 22 April 1942.

33. D'Ann Campbell, *Women at War with America: Private Lives in a Patriotic Era* (Cambridge, MA, 1984), 69.

Regardless of whether the women's work was a real necessity, wartime service organizations became a way to extract surplus value from women s unpaid work. Because of many women's general patriotism and concern for U.S. soldiers, they supported agencies that concentrated their resources for uses which they themselves only vaguely comprehended.

Beyond material work contribution, voices from all sides told women to strengthen home and community life so that the population would be mentally ready to dedicate itself to the war. As the Secretary of Agriculture Claude R. Wickard said in a speech, "Another thing that's up to the women is the matter of morale; holding the family together and keeping everyone cheerful in spite of difficulties."[34] Women frequently heard and read instructions on personal behavior that told them not to display the stereotypically female faults. According to an extension lesson, women needed to be calm, to contain fears rather than passing them on, to learn to accept sacrifices and losses without worry, self-pity and bitterness, to invest their increased war income into war bonds, and to be "facing changes without surprise and fear, to build up a sense of humor to meet trivial difficulties."[35] The League of Women Voters material submitted to the local newspaper asked each woman to vow to "curb my tongue, . . . not spread foolish stories, not criticize allies and not jump to hasty conclusions."[36]

The model woman was a mother or wife who gave moral and material support to her son or husband who was doing the real work of the war. A *Wallaces' Farmer* story told of a woman who raised poultry, but not for her own profit: "[She] has doubled her poultry production this year. She has a special reason for this increase. Her son Hilmar is in the army and may someday eat these eggs in powdered form."[37] Another woman who did farm work while her husband and brother were in the service disclaimed any credit for her contribution: "Work, she says, helps to keep her from thinking of the danger her husband, an officer on a flagship in the Pacific area, faces daily. "'I can't do enough to equal his service. I'm just trying to take my brother's place on the farm where I know I am needed.'"[38] When a 58-year-old woman helped detassel corn, the newspaper story related this to her role as a mother as it presented her as a model for other women: "[She] has five sons in service, four of them in the army and one in the navy. . . . She never detasseled corn before in her life, and altho she is 58 years of age, she said that this year was a good time to start. It is another way of doing her part to help win the war."[39] The ideal wartime woman worked without expecting any return other than the

---

34. Quoted in USDA, *Farm Women on the Home Front,* Extension Service Circular 390 (Washington, DC, 1942), 10.
35. *Open Country Bulletin,* 17 June 1942.
36. *Open Country Bulletin,* 15 April 1942.
37. *Wallaces' Farmer* 68 (1943), 118.
38. *Des Moines Register,* 12 May 1943.
39. *Grundy Center Register,* 29 July 1943.

satisfaction of knowing that she was supporting her men. Although she accepted the money that came to her, she did not question the amount. She did not seek rewards for herself; rather, she sought new ways that she could help.

The gender specificity in acceptable wartime goals becomes apparent when the configuration of appeals made to women is compared to those made to men. Enlisting in the military, besides being a patriotic duty, took a man around the world and showed him places and things he had never seen before; it was an opportunity. An Open Country school superintendent, commissioned as a naval officer, found that his training included radar instruction at Princeton University and further training at Massachusetts Institute of Technology. Affirming the superintendent's good fortune, the local newspaper editor wrote: "[He] said he was thrilled over his appointment and that it seemed like a dream too good to be true—getting to attend Princeton and M.I.T. both. His training in radar will be invaluable to him after the war."[40] A man did not risk public scorn for seeking his fortune in the war. He became a hero to local people, who followed his letters and news in weekly newspapers' special columns. Acceptable women were supportive and helpful; they did not seek personal gain or public recognition.

Some women left Open Country for jobs in industry or to join the military, but even those who left were encouraged to think in terms of sacrifice, not personal gain. A local notice of training opportunitites with stipends and living allowances for women learning aircraft construction ended with the statement, "No single and unattached trainees will be given subsistence," the implication being that a proper woman war worker was married and stable and that single women should not view the war as a chance to establish their independence or to seek adventures.[41]

Open Country women who responded to the pleas of the government for wartime service were entering a system that viewed men's activities, both on the battlefield and on the homefront, to be inherently more worthy. Contrary to the attitude toward men, the government valued women according to their usefulness, not as people who had intrinsic value and rights to work or to have their needs considered. While the wartime crisis happened differently in Open Country than in the cities, it must be considered in the context of a national and local spirit glorifying the male as warrior and subordinating the personhood of women.

ONE WAY of assessing the cumulative effects of World War II is to compare the situation in 1950 with that in 1940. The 1940s saw a significant movement of women from the farms, a movement not solely the result of the decline in the number of farms. In 1950, Open Country had 25 fewer farms than in 1940, but Table 14.2 indicates a decline of 472 adult women on farms. In spite of

---

40. *Open County Bulletin,* 18 August 1943.
41. *Open Country Bulletin,* 11 March 1942.

TABLE 14.2
NUMBER OF OPEN COUNTRY WOMEN OLDER THAN AGE 14, 1940–1950

Year	Farm	Nonfarm	Total
1940	2,899	2,698	5,597
1950	2,427	2,869	5,296

SOURCE: U.S. population censuses.

the encouragement for women to be more interested in others' needs than in their own, some of the women were ready and willing to leave the area in search of better prospects elsewhere. In fact, women who did hard, grimy work on farms before the war fit in well with the "non-traditional" work found in urban war industries. Karen Beck Skold cited an Idaho farm woman who felt that her wartime job in a Portland shipyard was less grueling than the hard work and cold weather she endured on the farm.[42] The number of farm women in Open Country decreased 16 percent from 1940 to 1950, and part of this decline can be attributed to those who left for more promising careers and did not return after the war. About one-half of this migrating farm population can be accounted for in the increased number of women in Open Country towns.

The Open Country farm population decreased slightly in the 1930s, and this trend was intensified in the 1940s and later. As shown in Table 14.3, Iowa population statistics show a net decline in the farm population and an increase in both the urban and rural nonfarm populations, thereby indicating an overall urbanization process which the war intensified.

The war increased the mobility of the U.S. population. Further, it expanded the populations of coastal cities and major midwestern industrial cities such as Detroit and Chicago, while it drained the rural areas of Iowa. The Depression slowed the process of urbanization in Iowa, both because adults and children were needed for the survival of farms and because of the lack of opportunity elsewhere.[43] However, many farm youths were ready to leave as soon as they could. Curtis Harnack wrote of his mother's determination that her children not remain on the farm: "Almost mystically, she had a sense of launching us into the mainstream of future American life, for we would die if we remained where we were born."[44] Harnack, his siblings, and all but one cousin left in the war years and after. The future of American life did not lie in the backwaters of rural Iowa, and the war meant that many rural youths such as Harnack did not have to go home—and they did not.

The net decline of farm population is only a partial description of the demographic change. While many people were leaving the area, people were

---

42. Karen Beck Skold, "American Women in the Shipyards During World War II," in *Women, War, and Revolution,* ed. Carol R. Burkin and Clara M. Lovett (New York, 1980), 65.

43. Cochrane, *Development of American Agriculture,* 123.

44. Curtis Harnack, *We Have All Gone Away* (1973; Ames, reprint, 1981), 187.

TABLE 16.3
RURAL AND URBAN POPULATION OF IOWA, 1930–1950*

Residence	1930	1940	1950
Urban	979	1084	1251
Rural	1515	1454	1370
Nonfarm	527	537	587
Farm	985	917	783

*Figures expressed in thousands.
SOURCE: U.S. population censuses.

also moving into Open Country, particularly in the years immediately after the war. Martha, for example, was raised in a city in Ohio and met Henry, a young man from an Open Country farm, when they were both in school. Henry was drafted, but he kept in touch with Martha and saw her whenever his service schedule allowed. After Martha received her B.A. in biology, she and Henry were married while he was still in the service. Martha accepted a secretarial position in Philadelphia so that she could work and be near Henry. When Henry left the service, they moved to Ames, Iowa, where Henry finished college and Martha continued to work as a secretary. In 1949, they moved to Open Country, where Henry took over his parents' farm. His three sisters, who also grew up on the farm, had already left Open Country, married, and settled with their husbands in other states. Thus, while Henry returned to his farming roots, his three sisters moved. Martha, as a new wife, had none of the Open Country enculturation that her sisters-in-law had.

There were numerous similar cases of farmer-soldiers returning with wives who had no experience in farming. Farm women like Martha came from the world outside of Open Country. Conversely, one-time farm girls, like Henry's sisters, often left to study, work, marry, and settle outside of Open Country. This pattern, which came to prevail in postwar years, represented a major discontinuity in the kinship relations and in the practical and emotional attachment of farm women to farming. In fact, in 1950 the extension service listed the scarcity of local marriageable women in rural areas as a particular postwar farm problem.[45] Men had to seek wives outside their home communities. Whether as soldiers, students, workers, or travellers, men as well as women were reaching outside the community for marriage partners. In 1950, approximately 7 percent of the Open Country population had lived outside the county the previous year.[46] While determining the number of returning natives and the number of newcomers is impossible, if this degree of mobility held constant for 10 years, approximately 70 percent of the people

---

45. Iowa State Extension Service, *Plan of Work: Cooperative Extension Work in Agriculture and Home Economics* (Ames, 1950), A10.
46. Census Bureau, *County and City Data Book 1952* (Washington, DC, 1953), 103.

would have lived outside the county, and this would almost certainly include a substantial number of non-natives. A man who married outside the community and brought his wife home was the partner with the stronger community and family ties, while his wife usually came as a stranger to the community, with her only link being through her husband.

European and American history shows a patrilineal tendency in farm land inheritance.[47] After World War II, however, with farm daughters leaving in greater numbers, patrilineal inheritance produced a distinct "patrilocal" type of residence pattern, in which the husband was living close to his kin and the wife was often far removed from her kin. Both the nature of military service and the GI Bill, which gave veterans support for college educations after the war, in addition to the land inheritance system, reinforced the patriarchal custom by which married couples planned their lives according to the career development contingencies and the family imperatives of the men. The "imported" wife was a stranger in her husband's community, inexperienced in farming, and had scant extended kin ties within the community.

The degree of their involvement with the farm varied among the transplanted farm women. Martha, the city woman who came to Open Country as a wife in 1949, spent much of her time at Henry's side learning to be a farmer. One of the first tasks, in the coldest period of the winter they arrived, was to remove the dead trees from their shelterbelt. Martha, the only help that Henry had, was needed, and she *wanted* to be part of the farm operation. She read extension brochures and farm journals and relied heavily on the friendship and help of an older, more experienced farm woman, as well as a close circle of four transplanted wives who came to the community at the same time she did. She started her own poultry enterprise and did substantial work with other livestock. Other such women had less interest in doing farm work, but they were all called upon to run errands, drive tractors, help sort cattle, or help with other work when an extra pair of hands was needed. Indeed, Henry said that Martha had the advantage of not having the "bad habits" of some women who had grown up on the farm—she did not refuse to do any particular tasks because women in her family had never done them. Farm women continued to fill the void left by hired farm laborers and children who never returned after the war. Few of these women had jobs off the farm.

Among the Open Country women living on farms, the number working in nonfarm jobs dropped from 171 to 85 between 1940 and 1950.[48] Table 14.4 indicates that professional and domestic services experienced the greatest decreases. Part of the decrease can be attributed to escape. Working daughters

---

47. Bengt Ankarloo, "Agriculture and Women's Work: Directions of Change in the West, 1700–1900," *Journal of Family History* 4 (1979), 111–20; Carolyn E. Sachs, *The Invisible Farmers: Women in Agricultural Production* (Totowa, NJ, 1983).

48. Census Bureau, *Sixteenth Census of the United States: 1940. Population,* vol. 3, *The Labor Force,* part 3, *Iowa–Montana* (Washington, DC, 1943), 925; Census Bureau, *1950 Census of Population,* vol. 2, *Characteristics of the Population,* part 15, *Iowa* (Washington, DC, 1952), 137.

TABLE 16.4
CHANGE IN NUMBER OF OPEN COUNTRY FARM AND NONFARM WOMEN
WITH NONFARM EMPLOYMENT, 1940–1950

Occupation	Farm	Nonfarm
Professional	-27	-3
Managerial	-3	+9
Clerical, sales	+2	+82
Operatives	-5	+34
Domestic service	-72	-38
Other service	+1	+42
Other, unreported	+18	-1
Total	-86	+125
Percent change	-50%	+24%

SOURCE: U.S. population censuses.

who were forced by economic necessity to live at home during the Depression accumulated enough resources to leave during the war, and their families were no longer dependent on their incomes. The ongoing consolidation of rural schools decreased the need for rural teachers, who constituted the majority of the professional women living on farms before World War II. The most drastic decline, however, was in the number of domestic service workers living on farms, again reflecting the increasing nonfarm job opportunities for those women who were mobile. Some of the new Open Country women were, like Martha, busy learning farming and helping their husbands establish farm operations, and they are not counted as workers in any of the government's labor force statistics. These factors notwithstanding, the 50 percent decline in farm women in nonfarm employment is significant, particularly in light of the continuing improvement of highways and automotive transportation and the increasing number of farm women with nonfarm backgrounds. The conclusion that farm women were more universally identifying as wives and subsuming their work lives under that of their husbands is justified.

Compared to the prewar period, an increasing percentage of postwar farm women were married. Statistics regarding the marital status of Iowa farm women are not available for all of the census periods, but federal census figures indicate that 25 percent of Iowa farm women over age 15 had never been married in 1930, but the corresponding number was 15 percent in 1960. Considering only those women older than age 20, 5 percent of Iowa's farm women, compared to 11 percent of its nonfarm women, had never been married in 1960.[49]

---

49. Census Bureau, *Fifteenth Census of the United States, 1930. Population*, vol. 3, part 1, *Alabama–Missouri* (Washington, DC, 1932), 774; Census Bureau, *Census of the Population: 1960*, vol. 1, *Characteristics of the Population*, part 17, *Iowa* (Washington, DC, 1963), 342, 343.

For farm women, even more than for other women, the postwar family came to mean the nuclear family of husband, wife, and children. Their own parents and siblings lived elsewhere. In contrast to the prewar situation in which the nucleus of a farm woman's social circle was her extended kin network, the postwar farm woman's link to local society was through her husband and her in-laws. Thus, the husband found himself assuming not only a more central role in teaching his wife the farming trade, but he was also assuming some of the intimate emotional and social functions that had previously been in the domain of a woman's extended kin. More than ever, a wife expected her husband to be her best friend as well as a compatible business partner and companion. Those farm women who did not marry left for the towns and cities.

As illustrated in Table 14.4, Open Country town women increased their participation in nonfarm employment during the 1940s. As mentioned, part of this increase can be interpreted as the movement of employed women from the farm to town. The number of professional women, mainly teachers, living in town decreased, again a product of school consolidation and the general rural-to-urban population shift. Throughout the country, the number of domestic workers decreased drastically in response to the newly available industrial jobs. The number of women managers increased slightly and the number of women working in factories doubled. The increase in jobs for women in retail businesses is directly related to the thriving rural economy that the war brought in the form of the strengthened market for farm products.

The most striking trend was a concentration of women in clerical, sales, and other nonprofessional services, and it is consistent with the findings of Karen Anderson and Susan Hartmann, who described the postwar restructuring of the gender division in which women were concentrated in the service sector of the postwar labor force. While the overall number of women in the recognized labor force rose, the status of women as workers in the prestigious managerial and professional fields did not.[50]

The total number of Open Country farm and nonfarm women working off the farm rose by only 39 between 1940 and 1950. Adding one farm woman per farm to approximate the number of actual working women results in a substantially higher estimate of working women throughout the decade of the 1940s: 2,675 in 1940 and 2,689 in 1950, representing approximately 50 percent of the total number of working aged women. The major change was not that many women moved into the workforce, but rather that they shifted from self-employed farm work and professional jobs to service work.

The postwar extension service highlighted and elaborated its material on women's housekeeping. Rather than the wartime housekeeping advice on whole wheat flour and canning, the 1946 Open Country women's food and nutrition

---

50. Karen Anderson, *Wartime Women: Sex Roles, Family Relations, and the Status of Women During World War II* (Westport, CT, 1982); Susan Hartmann, *Home Front and Beyond: American Women in the 1940s* (Boston, 1982).

program featured a unit called "Gracious Family Living" that instructed women in how to plan a meal with "English Family Service," including appropriate table decor and etiquette. In the same year, the local women's program planning committee selected units on the better groomed homemaker, the home water supply, maintaining a standard of living, child development, care of equipment, salads, and preservation for the following year's work.[51] The Iowa State Home Economics circular series begun in 1948 had topics dealing with home decoration, cooking, sewing, entertaining, child rearing, grooming, dieting, consumer information, and laundry hints. Typical of the postwar focus on elaborate housekeeping was a 1950 circular entitled "Let's Do Dishes," which gave a detailed description of the proper way to wash dishes.[52]

None of these postwar extension themes reflected conditions specific to farm women. They seemed, instead, to constitute a denial that farm women did farm work and that their role in a family economy was in any way different from that of the majority of nonfarm women. Accordingly, in the years after World War II, home economics extension ceased to address only rural women and directed increasing resources toward reaching urban women.[53] As one extension circular maintained, home economics extension logically reached out to urban women because making a division between farm and city women's lives was no longer possible.[54] Extension clearly envisioned women spending most of their time and energy in the home and leaving the major part of the farm work to their husbands. This change of focus in women's extension promoted the removal from farming of even the diminished number of women who remained in residence on farms.

While women took care of the home after the war, men were in charge of the farming. Anderson and Hartmann, in separate analyses of the nontraditional work done by women in manufacturing industry during World War II, found that the majority of these women lost their jobs after the war. Rather than retreating from the labor force, however, women moved into an already overcrowded, poorly paid female sector of the labor market. Rather than welding and riveting, women were typing and clerking and doing other work that soon came to be associated with women.[55] Not only did a similar process occur in Open Country towns, a parallel development occurred among Open Country farm women. The women who stayed on the farms expanded and intensified their work as farmers during the war, but this ended with the war. While no valid statistics are available comparing farm women's work with that

---

51. Open Country Extension, Annual Narrative Report, County Extension Activities, 1946.

52. M. Kagerice, "Let's Do Dishes," Home Economics Circular HE-17 (Ames, 1950).

53. Amelia S. Gordy and Gladys S. Gallup, *Progress in Home Demonstration Work: A Statistical Analysis of Trends, 1910–1950,* USDA Extension Service Circular 479 (Washington, DC, 1952), 1.

54. USDA, *Extension Work in Urban Areas,* Extension Service Circular 462 (Washington, DC, 1950).

55. Anderson, *Wartime Women*; Hartmann, *Home Front and Beyond.*

of women working in nonfarm jobs, indications are found that farm women also gave up some of their work after the war and retreated into stereotypically female roles, including the role as helper to the husband rather than independent producer.

For example, women, who had been the major poultry producers, lost ground after the war. The cash economy that prevailed during wartime effectively did away with the barter system, which was the most common way of marketing eggs even as late as 1940. The wartime poultry boom was, however, short-lived. Even given the heightened wartime demand, as early as 1944 there was a surplus of eggs and production diminished by 10 percent.[56] After the war, egg production was adjusted further, and this presented the opportunity for the restructuring and modernizing of the egg market, a development that the extension service had envisioned before the war. Extension articles encouraged farmers either to produce eggs solely for their own households or to have large poultry enterprises. The enlarged enterprises were to be run by men.[57]

All of the Open Country extension farm planning program committees were limited to men. After the intense physical and emotional energy needed to meet wartime crises, women's farm production saw a pronounced deflation toward the end. The Depression preceding the war was not a viable model for postwar normalcy and even if it had been, return to prewar patterns would not have been easy. The war made lasting social and economic changes, not only in what people did, but also in the way they viewed themselves in relation to the rest of the world, the way they organized their lives, and where they looked for direction.

The role of the government in the lives of rural people changed qualitatively during the 1940s. Once remote to the people of Open Country, government now entered into many aspects of local life. Even during the war, the extension service, which established the rural information system to change the habits of rural people, saw in this network a wider potential for reaching them readily — and permanently — for postwar educational programs.[58] After the war, production expanded, people were richer, and more people had seen the world outside of Open Country. They had the government (and the war) to thank for freedom and prosperity, and most were ready to receive further direction from the same source.

Americans exalted Americanism and demanded the same strong, unified expression of patriotism in peace that they had during the war. But the tide of postwar patriotism took the form of a standard ideology rather than the overt action of the war period. The Farm Bureau, which before the war had

---

56. Iowa State Extension Service, *What's Ahead for the Livestock Farmer,* Pamphlet 92 (Ames, 1944).

57. See Deborah Fink, *Open Country, Iowa: Rural Women, Tradition and Change* (Albany, NY, 1986), chap. 6, "Eggs: A Case in Point," 135–60.

58. Wilson, *Progress of the Neighborhood Leader Plan,* 11.

restricted itself to largely nonpolitical administration of the extension service, became the rural voice of the political right.[59] Departing from the original aim of teaching practical skills, its popular 4-H program, for example, initiated programs to instill religion and patriotism by means of special ceremonies involving prayer, candles, ritual drama, speeches, songs, pledges, and display of flags.[60] Prayer and the Pledge of Allegiance became standard at all Farm Bureau–Extension meetings. Another example of the new patriotism was the pervasive isolation and prejudice against the Open Country Friends Meeting, which had not supported the war. While some Quakers were conscientious objectors during World War I, they and others had been prominent Farm Bureau leaders in the period between World War I and World War II. Quakers never again assumed these central positions even though they were stable, respectable, and prosperous farmers, and most retained their membership.

The Quakers were forced into greater awareness of a phenomenon that touched on other Open Country people in more subtle ways: the focus on "the boys" was nearly as pervasive after the war as during the war. The social perceptions of gender underwent an emotional and cognitive shift, and the Quaker men had not done their duty in being men. Many of the women who came to Open Country after the war had varying war experiences and those who stayed at home certainly did their share to win the war, but no one could match the honor and prestige of a returning soldier. The small rural community fully extended itself in offering a fitting hero's welcome and in offering him the job or opportunity he needed. As Wherry wrote in her "Country Air" column: "It will be important when they (the soldiers) return for the boys to find an interest at once, to be busy. That is, after that eon of sleep has been caught up on. That's why there must be jobs and little businesses that they can get into."[61] Throughout the United States, returning soldiers were greeted first with celebrations and later with preferential access to jobs, housing, and education. Of the farm machinery that appeared on the market after the war rationing ended, 20 percent was earmarked for returning veterans. Farmtown Presbyterian women gave the returning servicemen red carnations in a ceremony of appreciation.

War distinguished a young man in a qualitatively different way than anything else could. When a rural woman wrote to the *Wallaces' Farmer* editor about her son's problems adjusting to civilian life, she received this advice: "Better not tell him about the 'hardships' civilians had to endure. Service men look at these things differently. And civilians who keep talking about the minor difficulties of war-time life at home simply make a veteran sure that civilians don't know anything about war, can't understand what he has been thru, and aren't worthy of his confidence. . . . You can help him a lot by your patience,

---

59. See Samuel R. Berger, *Dollar Harvest: The Story of the Farm Bureau* (Lexington, MA, 1971).
60. USDA, *Ceremonials,* Extension Service Circular 443 (Washington, DC, 1945).
61. Elizabeth Wherry, "Country Air," *Wallaces' Farmer* 70 (1945), 811.

your affection, and your willingness to let him alone."[62] Or, as the "Country Air" column apologized to the returning heroes: "[W]e'll be dumb—so dreadfully dumb! We just won't have the background to understand. . . . We'll try, fellows, but we'll miss the boat a lot of times. Be as patient with us as you can."[63]

Just as during the war, Open Country women received frequent and persuasive messages about their proper roles, but the emphasis shifted from making sacrifices for the war to making the necessary adjustments for the returning servicemen and structuring the postwar society. Women found many new situations to face after the war, most of which centered around home and family. Articles in *Wallaces' Farmer* in postwar years showed an unmistakable shift in tone. War messages had celebrated the almost infinite resilience and adaptability of the Iowa farm woman: she could rise to virtually any challenge, she adjusted to wartime shortages, and she helped maintain the morale of both her family and her community. Even if these were not always seen as natural female traits, for the most part, women did what they were called upon to do. After the war, the message was more complicated and ambivalent.

Beginning in 1945, *Wallaces' Farmer* had a steady run of pictures and short news items on farm women who were buying new kitchen equipment. As one woman wrote:

> During the depression years, farm women didn't have the money to improve their homes. When things began to get better, it seemed every extra dollar on the farm was needed to buy new stock, repair machinery or build new fences.
> To farm women, it has seemed it has just been year after year of hard work with not much coming our way, but now at last we feel free to make some of those home improvements for which we've waited so long. . . .
> Am I dreaming? If I am, don't wake me up![64]

The lead story of the November 3, 1945 issue discussed what women would buy with their Victory Bond money. Farm women reported plans to buy the following equipment: 34 percent would buy refrigerators; 27 percent, stoves; 26 percent, vacuum sweepers; 21 percent, new water systems; 20 percent, washing machines; 19 percent, linoleum; 16 percent, wallpaper; 14 percent, carpets; 18 percent, pressure cookers; 14 percent, bathroom fixtures; 19 percent, radios; 15 percent, electric irons; 10 percent, furnaces.[65] Other articles gave instruction in remodeling farm homes, buying home freezers, and using the new food mixes that made cooking easier and faster.[66] In the 1940s, many

---

62. "When Frank Gets Back," *Wallaces' Farmer* 70 (1945), 611.

63. Elizabeth Wherry, "Country Air," *Wallaces' Farmer* 70 (1945), 811.

64. Mrs. Virgil York, "Don't Wake Me Up" (letter to Homemaking Editor), *Wallaces' Farmer* 70 (1945), 846.

65. "What'll You Buy?" *Wallaces' Farmer* 70 (1945), 785.

66. Zoe Murphy, "We Have a Freezer," *Wallaces' Farmer* 73 (1948), 28; Elizabeth Wherry, "Country Air," *Wallaces' Farmer* 73 (1948), 83.

farm homes installed electricity, running water, and other conveniences, which greatly eased women's housework. By 1950, only 151 farm homes in Open Country were without electricity, as compared to 802 homes in 1940.[67]

In the face of the outmigration of so many farm women and the consequent necessity of attracting nonfarm women as wives, modernizing farm homes could not have been easily sidestepped. Henry said that his parents first installed an indoor water system so that Martha, who they hoped would be their daughter-in-law, would not be discouraged by the thought of farm life. They need not, however, have worried: Martha's attraction was to Henry. In the prevailing norms of the postwar period, woman's role as wife superseded concerns for physical comfort, as well as career plans and relations with other women, whether they were sisters, mothers, or friends.

The pervasiveness of male-female sexual ties has, since World War II, come to be so commonplace that it passes almost without comment. One early manifestation of this pervasiveness was the theme of sex appeal in advertisements for household products which had no obvious or direct connection to sex. While advertisements in *Wallaces' Farmer* were still directing women to buy poultry feed and equipment, some of the new advertisements showed thin and glamorous women in ecstasy over household products. A young woman was shown on a full page hugging a box of Tide detergent. Another full page advertisement showed a woman floating in space, ecstatic over Breeze dishwashing detergent, which was "MILDER than the MILDEST Beauty Soaps!"[68] The point of wanting dishwashing detergent to be like mild beauty soap was obviously to please a man.

The silliness of these advertisements and the selfishness implied in the consumer mentality was not lost on anyone. Alongside this image of luxury and ease was a new and overt expression of scorn for the pampered woman. A hired man wrote a bitterly humorous letter complaining about the scatterbrained farm woman who would not prepare the quality of food he deserved. She had a brand new stove, but this did no good, because she was always running off to town and never stayed home to cook carefully. Although she bought prepared foods, she managed to ruin them. As soon as she put something on her new stove, she would talk on the telephone or read women's magazines until it burned. The hired man reported that he had seeded a fine vegetable garden that she could not be bothered to cultivate or harvest.[69] The inept woman who could not handle her housekeeping was the butt of derisive jokes. In a *Wallaces' Farmer* cartoon, an obviously bored man was sitting at the table saying to his frowning mate, "Just like mother used to make—and

---

67. Census Bureau, *Sixteenth Census of the United States: 1940. Housing,* vol. 1, *Data for Small Areas,* part 1, *United States Summary for Alabama–Nebraska* (Washington, DC, 1943), 495; Census Bureau, *County and City Data Book, 1952* (Washington, DC, 1953), 184.
68. *Wallaces' Farmer* 73 (1948), 250, 211.
69. "Country Cooking? I Eat It!" *Wallaces' Farmer* 73 (1948), 281.

oh, boy, was she a lousy cook!"[70] These are just two examples that represent the rural manifestation of the postwar misogyny which was more generally displayed in the work of Philip Wylie, who coined the word "momism" to describe the disdain felt for the roles of women.[71]

The women remodelling houses and keeping everyone happy and the men farming might have constituted a system in which parallel spheres of equal value existed for women and men, but this was not the case. While some attempt was made to portray the housewife's role as an extremely important one for society, there were material indications that men's work was more highly valued. On the farm new machinery, chemicals and hybrids changed the nature of farming and the skills required. Men needed training and development to do their work. A *Wallaces' Farmer* article on education for farmers discussed the increasing complexity and "scientific" nature of farming and found that successful farmers felt the need for two years of agricultural training in college.[72] No mention was made that women received any formal education. Iowa State College had a substantial home economics program, but few claimed that this training was essential for a successful farm women. While a good wife was an asset on the farm (farming was, after all, becoming a complicated and intricate operation), she was strictly an assistant. An article entitled "Farm Records Are Important" told of the careful records one farmer kept: "He calls on his wife to look over the final figures on his record. Sure enough, he had forgotten all about the chickens; [he] has to start over."[73] The article did not broach the possibility that the wife herself might have been in a better position to account for the chickens.

A sense of deflation in farm women's lives was most poignant in the "Sarah Jane Says" column, the on-going tale of Sarah Jane's poultry enterprise and a good-natured encouragement for other women in dealing with their poultry flocks. Still writing in 1948, Sarah Jane said, "I have felt for some time that I have hardly enough to say to warrant writing a letter. But I will try to write once more, anyhow."[74]

Rose, who kept the detailed records of her wartime cream and egg accounts, made fewer and less reliable entries after the war, and her last entry was in 1946. Although she kept a laying flock for many years afterwards, she never again kept written records.

For men, the intensity of feeling associated with the war lasted long after the immediate postwar years: men's war stories are still told and retold. In 1982, a conversation involving a local farmer and a Farmtown business-

---

70. *Wallaces' Farmer* 73 (1948), 297.
71. Philip Wylie, *Generation of Vipers* (New York, 1955).
72. "What Education Do Farmers Need?" *Wallaces' Farmer* 73 (1948), 134.
73. "Farm Records Are Important," *Wallaces' Farmer* 73 (1948), 185.
74. "The Farm Flock," *Wallaces' Farmer* 73 (1948), 360.

man turned rather naturally to a favorite subject — World War II experiences. When asked about the centrality of the war, both said they found themselves thinking about the war years much more than their duration suggested. Both said that their lives were greatly enriched by the travel and informal education received during their service. Although neither had actually been in combat, they recounted in detail where they were stationed and what they did. Also in 1982, a World War II veteran who led the parade and gave the Farmtown Centennial celebration opening speech chastised the Centennial Steering Committee for not orienting the yearlong festivities around veterans, stating that Farmtown would not exist if the veterans had not served their country. Many of the World War II servicemen maintained continuing close ties with their former comrades. One reported a continuing "round-robin" letter among a group of 20 former servicemen; another said that he and his war buddies got together for a three- to four-day annual reunion; another who rarely got as far from home as Minneapolis or Des Moines took a vacation to New York to visit with an old army friend. Few women maintained these kinds of close ties with those they had known during the war, unless the women happened to be married to men who had maintained those ties.

When asked about their wartime activities, servicemen's wives invariably responded with further details about what the men had done. This is partially understandable in light of the realities of military life. Having no control over his orders, a man by necessity was the independent variable in a couple's plans. The date of marriage, the place of residence, and the amount of time spent together depended on the contingencies of a serviceman's life rather than on the needs of the woman. The GI Bill, passed after the war to finance college educations for veterans, was the first impetus for many veterans to attend college. Of the veterans eligible for the benefits, 97 percent were male. Since a large number of veterans married and the GI Bill did not provide sufficient money to support a family, veterans' wives found themselves working at supplementary jobs. As Anderson wrote of wives of World War II veterans, "[T]he essential challenge was to reconcile the autonomy and competence they had demonstrated while on their own with the needs and wishes of their returning husbands. In order to promote domestic harmony they were told to subordinate their interests and needs to those of their husbands."[75]

As with military service, the man's education also meant that the place of residence, the length of time spent in the college city, and the amount of time spent together also depended on the husband's needs. Those Open Country farmers who returned after serving in the military and (occasionally) receiving college educations were coming home to farms, a residence again determined by their occupations and foreign to the experiences of many of their wives.

The extension service gave rural women advice with regard to adjusting to returning soldiers after the women themselves were accustomed to coping

---

75. Anderson, *Wartime Women*, 174–75.

independently. One extension circular told the story of Mrs. Green and her preparations to relinquish her own authority, to ease her four children into accepting the father in the home again, and to help Mr. Green adjust. While everyone had to change, the responsibility for orchestrating and monitoring the process clearly rested with Mrs. Green, not Mr. Green. To keep her family happy, Mrs. Green had to be watchful and willing to change her approach: "I must plan for signs of irritability in both children and father. I must immediately notice signs of fatigue. I must notice whether the children are avoiding their father or are spending most of their free time away from home. For, if I'm not getting results I must change my plan."[76] While this may be read as a statement that a woman was capable and emotionally stable, it also may be read as a statement that a woman's place was in the home, making her husband's job as the breadwinner as easy as possible. Thus, her capability was used to make herself dependent on the returning serviceman.

Experts in family focussed on the nuclear family in the postwar period. A study done at Iowa State College on Iowa families' adjustments to wartime separations and reunions began by reducing the question of family adjustment to marital adjustment: "The literature on dismemberment is scanty as far as reference to family adjustment *as families* is concerned. Most or our hypotheses will, therefore, be drawn from the studies of marriage adjustment and the crises of demoralization and change of status.... Certainly a good marriage adjustment between man and wife is the foundation of family adjustment."[77]

Moreover, the study found that a woman's independence or close associations with extended family were negatively correlated with a good reunion adjustment with her husband. A woman's happiness in childhood and adolescence and a "low neurotic score" were associated with a good adjustment to separation, but not to reunion with her husband. The report established as a model the woman who sacrificed her personal goals for those of her mate and denigrated the woman who "wanted to be boss."[78] Women were needed for the war effort, but they were not supposed to take advantage of the national crisis by being bossy; they were not supposed to assume that because they had men's jobs and temporary independence they now had the same prerogatives as men.

The record from rural Iowa is consistent with what happened nationally in women's recruitment into the war effort. Although women, as typified by the Rosie the Riveter figure, did enter traditional male jobs, they did not enter as equals of men. As Doris Herrick Cochrane of the Business and Professional Women's Federation warned during the war, "Equality for the woman worker

---

76. USDA, *You Can Work It Out Yourself,* Extension Service Circular 430 (Washington, DC, 1945), 8.

77. Reuben Hill and Elise Boulding, *Families Under Stress: Adjustment to the Crises of War Separation and Reunion* (New York, 1949), 16.

78. Ibid., 154, 179.

during the war is essential if we are to have equality in the postwar world."[79] In the nation as a whole, women were recruited into heavy industry only when manpower was clearly insufficient, and they lost their "men's" jobs after the war when confronted with a re-entrenched gender division.[80]

The national government itself was a model for the ambiguous position of women in wartime and the ensuing re-entrenchment. Eleanor Straub, who studied women's equity issues in the intragovernmental political process during World War II, found that the Women's Bureau of the Department of Labor was largely ignored and without real power. In articulating women's interests, the women in the government found themselves shunted to the side. The Women's Advisory Committee (WAC), established to represent women's interests in the War Manpower Commission (WMC), never achieved an effective voice, in spite of straightforward resolutions passed requesting that women be part of the WMC process. In effect, the WAC functioned solely for publicity and propaganda. Thus, while women were needed for the war effort, the government allowed no powerful advocate for women's interests either during or after the war.

Straub attributed the women's weakness in setting policy to the diffuseness of their plans, the lack of an organized constituency, and the continual care to deny that they wanted anything for women in their own right. In other words, the pains they took to distance themselves from feminism guaranteed that women would not emerge in powerful positions. Straub concluded: "No evidence indicates that a more avowedly feminist stance would have improved the WAC's record, but in hewing a middle course, the committee undoubtedly made it easier for the WMC to ignore its presence."[81]

A parallel conclusion emerges from the experiences of Open Country women: No evidence indicates that a more avowedly feminist stance would have enhanced the position of Open Country women, but in failing to articulate their position as women, they undoubtedly made it easier for everyone to assume that they existed first and foremost to solve the problems of their husbands.

WORLD WAR II made vast changes in the lives of rural Iowa women. Many left the area as outside opportunities arose, but those who stayed intensified their work, whether on the farm or in town. They made more money than before, which eventually translated into material improvements in their living standards. In spite of these gains and a small increase in the number of women in the workforce, they achieved no lasting political or economic power from their war experience. Instead, the war brought a renewed emphasis on men and

---

79. Doris Herrick Cochrane, "Equal Pay for Comparable Work," *Independent Woman* 22 (1943), 216.

80. Anderson, *Wartime Women*; Hartmann, *Home Front and Beyond.*

81. Eleanor F. Straub, "United States Government Policy Toward Civilian Women During World War II," *Prologue* 5 (1973), 254.

the value of male experiences. Open Country women learned a new and more intense lesson that their value lay primarily in supporting and enabling men to do the critical work of protecting and leading society.

BIBLIOGRAPHICAL NOTE

Rural women, long overlooked by historians, have finally been receiving serious scholarly attention in the past decade. Joan Jensen was perhaps most responsible for raising historians' level of consciousness regarding the importance of rural women; see especially *Promise to the Land: Essays on Rural Women* (Albuquerque, NM, 1991). Deborah Fink's *Open Country Iowa: Rural Women, Tradition, and Change* (Albany, NY, 1986) is among the most frequently cited works in this new area of research. Her *Agrarian Women: Wives and Mothers in Rural Nebraska, 1880–1940* (Chapel Hill, NC, 1992) challenges agrarian myths about opportunities for rural women. She combined her perspective with Dorothy Schwieder's in "Iowa Farm Women in the 1930s: A Reassessment," *Annals of Iowa* 49 (1989), 570–90. Somewhat contrasting views appear in three important books published in the 1990s: Katherine Jellison, *Entitled to Power: Farm Women and Technology, 1913–1963* (Chapel Hill, NC, 1993); Mary Neth, *Preserving the Family Farm: Women, Community, and the Foundations of Agribusiness in the Midwest, 1900–1940* (Baltimore, 1995), which contains an excellent, broad-ranging bibliographical note; and, in a particularly positive assessment of rural women's experience in another region, Nancy Grey Osterud, *Bonds of Community: The Lives of Farm Women in Nineteenth-Century New York* (Ithaca, NY, 1991).

Rural history has been given a recent boost by the establishment of three series with prominent rural historians at the helm: the University of North Carolina Press's Studies in Rural Culture, edited by Jack Temple Kirby; Johns Hopkins University Press's Revisiting Rural America series, edited by Pete Daniel and Deborah K. Fitzgerald; and the University Press of Kansas's Rural America series, edited by Donald Worster, Kathleen Neils Conzen, Hal S. Barron, Cornelia Butler Flora, David L. Brown, and Carville Earle. A particularly noteworthy earlier work is David B. Danbom, *The Resisted Revolution: Urban America and the Industrialization of Agriculture, 1900–1930* (Ames, 1979). Now Danbom, apparently sensing that the secondary literature base in the new rural history is sufficiently broad and deep, has synthesized American rural history in *Born in the Country: A History of Rural America* (Baltimore, 1995). A valuable earlier survey is John T. Shover, *First Majority–Last Minority: The Transforming of Rural Life in America* (DeKalb, IL, 1976).

15

The Modernization of Iowa's Agricultural Structure in the Twentieth Century

MARK FRIEDBERGER

In the 1980s, as in the 1920s and 1930s, the bottom fell out of Iowa's agricultural sector. Among the many discussions of the farm crisis of the 1980s, it is good to have the perspective of a historian. Mark Friedberger traced the long-term changes in agriculture in his book Farm Families and Change in Twentieth-Century America *(Lexington, KY, 1988). Then he took a closer look at the 1980s farm crisis in* Shake-Out: Iowa Farm Families in the 1980s *(Lexington, KY, 1989). In this chapter from the latter book, he summarizes the changes in the structure of agriculture that set the stage for the farm crisis.*

THROUGHOUT THE TWENTIETH CENTURY agriculture has been undergoing a modernization whose primary goal is the substitution of technology for human labor. Supporters of modernization see agriculture as a business and believe that, like any other industry, it is driven by the profit motive. This philosophy stands in opposition to an agrarian tradition whose advocates believe strongly that farming is a way of life and that the people who live on the land, and the land itself, should be given highest priority in the formulation of policy.

In the past twenty-five years modernization proceeded rapidly, and the power of agribusiness grew considerably. Great changes occurred in the structure of agriculture, nowhere more so than in the distance put between those who grew food and fiber and those who served farmers or manufactured the final product for the consumer. A few large corporations came to control the grain trade, and increasingly these firms bought up companies that supply fertilizers, herbicides, and seed. In the seventies, oil and chemical companies began to buy up sectors of the food-processing industry in order to capture a

---

Reprinted from Mark Friedberger, *Shakeout: Iowa Farm Families in the 1980s* (17–41), copyright © 1989 by the University Press of Kentucky, by permission of the publishers.

share of the new industry based on agrigenetic technology. The newly created divisions of these corporations possessed the power to consolidate food production into even fewer hands. By the middle seventies large agribusinesses and chemical and pharmaceutical companies accounted for as many inputs in the production of farm commodities as farmers themselves. Similarly, the growing sophistication of agricultural service industries, such as finance, marketing, and computing, widened the gap between farmers and those who offered them services.[1]

By the seventies the structure of agriculture was also divided into several tiers. The first was the government in Washington, which had played a significant role in farming since the thirties. Its role would grow more important in the eighties. A second tier consisted of a technologically driven sector composed of nationally and internationally based agribusiness firms (grain companies, meat packers, chemical manufacturers, etc.). The third and fourth tiers were agri-finance and educational institutions such as the land-grant colleges. A fifth was composed of establishment farm organizations (the Farm Bureau and National Corn Growers Association) and farm cooperatives, which though they were nominally controlled by local membership were affiliated with large parent cooperatives such as Land of Lakes. Finally came the producers of food and fiber, the farmers and ranchers themselves. Large organizations like seed companies, meat packers, machinery manufacturers, and the government reached down into the local community through salesmen, dealers, and agents. This system had a tendency to confuse loyalties and made the relationship between farm families and agribusiness more complex in a time of economic stress.

It would be disingenuous, however, to claim that the farm population itself is an undifferentiated mass. Sharp divisions exist among farmers and ranchers in the character of their operations, their educational levels, the time spent on the job, and their desire to modernize. Even among the sample families in this study — a select group to start out with — there were divisions.

While rural Iowa was an especially tricky locale in which to classify farmers by status, and the downturn further blurred differentiation, three groups could be distinguished in the sample. There was a tiny group of well-educated upper-class families (n = 8), in which both husband and wife had college degrees. They were usually more cosmopolitan in their professional and social contacts. Their world stretched farther than the village and clan orientation of their neighbors, who often farmed as much ground and had comparable assets. The second group (n = 108) — the vast majority of these two-generation farm families — came out of a tradition of stability and long-term ownership in their communities. Their families had lived in the neighborhood for several genera-

---

1. Jack Doyle, *Altered Harvest* (New York: Viking, 1985), 29–30; John M.Conner et al., *The Food Manufacturing Industries: Structure, Strategies, Performance and Policies* (Lexington, Mass.: Lexington Books, 1985), 163–65; Larry W. Waterfield, *Conflict and Crisis in Rural America* (New York, Praeger, 1986), 56–59.

tions; they were often related to half a dozen other families round about; and their frugality and stability were rewarded until 1981 by the steady increase in the worth of their land. The third group (n = 19) came from a less stable tradition, often a tenant background; their families had moved around during the Depression and its aftermath. With little assistance from parents, they had had to make their own way, utilizing borrowed capital. Their desire to bring children into farming in the seventies made them especially vulnerable to possible economic dislocation.

Some have argued that the waste of human capital—the failure of the best and brightest in farming—could have a severe impact on local communities and leave agriculture as a whole in a less competitive position.[2] The "missing generation" thesis will be given some attention later; what needs to be underlined here is that some of the master farmers in the state of Iowa found that they had ceased to be the masters of their own destinies. The actual producers of food had allowed themselves to become the handmaidens of the idea of big agriculture, which fostered expansion through the use of large amounts of credit, undue attention to monoculture, and the substitution of machinery for labor. The technological and financial segment of food production—lenders, the grain trade, chemical companies, machinery manufacturers, government, and educators—so dominated the industry by the late seventies that there was little in the way of opposition to offer alternatives.[3]

How did this state of affairs come about, and what effect did this unequal relationship between farmers and the government and agribusiness have on the downturn? This chapter places farm families in the context in which they operated in the late seventies and early eighties and explores their relationships to the large institutions that catered to them.

CORN-BELT AGRICULTURE was integrated into national markets almost from the time the Midwest was settled. Grain and livestock prices fluctuated according to national and international events: wars were particularly profitable for Iowa farm families, whose products sharply increased in price during world conflicts. Unlike farmers in the wheat belt, who had to ship their grain very long distances and were beholden to variable transportation costs, corn-belt farmers usually fed their grain to their own animals and sold their livestock to terminal markets within 250 miles of the shipping point. Nevertheless, even though the farm family was dependent on outside forces for transportation, credit, and marketing, it remained physically isolated on its homestead. Most

---

2. Carlisle Ford Runge, "Technological and Financial Adjustment in American Agriculture: Who Will Quit and Why?" in *Public Policy and Agricultural Technology*, ed. Don Hadwiger and William P. Browne (New York: St. Martins Press, 1987), 33–51.

3. Marty Strange, "The Economic Structure of a Self Sustainable Agriculture," in *Meeting the Expectations of the Land: Essays in Sustainable Agriculture*, ed. Wes Jackson et al. (San Francisco: North Point Press, 1985), 116–20.

farm inputs were furnished by the family. The farm provided a third of its own food needs. Even education for the children was supplied through local resources in thousands of small school districts whose one-room schools were supported by real estate taxes and controlled by the immediate neighborhood.

The traditional family unit lived on land it could work with family labor and horse power. It employed a foolproof circular system—growing crops that were fed to livestock whose manure was then spread on the land. Before the introduction of chemical fertilizers and pesticides, strict crop rotation rejuvenated the soil and nature took care of pest control. In order to grow crops and raise animals on a 160-acre farm, the family head often had to toil twelve hours a day in summer and nine hours in winter, with the remainder of the family undertaking as much as 25 percent of the work load. Wives usually kept poultry flocks, did some of the milking, and planted and looked after the garden. Children worked at farm and household tasks as their age permitted. As late as the 1930s many wanted large families because of their labor value.[4]

The collapse of farming in the Great Depression brought change. Agriculture saw the beginnings of encroachment by government and other large organizations. First came government programs designed to cut production and raise income. Later, agribusiness began to influence the way crops were grown and livestock was raised. Slowly farm families became more dependent on outside inputs to make a living. The introduction of hybrid corn in the late thirties, the availability of electricity, the use of hydraulics, tractors, and other more sophisticated machinery, the discovery of antibiotics had produced a revolution in corn-belt agriculture by the forties. Although there was never an official policy of rural development, farmers migrated into urban occupations with increasing frequency in the late forties and fifties. They took advantage of jobs in farm-related industries like meat packing, agricultural implements, and grain processing. Out-migrants sold out to neighbors, and farms grew large enough to make efficient use of farm machinery. Industrialization was furthered to increase feed grain production for export out of the immediate area. The leveling and tiling of hitherto unproductive land and the introduction of larger machinery, improved strains of seed, and chemical fertilizers and pesticides helped increase both productivity and size of farms. For many farm families, the fifties were a time of transition. Specialization in one or two enterprises became common, and diversification as a means of risk avoidance was given less emphasis. Farmers pursued part ownership—owning some land but renting more—as one method of growing larger.[5]

---

4. Deborah Fink, *Open Country Iowa: Rural Women, Tradition and Change* (Albany: State Univ. of New York Press, 1986), 59–60.

5. The classic empirical study of changes in family farming in the upper Midwest after World War II is Peter Dorner, *Economic and Social Changes on Wisconsin Family Farms (A Sample of Wisconsin Farms—1950, 1960, 1975)* (Madison: College of Agricultural and Life Sciences, Univ. of Wisconsin, R3105, Feb. 1981). For Iowa, see Friedberger, *Farm Families and Change*, 20–22.

TABLE 15.1
AVERAGE ACREAGE AND LIVESTOCK PER FARM, BY REGION, 1971–1983

Year	Acres per Farm	Acres per Farm in Row Crops	Pigs Weaned per Farm	Cattle Sold per Farm
Northwest Iowa				
1971	289	198	448	182
1973	302	227	408	215
1975	304	233	472	172
1977	373	293	627	271
1979	360	307	607	142
1981	365	205	611	144
1983	366	320	718	99
Northeast Iowa				
1971	274	158	364	44
1973	280	176	320	29
1975	279	209	304	30
1977	335	230	491	48
1979	333	281	614	49
1981	347	299	453	69
1983	335	289	791	27
East Central Iowa				
1971	289	176	441	49
1973	295	202	356	44
1975	292	248	273	35
1977	367	279	542	57
1979	382	313	649	48
1981	398	358	641	42
1983	370	320	599	35

SOURCE: Cooperative Extension Service, Iowa State Univ., *Iowa Farm Costs and Returns* (Ames, 1972–84).

It was no longer easy to begin farming without assistance from relatives, and young men who wanted to farm needed considerable monetary and in-kind help in order to begin a farm career. Modernization continued apace from 1954 through 1974, but the Extension Service and the agricultural press, which had dominated the diffusion of techniques in earlier decades, were supplanted by agribusiness. Seed, feed, and machinery dealers influenced farmers' attitudes, the way they farmed, and even how they spent their leisure. This trend was succinctly symbolized by farmers' wholesale adoption of baseball caps emblazoned with the logos of companies with which they did business.

To illustrate this gradual but appreciable change in farming in the recent past, Table 15.1 shows the increase in farm size in the regions in Iowa where this study took place. The important trend was not acreage increase. Farms grew, but not at a great rate. Rather, the most marked change was the increase in the amount of land devoted to row crops, even in three regions where diversified farming was still strong. The modernization of the hog industry kept it strong and growing across Iowa, but competition from the West and heavy losses produced a decline in cattle production over the period.

Unquestionably, agriculture has changed drastically in the twentieth century, but farmers for the most part have resisted modernization at every turn. During the Progressive era, they were slow to take up the challenge of the Country Life movement.[6] Later, in the 1950s the diffusion of new techniques for animal production, such as routine use of antibiotics, took several years.[7] Thus, the expansion that occurred in the seventies, when land was bought, livestock enterprises expanded, elaborate buildings constructed, machinery purchased, and homes built and remodeled, was something of an aberration in farmer behavior and a tribute to the persuasiveness and growing influence of agribusiness. That the end result would be disaster for thousands of so-called progressive farmers in the mid-1980s underlined the gulf that separated those engaged in the production of food in the field—the family farmer—and those continuing and completing the process of bringing food to the table, in the bank, office, packing plant, factory, and supermarket.

WHY HAS FAMILY FARMING been so durable in the corn belt? A number of scholars have offered explanations for its long domination, despite the great changes in other areas of the food-production chain. The most important reason has to do with what some have called the dialectic of the family farm.[8] The farm family, after all, provides its own labor and management, to a great extent controlling its own destiny. In short, it is very flexible. Decisions about investment and consumption are made internally and not by some manager hundreds of miles away. A sudden drop in wages and a period of frugality instituted for benefits in the long term are easily understood by family members, but less so by hired hands. This adaptability is valuable because farming is at the mercy of the weather and market cycles; and timing is crucial. The inherent risks have made farming less attractive to large, bureaucratic business interests, but farmers have learned to accept the rewards and risks as they come. Every day is a new day on the farm, and rigid timetables are given little priority except in caring for livestock. Farmers remain generalists in a world of increasingly narrow job descriptions. They are managers, laborers, mechanics, and veterinarians. When problems occur they must deal with them directly and immediately. There are no staff channels of communication to follow. Despite relatively low monetary returns, farming provides many intangible rewards for

---

6. David B. Danbom, *The Resisted Revolution: Urban America and the Industrialization of Agriculture* (Ames: Iowa State Univ. Press, 1979).

7. George M. Beal, *The Adoption of Two Farm Practices in a Central Iowa County*, Iowa Agricultural Experiment Station, Special Report 26 (1960): 7–12.

8. William L. Flinn and Frederick H. Buttel, *Sociological Consequencs of Farm Size: The Family Farm and Ideological and Social Consequences of Scale in Agriculture*, Cornell Rural Sociology Bulletin 114 (1980): 28–29.

the family. The vaunted independence of farmers should not be scoffed at. Farmers are among the few allowed to work at their own pace and to retain a self-image "rooted in a sense of self mastery."[9]

Because of its unique configuration, blending work and family roles, the farm family has always needed a special chemistry to operate successfully.[10] Indeed, it could be argued that the key ingredient for success is the willingness to engage in self-exploitation. The constant need to care for animals and to perform hundreds of mundane tasks in unpleasant conditions requires a special dedication. Those not raised to follow such a regimen might find this ethic of hard work difficult to tolerate. Not surprisingly, farming has always been an occupation passed on from generation to generation in a family.

By the 1970s, full-time farm operators like the ones studied here had become a kind of landed gentry as rising land prices gave them considerable wealth, on paper at any rate. For the first time, there was some equality in status among small-town businessmen, professionals, and farmers. At the same time, there was an increasingly large gulf in small service communities between these three groups and those small-town residents who labored for wages. The latter would be particularly hard hit once the recession in agriculture hit Main Street.

The rapid changes that occurred in corn-belt agriculture from the fifties onward—the gradual switch to grain farming, the use of large machinery, and more specialized and efficient livestock management—tended to deemphasize the work ethic and to steer families away from the kind of self-absorption in farm-related tasks that so characterized earlier decades. A number of phenomena began to have an impact on the structure and organization of the farm family. First, family cooperation between generations became more popular, eventually leading to the formalization of farm organization into partnerships and family corporations. Estate planning became more important as land prices rose and created a need to shelter heirs from estate tax burdens.[11] Wives began to be involved in decision making in a new way; younger couples and those with larger farms formed what might be called husband-and-wife teams. According to one observer, it was quite common for women to act as business managers. "It used to be that wives came into our office to sign mortgages without knowing what's going on. Now they not only know, they are an important link in making it work." The likelihood of such participation depended, he said, "on how chauvinist the husband might be. Some men don't let loose the reins to the wife, or the children, for that matter."[12]

---

9. Philip Raup, *Family Farming: Rhetoric and Reality*, Miscellaneous Journal Series, Minnesota Agricultural Experiment Station Paper 2147 (1986): 6.

10. John W. Bennett, *Of Time and the Enterprise* (Minneapolis: Univ. of Minnesota Press, 1982); Seena B. Kohl, *Working Together: Women and Family in Southwestern Saskatchewan* (Toronto: Holt, Rinehart and Winston, 1976).

11. Sonya Salamon and Kathleen Markan, "Incorporation and the Farm Family," *Journal of Marriage and the Family* 46 (1984): 167–78.

12. Quoted in Des Moines *Sunday Register*, April 8, 1979.

Technological progress allowed women to contribute in a different way from that of fifty years before. They drove tractors and assisted with livestock raising, as well as taking part in more traditional activities.[13] These changes tended to make the larger farm, particularly those with an intergenerational dimension, resemble a small urban business concern, while retaining its unique ability to meld work and family roles.

Intergenerational cooperation among farm families had gone on in Iowa for many generations, but it had sometimes been a struggle to make a smooth transition from one generation to another.[14] The pressures of production agriculture made the task no easier. Research in the seventies tended to emphasize the friction in families over power and authority,[15] conflict that was exacerbated by the increase in the value of land. With land selling for several thousand dollars an acre, many families became millionaires on paper, and very often the larger the stakes, the greater the conflict. Off-farm heirs and women were more likely to exert their rights than was previously the case.[16]

The desire to bring family members into an operation as full working partners required a number of strategic decisions. The family had to decide whether to expand and how. Should they buy more land, more livestock, or both; should they rent more acres? Should they finance expansion with a private contract, a long-term loan from the Land Bank, or funds accumulated by the family over many years? Finally, should the organization of the operation change in any way? These were just some of the questions to be answered. Some families looked at their options and went their separate ways. Sons farmed by themselves and worked with parents and other relatives only when the need arose. Others formalized their business relationships into partnerships, with strictly drawn lines of ownership, rental, and income. Still others opted for a closely held corporation, in which land, machinery, and other assets were pooled under a corporate umbrella, and shares were issued to family members in proportion to their involvement in the running and ownership of the farm.

One advantage of a family corporation was that it eliminated the concern a family had for heavy estate tax penalties when the elder generation died. The steady inflation of land values in the seventies made this an issue among

---

13. L. Bharaswaj and E. A. Wilkening, "Occupational Satisfaction of Farm Husbands and Wives," *Human Relations* 27 (1974): 739; Janet Bokemeier and Lorraine Garkovich, "Assessing the Influence of Farm Women's Self-Identity on Task Allocation and Decision Making," *Rural Sociology* 51 (1987): 13–36.

14. Mark Friedberger, "The Farm Family and the Inheritance Process: Evidence from the Cornbelt, 1870–1950," *Agricultural History* 57 (1983): 1–13; Mark Friedberger, "Handing Down the Home Place: Farm Inheritance Strategies in Iowa, 1870–1945," *Annals of Iowa* 47 (1984): 518–36.

15. Paul C. Rosenblatt and Roxanne Anderson, "Interaction in Farm Families: Tension and Stress," in *The Family in Rural Society*, ed. R. T. Coward and M. W. Smith (Boulder, Colo.: Westview Press, 1981), 147–66; Paul C. Rosenblatt and L. O. Keller, "Economic Vulnerability and Economic Stress in Farm Couples," *Family Relations* 32 (1983): 567–73.

16. Friedberger, *Farm Families and Change*, 90–97; Paul C. Rosenblatt and Roxanne Anderson, "Family Conflict over Inheritance of Property" *Family Coordinator* 28 (1979): 337–46.

farmers, and just before the downturn their lobbying efforts were rewarded. The passage of legislation incorporated into the Economic Recovery Act of 1981 greatly increased exemptions, lowered land values for the calculation of the tax, and made estate taxes payable over many years. By 1985, with land values plunging markedly, these changes no longer made much difference. Even so, some families could point to the payment of high estate taxes as one reason for their demise in the farm crisis.[17]

Much of the expansion in the seventies was undertaken with the younger generation in mind. Researchers have noted that sons and especially daughters-in-law often found their position in an intergenerational farm operation unsatisfactory. The daughter-in-law was particularly vulnerable in that she often had to maintain a far closer physical relationship with her in-laws than was the case in a nonfarm family. Sometimes she did not come from a farm background. The difficulties were complicated when two or more married sons were farming together, and sibling rivalries as well as intergenerational differences emerged. Income division, schedules, vacations, and the purchase of expensive consumer items could all cause contention among family members. Daughters-in-law could be entirely left out of major strategic decisions, such as the purchase of land.[18] The younger generation, unless it was a full partner in an operation, felt less secure because the seniors usually owned most of the land and retained much management control.[19] Not surprisingly, when the downturn hit and an intergenerational operation seemed headed for failure, the young proved more willing to abandon farming and seek other employment.

The elderly are in an especially strategic position in farm families because of their continued control of land after they retire. In some townships in this study elderly women owned up to one-third of all tracts of land—testimony not only to their longevity but also to how the inheritance system operated. On small and medium-sized farms the usual method of taking care of a spouse after the death of her husband was to provide her with a life estate on a parcel of land. The rental from the land gave her an annuity for the rest of her life. Farmland was an ideal vehicle for this purpose, for the steady rise in land prices correlated with that of rents. By the seventies elderly widows were being handsomely reimbursed by tenants eager to rent more land. It was not unusual for a 160-acre tract to gross between fifteen and twenty thousand dollars in yearly income for the owner. Such sums were impressive particularly if they were invested in savings accounts paying high interest. No wonder the elderly sometimes relished their power over their younger relatives. Some

---

17. One sample family was paying out a quarter of a million dollars in estate taxes as a result of the death of a parent just before the change in the law. Their difficulties in 1986 were partly caused by the need to make these stiff payments.

18. Candyce Russell et al., "Coping Strategies Associated with Intergenerational Transfer of the Family Farm," *Rural Sociology* 50 (1985): 361–76.

19. Randy R. Weigel, Daniel J. Weigel, and Joan Blundall, "Stress, Coping, and Satisfaction: Generational Differences in Farm Families," *Family Relations* 36 (1987): 45–48.

indulged a kind of gamesmanship over sons and daughters who were interested in renting and inheriting land.[20] The attitude of elderly landowners in a climate of high land prices and inflation had an important bearing on the way many families operated.

SOME NATIONAL FIGURES that chart change in the number of inputs farmers utilized over the past sixty years illustrate how farming has moved from relative self-sufficiency to dependence on outside sources. In 1920 exactly half of all inputs on the farm were made up by the labor of the family itself, with machinery providing almost 12 percent and chemicals 2 percent. By 1980 machinery made up one-third of all inputs; meanwhile labor had fallen to only 14 percent of the total, and chemicals had increased to 11 percent.[21] By the late 1970s most of the resources needed to farm came from the outside.

In order to run a farm in the seventies, the typical two-generation family had both a long- and a short-term lender. The former was often the Land Bank, although it could be an insurance company. In addition, a certain percentage of land was bought on contract from individuals—often parents or other close relatives. Short-term lending for routine operations had a more varied base, with local banks being the main source. However, as families expanded they often outgrew the lending limits of the smaller country banks. The Production Credit Association within the Farm Credit System took over the business that required larger lines of credit in the short term. The lender of last resort, the Farmers' Home Administration, had less involvement with larger operations before the late seventies, but as the economy worsened, loan guarantees were introduced, and lending policies became more stringent, larger farmers turned to the FmHA more often. Infrequent visits to the bank to make principal and interest payments were usually the only contact a farmer had with a loan officer. Paperwork in planning a loan and assessing a client's ability to repay was minimal. In small local banks overdrafts were common, and one telephone call from a customer was enough to cover the purchase of livestock which in many cases had already occurred. The key elements here were a trusting relationship built up between the parties over an extended period of time and the ever-increasing equity of a farmer's land, which provided the collateral for the borrowed funds. At the same time, the Depression experience gave farmers a fear of going deeply into debt. Generally they repaid their loans on time, and there were universally good relations between farmers and lenders before the eighties.[22]

---

20. Sonya Salamon and Vicki Lockhart, "Land Ownership and the Position of Elderly in Farm Families," *Human Organization* 39 (1980): 324–30.

21. Philip Raup, *What Prospective Changes May Mean for Agriculture and Rural America in Farm Policy: The Emerging Agenda*, Missouri Agricultural Experiment Station, Special Report 338 (1985): 38.

22. Friedberger, *Farm Families and Change*, 121–25.

Farmers had financial obligations with a number of other businesses in the local area. These included notes for machinery purchases, and accounts at the feed and seed store. Feed bills were normally taken care of through regular thirty-day payments. In the boom local merchants, like bankers, were liberal in extending credit, even though much of it, unlike bank loans, was unsecured. When a reversal in the farm family's fortunes came, there was no collateral to cover a merchant's losses.

As price "takers" rather than price "makers," farmers sold their grain to the elevator and their livestock to the packer or collection point and took the going price. While there was some flexibility in where livestock or grain could be sold, for the most part, farmer autonomy in marketing decisions was an illusion. By the seventies, government programs and the intrusion into the grain business of the Board of Trade and a handful of multinational corporations were largely responsible for grain pricing. The concentration of cattle feeding in the vast lots of the plains and Southwest and the continued turmoil of the meat-packing industry in the seventies and eighties did not work in farmers' favor. The risk involved in marketing farm products also had an important bearing on farmers' ability to make money. The rapid computerization of futures trading revolutionized agricultural marketing and placed the average farmer at an even greater disadvantage compared to large institutional players. A farm family's ability to hedge its risks both through diversification of product and on the Board of Trade and Mercantile Exchange often had a bearing on performance. Unfortunately, many farmers used these newer methods to hedge and speculate unwisely and only added to their woes.

The boom allowed farm families and local agriculture-related business to make more money — at least before expenses were paid. Old ways of operating were sometimes forgotten in order to take advantage of the bonanza conditions that prevailed for a few years. The world food crisis of the seventies suggested that farmers, like oilmen, possessed considerable power. In the words of one ebullient editor, there was "a new realization by farm people of the vast economic power they have abroad as well as at home."[23] Such sentiments by a cheerleader for what was called the "new era for agriculture," masked the true picture of where farm families stood with their business partners once the boom collapsed.

ONE OF THE ROLES of the land-grant university is to train young people — particularly farm children — to assume positions in agricultural extension, finance, and agribusiness. The people so trained, though often from a farm background, have distanced themselves from the land; they have different loyalties and values from those of the farmers they are meant to serve. In the words of Wendell Berry, these kinds of jobs "were a means to escape farming,"

---

23. Roe C. Black, "A New Era for Agriculture," *Farm Journal* (March 1977): 21.

not to serve farmers. Those who took this route were "old farm boys," who, it was said, had gone "on to better things."[24] In Iowa there is a strong connection between lending institutions and Iowa State University, the land-grant college, which also administers the Cooperative Extension Service. Hundreds of graduates with agricultural education degrees have gone into positions in private banks, the Farm Credit System, and the Farmers' Home Administration. While the land-grant college graduates do not possess a monopoly of these jobs, the fact remains that no industry is more inbred than agriculture and agribusiness, and the old-farm-boy land-grant network reaches deeply into all corners of agri-finance and agribusiness. The brain drain from farming by this route is nothing new. Nevertheless, at a time when agriculture required more ability in finance and marketing than ever before, much of its homegrown talent sat on the other side of the desk from the farmer and pushed loans, larger machinery, and the illusion of wealth across to those who still grew the crops and raised the livestock.

Rural banking, like agriculture, witnessed great changes in the decade of the seventies. Banking was severely regulated in the Depression. Interest rates were pegged to savings accounts, and country lenders were largely isolated from national financial developments. They mostly relied on internal sources of capital to finance investment in livestock and equipment by farmer borrowers. The Land Bank provided much of the long-term credit for agriculture at interest rates of 5 percent or a little less. By the end of World War II, funds for this purpose were generated by borrowers themselves through stock purchases. Government sources for loans through the Farmers' Home Administration were severely restricted and regulated.

This conservatively run and stable business climate was destroyed with the deregulation of banking in the seventies. During that decade banks were allowed to utilize money market mutual funds and certificates of deposit for the first time. Customers took advantage of these changes by switching their deposits from low-yielding savings accounts to the more profitable investments, whose annualized yields often exceeded 10 percent. As a result rural banks lost their old reliable source of the funds that had traditionally been used for agricultural loans. The new sources of funds were more expensive. As banks paid out higher and higher interest to depositors, they charged their farmer borrowers correspondingly higher rates. The deregulation that revolutionized banking all over the country had an especially insidious effect on agricultural lenders.[25]

Competition between banks had not been a factor in the past. Interest rates were uniform, and farmers generally supported their local bank because it was

---

24. Wendell Berry, "A Defense of the Family Farm," in Gary Comstock, ed., *Is There a Moral Obligation to Save the Family Farm?* (Ames, 1987), 354.

25. Ian R. M. Bain and JoAnn Paulson, "Financial Stress in Agriculture: Its Causes and Extent," *Minnesota Agricultural Economist* 651, Special Issue 1 (1986): 1–12.

convenient. In the 1970s, however, lenders began to seek out new customers. The Farm Credit System and later the FmHA became competitive with commercial banks to attract new accounts. Dangerous practices, rare in the days of strict regulation, such as pyramiding long-term on short-term debt, became common. These questionable transactions, based on inflated land values, collapsed as soon as land prices fell, and lenders began to demand a balance sheet with what in the business was called "a healthy cash flow."

During the boom, lenders seemed like partners to farmers, and often they encouraged the plunging binge. Two illustrations should be sufficient to demonstrate the kind of reckless policies adopted by both commercial institutions and those supported by tax dollars. During the seventies and early eighties, the Hawkeye Bank Corporation, a Des Moines–based holding company, took advantage of the Iowa law that permitted branch banking. The bank grew until it owned an interest in thirty-six banks around the state, many of them in questionable condition. The bank pursued a deliberate plan to purchase agricultural banks between 1978 and 1982.[26] By 1984 these agricultural banks were beginning to suffer severe losses. In 1985 the holding company was teetering on the brink of bankruptcy, and its affairs were being overseen by a review committee appointed by its creditors. Between January and September 1985 Hawkeye lost more money ($83.8 million) than it had made during the previous ten years combined. Ten of its banks were put up for sale in an effort to prevent further losses. Hawkeye's problems were partly caused by deregulation and the bonanza atmosphere it created, for its expansion was financed not from Iowa sources but from loans by large Chicago banks and insurance companies around the country. These companies treated Iowa like another Latin America. Hawkeye bank officers in turn spurned the golden rule of bankers, which is to maintain reserves equal to 8 percent of assets.[27]

The Farmers' Home Administration, since the forties considered the "lender of last resort," also altered its style of lending in the seventies. In 1960 this agency administered eight national programs; 64 percent of its funds went to farm operating loans, and 14 percent to farm ownership loans with the remainder to other programs. By 1979 FmHA operated at least twenty-three programs, and farm ownership and operating loans had shrunk to under 10 percent of all funds dispensed. New programs now dominating the agency's portfolio included disaster emergency, economic emergency, housing, rural rental housing, water and waste, and business and industrial loans. Although absolute levels of funding for operating and ownership had not declined, the general perception of the agency had changed: it had become a major provider of subsidized credit and emergency loans. This policy tended to expand farmers' perceptions of their capacity to borrow money safely, encouraging them to pursue riskier

---

26. Des Moines *Register*, July 15, 1982.

27. Des Moines *Sunday Register*, Jan. 12, 1986, Feb. 15, 1987. For national trends in agricultural bank failures, see *Business Week*, Sept. 30, 1985, 90–91.

production and marketing strategies and more aggressive financial plans. Thus while 50 percent of all farm operation loans in 1979 went to farmers below the age of thirty, and 68 percent of loans were dispensed to farms with less than $120,000 net worth, one-third of all emergency loans were given to farms with more than $500,000 in assets.[28]

In Iowa this policy was reflected in the middle eighties by the number of loans past due and the large amounts of some of these loans. For instance, in one sample county one past-due loan totaled over $700,000. In the two western counties of Ida and Sac 34 percent and 29 percent of FmHA agricultural borrowers were past due. Much of this delinquency was due to the livestock losses and crop failures farmers had suffered in the previous decade. Other counties, like Fayette, had very low agricultural losses, but their housing programs in the towns were under severe strain because mortgage holders had lost their jobs in agriculture-related industry.[29] The performance of the Farm Credit System in the 1970s and early 1980s duplicated many of these trends. The Omaha District, of which Iowa was part, suffered crippling losses after 1984.

Like the farmers, these lending institutions collapsed or were badly crippled when the boom ended. Many factors contributed to their failure; most obvious were actions by the Federal Reserve that caused the decline in inflation, the fall of farm prices, and the steep loss in the value of land. Lapses in judgment, bad management, and ill-advised expansion were all partly to blame. Certainly the deregulation that encouraged formerly conservative professionals to take risks had an important impact.

For many years the Cooperative Extension Service was a voice for change in the countryside. County agents pleaded with farmers to adopt modern techniques, and home economists did the same for farm women in the home. This missionary activity made its mark by the 1950s, but by then commercial firms had taken over many of the functions of the county agent and his staff. Commercial enterprises now held their own demonstrations, attracting farmers and their families with free meals and handouts of clothing, feed, and seed. At the same time the Extension Service pamphlet, used to such great effect in an earlier time, became outdated. It took several years for the institution to adopt new electronic techniques for mass instruction. As a result, under 30 percent of all Iowa farm households used the Extension Service on a regular basis by the mid-1970s.[30]

---

28. U.S. Department of Agriculture, *A Time to Choose: Summary Report on the Structure of Agriculture* (Washington, D.C.: Government Printing Office, 1981), 118, 122; William McD. Herr and Eddy La Due, "The Farmers' Home Administration's Changing Role and Mission," *Agricultural Finance Review* 41 (1981): 58–72.

29. Des Moines *Sunday Register*, Sept. 14, 28, 1986.

30. Eric O. Hoiberg and Wallace Huffman, *Profile of Iowa Farms and Farm Families, 1976*, Iowa Agricultural Experiment Station Bulletin P141 (1978): 13; national trends can be found in Paul D. Warner and James A. Christensen, *The Cooperative Extension Service: A National Assessment* (Boulder, Col.: Westview, 1984), 61.

As an arm of the United States Department of Agriculture, the Extension Service had little alternative in the seventies but to follow the dictates of Washington and bolster big agriculture. Much work was done in estate planning, livestock confinement, new marketing techniques, and above all, pushing production agriculture to higher and higher levels. In light of what happened in the eighties, it is a pity that the service did not demonstrate more leadership and question some of the trends of the seventies. In its support of an agribusiness philosophy, the Extension Service forgot that one of its tasks was to give an objective appraisal of change in agriculture, not to lock step with agribusiness. Apparently farmers were aware of these developments, for according to an Iowa Poll, 34 percent thought the Extension Service was dedicated to serving agribusiness, whereas only 28 percent believed it looked after the interests of the family farmer.[31]

Extension paid too much attention to the needs of the larger production-oriented farm families and not enough to smaller and part-time operations. Ironically, in the farm crisis many of the plungers who had followed the gospel of big agriculture and, by inference, the Extension Service, were severely affected. A little later a clientele that desperately needed assistance in the worst period of the downturn — older farmers with smaller holdings — had considerable difficulty making contact with the service. They had either lost touch with the Extension Service years before or had never had a relationship with the county agent in the first place.

NOWHERE is the gap in financial and marketing expertise between the individual farmer-businessman and those who process his product more pronounced than in the huge multinational grain companies, the "merchants of grain," who came into their own in the seventies with the explosion in grain exports.[32] And no firm better characterizes the mysterious activities of the grain traders than the largest of them all, Cargill, the Minnesota giant that had $32 billion in revenues in 1986. Cargill originated in Iowa, but its founders quickly saw the importance of the Minnesota Twin Cities for the milling business and moved there before the turn of the century. By any standards Cargill is an extraordinary American business. It remains privately held, has been largely self-financed, and puts great stock in long-term strategic planning.[33]

Until the 1970s Cargill concentrated on the grain business and grew relatively slowly. However, in the next ten years the firm turned itself into the classic multinational conglomerate. Revenues of $2.1 billion in 1971 grew to $29 billion ten years later. The company diversified into fifty different

---

31. Des Moines *Register*, April 10, 1979.

32. Bruce Marion, *The Organization and Performance of the U.S. Food System* (Lexington, Mass.: Lexington Books, 1986).

33. Roger Burbach and Patricia Flynn, *Agribusiness and the Americas* (New York: Monthly Review Press, 1980), 221–52.

bulk commodities—in the best of times a very risky enterprise. It became first in grain exports, egg production, and soybean crushing, second in beef packing, third in corn and wheat milling, a top cotton and coffee trader, and important in feed, seed, fertilizer, steel, wool, zinc, and corn syrup, as well as financial services. Cargill employed forty-two thousand people in forty-six countries and maintained its position by continued reinvestment in the firm and continued diversification. While grain exports slumped in the eighties, salt, animal feed, poultry, coffee, and financial services prospered. Nevertheless, inasmuch as Cargill exported 20 percent of the nation's grain in the early eighties, the farm slump and the problems of maintaining farm exports remained a concern.

Evidence came to light in the spring of 1987 that Cargill and other large grain companies were helping to orchestrate a defeat of legislation that would put controls on production and so raise prices for farmers. With its extensive lobbying apparatus in Washington, Cargill became a major player in the formation of the 1985 farm bill. Calling their efforts "a sham and a scandal," the president of the National Farmers Union declared, "These companies recognize that their profit is substantial and that it results from their handling of farm products. They are involved in a deliberate effort to force prices down. This is pure exploitation."[34]

Cargill claimed that its interests were the same as the farmers' and that its work in building up exports and keeping costs low in order to undersell competitors would help farmers. It would seem that the firm achieved the best of both worlds. The bill steered the economy toward "market clearing" prices that made American grain more attractive to foreign buyers. At the same time, though exports did not increase, Cargill and other grain merchants made large sums of money storing surplus commodities for the Commodity Credit Corporation.[35]

At first sight it would seem that the farm cooperative movement would run counter to the thesis that farmers are at the mercy of large-scale business organizations. The Rochdale system, adopted by hundreds of small farmer-owned cooperatives from the turn of the century onward, was designed to market crops and reduce the price of farm inputs for members by avoiding the middleman. However, by the seventies most cooperatives were affiliated with large parent institutions and were run like any other big business. AGRI industries, which was once called the Farmers'-Grain Dealers Association, grew into the largest grain cooperative in Iowa. Rapid expansion in the seventies was followed by substantial losses by the early eighties. The cooperative was saved only when Cargill bought 51 percent of its stock in 1986 with a view

---

34. Quoted in Des Moines *Sunday Register*, April 6, 1986; for commodity groups' participation in the writing of the 1985 Farm Bill, see William P. Browne, *Private Interests, Public Policy, and American Agriculture* (Lawrence: Univ. Press of Kansas, 1988), 233–34.

35. *Fresno Bee*, May 24, 1987.

to running AGRI's main business, its grain market.[36] Such a turn of events showed elements of bitter irony, in that a farmer-owned business was forced to sell out to a commercial competitor, making a mockery of the concept of cooperation designed to reduce farmers' disadvantage in the grain trade. As in the debacle of the Farm Credit System—also nominally owned by farmer shareholders—when difficulties arose in a large organization, it was the organization, not the shareholders, that received most attention. Unfortunately, the AGRI experience demonstrated the powerlessness of the farm cooperative movement and its dominance by agribusiness.

Meat packing, another industry with close farm relations, also underwent major structural changes in the past twenty-five years. In 1947 the four biggest meat packers, Armour, Morrell, Swift, and Wilson, accounted for 41 percent of the value of meat added by manufacture. In 1963 this share had declined to 31 percent. By the seventies only one of these firms was still in business, and slaughtering no longer took place in terminal markets like Chicago, but in small, dispersed plants much closer to where livestock was raised.[37]

Meat cutting is a tough occupation with a long history of union militancy and strike activity. Since the movement of the industry to smaller communities, unions have attempted to organize plants in areas where antiunion sentiment was strong. Their most important target was Iowa Beef Processors, or IBP, a division of Occidental Petroleum, now the country's largest meat packer. IBP has thirteen plants, four of them in Iowa, and all the Iowa plants are nonunion. The company was able to take advantage of the need for jobs in a state where off-farm employment is at a premium in small towns. With starting wages at $5.25 per hour, the union has some justification in claiming that IBP is "exploiting workers while making millions." IBP also was able to use the "speedup" in the cutting line so graphically depicted in Upton Sinclair's *The Jungle*. According to the union, which said it had trouble documenting many of its facts because of the intimidation of workers by the firm, the work force in many plants had a turnover of 100 percent a year. In one new Iowa location an average of forty workers a week left because conditions were "brutal." Some had knife wounds, ammonia burns, or other injuries. To counter union influence, the company sent new workers to an eight-hour orientation program designed to present the company's program in the best light and to discourage union sentiment.[38]

The IBP situation is indicative, albeit to an exaggerated degree, of the conditions in rural America in the deflationary slide of the eighties. Workers

---

36. Des Moines *Sunday Register*, Jan. 25, 1987.

37. National Commission on Food Marketing, *Organization and Competition in the Livestock and Meat Industry* (Washington, D.C.: Government Printing Office, 1966), 9.

38. IBP was founded in the 1960s with a $300,000 loan from the Small Business Administration. See Jimmy M. Skaggs, *Prime Cut: Livestock Raising and Meat Packing in the United States, 1607–1983* (College Station: Texas A&M Univ. Press, 1986), 190; Des Moines *Sunday Register*, Jan. 25, 1987.

want good wages, safe working conditions, and the ability to raise a family in a small community. Management, employed by a huge absentee oil company, is concerned with profit maximization, with turning out nine hundred butchered hogs an hour, and paying the lowest possible wages for a work week that includes Saturdays.

The lack of work-force stability had consequences that went beyond the employees themselves, for although most Iowa communities were desperate for jobs, IBP's reputation as an employer made it difficult for the company to build other plants in the state. When the firm tried to set up a plant in an eastern Iowa community, opposition surfaced not only from townspeople but from farmers as well. Some were concerned that any more competition in the hog-slaughtering industry in their part of the state would lower prices for their product. Moreover, the farm crisis tended to cement relations between farmers and union members, and IBP's bad press made its mark, whereas a decade before farmers would likely have supported IBP's efforts at expansion.[39]

Other businesses close to farmers, such as implement dealers and their parent companies, the manufacturers, met disaster in the farm crisis. Their failure demonstrated the folly of a business mentality that stressed short-range profit in place of a balanced long-range sales program. Farmers had been persuaded to trade in tractors and other machinery once a year during the seventies, when capital was cheap. The practice was perfectly rational when the rate of inflation was higher than the cost of borrowing money; then, farmers bought tractors as an investment. Unfortunately, competition between dealers, and between lending institutions eager to write loans that would finance farm machinery, allowed some customers to make unwise purchases. As with expensive farmland bought on credit, once deflation occurred, many farmers could not keep up with their payments.[40]

In the 1970s tractor manufacturers possessed a special aura; farmers held them in high esteem. John Deere, for example, maintained 173 dealerships in the state and had 30 percent of the market for large machines. A typical dealer employed six mechanics and had annual sales of $1 million to $6 million, $250,000 in used inventory, and $80,000 in parts. Competition was keen not only with other kinds of dealerships, but within the Deere family itself.[41] Between 1980 and 1986 Iowa lost 265 implement dealers, and their attrition caused hardships to farmers, who not only lost the advantage of a competitive business climate but now had to drive far longer distances for repairs and service. The impact of the downturn in farm machinery sales was as severe

---

39. Partly as a result of union efforts and national publicity, IBP was fined a record $2.6 million by the Occupational Safety and Health Administration for violations of health and safety regulations at one of its plants in Nebraska. The evidence suggested that workers in Iowa plants labored under similar conditions. See Des Moines *Sunday Register*, July 26, Aug. 2, 1987.

40. Ibid., Oct. 12, 1986.

41. Ibid., Sept. 7, 1977.

in urban Iowa as the farm downturn was for small towns, for it entailed the loss of thousands of jobs in manufacturing plants located in Iowa cities.

The saga of Harvestores, the tall blue grain silos commonly to be found on livestock farms in the corn belt, was symbolic of the boom and bust that agribusiness firms experienced between 1975 and 1985. The Harvestore was a mark of status. Several in a row added even more prestige. In the boom years dealers organized Harvestore clubs for owners. Members attended steak dinners and went on tours to visit others who used the "Harvestore system." Potential customers were wooed with "seminars at sea" or trips to Las Vegas. According to one observer, "There was a sort of well-to-do air or 'country club' attitude among those who 'belonged.'" Five years later the world of "expensive blue" had turned to rust. In many instances, the Harvestore became the symbol of failure.[42]

In sum, agribusiness had a mixed record in the seventies and eighties. Some sectors suffered as much, if not more, than farmers. Those that had diversified under good management were not hurt as badly. But regardless of their record, their influence and power was such that farmers had little recourse but to meekly follow in their wake.

ONE OF FEW FARM ORGANIZATIONS with any hope of competing with agribusiness, the National Farmers Organization, lost much of its credibility among larger more conservative farmers when it resorted to withholding products from the market in the fifties and sixties. Nor did the American Agriculture Movement attract much of a following in Iowa in the late seventies, partly because of the preeminence of the Iowa Farm Bureau Federation.[43] The Farm Bureau was formed just after World War I as an organizational and farm representative arm of the Cooperative Extension Service. Establishment oriented and conservative, the Farm Bureau achieved most of its success through such business activities as a group insurance program open to nonfarmers as well. Wary of federal farm programs, the bureau led the drive for "free-market" agriculture and even as late as 1985 continued to endorse this concept, while attempting to recoup its position, having lost face in the farm crisis.[44]

The bureau was slow to recognize and react to the farm crisis mainly because of its own conservatism. Traditionally it operated by consulting with its membership and reaching consensus before embarking on a change of policy. Many members, however, clearly did not want to recognize the symptoms of the downturn. Unlike other farm organizations, the Farm Bureau was relatively well-heeled. Membership fees of sixty dollars a year supported a national headquarters staff of two hundred, in addition to eight regional offices around the

---

42. Ibid., April 6, 1986.
43. Des Moines *Register*, Jan. 30, 1979.
44. Iowa Farm Bureau *Spokesman*, Sept. 25, 1985.

country. Like other mainstream farm organizations, such as the National Corn Growers Association and American Soybean Association, the Farm Bureau placed great emphasis on making its voice heard in Washington. In the 1980s it began endorsing political candidates, formed political action committees, and developed a computer information system called Speedline, which allowed members to communicate directly with Washington to express their views on important issues. Other Farm Bureau programs dealt with marketing information and education, and there were programs for women and children too. These, together with financial stability, gave it formidable strength and credibility compared to other farm organizations that challenged its hegemony.[45]

Still, for all its vigor, its ability to organize in every township in Iowa, and its strong voice in the state legislature, the Farm Bureau remained unpopular among farmers because of its business orientation. If critics claimed the bureau did not pay enough attention to the needs of dirt farmers, they were correct. But then, the Farm Bureau epitomized how the structure of agriculture had changed in twenty-five years, and how a business orientation had prevailed.

A GOOD CASE could be made that government intervention was the principal force behind structural change in agriculture. Farm programs and tax policy are usually cited as instrumental in initiating change since the Depression and particularly after 1970. Historically, Iowa farmers did not make great use of farm programs. As late as 1954 farmers in the state voted down an option for the mandatory retirement of land. Farmers resented government dictation of policy, but perhaps more important, they believed the withdrawal of land would handicap the small farmers of the day. Most still fed much of their corn to livestock, and many feared that prices would rise if they had to buy corn for feed on the market.[46] Even in 1986 after the passage of the most controversial farm bill ever, the average payments to corn growers were relatively modest. The controversy concerned the legal ability of larger farmers to manipulate the rules of programs in order to receive the maximum payment possible. Larger operators were invariably able to take greater advantage of the farm program than the smaller operators, who needed support payments to retain economic viability. In Iowa, then, farm programs did not become a key issue until after 1980, and are best dealt with later.

Tax policy, on the other hand, had a fairly strong cumulative effect. The income tax system encouraged farmers to take advantage of depreciation and investment tax credits, instead of saving their excess income as they would have done a generation before. In addition, the system made it advantageous for nonfarmers to use farming as a tax shelter in the sixties and seventies. Nonfarmer investment damaged the Iowa cattle industry and influenced the

---

45. *Association Management* (Nov. 1986): 28–33.
46. Friedberger, *Farm Families and Change*, 119–20.

westward migration of this important segment of the state's farm economy. Iowa farmers took advantage of provisions that allowed them to write off the costs of land improvement, the purchase of machinery, and the construction of buildings where livestock were reared. Generally, the greater the income of a farmer, the higher the value of these tax code rules to his operation. There was a tremendous incentive to continue enlarging the farm and to substitute capital for labor, in order to reach income tax brackets that would be of maximum advantage to the farm family.[47]

In the 1970s, thus, large organizations assumed an increasingly powerful role, changing the structure of agriculture and deciding the direction farming would take. Urged by lenders, the government, and agribusiness, many operators undertook rapid modernization and expansion. Theirs was a rational approach, perhaps, in an inflationary environment, but the risks were great. Once a deflationary economy was triggered by a recession after 1981, disaster struck.

BIBLIOGRAPHICAL NOTE

There has been no shortage of analysis of the farm crisis of the 1980s. For a comprehensive guide to the literature, see Earl M. Rogers and Susan H. Rogers, *The American Farm Crisis: An Annotated Bibliography* (New York, 1989). An important book that reached a broad audience is Osha Gray Davidson, *Broken Heartland: The Rise of America's Rural Ghetto* (New York, 1990). Rural social history has also received increased attention in recent years, to supplement an ongoing interest in the history of agricultural policy. (That work is noted in the bibliographical notes to the essays by Dorothy Schwieder and Joseph Wall and by Deborah Fink.)

What is lacking is the kind of critical look at the twentieth-century history of institutions that affected agriculture and rural life that Friedberger's essay begins in a general way. Kimberly Porter has completed a dissertation at the University of Iowa on the Iowa Farm Bureau, and William Pratt has published a number of articles about the Farmers' Union. Philip J. Nelson, "The Rockwell Co-operative Society and the Iowa Farmers' Elevator Movement, 1870–1920," *Annals of Iowa* 54 (1995), 1–24, is a good look at the early development of the cooperative movement in Iowa. Dorothy Schwieder, *Seventy-Five Years of Service: Cooperative Extension in Iowa* (Ames, 1993), traces the history of that important agricultural institution. Wilson Warren calls attention to the efforts to build coalitions between farm and labor organizations in "The 'People's Century' in Iowa: Coalition-Building among Farm and Labor Organizations, 1945–1950," *Annals of Iowa* (1988), 371–93. Wilson

---

47. USDA, *A Time to Choose*, 92; for the implications of the 1986 tax revisions for farming, see Marty Strange, *Family Farming: A New Economic Vision* (Lincoln, Ne.: University of Nebraska Press, and Institute for Food and Development Policy, 1988), 163.

Warren's series of articles in the *Annals of Iowa* about the Morrell meatpacking company in Ottumwa traces the changes in the meatpacking industry in the twentieth century. (See the note to Shelton Stromquist's essay for more on the meatpacking industry and its workers.) For the most recent developments in that industry, see Warren's "When 'Ottumwa Went to the Dogs': The Erosion of Morrell-Ottumwa's Militant Unionism, 1954–1973," *Annals of Iowa* 54 (1995), 217–43; and Mark A. Grey, "Turning the Pork Industry Upside Down: Storm Lake's Hygrade Work Force and the Impact of the 1981 Plant Closure," ibid., 244–59. A recent — and massive — history of a native Iowa agribusiness that evolved into a huge multinational corporation is Wayne G. Broehl, Jr., *Cargill: Trading the World's Grain* (Hanover, NH, 1992).

16

The Evolution of the Iowa Precinct Caucuses

HUGH WINEBRENNER

> One of the most important questions history answers is, "How did we get to be the way we are?" Even recent developments can quickly take on an aura of "that's the way we've always done it." Such is the case with Iowa's most noted (and notorious) political event: the presidential precinct caucuses. In this essay Hugh Winebrenner describes the origins and evolution of this nationally prominent event.

IOWA'S EMERGENCE as a weather vane in presidential politics is a recent development. Prior to 1972, the Iowa caucuses were just another electoral event in the middle of the national caucus and primary schedule. When the Iowa Democratic Party decided to schedule their caucuses in January rather than March or April, they began a chain of events which resulted in the caucuses becoming a national phenomenon.

The Iowa caucuses have evolved from the early scandal-plagued days of the nineteenth century to their present position of national prominence. In those early days, small groups of individuals attempted to control the local parties by limiting participation in the caucuses. Throughout the early twentieth century various state legislatures enacted measures which brought the previously unregulated caucuses under the rule of law. In the last decade the Iowa Republican and Democratic parties made a number of changes in the conduct of the caucuses which eventually brought them national media attention far in excess of what might be expected for state parties electing so few delegates to their respective national conventions.

Theoretically, the caucus and convention system begins with precinct caucuses open to all party voters. The local caucuses elect delegates to county conventions which, in turn, elect delegates to district and state conventions

---

Originally published as Hugh Winebrenner, "The Evolution of the Iowa Precinct Caucuses," *Annals of Iowa* 46 (1983), 618–35. Copyright © 1983 by the State Historical Society of Iowa. Reprinted by permission of the publisher.

where the delegates to the national party conventions are selected. The system is a product of Jacksonian democracy of the early 1830s which, by 1840, had replaced the congressional and legislative caucuses as the method of nominating public officials in the United States. Since it "was neither recognized nor regulated by law," party bosses gained control of the system during the latter half of the nineteenth century.[1]

Iowa joined the Union in 1846 and the state's political parties immediately adopted the national practice of a caucus and convention system. As in other states, charges of manipulation soon emerged. Emory H. English, in an excellent article on voting practices in Iowa, outlines a number of common caucus abuses. Generally, cliques or special-interest groups dominated within party organizations and did their best to limit participation by opposing factions or the general public. The times and locations of caucuses often were closely guarded secrets, and "snap" caucuses were a favorite device of those "in the know." The knowledgeable would assemble on short notice, elect a slate of delegates to the county convention, and quickly adjourn. When outsiders knew caucus times, a caucus might be packed with supporters of a particular candidate or slate of delegates, or a "competing event" might be organized. English recounts an example of a "competing event" held in northern Iowa in which "the 'fortunate' burning of an old shed in the outskirts of a small town at exactly the advertised hour . . . of the caucus attracted nine-tenths of the people of the village, including members of the volunteer fire department. In the meantime, those in the 'know' assembled at the caucus . . . , selected a 'slate' of delegates without opposition and adjourned."[2]

Frequent abuses of the caucus process led to calls for reform, but the Iowa General Assembly acted slowly: The first reform bill was not introduced until 1896. Reformers focused on developing a system of primary elections in Iowa rather than taking the less radical step of revising the caucus and convention system. Three reform bills were introduced and rejected by the 26th General Assembly in 1896, but in 1898 the 27th General Assembly enacted a "voluntary" primary election law for counties. The first "compulsory" primary election law passed the 30th General Assembly in 1904, but it applied to counties with populations in excess of 75,000 people and Polk was the only county affected.[3]

In 1907, eleven years of reform efforts in the General Assembly culminated with the passage of a statewide primary election law. The law provided for primary elections to nominate candidates for any office filled by direct

---

1. Frank E. Horack, "Primary Elections in Iowa," in *Applied History*, Iowa Applied History Series, vol. 1 (Iowa City, 1912), 266.

2. Emory H. English, "Evolution in Iowa Voting Practices," *Annals of Iowa* 29 (April 1948), 257.

3. James J. Crossley, "The Regulation of Primary Elections by Law," *Iowa Journal of History and Politics* 1 (April 1903), 174–5; Iowa, *Acts and Resolutions*, 27th General Assembly, 1898, Chap. 111, 59; Iowa, *Acts and Resolutions*, 30th General Assembly, 1904, Chap. 40, 29.

popular vote in the general election with the exception of judges. It also required that delegates to the party county conventions, members of the county central committees, and presidential and vice-presidential electors be nominated by primary election. Finally, it required a preference poll for United States senators who at that time were chosen by the state legislature. Since the 1907 law only affected offices filled by direct popular vote, it did not provide for the nomination of presidential candidates. Moreover, the district and state conventions, not popular vote, still selected candidates to the national presidential conventions. The 1907 law, however, did represent a major change in Iowa electoral politics since it opened the previously closed party system to the voters and limited party control over the nominating process.[4]

Although amended several times, the 1907 law remained substantially intact until 1963. There were, however, changes in 1913 and 1917 worthy of examination. In those years Iowa initiated, and then abolished, a presidential primary election.

In 1913 the 35th General Assembly amended Iowa's primary election law to include the selection of delegates and alternate delegates to national conventions of all political parties, the selection of national committee members for each party, and a presidential preference poll "for the purpose of ascertaining the sentiment of voters of the state in the respective parties as to candidates for president and vice-president of the United States."[5]

Iowa held its only presidential primary election on April 10, 1916, with mixed results. None of the major presidential candidates entered the primary and less than one-third of the eligible electorate voted. The primary election process cost the state $122,000. Governor George W. Clarke, who, in his inaugural address of January 16, 1913, had called for the passage of a presidential preference primary law, now branded the 1916 presidential preference poll a farce. In his final biennial message to the General Assembly in 1917, he urged the repeal of the entire direct primary law and called for the return to the caucus and convention system of selecting candidates for public office.[6]

The 37th General Assembly was not willing to abolish the direct primary law in its entirety, but did agree with Governor Clarke's assessment of the presidential preference primary election. A bill to repeal this section unanimously passed both houses in early 1917 and the newly inaugurated governor, William G. Harding, signed it into law on February 16, 1917.[7] The next major

---

4. Iowa, *Acts and Resolutions*, 32nd General Assembly, 1907, Chap. 51, 51.

5. Iowa, *Acts and Joint Resolutions*, 35th General Assembly, 1913, Chap. 111, 99.

6. Steven E. Schier, *The Rules of the Game: Democratic National Convention Delegate Selection in Iowa and Wisconsin* (Washington, D.C., 1980), 58, fn 49; Des Moines *Register*, 30 January 1917, 2; Iowa, *Inaugural Address of Governor George W. Clarke to the Thirty-Fifth General Assembly*, 16 January 1913, 19–20; Iowa, *Biennial Message of Governor George W. Clarke to the Thirty-Seventh General Assembly*, 9 January 1917, 27.

7. Iowa, *Acts and Joint Resolutions*, 37th General Assembly, 1917, Chap. 14, 32.

modification of the caucus and convention system occurred in 1963 when the General Assembly amended Iowa's primary election law and returned the selection of county convention delegates to the precinct caucuses. Two years later, lawmakers also removed the selection of party county committee members from electoral politics and provided for their selection at precinct caucuses. Several factors contributed to these changes including the high cost of printing separate ballots for each precinct, the low visibility of party offices, and a movement in Iowa for a shorter ballot.[8] No additional substantive changes to the Iowa primary law occurred after 1965. The current law requires primary elections to nominate candidates for all elective officials below the office of president with the exception of judges, and provides for a caucus and convention system for selecting delegates to the presidential conventions.

When the General Assembly returned Iowa to the caucus and convention system for selecting delegates and committee members, it placed the caucuses on sound statutory footing. Iowa law provides that "delegates to county conventions of political parties and party committee members shall be elected at precinct caucuses not later than the second Monday in February on each even-numbered year."[9]

The actual date for precinct caucuses is set by the state central committee of each party, and since 1976 the Republican and Democratic parties have held their caucuses on the same day. The principal motivation for this unusual example of party cooperation in Iowa is to gain maximum media exposure, and in that regard they have succeeded.[10] The state central committee determines a uniform starting time for all Democratic caucuses. The county central committees control the starting time for Republican caucuses in each county, which results in some variation in the evening starting times. Iowa law also requires that "the date, time, and place of each precinct caucus of a political party shall be published at least twice . . . not more than thirty days and not less than five days before the date of the caucuses." In addition the notice must state in substance that each voter affiliated with the specified political party may attend the precinct caucus. Finally, whenever possible, precinct caucuses are to be held in publicly owned buildings or in places used for holding public meetings.[11]

The requirements are intended to ensure an open and well publicized caucus process and have succeeded in eliminating most of the earlier abuses. It is still possible, however, to pack a caucus with supporters of a particular

---

8. Iowa, *Acts and Joint Resolutions*, 60th General Assembly, 1963, Chap. 78, 117; Iowa, *Acts and Joint Resolutions*, 61st General Assembly, 1965, Chap. 89, 158; interview with Clifton Larson, former chairman, Iowa Democratic Party, 23 February 1981.

9. Iowa *Code*, Sec. 43.4.

10. Interview with Tim Hyde, 8 October 1982. Hyde, former executive director of the Republican Party of Iowa, provided two additional reasons for the Republicans' willingness to initiate a common caucus date: to maximize caucus participation through joint announcements and to prevent people from participating in both the Republican and Democratic caucuses.

11. Iowa, *Code*, Sec. 43.92, Sec. 43.93.

candidate or slate of delegates, but greater media coverage and the correspondingly higher salience of the caucuses make the use of this tactic increasingly difficult, especially in presidential election years.

The legislation of 1965 also determined rules of eligibility for caucus participation. The law requires that caucus participants reside within the precinct and that they are or will be eligible electors by the next general election. The law permits seventeen-year-olds who will be eighteen by the time of the general election to participate in the caucuses. Since the precinct caucuses are party-sponsored events, the parties can have, and each has, additional requirements for participation. Neither party requires that participants be registered to vote, but the Iowa Republican party requires that participants "declare" themselves Republicans and authorizes the resolution of eligibility disputes at caucuses by majority vote. The Democratic party limits participation to those who are "supporters of the purpose of the Democratic party and are not members of any other political party." Although the goal of these requirements is to prevent raiding, it is very unlikely that persons willing to "declare" themselves supporters of the party on the evening of the caucus will be prevented from participating by either party.[12]

Voting procedures within caucuses are at the discretion of each caucus gathering, although the Republican State Central Committee suggests votes be taken by secret ballot. Moreover, any questions not covered in state law or by party rules are resolved by majority vote of the caucus voters.

THE PRINCIPAL CONCERNS of the precinct caucuses are delegate selection and the development of issues for the party platforms, but the parties vary somewhat in their conduct of business. Both normally elect two precinct committee members to represent their precinct on the county central committees. Each begins the platform-building process by developing and discussing issues which are then forwarded to the county platform committees. Republican caucuses "take stands" and Democrats "prioritize" the issues. The Democratic caucuses elect members and alternates to serve on the Platform Committee and the Committee on Committees planning the county conventions. The Republican County Committees determine the procedures for filling these positions and they vary by county. The foremost concern of the party caucuses is the election of delegates to their respective county conventions, and in presidential years, Democratic and Republican procedures differ significantly.

The Democrats practice a system of proportional representation: Delegates to the county conventions are elected in proportion to the levels of support for presidential candidates in each caucus. There may be, and usually is, an uncommitted group. A candidate preference or uncommitted group is viable —

---

12. Ibid., Sec. 43.90; Republican Party of Iowa, "Suggested Procedure for Precinct Caucuses, January 21, 1980," mimeographed (Des Moines, 1980); Iowa Democratic Party, "Precinct Caucus Kit, 1980," mimeographed (Des Moines, 1980).

eligible to elect delegates to the county convention—only if it includes a minimum of 15 percent of the total caucus voters. If more than 85 percent of those voting at a caucus support one presidential candidate, or are uncommitted, they are entitled to elect the entire slate of delegates to the county convention.[13]

Delegate selection at Democratic caucuses is a multi-step process with opportunities for bargaining and politicking at each stage. After the chair determines the number of eligible voting members in attendance, caucus participants divide into presidential preference groups. When that stage is completed, groups are counted for purposes of determining viability, and preference groups that fail to meet minimum viability standards have the opportunity to reassociate with other groups. At this point, politicking increases in intensity as viable groups seek to proselytize the "groupless" voters in order to increase the number of delegates for which they qualify. When all voters are members of a viable candidate preference or uncommitted group, the caucus chair again counts the groups and determines the number of delegates to the county convention which each is entitled to elect. The chair informs county headquarters of the number of delegates committed to each candidate, as well as the number selected as uncommitted, and the final step of delegate selection begins. Delegate selection within groups is usually a lively and spirited process which frequently involves speechmaking, bargaining, and vote trading.

Party officials claim that the system of proportional representation makes it possible to project the number of delegates that each Democratic presidential candidate will have among those ultimately comprising the Iowa delegation to the national convention. In 1972, Iowa Democratic officials responded to national media requests for "results" of the caucus process by preparing a list of sample precincts for purposes of projecting statewide caucus candidate support. In 1976, under State Chairman Tom Whitney, the Democrats established a "caucus returns headquarters" at the Des Moines Hilton with a phone reporting system by party chairs from Iowa's ninety-nine counties. A party staffer was present and provided immediate analysis of support patterns from around the state. The enterprising Whitney charged all present ten dollars for the service.[14]

The projections resulting from these Democratic efforts are highly tentative since some delegates are selected as "uncommitted," none is legally bound at succeeding steps in the process, and possibly, indeed probably, one or more of the presidential hopefuls will drop out of the race prior to the county conventions leading to realignments of delegates previously supporting those candidacies. The 1976 and 1980 caucuses provide interesting contrasts as to the accuracy of national convention delegate strength projections based on caucus

---

13. The 15 percent rule applies to caucuses electing four or more delegates. The minimum figures for viability in caucuses electing fewer delegates are: three delegates — 16⅔ percent, two delegates — 25 percent, and one delegate — 50 percent plus one.

14. Schier, *Rules of the Game*, 145, 316.

outcomes. The 1976 projection indicated that Jimmy Carter would control 13 of Iowa's 47 national convention delegates, Morris Udall 3, others 13, and "uncommitted" 18. On the first ballot, Iowa's delegates gave Carter 25 votes, Udall 20, Jerry Brown 1, and Ted Kennedy 1, which certainly calls the accuracy of the caucus projections into question. In 1980, with an incumbent president and fewer candidates for the nomination, the projections of future delegate strength proved to be very accurate. Democratic officials projected that the Iowa delegation would include 31 Carter supporters, 16 Kennedy, and 5 uncommitted delegates. The totals of those ultimately selected, and bound by the 1980 national convention rules, were Carter 31, Kennedy 19, and 2 uncommitted.[15]

The Republican delegate selection process in presidential caucus years is less complex than the Democrats' system. The Republicans generally select their delegates on an "at large" basis, although individual caucuses determine their selection procedures, and should they desire, elect delegates on a proportional basis. A precinct electing six delegates at large would allow each caucus participant to vote for as many as six delegates, and the persons receiving the most votes are elected regardless of their presidential preference. A well organized candidate organization possibly could pack a caucus and with a simple majority control all the delegates elected, a feat requiring 85 percent at Democratic caucuses. The Republican delegate selection process probably leads to the selection of more party regulars to the county convention than the proportional system used by the Democrats.

The Republican at-large system does not lend itself to projecting the composition of the delegation to the national convention. In response to media pressure for concrete outcomes from the caucus process and the desire to maximize the attention given to the Iowa caucuses, the Iowa Republicans initiated a presidential preference poll in 1976. Beginning modestly, sixty-two scientifically selected precincts conducted the poll; by 1980, all caucuses did so.

The poll occurs prior to the delegate selection process, but there is no requirement that delegates elected later in the evening reflect the sentiments expressed by the poll. Delegates are not committed or bound to any candidate. Consequently, the poll has little scientific basis for predicting candidate support among the Iowa delegation to the Republican National Convention. Republican officials, however, note that in 1976 the poll predicted very accurately the breakdown within the delegation to the national convention. In that year, the poll results indicated that 45.3 percent of those attending Republican caucuses supported President Gerald Ford, 42.5 percent favored Ronald Reagan, and 10.6 percent were undecided. The Iowa delegation split 19 for Ford and 17 for Reagan on the first ballot at the convention. In 1980 the poll was a complete failure as a predictor. George Bush was favored by 32 percent of the

---

15. Interview with Marie Menne, former caucus chairperson, Iowa Democratic Party, 23 February 1981.

caucus participants, Ronald Reagan by 30 percent, and several other candidates divided the remaining votes. The Bush advantage increased at the county conventions, but by the national convention, Reagan supporters were in complete control of the Iowa delegation and cast a unanimous vote for Reagan.

FROM A POSITION of relative obscurity, the Iowa precinct caucuses moved toward national prominence in 1972 when the Iowa Democratic Party moved its caucus date forward to January 24, making it the first primary event in the nation. The early date for the caucuses is the result of an interesting series of events. The Iowa General Assembly first passed legislation governing the date of precinct caucuses in 1969. The law required that caucuses be held "not later than [the] second Monday in May in each election year," but did not limit how early they might be held. Prior to 1972, the Iowa parties tended to hold their precinct caucuses in late March or in April, which fell in the middle of the national primary schedule. The Democratic National Committee prompted the move by deciding to hold its national convention on July 9, 1972, which was somewhat earlier than usual. The Iowa Democratic Party constitution included a clause requiring thirty days between party functions (precinct caucuses, county conventions, congressional district conventions, the state statutory convention, the state presidential convention, and the national convention), and due to the early date for the national convention, the latest possible date for the caucuses in 1972 was January 24. The January date moved the Iowa Democratic Party caucuses ahead of the New Hampshire primary election which was traditionally the nation's first primary event.[16]

The thirty-days-between-events clause in the party constitution arose from practical rather than philosophical considerations. According to Cliff Larson, Democratic state chair from 1970 to 1973, the party wanted to include as many Democrats as possible in the caucus process and to provide delegates to the next set of party functions with good sources of information. Unfortunately, the state party headquarters had severe physical limitations and very poor office equipment, so to complete the paper work and arrangements required for each level of meetings, a month interlude between party functions was necessary. Larson maintains there was no political intent in moving the caucus date forward, and confesses that he was unaware the Iowa Democratic caucuses would be the nation's first as a result of the move. He hastens to add, however, that it did not take Iowa Democrats long to realize what they had done, and although surprised by the magnitude of the media attention, the Iowa Democratic Party set out to capitalize on its new position of prominence.[17]

---

16. Iowa, *Acts and Joint Resolutions*, 63rd General Assembly, 1969, Chap. 90, 124; James Flansburg, "Iowa Caucus Date is First," Des Moines *Register*, 21 November 1971, Sec. B, 1.
17. Interview with Clifton Larson.

The early date for the Iowa precinct caucuses changed their character completely. Prior to 1972, they attracted no national attention. Generally, caucus attendance was poor, and often a handful of party regulars were the only persons present. Thus, even though the meetings were open and the Iowa press and other media publicized them extensively, party regulars dominated the precinct caucuses and the candidate selection process. Although empirical evidence is not available, probably many party regulars were happy with limited public participation.

Being the first primary event brought the Iowa Democratic caucuses to the attention of Democratic presidential candidates as well as to the media. When the major Democratic hopefuls campaigned extensively in the state in 1972, increased attention given the caucuses by the candidates and media stimulated voter participation: Turnout for the Democratic caucuses increased from 38,000 people in 1968 to 60,000 in 1972.[18]

The caucuses received an immediate boost in media attention when the McGovern campaign decided to make a major effort in the state. Muskie also campaigned in Iowa in 1972. The prominence of being first, and frequent visits by the major Democratic candidates, focused a great deal of media attention on the precinct caucuses.

The national attention in 1972 prompted the parties to take steps to further expand interest in, and publicity for, the Iowa caucuses. The Republicans, who missed out on the headlines in 1972 by holding their caucuses in April, were anxious to share the limelight with the Democrats. Both parties realized the necessity of a common caucus date to maximize media coverage. The two parties successfully negotiated an agreement to hold the Republican and Democratic caucuses in 1976 on January 19, and have continued the practice of a common date since that time. The Republicans also initiated a presidential poll in 1976.[19]

The common date for the Republican and Democratic caucuses in 1976 set the stage for a real media event and Iowa's party leaders were not disappointed. Jimmy Carter targeted Iowa as a testing ground for his campaign and Ronald Reagan challenged President Gerald Ford in the state. The candidates and media representatives visited the state in large numbers and Iowa's caucuses gloried in national attention. Surprisingly, participation in the caucuses was low in 1976. Party officials estimate that 4 percent (22,000 to 26,000) of the registered Republicans and 7 percent (38,500) of the eligible Democrats attended. The success of the Carter campaign, and the credit given the Iowa caucuses for his good start virtually guaranteed greater media attention for the 1980 Iowa caucuses.

---

18. Levels of participation are very rough estimates by state party officials and should be treated carefully.
19. Interview with Steve Roberts, former chairman, Republican Party of Iowa, 25 March 1981.

Yet, not everyone was pleased with the consequences of the early caucuses. In late 1977, the Democratic National Committee, concerned about the length and cost of a primary and caucus process that was over five months in duration, began examining alternatives to the drawn out process. When Iowa legislators learned that compression of the primary schedule was a possibility, they reacted to the perceived threat to their now famous caucuses by enacting legislation on March 31, 1978, which required precinct caucuses to be held no later than the second Monday in February in even-numbered years. The Democratic National Committee ultimately included in its procedures for the 1980 National Convention a rule (number 10) requiring caucuses or primaries to be held between the second Tuesday in March and the second Tuesday in June, but included an appeal process for states who had held caucuses or primaries earlier in 1976.[20]

In 1979, Iowa Democrats requested a variance to Rule 10, and after demonstrating that they attempted without success to persuade the Iowa General Assembly to change the caucus law and permit a date which fell within the March to June Democratic National Committee guidelines, received permission to conduct their precinct caucuses in January again.[21]

The candidates and media arrived in Iowa in late 1979 in preparation for the 1980 precinct caucuses. The early date of the Iowa caucuses had the effect of moving the entire national caucus and primary process forward, thus lengthening the campaign and increasing the costs to candidates. Although campaign expenses, and particularly media costs, are relatively low in Iowa, success in a caucus state is largely dependent on good grass-roots organizing. The successful 1980 campaigns of Jimmy Carter and George Bush again demonstrated this in Iowa. Both spent months putting together their organizations. John Connally, on the other hand, had little or no organization in Iowa and invested heavily in television time with few positive results.[22]

Media coverage of the precinct caucuses was immense. On Iowa caucus night in 1980, all three network national news programs originated from Des Moines. Democratic party leaders estimate media expenditures of over $3.5 million to cover the Iowa caucuses, with over two hundred national press people on hand.[23]

The early and sustained attention given the caucuses stimulated interest and officials reported record voter participation throughout the state. The Republican poll indicated that 106,000 persons participated, and the Democrats estimated that 100,000 people attended their meetings. The large turnout in-

---

20. Iowa, *Acts and Joint Resolutions*, 67th General Assembly, 1978, Chap. 1042, 207; Democratic National Committee, "Delegate Selection Rules for the 1980 Democratic National Convention," mimeographed (Washington, D.C., June 9, 1978), 10.
21. Interview with Marie Menne.
22. Ibid.
23. Ibid.

cluded many political amateurs attending their first caucus and some of the usually well-orchestrated events degenerated into rather chaotic affairs. Organizational efforts faltered as meetings spilled over into second and third rooms and supplies ranging from registration forms to ballots were in short supply. The results of large-scale citizen participation in the caucuses produced mixed results. Many meetings elected persons attending their first caucus as delegates to county conventions, and others were at best examples of symbolic democracy as citizens unfamiliar with caucus procedure had little impact. An interesting example of the latter occurred in Republican Caucus 74 in Des Moines, where 474 people attended and participated in the straw poll, but upon completion of the poll approximately half of those present left before the real business of delegate selection took place.[24]

After the 1980 caucuses and primaries, the Democratic Party's National Rules Committee made another move to compress the caucus and primary schedule at a meeting on July 9, 1980. The committee defeated by an 80 to 55 margin an effort to force all precinct caucuses and primary elections into a fourteen-week period between the first Tuesday in March and the second Tuesday in June. They did approve, however, a resolution asking the party's national executive committee to study the length of the presidential selection process.[25]

The Democratic National Committee responded to that recommendation by appointing the Commission on Presidential Nominations (called the Hunt Commission after its chair, North Carolina Governor James Hunt) to consider a number of changes in the nominating process. Their report, dated January 15, 1982, included a recommendation that the length of the Democratic primary season be compressed into a thirteen-week period between the second Tuesday in March and the second Tuesday in June. In deference to Iowa and New Hampshire, they granted permanent exemptions from the time limits for the Iowa caucuses and the New Hampshire primary election, although both must be held later than in 1980: Iowa may hold its Democratic caucuses no earlier than fifteen days before the start of the thirteen-week period and New Hampshire seven days. The exception will give Iowa and New Hampshire the opportunity to focus national attention on their primary events as in the past, but may lessen the long-term impact, as candidates will have the opportunity to tumble more quickly from victories (or rebound more quickly from defeats) in Iowa and New Hampshire.[26] Due to the widespread national attention, the Iowa caucuses have an impact on presidential races far beyond their real significance. Iowa is a small, homogeneous midwestern farming state of small

---

24. Interview with Scott Bittick, caucus member, 23 January 1980.

25. Larry Fruhling, "Move to Push Back Iowa's January Caucuses is Killed," Des Moines *Register*, 10 July 1980, 1.

26. The Democratic National Committee accepted the Hunt Commission's recommendations on March 26, 1982.

towns and rural areas. In 1980, only 123 of Iowa's municipalities had populations in excess of 2,500 people, 17 cities exceeded 25,000 persons, and Des Moines, the largest city in the state, had fewer than 200,000 residents. The state's 1980 population of 2,913,808 was 97 percent white. It sent fifty delegates to the Democratic National Convention and thirty-seven to the Republican Convention in 1980 which was 1.5 percent and 1.9 percent of the total at the respective conventions. Participation in the caucuses is typically less than 10 percent of the electorate, although it grew to about 20 percent in 1980 which was comparable to the turnout for the New Hampshire primary election. Iowa has eight electoral votes. Party competition in Iowa is high, but in presidential elections the state supported the Republican candidate in seven of the last nine races, the exceptions being 1948 and 1964.

Although no state legitimately can claim to mirror the national electorate, Iowa is less representative than many. Larger states legitimately complain that Iowa influences the candidate selection process far more than it should given its lack of demographic and political representativeness. There is a certain irony in the Iowa caucuses twice playing a major role in the nomination of Jimmy Carter and then supporting Gerald Ford and Ronald Reagan in the 1976 and 1980 presidential races.

Perhaps more important in placing the Iowa caucuses in perspective is the fact that the "results" have little meaning. As previously noted, the caucuses are the first in a multi-step process and the delegates selected at those meetings are not bound to support a particular candidate at the county conventions, nor are delegates from the county to the state conventions bound. (A Hunt Commission recommendation also accepted by the Democratic National Committee at its March 26, 1982, meeting will abolish the 1980 Democratic party practice of binding state delegates at the national convention.) As the field of presidential candidates narrows and as the political process is played out at the county, district, and state conventions, there is always fluctuation in candidate support. Projecting levels of delegate strength—referred to as "national delegate equivalents" by state party officials and the national media—after the first step in a fluid multi-step process is untenable. The "national delegate equivalents" are little more than guesses.

Even so, as long as the Iowa precinct caucuses are the earliest event in the primary season, they undoubtedly will attract a great deal of national attention. It matters little that the "results" of the Iowa caucuses are meaningless as predictors of delegate preference within the Iowa delegations to the national conventions. They are significant because they are first and the national media choose to assign importance to them. Media interpretation of caucus "outcomes" in Iowa is crucial to the campaigns of presidential aspirants. The broad coverage of the media advances the campaigns of the "winners" by featuring them on the evening news, the front pages of newspapers, and on the covers of national magazines. They also make it difficult for the less fortunate candidates, branding them "also rans" or "losers." The winners experience renewed vigor in their campaigns and increased success in fund-raising efforts, while the losers' campaigns are set back and they find it more difficult to raise money. In 1976 for example, R. W. Apple of the New York *Times* in a post-caucus story headline declared that "Carter is Regarded as Getting Big Gains From Iowa Results," an interpretation that "was prevalent on major networks and in major newspapers."[27] The CBS Morning News of January 20, 1976, declared Carter the victor and conducted a rather lengthy interview with him in which they permitted Carter to interpret the impact of the caucuses on his and the other candidates' campaigns. The only other candidate shown during the program was Fred Harris, and he was represented as having finished a poor third. The Washington *Star* declared Udall's campaign "damaged" on the basis of his fifth-place finish in Iowa with only 5.8 percent of the caucus vote.[28] Yet, at the Democratic National Convention in 1976 Carter, the media winner, received 25 votes and Udall, the loser, 20 votes on the first ballot.

In 1980, the Iowa caucuses provided a tremendous boost to the candidacy of George Bush who shaded the front-runner and heavily favored Ronald Reagan in the Republican poll by a margin of 32 to 30 percent. The media trumpeted his "victory" around the nation. Reagan underestimated the importance of Iowa and chose not to devote his personal energy to campaigning in the state. Bush's star rose dramatically after the victory in Iowa, and he rode the momentum all the way to the Republican vice-presidential nomination.

The national media and officials of both state parties cooperated in selling the caucuses as a weathervane in the presidential selection process. The actions taken by the Democrats in 1972 and 1976 and by Republicans in 1976 and 1980 made possible a media event by providing "results" or "outcomes" of the caucuses, even though the "results" are of little scientific value and actually may be very misleading.

The 1984 caucuses will again be the first event in the national primary season and will be conducted under the microscope of the media. Presidential candidates will be in Iowa very early, and large sums of money will be expended by the candidates and the media. The national attention tends to increase participation in the caucus process, and state officials of both parties are pleased to be able to identify potential sources of party support nine or ten months prior to the November elections. Because of the media attention, the Iowa local meetings which were designed to generate platform issues and select delegates to the county conventions will make or break presidential candidacies and must be taken seriously by all presidential candidates.

27. R. W. Apple, New York *Times*, 20 January 1976, quoted in Schier, *Rules of the Game*, 336.
28. Schier, *Rules of the Game*, 336.

BIBLIOGRAPHICAL NOTE

Post–World War II political history is nearly invisible to interpreters of Iowa history. The most reliable guide to Iowa's political history, Leland Sage's *History of Iowa* (Ames, 1979), gives only the briefest overview of the years following the New Deal. James Larew describes the rebirth of Iowa's Democratic Party in *A Party Reborn: The Democrats of Iowa, 1950–1974* (Iowa City, 1980). Thomas G. Ryan analyzed election returns and census data to call into question some of Larew's explanations for the Democratic revival in "The Early Years of the Iowa Democratic Revival, 1950–1956," *Annals of Iowa* 46 (1981), 43–63. Iowa's increasing urbanization (one of the debatable factors in the Democratic revival) led to a decade-long battle over reapportionment which is chronicled in Charles Wiggins, "The Post World War II Legislative Reapportionment Battle in Iowa Politics," in *Patterns and Perspectives in Iowa History,* ed. Dorothy Schwieder (Ames, 1973), 403–30. For profiles of postwar Iowa politicians, see Edward L. Schapsmeier and Frederick H. Schapsmeier, "A Strong Voice for Keeping America Strong: A Profile of Senator Bourke Hickenlooper," *Annals of Iowa* 47 (1984), 362–76; and Jon Bowermaster, *Governor: An Oral Biography of Robert D. Ray* (Ames, 1987). A welcome addition to the literature is Suzanne O'Dea Schenken, *Legislators and Politicians: Iowa's Women Lawmakers* (Ames, 1995).

For a fascinating account of the emerging influence of Christian evangelicals in the Iowa caucuses by a historian of American religion, see Randall Balmer, "Campaign Journal," in *Mine Eyes Have Seen the Glory: A Journey into the Evangelical Subculture in America* (New York, 1989), 109–137.

17

Iowa's Abortion Battles of the Late 1960s and Early 1970s: Long-term Perspectives and Short-term Analyses

JAMES C. MOHR

Like the caucuses, it seems difficult to imagine a time when the intractable social and political debates over abortion were not a part of our political discourse. In the following essay, historian James Mohr offers a welcome historical perspective on this contentious issue.

THE FIRST SESSION of the Iowa territorial legislature passed a general criminal code that contained language designed to permit the punishment of people who poisoned their fellow citizens. Among the poisons proscribed were abortifacients.[1] That section of the original territorial code proved to be the first formal mention of abortion in Iowa law. When the territorial code was revised in 1843, the attempt to abort a pregnant woman by any means (not just by poisons) became criminal, but only if the attempt was made after "quickening."[2] Quickening was the first perception of fetal movement by the mother herself, and the legislators who drafted and passed these early statutes surely knew that quickening usually takes place near the midpoint of a normal gestation, at the end of the fourth or the beginning of the fifth month of pregnancy. In adopting this policy, Iowa lawmakers were following long-established

---

1. The section is reprinted in Eugene Quay, "Justifiable Abortion — Medical and Legal Foundations," *Georgetown Law Review* 49 (1961), 470–71.

2. Ch. 48, 1843 *Iowa Territorial Revised Statutes* 162–63.

Originally published as James C. Mohr, "Iowa's Abortion Battles of the Late 1960s and Early 1970s: Long-term Perspectives and Short-term Analyses," *Annals of Iowa* 50 (1989), 63–89. Copyright © 1989 by the State Historical Society of Iowa. Reprinted by permission of the publisher.

precedent, for the quickening doctrine had been in effect in American law, both common and statute, since the founding of the republic.³

Modern analysts might conclude from these early actions that Iowa policymakers have opposed abortion since territorial days. The argument would be true, but only to a very limited extent. Iowa lawmakers did not want apothecaries poisoning their women, and they did not want anyone trying to induce abortions on women with fairly advanced pregnancies, partly because they believed that the potential for harm from an abortion increased with the length of the pregnancy. But it would be equally true to conclude that Iowa policymakers during the territorial period were remarkably tolerant of abortion, provided it was undertaken early, since the territorial codes that made late abortions subject to indictments for manslaughter also, in a sense, reaffirmed the longstanding legality of abortions performed prior to quickening. Subsequent events support the second interpretation.

The first of those events was the enactment of Iowa's state code in 1851. That compilation dropped the criminal sanctions against late abortions which had appeared in the territorial laws, and Iowa entered the Union without any statutory policies on the subject of abortion, hardly evidence of deep concern about the practice.⁴ The second revealing event was a court case known as *Abrams v. Foshee and Wife* (1857). The case was an action for slander: Mrs. Foshee was alleged to have publicly accused Mrs. Abrams of aborting herself. On appeal before the Iowa Supreme Court, attorneys for the Foshees conceded that an accusation like the one Mrs. Foshee made "might injure [a woman] in the estimation of the community," but it was not formally slanderous. It was closer, they argued, to accusations that Mrs. Abrams "was a common tattler, or liar, or that she indulged in the use of profane or vulgar language; that she was a drunkard, or the like." The Iowa Supreme Court agreed. To accuse someone of practicing abortion was unpleasant but not slander, and the justices stated explicitly that abortion before quickening was no crime in Iowa.⁵

The *Abrams* decision was published in 1857, and the following year a Keokuk physician, upset by the result, wrote his state senator urging enactment of a law against feticide.⁶ The legislature complied, but in limited fashion. The 1858 Iowa abortion law made the administration of drugs or the use of instruments on "any pregnant woman, with the intent thereby to procure the

---

3. For two different perspectives on the history of the quickening doctrine, see Cyril C. Means, Jr., "The Law of New York Concerning Abortion and the Status of the Foetus, 1664–1968: A Case of Cessation of Constitutionality," *New York Law Forum* 14 (Fall 1968), 411–26, and John T. Noonan, Jr., "An Almost Absolute Value in History," in John T. Noonan, Jr., ed., *The Morality of Abortion* (Cambridge, MA, 1970), 1–59. On the doctrine in the United States during the first half of the nineteenth century, see James C. Mohr, *Abortion in America: The Origins and Evolution of National Policy, 1800–1900* (New York, 1978), 1–146.

4. See *Iowa Code* § 4.28 (1851), cited by Quay, "Justifiable Abortion," 471.

5. *Reports of Cases in Law and Equity, Determined in the Supreme Court of the State of Iowa* (New York and Albany, 1857), 3: 274–81.

6. See the "momorial" of Dr. D. L. McGugin in 1858 *Iowa Senate Journal* 284.

miscarriage of any such woman" a crime punishable by up to a year in jail and up to a one-thousand-dollar fine.[7] But the word *pregnant* meant quickened, and the word *intent* made the crime virtually impossible to prove. Moreover, the Iowa Supreme Court ruled in 1863 that the 1858 statute could not be invoked against women who attempted to abort themselves by any means. "It is clear to us from the wording" of the 1858 law, ruled the court, "that it was the person who used the means with the pregnant woman to procure the abortion, and not the woman herself, that the legislature intended to punish."[8] Irregular abortionists and local midwives who performed abortions could be harassed under the 1858 law, which is quite probably what the state's established physicians wanted in any event, but the state made clear that the women of Iowa themselves would not be indicted for actions they took to end unwanted pregnancies.[9]

The overall result of these early abortion-related laws and decisions created in Iowa a sort of benign neglect toward the practice. Abortions early in pregnancy were tolerated, and the practice was almost certainly widespread in the state by the 1860s. No Iowa-specific data exist from that era, but in the nation as a whole the abortion rate probably rose to one abortion for every four or five pregnancies.[10] A special report on abortion presented to the Iowa State Medical Society in 1871 maintained that Iowa was keeping up with the nation in this respect, for abortion had become a significant means of family limitation throughout the state.[11] Abortions performed after the midpoint of a pregnancy were technically illegal, but the crime was virtually impossible to prove and authorities made no apparent effort to enforce the letter of the law. When the General Assembly decided to revise the state code in 1873, legislators asked the secretary of state to compile for them the last two years of criminal convictions in Iowa, complete with sentences, the types of persons involved, and similar information. That official did not report a single conviction for abortion during 1872 or 1873.[12] Nor did the new code alter the state's abortion policy.[13]

---

7. Ibid., 425; 1858 *Iowa House Journal* 612–13; Quay, "Justifiable Abortion," 471.

8. *Hatfield et. ux. v. Gano* in *Reports of Cases Argued and Determined in the Supreme Court of the State of Iowa* (Des Moines, 1864), 15: 177–79. This case was also a slander case.

9. On the role of the regular physicians in the origin of anti-abortion legislation during the nineteenth century, see Mohr, *Abortion in America*, 147–70.

10. Ibid., 46–118.

11. J. C. Stone, "Report on the Subject of Criminal Abortion," *Transactions of the Iowa State Medical Society* (1871), 1: 26–34.

12. Secretary of State, *Report in Relation to Criminal Returns*, in *Iowa Legislative Documents*, 1874, vol. 1.

13. 1873 *Iowa House Journal*. In considering the absence of tougher abortion clauses in the Iowa revisions of 1873, when other states were enacting them, it may have been significant that the General Assembly appeared to contemporary observers to have a decidedly pro-feminist tone. On January 25, 1874, for example, the *Burlington Hawk-Eye* noted that "the Legislature seems disposed to give [women] everything but the ballot."

Elsewhere in the nation, organized physicians, operating under the banners of the AMA and state medical societies, pushed during the 1870s for abandonment of the ancient quickening doctrine and for new statutes that would make abortion at any time during pregnancy a crime.[14] These anti-abortion physicians were remarkably successful in most states, but made little headway in the Iowa legislature. They won a major victory in the courts, however, in 1878, when the Iowa Supreme Court upheld a conviction under the 1873 code for an abortion performed prior to quickening. In essence, this decision, known as *State v. Fitzgerald* (1878), introduced in Iowa the policy that legislative pressure had produced elsewhere.[15] To attempt to abort a woman at any point in gestation would henceforth be an act liable to criminal prosecution in Iowa.

Four years later, in 1882, the medical establishment, as if to emphasize the new policy, spearheaded a successful effort in the General Assembly to lengthen the possible sentence for performing an abortion from one year to five years.[16] In 1886 the Iowa Supreme Court sustained the principle that death resulting from an abortion would be treated as second degree murder.[17] This ruling would remain in effect in Iowa through the first half of the twentieth century, which placed the state in the middle of national trends. Fifty years later, in 1936, eleven states would be punishing abortion-related deaths more severely; twenty would be punishing them less severely; and fifteen would be treating them just as Iowa did.[18] Finally, in 1915, the word *pregnant* was dropped from the abortion section of the criminal code, and with it went all ambiguity about the question of quickening: a formal, if somewhat belated, recognition that Iowa law had changed from territorial days.[19]

Even with the dramatic legal shifts of the late nineteenth century, however, substantial evidence suggests that abortion remained a reasonably widespread practice in Iowa, just as it did in other states, criminal statutes notwithstanding. Court records from the turn of the century indicated the existence of sanitariums where various operators, including some trained doctors, performed abortions on a regular and quite openly business-like basis.[20] The most famous abortionist in Des Moines, Carrie Rowley, practiced from the teens through the

---

14. This crusade is discussed in Mohr, *Abortion in America*, 147–225.

15. *State v. Fitzgerald*, 49 Iowa 260, 31 Am. Reports 148 (1878).

16. 1882 *Iowa Senate Journal* 46, 65, 73, 84, 195, 204, 206, and 1882 *Iowa House Journal* 104, 118, 123, 238–39, 260. The role of the state's established physicians became obvious when the bill was referred not to the Judiciary Committee, which would normally have jurisdiction over changes in the state code, but to the Committee of Medicine and Surgery.

17. *State v. Leeper*, 70 Iowa 748 (1886).

18. Frederick J. Taussig, *Abortion: Spontaneous and Induced: Medical and Social Aspects* (St. Louis, 1936), 434. Taussig's book, prepared for the National Committee on Maternal Health, ranks as one of the most impressive works on the subject of abortion ever published.

19. 1915 Iowa Acts at 69, in Quay, "Justifiable Abortion," 472.

20. For testimony about such a clinic in Lamoni, Decatur County, see *State v. Crofford*, 121 Iowa 395 (1903).

1930s. In 1933 she claimed that she would be rich if she had been paid for all the abortions she had performed, that she "produced abortions to save disgraced girls," and that she "was glad to do it."[21] As a rule, even people like Rowley, who was not a trained or licensed physician, encountered the authorities only when a patient died.

The best figures on abortion rates in Iowa specifically during the first three decades of the twentieth century were amassed by E. D. Plass in 1931. Plass, a physician, wanted to find out whether abortion was as common in rural areas as it was in urban areas, and fortunately for present purposes, he decided to look at the situation in Iowa. Plass surveyed eighty-one doctors who had rural practices. Altogether, they had overseen approximately 51,000 deliveries. They also reported seeing over 6,600 induced abortions, at least 90 percent of which were technically criminal (a few were therapeutic and hence legal under a ruling that allowed abortion to save the life of the mother). More than half of the doctors surveyed saw those rates as holding steady in Iowa; 27 percent thought the incidence of abortion was rising as the Great Depression set in. Moreover, the Iowa doctors considered their figures conservative because they simply did not see the large number of autoabortions and midwife abortions that progressed perfectly well and required no physician's aid or intervention afterward.[22]

Decisions of the Iowa Supreme Court through the same period further confused the legal status of abortion in the state. While the court remained firm on the issue of abortion-related deaths, it made the crime of abortion itself, as distinguished from actions arising from abortion-related deaths, difficult to prove. Between 1899 and 1928 a series of rulings made clear that the death or even the presumed death of an unborn fetus was considered a threat to the life of the woman carrying it and therefore justified an abortion; that anyone could attempt an abortion as long as the life of the woman appeared to be at stake; and, most importantly, that the state had the burden of proof to demonstrate that the abortion was *not* necessary.[23]

Those rulings help explain why people performing abortions in Iowa rarely encountered the authorities unless a patient died. Even then, conviction was difficult if the practitioner was a licensed physician. The state's attorneys-general from 1927 through 1932 reported only one indictment in Iowa for violation of the state's anti-abortion statute. Neighboring Minnesota, by com-

---

21. *State v. Rowley*, 216 Iowa 140; 248 N.W. 340 (1933). Quotes are from 216 Iowa 143. The case in which Rowley made these statements, however, actually involved a married woman who already had a seven-month-old child at home and did not want another pregnancy so quickly in the face of the worsening depression. Rowley had been before the Iowa Supreme Court a decade earlier, in 1922, when Polk County authorities, almost certainly abetted by the local medical society, set her up. See *State v. Rowley*, 198 Iowa 613; 198 N.W. 37 (1924).

22. Survey data of E. D. Plass as reported to and summarized by Taussig, *Abortion*, 366, 378.

23. *State v. Aiken*, 109 Iowa 643 (1899); *State v. Shoemaker*, 157 Iowa 176 (1912); *State v. Rowley*, 198 Iowa 613 (1924); and *State v. Dunklebarger*, 206 Iowa 971 (1928).

parison, where anti-abortion statutes were more continuously and aggressively enforced by state authorities, brought one hundred indictments (which resulted in thirty-one convictions) in the period from 1911 to 1930.[24]

Thus, following a century of somewhat contradictory legal activity on the subject of abortion, Iowa emerged from World War II facing a situation common to almost all of the other states as well: abortion was formally illegal, though quite widely practiced in a semi-clandestine fashion and quite rarely prosecuted. As interpreted by the courts, Iowa's anti-abortion statutes functioned as something akin to malpractice indictments in advance. If bona fide physicians were willing, for whatever reasons, to undertake occasional discreet abortions they could probably do so with impugnity. Even non-physicians and pregnant women themselves could try to induce abortions and seldom risk punishment, provided the procedure went well. But if the procedure was botched, and especially if a woman died as the result of an attempted abortion, hard questions would have to be answered and stiff penalties from the state courts were likely.

EARLY IN THE 1950s the Iowa Supreme Court sent a signal that this paradoxical and inconsistent situation might no longer be so lightly tolerated. Dr. J. A. Snyder, an elderly physician from Roland, was indicted for violation of the abortion statutes, even though all the procedures he was accused of performing went well. The prosecutor who brought the indictment had assembled fifteen women who were willing to testify that they had received abortions from Dr. Snyder during 1950 and 1951. When the local judge refused to grant the witnesses immunity, all but one of them withdrew. On the testimony of the lone remaining woman, however, Dr. Snyder was convicted. On appeal in 1953, the Iowa Supreme Court upheld the conviction, notwithstanding the fact that Snyder had been a duly licensed physician in the state for more than forty years. Because Snyder had the woman return to his office after dark, and because he did not give her a general physical examination, the court reasoned that he was merely providing an abortion, and was not really concerned about her health, much less fearful for her life.[25] Delivered in a climate of conservative politics and in a period of resurgent domesticity, the decision presaged an era when abortions might become difficult to obtain, even for sophisticated women with access to friendly and well-paid physicians, let alone for poor or desperate women.

While legal authorities moved during the 1950s to resolve the inconsistencies in Iowa's abortion policy by stepping up enforcement of the letter of the law, other people in the state were beginning to consider resolving the inconsistencies not by enforcing the law more vigorously but by redrafting it. The advocates of change in Iowa and elsewhere held many different views

---

24. Taussig, *Abortion*, 441.
25. *State v. Snyder*, 244 Iowa 1244; 59 N.W.2d 223 (1953).

through the late 1950s and early 1960s, but most agreed by the middle of the latter decade that abortions performed early in pregnancy by competent physicians for reasons they deemed physically or mentally appropriate should no longer be proscribed as criminal acts.[26]

In the General Assembly of 1967 State Senator John M. Ely, Jr., of Cedar Rapids, chairman that year of the Senate Public Health and Welfare Committee, introduced a bill that would have brought about such a change. Ely's bill, the first formal legislative proposal of its sort in Iowa in over a century, eventually expired with the Sixty-second General Assembly.[27] But it proved in retrospect to be the opening round of what would become from 1969 through 1973 one of the most tumultuous and emotional battles in Iowa political history.[28]

The General Assembly did not meet in 1968, but in 1969 the advocates of abortion reform returned to Des Moines, stronger than ever before and determined to alter Iowa policy on the subject.[29] Senator Minnette Doderer of Iowa City and Representative Richard Radl of Linn County submitted liberalizing proposals, but legislative activity in 1969 centered on a bill that emerged from the Senate Committee on Social Services.[30] That committee bill brought to the fore a Cedar Falls Republican, W. Charlene Conklin, who quickly became a key figure in the struggles of the early 1970s. Conklin did not like the 1969 committee draft for a host of substantive and procedural reasons, and helped defeat it.[31] But she announced her intent to submit a proposal of her own in 1970, which she did, and she became in some sense the legislative point person for Iowa abortion reform.[32]

The General Assembly debated and defeated efforts to liberalize Iowa abortion policy in 1970 and 1971. In both years the battles were bitter and

---

26. For information on shifting positions through 1967, see David T. Smith, *Abortion and the Law* (Cleveland, 1967); Lawrence Lader, *Abortion* (Indianapolis, 1966), and *Abortion II: Making the Revolution* (Boston, 1973); reprint of the American Law Institute's model code of 1959 in Quay, "Justifiable Abortion," 173–74; and *Report of the Governor's Commission Appointed to Review New York State's Abortion Law* (Albany, 1968).

27. See Index for *Iowa State and House Journals,* 1967 (hereafter cited as *Index*). The bill died in committee, but not without a public hearing that allowed Ely and his supporters to make their points publicly for the media.

28. John M. Ely, Jr., to Charlene Conklin, 30 January 1971, and Conklin to Ely, 3 February 1971, Charlene Conklin Papers, Special Collections, University of Iowa Libraries, Iowa City, Iowa (hereafter referred to as CCP). There is a copy of Ely's original bill, dated 27 March 1967, in box 2, CCP.

29. *Des Moines Register,* 6, 18, 28 January 1969.

30. *Index* (1969); draft of the bill, dated 7 February 1969, in box 2, CCP.

31. Conklin to James P. Schmitz, 19 February 1969; Conklin to James H. Polacek, 28 February 1969; Conklin to Cynthia Wessel, 10 April 1969, all in CCP. *Des Moines Register,* 7, 19, 22, 23 February 1969.

32. A copy of the 1970 bill, No. 1052, is in box 1, CCP. See also Corinne Miller, Co-Vice-Chairman, Winnebago County Republican Party to Conklin, 21 January 1970; Blain C. Wood, Tenth District Judge, to Conklin, 20 January 1970, both in box 1, CCP; *Index* of the 63rd General Assembly; *Des Moines Tribune,* 30 December 1970.

closely contested.³³ Following the respite of 1972, the General Assembly reconvened in January 1973. Many observers believed that the advocates of liberalization were on the brink of success at the state level, for they had made significant gains in each of the previous three years.³⁴ Hardly had the battle been reengaged, however, when the decision of the United States Supreme Court in the case of *Roe v. Wade* (1973) summarily ended the struggle. Ironically, that decision gave advocates of reform at the state level a victory they had not yet been able to win in the Iowa legislature.

THE BATTLES that raged in the Iowa legislature in the late 1960s raise for us twenty years later a host of intriguing historical issues. Not the least of them is the deceptively obvious question of why they broke out at all. Why had so many Iowans decided after a century of living with paradox, inconsistency, and benevolent neglect that they would like formally to alter the laws proscribing abortion? Why, in turn, did so many other Iowans rise to such passionate and politically powerful defense of the state laws, when most of their fellow citizens for a hundred years had apparently paid little or no attention to the policy one way or the other? Manuscript collections from the files of prominent state legislators during the late 1960s and early 1970s, which are now available in the University of Iowa Special Collections, provide some illuminating answers to these questions and help us place those battles into a longer historical perspective.

Four broad factors seem to have energized the proponents of liberalization. The first was a growing national concern about overpopulation. The administration of President Lyndon B. Johnson, which spanned the middle years of the 1960s, was the first one to spend substantial amounts of federal money on programs of fertility control. Iowans clearly shared the national concern about overpopulation. Richard Radl, who had cosponsored one of the unsuccessful liberalization bills in 1969, had stressed the threats of overpopulation. "All of our current environmental problems," he argued, "are closely related to the issue of over-population." Iowans had to "enact meaningful legislation" on subjects like abortion in order "to keep ourselves from being inundated."³⁵

---

33. *Index* (1970, 1971); *Des Moines Register*, 2 January, 14 February, 3, 4 April 1970; 4 January, 6, 7, 8, 10, 11, 12 February 1971. The legislative activities of 1971 are well documented in the Philip B. Hill Papers (hereafter PHP), Special Collections, University of Iowa Libraries, Iowa City, Iowa. The PHP contain roll calls, proposed amendments, tear sheets from the *House Journal*, and similar materials. There is also a superb summary of legislative activity in the form of a scholarly paper in the Earl M. Willits Papers (hereafter EWP), Special Collections, University of Iowa Libraries, Iowa City, Iowa. The paper has no listed author, though it is most likely by Willits himself and certainly prepared for his use.

34. Details of the early maneuvering in the 1973 session are fully documented in CCP, EWP, and especially in PHP, which are full of letters, tear sheets, proposed positions, and the like from the first weeks of the 1973 session.

35. Planned Parenthood of Iowa, *Newsletter* (March 1970), 2.

Senator Conklin's files contain copies of President Richard Nixon's 1969 special message to Congress, "Relative to Population Growth," and Morris K. Udall's influential article, "Standing Room Only on Spaceship Earth," which appeared in *Reader's Digest* that same year.[36]

The question of population was so closely linked to the question of abortion in Iowa that the *Des Moines Register*'s most famous and most often cited Iowa Poll on abortion, the one of January 1971 which revealed a clear majority in the state for liberalization, also asked people whether they thought the legislature should set legal limits on family size.[37] More telling still was the response of Iowa citizens to abortion-related appeals from population control groups. In February 1971, for instance, the Black Hawk chapter of Zero Population Growth ran a piece in the *Waterloo Courier* urging citizens to support abortion reform for population reasons. The announcement contained a section that readers were to clip out, fill in, and send to their state legislator. The positive response generated by this ad was the largest of its sort in the Conklin papers, clear evidence that appeals for a liberal abortion policy in the context of concern for overpopulation had substantial impact at the grassroots level in Iowa.[38]

Equally telling were the frequent allusions to population concerns expressed in hundreds of letters to other legislative supporters of abortion reform.[39] Earl M. Willits, a careful and almost scholarly state legislator from Ankeny, eventually concluded that population control was one of the two most important reasons why so many Iowans favored legalization, or re-legalization, of abortion by 1970.[40] No wonder, when Willits received letters like the following: "As young Catholics both my wife and I believe the church's stand [against abortion] is not in keeping with the times. We are concerned with the population problem and think each child brought into the world should be wanted and planned for."[41]

A second factor that proved important both in the nation as a whole and in the state of Iowa in particular was related to perceptions of fairness. The poor and the unsophisticated had a much harder time obtaining abortions under the old system of benign neglect than did the wealthy and the well connected. This inequity appears to have influenced several prominent groups around the state, especially social workers and mission-oriented clergy.[42] Fairness was

---

36. Nixon's message is in *Congressional Record*, 91st Cong., 1st sess., doc. # 91-139. The Udall piece appeared in December 1969. Both in CCP.

37. *Des Moines Register*, 10 January 1971, clipping in EWP.

38. The constituent forms are in box 3, CCP.

39. Many such references occur in PHP and EWP.

40. "Attempts to Liberalize Abortion Laws," p. 1, in EWP.

41. G. T. Nichols to Willits, 23 January 1971, EWP.

42. See Central Iowa Chapter, National Association of Social Workers, to Hill, 31 January 1973, PHP, and several different communications from the Iowa Clergy Consultation Service on Problem Pregnancy, Adoption, and Abortion to Conklin in box 3, CCP.

also an important issue in the decision of the Iowa YWCA to support repeal of the old law, a decision the YWCA reached as early as 1966.[43] The Iowa Conference of the United Church of Christ urged all of its pastors to favor repeal of the state's anti-abortion law in part because "the rich and middle class can terminate a pregnancy safely (legally *or* illegally) because they can afford to pay for it, while pregnancy termination is not readily available to the poor because of its cost (introducing another form of discrimination)."[44]

Abortions were expensive. Dr. Snyder, the man whose conviction in 1953 had signaled the possibility of stronger enforcement of the law, was charging his patients fifty dollars in 1950, a substantial sum indeed for that year. Iowa college students were also sensitive to the question of fair access. The student government in Iowa City raised conservative hackles in the fall semester of 1971 by voting funds for abortion counseling and abortion services to students who could not afford them. When their actions were overruled by university authorities under pressure from Des Moines, the students created a special loan fund for the same purpose.[45] Similar concerns were expressed at Drake University, Iowa State University, and the University of Northern Iowa.[46] The inequities of the old system played an important role in forcing the issue before the legislature.

Medical opinion proved to be a third critical factor in precipitating the abortion debate twenty years ago. During the 1950s, just as the state's anti-abortion laws began to be more vigorously enforced, even against physicians, medical statisticians demonstrated that abortions had actually become safer for pregnant women than going full term and bearing a child. Though no one, of course, was prepared to argue that all pregnant women should therefore be required to undergo abortions to protect their health, these figures undermined the female safety justifications that had once proved important to nineteenth-century legislators and jurists.

More crucial still was a dramatic shift in medical opinion that became manifest during the 1960s. Physicians were no longer defensive members of a struggling profession, looking to the state to prosecute their competitors, such as midwives. Instead, they were now at the height of their power and prepared to assert their right to make sensitive and tolerant decisions without

---

43. Statements from the YWCA appear prominently in the files of all of the leading abortion reformers; the earliest statements in CCP are from 1966.

44. Circular letter "To pastors" from the Christian Social Action Committee of the Iowa Conference of the United Church of Christ, 27 January 1971, box 1, CCP (parentheses and emphasis in original).

45. *Des Moines Tribune*, 8 October, 18 November 1971; *Daily Iowan*, 19 November, 14 December 1971, box 1, CCP; *Cherokee Daily Times*, n.d., clipping in CCP.

46. L. Wayne Bryan, campus minister at Drake, to Hill, 10 February 1971; Janet Jepeway-David to Hill, 19 February 1973, both PHP; Gary Sanders to Conklin, 18 January 1970; Linda Marshall to Conklin, 19 January 1970, both CCP; Charles E. Landis, United Campus Ministry at U.N.I., to James Gallagher, 22 January 1973, James Gallagher Papers (hereafter JGP), Special Collections, University of Iowa Libraries, Iowa City, Iowa.

the state looking over their shoulders. To put it crassly, now that they had finally cornered the medical market, physicians sought to reduce the market's restrictions; to put it less crassly, physicians went public with their desire for a nearly absolute degree of flexibility in providing what they thought, not what the state thought, their patients wanted or needed. The decision to have or not to have an abortion, they believed, should be made in a private, medical context.

By 1967, according to a survey conducted by *Modern Medicine* magazine, some 87 percent of all American physicians favored more permissive abortion laws than prevailed in their states.[47] It is not possible to determine whether that figure would have held steady in Iowa specifically, but there is no question that Iowa physicians played a major role in the drive to alter their state's abortion statutes. It is surely no accident that the abortion files of leading reform legislators are full of medical articles and physicians' letters urging liberalization, articles and letters that presumably influenced the thinking of those legislators. Nor is it a coincidence that Senator Conklin's husband was a physician. The senator herself was significantly influenced by a session she attended with her husband at the Denver meetings of the American Medical Association in 1969: a panel on "How the Abortion Law Has Worked."[48]

Physicians worked hard to change Iowa abortion laws during the six years of open struggle between 1967 and 1973. One of the principal pressure groups favoring liberalization astutely called itself the Iowa Association for the Medical Control of Abortion.[49] Many influential doctors in private practice wrote letters of support to the champions of reform, as did key professors and researchers at the state's two medical colleges. A letter from Dr. Wendell K. Downing of Des Moines to Philip Hill assured the representative that a majority of Iowa physicians favored legalizing abortion.[50] A letter from Dr. Hans Zellweger of the Department of Pediatrics at the University of Iowa urged legal abortions where amniocentesis indicated abnormality.[51]

---

47. "Abortion: The Doctor's Dilemma," *Modern Medicine*, 24 April 1967, 12–32, and L. M. Cohen, editorial director of *Modern Medicine*, to Martin M. Cummings, director of the National Library of Medicine (NLM), 2 May 1967, explaining the questionnaire and the responses upon which the article was based. The letter is attached to the NLM's reprint copy of the article in its Miscellaneous Collections, NLM, Bethesda, MD.

48. Conklin to Mrs. John L. Beattie, 5 February 1970, CCP. See also *Council Bluffs Nonpareil*, 15 February 1970.

49. This was not a medical organization per se, but it took full advantage of the fact that physicians were tacitly, and in many cases overtly, in support of its programs. The activities of this organization are well documented in PHP and CCP. The group claimed an extensive local following, generated a great deal of literature in favor of reform, and sent representatives to testify at virtually all of the public hearings held by the legislature on the subject of abortion law. Barbara Madden, head of the IMCA, actually served as secretary at one of the key hearings, 2 April 1970; see hearing notes in box 2, CCP, and Conklin to Madden, 7 April 1970, box 2, CCP.

50. Wendell K. Downing to Hill, 9 February 1971, PHP. Hundreds of letters like this one could be cited, but they are far too numerous to be listed separately.

51. Zellweger to Conklin, 5 March 1970, CCP; Zellweger and Jane Simpson to Hill, 2 January 1973, PHP. Zellweger also testified to the legislature on this subject.

Dr. George D. Aurand of Clinton, who testified to the legislature in favor of reform, also sought to persuade the Iowa county attorneys to favor liberalization of the state's abortion laws.[52] The Clinton and Scott County medical societies were but two of several local medical associations in Iowa to endorse the need for a more liberal abortion policy.[53] Most striking of all, the chairman of the Iowa Medical Society's Commission on Legislation testified to the state senate in favor of legalizing abortions performed by licensed physicians, a dramatic reversal of the stance taken by the state's doctors a century earlier.[54] Since Iowa had historically debated the abortion issue in the context of medicine and health, there can be little doubt that the activity of the medical community during the 1960s and early 1970s in behalf of legal abortions had a major impact in bringing the issue to public and legislative attention.[55]

The fourth major factor behind the abortion debate in Iowa in the late 1960s and early 1970s was the tremendous force of the women's movement. This is not the place to chronicle the revolutionary and remarkably rapid surge of modern feminism during the 1960s, but that surge certainly played a tremendous part in the Iowa abortion debates. At the grassroots level, abortion became a quintessentially women's issue, perhaps *the* quintessentially women's issue in Iowa for the period 1967 to 1973.[56]

During the late 1960s and early 1970s, a large proportion of the letters written to legislators in Des Moines urging reconsideration of the state's abortion policies were written by women. The phenomenon was really quite astonishing. It is hard to imagine that any issue in Iowa history to that point had ever generated either more letters to state legislators specifically from women or a higher percentage of letters from women than did the abortion issue between 1967 and 1973. Taken together those letters constitute a rich source of social history for future researchers, because many of the women who wrote their state legislators poured out private stories in great detail. They told Charlene Conklin things they had never dared to tell their husbands.[57]

---

52. Aurand to Hill, 17 August 1971, and attached paper, PHP.

53. *Des Moines Register,* 25 January 1970, and *Davenport-Bettendorf Times-Democrat,* 10 February 1970. The former vote, engineered by George Aurand, drew protests from Catholic physicians.

54. See notes on the Senate hearing of 2 April 1970, in box 2, CCP.

55. The attitude of private practitioners toward legal abortions has recently been examined by Jonathan B. Imber in *Abortion and the Private Practice of Medicine* (New Haven, CT, 1986). Though Imber's material came from a survey conducted in New England rather than Iowa, the analyses offered there are germane to anyone interested in the relationship between the abortion issue and the professional community of physicians.

56. In February 1971 the *Cherokee Daily Times* asked readers to complete a questionnaire concerning their attitudes toward abortion. Of the 815 people who responded, 79 percent were women.

57. This raises the whole question of confidentiality in recent history. Though the letters were obviously intended to be personal and private, virtually all of them are signed, and return addresses are given. Most of the women who wrote those almost intensely intimate letters are still alive and would probably be appalled to see them quoted in learned publications around the state and nation. This paper has deliberately avoided citing deeply personal matters.

Women's organizations seized upon the abortion issue as well. The Iowa YWCA took an overtly feminist position in 1969 in favor of reform. "One of the Imperatives for Action in the 1970–73 period is to revolutionize society's expectations of women and their own self-perception. Therefore, we must undertake intentional actions which will support, in public policy, the greater liberation of women. Among these actions, we will give special emphasis to the repeal of all laws restricting or prohibiting abortions performed by a duly licensed physician."[58] By 1970 the women of the Y had been joined by many other gender-based organizations urging repeal or reform of the criminal statutes against abortion. Included in the list were the Iowa Division of the American Association of University Women, which in 1970 considered "the present laws regarding abortion . . . outdated," and called for their repeal;[59] local YWCA branches, including the large ones in Des Moines and Waterloo;[60] the Class in Literature, one of the oldest of the federated women's clubs in the state;[61] the Status of Women Council of the Greater Des Moines Area;[62] the four hundred women of the Tifereth Israel Women's League in Des Moines;[63] and the Iowa Nurses' Association.[64]

Also influential were the actions of women in political life. Governor Robert Ray appointed a special Commission on the Status of Women in 1969, and from 1970 through 1973 the commission endorsed abortion reform in no uncertain terms. When the commission issued its first formal report in May 1970, a majority of the commissioners believed that the state's abortion laws were "antiquated and restrictive." The "principle" that should guide legislative action, according to the Women's Commission, was the idea "that a woman is a free being and as such has a right to control her own life, her own property, and her own physical being."[65] In December 1972 the commission reiterated its strong stand with only one vote opposed, that of a nun who sat on the commission. During the legislative session of 1973, the Iowa Women's Commission was pressing actively for repeal, when the *Roe* decision intervened.[66] Around the state women organized petition drives in favor of liberal abortion laws.[67]

---

58. Excerpt from Iowa Association for Medical Control of Abortion handbills, 1 January 1970, copies in PHP and CCP.

59. Ibid.

60. Box 2, CCP.

61. Mrs. Leland Beneke and Mrs. Robert LaGrange to Conklin, 14 January 1971, box 1, CCP.

62. Mrs. Linda L. Archibald to Conklin, 26 January 1970, box 1, CCP.

63. Mrs. Harold Pidgeon to Hill, 19 January 1973, PHP.

64. See statement sent to Hill, 2 February 1971, PHP.

65. Statement by the Governor's Commission on the Status of Women Before the Democratic and Republican Platform Committees, May 1970, PHP.

66. Christine Wilson, Chair of the State Commission on the Status of Women, to Hill, 5 January 1973 and 16 January 1973, PHP.

67. For an example, see Mary Schreiber to Conklin, n.d., but almost certainly January 1971, with attached petition of 238 signatures from Iowa City, box 3, CCP.

Women delegates and committeewomen in the Democratic and Republican parties likewise helped push the abortion issue into the open. Both parties adopted platform planks supporting abortion reform. The Republican resolution was the stronger of the two, asserting that "the decision to terminate a pregnancy is a matter of conscience and health, not of law. Laws are appropriate in this area only to assure proper safeguard for such procedures. We recommend Iowa's laws be revised to acknowledge these facts."[68] The Democratic resolution likewise recognized the decision as one of "conscience" involving a woman and her physician, but hedged with a statement that "the highly personal and non-partisan nature" of the issue "will not permit universal acceptance" of the liberal position.[69] That was a bow to the strong Catholic core in the Iowa Democratic party. Moreover, there is evidence that local party women took their parties' resolutions seriously. The Johnson County Women Democrats formally endorsed repeal of Iowa's anti-abortion laws in 1970 and worked to keep their party's position on abortion as liberal as its Catholic core would permit.[70] Rosalee Hillman, a Republican committeewoman from Essex, wrote Senator Conklin to let her know that Hillman would "no longer support Senator Bass [an Essex senator who voted against abortion reform], if he will not represent women as well as men in his area."[71]

In view of the foregoing, two facts bear repeating. First, efforts to re-legalize abortions in Iowa repeatedly failed through 1973; the United States Supreme Court, not the Iowa legislature, overturned the state's nineteenth-century anti-abortion statutes. Those who forced abortion reform into the open and onto the agenda of the General Assembly never really prevailed at the state level. Second, while the abortion issue became a quintessentially women's issue in Iowa, the state's women were far from unanimous on the question of whether to liberalize the law or to enforce it as it stood. In short, any effort to understand the Iowa abortion battles of the late 1960s and early 1970s must take seriously those people who rose to defend the anti-abortion policies already in place. Who were they and why would they do it?

THE CONVENTIONAL ANSWER identifies the defenders of the old criminal statues primarily as people who acted from *a priori* assumptions, either religious or scientific, that human life begins at conception. To interrupt the process of gestation was, in that view, tantamount to murder. Life has always been and still remains an absolute, and the state should not permit citizens to destroy it under any circumstances whatsoever. The chief example invariably cited is the position of the Roman Catholic church, which played essentially no role in the origin or evolution of Iowa's anti-abortion policies in the nine-

---

68. See excerpt of the IMCA handbill, 1 January 1971, box 3, CCP.
69. Ibid.
70. *Iowa City Press-Citizen*, 4 April 1970.
71. Rosalee Hillman to Conklin, 27 January 1971, box 1, CCP.

teenth century, but defended them fiercely as moral absolutes once they came under attack in the second half of the twentieth century.

Like most bits of conventional wisdom, this one has a great deal of truth in it, and it is substantiated in the manuscript collections of the state legislators of the period. The files are full of letters arguing fine points about the origins of life, full of anguished concern on the part of citizens clearly committed to what they considered a moral imperative. Discussions in newspaper editorials, commentaries on radio and television, and hearings before the legislature often sought to address the issue of when life begins.[72] When the Catholic parishes of Iowa systematically began to generate action on the part of their members against abortion reform, they distributed sheets in church explaining the most effective ways to write letters to legislators. Those sheets were unambiguous about the essential point to make: "The basic question is: When does life begin?"[73]

There is little question that the Catholic parishes in Iowa took the early lead in defending the state's already existing anti-abortion policies against the forces of repeal and reform. The first public efforts at liberalization were countered with massive letter-writing and telegram-sending campaigns from Catholics; hundreds and hundreds of those letters and telegrams are now in the archives. Legislative leaders of the anti-abortion forces kept closely in touch with the Catholic hierarchies in their districts, especially with Catholic educators.[74] The Catholic commitment to life from the instant of conception was clearly a crucial factor, and Catholics were remarkably effective as a pressure group considering they were well under 20 percent of the state's population during the late 1960s and early 1970s. Certainly their opponents had a grudging respect for them, as many bitter letters testified. Mrs. R. E. Christiansen of West Des Moines, an active member of the Iowa Association for the Medical Control of Abortion, expressed a widely held sentiment when she wrote Representative Hill after the defeat of the reform bill in 1971: "It seems that no matter what the political parties, the Medical Society, the A.A.U.W., the Y.W.C.A., the Council of Churches, or the people of Iowa want, the Catholic Church has the money and the muscle to impose its will on the rest of society."[75]

Clearly, however, the abortion debates in Iowa involved far more than the *a priori* commitments of specific groups, regardless of their size, influence, or

---

72. The editorials and the hearings are easily documented. For transcripts of radio and television editorials, see Edwin J. Lasko, general manager of the KCRG stations, to Conklin, 18 November 1971, Dan Yates, news director, KCFI, to Conklin, 9 February 1971, and WMT-TV, WMT-Radio editorials of 9 February 1971, all in CCP; John A. Moline, general manager, KOUR Radio, to Gallagher, 19 February 1973, JGP.

73. See handbill passed out in the Des Moines Catholic parishes in December 1970, attached to a letter from Robert Gorsuch to Willits, 22 December 1970, EWP.

74. For a good example, see the Reverend Carl L. Schmitt, Metropolitan Coordinator, Dubuque Metropolitan System of Catholic Education, to Gallagher, 23 January 1973, JGP.

75. Mrs. R. E. Christiansen to Hill, 15 February 1971, PHP.

effectiveness. More seemed to be at stake than difficult distinctions between life as an absolute, life in the process of becoming, life not yet realized, and life already manifest. Much broader concerns were evident: concerns about the fundamental tone of what life would be like in the future and how men and women, but especially women, would relate to the new world ahead. Ultimately, the abortion battle was about where American society seemed to headed.

The abortion battle did not emerge from a contextual vacuum, after all, but from a decade that included civil rights, affirmative action, urban rioting, cities burning, much talk about perpetual welfare and fatherless families, national leaders being assassinated, a terrifying surge in the use of illegal drugs and chemicals, the free speech movement on college campuses, draft resistance, bitter debates (especially in Iowa) over the righteousness of the Vietnam War, and similarly unsettling developments. Many of the people who wrote their state legislators saw in the drive to liberalize abortion a sort of symbolic last straw. Some lines had to be drawn somewhere, and abortion, an issue that could be presented in clear-cut life-and-death terms, seemed to be the place to draw one. If the state permitted abortion "on demand," as the opponents of liberalization put it, even the sanctity of motherhood might disappear. The basic idea of the family would be undermined, and with it might go all traditional social values.

In a decade of near-revolutionary change, many Iowa women clung to the bedrock of traditional reproductive arrangements. As a woman from Estherville put it to Senator Conklin, "From the small cell of the family to the complex organization of the society, women play a basic role. . . . Where is your womanly dignity?"[76] The same feminism that galvanized unprecedented numbers of Iowa women into the movement to liberalize the state's abortion laws, it now appears, drove others to fear for their own futures and for the future of society. Without traditional values, argued another woman, "men will get ideas of abusing women," since their own male responsibilities would be stripped by the proposed laws.[77] A couple from Iowa City saw the feminist issue of autonomy as unrealistic. "In the abstract, man or woman has an absolute right over their body and its life; however, in the practical order of civilized societal living, this right has been modified by human laws throughout the ages. Modern woman must still reside in our society, and she needs to modify her right over her body for the good of the group, the same as everyone else."[78] In the words of the sociologist Kristin Luker, the abortion debate that broke out in the 1960s was in large part "about women's contrasting obligations to themselves and others. . . . a *referendum on the place and meaning of motherhood.*"[79]

---

76. Agnes Fitzgibbons to Conklin, [February 1971], CCP.
77. Mrs. B. H. Meinar to Conklin, 29 January 1971, CCP.
78. Floyd and Charlene Sarff to Conklin, 30 January 1970, CCP.
79. Kristin Luker, *Abortion and the Politics of Motherhood* (Berkeley, 1984), 193 (emphasis in the original).

In this respect, there was a striking parallel between the abortion battles of the late 1960s and early 1970s, on the one hand, and a similarly searing issue of the nineteenth century: slavery in the territories. The parallel was not one of substance, but one of cultural and political process. Slavery in the territories was an inherently important issue in and of itself, of course, just as abortion was. But slavery in the territories *per se* did not by itself provoke guerrilla warfare in Kansas or bring about a revolution in the political party structure of the nation. Instead, slavery in the territories became the symbolic or surrogate question upon which was focused a much wider range of more difficult but less well defined problems separating the North and the South.

The abortion debates of the late 1960s had much of the same ring to them. They were especially intense because they turned not on the specific issue alone, important as it was, but also on a much wider range of more difficult but less well defined problems separating those who welcomed the cultural revolutions of the 1960s (or were willing to try to accommodate them), on the one hand, and those who defended traditional virtues (or the virtues of traditionalism), on the other. That parallel helps to explain why the most fundamental Protestant sects in Iowa tended to side with the Catholics on the abortion issue, though on the face of it they would stand doctrinally and socially a long distance from the papacy.[80]

For many Iowans, abortion came to be the great symbolic or surrogate issue of the late 1960s and early 1970s. Upon it they focused a host of related misgivings about the general direction of society.[81] Legal abortion was a first step to larger "moral corruption."[82] The "entire state" was on the brink of becoming "a tainted, shamed land."[83] In a decade when "co-ed dorimtories [sic] are already starting," some envisioned, at least hyperbolically, "sexual relations . . . taking place on the street corners."[84] A surprisingly large number of older people feared that abortion would lead to other forms of social killing and that they would become logical victims. Phoebe Stewart of Des Moines saw "the next move as Mercy killing of the aged, sick, deformed, and mentally ill. What assurance do we have that we will not fall into one of the other cate-

---

80. See, for example, Raymond W. Fletcher, public relations officer for the Lutheran Church–Missouri Synod (which claimed 126,500 members in Iowa) to Hill, 28 January 1971, with attached 25-page statement: "A Position Paper on Induced Voluntary Abortion, by A Committee Appointed by the President of the Iowa District West of the Lutheran Church–Missouri Synod, By Order of the 1970 District Convention"; and Calvin Rumley, pastor of Ankeny Baptist Church, to Hill, 4 February 1971, in which the pastor states that "many hundreds of non-liberal, Bible believing churches" in Iowa opposed liberalization of the state's abortion policies, both in PHP.

81. For data that strongly support this argument in the context of the ERA battle of the 1970s and 1980s, see Louis Bolce, Gerald DeMaio, and Douglas Muzzio, "ERA and the Abortion Controversy: A Case of Dissonance Reduction," *Social Science Quarterly* 67 (June 1986), 299–314.

82. See telegram of John Craig et al. to Conklin, 20 February 1969, CCP.

83. Mrs. Bernard Zimmerman to Conklin, 28 January 1971, CCP.

84. Mrs. Dwayne Van Ort to Willits, 20 January 1971, EWP.

gories? You may be signing your own death warrant," she warned Representative Hill, "if you approve" the liberal abortion bill.[85] References to euthanasia were extremely common in the letters of those who opposed reform. Opinion polls in Iowa during the late 1960s and early 1970s consistently indicated that liberalized abortion was more likely to be opposed by the elderly than the young, the poor than the wealthy, and the least well educated than those with solid schooling.[86] Put differently, this suggests strongly that those least confident of their abilities to adapt to revolutionary change in the basic fabric of society —the vulnerable, the poor, and the poorly prepared—were the groups most skeptical about abortion reform.

THIS WAY OF VIEWING THE ABORTION ISSUE—as one of the great symbolic issues of its time, a political focal point for Iowans dismayed by the cultural tumult of the 1960s—may throw some light on an aspect of the abortion controversy that has always stood out as a troubling anomaly in this whole business: the apparent inconsistency between public opinion polls of the period, on the one hand, and political action (or lack of action), on the other. Beginning in 1967, opinion polls consistently made clear that a majority of Iowans favored some degree of legal tolerance toward the practice of abortion. The respected "Iowa Poll" reported in the fall of that year that 68 percent of the state's citizens favored liberalization of the Iowa abortion laws, 21 percent opposed liberalization, and 11 percent expressed no opinion.[87] In the state's best-known survey of public attitudes on this subject, the *Des Moines Register*'s "Iowa Poll" of January 1971, 21 percent of Iowa citizens favored the legalization of all abortions, 54 percent favored the legalization of abortions that threatened the physical or mental well-being of the mother (for a total of 75 percent in favor of liberalization), and only 11 percent opposed abortion under any circumstances.[88] A *Cherokee Daily Times* survey a month later registered 57 percent in favor of liberalization.[89] A "Voter's Lobby" poll that same year was two to one in favor of liberal legislation, and a KDMI survey showed 64 percent for reform.[90] The *Davenport-Bettendorf Times-Democrat* also ran a "Viewpoint Poll" on the subject that year. Well over one thousand people responded, and 73 percent favored liberalizing the state's abortion pol-

---

85. Phoebe Stewart to Hill, 27 January 1971, PHP.

86. See the "Iowa Polls" in the *Des Moines Register*, 10 December 1967, 28 February 1969, and 10 January 1971; *Cherokee Daily Times*, 10 February 1971; *Davenport-Bettendorf Times-Democrat*, 15 February 1971. These Iowa patterns were consistent with surveys elsewhere in the country.

87. See recapitulation in *Des Moines Register*, 28 February 1969.

88. Clipping in EWP.

89. *Cherokee Daily Times*, 10 February 1971.

90. Both surveys are noted in PHP.

icies.[91] When Representative Willits polled his constituents in January 1972, he continued to receive similar figures: 68 percent for liberal legislation, 26 percent opposed to legalizing abortions, and 6 percent without an opinion on the subject.[92]

In the face of such strikingly consistent figures, why was the legislature so reluctant to act? Why did the lawmakers at Des Moines drag their feet until the issue was resolved for them from Washington in the form of a Supreme Court decision? Some feminists have argued that this was a case of male reluctance to pass feminist legislation. Because public opinion surveys indicated that men consistently favored liberal abortion policies more strongly than women, this charge is difficult to assess.[93] The charge may have some validity, for the paradoxical reason that so many Iowa women opposed the feminist position on this issue, but a thorough evaluation of the gender argument in this context will have to await evidence of a different sort from what is presently available in the archives.

Other analysts hinted darkly at the power of special interests, especially the Catholic church, or at the ability of single-issue activists to clog and confuse the expression of majoritarian sentiment in the American political process, especially at the state and local level. Both are fundamentally structural arguments that merit serious consideration. But neither fully explains the inconsistencies between public opinion polls on abortion and official public policy on the subject.

The inconsistencies may also have resulted from the fact that the polls were measuring something different from what the legislators sensed in their mail. By their nature, opinion polls artificially isolated abortion as a separate and distinct issue. And as a separate and distinct issue, divorced from the cultural and social context of the late 1960s and early 1970s, Iowans confirmed what had been, after all, their long-term behavioral response toward abortion: a tolerant, if uneasy and even unofficial, permissiveness. Because that basic pattern had been sustained from territorial days, the polls should not have surprised anyone familiar with the history of the issue in the state.

Politicians of the day, however, did not face the question as a separate issue. They faced an emotional surrogate, freighted with a great deal of cultural baggage. They faced an issue that could no longer be dealt with in issue-specific terms. They faced a sort of symbolic referendum on the social revo-

---

91. *Davenport-Bettendorf Times-Democrat*, 15 February 1971. An editorial noted that surveys conducted in area high schools were even more lopsided. At West High School in Davenport the students favored liberal abortion laws 79 percent to 21 percent.

92. The abortion issue was the twelfth of fifteen issues about which Willits sought his constituents' opinions. See *Ankeny Press-Citizen*, 13 January 1972, and Willits to constituents, form letter, 3 February 1972, EWP.

93. This is not the place to pursue this argument in detail, but the surveys referred to in the footnotes above revealed a consistently more liberal view toward legal abortions on the part of men than women.

lutions of the 1960s, and that made the abortion issue political dynamite. No wonder there was something of a sigh of relief in Des Moines in the early weeks after the *Roe* decision, even on the part of those who had opposed reform.[94] No wonder the legislature quickly agreed to a moratorium on the issue, pending action of the Iowa Attorney General on the impact of the decision at the state level.[95]

Two days after the *Roe* decision was announced by the United States Supreme Court, the author of that decision, Mr. Justice Harry Blackmun, came to Iowa to address the Cedar Rapids–Marion Area Chamber of Commerce. He was greeted that night by fifty-one anti-abortion demonstrators outside the meeting place. Later in his career he would become inured to such treatment, but their presence clearly bothered Blackmun less than forty-eight hours after the decision. He devoted most of his after-dinner speech to a canned history of the Supreme Court and how it worked, but turned at the end of his talk, "with seeming anguish," according to the *Cedar Rapids Gazette*, to the abortion question. He expressed a deep frustration, for he had known all along that the members of the court would "be excoriated from one end of the country to the other," regardless of how they decided the abortion issue. Blackmun "really resent[ed]" that evening in Cedar Rapids "the bitter nights" the issue had already given him and the many more he knew would follow. Indirectly, at least, he blamed the nation's state legislatures for their unwillingness, or inability, to face up to abortion as a separate issue the way they faced other issues.[96]

TO CONCLUDE by returning to the subtitle of this essay, "Long-term Perspectives and Short-term Analyses," two overriding observations emerge. First, debate over the abortion issue broke out in the late 1960s, after more than a century of quiescence, because abortion policy figured centrally in a concatenation of concerns that came to the surface of American public consciousness during that decade: concerns about population growth, concerns about fairness, concerns about the place and power of the professions, and above all, concerns about the future of women. Second, once the issue reemerged, it became unresolvable in the Iowa legislature not merely because it created serious policy disagreements in and of itself (though it most certainly did), but also in part because it became the symbolic surrogate for profound cultural misgivings that already existed. An outpouring of material from constituents reenforced that conclusion, and for six years Iowa legislators were unable in practice to disentangle the abortion question from its cultural context the way opinion polls could do in theory.

---

94. See, for example, Gallagher to James J. Milbach, 23 January 1973, Gallagher to V. G. McSweeney, 23 January 1973, and Gallagher to Janice Edred, 9 March 1973, all in JGP.

95. See *Des Moines Register*, 23 January, 28 February, 15 March 1973; *Waterloo Courier*, 2 February 1973.

96. *Cedar Rapids Gazette*, 25 January 1973.

BIBLIOGRAPHICAL NOTE

The State Historical Society of Iowa was founded in 1856 — only a decade after the state joined the union — to begin preserving and recording Iowa history that the founders feared was in danger of being lost to succeeding generations. Historians now need to begin recording Iowa's recent history, humbly acknowledging that succeeding generations will reinterpret events based on the questions they need to answer. But early reflection provides a firm basis for reinterpretation. An outstanding example of the value of such work, besides the preceding essay by James Mohr and Mark Friedberger's work on the farm crisis of the 1980s, is James F. Findlay, "Religion and Politics in the Sixties: The Churches and the Civil Rights Act of 1964," *Journal of American History* 77 (1990), 66–92. For additional details about legislative battles over issues of special concern to women — and the role of women legislators in those and other battles — see Suzanne O'Dea Schenken, *Legislators and Politicians: Iowa's Women Lawmakers* (Ames, 1995).

INDEX

Abolitionist movement, birth of, 88
Abortion, xi, 411–430
  battles of, in Iowa legislature, 417–424
  Catholic Church on, 424–425
  medical opinion on, 420–422
  Roe v. Wade on, 418, 423, 430
  rulings by Iowa Supreme Court on, 416
  women on, 422–424, 426–428
Abrams v. Foshee and Wife, 412
Adams, Charles Francis, Jr., 216–217, 221
Adams, R. S., 172
Adams, W. P. C., 164
Adorno, T. W., 150
African Americans
  community of, in Iowa, 129, 130–131
  education of, 9
  enlistment of, as soldiers, 137–138, 152
  granting of suffrage to, 9, 132
  migration from South, 2
  population of, 15
  and prohibition issue, 279–280
  terms used for, 296
Agribusiness firms, 379
  growth of power of, 375–376
Agricultural Adjustment Act, 343
Agriculture. *See* Farming
Agriculture, U.S. Department of, War Board, 355
Agri-finance institutions, role of, in farming, 376
Agrigenetic technology, 376
AGRI industries, 390–391
Allen, James, 28
Allen, Mrs. C. D., 120
Allison, William Boyd
  as GOP leader, 250, 253, 256
  power of, as senator, 324
  and prohibition, 264, 269, 272, 273, 275, 282–283
  and railroad regulation, 231
Allport, Gordon W., 150–151, 152, 153–154
Amana colonies, xv, 11
American Agriculture Movement, 393
American Association of University Women (AAUW), Iowa Division of, 423, 425
American Dilemma, An (Myrdal), 149–150
American Farm Bureau Federation, 338–339
American Farmers: The New Minority, The (Fite), 328–329
American Gothic (Wood), 1–2, 3
American political system, 87
American Soybean Association, 394
Anderson, Albert R., 251–252
Anderson, Karen, 364, 365, 371
Annals of Iowa, The, xvi
Anti-Keokuk party, 26
Anti-Monopoly party, 11, 212, 265
Anti-Nebraska party, policy battles over black equality in, 131
Apple, R. W., 409
Argersinger, Peter H., 258
Armour Company, 391
Ashby, Newton B., 255, 257
Atherton, Lewis, 7, 291, 310–311, 329
Athletics, integration in, 294–295
Aurand, George D., 422
Automobiles, and rural life style, 328, 331

Baker, Jean H., 132
Baker, Margaret McCormick, 303
Baptists
  beliefs of, 9
  membership in, 301, 302
  political affiliation of, 97, 147
  and prohibition, 277
Barlow, Lester, 340–341
Barr, Cleve, 311, 312
Bass, Senator, 424
Beach, John, 29, 30
Beard, Charles, 298
Beecher, Catharine, 47
Belknap, George, 43
Belknap, Kitturah, 42, 43, 45, 49, 52, 54–55, 56
Belknap family, 44
Bellows, Henry, 125–126

433

Beltman, Brian, xiv
Benson, Lee, 87
Benton, Thomas Hart., Jr., 138
Berkhofer, Robert F., Jr., 19
Berry, Wendell, 385–386
"Bill of Rights for Iowa Children," 334
Birkbeck, Morris, 79
"Birth of a Nation," 296
Black Bears, 26
Black code in Iowa, 131, 149
Black Hawk, 20, 22–23, 25
Black Hawk Purchase (1832), 90
Black Hawk War (1832), 23–24, 25, 26
Blackmun, Harry, 430
Blaine, James, 288
Bloomer, Amelia, 121
Bloor, "Mother" Ella, 340
Blue laws, 95
Blythe, Joseph W., 231, 233, 256
Bogue, Allan G., xi, 61–84, 129
Boies, Horace, and prohibition, 255–256, 275, 277–283
Bootlegging, 271
Bosch, John, 342
Bradley, Charles, 13, 341, 342–343
Bradley, Eva, 316
Brainard, Helen, 331
Brainerd, N. H., 122
Brewer, David J., 234
Brewers' Association, opposition to prohibition, 267
Brewster, S. A., 187–188
Brookhart, Smith Wildman, x
Brooks, Elisha, 52
Brotherhood of Locomotive Engineers, 191, 273
Brown, Jerry, 403
Brown, John, 268
Brown v. Board of Education, 153–154
Brunner, Mike, 307
Bryan, William Jennings, 322, 325
Buchanan, James, 147
Burlington
  Board of Trade in, 179
  development of, as urban area, 91
  economy of, 173–174
  effect of railroad strikes on, 178–179, 181–184, 185, 190
  elite in, 180–181
  growth of, 185
  railroad ambitions of, 173
  and railroad rate regulation, 207–208
  relationship with Burlington & Missouri Railroad, 174–176
  relationship with Chicago, Burlington & Quincy Railroad, 174–176, 178
  retail in, 172
  size of, 172
  stagnation of, 185
  and transportation, 172–173
Burlington and Missouri River Railroad, xi, 171, 172, 174–176, 198–199, 205, 206
Burlington Gazette, 222
Burlington Hawk-Eye, 190, 201, 205, 208, 214–215
Burlington Lumber Company, 176
Burlington Voluntary Relief Association, 191
Burrows, Jay, 260
Bush, George, 403–404, 406, 409
Butler, David, 21
Byers, S. H. M., 105

Campbell, D'Ann, 357
Campbell, James, and prohibition, 285
Capital, power of, in farming, 79–80
Capitalism
  commercial, 88, 90
  free labor, 92
  industrial, 88
  merchant, 201
Cargill, 389–390
Carpenter, Cyrus Clay, 209–210, 212–213, 220
Carter, E. H., 311
Carter, Jimmy, 403, 405, 406, 408, 409
Catholics, 6
  in abortion debate, 424–425
  beliefs of, 9
  colleges set up by, 6
  Ku Klux Klan opposition to, 305–308
  membership in, 301, 302
  political affiliation of, 97, 142, 147, 148
  schism between protestants and, in small towns, 301–309
Catt, Carrie Chapman, 9
Cattle feeders in farming, 73, 74–75
Cedar Rapids, industrial development of, 10
Central Pacific Railroad, 171
Chamberlain, Elisha, 175
Chambers, John, 28

INDEX 435

Chenault, John R., 30
Chicago, Burlington & Quincy Railroad,
 166, 173, 175, 198, 205
 Burlington's difficulties with, 178
 concern over growth of Knights of Labor,
  186
 strikes of, 163, 182–185
 workforce of, 191
Chicago, prohibition fight in, 286
Chicago, Rock Island & Pacific Railroad,
 166
Chicago, University of, Fox Project, 20
Chicago and Aurora Railroad, 173
Chicago & Northwestern (C&NW), 166,
 205
Chicago Farmers Convention (October
 1873), 212
Children in frontier settlement, 42, 51–52
Christians (Disciples), membership of, 301,
 302
Christiansen, Mrs. R. E., 425
Cincinnati Commercial-Gazette, 285, 287
Cincinnati Freie-Presse, 286
Cincinnati Times-Star, 286
Cincinnati Volksblatt, 286
Civil Rights Act (1964), 155
Civil War, xi, 2, 4
 in Iowa, 7, 9–10
 relief organizations in, 105–126
Clarke, George W., 399
Clarkson, Coker F., 218
Clarkson, James S.
 and the antimonopoly coalition, 250
 as GOP leader, 264, 269, 275
 and protectionism, 272
 and railroad regulation, 210, 212, 213,
  232–233, 253
Class, role of, in Iowa politics, 97–98
Clay, Henry, 87
Clerical positions, women in, 320
Cleveland, Grover, 264–265, 269, 272
Clinton, and railroad rate regulation, 207
Coal mining, 10
Cochrane, Doris Herrick, 372–373
Cochrane, Willard, 349
Colbert, Tom, x
Cole, C. C., 134, 138
Colleges
 land-grant, 376, 385–389
 religious affiliation of, 6
Collins Radio, 10

Commercial capitalism, 90
Commercial-industrial capitalism, 88
Commission on Presidential Nominations,
 407
Commission on the Status of Women, 423
Committee of Five Hundred (Cincinnati),
 284, 286
Commodity Credit Corporation, 390
Communists, 340, 341
Communities, basic types of, 161–162
Community clubs, formation of, 335
Compromise of 1850, 100
Conard, Rebecca, xvi
Congregationalists
 beliefs of, 9
 political affiliation of, 97, 147, 151
 and slavery, 8
Conklin, W. Charlene, 417, 419, 421, 422,
 424, 426
Conservative Republican coalition parties,
 152
Constant open moralizing, 6
Contributions to farming, by women, 382
Cook, Robert, xi, 86–104
Cooke, Jay, & Co., failure of, 206
Cooke, Lucy, 56–57
Cooke, William, 57
Cooperative Extension Service, xiii,
 371–372, 393
 as arm of U.S. Department of Agricul-
  ture, 389
 at Iowa State College, 13, 386
 as voice for change, 388
Cordier, Mary Hurlbut, xiii
Corn belt, 61, 69, 73, 79, 83–84
Corse, Mayor, 174
Coughlin, Father, 340
Council Bluffs, 171, 205
 Soldiers' Aid Society in, 121
Council of Churches, 425
Country Life Commission, 12–13, 329
Country Life Movement, 327
Country People (Suckow), 313, 315
Covered wagons in frontier settlement, 41,
 42
Cow War (1931), 13, 341
Cox, George, 284
Coyne, Michael, 305
Craig, John, and prohibition, 275
Credit, availability of, in farming, 80
Crédit Mobilier scandal, 206

Creston, 171
  Board of Trade in, 178, 179
  business stagnation in, 188
  concern over, 177–178
  development of, 176–179
  effect of railroad strike on, 178–179, 181–182, 184–185, 188–189, 191
  elite in, 180, 181
  growth of, 185
  population of, 177, 179–180
  railroad employment in, 177
  stagnation of, 185
  urban ambitions of, 191–192
Creston Daily Advertiser, The, 189, 191
  strike of, by Typographical Union No. 131, 186–187
Crim, Charles, 330–331, 332
Crim, Lola, 330
Crim, Mildred Erickson, 331–332
Cromwell, 176
Cronon, William, xvi
Cudahy, Frank, 308
Cudahy, Margaret Minnihan, 308
Cullom, Shelby M., 224, 227
Cult of the Immediately Useful and Practical, 14
Cultural influences, on farming, 70–72
Cultural values in Iowa, 15
Cummins, Albert, 9
Currency deflation, 200
Curtis, Charles, 336, 337
Curtis, Roy, 311

Danish immigrants, farming by, 71
Davenport
  development of, as urban area, 91
  and railroad rate regulation, 207
Debt-to-property-value ratio, 246–247
Declaration of Independence, 152
Democratic party, 8, 15, 101
  on abortion, 424
  appeal of, 93–94
  equal rights issue in, 132–134
  and evolution of Iowa precinct caucuses, 397–409
  immigrant affiliation with, 97
  issues in, 101, 103–104
  Jacksonian, 89, 93–94
  and land distribution, 98–99
  leadership in late 1800s, 264–265
  nature of constituencies in, 96–97
  as Negrophobic, 95–96

  New Departure policy of 1870s, 141
  and prohibition, 266, 277, 282
  race as issue in, 131
  and religious affiliation, 321–324
Denison, John N., 202
Derr, Nancy, xiv
Derry, Fred, 311
Des Moines
  educational institutions in, 6
  Methodist Conference in, 276–277
  population in, 14
Des Moines Plan, 9
Dey, Peter A.
  and prohibition, 275
  and railroad regulation, 220, 273–274
  and the Republican vote, 277
Dillon, John F., 123
Dinner for Threshers (Wood), 1
Disciplines, political affiliation of, 142
Disease in Mesquakie people, 30
Division of labor in frontier settlement, 41–45
Dixiecrats, 154
Doderer, Minnette, 417
Dodge, Grenville M., 136–137
Dolliver, Jonathan P., 263, 322, 324
Domestic servants, women as, 318
Donahue, Robert, 184
Douglas, Stephen, 101, 104
Douglass, Frederick, 155
Downes, Wilma, 316, 320
Downing, Wendell K., 421
Dragoons, 28, 29
Drake, St. Clair, 155
Dred Scott decision, 104
Dubuque
  as center of Catholicism, 6
  creation of Catholic diocese in, 6
  development of, as urban area, 91
  and railroad rate regulation, 207
Dubuque & Pacific Railroad, 166
"Dubuque's Mines," 24
Dunham, E. Allene, 56, 57
Dutch immigrants, xiv, xv
Dykstra, Robert R., xi, 129–156

Eckerson, C. W., 186
Economic Recovery Act (1981), 383
Economy. *See also* Capitalism
  and early settlement, 90–91
  as factor in rise of Populist party, 242–262

and farming, 13
  in Iowa, 9–10, 13, 14, 92
  and party affiliation, 87
Education, 16
  of African Americans, 9
  desegregation of, 153–154
  of farm children, 378
  history of, xiii–xiv
  institutions for, 6–7, 376
  in Iowa, 9–10, 15, 16
  rural, 328, 331–332
Egbert, Eliza Ann, 56, 57
Elderly, position of, in farm families, 383–384
Election of 1892, 241–242
  Populist voting in, 243
Elite in market cities, 162–163
Elkins Act (1903), 237
Ellsworth, John, 61–62
Ellsworth, Oliver, 61–62
Ely, John M., Jr., 417
Emancipation Proclamation, 152
Emergency Farm Mortgage Act, 343
Emmet, Robert, 135
Emonds, Reverend, 121–122
Engelhardt, Carroll, xiii
English, Emory H., 398
English immigrants, 4
  farming by, 70
Episcopalians
  attitude toward equal rights, 142, 147
  beliefs of, 9
  political affiliation of, 142
Epworth League, 309
Equal rights, correlation with religion, 142, 147–148
Equal suffrage, as issue in Iowa, 9, 132–136
Erie Railroad, strikes on, 163
Estate planning for farm families, 381
Ethnicity. *See also specific ethnic groups*
  growth of, 14–15
  influences on farming, 70–72
  in Iowa, 2, 70–72
Evangelical Association (Cincinnati), 284
Evangelical Protestantism, 292, 303
Evergreen Sporting Association, 335
Extension home economists, role of, in rural Iowa, 350

Factionalism as consequence of spoils system, 99–100
Failure rates in farming, 82–83

Fairbanks, Charles, 287
Fairfield, educational institutions in, 6
Families. *See also* Farm families
  in frontier settlement, 39, 41
  and rural life style, 330–331
Farm Bloc, 339, 340
Farm Bureau, 334–335, 366–367, 376. *See also* American Farm Bureau; Iowa Farm Bureau
Farm Credit Act, 343
Farm Credit System, 384, 386, 387, 388, 391
Farmers. *See also* Families; Farm families
  demographics of, 62
  impact of transportation costs on, 245–246
  mobility of, 62–63
  in social order, 312–314
  turnover patterns in, 63–64
Farmers' Alliance, 252–257, 273
  and Industrial Union, 257
Farmers'-Grain Dealers Association, 390
Farmers' Holiday Association, 13, 342
Farmers' Home Administration (FmHA), 384, 386, 387–388, 388
Farmers' Union, 334–335, 339
Farm families. *See also* Families; Farmers; Farming
  durability of, 380–384
  formation of corporation by, 381, 382–383
  intergenerational cooperation among, 382–384
  need for outside input, 378, 384–385
  position of elderly in, 383–384
  and pursuit of part ownership, 378
Farm Families and Change in Twentieth-Century America (Friedberger), 375
Farming, 14. *See also* Farmers; Farm families
  and breaking of prairie sod, 66–67
  cattle feeders in, 73, 74–75
  corn in, 61, 69, 73, 75, 79, 83–84, 84
  credit in, 80
  crop production patterns in, 69
  cultural influences on, 70–72
  and downturn in machinery sales, 392–393
  and economy, 13, 243–244, 246–249
  ethnic influences on, 70–72
  expansion of interest groups, 334–335
  failure rates in, 82–83

Farming (*continued*)
  fencing as problem in, 65–66
  general, 72–73
  and Grange movement, 11
  and herd law, 65
  hogs in, 69, 72, 74
  horses in, 77
  impact of World War II on, 348–349
  innovators in, 79
  integration of, into national markets, 377–380
  in Iowa, 11–15, 61–84
  as labor intensive, 12–13
  and lack of timber, 64
  land speculation in, 80–81
  and Mesquakie people, 21, 30–31
  milk cows in, 68
  modernization of, 375–395
  and net decline of population, 360–361
  nonfamily labor in, 77
  power of capital in, 79–80
  practices of, xi
  prices in, 90–91
  production patterns in, 68–69, 73–74
  products of, 246
  steers in, 74–75
  technology in, 75–77, 80
  tenants in, 81–82, 83, 313–314
  and transportation facilities, 69–70
  of wheat, 69, 73–74
  women in, 12–14
Farmington Township, 268
Farm-Labor party, 339
Farmtown Presbyterian Women's Guild, 357
Feagin, Joe R., 149
Federal Farm Loan System, 339
Fencing as problem in farming, 65–66
Ferrin, Mary Ann, 47
Field, S. E., 252
Finch, Roy, 312
Fink, Deborah, xi, 347–374
Finn, A. J., 303, 321–322
Finn, George, 256
Fite, Gilbert, 328, 337
Foner, Eric, 87
Food for Freedom program, 350, 351
Food for Victory, 355
Foote, John G., 174
Foraker, Joseph B., 284
Forbes, John Murray
  belief in natural laws of trade, 201–202
  on Grange movement, 211, 213, 214
  and passage of Interstate Commerce Act (1887), 226
  and railroad development, 174–175, 199–200, 204, 205, 221–222, 235
  and railroad rate regulation, 215, 216, 217, 225–226, 232, 235
Ford, Gerald, 403–404, 405, 408
Foreclosure of rural mortgages, 82–83
Foreign policy and issue of race, 296–297
Formisano, Ronald, 87
Fort Des Moines, 29
Fort Laramie, 57, 58
Fort Leavenworth, 29, 32
Fort Pillow (Kentucky), 152
Fort Sumter, 107
4-H program, 367
Fox-Wisconsin waterway, 21
Franklin, Benjamin, 152
Frazier-Lemke Bankruptcy Act, 343
Free labor capitalism, 92
Free Soil, Free Labor, Free Men (Foner), 87
Free Soil Whigs, 101, 102, 103
Frémont, John C., 132
Friedberger, Mark, xi, 375–395
Friendship patterns and occupation, 310
Frontier settlement, 37–38
  children in, 51–52
  covered wagons in, 41, 42
  division of labor in, 41–45
  families in, 39, 41
  migrants in, 38, 39–40, 46
  and Native Americans, 40
  railroads in, 40–41
  riverboats in, 40
  squatters in, 39
  thesis of, 92
  trail life in, 37–38, 39–40, 44–46, 48–52
  women in, 38–39, 46–49, 51–59
Fugitive Slave Law (1850), 102, 131
Furrow, J. B., 255

Galesburg, Illinois, 173
Gallaher, Ruth, 317–318
Garland, Hamlin, 5, 16
Gender. *See also* Women
  and division of labor, in frontier settlement, 41–45
General Assembly, opening of, to blacks in Iowa, 132
Genetic inheritance, 293
Geography, 2, 5, 16

INDEX 439

and farming, 69–70
German immigrants, 4
    farming by, 71–72
    political affiliation of, 97, 147, 148
    religious beliefs of, 9
    and temperance issue, 8, 265–266, 269, 270, 274–275, 278, 280, 285–286
GI Bill, 371
Gillett, John Dean, 74
Gilmore, Quincy A., 199
Godkin, E. L., 211–212, 214, 216, 220
Good Templars, 277
Goodwyn, Lawrence, 243, 254
Gould diary, 51, 55
Government, role of, in farming, 376
Grain Futures Act, 339–340
Grange movement, 11, 79, 197, 205
    and demand for railroad regulation, 208–221
    and farming, 11
    growth in number of local chapters, 209
    and struggle for railroad control, 200
Granger, R. S., 29
Granger laws, 198, 213–219, 250, 272
    U.S. Supreme Court ruling on, 219–221
Grant, Ulysses S., 134, 135, 141, 147, 149, 154, 266
Great Depression, collapse of farming in, 378
Great Northern Railroad, strike on, in 1894, 163, 164
Green, Michael D., xi, 19–35
Greenback party, 11, 180, 265
Griffith, D. W., 296
Grimes, James W.
    as antislavery Whig, 101–102
    election of, as Whig governor, 8
    and Grange movement, 208–209
    and Mesquakies, 3–4, 33–34
    and proliferation of federal agencies, 199
    and railroad development, 96–97
    and railroad regulation, 214, 230, 236
    realignment of, as Republican, 8
    and Reconstruction, 199–200
Grimmell, Gus, 317
Grinnell, Josiah Bushnell, 33, 34, 151
Grinnell College, 9
Gutman, Herbert, 164–165, 181

Half-Breed Tract, 39
Halstead, Murat, 285
Hamilton, Carl, 313–314

Hanna, Mark, 287
Hardfish, 26
Harding, Bess, 316
Harding, William G., 399
Harding, Winifred, 316
Harlan, James, 134
Harnack, Curtis, xiv, 13–14, 331, 360
Harris, Fred, 409
Harris, Lem, 340
Harris, Orville, 323
Harris, Robert, 183, 184, 211, 216, 218–219, 220
Harris family, 40, 46, 48–49
Harrison, William Henry
    in election of 1888, 280
    and Native American treaties, 22
    and prohibition, 285, 286, 287–288
    and protective tariff, 277
Harsh, J. B., 179, 186
Hartmann, Susan, 364, 365
Hartshorn, Elden J., 135
Harvestores, 393
Harvey, Thomas, 31
Haun, Catherine Margaret, 44, 52, 56, 58
Hawk-Eye, The, 76
Hawk-Eye Bank Corporation, 387
Henderson, David B., 264, 269, 275, 324
Hepburn, William, 251
Hepburn Act (1906), 237
Herd law and farming, 65
High-License League of Indiana, 286
Hill, Philip, 421, 428
Hillman, Rosalee, 424
Hird, Charles, 307–308
Hired hands in social order, 314–315
Hispanic Americans, growth of, 14
Historic preservation movement, xvi
History
    as interpretation, ix–x
    of Mesquakie people, 19–35
Hoboes in social order, 315–316
Hogs
    in farming, 69, 72, 74
    modernization of industry, 379–380
Holiday movement, farmers', 13, 342, 343
Holt, Michael, 87, 100–101
Homestead Act (1862), 4–5
Hoover, Herbert, x, 268
Horses in farming, 77
Howell, Mrs. J. B., 114, 116
Hubbard, Nathaniel M., 256
Huftalen, Sarah Gillespie, xiii
Hughes, Harold, x

Human differences, genetic theories of, 293
Humphrey, Lyman U., 260
Hungarian immigrants, farming by, 70
Hunt, James, 407
Hunt Commission, 407, 408
Hutchinson, Fred, 312
Hutchison, Joseph G.
  and GOP nomination for governor, 255
  and prohibition, 276, 280–282

Illinois and Michigan canal, 70
Illinois Industrial University, 79
Illinois Military Tract, 69
Illinois system of feeding cattle or hogs, 76
Immigrants. *See also specific group*
  in frontier settlement, 38, 39–40, 46
  in Iowa, 4, 8–9, 10
  issue of Southern and Eastern European, 297–298
  labor unions as spokesman for, 298–299
  and political affiliation, 147
  and prohibition issue, 280–281
  and religious affiliation, 147
  as threat to traditional values, 299–301
Indianapolis, prohibition fight in, 286–287
Industrial development in Iowa, 10–11
In No Time at All (Hamilton), 313–314
Innovators in farming, 79
Integration in athletics, 294–295
Interstate commerce, problem of, 224
Interstate Commerce Act (1887), 198, 226–228, 229, 272
Iowa
  African American community in, 129, 130–131
  agriculture in, 14
  black code in, 131, 149
  and Civil War, xi, 2, 4, 7, 9–10
  cultural values in, 15
  economy in, 9–10, 14, 92
  education in, 6–7, 9–10, 15, 16
  1857 referendum in, 139
  1868 referendum in, 135, 136, 139, 141, 154
  1880 referendum in, 135–136, 139, 141, 154
  equal suffrage issue in, 132–136
  ethnic groups in, 2, 70–72
  evolution of precinct caucuses in, 397–409
  farming in, 11–15, 61–84
  geography of, 2, 5, 16
  history of, ix
  immigrants in, 4, 8–9, 10
  industrial development, 10–11
  Irish Catholics in, 91
  kinship networks in, 15
  land cessions in, 23
  middle class in, 91
  minorities in, 14–15
  Native Americans in, 3–4, 40
  nineteenth-century legacy, 3
  opening of General Assembly to blacks, 132
  opposition to slavery in, 131
  political affiliations in, 15
  political culture of, 86–104
  political parties in, 8–9, 93–100
  politics of race in, 129–156
  population of, 2, 12, 14, 27
  primary values in, 92
  prohibition in, 7–8, 9
  and railroad regulation, 197–238
  reforms in, 7–8, 9–10
  relief organization in, 105–126
  religious patterns in, 5–6, 8–9, 142, 147
  removal of Native Americans from, 27–28, 29–30, 90
  Republicanism in, 8
  role of class in politics in, 97–98
  role of race in politics in, 95–96, 129–156
  rural life in, 1, 2–3, 16, 327–344
  secondary values in, 92
  settlement of, 4–5
  slavery in, 7, 8
  social structure of, 91–92
  society that evolved in, 5–7
  statehood for, 2, 8, 90
  transportation in, 10, 13, 40–41, 69–70, 88, 94
  women in, 9, 13, 37–59
  World War II in, 14
  YWCA in, 420, 423
Iowa Association for the Medical Control of Abortion, 421, 425
Iowa Beef Processors (IBP), 391–392
Iowa Board of Control, 357
Iowa Board of Railroad Commissioners, 226, 230, 234, 273
Iowa Business and Professional Women's

INDEX

Federation, 372–373
Iowa Commissioner Law (1878), 227
Iowa Constitution (1846), 94
Iowa Department of Public Instruction, xiii
Iowa Farm Bureau Federation, 355, 393–394
Iowa Farmers' Alliance (I.F.A.), 257–258
Iowa Farmers' Union, 336, 342
Iowa Federation of Women's Clubs, 355
Iowa Homestead, 212, 251, 273
Iowa Medical Society Commission on Legislation, 422
Iowa Nurses' Association, 423
Iowa State Agricultural Society, 208–209
Iowa State Army Sanitary Commission, 123
  anger of Keokuk Society over establishment of, 112–113
  conflict between Keokuk Ladies' Soldiers' Aid Society and, 113–114, 121–122, 125
  creation of, 110–111
  efforts of, 121
Iowa State Leader, 251
Iowa State Register (Des Moines), 210, 218, 264, 279
Iowa State Teachers Association, xiii
Iowa State Temperance Alliance, 266–267
Iowa State University, 9
  Cooperative Extension Service at, 13, 386
  Home Economics Department at, 334, 365
Iowa Young Women's Christian Association, 423, 425
Ioway people, 3
Irish, John P., 265
Irish immigrants, 4
  political affiliation of, 96, 97
  and prohibition, 274–275, 278
  religious affiliation of, 91, 96, 274–275, 278
  settlement of, in Iowa, 91
Irish Trappist monastery, 6
"Ironic" approach to history of American race relations, 148
Irons, Martin, 190
Issues, role of, in political culture, 99
Ivins, Virginia, 56, 58–59

Jackson, Andrew, 8, 40

Jacksonian Democrats, 89, 93–94
Jefferson, Iowa, social identity of, xi, 291–325
Jefferson, Thomas, 12, 22, 90, 152
Jefferson Bee, 293, 295, 296, 297
Jefferson Country Club, 303
  membership in, 310
Jensen, Richard, xi, xiv, xv, 263–288, 302, 321
John Deere Company, 79, 392
Johnson, Keach, xiii
Johnson, Lyndon B., 418
Joint stock corporations, 88
Jones, William, 20
Journal of History and Politics (Iowa), x
Joy, James F., 173, 206
Jungle, The (Sinclair), 391

Kansas Farmer, 259
Kansas-Nebraska Act, 99, 101, 102
Kaufman, Polly Welts, xiii
Kawkawke, 29
Kelly, Oliver Hudson, 208
Kennedy, Ted, 403
Keokuk, as chief of Mesquakie people, 20, 22, 24, 25, 26, 31, 107
Keokuk Ladies' Soldiers' Aid Society, 107–122
  anger of, over establishment of Iowa State Army Sanitary Commission, 112–113
  and conflict between Iowa State Army Sanitary Commission, 113–114, 121–122, 125
  establishment of, 107
  need for financial support, 118
  purpose of, 107–108
  recordkeeping by, 114–116
  resistance to United States Sanitary Commission control, 109
  successes of, 111
  support for, in Iowa, 117–118
Keokuk (town), 107. *See also* Keokuk Ladies' Soldiers' Aid Society
  development of, as urban area, 91
  military hospital at, 108
  and railroad rate regulation, 207
  soldiers in, 107
Kickapoo people, 22, 32
Kinship networks in Iowa, 15

Kirkendall, Richard, x
Kirkwood, Samuel J., and fight between
    Iowa State Sanitary Commission and
    Keokuk Ladies' Soldiers Aid Society,
    110–111, 113, 117, 118, 120, 134, 269
Kirschner, Don, 298, 300
Kleppner, Paul, 87
Knights of Labor, 180
    representation of railroad workers by,
        186
Knowles, Lucretia, 114, 115–116, 120
Know Nothing party, 137
    support for, 102
Kousser, J. Morgan, 155–156
Kramer, Dale, 342
Ku Klux Klan and anti-Catholicism,
    305–308
Kynett, A. J.
    as Iowa State Sanitary Agent, 111,
        113–114, 118, 119, 121, 123, 124
    relationship with Wittenmyer, 113

Laborers in social order, 311–312
Labor intensive, farming as, 12–13
Labor unions as spokesman for immigrants,
    298–299
Lamoni, educational institutions in, 6
Land Bank, 384, 386
Land cessions in Iowa, 23
Land distribution, Whig support for, 98–99
Land-grant colleges, role of, in farming,
    376, 385–389
Land negotiations and Mesquakie people,
    27–29
Land O Lakes, 376
Land speculation in farming, 80–81
Larew, James, x
Larrabee, William
    and railroad development, 166
    and railroad regulation, 228–239, 256,
        272–273
    and reforms, 252, 253
    as state senator, 269
    support for prohibition, 271
Larson, Cliff, 404
Larson, John Lauritz, xi, 197–238
Lead deposits, 24, 90
League for the Preservation of Citizens'
    Rights (Cincinnati), 284–285
League of Women Voters, 358
Legal and Political Status of Women in

    Iowa (Gallaher), 317–318
Legal code (1851), 94
Le Mars, 13, 342–343
Le Mars Globe-Post, 342–343
Leonard, Elizabeth D., xi, 105–126, 347
Levine, Bruce, 87
Lewis, Bernard, 155
Lincoln, Abraham, 104, 107, 116, 149, 325
Livestock, value of, 246
Long, Huey, 341
Loras, Mathias, 6
Louisiana Purchase, 90
Lovejoy, Vic, 293, 323, 324
Luker, Kristin, 426
Lutherans
    membership in, 301
    political affiliation of, 147, 148
Lyon, "Cap," 311

Mackintosh, Jette, xiv
Madison, James, 152
Mahin, John, 273–274
Main Street on the Middle Border (Atherton), 7, 291, 329
Main Traveled Roads (Garland), 16
Mann-Elkins Act (1910), 237
Market economy, influence of, 93
Market revolution
    impact of, on trans-Mississippi West,
        89–91
    social impact of, 87–88
Market towns
    attributes separating railroad towns and,
        168
    economic diversification of, 169–170
    elite in, 162–163
    growth rates of, 169
    manufacturing in, 170
    size of, 170
    wholesaling in, 170
Marriage
    and careers for women, 47, 319–320
    problem of mixed, 308
    for rural women, 47, 363
Marsh, A. S., 113–114
Mason, Charles, 96–97
Maytag, Frederick, 10, 11
McCaffery, John, 189
McCormick, Billy, 321–322
McDaniel, George, x
McDill, James W., 220, 226, 227, 230, 233,

INDEX   443

253
McGovern, George, 405
McGuffey, William Holmes, 6
McGuffey's Readers, 6
McKinley, William, 285, 287, 322, 324, 325
McKinley tariff, 282, 283
McLaughlin, Mary Moore, 44, 46, 47, 49
McLaughlin, Pete, 312
McNary-Haugen Bill, 340
McTaggart, Fred, 20
Meat cutting, 391
Meat packing, 391
Mechanics in social order, 311–312
Media coverage of precinct caucuses, 406, 408
Meier, August, 149
Melson, Gene, 309
Men, role of, in frontier settlement, 41–45
Menace, 305
Mendota, 173
Merchant capitalism, 201
Merton, Robert K., 150
Mesquakie people, 3–4, 90
   adaptation of annual life cycle by, 31–32
   and Black Hawk War, 23–24
   disease in, 30
   efforts to win separate status from government, 32–33
   farming by, 21, 30–31
   history of, 19–35
   Keokuk as head chief of, 24
   and land negotiations, 27–29
   and lead deposits, 24
   opposition to "money chiefs," 26–27
   relations between Sauk people and, 24–26
   relations between Sioux people and, 27–28
   removal of, 29–30
   and right to buy land, 33–34
   and Sauk alliance, 34–35
   and treaty violations, 32
Mesquakie Settlement, 3–4
Methodists
   beliefs of, 8–9
   colleges set up by, 6
   membership of, 301, 302
   political affiliation of, 97, 142, 147
   and temperance issue, 8–9, 266, 268, 276–277
Mexican immigrants, 14
Mexican War, 100

Mexico, stability of government, 297
Michelson, Truman, 20
Michigan Central Railroad, 173
Middle class in Iowa, 91
Middle land, 2
Military Tract, 68
Milk cows in farming, 68
Mills bill, 272
Miners' Bank of Dubuque, 93, 95, 100
Minorities in Iowa, 14–15. *See also specific groups*
Missing generation thesis, 377
Missouri Compromise, 8, 101
Missouri people, 3
Mohr, James C., xi, 411–430
Morain, Frederick, 312
Morain, Thomas J., xi, 291–325
Moral standards for teachers, 319
Morden, Elizabeth Ann, 317
Morden, Leone, 317
Morden, Roy, 317
Morley, Maxine, 319
Morrell, John, 10
Morrell Company, 391
Morrill Act, 9
Mortgages, foreclosure of, 82–83
Mosby, John, and prohibition, 284–285
Mosteller, Roy, 303, 307, 309
Mott family, 40–41
Mount Pleasant, 172
Multiculturalism, ix
Murphy, Peter, 309
Muscatine and railroad rate regulation, 207
Muskie, E., 405
Myrdal, Gunnar, 149–150, 154
Myrdal hypothesis, 152

Naipaul, V. S., 129
National Corn Growers Association, 376, 394
National Farmers' Alliance, 260
National Farmers Organization, credibility of, 393–394
National Farmers Union, 390
National Live Stock Journal, 84
National State Bank, 174, 176
Native Americans. *See also* Mesquakie people; Sauk people
   in frontier settlement, 40
   in Iowa, 3–4, 40
   removal of, from Iowa, 27–28, 29–30, 90

Nature of Prejudice, The (Allport), 150–151
New Deal, 343–344
New England belt, 5
Newhall, 47
New Hampshire primary election, 407–408
New Providence, 8
Newton family, 40
Nineteenth-century legacy of Iowa, 3
Nixon, Richard, 419
Noble, Patrick, 29
Noble and Holy Order of the Knights of Labor, 186
Nonfamily labor in farming, 77
Non-Partisan League, 339, 340
Northern Pacific Railroad, 163
Northwest Ordinance, 8
Norwegian immigrants, 4
  farming by, 71
Noun, Louise, x

Occidental Petroleum, 391
Occupations
  as factor in social order, 309–316
  to friendship patterns, 310
  and opportunities for women, 47, 316–320
Ohio, struggle over prohibition in, 284–286
Omaha people, land treaties with, 3
Omaha *World Herald,* 325
Open Country Friends Meeting, 367
Oquawka, Illinois, 173
Order of Good Templars, 266
Osage River, 28
  reservation of, 33
Osgood, Bess, 322
Oskaloosa, educational institutions in, 6
Ostler, Jeffrey, xi, 241–262
Oto people, land treaties with, 3
Ottumwa and railroad rate discrimination, 207
Overton, Richard C., 174

Packers and Stockyard Act, 339
Parks, Rosa, 342
Parochialism, xi
Partnerships for farm families, 381, 382
Patterson, J. E. (Pat), 322
Patterson, William, 151
Peasley, F. J. C., 174, 176
Peasley, J. C., 176

Peck, John M., 71
Peffer, William, 260–261
Pelley, William Dudley, 340
People's party. *See* Populist party
Peoria & Oquawka Railroad, 172
Perkins, Arozina, xiii
Perkins, Charles, and railroad rate regulation, 174–176, 182–185, 204–206, 212, 213, 215, 216, 218–219, 220, 221–222, 224–226, 226, 230, 234–235
Persons, Stow, xiii
Petersen, Peter, xiv
Pettigrew, Thomas Fraser, 151, 154
Phelps, Caroline, 53
Philippines, United States intervention in, 297
Physicians, women as, 317–318
Pillow, Fort (Kentucky), 152
Plains states, Populist party in, 242
Planting Corn Belt Culture (Power), 5
Plass, E. D., 415
Political affiliations. *See also* Democratic party; Populist party; Republican party; Whig party
  factors in establishing, 320–324
  in Iowa, 15
  roots of, 87–88
Political correctness, ix
Political culture
  in antebellum Iowa, 86–104
  in Iowa, 92–93
  race as element of, 95–96, 129–156
Political parties, 8–9, 93–100. *See also* Democratic party; Republican party; Whig party
  affiliation with, and link between economic change, 87
  breakdown of second system, 89
  emergence of third system, 89
  and religious affiliation, 97, 263
  and religious orientation, 96, 97, 263, 321–324
Pooling, prohibition of, 226
Population of Iowa, 2, 12, 14, 27
Populism, level of support for, 244–245
Populist party, 241–262
Post, August, 255
Potawatomi people, 3, 32, 90
Potter, Thomas J., 185, 230
Power, Richard, 5
Poweshiek, 20, 25, 26, 29, 30, 32
Prairie Farmer, 66–67, 79, 177

INDEX 445

Prairie schooner, 43
Prairie sod, breaking of, 66–67
Pregnancy, public inhibition about, 320
Presbyterians
  attitude toward equal rights, 142, 147
  beliefs of, 9
  membership in, 301, 302
  political affiliation of, 97
  and prohibition, 277
Price, George, 184
Price, Hiram, 134
Primary values in Iowa, 92
Production Credit Association, 384
Production patterns in farming, 68–69, 73–74
Progressive evolution, 293–294
Progressive movement, 9
Prohibition, 7–8, 9, 263–288
  early laws on, 7
  and political activism of churches, 321
Prohibition Club, 335
Prohibition party, 266, 267
Property value, 246
Proposition 1, 133
Proposition 2, 133–134, 139, 141, 148
Pro rata movements of East, 197
Protective tariff, 279
Protestant-Catholic schism in small towns, 301–309
Protestant work ethic, 6–7
Pullman boycott, 163

Quaker Oats, 10
Quakers, 8
  attitude toward equal rights, 142
  membership in, 301
  political affiliation of, 142, 147, 151
  and slavery, 8
  and temperance issue, 268
  and World War II, 367
Quarles, Benjamin, 152
Quick, Herbert, 13, 76, 329
Quickening, abortion and, 411

Race, xi
  as factor, in social order, 294–301
  politics of, in Iowa, 95–96, 129–156
Radl, Richard, 417, 418
Railroads, 40–41
  benefits of, 99

  construction of, 10
  expansion of, 10
  in frontier settlement, 40–41
  and growth of coal industry, 10
  impact of, on urban development, 160–163, 165–171
  and production patterns, 70
  regulation of, 197–238, 272
  sell of land by, 4
Railroad strike of 1877, 182–185
Railroad strike of 1888, effect of, on retail operations, 178
Railroad towns, 161, 162, 163
  attributes separating market cities from, 168
  characteristics of, 192–193
  class relations in, 165
  creation of network of, 166–168
  economic diversification of, 169–170
  growth rates of, 169
  manufacturing in, 170
  size of, 162, 170
  social structure of, 162
  wholesaling in, 170
Raver, Berniece, 311
Raver, Earl, 312
Reagan, Ronald, 403–404, 405, 408, 409
Reconstruction, 199–200
Red Cross, 357
Red Rock boundary line, 28
Referendum of 1857, 139
Referendum of 1868, 135, 136, 139, 141, 154
Referendum of 1880, 135–136, 139, 141, 154
Religion. *See also specific denominations*
  as factor in social order, 301–309
  institutions, in Iowa, 8–9, 142, 147
  patterns, in Iowa, 5–6
  and political affiliation, 96, 97, 263, 321–324
  and rural life, 331–332
  in shaping world view, 92, 93
  and voting behavior, xv
Religious groups, attitudes toward equal rights, 142, 147–148
Reno, Milo, 336–337, 342, 343–344
"Report of the Ladies' Soldiers' Aid Society," 110
Republican party, 8, 15
  on abortion, 424
  and agrarian discontent, 249–252

Republican party (*continued*)
  and anti-monopoly issue, 252–253
  antirailroad stand of, 212
  1865 convention of, 153
  equal rights issue in, 132–136
  and evolution of Iowa precinct caucuses, 397–409
  immigrant affiliation with, 97
  issues in, 103
  origin of, 102
  policy battles over black equality in, 131
  position on equal rights, 153
  and prohibition, 263–288
  and racial attitudes, 139, 140, 141
  and railroad regulation, 208
  and religious affiliation, 321–324
  slave issue in, 102–103
  and temperance movement, 8–9
  use of, 8–9
Resolution 4, 134, 137, 138
Reynolds, John, 23
Rhodes, G. W., 186
Richardson, Anna E., 334
Richardson, Guy, 323
Riley, Glenda, xi, 37–59
Risius, Andrew, 330
Riverboats in frontier settlement, 40
River towns, 162
Rochdale system, 390
Roche, John, 286
Rock River, 21
Rock River valley, 22–23
Rockwell International, 10–11
Rocky Mountain, Populist party in, 242
Roe v. Wade, 418, 423, 430
Roosevelt, Franklin, 13, 324, 343, 348
Roosevelt, Theodore, 287, 322, 329
Rouse, Clara, 175
Rowley, Carrie, 414–415
Rudwick, Elliott, 149
Rural Americans, immigrants as threat to traditional values of, 299–301
Rural banking, changes in, 386–388
Rural Electrification Act (1935), 13
Rural legacy in Iowa, 16
Rural life, 1, 2–3
  and education, 328
  exodus from, to city, 329–330
  in Iowa, 1, 2–3
  shortcomings of, 328
Russell, Pauline McCormick, 306, 309
Rutter, Bertha, 316
Rydings, May Dunham, 316

Sac and Fox Agency, 29–30, 32
Sac and Fox tribes, 22, 24, 34–35. *See also* Mesquakie people
  factionism in, 20, 24
Sage, Leland, 324, 327
Salaried employees in social order, 311
Salem, 8
Sandoz, Mari, 5
Sanford, Nettie, 124–125
Santee Sioux people, 3
  land treaties with, 3
Saukenuk, 22–23
Sauk people, 3, 4, 20, 21, 25, 34, 90. *See also* Mesquakie people
  relations with Mesquakie people, 24–26, 34–35
Scandinavian immigrants
  farming by, 71–72
  religious beliefs of, 9
Scarpino, Philip, xvi
Schenken, Suzanne, xiv
Schuman, Howard, 154
Schwieder, Dorothy, ix, xi, xiii, xiv, xvii, 1–16, 327–335
Scott, John, 209
Scott, William, 185
Scott, Winfield, 23–24, 34
Scott County Hydraulic Company, 100
Secondary values in Iowa, 92
Second Bank of the United States, 93
Sellers, Charles, 87
Seventy-Sixers club, 341
Shake-Out: Iowa Farm Families in the 1980s (Friedberger), 375
Share the Wealth program, 341
Shaw, Leslie, 324
Sheaffer Company, 10
Sherman, John, 285, 287
Shover, John, 342
Shutes, Ann, 44
Shutes, Hiram, 45, 46, 53
Shutes, Mary Alice, 45, 49–50, 52
Shutes family, 49, 53
Simpson, John, 337, 342
Sinclair, Upton, 391
Sinclair Meat Packing, 10
Sioux City, industrial development of, 10
Sioux City Community House, xiv
Sioux people, relations between Mesquakie people and, 27–28
60th U.S. Colored Infantry, 138, 152
Skold, Karen Beck, 360
Slavery

INDEX 447

in Iowa, 7, 8
opposition to, in Iowa, 131
Slothower, A. E., 303
Smedley, A. B., 212
Smith, Adam, 201
Smith, Al, 299
Smith, R. P., 179, 185
Snowden, Frank M., 155
Snyder, J. A., 416, 420
Social equality, avoiding issue of, 295–296
Social evolution, theory of progress through, 293
Social identity of Jefferson, Iowa, 291–325
Social order
  occupation as factor in, 309–316
  race as factor in, 294–301
  religion as factor in, 301–309
Social structure in Iowa, 91–92
Society that evolved in Iowa, 5–7
Soike, Lowell, xiv
Soldiers' aid society. *See* Keokuk Ladies' Soldiers' Aid Society
Sons of Temperance, 266
South, Populist party in, 242
Southern Alliance, 257
Sovereign, James, 279
Spanish Speaking Peoples' Committee, 14–15
Spirit Lake Massacre, 3
Springdale, 8, 268
Spring in Town (Wood), 1
Squatters in frontier settlement, 39
Stanton, Edwin, 116
Starzl, Rome, 342–343
State v. *Fitzgerald,* 414
Status of Women Council of the Greater Des Moines Area and abortion issue, 423
Steers, 74–75
Stevenson, John, 323
Stewart, O. E., 190
Stewart, Phoebe, 427–428
Stillman, Frank, 295
Stillman, Paul, 323
Stone, William M., 137–139, 152, 154, 191
Strange Career of Jim Crow, The (Woodward), 148
Straub, Eleanor, 373
Stromquist, Shelton, x, xi, 159–193, 197
Strong, Josiah, 292
Strong, Mary, 114–115, 118, 119, 120
Stuntz, A. L., 256
Suckow, Ruth, xvii, 313, 315

Sumner, Charles, 104
Sumptuary laws, 266
  opposition to, 267
Sunday laws, 288
Swedish immigrants, 4
Sweeney, J. H., 253
Swift meat packer, 391

Taft, William, 324
Tama County, 3
  settlement of, 34
Tax, Sol, 20
Tax policy, cumulative effect on farming, 394–395
Taylor, F. J., 188
Taylor, George R., 88
Teachers, women as, 318–320
Technology in farming, 75–77, 80
Temperance. *See* Prohibition
Temperance Alliance, 267, 268
Temple, A. D., 185
Tenant farming, 81–82, 83, 313–314
Thayer, John M., 259–260
Thomas, Kellogg, 305, 308–309
Tifereth Israel Women's League in Des Moines, 423
Tillman, Ben, 294
Timber shortage, 64–65
Titus, Lydia, 50, 51
Titus, Sarah, 50
Titus party, 48
Topeka Capital-Commonwealth, 258–259
Townley, A. C., 337
Towns. *See also* Market towns; Railroad towns
  social identity of small, 291–325
Trail life in frontier settlement, 37–38, 39–40, 44–46, 48–52
Tramps in social order, 315–316
Trans-Mississippi West, impact of market revolution on, 87–91
Transportation. *See also* Railroads; Riverboats
  and farming, 69–70
  forms of, in Iowa, 10, 13, 40–41, 69–70, 88, 94
  impact of costs of, on economic condition of farmers, 245–246
Treglia, Mary, xiv
Truman, Harry S., 154
Tucker, Bert, 311
Turner, Frederick Jackson, 64, 92

Turner, Jonathan B., 79
Turnerian frontier utopia, 99
Tuskegee Institute and issue of social equality, 295–296
Typographical Union No. 131, strike of *Creston Advertiser* by, 186–187

Ubbelohde, Carl, xii
Udall, Morris K., 403, 409, 419
Underground railroad, 8
Under the Guns: A Woman's Reminiscences of the Civil War (Wittenmyer), 106
Union Anti-Negro Suffrage party, 152, 265
Union Labor party, 180, 189, 273, 277
Union Pacific Railroad, 171
Unitary ballot, 135
United States Sanitary Commission (USSC)
  establishment of, 109
  resistance of Keokuk Society to, 109
University of Iowa, xiii, 9
Upper Mississippi Valley, 3
Urban areas, creation of ethnic pockets in, 298
Urban development, effects of railroad development on, 165–171

Values, immigrants as threat to traditional, 299–301
Vassady, Béla, xiv
Voting behavior, and religious affiliation, xv
Voting Rights Act (1965), 155

Wadsworth, Grace, 316, 320
Walker, James M., 208, 213, 214, 215
Wall, Joseph Frazier, xi, xvii, 16, 292, 312, 327, 336–344
Wallace, Henry, x, 6–7, 251, 253, 273, 293, 327, 333–334, 348
Wallaces' Farmer, 6–7, 293, 333–334, 348, 355
  advertisements in, 12, 351, 369
  articles in, 350–351, 368–369, 370
  cartoons in, 369–370
  "Country Air" column of, 347, 352, 353–354, 356–357, 367
  "Letters to Farm Folks" column in, 7
  "Sarah Jane Says" column in, 370
  stories in, 358–359
Wapello (Mesquakie), 20, 25, 26

Ware, Harold, 340
War effort, women's recruitment in, 372–373
War Manpower Commission (WMC), 373
Wartburg, educational institutions in, 6
Washington, Booker T., 295
Watson, Harry, 87
Weaver, James B., x, 11, 13, 241–242, 249, 257
  and prohibition, 267
We Have All Gone Away (Harnack), 13–14, 331
West Branch, 8
Western Live Stock Journal, 74
Wetemah, 29, 30
What Would Lincoln Do? (Barlow), 340
Wheat farming, 69, 73–74
Wheeler, Hiram C., 255
Wherry, Elizabeth, "Country Air" column of, 347, 352, 353–354, 356–357, 367
Whig party, 8, 101, 103
  appeal of, 94–95
  attitude toward blacks in, 95–96
  collapse of, 101–102
  Free Soil, 101, 102
  immigrant affiliation with, 97
  and land distribution, 98–99
  nature of constituencies in, 96–97
  policy battles over black equality in, 131
  and prohibition, 265
Whiskey Ring scandals, 266
Whiting, Charles E., 250
Whitney, Tom, 402
Wickard, Claude R., 358
Wiggins, Charles, 15
Wilcox, Lumund, 321, 323–324
Wilcox, Nancy, 321
Willits, Earl M., 419, 429
Wills, Herman, 273
Wilmot Proviso, 131
Wilson, James "Tama Jim," 11, 12, 256, 257, 324
Wilson, Minnie, 316
Wilson, Ned, 312
Wilson Company, 391
Winebrenner, Hugh, xi, 397
Winey, Wayne, 307
Winnebago Industries, 11
Winnebago people, 90
  and treaty violations, 32
Winning of the Midwest (Jensen), 321
Wishecomaque, 26

Wittenmyer, Annie, xi, 105, 347
  appointment of, as Iowa State Sanitary Agent, 118, 119
  as corresponding secretary of Keokuk Society, 107, 110
  efforts to cooperate with Iowa Commission, 119
  as general agent, 110
  as Iowa State Sanitary Agent, 123–124
  leveling of scandalous charges against, 121–122
  relationship with Reverend Kynett, 113
  soldier relief efforts of, 106–107
Wittenmyer, William, 106
Wolf, Mort, 312
Wolfskin, 29
Woman's Christian Temperance Union (WCTU), 266, 276
Women
  career opportunities for, 47, 316–320
  discontent of farm, 330
  in farming, 12–14, 382
  in frontier settlement, 38–39, 41–45, 46–49, 51–59
  as physicians, 317–318
  rights of, 9
  role of, xi
  rural, and World War II, 347–374
  settlement of single, in Iowa, 47–48
  and soldiers' aid in Civil War, 105–126
Women's Advisory Committee (WAC), 373
Women's movement, force of, in abortion debate, 422–424
Wood, Grant, 1–2, 3
Woodward, C. Vann, 148
Work-force stability, consequences of lack of, 392
Workingmen's Advocate, The, 187
World War II, xi
  effect of, on Iowa, 14
  and rural women, 347–374
Wrede, Steven, xiv
Wylie, Philip, 370

Yankee Confession, 304
YWCA, 423, 425

Zellweger, Hans, 421
Zero population growth, 419